AMERICAN POLITICAL, ECONOMIC, AND SECURITY ISSUES

ECONOMIC, POLITICAL AND SOCIAL ISSUES OF NORTH AMERICA

AMERICAN POLITICAL, ECONOMIC, AND SECURITY ISSUES

Additional books in this series can be found on Nova's website
under the Series tab.

Additional E-books in this series can be found on Nova's website
under the E-books tab.

AMERICAN POLITICAL, ECONOMIC, AND SECURITY ISSUES

ECONOMIC, POLITICAL AND SOCIAL ISSUES OF NORTH AMERICA

MICHELLE L. FERGUSSON
EDITOR

Nova Science Publishers, Inc.
New York

For permission to use material from this book please contact us:
Telephone 631-231-7269; Fax 631-231-8175
Web Site: http://www.novapublishers.com

NOTICE TO THE READER

The Publisher has taken reasonable care in the preparation of this book, but makes no expressed or implied warranty of any kind and assumes no responsibility for any errors or omissions. No liability is assumed for incidental or consequential damages in connection with or arising out of information contained in this book. The Publisher shall not be liable for any special, consequential, or exemplary damages resulting, in whole or in part, from the readers' use of, or reliance upon, this material. Any parts of this book based on government reports are so indicated and copyright is claimed for those parts to the extent applicable to compilations of such works.

Independent verification should be sought for any data, advice or recommendations contained in this book. In addition, no responsibility is assumed by the publisher for any injury and/or damage to persons or property arising from any methods, products, instructions, ideas or otherwise contained in this publication.

This publication is designed to provide accurate and authoritative information with regard to the subject matter covered herein. It is sold with the clear understanding that the Publisher is not engaged in rendering legal or any other professional services. If legal or any other expert assistance is required, the services of a competent person should be sought. FROM A DECLARATION OF PARTICIPANTS JOINTLY ADOPTED BY A COMMITTEE OF THE AMERICAN BAR ASSOCIATION AND A COMMITTEE OF PUBLISHERS.

Additional color graphics may be available in the e-book version of this book.

LIBRARY OF CONGRESS CATALOGING-IN-PUBLICATION DATA

Economic, political, and social issues of North America / editor, Michelle
L. Fergusson.
    p. cm.
  Includes index.
  ISBN 978-1-61122-555-6 (hardcover)
 1. United States--Politics and government--2009- 2. United
States--Foreign relations--2009- 3. United States--Economic policy--2009-
4. Presidents--United States--Election. 5. Vice-Presidents--United
States--Election. 6. Border security--North America. 7. National
security--United States. 8. Finance, Public--United States. 9. Health care
reform--United States. I. Fergusson, Michelle L.
  JK275.E36 2010
  320.60973--dc22
                        2010038633

Published by Nova Science Publishers, Inc. ✛ *New York*

CONTENTS

PREFACE

This book presents and discusses important political and economic changes in North America. Topics discussed herein include security and prosperity partnership of North America; border security; foreign aid; the global financial crisis; the electoral college and presidential elections; the budget resolution and spending legislation; immigration of foreign workers; and the National Security Council.

Chapter 1 – The Security and Prosperity Partnership of North America (SPP) is a three-country initiative that is intended to increase cooperation and information sharing in an effort to increase and enhance prosperity in the United States, Canada, and Mexico. The SPP was endorsed by the leaders of the three countries, but it is not a signed agreement or treaty and, therefore, contains no legally binding commitments or obligations. The goals of the prosperity components of the SPP are to increase cooperation and sharing of information in order to improve productivity, reduce the costs of trade, and enhance the quality of life. The goal of the security components of the SPP is to coordinate the security efforts undertaken by each of the three participating nations to better protect citizens from terrorist threats and transnational crime while promoting the safe and efficient movement of legitimate people and goods. Congressional interest in the SPP concerns possible implications related to national sovereignty, transportation corridors, cargo security and border facilitation. This report will not be updated.

Chapter 2 – This report outlines the issues involved with DHS's construction of the San Diego border fence and highlights some of the major legislative and administrative developments regarding its completion. Congress first authorized the construction of a 14-mile, triple-layered fence along the U.S.-Mexico border near San Diego in the Illegal Immigration Reform and Immigration Responsibility Act (IIRIRA) of 1996. By 2004, only nine miles had been completed, and construction was halted because of environmental concerns. The 109th Congress subsequently passed the REAL ID Act (P.L. 109-13, Div. B), which contained provisions to facilitate the completion of the 14-mile fence. These provisions allow the Secretary of Homeland Security to waive *all legal requirements* determined necessary to ensure expeditious construction of authorized barriers and roads. In September 2005, the Secretary used this authority to waive a number of mostly environmental and conservation laws. Subsequently, the Secure Fence Act of 2006 (P.L. 109-367) *removed* the specific IIRIRA provisions authorizing the San Diego fence and added provisions authorizing five stretches of two-layered reinforced fencing along the southwest border. While the specific authorization of the San Diego fence was deleted, the project appears permissible under a separate, more general authorization provision of IIRIRA. In the 110th Congress,

S.Amdt. 1150, the Secure Borders, Economic Opportunity, and Immigration Reform Act of 2007, which has been proposed in the nature of a substitute to S. 1348, the Comprehensive Immigration Reform Act of 2007, would amend § 102 of IIRIRA to once again expressly authorize the construction of the San Diego fence.

Chapter 3 – Statutory offices of inspector general (OIG) consolidate responsibility for audits and investigations within a federal agency. Established by public law as permanent, nonpartisan, independent offices, they now exist in more than 60 establishments and entities, including all departments and largest agencies, along with numerous boards and commissions. Under two major enactments — the Inspector General Act of 1978 and its amendments of 1988 — inspectors general are granted substantial independence and powers to carry out their mandate to combat waste, fraud, and abuse. Recent laws have added offices, funding for special operations, and law enforcement powers to OIGs in establishments. Recent initiatives have set up mechanisms to oversee the Gulf Recovery Program, while various legislative proposals in the 110th Congress are designed to strengthen the IGs' independence and establish new posts, among other matters.

Chapter 4 – This paper seeks to consider the role of deliberative social justice, how author think about health care, and the general presumption that there exists some unspoken, natural right or rights to the services and goods provided by the health care scheme within the United States. While it is perhaps possible to establish such a theoretical right, at present the current system within the U.S. excludes any such notion. It is also the intent of this article to support the claim, from a utilitarian position, that rights do not legitimately exist apart from the recognition and willingness of the general populace to support such a right, and the existence of reciprocal moral responsibility by the individual who exercises the right. Faced with significant inequalities in the distribution of health care services and resources, in the United States, there is an inclination to assert that a violation of basic human rights is involved by such a denial or constraint. The attempt to adjudicate the notions of social justice with the alleged notion of a right to health care is an ever present problem and reality that will be examined. While numerous political promises and various proposed business schemes may present hopeful solutions, the examination and clarification of the idea of a perceived right and the associative obligations must be examined in order to attempt to qualify the notion of such a right.

Chapter 5 – Foreign assistance is a fundamental component of the international affairs budget and is viewed by many as an essential instrument of U.S. foreign policy. The focus of U.S. foreign aid policy has been transformed since the terrorist attacks of September 11, 2001. This report provides an overview of the U.S. foreign aid program, by answering frequently asked questions on the subject.

There are five major categories of foreign assistance: bilateral development aid, economic assistance supporting U.S. political and security goals, humanitarian aid, multilateral economic contributions, and military aid. Due largely to the implementation of two new foreign aid initiatives—the Millennium Challenge Corporation and the HIV/AIDS Initiative—bilateral development assistance has become the largest category of U.S. aid.

In FY2008, the United States provided some form of foreign assistance to about 154 countries. Israel and Egypt placed among the top recipients in FY2008, as they have since the late 1970s, although on-going reconstruction activities in Iraq and Afghanistan now place those nations near the top as well. The impact of the terrorist attacks on September 11, 2001, and the subsequent use of foreign aid to support the war on terrorism are clearly seen in the estimated country-aid levels for FY2008. Pakistan and Jordan are key partners in the war on terrorism and major beneficiaries of U.S. assistance. Also among the leading recipients are some African countries that are the focus of the multi-billion dollar HIV/AIDS initiative.

By nearly all measures, the amount of foreign aid provided by the United States declined for several decades but has grown in the past few years. After hitting an all-time low in the mid-1990s, foreign assistance levels since FY2004, in real terms, have been higher than any period since the early 1950s, largely due to Iraq and Afghanistan reconstruction and HIV/AIDS funding. The 0.19% of U.S. gross national product represented by foreign aid obligations for FY2008 is consistent with recent years, but quite low compared to the early decades of the foreign assistance program. The United States is the largest international economic aid donor in absolute dollar terms but is the smallest contributor among the major donor governments when calculated as a percent of gross national income.

Chapter 6 – Science and engineering activities have always been international. Scientists, engineers, and health professionals frequently communicate and cooperate with one another without regard to national boundaries. This report discusses international science and technology (S&T) diplomacy, instances when American leadership in S&T is used as a diplomatic tool to enhance another country's development and to improve understanding by other nations of U.S. values and ways of doing business. According to the National Research Council, five developmental challenges where S&T could play a role include child health and child survival, safe water, agricultural research to reduce hunger and poverty, micro-economic reform, and mitigation of natural disasters.

Title V of the Foreign Relations Authorization Act, FY1979 (P.L. 95-426) provides the current legislative guidance for U.S. international S&T policy. This act states that Department of State (DOS) is the lead federal agency in developing S&T agreements. The National Science and Technology Policy, Organization, and Priorities Act of 1976 (P.L. 94-282) states that the director of the White House Office of Science and Technology Policy (OSTP) is to advise the President on international S&T cooperation policies and the role of S&T considerations in foreign relations.

DOS sets the overall policy direction for U.S. international S&T diplomacy, and works with other federal agencies as needed. Within DOS, the Bureau of Oceans and International Environmental and Scientific Affairs (OES) coordinates international S&T activities. The Science and Technology Advisor to the Secretary of State (STAS) provides S&T advice to the Secretary and the director of the U.S. Agency for International Development (USAID). OSTP acts as a interagency liaison. A number of federal agencies that both sponsor research and use S&T in developing policy are involved in international S&T policy.

A fundamental question is why the United States should invest in international S&T diplomacy instead of domestic research and development (RandD) and science, technology, engineering, and mathematics education (STEM) activities, which are facing budget constraints. If Congress should decide that funding international S&T activities is important, agreeing on a policy goal beyond enhancing the country's development, such as improving U.S. relations with other countries, or enhancing popular opinion of the United States may help set priorities.

Policy options identified for Congress by expert committees who have assessed U.S. international S&T diplomacy efforts include ensuring a baseline of science, engineering, and technical (SET) literacy among all appropriate DOS personnel, increasing the presence overseas of personnel with significant SET expertise, and expanding the Department's engagement within global SET networks through exchanges, assistance, and joint research activities addressing key global issues. Other proposed actions include increasing USAID support that builds S&T capacity in developing countries, and orienting other departments and agencies S&T developing country programs to support the development priorities of the host countries. Another proposal would establish a new U.S. government organization, modeled on the Defense Advanced Research Projects Agency (DARPA) known for its risk-taking and innovation, called the "Development Applications Research Institute" (DARI) to develop and apply innovative technologies to development problems. In all of these efforts, Congress might wish to consider enhancing the prominence of the STAS, and coordination among S&T leaders at OES, STAS, and OSTP.

Chapter 7 – The United States and Soviet Union signed the Strategic Arms Reduction Treaty in 1991; it entered into force in December 1994 and is due to expire in December 2009. The United States and Russia have held several meetings to discuss options for continuing their arms control relationship, but have not agreed on whether to extend START or how to replace it.

START counts each deployed ICBM, SLBM, bomber as a single delivery vehicle under the Treaty limit of 1,600 delivery vehicles and attributes an agreed number of warheads to each deployed delivery vehicle. This attribution rule provides the total number of warheads that count under the 6,000 warhead limit in the Treaty. To verify compliance with START, each side monitors the numbers and locations of ballistic missiles, launchers and heavy bombers deployed by the other country. The parties use a wide variety of means to collect information—or monitor—these forces and activities. Some of these monitoring systems, such as overhead satellites, operate outside the territories of the treaty parties. They also have also been required to exchange copious amounts of data on locations, operations, and technical characteristics of the treaty-limited items. This verification regime has allowed the parties to remain confident in each other's compliance with the Treaty.

The United States and Russia began to discuss their options for arms control after START expired in mid-2006. They have, however been unable to agree on a path forward. Neither side wants to extend START in its current form, as some of the Treaty's provisions have begun to interfere with some military programs on both sides. Russia wants to replace START with a new Treaty that would further reduce deployed forces while using many of the same definitions and counting rules in START. The United States initially did not want to negotiate a new treaty, but, under the Bush Administration, would have been willing to extend, informally, some of START's monitoring provisions. In 2008, the Bush Administration agreed to conclude a new Treaty, with monitoring provisions attached, but this Treaty would resemble the far less formal Strategic Offensive Reductions Treaty that the two sides signed in 2002. In December 2008, the two sides agreed that they wanted to replace START before it expired, but acknowledged that this task would have to be left to negotiations between Russia and the Obama Administration.

The United States and Russia could choose from a number of options for the future of their arms control relationship. They could allow START to lapse or they could extend START for five years. They could extend START, then amend it to ease some of the outdated provisions. They could negotiate a new Treaty, or they could pursue less formal arrangements to manage their nuclear forces. Moreover, if a new treaty included further reductions in nuclear weapons, it could use some START definitions and counting rules or the less formal Moscow Treaty declarations.

This report will be updated as needed.

Chapter 8 – This report discusses two potential roles the International Monetary Fund (IMF) may have in helping to resolve the current global financial crisis: (1) immediate crisis control through balance of payments lending to emerging market and less-developed countries and (2) increased surveillance of the global economy through better coordination with the international financial regulatory agencies.

Chapter 9 – The Office of Infrastructure Protection (OIP) in the Department of Homeland Security (DHS) has been developing and maintaining a National Asset Database. The Database contains information on over 77,000 individual assets, ranging from dams, hazardous materials sites, and nuclear power plants to local festivals, petting zoos, and sporting good stores. The presence of a large number of entries of the latter type (i.e. assets generally perceived as having more local importance than national importance) has attracted much criticism from the press and from Members of Congress. Many critics of the Database have assumed that it is (or should be) DHS's list of the nation's *most* critical assets and are concerned that, in its current form, it is being used inappropriately as the basis upon which federal resources, including infrastructure protection grants, are allocated.

According to DHS, both of those assumptions are wrong. DHS characterizes the National Asset Database not as a list of critical assets, but rather as a national asset inventory providing the 'universe' from which various lists of critical assets are produced. As such, the Department maintains that it represents just the first step in DHS's risk management process outlined in the National Infrastructure Protection Plan. DHS has developed, apparently from the National Asset Database, a list of about 600 assets that it has determined are critical to the nation. Also, while the National Asset Database has been used to support federal grant-making decisions, according to a DHS official, it does not drive those decisions.

In July 2006 the DHS Office of the Inspector General released a report on the National Asset Database. Its primary conclusion was that the Database contained too many unusual and out-of-place assets and recommended that those judged to be of little national significance be removed from the Database. In his written response to the DHS IG report, the Undersecretary of DHS did not concur with this recommendation, asserting that keeping these less than nationally significant assets in the Database gave it a situational awareness that will assist in preparing and responding to a variety of incidents.

Accepting the DHS descriptions of the National Asset Database, questions and issues remain. For example, the National Asset Database seems to have evolved away from its origins as a list of critical infrastructures, perhaps causing the differences in perspective on what the Database is or should be. As an inventory of the nation's assets, the National Asset Database is incomplete, limiting its value in preparing and responding to a wide variety of incidents. Assuring the quality of the information in the Database is important and a never-ending task. If DHS not only keeps the less than nationally significant assets in the Database but adds more of them to make the inventory complete, assuring the quality of the data on these assets may dominate the cost of maintaining the Database, while providing uncertain value. Finally, the information currently contained in the Database carries with it no legal obligations on the owner/operators of the asset. If, however, the Database becomes the basis for regulatory action in the future, what appears in the Database takes on more immediate consequences for both DHS and the owner/operators.

Chapter 10 – Concerns over financing federal elections have become a seemingly perennial aspect of our political system, long centered on the enduring issues of high campaign costs and reliance on interest groups for needed campaign funds. Rising election costs had long fostered a sense in some quarters that spending was out of control, with too much time spent raising funds and elections "bought and sold." Debate had also focused on the role of interest groups in campaign funding, especially through political action committees (PACs). Differences in perceptions of the campaign finance system were compounded by the major parties' different approaches. Democrats tended to favor more regulation, with spending limits and public funding or benefits a part of past proposals. Republicans generally opposed such limits and public funding.

The 1996 elections marked a turning point in the debate's focus, as it shifted from whether to further restrict already regulated spending and funding sources to addressing election-related activities largely or entirely outside federal election law regulation and disclosure requirements (i.e., soft money). While concerns had long been rising over soft money in federal elections, its widespread and growing use for so-called issue advocacy since 1996 raised questions over the integrity of existing regulations and the feasibility of any limits at all. Following 1996, reform supporters offered legislation whose primary goals were to prohibit use of soft money in ways that could affect federal elections and to bring election-related issue advocacy communications under federal regulation. In both the 105th and 106th Congresses, the House passed the Shays-Meehan bill, but the Senate failed to invoke cloture to allow a vote on the companion McCain-Feingold bill. The 106th Congress did, however, agree on an aspect of campaign reform, in passing P.L. 106-230, to require disclosure by certain tax-exempt political organizations organized under Section 527 of the Internal Revenue Code. Such groups exist to influence elections, but many had not been required to disclose financial activity (to the FEC or IRS).

In the 107th Congress, the Senate passed McCain-Feingold, as amended, and the House passed the companion Shays-Meehan bill, as amended. The Senate then passed the House bill, which was signed into law by President Bush as the Bipartisan Campaign Reform Act of 2002 — BCRA (P.L. 107-155), constituting the first major change to the nation's campaign finance laws since 1979.

In the 2004 elections, more than $400 million was raised and spent by "political organizations" organized under Section 527 of the Internal Revenue Code but outside of federal election law regulation. In response to this perceived circumvention of election law regulation, the 109th Congress has examined the role of 527 groups in federal elections, and the House has passed legislation to address it.

This report (formerly CRS Issue Brief IB87020) provides an overview of campaign finance law governing federal elections, issues raised in recent years by campaign finance practices, and recent legislative activity and proposals in Congress, with a focus on the current (109th) Congress.

Chapter 11 – American voters elect the President and Vice President of the United States indirectly, through an arrangement known as the electoral college system. The electoral college system comprises a complex mosaic of constitutional provisions, state and federal laws, and political party rules and practices.

Although the electoral college system has delivered uncontested results in 46 out of 50 presidential elections since it assumed its present constitutional form in 1804, it has been the subject of persistent criticism and frequent proposals for reform. Reform advocates cite several problems with the current system, including a close or multi-candidate election can result in no electoral college majority, leading to a contingent election in Congress; the current system can result in the election of a President and Vice President who received a majority of electoral votes, but fewer popular votes, than their opponents; the formula for assignment of electoral votes is claimed to provide an unfair advantage for less populous states and does not account for population changes between censuses; and the winner-take-all system used by most states does not recognize the proportional strength of the losing major party, minor party, and independent candidates. On the other hand, defenders assert that the electoral college system is an integral and vital component of federalism, that it has a 92% record of non-controversial results, and that it promotes an ideologically and geographically broad two-party system. They maintain that repair of the electoral college system, rather than abolition, would eliminate any perceived defects while retaining its overall strengths. Proponents of presidential election reform generally advocate either completely eliminating the electoral college system, replacing it with direct popular election, or repairing perceived defects in the existing system. The direct election alternative would replace the electoral college with a single, nationwide count of popular votes. That is, the candidates winning a plurality of votes would be elected; most proposals provide for a runoff election if no candidates received a minimum of 40% of the popular vote. Electoral college reform proposals include (1) the district plan, awarding each state's two at-large electoral votes to the statewide popular vote winners, and one electoral vote to the winning candidates in each congressional district; (2) the proportional plan, awarding electoral votes in states in direct proportion to the popular vote gained in the state by each candidate; and (3) the automatic plan, awarding all of each state's electoral votes directly on a winner-take-all basis to the statewide vote winners. Major reforms of the system can be effected only by constitutional amendment, a process that requires two-thirds approval by both houses of Congress, followed by ratification by three-fourths (38) of the states, usually within a period of seven years. For further information, please consult CRS Report RL32611, The Electoral College: How It Works in Contemporary Presidential Elections, by Thomas H. Neale, and CRS Report RL32612, The Electoral College: Reform Proposals in the 108th Congress, by Thomas H. Neale.

Chapter 12 – When Americans vote for a President and Vice President, they actually vote for presidential electors, known collectively as the electoral college. It is these electors, chosen by the people, who elect the chief executive. The Constitution assigns each state a number of electors equal to the combined total of its Senate and House of Representatives delegations; at present, the number of electors per state ranges from three to 55, for a total of 538, a figure which includes three electors for the District of Columbia. Anyone may serve as an elector, except for Members of Congress, and persons holding offices of "Trust or Profit" under the Constitution. In each presidential election year, a group (ticket or slate) of candidates for elector is nominated by political parties and other groups in each state, usually at a state party convention, or by the party state committee. It is these elector-candidates, rather than the presidential and vice presidential nominees, for whom the people vote in the election held on Tuesday after the first Monday in November (November 2, 2004).

In most states, voters cast a single vote for the slate of electors pledged to the party presidential and vice presidential candidates of their choice. The slate winning the most popular votes is elected; this is known as the winner-take-all, or general ticket, system. Maine and Nebraska use the district system, under which two electors are chosen on a statewide, at-large basis, and one is elected in each congressional district. A second alternative, the proportional system, would award electors to presidential tickets in direct proportion to the percentage votes they received in a particular state. Electors assemble in their respective states on Monday after the second Wednesday in December (December 13, 2004). They are pledged and expected, but not required, to vote for the candidates they represent. Separate ballots are cast for President and Vice President, after which the electoral college ceases to exist for another four years. The electoral vote results are counted and declared at a joint session of Congress, held on January 6 of the year succeeding the election. A majority of electoral votes (currently 270 of 538) is required to win. Constitutional amendments to abolish or reform the electoral college system are regularly introduced in Congress. For information on legislative activity in the current Congress, please see CRS Report RL32612, The Electoral College: Reform Proposals in the 108th Congress, by Thomas H. Neale.

A proposal to establish the proportional system in Colorado will appear on that state's ballot on November 2, 2004. If the voters of that state approve it, and if it is found to be constitutional, Colorado's electoral votes for the current election could be allocated according to this plan.

Chapter 13 – This report describes the four stages of the presidential election process: the pre-nomination primaries and caucuses for selecting delegates to the national conventions; the national nominating conventions; the general election; and voting by members of the electoral college to choose the President and Vice President. The report will be updated again for the 2004 presidential election.

Chapter 14 – The 12th Amendment to the Constitution requires that candidates for President and Vice President receive a majority of electoral votes (currently 270 or more of a total of 538) to be elected. If no candidate receives a majority, the President is elected by the House of Representatives, and the Vice President is elected by the Senate. This process is referred to as contingent election. It has occurred only twice since the adoption of the 12th Amendment in 1804: for President in 1825, and for Vice President in 1837. In the House, the President is elected from among the three candidates who received the most electoral votes. Each state casts a single vote for President, and a majority of 26 or more state votes is required to elect. In 1825, the House decided that a majority of votes of Representatives in each state was required to cast the state's vote for a particular candidate, or the state's vote would be forfeit for that round of voting. This and other decisions reached in 1825 would have precedent, but would not be binding in future contingent elections. In cases where a state has only one Representative, that Member decides the state vote. In the Senate, the Vice President is elected from among the two candidates for Vice President who received the most electoral votes, with each Senator casting a single vote. A majority of the whole Senate, 51 or more votes, is necessary to elect. The District of Columbia does not participate in contingent election of either the President or Vice President. Contingent election would be conducted by the newly elected Congress immediately following the joint session (held on January 6 of the year following a presidential election) that counts electoral votes. If the House is unable to elect a President by January 20 (when the new presidential and vice presidential terms begin), the Vice President-elect serves as Acting President until the impasse is resolved. If the Senate is unable to elect a Vice President by January 20, then the Speaker of the House serves as Acting President.

Chapter 15 – On May 9, 2007, President George W. Bush issued National Security Presidential Directive (NSPD) 51, which is also identified as Homeland Security Presidential Directive (HSPD) 20, on National Continuity Policy. The directive updates longstanding continuity directives designed to assure that governing entities are able to recover from a wide range of potential operational interruptions. Executive branch efforts to assure essential operations are similar to those that are broadly integrated into many private sector industries. Government continuity planning also incorporates efforts to maintain and preserve constitutional government, based on the assumption that certain essential activities typically provided by government must be carried out with little or no interruption under all circumstances.

Chapter 16 – The National Security Council (NSC) was established by statute in 1947 to create an interdepartmental body to advise the President with respect to the integration of domestic, foreign, and military policies relating to the national security so as to enable the military services and the other departments and agencies of the Government to cooperate more effectively in matters involving the national security. Currently, statutory members of the Council are the President, Vice President, the Secretary of State, and the Secretary of Defense; but, at the President's request, other senior officials participate in NSC deliberations. The Chairman of the Joint Chiefs of Staff and the Director of National Intelligence are statutory advisers. In 2007 the Secretary of Energy was added to the NSC membership.

The President clearly holds final decision-making authority in the executive branch. Over the years, however, the NSC staff has emerged as a major factor in the formulation (and at times in the implementation) of national security policy. Similarly, the head of the NSC staff, the National Security Adviser, has played important, and occasionally highly public, roles in policymaking. This report traces the evolution of the NSC from its creation to the present.

The organization and influence of the NSC have varied significantly from one Administration to another, from a highly structured and formal system to loose-knit teams of experts. It is universally acknowledged that the NSC staff should be organized to meet the particular goals and work habits of an incumbent President. The history of the NSC provides ample evidence of the advantages and disadvantages of different types of policymaking structures.

Congress enacted the statute creating the NSC and has altered the character of its membership over the years. Congress annually appropriates funds for its activities, but does not, routinely, receive testimony on substantive matters from the National Security Adviser or from NSC staff. Proposals to require Senate confirmation of the Security Adviser have been discussed but not adopted.

The post-Cold War world has posed new challenges to NSC policymaking. Some argue that the NSC should be broadened to reflect an expanding role of economic, environmental, and demographic issues in national security policymaking. The Clinton Administration created a National Economic Council tasked with cooperating closely with the NSC on international economic matters. In the wake of the 9/11 attacks, the George W. Bush Administration established a Homeland Security Council. Both of these entities overlap and coordinate with the NSC, but some observers have advocated more seamless organizational arrangements.

Chapter 17 – The State, Foreign Operations, and Related Programs appropriations legislation provides annual funding for almost all of the international affairs programs generally considered as part of the 150 International Affairs Budget Function (the major exception being food assistance). In recent years, the legislation has also served as a vehicle for Congress to place conditions on the expenditure of those funds, and express its views regarding certain foreign policy issues.

This report briefly discusses the legislation generally and then provides a short description of the various funding accounts as they appear in Division H, "Department of State, Foreign Operations, and Related Programs Appropriations Act, 2009," of the Omnibus Appropriations Act, 2009 (P.L. 111-8).

Chapter 18 – The budget resolution sets forth aggregate levels of spending, revenue, and public debt. It is not intended to establish details of spending or revenue policy and does not provide levels of spending for specific agencies or programs. Instead, its purpose is to create enforceable parameters within which Congress can consider legislation dealing with spending and revenue.

The spending policies in the budget resolution encompass two types of spending legislation: discretionary spending and direct (mandatory) spending. Discretionary spending is controlled through the appropriations process. Appropriations legislation is considered each fiscal year and provides funding for numerous programs such as national defense, education, and homeland security. Direct spending, alternately, is provided for in legislation outside of appropriations acts. Direct spending programs are typically established in permanent law and continue in effect until such time as revised or terminated by another law.

During the week of March 23, 2009, both the House Budget Committee and the Senate Budget Committee approved their respective versions of a FY20 10 budget resolution. The budget resolution establishes congressional priorities by dividing spending among the 20 major functional categories of the federal budget. These 20 categories do not correspond to the committee system by which Congress operates, and as a result these spending levels must be "crosswalked" to the House and Senate committees having jurisdiction over both discretionary and direct spending. These amounts are known as 3 02(a) allocations and hold committees accountable for staying within the spending limits established by the budget resolution.

Each Appropriations Committee is responsible for subdividing its 302(a) allocation among its 12 subcommittees. These allocations, referred to as 302(b) subdivisions, establish the maximum amount that each of the 12 appropriations bills can spend.

It is inevitable that Members will consider the impact on particular programs or agencies when they consider a budget resolution. While the budget resolution does not allocate funds among specific agencies or programs, congressional assumptions or desires underlying the amounts set forth in the functional categories are frequently communicated through the budget resolution. Report language accompanying the budget resolution, as well as certain provisions in the budget resolution, can sometimes express non-binding programmatic assumptions and desires.

Budget resolutions also often include procedural provisions such as reserve funds or reconciliation instructions. These provisions may also reflect underlying program assumptions or desires of Congress.

Chapter 19 – The Federal Deposit Insurance Corporation (FDIC) was established as an independent government corporation under the authority of the Banking Act of 1933, also known as the Glass- Steagall Act (P.L. 73-66, 48 Stat. 162, 12 U.S.C.), to insure bank deposits.

This report discusses recent actions taken by the FDIC in support of financial and housing markets, which include restoration of the Deposit Insurance Fund, the development of the Temporary Liquidity Guarantee Program, efforts to reduce foreclosures, and establishment of the proposed Public-Private Investment Fund. Legislation such as H.R. 786 (introduced by Representative Barney Frank); H.R. 1106, Helping Families Save Their Homes Act of 2009 (introduced by Representative John Conyers, Jr., with 24 co-sponsors); and S. 541, The Depositor Protection Act of 2009 (introduced by Senator Christopher Dodd with 12 co-sponsors) have also been introduced to increase the effectiveness of the FDIC's efforts to respond to recent market weaknesses.

Chapter 20 – At present, the United States has two main programs for temporarily importing low-skilled workers, sometimes referred to as guest workers. Agricultural guest workers enter through the H-2A visa program, and other guest workers enter through the H-2B visa program. Employers interested in importing workers under either program must first apply to the U.S. Department of Labor for a certification that U.S. workers capable of performing the work are not available and that the employment of alien workers will not adversely affect the wages and working conditions of similarly employed U.S. workers. Other requirements of the programs differ.

The 109th Congress revised the H-2B program in the FY2005 Emergency Supplemental Appropriations Act (P.L. 109-13). Among the changes, a temporary provision was added to the Immigration and Nationality Act (INA) to exempt certain returning H-2B workers from the H-2B annual numerical cap. The FY2007 Department of Defense authorization P.L. 109-364) extended this exemption through FY2007. Other bills before the 109th Congress proposed to make changes to the H2A program (S. 359/H.R. 884, H.R. 3857, S. 2087, Senate-passed S. 2611), the H-2B program (S. 278, H.R. 1587, S. 1438, S. 1918), and the "H" visa category generally (H.R. 3333), and to establish new temporary worker visas (S. 1033/H.R. 2330, S. 1438, S. 1918, H.R. 4065, Senate-passed S. 2611). Some of these bills also would have established mechanisms for certain foreign workers to become U.S. legal permanent residents (LPRs). None of these bills were enacted. President George W. Bush proposed a new, expanded temporary worker program in January 2004 when he announced his principles for immigration reform. In a May 2006 national address on comprehensive immigration reform, he reiterated his support for a temporary worker program.

Guest worker bills before the 110th Congress include proposals to reform the H2A program (S. 237/S. 340/H.R. 371, S. 1639, H.R. 1645) and the H-2B program (S. 1639), and to establish new temporary worker visas (S. 330, S. 1639, H.R. 1645). Some of these bills also would establish mechanisms for certain foreign workers to become LPRs.

The current discussion of guest worker programs takes place against a backdrop of historically high levels of unauthorized migration to the United States. Supporters of a large-scale temporary worker program argue that such a program would help reduce unauthorized immigration by providing a legal alternative for prospective foreign workers. Critics reject this reasoning and instead maintain that a new guest worker program would likely exacerbate the problem of illegal migration.

The consideration of any proposed guest worker program raises various issues, including how new program requirements would compare with those of the H-2A and H-2B programs, how the eligible population would be defined, and whether the program would include a mechanism for participants to obtain LPR status.

Chapter 21 – The Committee on Foreign Investment in the United States (CFIUS) is comprised of 12 members representing major departments and agencies within the federal Executive Branch. While the group generally operates in relative obscurity, the proposed acquisition of commercial operations at six U.S. ports by Dubai Ports World in 2006 placed the group's operations under intense scrutiny by Members of Congress and the public. Prompted by this case, some Members of the 109th and 110th Congresses have questioned the ability of Congress to exercise its oversight responsibilities given the general view that CFIUS's operations lack transparency. Other Members revisited concerns about the linkage between national security and the role of foreign investment in the U.S. economy. Some Members of Congress and others argued that the nation's security and economic concerns have changed since the September 11, 2001 terrorist attacks and that these concerns were not being reflected sufficiently in the Committee's deliberations. In addition, anecdotal evidence seemed to indicate that the CFIUS process is not market neutral, instead a CFIUS investigation of an investment transaction may be perceived by some firms and by some in the financial markets as a negative factor that adds to uncertainty and may spur firms to engage in behavior that is not optimal for the economy as a whole.

As a result of the attention focused on the Dubai Ports World transaction, Members of Congress introduced more than two dozen measures on foreign investment in the 109th Congress. These measures reflected various levels of unease with the broad discretionary authority Congress has granted CFIUS. In the 1st session of the 110th Congress, Congresswoman Maloney introduced H.R. 556, the National Security Foreign Investment Reform and Strengthened Transparency Act of 2007, on January 18, 2007. The measure was approved by the House Financial Services Committee on February 13, 2007 with amendments, and was approved with amendments by the full House on February 28, 2007 by a vote of 423 to 0. On June 13, 2007, Senator Dodd introduced S. 1610, the Foreign Investment and National Security Act of 2007. On June 29, 2007, the Senate adopted S. 1610 in lieu of H.R. 556 by unanimous consent. On July 11, 2007, the House accepted the Senate's version of H.R. 556 by a vote of 370-45 and sent the measure to the President.

Chapter 22 – Economic indicators confirm that the economy is in a recession. Historically, international migration ebbs during economic crises; e.g., immigration to the United States was at its lowest levels during the Great Depression. While preliminary statistical trends hint at a slowing of migration pressures, it remains unclear how the current economic recession will effect immigration. Addressing these contentious policy reforms against the backdrop of economic crisis sharpens the social and business cleavages and narrows the range of options.

Even as U.S. unemployment rises, some employers maintain that they continue to need the "best and the brightest" workers, regardless of their country of birth, to remain competitive in a worldwide market and to keep their firms in the United States. While support for increasing employment-based immigration may be dampened by the economic recession, proponents argue that the ability to hire foreign workers is an essential ingredient for economic growth.

Those opposing increases in foreign workers assert that such expansions—particularly during an economic recession—would have a deleterious effect on salaries, compensation, and working conditions of U.S. workers. Others question whether the United States should continue to issue foreign worker visas (particularly temporary visas) during a recession and suggest that a moratorium on such visas might be prudent.

The number of foreign workers entering the United States legally has notably increased over the past decade. The number of employment-based legal *permanent* residents (LPRs) grew from under 100,000 in FY1994 to over 250,000 in FY2005, and stood at 163,176 in 2007. The number of visas for employment-based *temporary* nonimmigrants rose from just under 600,000 in FY1994 to approximately 1.4 million in FY2007. In particular, "H" visas for temporary workers tripled from 98,030 in FY1994 to 424,369 in FY2007.

The Immigration and Nationality Act (INA) bars the admission of any alien who seeks to enter the U.S. to perform skilled or unskilled labor, unless it is determined that (1) there are not sufficient U.S. workers who are able, willing, qualified, and available; and (2) the employment of the alien will not adversely affect the wages and working conditions of similarly employed workers in the United States. The foreign labor certification program in the U.S. Department of Labor (DOL) is responsible for ensuring that foreign workers do not displace or adversely affect working conditions of U.S. workers.

In the 110th Congress, Senate action on comprehensive immigration reform legislation, which included substantial revisions to employment-based immigration, stalled at the end of June 2007 after an intensive floor debate. The House, however, did not act on comprehensive legislation in the 110th Congress. During his time in the Senate, President Barack Obama supported comprehensive immigration legislation that reformed employment-based immigration. Similar views have been expressed by Secretary of Homeland Security (and former Arizona Governor) Janet Napolitano.

The 111th Congress addressed one element of this issue in §1611 of P.L. 111-5, the American Recovery and Reinvestment Act of 2009, which requires companies receiving Troubled Asset Relief Program (TARP) funding to comply with the more rigorous labor market rules of H-1B dependent companies if they hire foreign workers on H-1B visas. This report does not track legislation and will be updated if policies are revised.

Chapter 23 – Given its relatively low savings rate, the U.S. economy depends heavily on foreign capital inflows from countries with high savings rates (such as China) to help promote growth and to fund the federal budget deficit. China has intervened heavily in currency markets to limit the appreciation of its currency, especially against the dollar. As a result, China has become the world's largest and fastest growing holder of foreign exchange reserves (FER). China has invested a large share of its FER in U.S. securities, which, as of June 2008, totaled $1,205 billion, making China the 2nd largest foreign holder of U.S. securities (after Japan). These securities include long-term (LT) Treasury debt, LT U.S. agency debt, LT U.S. corporate debt, LT U.S. equities, and short-term debt.

U.S. Treasury securities are issued to finance the federal budget deficit. Of the public debt that is privately held, about half is held by foreigners. As of December 2008, China's Treasury securities holdings were $727 billion, accounting for 23.6% of total foreign ownership of U.S. Treasury securities, making it the largest foreign holder of U.S. Treasuries (replacing Japan in September 2008).

Some U.S. policymakers have expressed concern that China might try to use its large holdings of U.S. securities, including U.S. public debt, as leverage against U.S. policies it opposes. For example, in the past, some Chinese officials reportedly suggested that China could dump (or threaten to dump) a large share of its holdings to prevent the United States from imposing trade sanctions against China over its currency policy. Other Chinese officials reportedly stated that China should diversify its investments of its foreign exchange reserves away from dollar-denominated assets to those that offer higher rates of returns. The recent global financial crisis has heightened U.S. concerns that China might reduce its U.S. asset holdings.

A gradual decline in China's holdings of U.S. assets would not be expected to have a negative impact on the U.S. economy (since it could be matched by increased U.S. exports and a lower trade deficit). However, some economists contend that attempts by China to unload a large share of its U.S. securities holdings could have a significant negative impact on the U.S. economy (at least in the short run), especially if such a move sparked a sharp depreciation of the dollar in international markets and induced other foreign investors to sell off their U.S. holdings as well. In order to keep or attract that investment back, U.S. interest rates would rise, which would dampen U.S. economic growth, all else equal. Other economists counter that it would not be in China's economic interest to suddenly sell off its U.S. investment holdings. Doing so could lead to financial losses for the Chinese government, and any shocks to the U.S. economy caused by this action could ultimately hurt China's economy as well.

The issue of China's large holdings of U.S. securities is part of a larger debate among economists over how long the high U.S. reliance on foreign investment can be sustained, to what extent that reliance poses risks to the economy, and how to evaluate the costs associated with borrowing versus the benefits that would accrue to the economy from that practice.

Versions of these chapters were also published in *Current Politics and Economics of the United States, Canada, and Mexico* Volume 10, published by Nova Science Publishers, Inc. They were submitted for appropriate modifications in an effort to encourage wider dissemination of research.

In: Economics, Political and Social Issues ...
Editor: Michelle L. Fergusson

ISBN: 978-1-61122-555-6
©2011 Nova Science Publishers, Inc.

SECURITY AND PROSPERITY PARTNERSHIP OF NORTH AMERICA: AN OVERVIEW AND SELECTED ISSUES[*]

M. Angeles Villarreal and Jennifer E. Lake

ABSTRACT

The Security and Prosperity Partnership of North America (SPP) is a three-country initiative that is intended to increase cooperation and information sharing in an effort to increase and enhance prosperity in the United States, Canada, and Mexico. The SPP was endorsed by the leaders of the three countries, but it is not a signed agreement or treaty and, therefore, contains no legally binding commitments or obligations. The goals of the prosperity components of the SPP are to increase cooperation and sharing of information in order to improve productivity, reduce the costs of trade, and enhance the quality of life. The goal of the security components of the SPP is to coordinate the security efforts undertaken by each of the three participating nations to better protect citizens from terrorist threats and transnational crime while promoting the safe and efficient movement of legitimate people and goods. Congressional interest in the SPP concerns possible implications related to national sovereignty, transportation corridors, cargo security and border facilitation.

BACKGROUND

The Security and Prosperity Partnership of North America (SPP) is a trilateral initiative, launched in March 2005, that is intended to increase cooperation and information sharing in an effort to increase and enhance prosperity in the United States, Canada, and Mexico. The SPP is a government initiative that was endorsed by the leaders of the three countries, but it is not a signed agreement or treaty and, therefore, contains no legally binding commitments or obligations. It can, at best, be characterized as an endeavor by the three countries to facilitate communication and cooperation across several key policy areas of mutual interest. Although the SPP builds upon the existing trade and economic relationship of the three countries, it is not a trade agreement and is distinct from the existing North American Free Trade Agreement (NAFTA). Some key issues for Congress regarding the SPP concern possible implications related to national sovereignty, transportation corridors, cargo security, and border security. These issues are discussed in various sections of the report.

---

[*] Excerpted from CRS Report RS22701, dated August 2, 2007.

On March 23, 2005, President George W. Bush met with former Prime Minister Paul Martin of Canada and former President Vicente Fox of Mexico in Waco, Texas to discuss a number of issues including trade and economic collaboration. A major outcome of the summit was the announcement of the SPP. The government fact sheet on the SPP states that the SPP "energizes other aspects of our cooperative relations, such as the protection of our environment, our food supply, and our public health."[1] The initial plan for the SPP was to establish a number of security and prosperity working groups in those two separate categories. The security working groups would be chaired by the Secretary of Homeland Security and the prosperity working groups would be chaired by the Secretary of Commerce.

WORKING GROUP PROPOSALS AND INITIATIVES

In June 2005, the SPP working groups offered their initial proposals to the North American leaders on how to accomplish the goals of the SPP. In their report, the working groups announced the completion of several proposals to increase collaborative efforts to improve certain sectors of the economy; develop higher standards of safety and health; and address environmental concerns. The proposals related to trade and commerce included a signed Framework of Common Principles for Electronic Commerce; liberalization of Rules of Origin; a Memorandum of Understanding between Canada and the United States to exchange information and cooperate on activities relating to consumer product safety and health; harmonization of the use of care symbols on textiles and apparel labeling; and a document clarifying each country's domestic procedures for temporary work entry of professionals under NAFTA.[2]

In March 2006, the three countries agreed to continue to advance the agenda of the SPP by focusing on five high priority initiatives: 1) increasing private sector engagement in the SPP through the North American Competitiveness Council; 2) advancing cooperation on avian and pandemic influenza management; 3) ensuring a secure and sustainable energy supply through the North American Energy Security Initiative; 4) developing a common approach to emergency management in all three countries; and 5) contributing to smart and secure borders by increasing collaboration on standards and processes.

PROSPERITY COMPONENTS OF THE SPP

Goals of the SPP in the area of prosperity are to increase cooperation and sharing of information in order to improve productivity, reduce the costs of trade, and enhance the quality of life. The three countries agreed to establish a series of working groups to "consult with stakeholders; set specific, measurable, and achievable goals and implementation dates; and identify concrete steps the governments can take to achieve these goals." The prosperity working groups were established to cover the following range of issue areas: 1) Manufactured Goods and Sectoral and Regional Competitiveness; 2) Movement of Goods; 3) Energy; 4) Environment; 5) E-Commerce & Information Communications Technologies; 6) Financial Services; 7) Business Facilitation; 8) Food and Agriculture; 9) Transportation; and 10) Health.[3]

SECURITY COMPONENTS OF THE SPP

The goal of the security components of the SPP is to coordinate the security efforts undertaken by each of the three participating nations to better protect citizens from terrorist threats and transnational crime while promoting the safe and efficient movement of legitimate people and goods. Working groups were established to address the security aspects of the SPP. The security working groups address three broad themes: (1) external threats to North America; (2) streamlined and secured shared borders; and (3) prevention and response within North America. Ten individual security working groups have been established to address specific portions of the security agenda and include traveler security; cargo security; border facilitation; aviation security; maritime security; law enforcement; intelligence cooperation; bio-protection; protection, preparedness and response; and science and technology.[4]

THE SPP AND MEMBER ECONOMIES

The SPP is not a trade agreement, nor a form of economic integration, and goes only as far as leading to some measure of regulatory harmonization among the United States, Canada, and Mexico. The SPP working groups are not contemplating further market integration in North America. Such a move would require a government approval process within each of the three countries. In the United States, such an agreement would require the approval of the U.S. Congress.

A free trade agreement (FTA), such as NAFTA, is the most common form of regional economic integration. Generally, in an FTA, member countries agree to eliminate tariffs and nontariff barriers on trade and investment within the specified free trade area. Under an FTA, each country maintains its own trade policies, including tariffs on trade outside the region.

In addition to FTAs, other forms of economic integration are customs unions, common markets, and economic unions. Such agreements sometimes imply a greater loss of autonomy over the parties' commercial policies and require longer and more complex negotiations and implementation periods than FTAs. Customs unions are agreements in which members conduct free trade among themselves and maintain a common trade policy towards non-members. These agreements require the establishment of a common external tariff and harmonization of external trade policies. Common markets are those in which member countries go beyond a customs union by eliminating barriers to labor and capital flows across national borders within the market. The European Union is the most prominent example of a common market. In economic unions, member countries merge their economies even further than common markets by establishing a common currency, and therefore a unified monetary policy, along with other common economic institutions. The 12 members of the European Union that have adopted the euro as a common currency is the most significant example of a group of countries that has moved forward from a customs union to an economic union.

Some proponents of economic integration in North America have maintained that the emergence of China and India in the global marketplace may be putting North America at a competitive disadvantage with other countries and that NAFTA should go beyond a free trade agreement. Some observers have written policy papers proposing that the U.S. government consider the possibility of forming a "NAFTA-Plus," a "North American Union," or even a common currency called the "Amero."[5] Critics of this level of economic integration believe that NAFTA has already gone too far and that it has harmed the U.S. economy and undermined democratic control of domestic policy-making.[6] Others suggest that the SPP may be more than an initiative to increase cooperation and that it could lead to the creation of a common market or economic union in North America.[7] However, as previously noted, if the United States were to potentially consider the formation of a customs union or common market with its North American neighbors, it would require approval by the U.S. Congress.

TRANSPORTATION CORRIDORS

One of the stated goals of the SPP is to improve the safety, security, and efficiency of the flow goods between the three countries. The majority of trade between the United States, Canada and Mexico is transported by land modes (truck, rail, and pipeline). U.S. freight trade with Canada and Mexico more than doubled in value between 1996 and 2006, growing from $419 billion in 1996 to $866 billion in 2006.[8] Trucks are the dominant mode for transporting goods between the United States. and its NAFTA partners, accounting for 62% ($534 billion) of the value, and 26% of the weight of total trade in 2006.[9] This growth in the volume of freight is placing and increasing burden on transportation systems, and particularly the road network.

Some observers contend that the SPP may ultimately lead to a so-called "NAFTA Superhighway" that would link the United States, Canada, and Mexico with a 'supercorridor'.[10] The federal government however, has stated that there are no plans to build a "NAFTA Superhighway," and that no super-corridor initiative of any sort is a part of the SPP.[11] Further, no legal authority exists and no funds have been appropriated to construct such a superhighway, nor are there current plans to seek such authority or funding.[12]

States regularly undertake highway construction and improvement projects independently of the SPP. As noted above, the nation's freight transportation system is being exposed to an increasing burden from cross-border trade.[13] States and localities undertake highway projects to address the impacts of this increasing burden on the roadways, particularly in border states. Planning for these projects along the border often requires consultation with the neighboring NAFTA partner, as expansions of port access roads, additional lanes and bigger plazas, impact the flow of traffic through the port, and therefore the flow of traffic entering the neighboring country. Among other efforts, the SPP Transportation Working Group is analyzing border trade and traffic flows to support border infrastructure planning and prioritization.

CARGO SECURITY AND BORDER FACILITATION

One of the central tensions in border management policy concerns how to design policies that facilitate the efficient entryof legitimate cargo while simultaneously ensuring that a sufficient level of security and scrutiny is applied to deny the entry of illegitimate cargo. Two of the ten SPP security working groups are devoted to cargo security and border facilitation. In the immediate aftermath of the terrorist attacks of September 11, 2001, the U.S. border was virtually closed. The U.S. Customs Service went to its highest state of alert and began searching every vehicle entering the U.S. from Canada and Mexico. Delays of up to 12 hours were experienced at some ports of entry in Michigan and New York.[14] Since 9/11, the U.S. government has undertaken a number of initiatives aimed at improving cargo security and the facilitation of legitimate or low-risk cargo. Programs such as the Free and Secure Trade (FAST) program (a joint U.S.-Canada, and U.S.-Mexico program), and the Customs-Trade Partnership Against Terrorism (C-TPAT) program (a public-private supply chain security initiative) are two well-known examples of post-9/11 initiatives that seek to provide increased security while also providing expedited customs-clearance to pre-vetted shipments.

One initiative being considered under the SPP is known as pre-clearance, which has long been in place at airports, but which has remained difficult to implement at the land border. A related concept is known as reverse inspections which is essentially preclearance conducted on both sides of the border. Under the reverse inspection scenario, U.S. customs officials would be stationed in Canada to process and clear cargo en-route to the U.S. before the cargo reaches the U.S. border. Similarly, Canadian customs officials would be stationed in the U.S. to process cargo en-route to Canada from the United States. Proponents of reverse inspections maintain that this process offers increased security because it would allow, for example, U.S. customs officers the opportunity to intercept high-risk cargo before the truck reaches the bridge or the booth at the on the U.S. side of the border. Critics of the reverse inspection proposal cite sovereignty issues as a primary obstacle, but there are a host of other issues including the different authorities held by each country's customs agencies, and a variety of different legal issues.[15]

Progress was made, under the U.S.-Canada Shared Border Accord and the SPP, towards developing a pilot program to test reverse inspections at two different land border ports along the U.S.-Canada border.[16] To date however, the pilots have not gone forward[17], and it is unclear whether or not the obstacles to reverse inspections can be overcome in the future.

REFERENCES

[1]   See Security and Prosperity Partnership of North America (SPP) website [*http://www.spp.gov/*].

[2]   Security and Prosperity Partnership of North America (SPP), *Report to Leaders,* June 2005.

[3]   SPP.GOV: A North American Partnership, "Prosperity Working Groups: Security and Prosperity Partnership of North America," [*http:// www.spp.gov*].

[4]   Government of Canada, "Security and Prosperity Partnership of North America: Working Groups," accessed at [*http://www.psp-spp.gc.ca/ overview/working_groups-en.aspx*].

[5]   U.S. Council of the Mexico-U.S. Business Committee, Council of the Americas, *A Compact for North American Competitiveness,* April 2005; Grubel, Herbert G., The Fraser Institute, *The Case for the Amero: The Economics and Politics of a North American Monetary Union,* September 1999.

[6]   Public Citizen, Global Trade Watch, *North American Free Trade Agreement,* see [*http://www.citizen.org*].

[7]   Corsi, Jerome R., *The Plan to Replace the Dollar with the 'Amero',* May 22, 2006.

[8] Bureau of Transportation Statistics, *Increased Trade Spurs Growth in North American Freight Transportation*, May, 2007, accessed at [*http://www. bts.gov/publications/ bts_special_report/2007_05/pdf/entire.pdf*].

[9] Ibid.

[10] See for example, Corsi, Jerome, *I-69: Yet Another NAFTA Superhighway*, accessed at [*http://www.humanevents.com/article.php?id=16966*]; or Schlafly, Phyllis, *The NAFTA Superhighway*, August 23, 2006, accessed at [*http://www.eagleforum.org/column/ 2006/aug06/06-08-23.html*]; or for a rebuttal ofsome of these claims see for example, Dine, Philip, "Superhighway myth feeds on fear," *St. Louis Post-Dispatch*, May 19, 2007.

[11] Security and Prosperity Partnership of North America, *Myths vs. Facts*, accessed at [*http://www.spp.gov/myths_vs_facts.asp*].

[12] Ibid.

[13] See, Bureau of Transportation Statistics, *Increased Trade Spurs Growth in North American Freight Transportation*, May, 2007, accessed at [*http:// www.bts.gov/publications/bts_special_report/2007_05/pdf/entire.pdf*].

[14] Remarks of Customs and Border Protection Commissioner Robert Bonner, September 12, 2004, at the Customs World London Summit, at [*http://www.cbp.gov/xp/cgov/ newsroom/commissioner/speeches_statements/archives/2004/0 9212004_customs_world.xml*]

[15] See, Tower, Courtney. "Pre-clearance scrapped after U.S. breaks of Canada talks," *Journal of Commerce Online*, April 27, 2007, citing the concerns of the Department of Homeland Security regarding the restrictions Canadian law would have placed on U.S. searches, investigations, and fingerprinting. See also, Nakashima, Ellen. "Fingerprint Dispute Dooms Border Site," *Washington Post*, May 24, 2007.

[16] U.S. Department of Homeland Security. "Security and Prosperity Partnership: Implementation Report-Security Agenda," *Fact Sheet*, June 27, 2005. Accessed at [*http://www.spp.gov/SECURITY_FACT_SHEET. pdf?d Name=fact_sheets*].

[17] Tower, Courtney. "Pre-clearance scrapped after U.S. breaks of Canada talks," *Journal of Commerce Online*, April 27, 2007.

In: Economics, Political and Social Issues ...
Editor: Michelle L. Fergusson

ISBN: 978-1-61122-555-6
©2011 Nova Science Publishers, Inc.

BORDER SECURITY: THE SAN DIEGO FENCE[*]

Blas Nuñez-Neto and Michael John Garcia

ABSTRACT

This report outlines the issues involved with DHS's construction of the San Diego border fence and highlights some of the major legislative and administrative developments regarding its completion.[1] Congress first authorized the construction of a 14-mile, triple-layered fence along the U.S.-Mexico border near San Diego in the Illegal Immigration Reform and Immigration Responsibility Act (IIRIRA) of 1996. By 2004, only nine miles had been completed, and construction was halted because of environmental concerns. The 109th Congress subsequently passed the REAL ID Act (P.L. 109-13, Div. B), which contained provisions to facilitate the completion of the 14-mile fence. These provisions allow the Secretary of Homeland Security to waive *all legal requirements* determined necessary to ensure expeditious construction of authorized barriers and roads. In September 2005, the Secretary used this authority to waive a number of mostly environmental and conservation laws. Subsequently, the Secure Fence Act of 2006 (P.L. 109-367) *removed* the specific IIRIRA provisions authorizing the San Diego fence and added provisions authorizing five stretches of two-layered reinforced fencing along the southwest border. While the specific authorization of the San Diego fence was deleted, the project appears permissible under a separate, more general authorization provision of IIRIRA. In the 110th Congress, S.Amdt. 1150, the Secure Borders, Economic Opportunity, and Immigration Reform Act of 2007, which has been proposed in the nature of a substitute to S. 1348, the Comprehensive Immigration Reform Act of 2007, would amend § 102 of IIRIRA to once again expressly authorize the construction of the San Diego fence.

BACKGROUND

The United States Border Patrol (USBP) is the lead federal agency charged with securing the U.S. international land border with Mexico and Canada. The USBP's San Diego sector is located north of Tijuana and Tecate, Mexican cities with a combined population of 2 million people, and features no natural barriers to entry by unauthorized migrants and smugglers.[2] As part of the "Prevention Through Deterrence" strategy, which called for reducing unauthorized migration by placing agents and resources directly on the border abutting population centers, in 1990 the USBP began erecting a physical barrier to deter illegal entries and drug smuggling in the San Diego sector using the broad powers granted to the Attorney General (AG) to control and guard the U.S. border.[3] The ensuing "primary" fence was

---

[*] Excerpted from CRS Report RS22026, dated May 23, 2007.

completed in 1993 and covered the first 14 miles of the border, starting from the Pacific Ocean, and was constructed of 10-foot-high welded steel.[4] This fence (and the subsequent three-tiered fence, see discussion below) was constructed with the assistance of the Department of Defense's (DOD's) Army Corps of Engineers.

According to the Bureau of Customs and Border Protection (CBP), the primary fence, in combination with various labor intensive USBP enforcement initiatives along San Diego border region (i.e., Operation Gatekeeper), proved to be quite successful but fiscally and environmentally costly.[5] For example, as undocumented aliens and smugglers breached the primary fence and attempted to evade detection, USBP agents were often forced to pursue the suspects through environmentally sensitive areas. It soon became apparent to immigration officials and lawmakers that the USBP needed, among other things, a "rigid" enforcement system that could integrate infrastructure (i.e., a multi-tiered fence and roads), manpower, and new technologies to further control the border region. The concept of a three-tiered fence system was first recommended by a 1993 Sandia Laboratories study commissioned by the Immigration and Naturalization Service (INS). The study concluded that aliens attempting to enter the United States from Mexico had shown remarkable resourcefulness in bypassing or destroying obstacles in their path, including the existing primary fence, and postulated that "[a] three-fence barrier system with vehicle patrol roads between the fences and lights will provide the necessary discouragement."[6] Congress responded to these enforcement needs, in part, with the passage of the Illegal Immigration Reform and Immigration Responsibility Act (IIRIRA) of 1996.[7] This comprehensive law, among other things, expanded the existing fence by authorizing the INS to construct a triple-layered fence along the same 14 miles of the U.S.-Mexico border near San Diego.

SECTION 102 OF IIRIRA — IMPROVEMENT
OF BARRIERS AT THE BORDER

Section 102 of IIRIRA concerns the improvement and construction of barriers at our international borders. As described later, several of the provisions in §102 were amended in the 109th Congress to facilitate the construction of the San Diego fence, as well as other border barriers. The following paragraphs, however, discuss §102 as originally passed in IIRIRA to provide a historical perspective and comparative analysis.

Section 102(a) appears to give the AG[8] broad authority to install additional physical barriers and roads "in the vicinity of the United States border to deter illegal crossings in areas of high illegal entry into the United States." The phrase *vicinity of the United States border* is not defined in the Immigration and Nationality Act (8 U.S.C. §1101 *et seq.*) or in immigration regulations. The section also does not stipulate what specific characteristics would designate an area as one of *high illegal entry*. This subsection has not been amended.

Section 102(b) — before its amendment in the Secure Fence Act of 2006 (P.L. 109367) — mandated that the AG construct a barrier in the border area near San Diego. Specifically, §102(b) directed the AG to construct a three-tiered barrier along the 14 miles of the international land border of the United States, starting at the Pacific Ocean and extending eastward. Section 102(b) ensured that the AG would build a barrier, pursuant to his broader authority in §102(a), near the San Diego area. Other non-amended provisions in §102(b) provide authority for the acquisition of necessary easements, require that certain safety features be incorporated into the design of the fence, and authorize an appropriation not to exceed $12 million.

Section 102(c) — before its amendment in the REAL ID Act as part of P.L. 109-13 — waived the Endangered Species Act (ESA) of 1973 (16 U.S.C. §§1531 *et seq.*) and the National Environmental Policy Act (NEPA) of 1969 (42 U.S.C. §§4321 *et seq.*), to the extent the AG determined necessary, in order to ensure expeditious construction of the barriers authorized to be constructed under §102.[9] The waiver authority in this provision appears to apply both to barriers that may be constructed *in the vicinity of the border* under §102(a) and to the barrier that is to be constructed near the San Diego area under §102(b).

SAN DIEGO SECTOR APPREHENSIONS

Apprehension statistics have long been used as a performance measure by the USBP. However, the number of apprehensions may be a misleading statistic for several reasons, including the data's focus on events rather than people[10] and the absence of reliable estimates for how many aliens successfully evade capture. These factors aside, however, apprehensions data remain the best way to gain a glimpse into the reality facing USBP agents and the trends in unauthorized migration along the border. As figure 1 shows, apprehensions remained stable during the early 1990s in the San Diego sector despite the construction of the "primary" fence in 1993.

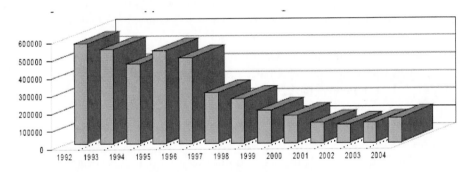

Figure 1. USBP Apprehensions, San Diego Sector, FY1992-FY2004.

After the IIRIRA's mandate for increased enforcement along the Southwest border in 1996, including construction of the triple-fence, apprehensions dropped rapidly in the San Diego sector in the late 1990s — from 480,000 in FY1996 to 100,000 in FY2002. The reduction in apprehensions was even more marked in the areas where fencing was constructed within San Diego sector. The USBP's Imperial Beach and Chula Vista stations saw their apprehensions decline from 321,560 in FY1993 to 19,035 in FY2004 — a reduction of 94% over the 12 year period. Although much of this reduction in apprehensions in those stations and in San Diego sector may have been due to the construction of the triple-fence, the sector also saw an increase in other resources that may account for part of the reduction. For example, the number of agents assigned to the San Diego sector increased significantly during this period — from 980 agents in 1993 to 2,274 in 1998.[11] Additionally, the number of underground sensors deployed in the San Diego sector almost tripled from 1993 to 1998, and the fleet of vehicles increased by over 150% over the same period.[12]

The increase in manpower and resources reflected the USBP's policy of re-routing unauthorized migration away from population centers to remote border regions where their agents have a tactical advantage over border-crossers. Other sectors, especially the remote Tucson sector in Arizona, saw apprehensions increase significantly in the late 1990s. Proponents of border fences point to the drastic reduction in apprehensions along the San Diego sector as tangible proof that these fences succeed in their goal of reducing cross-border smuggling and migration where they are constructed. Opponents attribute part of the decrease in apprehensions to the increase in manpower and resources in the sector and (pointing to the increase in apprehensions in less-populated sectors) contend that the fence only succeeds in re-routing unauthorized migration.

RECENT DEVELOPMENTS

The Controversy

By 2004, only nine miles of the 14 miles of fence authorized to be constructed had been completed. Two sections, including the final three-mile stretch of fence that leads to the Pacific Ocean, were not finished because of environmental concerns and litigation.[13] In order to finish the fence, the USBP proposed to fill a deep canyon known as "Smuggler's Gulch" with over 2 million cubic yards of dirt. The triple-fence would then be extended across the filled gulch. California's Coastal Commission (CCC), however, essentially halted the completion of the fence in February 2004. The CCC determined that the CBP had not demonstrated, among other things, that the project was consistent "to the maximum extent practicable" with the policies of the California Coastal Management Program — a state program approved under the federal Coastal Zone Management Act (CZMA) (16 U.S.C. §§1451-1464).[14] Specifically, the CCC was concerned with the potential for significant adverse effects on (1) the Tijuana River National Estuarine Research and Reserve; (2) state and federally listed threatened and endangered species; (3) lands set aside for protection within California's Multiple Species Conservation Program; and (4) other aspects of the environment. The CCC held that Congress did not specify a particular design in the IIRIRA and that the CBP failed to present a convincing argument that the less environmentally damaging alternative projects it rejected would have prevented compliance with the IIRIRA.

Congressional Action

Although the IIRIRA initially allowed DHS to waive two major environmental laws, it did not include the CZMA in its purview. Congress, accordingly, attempted to pass legislation to facilitate the completion of the fence. The 107th Congress, in §446 of the Homeland Security Act (P.L. 107-296), expressed its sense that completing the 14-mile border project should be a priority for the Secretary of DHS. The 108th Congress considered measures that would have allowed the Secretary of DHS to waive the CZMA and other environmental laws, but no bill passed both chambers.[15] However, the 109th Congress subsequently passed the REAL ID Act of 2005 (P.L. 109-13, Div. B), which authorized the Secretary of Homeland Security to waive *all legal requirements* determined necessary to ensure expeditious construction of barriers and roads authorized under IIRIRA § 102. Such waivers are effective upon publication in the Federal Register. Federal district courts are provided with exclusive jurisdiction to review claims alleging that the actions or decisions of the Secretary violate the U.S. Constitution, and district court rulings may only be reviewed by the Supreme Court. Because the REAL ID Act amended only the waiver provision of §102 of IIRIRA, the new waiver authority appears to apply to all the barriers that may be constructed under IIRIRA — that is, both to barriers constructed in the vicinity of the border and to the barrier that is to be constructed near the San Diego area.

The 109th Congress also passed the Secure Fence Act of 2006 (P.L. 109-367), which *removed* the specific provisions authorizing the San Diego fence and added provisions authorizing five stretches of two-layered reinforced fencing along the southwest border. CBP has estimated that this fencing will total roughly 850 miles.[16] While the specific authorization of the San Diego fence was deleted, the project appears permissible under the general fence authorization in §102(a) of IIRIRA. In the 110th Congress, S.Amdt. 1150, the Secure Borders, Economic Opportunity, and Immigration Reform Act of 2007, which has been proposed in the nature of a substitute to S. 1348, would amend § 102 of IIRIRA to once again expressly authorize the construction of the San Diego fence.

Waivers, Costs, and Construction

CBP, in conjunction with the Army Corps of Engineers and the National Guard, have now begun the process of acquiring the land required to finish building the San Diego border fence. On September 22, 2005, DHS published a *Federal Register* notice declaring the waiver of, in their entirety: (1) the NEPA; (2) the ESA; (3) the CZMA; (4) the Federal Water Pollution Control Act (33 U.S.C. §§1251 *et seq.*); (5) the National Historic Preservation Act (16 U.S.C. §§470 *et seq.*); (6) the Migratory Bird Treaty Act (16 U.S.C. §§703 *et seq.*); (7) the Clean Air Act (42 U.S.C. §§7401 *et seq.*); and (8) the Administrative Procedure Act (5 U.S.C. §§551 *et seq.*).[17] DHS predicts that the San Diego fence will have a total cost of $127 million for its 14-mile length when it is completed — roughly $9 million a mile.[18] Construction of the first 9.5 miles of fencing cost $31 million, or roughly $3 million a mile, while construction of the last 4.5 miles of fencing is projected to cost $96 million, or roughly $21 million a mile.[19] DHS is proposing to hire private contractors to expedite the construction of the remaining 4.5 miles of fencing; this fact, and the complex construction project of filling Smuggler's Gulch, may account for part of the difference in cost. The FY2006 DHS Appropriations Act (P.L. 109-90) provides $35 million for the construction of the border fence in San Diego. For FY2007, conferees for the DHS Appropriations Act (P.L. 109-295) recommended $30.5 million be allocated to the San Diego fence. Since 1990, Congress has also included language in DOD appropriations bills allowing the DOD to assist federal agencies in counter-drug activities, including the construction of fencing and roads to reduce the flow of narcotics into the country.[20]

REFERENCES

[1]   For more analysis of border fencing and other barriers, please see CRS Report RL33659, *Border Security: Barriers Along the U.S. International Border*, by Blas Nuñez-Neto and Michael John Garcia.

[2]   U.S. Department of Justice, Office of the Inspector General, *Operation Gatekeeper: An Investigation Into Allegations of Fraud and Misconduct*, July 1998.

[3]   See e.g., 8 U.S.C. §1103 (a)(5).

[4]   U.S. Government Accountability Office, *Border Control — Revised Strategy is Showing Some Positive Results*, GAO/GGD-95-30, January 31, 1995.

[5]   See California Coastal Commission, *W 13a Staff Report and Recommendation on Consistency Determination*, CD-063-03, October 2003, at 14-16 (stating that construction of the primary fence significantly assisted the USBP's efforts in deterring smuggling attempts via drive-throughs using automobiles and motorcycles). (Hereafter CCC *Staff Report*.)

[6]   Peter Andreas, "The Escalation of U.S. Immigration Control in the Post-NAFTA Era," *Political Science Quarterly*, vol. 113, no. 4, winter 1998-1999, p. 595.

[7]   See P.L. 104-208, Div. C. IIRIRA was passed as part of the Omnibus Consolidated Appropriations Act of 1997.

[8]   Although the law still cites to the Attorney General, the authorities granted by this section now appear to rest with the Secretary of DHS. See P.L. 107-296, §§102(a), 441, 1512(d) and 1517 (references to the Attorney General or Commissioner in statute and regulations are deemed to refer to the Secretary).

[9]   CBP never used this waiver authority and actually published a Final Environmental Impact Study and received a non-jeopardy Biological Opinion under the ESA. See Department of Homeland Security, Environmental Impact Statement for the Completion of the 14-mile Border Infrastructure System, San Diego, California (July 2003).

[10] If the same person is apprehended multiple times attempting to enter the country in one year, each apprehension will be counted separately by the USBP in generating their apprehension statistics. This means that apprehension statistics may overstate the number of aliens apprehended each year.

[11] CBP data provided to CRS on January 12, 2004.

[12] U.S. Citizenship and Immigration Services, "Operation Gatekeeper Fact Sheet," July 14, 1998, available at [*http://uscis.gov/graphics/publicaffairs/factsheets/opgatefs.htm*].

[13] A coalition of environmental groups had filed a lawsuit alleging that the government had not issued a proper environmental impact statement. The lawsuit was later dismissed because of the use of DHS's new waiver authority (see later discussion). Sierra Club v. Ashcroft, 04-CV-272 (S.D. Cal. February 10, 2004).

[14] See CCC, *Staff Report*, at 5-7. The CZMA requires federal agency activity within or outside the coastal zone that affects any land or water use or natural resource of the coastal zone to be carried out in a manner that is consistent to the maximum extent practicable with the policies of an approved state management program. 16 U.S.C. §1456(c).

[15] See, e.g., S. 2845 (108th Cong.), as passed by the House.

[16] From CBP Congressional Affairs, September 25, 2006.

[17] The waiver also includes all federal, state, or other laws and regulations deriving from the listed laws.

[18] See DHS FY2007 Congressional Budget Justifications.

[19] From the DHS FY2006 and FY2007 Congressional Budget Justifications.

[20] See P.L. 101-510, Div. A, Tit. X, §1004; codified, as amended, at 10 U.S.C. §374 nt. This authorization was recently extended through FY2011. See P.L. 109-364, Div. A, Tit. X, §1021.

In: Economics, Political and Social Issues …
Editor: Michelle L. Fergusson

STATUTORY OFFICES OF INSPECTOR GENERAL: PAST AND PRESENT[*]

Frederick M. Kaiser

ABSTRACT

Statutory offices of inspector general (OIG) consolidate responsibility for audits and investigations within a federal agency. Established by public law as permanent, nonpartisan, independent offices, they now exist in more than 60 establishments and entities, including all departments and largest agencies, along with numerous boards and commissions. Under two major enactments — the Inspector General Act of 1978 and its amendments of 1988 — inspectors general are granted substantial independence and powers to carry out their mandate to combat waste, fraud, and abuse.[1] Recent laws have added offices, funding for special operations, and law enforcement powers to OIGs in establishments. Recent initiatives have set up mechanisms to oversee the Gulf Recovery Program, while various legislative proposals in the 110th Congress are designed to strengthen the IGs' independence and establish new posts, among other matters.

RESPONSIBILITIES

The IGs' three principal responsibilities are:

- conducting and supervising audits and investigations relating to the programs and operations of the establishment;
- providing leadership and coordination and recommending policies for activities designed to promote the economy, efficiency, and effectiveness of such programs and operations, and preventing and detecting waste, fraud, and abuse in such programs and operations; and
- providing a means for keeping the establishment head and Congress fully and currently informed about problems and deficiencies relating to such programs and the necessity for and progress of corrective action.

---

[*] Excerpted from CRS Report 98-379, dated June 21, 2007.

AUTHORITY AND DUTIES

To carry out these purposes, IGs have been granted broad authority to: conduct audits and investigations; access directly all records and information of the agency; request assistance from other federal, state, and local government agencies; subpoena information and documents; administer oaths when taking testimony; hire staff and manage their own resources; and receive and respond to complaints from agency employees, whose confidentiality is to be protected. In addition, the Homeland Security Act of 2002 gave law enforcement powers to criminal investigators in offices headed by presidential appointees. IGs, moreover, implement the cash incentive award program in their agency for employee disclosures of waste, fraud, and abuse (5 U.S.C. 4511).

Notwithstanding these powers and duties, IGs are *not* specifically authorized to take corrective action themselves. Along with this, the Inspector General Act prohibits the transfer of "program operating responsibilities" to an IG. The rationale here is that it would be difficult, if not impossible, for IGs to audit or investigate programs and operations impartially and objectively if they were directly involved in carrying them out.

REPORTING REQUIREMENTS

IGs have reporting obligations regarding their findings, conclusions, and recommendations. These include reporting (1) suspected violations of federal criminal law directly and expeditiously to the Attorney General; (2) semiannually to the agency head, who must submit the IG report (along with his or her comments) to Congress within 30 days; and (3) "particularly serious or flagrant problems" immediately to the agency head, who must submit the IG report (with comments) to Congress within seven days. The CIA IG must also report to the Intelligence Committees if the Director or Acting Director is the focus of an investigation or audit. By means of these reports and "otherwise," IGs are to keep the agency head and Congress fully and currently informed. Other means of communication include testifying at congressional hearings; meeting with Members and staff of Congress; and responding to congressional requests for information and reports.

INDEPENDENCE

In addition to having their own powers (e.g., to hire staff and issue subpoenas), IG independent status is reinforced in other ways: protection of their budgets in the larger establishments, qualifications on their appointment and removal, prohibitions on interference with their activities and operations, a proscription on operating responsibilities, and fixing the priorities and projects for their office without outside direction. One exception to the IGs' rule occurs when a review is ordered in statute, while another is the contrary: in the few instances when an establishment head prevents or halts an audit or investigation. IGs, of course, may voluntarily conduct a review requested by the agency head, President, or congressional offices.

SUPERVISION

IGs serve under the "general supervision" of the agency head, reporting exclusively to the head or to the officer next in rank if such authority is delegated. With but a few specified exceptions, neither the agency head nor the officer next in line "shall prevent or prohibit the Inspector General from initiating, carrying out, or completing any audit or investigation, or from issuing any subpoena...." Under the IG Act, the heads of only six agencies — the Departments of Defense, Homeland Security, Justice, and Treasury, plus the U.S. Postal Service and Federal Reserve Board — may prevent the IG from initiating, carrying out, or completing an audit or investigation, or issuing a subpoena, and then only for specified reasons: to preserve national security interests or protect ongoing criminal investigations, among others. When exercising this power, the agency head must transmit an explanatory statement for such action within 30 days to the House Government Oversight and Reform Committee, the Senate Homeland Security and Governmental Affairs Committee, and other appropriate congressional panels. The CIA IG Act similarly allows the agency head to prohibit the inspector general from conducting investigations, audits, or inspections; but the director must then notify the House and Senate intelligence panels of his reasons, within seven days.

APPROPRIATIONS

Presidentially appointed IGs in the larger federal agencies — but not in designated federal entities (DFEs) — are granted a separate appropriations account (a separate budget account in the case of the CIA) for their offices. This restricts agency administrators from transferring or reducing IG funding once it has been specified in law.

APPOINTMENT AND REMOVAL

Under the Inspector General Act, IGs are to be selected without regard to political affiliation and solely on the basis of integrity and demonstrated ability in accounting, auditing, financial and management analysis, law, public administration, or investigations. The CIA IG, who operates under a different statute, is to be selected under these criteria as well as prior experience in the field of foreign intelligence and in compliance with the security standards of the agency. Presidentially nominated and Senate-confirmed IGs can be removed only by the President. When so doing, he must communicate the reasons to Congress.

However, IGs in the (usually) smaller DFEs are appointed by can be removed by the agency head, who must notify Congress in writing when exercising the power. In the Postal Service, by comparison, the governors appoint the inspector general, one of only two IGs with a set term (seven years) specified in law. The USPS IG, moreover, is the only one with qualified removal: only "for cause" and then with the written concurrence of at least seven of the nine governors. The other is in the Capitol Police (five years), who is appointed by and can be removed by the Capitol Police Board. Indirectly, the IG in the Peace Corps also faces an effective limited tenure, because all positions in the entity are restricted to a certain period (from five to 8½ years).

COORDINATION AND CONTROLS

Several presidential orders govern coordination among the IGs and investigating charges of wrongdoing by the IGs themselves and other top echelon officers. Two councils, now governed by E.O. 12993, are the President's Council on Integrity and Efficiency (PCIE), established in 1981, and a parallel Executive Council on Integrity and Efficiency (ECIE), in 1992. Chaired by the Deputy Director of the OMB, each is composed of the relevant statutory IGs plus officials from other agencies, such as the Federal Bureau of Investigation (FBI) and Special Counsel. Investigations of alleged wrongdoing by IGs or other high-ranking OIG officials (under the IG act) are governed by a special Integrity Committee, composed of PCIE and ECIE members and chaired by the FBI representative (E.O. 12993), with investigations referred to an appropriate executive agency or to an IG unit. An Intelligence Community Inspectors General Forum — a coordinative body of the inspectors general from the IC agencies along with observers from the FBI and several defense units — also exists.

ESTABLISHMENT

Statutory offices of inspector general been authorized in 64 current federal establishments and entities, including all 15 cabinet departments; major executive branch agencies; independent regulatory commissions; various government corporations and boards; and three legislative branch agencies. All but six of the OIGs — in GPO, LOC, Capitol Police, CIA, ODNI, and the Special Inspector General for Iraq Reconstruction (SIGIR) — are directly and explicitly under the 1978 Inspector General Act. Each office is headed by an inspector general, who is appointed in one of two ways:

1. 30 are nominated by the President and confirmed by the Senate in the federal establishments, including all departments and the larger agencies under the IG act specifically, plus the CIA under its separate statutory authority (table 1).
2. 34 are appointed by the head of the entity in the 28 designated federal entities — usually smaller boards and commissions — and in five other units, where the IGs operate under separate but parallel authority: SIGIR, ONDI, and three legislative agencies (i.e., GPO, LOC, and U.S. Capitol Police) (table 2).

**Table 1. Statutes Authorizing Inspectors General Nominated by the President and
Confirmed by the Senate, 1976-Present
(current offices are in bold)[a]**

Year	Statute	Establishment
1976	P.L. 94-505	Health, Education, and Welfare (now Health and Human Services)
1977	P.L. 95-91	Energy
1978	P.L. 95-452	Agriculture, Commerce, Community Services Administration,[b] Housing and Urban Development, Interior, Labor, Transportation, Environmental Protection Agency, General Services Administration, National Aeronautics and Space Administration, Small Business Administration, Veterans Administration (now the Veterans Affairs Department)
1979	P.L. 96-88	Education
1980	P.L. 96-294	U.S. Synthetic Fuels Corporation[b]
1980	P.L. 96-465	State[c]
1981	P.L. 97-113	Agency for International Development[d]
1982	P.L. 97-252	Defense
1983	P.L. 98-76	Railroad Retirement Board
1986	P.L. 99-399	U.S. Information Agency[b,c]
1987	P.L. 100-213	Arms Control and Disarmament Agency[b,c]
1988	P.L. 100-504	Justice,[e] Treasury, Federal Emergency Management Administration,[b,f] Nuclear Regulatory Commission, Office of Personnel Management
1989	P.L. 101-73	Resolution Trust Corporation[b]
1989	P.L. 101-193	Central Intelligence Agency[a]
1993	P.L. 103-82	Corporation for National and Community Service
1993	P.L. 103-204	Federal Deposit Insurance Corporation
1994	P.L. 103-296	Social Security Administration
1994	P.L. 103-325	Community Development Financial Institutions Fund[b]
1998	P.L. 105-206	Treasury Inspector General for Tax Administration[g]
2000	P.L. 106-422	Tennessee Valley Authority[h]
2002	P.L. 107-189	Export-Import Bank
2002	P.L. 107-296	Homeland Security[f]

a. All except the CIA IG are directly under the 1978 Inspector General Act, as amended.

b. CSA, Synfuels Corporation, USIA, ACDA, RTC, CDFIF, and FEMA have been abolished or transferred.

c. The State Department IG had also served as the IG for ACDA. In 1998, P.L. 105-277 transferred the functions of ACDA and USIA to the State Department and placed the Broadcasting Board of Governors and the International Broadcasting Bureau under the jurisdiction of the State IG.

d. The Inspector General in AID may also conduct reviews, investigations, and inspections of the Overseas Private Investment Corporation (22 U.S.C. 2199(e)).

e. In 2002, P.L. 107-273 expanded the jurisdiction of the Justice OIG to cover all department components.

f. P.L. 107-296, which established the Department of Homeland Security, transferred FEMA's functions to it and also granted law enforcement powers to OIG criminal investigators in establishments.

g. The OIG for Tax Administration in Treasury is the only case where a separate IG, under the 1978 IG Act, exists within an establishment or entity that is otherwise covered by its own statutory IG.

h. P.L. 106-422, which re-designated TVA as an establishment, also created, in the Treasury Department, a Criminal Investigator Academy to train IG staff and an Inspector General Forensic Laboratory.

**Table 2. Designated Federal Entities and Other Agencies with Statutory IGs Appointed
by the Head of the Entity or Agency
(current offices are in bold)[a]**

ACTION[b]	Interstate Commerce Commission[f]
Amtrak	Government Printing Office[a]
Appalachian Regional Commission	Legal Services Corporation
Board of Governors, Federal Reserve System	Library of Congress[a]
Board for International Broadcastingc	National Archives and Records Administration
Coalition Provisional Authority (in Iraq)a	National Credit Union Administration
Commodity Futures Trading Commission	National Endowment for the Arts
Consumer Product Safety Commission	National Endowment for the Humanities
Denali Commissionm	National Labor Relations Board
Corporation for Public Broadcasting	National Science Foundation
Election Assistance Commissionl	Office of Director of National Intelligencea[k]
Equal Employment Opportunity Commission	Panama Canal Commissiong
Farm Credit Administration	Peace Corps
Federal Communications Commission	Pension Benefit Guaranty Corporation
Federal Deposit Insurance Corporationd	Securities and Exchange Commission
Federal Election Commission	Smithsonian Institution
Federal Home Loan Bank Boarde	Special IG for Iraq Reconstruction[a]
Federal Housing Finance Boarde	Tennessee Valley Authority[h]
Federal Labor Relations Authority	U.S. Capitol Policea[j]
Federal Maritime Commission	U.S. International Trade Commission
Federal Trade Commission	U.S. Postal Service[i]

a. All these agencies — except SIGIR, ODNI, GPO, LOC, and Capitol Police — are considered "designated federal entities" and placed directly under the 1978 IG Act by the 1988 Amendments and subsequent acts. The CPA was dissolved in mid-2004 and its IG was converted to SIGIR.

b. In 1993, P.L. 103-82 merged ACTION into the new Corporation for National and Community Service.

c. The BIB was abolished by P.L. 103-236 and its functions transferred to the International Broadcasting Bureau within USIA, which was later abolished and its functions transferred to the State Department.

d. In 1993, P.L. 103-204 made the IG in FDIC a presidential appointee, subject to Senate confirmation.

e. In 1989, P.L. 101-73 abolished the FHLBB and placed the new FHFB under the 1988 IG Act.

f. The ICC was abolished in 1995 by P.L. 104-88.

g. The Panama Canal Commission, replaced by the Panama Canal Commission Transition Authority, was phased out with the transfer of the Canal to the Republic of Panama (22 U.S.C. 3611).

h. P.L. 106-422 re-designated TVA as a federal establishment.

i. In 1996, the U.S. Postal Service Inspector General post was separated from the Chief Postal Inspector. The separated IG is appointed by, and can be removed only by, the governors.

j. The Legislative Branch Appropriations Act, FY2006 (P.L. 109-55) added IGs to LOC, following the IG Act of 1978 closely, and the Capitol Police, whose IG has specialized responsibilities.

k. P.L. 108-458 grants the Director of National Intelligence (DNI) full discretion to create and construct an OIG in his Office (based on provisions in the IG Act). This occurred in 2006. ODNI, *Report on the Progress of the DNI in Implementing "the Intelligence Reform Act of 2004,"* May 2006; and House Select Committee on Intelligence, *Intelligence Authorization Act for FY 2007* (H.Rept. 109-411).

l. P.L. 107-252, the Help America Vote Act of 2002.

m. P.L. 105-277 (42 U.S.C. 3121), Denali Commission Act of 1998, as amended.

Table 3. Tabulation of Existing Federal Establishments, Entities, or Agencies with IGs Authorized in Law

Controlling statute	IGs nominated by President and confirmed by Senate	IGs appointed by head of entity or agency	Total
1978 IG Act, as amended	29	29	58
Other statutes	1a	5b	6
Total	30	34	64

a. CIA Inspector General.
b. SIGIR, GPO, LOC, U.S. Capitol Police, and ODNI inspectors general.

RECENT INITIATIVES

Initiatives in response to the 2005 Gulf Coast Hurricanes arose to increase OIG capacity and capabilities in overseeing the unprecedented recovery and rebuilding efforts: an initial coordinating team of IGs or deputies from affected agencies has evolved into the Homeland Security Roundtable, chaired by the IG in DHS; a Hurricane Katrina Contract Fraud Task Force, established by the Justice Department, includes relevant inspectors general; an official in the DHS office has been designated to direct its effort here; and an additional $15 million for the OIG in Homeland Security was approved (P.L. 109-62). Other proposals included setting up a long-term task force or coordinative mechanism of IGs from relevant agencies (H.R. 3737 and 3810, 109th Cong.), while another would have established an IG post in the office of the Architect of the Capitol (H.R. 5521, 109th Cong.). Other initiatives have called for consolidating DFE OIGs under one or more new presidentially appointed IGs or under a related establishment office (GAO-02-575) and granting law enforcement authority to DFE IGs.

Separate recommendations have arisen in the 110th Congress. H.R. 785 and S. 461 would establish an inspector general for the Judicial Branch, appointed by and removable by the Chief Justice for a renewable four-year term. H.R. 401 would create an IG in the Washington Metropolitan Area Transit Authority, while H.R. 2771, Legislative Branch Appropriations Act, 2008, would do so in the Architect of the Capitol office. A far-reaching proposal (H.R. 928), advanced to increase the IGs' independence and powers, calls for sending initial OIG budget estimates to Congress and OMB for later comparison with the final amount in the President's budget submission, removing an IG only for "cause," setting a term of office for IGs (seven years with possible reappointment), establishing a Council of Inspectors General for Integrity and Efficiency in statute (thus, replacing the PCIE and ECIE), revising the pay structure for IGs, allowing for IG subpoena power "in any medium," and granting law enforcement powers to qualified IGs in designated federal entities. Another proposal (S. 680) would increase the pay level for presidentially appointed IGs, prohibit cash awards or bonuses for them, set qualifications for the appointment and removal of IGs in designated federal entities, and grant IGs subpoena power in any medium.

REFERENCES

[1]   5 U.S.C. Appendix covers all but six of the statutory OIGs. See U.S. President's
        Council on Integrity and Efficiency, *A Strategic Framework, 2005-2010*
        [*http://www.ignet.gov*]; Frederick Kaiser, "The Watchers' Watchdog: The CIA
        Inspector General," *International Journal of Intelligence (*1989); Paul Light,
        Monitoring Government: Inspectors General and the Search for Accountability (1993);
        Government Accountability Office, *Inspectors General: Office Consolidation and
        Related Issues*, GAO-02-575, and *Highlights of the Comptroller General's Panel on
        Federal Oversight and the Inspectors General,* GAO-06-931SP; U.S. House
        Subcommittee on Government Efficiency, *25th Anniversary of the Inspector General
        Act*, and *Improving IG Functionality and Independence*, hearings (2003 and 2004); U.S.
        House Subcommittee on Government Management, Organization, and Procurement,
        Inspectors General: Independence and Accountability, hearing (2007); and Peter Stone,
        "The Watchdogs," *National Journal,* May 12, 2007, pp. 30-35.

In: Economics, Political and Social Issues ...
Editor: Michelle L. Fergusson

ISBN: 978-1-61122-555-6
©2011 Nova Science Publishers, Inc.

SOCIAL JUSTICE AND THE NOTION
OF A RIGHT TO HEALTH CARE

Harry Moore[*]
St. Gregory's University
Shawnee, OK 74804, USA

ABSTRACT

This paper seeks to consider the role of deliberative social justice, how we think about health care, and the general presumption that there exists some unspoken, natural right or rights to the services and goods provided by the health care scheme within the United States. While it is perhaps possible to establish such a theoretical right, at present the current system within the U.S. excludes any such notion. It is also the intent of this article to support the claim, from a utilitarian position, that rights do not legitimately exist apart from the recognition and willingness of the general populace to support such a right, and the existence of reciprocal moral responsibility by the individual who exercises the right. Faced with significant inequalities in the distribution of health care services and resources, in the United States, there is an inclination to assert that a violation of basic human rights is involved by such a denial or constraint. The attempt to adjudicate the notions of social justice with the alleged notion of a right to health care is an ever present problem and reality that will be examined. While numerous political promises and various proposed business schemes may present hopeful solutions, the examination and clarification of the idea of a perceived right and the associative obligations must be examined in order to attempt to qualify the notion of such a right.

INTRODUCTION

This is a paper on how we think about health care and the general presumption that there exists some unspoken natural right or rights associated to the services and goods provided by the health care scheme within the United States. In moral and political philosophy, rights have traditionally been understood as entitlements a person may have to some service, good, or liberty.[1] Faced with significant inequalities in the distribution of health care services and resources, in the United States, there is an inclination to assert that a violation of basic human rights is involved by such a denial or constraint. While any theoretical consideration may

---

[*] E-mail: hmoore@stgregorys.edu
[1] Tom L. Beauchamp and Ruth R. Faden, "The Right to Health and the Right to Health Care," *The Journal of Medicine and Philosophy*, vol. 4, no. 2 (1979): 119.

present some possible options to the resolution of conflicts and rights, it is only in a tangible context that the extent of the obligation associated with a particular right can be determined.

There is also a problem associated with the phrase "right to health care." This cliché encompasses a cluster of moral concerns often used to solicit support of some social program; but it is also a phrase that contains no clear sense of a moral foundation for entitlement.[2] If health care, or access to the health care system, is a "right," regardless of ability to pay for services rendered, then can it be considered a more legitimate right than the need for the basic necessities of life such as food, clothing, and shelter? Clearly, health care is a need, but the question of whether it is a right is questionable.

Accordingly, while it may be acknowledged that individuals have rights beyond "life and liberty such rights do not follow from some ideal conception of societal justice or humanity, but from a shared conception of social goods and a deliberative notion of social justice.[3] For the notion of "distributive justice has as much to do with being and doing as with having, as much to do with production as with consumption . . . [and the] multiplicity of goods is matched by a multiplicity of distributive procedures, agents and criteria."[4]

Though the design and claims of this article are stated primarily in terms of utilitarianism, admittedly, there are implicit elements of communitarian (social contract, deontological, and rights theories that have been incorporated. While the inclusion of these theoretical components may provide an impure form of a utilitarian theory, it is acknowledged that there are and will be decisions and standards of conduct independent of, or seemingly in conflict with, classical utilitarianism, or any other theory for that matter. And while the major premises are utilitarian, it is my hope to retain some features of these theoretical constructs and reconcile them with a more communitarian outlook.

Such a commingling of theoretical elements, under the claim of being utilitarian, may seem ambiguous. However, it is my contention that such inclusions only serve to enhance the plausibility of this sphere-specific form of utilitarianism and the adjudication of rights. Additionally, while there are components of other theories included the basis of utilitarianism still serves as the foundation by which all other actions, decisions, and values are judged.

CONCERNING THE NOTION OF RIGHTS

As Jeremy Bentham argued, a "Right . . . is the child of law: from *real* laws come *real* rights; but from *imaginary* laws, from laws of nature . . . come *imaginary* rights."[5] The misconception of the legitimacy of a right(s) seems to come from the failure to establish a clearly defined set of principles associated with an identified right relevant to a particular sphere, system or institution. Rather, claims of a right often come from the individual's desire or assumption of having a right to that particular thing, good, or service, or merely serve as an appeal to normative or ideal values.

---

[2] H. Tristram Engelhardt, "Rights to Health Care: A Critical Appraisal," *The Journal of Medicine and Philosophy*, vol. 4, no. 2, (1979): 113.

[3] Walzer, xv.

[4] Ibid., 3.

[5] Jeremy Bentham, *Anarchical Fallacies*, ed. John Browning, Vol. 2 (New York: Russell and Russell, 1962; as reproduced from the 1843 edition), 220.

Benevolent interests in justice are sustained in part because of inequalities among persons.[6] In the sphere of health care these inequalities become even more pronounced by virtue of the natural and social lotteries. The natural lottery, or those events that occur outside of human responsibility, for example, may bring good health to one person and poor health to another. Some individuals may be born healthy and remain so for most of their lives, and others may be born with genetic or congenital diseases which create life-long health problems. Then there are those who by virtue of an accident or serious illness become dependent on even more of the services and goods provided by a health care system.[7]

In the social lottery, some individuals have better fortune than others, that is, some have more advantages, more money, or more influence, and others are less fortunate, have less money, no influence, or become victim of the malevolent actions of others. Regardless of the circumstances, some will have greater need for health care services and resources, some will be able to afford more services, and some will have more choices regarding which doctor to see and which hospital to enter and others will not.

While the notion of specific rights and obligations of beneficence may presuppose a particular moral viewpoint, the idea of need does not necessarily create a right to particular services or goods. Only by the recognition and willingness of others to meet such a need, and the validation by institutional, governmental, and even legal support, can a right be considered legitimate.

Rights in this context, then, are contingent upon a balancing of individual need and social interests or the general willingness to support such a claim.[8] It must be realized that in this attempt at social equilibrium or a notion of social justice, claims of rights are prima facie rather than absolute, that is, while a particular right may be valid, it may also be overridden by more demanding claims.[9]

For example, if a hospital were evaluating the need to implement a new program that would allow for cardiac bypasses to be performed or use the money for existing services, competing needs would be a factor in the utility equation. If such a service exits at a nearby hospital, or even in a neighboring city, duplication of services may not be warranted. The decision not to offer such a program does not negate the right of an individual to receive a needed heart bypass, it only creates a potential inconvenience of location.

Conversely, the need for the immunization of children would necessitate the implementation of a program rather than the evaluation of a program. Furthermore, while not all parents/guardians may be able to afford such inoculations, the state may provide and cover the cost of the needed or required immunizations in seeking the best interest of the general community. Of course such a service is not "free" or without cost to someone.

The reimbursement may be indirectly realized by citizens of that state through taxation, and the funding is further supplemented by various state and federal programs such as Medicaid, wellness clinics and public health clinics, for those that cannot afford the cost and or do not have private health insurance.

---

[6] H. Tristram Engelhardt, Jr., *The Foundations of Bioethics,* Second Edition, (New York: Oxford University Press, 1996), 339.

[7] Ibid., 339-340.

[8] Beauchamp and Faden, 122.

[9] Ibid.

TECHNOLOGY, ECONOMICS AND ETHICS

Given the whirlwind advancement of health care over the past fifty years the tumultuous progress may best be epitomized in a written statement from Wilbur Wright. Referring to the multiplicity of events he experienced while flying the first airplane, he writes, "With the machine's moving forward, the air flying backward, the propellers turning sideways and nothing standing still, it seemed almost impossible to find a starting point from which to trace various simultaneous reactions."[10] Medical knowledge, procedures, pharmaceuticals, and technology continue to advance, driving up costs at astronomical rates. Expectations and demands by health care consumers continue to escalate, and the administration of the system seems out of control.

The sacrifice of a community or nation's infrastructure and well-being in the distribution of these created goods, for the sake and sanctity of the notion of autonomy and the individual's perceived right to this or that, in this case health care, is a no-win situation.[11] Deliberative justice in the distributive process calls for not only an ongoing discussion of how to address the problem of distribution but some social controls and "defined limits of freedom"[12] within the particular sphere of goods or services being distributed. The intersection of autonomy and interdependence, individual rights and mutual obligations, calls for a "natural sensibility which impels us to see ourselves in relationships of interdependence with other people and take responsibility both for our own lives and for what happens to others as well."[13] In this framework an individual's obligations precede any rights or notions of entitlement and conversely, rights presuppose obligations.

"All goods with which distributive justice is concerned are social goods.... [which] have shared meanings, because [the] conception and creation [of these goods] are [defined by] social processes."[14] It is from these social processes that social goods and personal qualities have their own spheres of operation, in which they work their effects "freely, spontaneously, and legitimately."[15]

It is from this notion that Spheres of Justice, by Michael Walzer, has been a major influence. I agree with his notion of a "distributive logic" which claims that "[health] care should be proportionate to illness and not to wealth."[16] I do, however, disagree with his view that "no single principle of distributive justice can govern all social goods and their distribution."[17] The principle of utility may serve as the benchmark by which all distributive actions, values, and consequences are judged.

However, even with the supposition that the traditional view of utilitarianism offers a standard for all areas of life, it fails to take into account the specific rights and responsibilities connected with the area of life being evaluated. The idea of examining a sphere or

---

[10] This quote comes from the Wilbur Wright exhibit at the Aerospace Museum, San Diego, California.

[11] Willard Gaylin and Bruce Jennings, *The Perversion of Autonomy: The Proper Uses of Coercion and Constraints in a Liberal Society* (New York: The Free Press, 1996), 6.

[12] Ibid., 7.

[13] Ibid., 4.

[14] Walzer, 7.

[15] Ibid., 19. It is from this statement that the notion of spheres of utility came to fruition.

[16] Ibid., 86.

[17] Tom L. Beauchamp and James F. Childress, *Principles of Biomedical Ethics*, Fourth Edition (Oxford: Oxford University Press, 1994), 338. (See Walzer's discussion in *Spheres*, pp. 3-10).

environment of utility, in this case, the utility associated with the sphere of health care, allows for the good to be more easily defined and translated into some semblance of success.

While classical utilitarianism is basically defined as achieving the "greatest good or happiness," it is further equated with achieving or experiencing the greatest "good," over the potential "bad," for the greatest number. The general concept of the "greatest good for the greatest number," however, is too obscure when not defined from a particular or intentional point of utility to be achieved.

Even when a particular scenario is presented, for example, sacrificing one individual for the benefit of several others, this context still omits two major elements. One is that while it is true that the initial defining of utilitarianism must start with the general and proceed to the more specific, the sphere of life or context in which the situation may take place has been ignored.

Second, while social utility is of primary importance in a utilitarian theory, the individual need not be sacrificed for the greater good or net benefit. The reason is, the scope of moral action is not fixed but fluid and based on a multiplicity of events, with varying degrees of moral interest which are relevant only to the participants' proximity of the sphere of utility being examined.

Conversely, one primary weakness of classical utilitarianism is that it ignores, or at least does not do full justice to, the notion of personal responsibility or sense of obligation. If the only duty or requirement is to produce some obscure sense of the "greatest good" the question of how the good is identified and who is to have the good remains unanswered by the traditional utilitarian construct.[18] Even with the assumption that the "greatest good" applies to any and all areas of life, the good or value intended must still be defined.

Another problem with the classical view of utilitarianism is that it is too broad in its scope of defining "the greatest good" or realm of value. But, to narrow the area of value to a particular sphere or environment allows for the utility and associated rights in question to be identified, the value measured, and the success more easily interpreted. Again, it is here that Walzer's notion of social goods having their own spheres of operation[19] comes into play, when identified with the rights contained within the particular sphere or environment of utility being evaluated.

It is my contention, therefore, that the "greatest good," in association with specific rights, must necessarily be defined or examined from within a particular sphere or environment, which serves as the focal point in which the theory is grounded. While maintaining the general premise of utilitarianism, that is, "the greatest good for the greatest number," the notion is not from some nebulous concept or subjective position about life, fairness, or feelings in general. This sphere-specific position also acknowledges and defines the "rights" of the individual within the particular sphere being considered, in this case, the sphere of health care.

To put it another way, what kind of algorithm can be applied in order to know if the results or the desire to achieve "the greatest good" is successful? For example, the value of any medical activity is to restore some semblance of health; it is not the thing (i.e., the

---

[18] Ross, W.D., "What Makes Right Acts Right?," *Ethical Theory: Classical and Contemporary Readings*, Louis P. Pojman, ed., (California: Wadsworth Publishing Co., 1989), 256.

[19] Walzer, 7.

medicine, test, procedure, or surgery) itself which defines the "good" or value, but it is the sphere or environment within a particular context which gives or defines the value.

Another example might be the availability or use of a CT scan (Computerized Axial Tomography) machine. The utility or value will be determined by the sphere or environment in which it is used, that is, it is the identified sphere or context which determines the value. Suppose there are three circumstances or arenas: one involves a person, the next involves the legal system, and the last involves a business. How will the value or utility be determined?

For the individual brought into the emergency room, after being injured in a motor vehicle accident, the CT scan may be of benefit in determining internal injuries not visible by routine x-rays. In this case, while the CT scan is important, it is not the machine that has value, but the results it produces. These results allow for the identification of certain sustained injuries, which provides the physician with the means to better know what treatment is needed, which, in turn, will help the person to regain a state of health.

From the perspective or sphere of the legal system, the use or availability of a CT scan machine has no value, unless it happens to be relevant to a particular case involving malpractice, which could have been avoided by the results produced by the test. However, if such a test was not warranted, then it is of no consequence to the value or sphere of litigation.

The last arena mentioned, the business environment or technological advancement, will have a totally separate means of determining the utility, based on the production of a particular product, good, or service, in this case, the production of the CT scan machine. If a particular company produces the CT machine, then the value, success, or utility to be measured will be the number of machines sold, not the number of CT scans, or the reason it was or was not used.

While there are some goods that are needed absolutely, such as medical care, "there is no good such that once we see it, we know how it stands vis-à-vis all other goods and how much we owe to one another. The nature of the need is not self-evident."[20] But, such need is somewhat determinable by virtue of the identified or particular sphere of utility, with its different conceptions, associated rights and experiences. This, in turn, leads to "different patterns of provision"[21] and notions of distributive justice related to that specific sphere of goods or services needed or in demand.

"Despite the inherent forcefulness of the word, needs are elusive. People don't just have needs, they have ideas about their needs;"[22] they have degrees and various priorities associated with their perception of need. These degrees and priorities are related not only to the concept of human nature but also to the history and culture of a particular society.[23] "Since resources are always scarce, hard choices have to be made.. . ;"[24] and while such choices are subject to philosophical elucidation, the idea of a need or a communal commitment to meet such a need does not yield any clear calculation of degrees or priorities. Clearly, every need cannot be met to the same degree, "or any need to the ultimate degree,"[25] but, by examining needs and the goods or services associated with those needs, in relation to

---

[20] Ibid., 65.
[21] Ibid.
[22] Ibid., 66.
[23] Ibid.
[24] Ibid.
[25] Ibid., 66-67.

the specific sphere in which the needs exist, perhaps a more precise form of distributive justice may be deliberatively attained.

Furthermore, it seems that the advancement of technology perpetuates a false notion of a right to the services and goods within the health care system; even at the expense of others. What many consumers seem to fail to realize is that,

> The role of medical care in preventing sickness and premature death is secondary to that of other influences; yet healthcare funding is based on the premise that medical care plays the major role. The public concept of health is that intervention by the doctor and early discovery of disease will prevent or cure disease, when in fact health is determined mainly by the lifestyles people choose to follow.[26]

Currently, there are more than two million Americans who lose their health care coverage each month; some will get it back, but the numbers continue to add to the more than 47 million who already go without health care coverage.[27] Many who have health insurance will lose their benefits due to unemployment, some because of their inability to continue making payments for medical insurance, and still others because benefits have been cut by their employer due to rising costs. Out of this 47 million, there are more than nine million children who are not covered under any form of a health care plan.[28]

In addition, procedural costs and technological capabilities have seemingly outstripped the affordability of health care for many individuals within the U.SThe system has also advanced to such complexity that the ethics of humane and reasonable treatment seems to have been lost to defensive medicine in many cases triggered by our litigious society. Just because the potential exists for prolonging the physiological characteristics of a person, do such possibilities and acts of vitalism always constitute the preserving of "life," thereby negating the responsible and realistic use of medical resources? I think not.

While many may choose to ignore the economic considerations of receiving and providing health care, it is by necessity a relevant factor which must be given equitable consideration. The issues of one person's so-called "right" to health care, that is, to receive the resources and equitable treatment must be evaluated in terms of benefit and burden.

Ethical concerns and health care reform have been, and continue to be, major political and economic "hot topics" of discussion. Attempts have been made to ensure that every citizen can access the system and receive medical treatment, regardless of the prognosis or ability to pay. The down side is that many individuals have come to view this as a guarantee of a "right" to health care, when in reality, health care in the current market is a commodity to be purchased and is not and never has been a "right" in the United States.

Only in the event of an emergency or evidence of some type of guaranteed financial reimbursement has medical care been considered a "right." The up side, and only clearly defined "right," which is recognized and supported legally and clinically, is the right of the individual to have input into his or her treatment. This right also includes the individual's

---

[26] Peggy S. Stanfield, Nanna Cross, and Y.H. Hui, *Introduction to the Health Professions*, 5th edition, (Jones and Bartlett Publishers, LLC, 2009), 5.

[27] Teddi Dineley Johnson, "Census Bureau: Number of U.S. Uninsured Rises to 47 Million Americans are Uninsured: Almost 5 Percent Increase Since 2005, *Nations Health*, October, 2007: 38.

[28] Walzer, 2.

right to decide whether or not to even receive treatment, and the right to declare, in advance, what he or she would want if in a terminal or persistently unconscious condition.[29]

In addition, there is minimal, if any, agreement among the key players (e.g., hospital administrators, politicians, and insurance companies) on how to correct or control the health care system. The technologic explosion in medicine makes it almost impossible to find a point of reference from which to explore the problems and potential resolutions, if any, of such a system in a constant state of change and confusion.

Additionally, many health care policies, proposed political and economic solutions and various types of health care reform have been laid on the altar, built by the health care industry, and offered up in smoke in an attempt to appease this behemoth god of medicine. Philosophical arguments and intricate theories have attempted to design plans that would minimize or eradicate the associated ethical problems of justice, rights, and equality for the recipients of health care.

UTILITARIANISM AND MAXIMIZING RIGHTS

Another consideration, from a utilitarian position, is the "problem of interpretation," which challenges the premise that the utility must be "'maximal' in every case,"[30] or that equal access means equal distribution. Seemingly unequal distribution does not mean a violation of or negate a clearly defined right, in this case, a right to health care services and resources. The right to receive health care will have value in varying degrees to different individuals and the services and resources will be determined by need.

It may also be claimed that a utilitarian position compromises the notion of fairness and justice in distribution. However, it should be recognized that health care needs cannot be satisfied in the same manner as other needs, such as those for food, clothing, or shelter. Regarding the utility maxim of "the greatest good for the greatest number," there are certain conditions under which the "greatest good" may be served. Immunizations for certain diseases certainly prove to be for the greater good, and the restoring of one's health may also prove to be beneficial to the aggregate well-being. Another example may be the person who has need of a heart bypass; while costly, such a procedure will, ideally, allow the individual to return to a productive life, contributing to the general welfare and minimizing the need for continuous demands on health care resources.

In this context, such a proposal, based on the notion of genuine need, while seemingly only serving to enhance distributive inequalities or injustices has actually created a more stable and equitable system. It must be remembered that not all inequalities are the same as inequities or that what seems unfortunate is always unfair.[31]

---

[29] These rights have been acknowledged and made a part of the legal system by the Patient Self-Determination Act of 1991, and are expressed in the Advance Directive, as related to the withholding or withdrawal of medical treatment if diagnosed as being terminally ill or persistently unconscious.

[30] C. L. Sheng, *A New Approach to Utilitarianism: A Unified Utilitarian Theory and Its Application to Distributive Justice* (Norwell, Main: Kluwer Academic Publishers, 1991), 38. While Sheng uses this phrase in terms of negative and positive duties (or rights), from a sphere-specific utility position, the notion is that while the maximal utility may not be achieved in every case, it can be realized through the maximizing of the identified sphere of utility. In this instance, the specific sphere is the provision of medical care and the utility to be realized is the greatest benefit in the overall distribution and use of health care resources for the greatest number of individuals.

[31] Engelhardt, 344.

Just by virtue of the natural lottery alone, a need for health care services will vary from person to person. Individual circumstances will also be another determining factor. Much like a triage system found in an emergency room, there would be those individuals with major trauma who take priority over others with cuts, colds, and minor injuries.

Another relevant point is that just because a particular medicine, test, or procedure may be available, it is not always the case that such treatment is warranted. Kenneth Arrow, Ph.D., and Nobel Prize laureate, has rightly pointed out that while consumers may be better educated to the ways of medicine, they are not well qualified to decide which tests, medications, or procedures they genuinely need.[32] Neither is the duplication of services necessary. For example, while having two, three, or even four MRI machines in a city may be more convenient, what purpose does it serve except to increase the cost of each test in order to pay for the equipment and man-hours?

It must also be realized that a major conflict exists between the notion of a right and the obligation of supporting that right. The claim of having a right is ineffectual by itself, but has validity only in relation to the corresponding obligation as recognized by others. For an obligation which goes unrecognized by others loses none of the full force of its existence, but a right unrecognized or unsupported has little value.[33]

RIGHTS AND THE INDIVIDUAL

It makes no sense to say that rights exist without the concept of preceding obligations which validate the rights, for the actual relationship between the two is as between object and subject. Case in point, a man in isolation has only a duty or obligation towards himself. In community, however, the idea of duty towards self is superseded by a two-fold concept of obligations and rights. That is, the individual has rights only when recognized as obligations by others, and in turn his participation in community calls for reciprocal recognition, responsibility and support.

A person alone in the universe would have only obligations toward himself, for genuine rights exist only when recognized and supported by others.[34] It may be argued that the lone individual has rights or the right to do as he pleases, but such a premise seems merely a matter of semantics with no theoretical or applicable substance. Only in relation to others can there be a genuine claim or identification of rights.

It is also the case that the ethics of utilitarianism makes us all members of the same moral community,[35] thereby creating the necessity of moral equality or humanitarian consideration. It is only out of a sense of community that rights get their force and meaning. In turn, the conferment of clearly defined rights provides the individual with the recognition of entitlement to participate in the community.[36]

---

[32] Eli Ginzberg, Ph.D., "A Cautionary Note on Market Reforms in Health Care," *JAMA*, (November 22/29, 1995), vol. 274, no. 20: 1633.

[33] Simone Weil, *The Need for Roots*, trans. A.F. Willis, with a Preface by T.S. Eliot (New York: Routledge, 1995), 3.

[34] Ibid.

[35] Harsanyi, 56.

[36] Jay Bernstein, "Right, Revolution and Community: Marx's 'On the Jewish Question,'" *Socialism and the Limits of Liberalism*, ed., Peter Osborne (New York: Verso, 1991), 103.

While it could be argued that rights exist whether fully endorsed or supported by all members of a particular group, the fact still remains that the existence of a genuine right is given meaning only by an acknowledged sense of obligation by others. An additional problem exists with the notion of obligation, for an obligation clearly undefined allows for arguments of how much or how often members of a particular community or society will be involved or support that identified right.

There is also the argument that rights and utility are incompatible. This notion, however, seems to stem from the idea that some notion of a particular right is considered to have a higher value or priority than the desired utility, except when the utility is extremely large, and only then is the utility given serious consideration. The problem with this position is that the starting point at which the utility becomes relevant is undefined and is predicated on the whimsical decisions of a few.

Another problem is that the guarantee of a right does not necessarily translate into an equal right, for such a notion of equality is defined more by the arena or sphere to which it is related, than to the ideal concept. To unmask the ideal abstractions tends to point to the realities in which individuals live their lives. For example, the guaranteed right to vote may be equal for all who meet the stipulated criteria of age, etc., but such a right does not guarantee an equal distribution of power. Neither does the right to equal treatment before the law translate into legal equality.[37]

While such concepts may be bolstered as the moral ideal, serving as rhetoric for equality, the existence of rights is in no way diminished for the individual by the utilitarian equation. The meshing of idealism with pragmatic reality does nothing to diminish the philosophical validity or stability of such a premise, even when the considerations of social and economic constraints are factored.

MORALITY AND THE NOTION OF RIGHTS

The morality of rights, therefore, is predicated on the idea of equality of opportunity, while the ethic of responsibility relies on the concept of justice, with consideration given to the differences of need. The reality is that the ethics of rights is a manifestation of equal respect, which attempts to balance the claims of others and self, creating an ethic of responsibility and reciprocity which rests on an awareness of and gives rise to an ethic of compassion and care.[38] It must also be recognized that reciprocity as an ideal is not a tallying sheet but a continuous contribution by both parties, both socially and individually, as one is able, in order to facilitate the idea of distributive justice. From the social equilibrium side, there ideally exists a feeling of obligation rather than a quantity or sum to be exacted from the person in need.

Even if the notion of equal rights and justice is fully supported, the need or desire to exercise a particular right, by an individual, is not going to be the same for all individuals at the same time. And, while there may be cases which seemingly compromise or negate a particular right, or theoretical scenarios which create exceptions to ideal principles of moral choice or behavior, the fact remains that the right still exists. The exercise of a particular right

---

[37] Anne Phillips, "'So What's Wrong with the Individual?' Socialist and Feminist Debates on Equality," *Socialism and the Limits of Liberalism*, edited by Peter Osborne (New York: Verso, 1991), 142.

[38] Carol Gilligan, *In a Different Voice* (Cambridge: Harvard University Press, 1982), 164-165.

not only perpetuates the idea of aggregate obligation, but also creates a sense of responsibility and accountability to those who give authenticity to that right.

Even in an ideal state of existence, the needs of one individual are not going to be the same as the need by others, if the concept of individual identity is to be maintained. The wants and desires of individuals vary, unless individuality is negated and all are programmed to desire the same things.

Accordingly, while it may be acknowledged that individuals have rights beyond "life and liberty," such rights do not follow from some ideal conception of societal justice or humanity, but from a shared conception of social goods.[39] For "the idea of distributive justice has as much to do with being and doing as with having, as much to do with production as with consumption . . . [and the] multiplicity of goods is matched by a multiplicity of distributive procedures, agents and criteria."[40]

"All goods with which distributive justice is concerned are social goods. . . [which] have shared meanings, because [the] conception and creation [of these goods] are [defined by] social processes."[41] It is from these social processes that social goods and personal qualities have their own spheres of operation, in which they work their effects "freely, spontaneously, and legitimately."[42]

The ethical implications of such a system, which acknowledges, defines, and supports the individual's right(s), will by necessity include the individual's responsibility in connection with the entitlement or right. Pragmatically, the balance between the notion of a right to health care and the associated responsibilities are as follows.

First, the rational and efficient use of resources is by necessity a primary component. Second, since the function of morality is to serve as a guide to ethical human conduct, the value or utility of the actions associated with health care are to achieve the greatest benefit for the largest number, with the resources available.

This, of course, does not mean that there are no negative or less than desirable outcomes, but the utility, intent, or "greatest good" or "benefit over burden" of the sphere of health care is maximized, decision-making or *prima facie obligations*[43] becomes clearer, and the resolution of conflict is strengthened. Such action calls for a reduction in the continued use of scarce medical resources for cases that are deemed futile, based on clinical evidence of prognosis and ability to respond to treatment.

Third, as argued by David Hume, the obligation to benefit others comes from the principle of reciprocity. That is, if there are benefits received from society, then by virtue of this principle, society can expect and the individual has an obligation in return to promote or contribute to that society's well-being or best interest.

Another consideration is that while the sick individual is a patient with rights to accept or reject treatment(s), he/she is also a citizen with responsibilities associated to that right. That is, the acknowledged right to make health care decisions should not be seen as an absolute or guaranteed right outside a given context. This context is bounded by the reality of the

---

[39] Walzer, Michael, *Sphere of Justice: A Defense of Pluralism and Equality*, (United States: Basic Books, A Division of Harper Collins Publishers, 1983), xv.

[40] Ibid., 3.

[41] Walzer, 7.

[42] Ibid., 19.

[43] W.D. Ross, *The Right and the Good* (Oxford: Clarendon Press, 1930), 19-36.

patient's ability to respond to the care received, and the reality of limited resources and a society that recognizes the competing rights of others.[44]

CONCLUSION

The fact remains that the issue of "rights" must be defined in conjunction with the idea of a particular system with established and clearly interpreted rights, rather than from the individual's purely subjective desire or claim of an assumed right. As stated previously, the one important element which is most often overlooked in most theories addressing the issue of rights is the participant's responsibility; the tendency is to discuss rights without mention of the recipient's obligation in relation to that particular, identified right.

Given the complexities of the concepts of equality and rights, the notion of distributive justice must be analyzed within a particular sphere or environment, in this case the environment of health care. Naturally, the development of any supporting policy will not work strictly within the micro realm of the individual or the macro realm of society at large. Clearly defined boundaries and consequences must be established in order to support a genuine right to health care at a more objective and equitable level.

Ideally, social justice seems to be a combination of empathy and responsibility rather than one's subjective impression of "fairness" and "justice" in relation to personal concern. While no health care system will ever be conceived as meeting everyone's needs or idea of justice, it seems possible that a system may be devised which will accommodate the "greatest good for the greatest number." This, of course, does not come without a price. Individualism in a deliberative social order will call for personal responsibility, and the input of additional resources.

BIBLIOGRAPHY

Beauchamp, Tom L. and Faden, Ruth R. "The Right to Health and the Right to Health Care." *The Journal of Medicine and Philosophy*. vol. 4, no. 2 (1979): 118-131.

Bentham, Jeremy. *Anarchical Fallacies*. John Browning, ed. Vol. 2. As reproduced from the 1843 edition. New York: Russell and Russell, 1962.

Bernstein, Jay. "Right, Revolution and Community: Marx's 'On the Jewish Question,'" *Socialism and the Limits of Liberalism*. Peter Osborne, ed. New York: Verso, 1991.

Churchill, Larry. "Autonomy and the Common Weal," *Hastings Center Report* (January-February, 1991): 25–31.

Engelhardt, H. Tristram. *The Foundations of Bioethics*. Second Edition. New York: Oxford University Press, 1996.

————. "Rights to Health Care: A Critical Appraisal," *The Journal of Medicine and Philosophy*, vol. 4, no. 2, (1979): 75–93.

Gaylin, Willard and Jennings, Bruce. *The Perversion of Autonomy: The Proper Uses of Coercion and Constraints in a Liberal Society*. New York: The Free Press, 1996.

Gilligan, Carol. *In a Different Voice*. Cambridge: Harvard University Press, 1982.

---

[44] Larry Churchill, "Autonomy and the Common Weal," *Hastings Center Report* (January-February, 1991): 28.

Ginzberg, Eli. "A Cautionary Note on Market Reforms in Health Care." *JAMA*. (November 22/29, 1995), vol. 274, no. 20: 1633–1634.

Johnson, Teddi Dineley. "Census Bureau: Number of U.S. Uninsured Rises to 47 Million Americans are Uninsured: Almost 5 Percent Increase Since 2005, *Nations Health*, October, 2007.

Nielsen, Kai. "Global Justice, Capitalism and the Third World." *Social Ethics: Morality and Social Policy*. Thomas Mappes and Jane Zembaty, eds. New York: The McGraw-Hill Companies, Inc., 1997.

Phillips, Anne. "'So What's Wrong with the Individual?' Socialist and Feminist Debates on Equality." *Socialism and the Limits of Liberalism*. Peter Osborne, ed. New York: Verso, 1991.

Ross, W. D. *The Right and the Good*. Oxford: Clarendon Press, 1930.

Sheng, C. L. *A New Approach to Utilitarianism: A Unified Utilitarian Theory and Its Application to Distributive Justice*. Norwell, Main: Kluwer Academic Publishers, 1991.

Stanfield, Peggy S., Cross, Nanna , and Hui, Y.H. *Introduction to the Health Profession.* 5th edition. Jones and Bartlett Publishers, LLC, 2009.

Walzer, Michael. *Spheres of Justice: A Defense of Pluralism and Equality*. United States: Basic Books, A Division of Harper Collins Publishers, 1983.

Weil, Simone. *The Need for Roots*. Trans., A.F. Willis, with a Preface by T.S. Eliot. New York: Routledge, 1995.

In: Economics, Political and Social Issues …
Editor: Michelle L. Fergusson

ISBN: 978-1-61122-555-6
©2011 Nova Science Publishers, Inc.

FOREIGN AID:
AN INTRODUCTION TO U.S. PROGRAMS AND POLICY[*]

Curt Tarnoff [#] *and Marian L. Lawson*
Foreign Affairs, Foreign Assistance

ABSTRACT

Foreign assistance is a fundamental component of the international affairs budget and is viewed by many as an essential instrument of U.S. foreign policy. The focus of U.S. foreign aid policy has been transformed since the terrorist attacks of September 11, 2001. This report provides an overview of the U.S. foreign aid program, by answering frequently asked questions on the subject.

There are five major categories of foreign assistance: bilateral development aid, economic assistance supporting U.S. political and security goals, humanitarian aid, multilateral economic contributions, and military aid. Due largely to the implementation of two new foreign aid initiatives—the Millennium Challenge Corporation and the HIV/AIDS Initiative—bilateral development assistance has become the largest category of U.S. aid.

In FY2008, the United States provided some form of foreign assistance to about 154 countries. Israel and Egypt placed among the top recipients in FY2008, as they have since the late 1970s, although on-going reconstruction activities in Iraq and Afghanistan now place those nations near the top as well. The impact of the terrorist attacks on September 11, 2001, and the subsequent use of foreign aid to support the war on terrorism are clearly seen in the estimated country-aid levels for FY2008. Pakistan and Jordan are key partners in the war on terrorism and major beneficiaries of U.S. assistance. Also among the leading recipients are some African countries that are the focus of the multi-billion dollar HIV/AIDS initiative.

By nearly all measures, the amount of foreign aid provided by the United States declined for several decades but has grown in the past few years. After hitting an all-time low in the mid-1990s, foreign assistance levels since FY2004, in real terms, have been higher than any period since the early 1950s, largely due to Iraq and Afghanistan reconstruction and HIV/AIDS funding. The 0.19% of U.S. gross national product represented by foreign aid obligations for FY2008 is consistent with recent years, but quite low compared to the early decades of the foreign assistance program. The United States is the largest international economic aid donor in absolute dollar terms but is the smallest contributor among the major donor governments when calculated as a percent of gross national income.

---

[*] Excerpted from CRS Report R40213 dated February 10, 2009.
[#] E-mail: ctarnoff@crs.loc.gov

INTRODUCTION

U.S. foreign aid is a fundamental component of the international affairs budget and is viewed by many as an essential instrument of U.S. foreign policy [1]. Each year, it is the subject of extensive congressional debate and legislative and executive branch initiatives, proposing changes in the size, composition, and purpose of the program. The focus of U.S. foreign aid policy has been transformed since the terrorist attacks of September 11, 2001. In 2002, a National Security Strategy for the first time established global development as a third pillar of U.S. national security, along with defense and diplomacy.

This report addresses a number of the more frequently asked queries regarding the U.S. foreign aid program, its objectives, costs, organization, the role of Congress, and how it compares to those of other aid donors. In particular, the discussion attempts not only to present a current snap-shot of American foreign assistance, but also to illustrate the extent to which this instrument of U.S. foreign policy has changed from past practices, especially since the end of the Cold War and the launching of the war on terror.

Data presented in the report are the most current, reliable figures available, usually covering the period through FY2008. Dollar amounts are drawn from a variety of sources, including the Office of Management and Budget (OMB), U.S. Agency for International Development (USAID), and from annual State, Foreign Operations and other appropriations acts. As new data become obtainable or additional issues and questions arise, the report will be modified and revised.

Foreign aid acronyms used in this report are listed in Appendix B.

A Note on Numbers and Sources

The numeric measures of foreign assistance used in this report come from a variety of sources. Different sources are necessary for comprehensive analysis, but can often lead to discrepancies from table to table or chart to chart.

One reason for such variation is the different definitions of foreign assistance used by different sources. The Budget of the United States historical tables data on foreign assistance, for example, includes only those programs that fall under the traditional 151 and 152 budget subfunction accounts. This excludes various programs run by federal agencies outside of the traditional State/USAID framework. USAID's U.S. Overseas Loans and Grants database (Greenbook), in contrast, uses a broad and evolving definition of foreign aid which in past years has included mandatory retirement accounts, Departments of Defense and Energy nonproliferation assistance, and other U.S. agency accounts that many would not classify as foreign assistance. Official Development Assistance (ODA), reported by the Organization for Economic Cooperation and Development (OECD), differs from both U.S. Budget and Greenbook numbers because it excludes all military assistance.

Apparent discrepancies also arise due to funding being recorded at different points in the process. U.S. Budget historic tables represent budget authority, funds appropriated by fiscal year, whereas the Greenbook reports funds obligated by fiscal year. The disparity this creates is apparent when comparing recent aid levels in Figures 7 and 9.

Figure 9 shows a sharp spike in appropriations in FY2004 for Iraq Reconstruction, but that appropriation was obligated over multiple years, resulting in the much less dramatic rise in FY2004 and FY2005 obligations depicted in Figure 7. The reporting calendar may result in discrepancies as well—ODA figures, unlike budget and Greenbook numbers, are reported by calendar year rather than fiscal year.

The differences between sources make precise comparisons difficult. For this reason, CRS has attempted not to mix sources within figures and tables, with the exception of Table A-3 (on which Figure 7 is based), which was necessary because no single source exists for data from 1946 through to 2008. Though imperfect, this compilation of data is useful for depicting long-term trends in U.S. foreign assistance levels.

FOREIGN AID PURPOSES AND PRIORITIES

What Are the Rationales and Objectives of U.S. Foreign Assistance?

Foreign assistance is predicated on several rationales and supports a great many objectives. Both rationales and objectives have changed over time.

Rationales for Foreign Aid

Since the start of modern U.S. foreign aid programs, the rationale for such assistance has been posited in terms of national security. From a beginning in rebuilding Europe after World War II under the Marshall Plan (1948-1951), U.S. aid programs reflected anti-communist Cold War tensions that continued through the 1980s. U.S. development assistance programs to newly independent states were viewed by policymakers as a way to prevent the incursion of Soviet influence in Latin America, Southeast Asia, and Africa. Military and economic assistance programs were provided to allies offering U.S. base rights or other support in the anti-Soviet struggle.

In the immediate aftermath of the dissolution of the Soviet Union in 1991, aid programs lost their Cold War underpinnings. Foreign aid programs reflected less of a strategic focus on a global scale and instead responded to regional issues, such as Middle East peace initiatives, the transition to democracy of eastern Europe and republics of the former Soviet Union, and international illicit drug production and trafficking in the Andes. Without an overarching theme, foreign aid budgets decreased in the 1990s. However, since the September 11, 2001, terrorist attacks in the United States, policymakers frequently have cast foreign assistance as a tool in the global war on terrorism. This has comprised an emphasis on aid to partner states in the terrorism war, including the substantial reconstruction programs in Afghanistan and Iraq. As noted, global development is now accepted, along with defense and diplomacy, as a key element of U.S. national security [2].

Even during periods when aid programs were framed in the context of anti-communism, and more recently in the context of anti-terrorism, foreign aid programs were justified for other reasons as well, primarily commercial and humanitarian. Foreign assistance has long been defended as a way to either promote U.S. exports by creating new customers for U.S. products or by improving the global economic environment in which U.S. companies compete. At the same time, a strong current has existed that explained U.S. assistance as a moral imperative to help poverty-stricken countries and those trying to overcome disasters or conflict. Providing assistance for humanitarian reasons or in response to natural disasters has generally been the least contested purpose of aid by the American public and policymakers alike.

Objectives of Foreign Aid

The objectives of aid are thought to fit within these rationales. Aid objectives include promoting economic growth and reducing poverty, improving governance, addressing population growth, expanding access to basic education and health care, protecting the environment, promoting stability in conflictive regions, protecting human rights, curbing weapons proliferation, strengthening allies, and addressing drug production and trafficking. The expectation has been that, by meeting these objectives, the United States will achieve its national security goals as well as ensure a global economic environment for American products and demonstrate the humanitarian nature of the U.S. people. Some observers have returned to the view that poverty and lack of opportunity are the underlying causes of political instability and the rise of terrorist organizations, much as poverty was viewed as creating a breeding ground for communist insurgencies in the 1960s, 1970s, and 1980s.

Generally speaking, different types of foreign aid support different objectives. Focusing on any single element of the aid program would produce a different sense of the priority of any particular U.S. objective. But there is also considerable overlap among categories of aid. Multilateral aid serves many of the same objectives as bilateral development assistance, although through different channels. Both military assistance and economic security assistance serve U.S. objectives in the Middle East and South Asia. Drug interdiction activities, backed in some cases with military assistance and alternative development programs, are integrated elements of American counter-narcotics efforts in Latin America and elsewhere.

Depending on how they are designed, individual assistance projects on the ground can also serve multiple purposes. A health project ostensibly directed at alleviating the effects of HIV/AIDS by feeding orphan children may also mobilize local communities and stimulate grassroots democracy and civil society while additionally meeting U.S. humanitarian objectives. Microcredit programs may help develop local economies while at the same time providing food and education to the children of entrepreneurs.

In an effort to rationalize the assistance program more clearly, the Director of Foreign Assistance (DFA) at the State Department developed a framework (Table 1) in 2006 that organizes U.S. foreign aid—or at least that portion of it that is managed by the State Department and/or USAID—around five strategic objectives, each of which includes a number of program elements, also known as sectors [3].

The five objectives are Peace and Security; Investing in People; Governing Justly and Democratically; Economic Growth; and Humanitarian Assistance. Generally, these objectives and sectors do not correspond to any one particular budget account in appropriations bills [4]

Table 1. Bilateral State/USAID Assistance by Objective: FY2006-FY2008
(in millions of current dollars)

Aid Objectives and Program Areas	FY2006	FY2007	FY2008
Peace and Security	$6,817.1	$8,684.6	$7,480.3
Counter-Terrorism	$157.0	$242.1	$178.5
Combating WMD	$229.9	$228.0	$247.8
Stabilization/Security Sector Reform	$5,178.0	$6,668.6	$5,579.5
Counter-narcotics	$1,007.1	$1,148.1	$1,125.1
Transnational Crime	$60.2	$51.2	$73.2
Conflict Mitigation	$184.8	$346.6	$276.4
Investing in People	$4,957.4	$6,659.4	$8,522.7
Health	$2,595.2	$5,705.1	$7,277.2
Education	$689.8	$754.5	$928.4
Social Services/Protection of Vulnerable	$136.9	$199.7	$317.0
Governing Justly & Democratically	$1,233.2	$2,141.3	$2,260.4
Rule of Law & Human Rights	$301.1	$532.0	$606.1
Good Governance	$354.2	$763.2	$818.9
Political Competition	$197.3	$305.4	$288.7
Civil Society	$380.6	$540.8	$546.8
Economic Growth	$2,826.2	$3,212.2	$2,920.6
Macroeconomic Growth	$409.1	$591.5	$330.5
Trade & Investment	$408.7	$331.6	$210.9
Financial Sector	$277.2	$176.8	$190.8
Infrastructure	$414.9	$723.9	$850.4
Agriculture	$562.0	$538.1	$487.7
Private Sector Competitiveness	$350.5	$385.4	$358.3
Economic Opportunity	$111.6	$127.0	$167.9
Environment	$292.1	$337.8	$324.0
Humanitarian Assistance	$1,808.4	$3,097.4	$3,157.8
Protection, Assistance & Solutions	$1,664.1	$2,963.7	$3,025.5
Disaster Readiness	$74.8	$78.2	$74.5
Migration Management	$69.6	$55.5	$57.7

Source: USAID and Department of State budget documents. Notes: Figures include Iraq funding and supplementals, with exception of FY2008 3 supplemental appropriation.

Peace and Security

The Peace and Security objective is composed of six program areas: counter-terrorism; combating weapons of mass destruction; stabilization operations and security sector reform; counter-narcotics; transnational crime; conflict mitigation and reconciliation. With an elevated level of engagement in the aftermath of 9/11, these types of programs have been emphasized by the Bush Administration as essential to the war on terrorism, and to promote stability in failing states that may become permissive environments for terrorism. For FY2008, the Peace and Security objective was funded at $7.5 billion. Major portions of these funds were allocated to Israel, Egypt, Afghanistan, Iraq, Pakistan, and Jordan. Were the DFA framework to include all foreign aid, regardless of source, the DOD training and equipping of Iraqi and Afghan security forces would add $5.8 billion in FY2008 under this objective.

Investing in People

The Investing in People objective is composed of three program areas: health; education; and social services and protection for vulnerable people. For FY2008, the objective was funded at $8.5 billion. Most of the funding falls in the health program area, particularly the President's Global AIDS Initiative.

Health programs also include funds for combating avian influenza, tuberculosis, and malaria. A significant portion of health funds are provided for maternal and child health, and family planning and reproductive health programs. The objective also includes education programs with the majority of funds focusing on basic education needs, especially in Africa, but increasingly in south and central Asia and the Middle East.

Governing Justly and Democratically

This objective includes a number of program areas related to promoting the rule of law and human rights, good governance, political competition, and civil society. The two largest components for FY2008 were the rule of law and good governance. Some aid experts believe that development is more effective when the recipient government is democratic in nature and respectful of citizens' rights. Program goals include strengthening the performance and accountability of government institutions, such as the judiciary and police, and combating corruption. Funding levels have grown somewhat in recent years; the objective totaled $2.3 billion in FY2008.

Economic Growth

The Economic Growth objective, amounting to $2.9 billion in FY2008, includes a wide range of program areas that are believed to contribute to economic growth in developing economies, including agriculture, the environment, infrastructure, and trade. Agriculture programs focus on science and technology advances that reduce poverty and hunger, trade-promotion opportunities for farmers, and sound environmental management practices for sustainable agriculture. Private sector development programs include support for business associations and microfinance services. Programs for managing natural resources and protecting the global environment focus on conserving biological diversity, improving the management of land, water, and forests, promoting environmentally-sound urban development, encouraging clean and efficient energy production and use, and reducing the threat of global climate change while strengthening sustainable economic growth. Were the DFA framework to encompass all foreign aid, regardless of funding source, the economic growth objective would likely include most of the Millennium Challenge Account, adding perhaps another $1.5 billion in FY08, and much of the Commander's Emergency Response Program (CERP), the latter funded by DOD at $1.8 billion in FY08.

Humanitarian Assistance

Humanitarian assistance responds to both natural and man-made disasters as well as problems resulting from conflict associated with failed or failing states. Responses include protection and assistance to refugees and internally displaced persons and provision of emergency food aid. Programs generally address unanticipated situations and are not integrated into long-term development strategies. In FY2008, humanitarian programs were funded at $3.2 billion.

What Are the Different Types of Foreign Aid?

The framework introduced by the DFA organizes assistance by foreign policy objective. But there are many other ways to categorize foreign aid. More commonly, Congress and others group traditional foreign aid by five major types of assistance, as illustrated in Figure 1 below. Each category of assistance is funded by discrete aid accounts in the U.S. budget. There are many such accounts, supporting different aid agencies, offices, and programs.

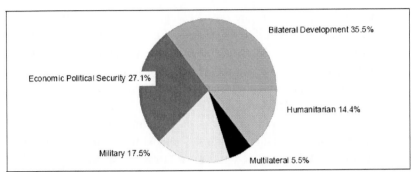

Source: U.S. Department of State, Summary and Highlights, International Affairs, Function 150, FY2009, House and Senate Appropriations Committees, and CRS calculations.

Figure 1. Aid Program Composition, FY2008.

Iraq and Afghanistan Reconstruction Funding

In recent years, reconstruction assistance to Iraq and Afghanistan has accounted for billions of dollars and has, perhaps, disproportionately shaped the portrait of the U.S. foreign aid program. Aid efforts in both countries have been mostly directed at improving the security capabilities of police and armed forces, at building and rehabilitating infrastructure, promoting governance, and stimulating economic growth.

Reaching a total of $49 billion in appropriations from all sources in the years FY2003 to FY2009, the U.S. assistance program to Iraq is the largest aid initiative since the 1948-1951 Marshall Plan. Nearly $21 billion of the total was funneled through an Iraq Relief and Reconstruction Fund in just two fiscal years, FY2003 and FY2004. About $22 billion has been provided under the DOD budget, not traditionally included in foreign aid totals, and, therefore, unless otherwise noted, not captured in the context of this report. The Afghanistan program to date accounts for about $11 billion in traditional foreign aid and another $15 billion in DOD-funded aid.

While traditional foreign aid amounts noted in this report include figures for Iraq and Afghanistan reconstruction, it is important to keep in mind that these aid efforts—running currently at $2-$3 billion a year—might overshadow and obscure key trends in changing aid budget and policy priorities for the period FY2002-2009. Therefore, at various points throughout the text, a notation may be made stating what a particular amount would equal if Iraq and/or Afghanistan assistance was excluded.

This methodology encompasses all traditional aid, a larger universe than that in the DFA framework [5] However, as noted, the Department of Defense and some other government agencies undertake assistance programs with funding outside traditional foreign aid budget accounts. These non-traditional programs are not captured in this discussion.

Bilateral Development Assistance

Development assistance programs are designed chiefly to foster sustainable broad-based economic progress and social stability in developing countries. For FY2008, Congress appropriated $10.3 billion in such assistance, an amount accounting for nearly 37% of total foreign aid appropriations. A significant proportion of these funds—largely encompassed by the Development Assistance and the Child Survival and Health accounts—is managed by the U.S. Agency for International Development (USAID) and is used for long-term projects in the areas of economic reform and private sector development, democracy promotion, environmental protection, population control, and improvement of human health. Development activities that have gained more prominence in recent years include basic education, water and sanitation, and support for treatment of HIV/AIDS and other infectious diseases. Other bilateral development assistance goes to distinct institutions, such as the Peace Corps, Inter-American Development Foundation, African Development Foundation, Trade and Development Agency, and Millennium Challenge Corporation.

Economic Aid Supporting U.S. Political and Security Objectives

For FY2008, Congress appropriated $7.8 billion, 27% of total assistance, for five major programs whose primary purpose is to meet special U.S. economic, political, or security interests. The bulk of these funds—$5.3 billion—was provided through the Economic Support Fund (ESF), designed to advance American strategic goals with economic assistance. ESF funds can be used for development projects, or in other ways, such as cash transfers, to help a recipient country stabilize its economy and service foreign debt. For many years, following the 1979 Camp David accords, most ESF funds went to support the Middle East Peace Process. Since 9/11, ESF has largely supported countries of importance in the war on terrorism. In FY2008, for example, about $1.8 billion in ESF was directed at Iraq and Afghanistan alone.

With the demise of the Soviet empire, the United States established two new aid programs to meet particular strategic political interests. The SEED (Support for East European Democracy Act of 1989) and the FREEDOM Support Act (Freedom for Russia and Emerging Eurasian Democracies and Open Markets Support Act of 1992) programs were designed to help Central Europe and the newly independent states of the former Soviet Union (FSA) achieve democratic systems and free market economies. In FY2008, SEED countries were allocated about $294 million while the FSA countries received $397 million in appropriated funds (not counting an emergency appropriation at the end of the fiscal year of $365 million specifically for Georgia). Both accounts have seen decreases as countries graduate from U.S. assistance, from a ten-year high of $676 million in 2001 for SEED and $958 million in 2002 for FSA countries.

Especially since 2001, policymakers have given greater weight to several global concerns that are considered threats to U.S. security and well-being—terrorism, illicit narcotics, crime, and weapons proliferation. They have addressed each concern with aid programs that provide a range of law enforcement activities, training, and equipment. In FY2008, the anti-narcotics and crime program accounted for about $1.3 billion in foreign aid appropriations—about a quarter of which was for an Andean anti-narcotics initiative. Anti-terrorism programs added another $150 million, and weapons proliferation-related activities, including humanitarian demining, were funded at $347 million.

Humanitarian Assistance

For FY2008, Congress appropriated $4.2 billion, 14.4% of assistance, for humanitarian aid programs [6]. Unlike development assistance programs, which are often viewed as long-term efforts that may have the effect of preventing future crises from developing, humanitarian aid programs are devoted largely to the immediate alleviation of humanitarian emergencies. A large proportion of humanitarian assistance goes to programs aimed at refugees and internally displaced persons administered by the State Department and funded under the Migration and Refugee Assistance (MRA) and the Emergency Refugee and Migration Assistance (ERMA) accounts. These accounts support, with about $1.4 billion in FY2008, a number of refugee relief organizations, including the U.N. High Commission for Refugees and the International Committee of the Red Cross. The International Disaster Assistance (IDA) and Transition Initiatives (TI) accounts managed by USAID provide relief, rehabilitation, and reconstruction assistance to victims of man-made and natural disasters, activities totaling $694 million in FY2008 [7]

Food assistance supplements both programs (about $2.1 billion in FY2008). The food aid program, generically referred to as P.L. 480 (after the law that authorizes it) or the Food for Peace program, provides U.S. agricultural commodities to developing countries. USAID-administered Title II (of the public law) grant food aid is mostly provided for humanitarian relief, but may also be used for development-oriented purposes by private voluntary organizations (PVOs) or through multilateral organizations, such as the World Food Program. Title II funds are also used to support the "farmer-to-farmer" program which sends hundreds of U.S. volunteers as technical advisors to train farm and food-related groups throughout the world. A new program begun in 2002, the McGovern-Dole International Food for Education and Child Nutrition Program, provides commodities, technical assistance, and financing for school feeding and child nutrition programs ($100 million in FY2008) [8]

Multilateral Assistance

A relatively small share of U.S. foreign assistance—5.5% in FY2008—is combined with contributions from other donor nations to finance multilateral development projects. For FY2008, Congress appropriated $1.6 billion for such activities implemented by international organizations, like the United Nations Children's Fund (UNICEF) and the United Nations Development Program (UNDP), and by multilateral development banks (MDBs), such as the

World Bank. On average, U.S. contributions represent about 23% of total donor transfers to the MDBs.

Military Assistance

The United States provides military assistance to U.S. friends and allies to help them acquire U.S. military equipment and training. Congress appropriated $5.1 billion for military assistance in FY2008, 17.5% of total U.S. foreign aid. There are three main programs, administered by the Department of State, but implemented by DOD. Foreign Military Financing (FMF), $4.7 billion in FY2008, is a grant program that enables governments to receive equipment from the U.S. government or to access equipment directly through U.S. commercial channels. Most FMF grants support the security needs of Israel and Egypt. The International Military Education and Training program (IMET), $85 million, offers military training on a grant basis to foreign military officers and personnel. Peacekeeping funds, $261 million in FY2008, are used to support voluntary non-U.N. operations as well as training for an African crisis response force. As noted earlier, since 2002, DOD appropriations, not included in counts of traditional foreign aid, have supported FMF and IMET-like programs in Afghanistan and Iraq at a level of nearly $6 billion in FY2008.

What Are the Funding Priorities and Trends in U.S. Foreign Assistance?

Tracking changes in the amount of funds distributed to each objective, sector, type of assistance, or funding account is one means of measuring the relative priority placed by the executive branch on any of the aid activities represented by that category of assistance. Because Congress closely examines the executive's distribution of bilateral economic resources and in a number of cases modifies the President's proposed budget plan, funding trends also characterize congressional aid priorities and areas of special concern [9]

Trends in Types of U.S. Aid

As shown in Figure 2 (and Table A-2), there have been shifts in the use of different types of U.S. assistance in response to world events and changing priorities. Funding a Middle East peace supplemental, the Andean Counter-narcotics Initiative and economic support for countries assisting U.S. efforts in the war on terrorism pushed strategic-oriented economic aid from a 26% share in FY1995 to an average 33% share from FY1997 through FY2002. The injection of significant assistance to Iraq raised political-strategic assistance to 50% in FY2004 [10]. Excluding the anomaly of Iraq, however, would lower the proportion of political-strategic aid to 29% in FY2004. Even with Iraq funding included in the following years, this grouping of aid drops to about 29% in the period FY2005 through FY2007, reflecting somewhat the impact of a continuing ten-year plan to reduce economic aid to Israel and Egypt, and, except in the case of Afghanistan, less robust aid for partner states in the war on terrorism. The growth of development-related aid in this period also diminished the relative proportion of other forms of assistance. The proportion of total aid represented by political-strategic assistance in FY2008 was 27%. For more than two decades, military assistance as a share of total aid obligations has declined, a trend that began after military aid peaked at 42% in FY1984.

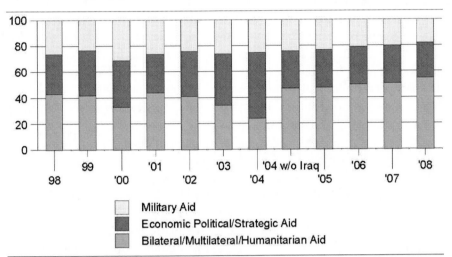

Source: U.S. Department of State and CRS calculations.

Notes: To illustrate the impact of Iraq funding on the aid program, the column "FY04 without Iraq" excludes $18.4 billion in Iraq Relief and Reconstruction Fund (IRRF) aid.

Figure 2. Shifts in Program Emphasis (FY1998-2008) (as % of total U.S. foreign assistance).

Despite increases in other forms of assistance in the period from 1998 through FY2004, military aid hovered in the 25% range as the United States provided additional security support to many of the partner states in the war on terrorism and other countries that might face new external threats due to the pending conflict in Iraq. From FY2005, however, its share continued to fall, largely due to the rise in prominence of the development assistance category. In FY2008, military assistance represented less than 18% of total aid. However, as discussed in a later section, foreign assistance provided by the Department of Defense, and not counted in estimates of traditional foreign aid, has been increasing with operations in Iraq and Afghanistan, with new authority to train and equip foreign militaries, and with anti-narcotics activities in Latin America and Afghanistan.

Perhaps the most striking trend in this period has been the growth in development-related assistance, including humanitarian aid, food aid, and contributions to multilateral institutions. Development-related aid rose steadily from a 38% share in FY1990 to nearly 48% by FY1995. The growth of more politically driven economic programs in central Europe and the former Soviet Union, plus sizable cuts to development aid in FY1996/1997 and increased emphasis on security assistance following the September 11 terrorist attacks, drove the share down to an average of 41% during the late 1990s through FY2002. If Iraq funding were excluded in FY2004, the proportion of development aid would jump to 47%, rather than the deep decline to 25% if Iraq is included. With the approval of significant amounts of funding for two new presidential aid priorities, the Millennium Challenge Corporation and the HIV/AIDS Initiative, development assistance grew to represent over half of total U.S. foreign aid by FY2005, the highest proportion in more than twenty years. This share has since continued to increase, reaching 55% in FY2008.

Trends in Programs and Sectors of Special Interest

There are multiple ways to define and categorize U.S. foreign assistance programs. At various times, congressional and public attention centers on one or another slice of the aid effort. For instance, the large community of non-governmental organizations (NGOs) working on international sustainable development activities most often concerns itself with what it calls "core development accounts," usually defined as including the USAID Child Survival and Health, USAID Development Assistance, Millennium Challenge, and HIV/AIDS accounts. Collectively, these have grown exponentially over the ten year period from 1998 to 2008, from $1.9 billion to $9.6 billion, largely due to the launching of the HIV/AIDS and MCA programs.

One of the most striking changes in the distribution of economic aid resources in recent years has been the sharp growth in funding for health programs, especially in the area of HIV/AIDS and other infectious diseases (see Table 1). In 2004, the Bush Administration launched a five-year Global AIDS Initiative, the President's Emergency Plan for AIDS Relief (PEPFAR), with the goal of treating two million HIV-infected individuals, and caring for ten million infected people and AIDS orphans that eventually provided over $18 billion. The program was re-authorized in 2008 (P.L. 110-293) at $48 billion for FY2009 through FY2013 to support prevention and treatment of HIV/AIDS, malaria, and tuberculosis. Spending on non-AIDS infectious diseases has increased by 400% since FY2001. Funding has also risen notably for Child Survival and Maternal Health projects that aim to reduce infant mortality, combat malnutrition, improve the quality of child delivery facilities, and raise nutritional levels of mothers. Funding for these activities has grown by 45% in the past seven years.

Public support and congressional and Administration action often raise the priority given to specific sectors or programs. In recent years, high profile programs include support for microenterprise, basic education, clean water and sanitation. For each of these specific interests, funding has been boosted by Congress in the form of legislative directives or earmarks in the annual foreign aid appropriations legislation. Funding for microenterprise, for instance, went from $58 million in FY1988 to $111 million in FY1996 and $216 million in FY2006. Congress mandated a level of $245 million for microenterprise assistance in FY2008. Basic education programs were funded at about $95 million in FY1997; they were set at $700 million in FY2008. Funding for water and sanitation projects was not closely tracked ten years ago; the directed level for FY2008 was $300 million.

Some sectors once strongly favored by Congress and the executive branch have lost out in the funding competition in recent decades. Agriculture programs have seen significant decreases since the 1970s and 1980s when they represented the bulk of U.S. development assistance. In FY1984, for instance, agriculture and rural development received an appropriation of $725 million from the development assistance account, compared to $315 million in FY1998 and $413 million in FY2008 from all USAID/State accounts. Programs managing natural resources and protecting the global environment fell from $504 million in FY2002 to $324 million in FY2008. The rapid rise in HIV/AIDS funding overshadows to some extent reductions for other health sectors. Spending on family planning and reproductive health programs has been flat during the past 15 years, with the FY2008 level of $457 million only slightly higher than the 15-year average of $444 million.

Which Countries Receive U.S. Foreign Aid?

In FY2008, the United States is providing some form of foreign assistance to about 154 countries. Figure 3 and Figure 4 identify the top 15 recipients of U.S. foreign assistance for FY1998 and FY2008, respectively [11]. Assistance, although provided to many nations, is concentrated heavily in certain countries, reflecting the priorities and interests of United States foreign policy at the time.

As shown in the figures below, there are both similarities and sharp differences among country aid recipients for the two periods. The most consistent thread connecting the top aid recipients over the past decade has been continuing U.S. support for peace in the Middle East, with large programs maintained for Israel and Egypt and a relatively smaller program for West Bank/Gaza. The commitment to Latin America counter-narcotics efforts is also evident in both periods, with Peru and Bolivia appearing in FY1998 and Colombia and Mexico among the top U.S. aid recipients a decade later. Assisting countries emerging from conflict, usually under more temporary circumstances, is another constant aspect of U.S. foreign aid. Haiti and Bosnia, leading recipients in FY1998, have been replaced currently by Sudan, Afghanistan, and Iraq.

But there are also significant contrasts in the leading aid recipients since FY1998. The impact of the terrorist attacks on September 11, 2001, and the subsequent use of foreign aid to support other nations threatened by terrorism or helping the U.S. combat the global threat is clearly seen in the country aid allocations for FY2008. Afghanistan, Pakistan, and Jordan, none of which was a top recipient in FY1998, are key partners in the war on terrorism.

Another relatively new feature of American assistance—the emphasis on HIV/AIDS programs— is evident in FY2008 aid figures with Ethiopia, Kenya, Nigeria, and South Africa among the top recipients, largely due to their selection as focus countries for the Bush Administration's HIV/AIDS Initiative. A further shift concerns the former Soviet states in which the United States invested large sums to assist in their transitions to democratic societies and market-oriented economies. In FY1998, Ukraine, Armenia, Georgia, and Russia were among the top fifteen U.S. aid recipients. By FY2008, only Georgia remains because of a U.S. reconstruction initiative following Georgia's recent conflict with Russia.

Finally, a striking feature of the more recent aid recipients is the robust level of assistance provided to those below the top-ranked two or three countries. Ten years previously, the gap between the second and third recipients, Egypt and Bosnia, was nearly $2 billion.

In FY2008, the gap between the second and fourth recipients, Afghanistan and Jordan, was less than $1 billion, and, on average, the bottom dozen recipients received more than four times what their counterparts received in FY1998.

On a regional basis (Figure 5 and Figure 6), the Middle East has for many years received the bulk of U.S. foreign assistance. With economic aid to the region's top two recipients, Israel and Egypt, declining since the late 1990s and overall increases in other areas, however, the share of bilateral U.S. assistance consumed by the Middle East fell from nearly 57% in FY1998 to nearly 34% by FY2008.

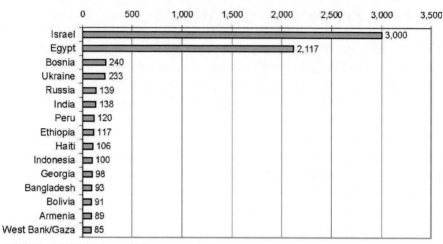

Source: USAID and Department of State.

Figure 3. Top Foreign Aid Recipients, FY1998 (appropriations in millions, US$).

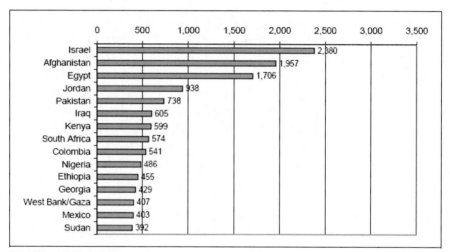

Source: USAID and State Department.

Figure 4. Top Foreign Aid Recipients, FY2008 (appropriations in millions, US$).

On a regional basis (Figure 5 and Figure 6), the Middle East has for many years received the bulk of U.S. foreign assistance. With economic aid to the region's top two recipients, Israel and Egypt, declining since the late 1990s and overall increases in other areas, however, the share of bilateral U.S. assistance consumed by the Middle East fell from nearly 57% in FY1998 to nearly 34% by FY2008.

Since September 11, 2001, South Asia has emerged as a significant recipient of U.S. assistance, rising from a 4% share ten years ago to about 17% in FY2008, largely because of aid to Afghanistan and Pakistan. Similarly, the share represented by African nations has increased from a little more than 13% to nearly 29% in 2008, largely due to the HIV/AIDS Initiative, that funnels resources mostly to African countries. Latin America, despite a renewed effort to deter illicit narcotics production and trafficking with large aid programs, is a region where the proportion of total U.S. assistance has remained level. With the graduation of several East European aid recipients in recent years and the phasing down of programs in Russia, Ukraine, and other former Soviet states, the Europe/Eurasia regional share has fallen significantly. The proportion of assistance provided to East Asia grew in the past decade, but the region remains the smallest area of concentration, accounting for 4% of U.S. foreign aid in FY2008.

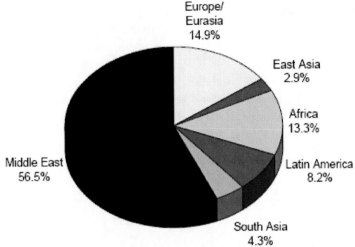

Source: USAID and Department of State. Note: Based on appropriated levels. Figures include supplemental appropriations and Iraq.

Figure 5. Regional Distribution of Aid, FY1998.

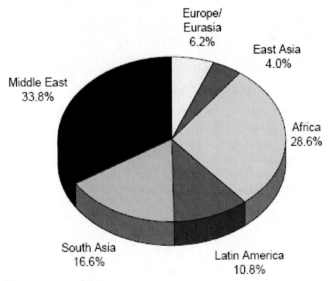

Source: USAID and Department of State.
Note: Based on appropriated levels. Figures include supplemental appropriations and Iraq.

Figure 6. Regional Distribution of Aid, FY2008.

FOREIGN AID SPENDING

How Large Is the U.S. Foreign Assistance Budget and What Have Been the Historical Funding Trends?

There are several methods commonly used for measuring the amount of federal spending on foreign assistance. Amounts can be expressed in terms of budget authority (funds appropriated by Congress), outlays (money actually spent), as a percent of the total federal budget, as a percent of total discretionary budget authority (funds that Congress directly controls, excluding mandatory and entitlement programs), or as a percentage of the gross domestic product (GDP) (for an indication of the national wealth allocated to foreign aid).

By nearly all of these measures, some of which are illustrated in Figure 7 and Figure 8, foreign aid resources fell steadily over several decades since the historical high levels of the late 1940s and early 1950s.

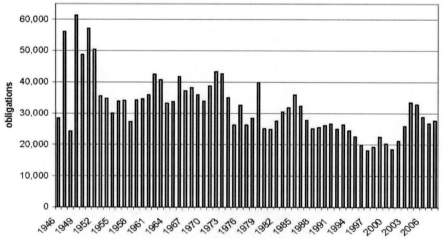

Source: U.S. Overseas Loans and Grants (Greenbook) July 1,1945-September 30, 2006; House and Senate appropriations legislation; CRS calculations.

Notes: This figure is based in the data from Table A-3. See the notes following Table A-3 for an explanation of the methodology used.

Figure 7. U.S. Foreign Aid: FY1946-FY2008 (obligations, in millions of constant 2008 US$).

This downward trend was sporadically interrupted, with spikes in the 1960s and early 1970s, 1979, and the mid-1980s, largely due to major foreign policy initiatives such as the Alliance for Progress for Latin America in 1961 and the infusion of funds to implement the Camp David Middle East Peace Accords in 1979. The lowest point in U.S. foreign aid spending came in 1997 when foreign operations appropriations fell near $18 billion (in constant dollar terms) and represented roughly 29% of the peak foreign aid committed during the Marshall Plan period.

Following the September 11 terrorist attacks, foreign aid became a key instrument in fighting the global war on terrorism and contributing to the reconstruction of Afghanistan and Iraq. See Figure 9 at the end of this section for a more detailed snapshot of foreign aid funding trends and related foreign policy events. As a percent of gross domestic product, prior to the mid-1960s, in most years foreign aid represented over 1%. Following the Vietnam War, foreign assistance as a percent of GDP ranged between 0.5% and 0.25% for the next 20 years. The program's share of GDP dropped to its lowest level ever in FY2001 (0.15%), but has risen somewhat in recent years, averaging about 0.20% between FY2006 and FY2008 (Figure 8).

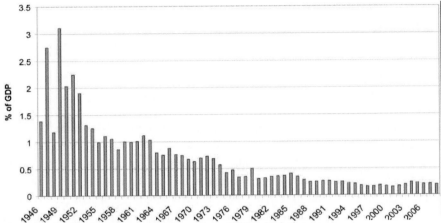

Source: Greenbook, U.S. Department of Commerce, CRS calculations.

Figure 8. Foreign Aid as % of GDP.

Congress appropriates most foreign aid money through annual State-Foreign Operations appropriations bill. That legislation represents the most direct congressional action on foreign assistance spending decisions, although small but growing amounts of foreign aid are funded in other legislation [12].

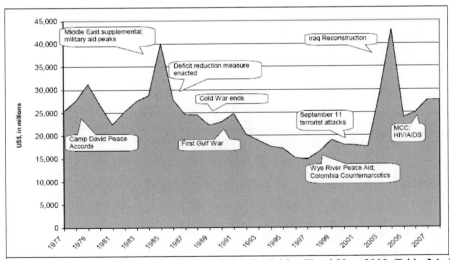

Source: Budget of the United States Government: Historic Tables Fiscal Year 2009, Table 5.1: Budget Authority by Function and Subfunction, 1976-2013; appropriations acts for FY2008.

Figure 9. Foreign Aid Funding Trends, FY1977-FY2008 (budget authority, in millions of constant 2008 US$).

Table 2. Foreign Operation Appropriations, FY1997-FY2008 (in billions of dollars)
FY97 FY98 FY99 FY00 FY01 FY02 FY03 FY04 FY05 FY06

	FY97	FY98	FY99	FY00	FY01	FY02	FY03	FY04	FY05	FY06	FY07	FY08
$ Current	12.3	13.2	15.4	16.4	14.9	16.5	23.7	39.0 (20.6)	22.3	23.2	26.08	27.7
$ Constant 2008	16.3	17.3	19.7	20.3	17.9	19.5	27.4	44.0 (23.2)	24.3	24.5	26.81	27.7

Source: Annual appropriations acts; CRS calculations.

Notes: FY1999 excludes $17.861 billion for the IMF because it is offset by a U.S. claim on the IMF that is liquid and interest bearing, resulting in no outlays from the U.S. treasury. The FY2004 figure in parenthesis shows the total without Iraq reconstruction funds to illustrate the significant but anomalous impact of those funds on total foreign assistance spending.

Like other measures of foreign assistance programs, State-Foreign Operations appropriations declined in the mid-1990s to near $16 billion in 2008 dollars, the lowest level during the past decade in real terms (Table 2). Appropriated amounts rose beginning in FY1998 and averaged about $19 billion in constant dollars through the next four years. The combination of additional funding for the war on terrorism, Afghanistan reconstruction, and new foreign aid initiatives focused on HIV/AIDS and the Millennium Challenge Corporation, have pushed average annual Foreign Operations appropriations well above $20 billion consistently since FY2003. Including Iraq funding, FY2004 was the largest Foreign Operations appropriations level, in real terms, in at least 30 years [13.

How Does Foreign Aid Compare with Other Federal Programs?

Foreign aid spending is a relatively small component of the U.S. federal budget. As part of the estimated total amount spent in FY2008 on all discretionary programs (those controlled by Congress through appropriations), entitlements, and other mandatory activities, foreign aid outlays represent an estimated 1%.

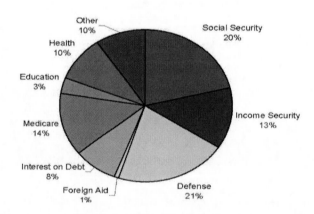

Source: Budget of the United States Government: Historic Tables Fiscal Year 2009, Table 3.2: Outlays by Function and Subfunction, FY2008 Estimates.

Figure 10. U.S. Budget Outlays, FY2008.

This figure is in line with typical foreign aid outlay amounts, which have generally equaled slightly less than 1% of total U.S. spending. Figure 10 compares foreign aid outlays for FY2008 with those of other major U.S. government spending categories.

How Much of Foreign Aid Dollars Are Spent on U.S. Goods?

Most U.S. foreign aid is used to procure U.S. goods and services, although amounts of aid coming back to the United States differ by program. No exact figure is available due to difficulties in tracking procurement item by item, but some general estimates are possible for individual programs, though these may vary from year to year. In FY2008, roughly 87%, or $4.1 billion, of military aid financing was used to procure U.S. military equipment and training. The remaining 13%, $614 million, was allocated to Israel for procurement within that country.

Food assistance commodities are purchased wholly in the United States, and most expenditures for shipping those commodities to recipient countries go entirely to U.S. freight companies. Under current law, [14] three-fourths of all food aid must be shipped by U.S. carriers. On this basis, a rough estimate suggests that more than 90%—or nearly $1.85 billion in FY2008—of food aid expenditures were spent in the United States.

Because U.S. contributions to multilateral institutions are mixed with funds from other nations and the bulk of the program is financed with borrowed funds rather than direct government contributions, the U.S. share of procurement financed by MDBs may even exceed the amount of the U.S. contribution, as occurred in 2003. However, no recent figures showing procurement on a nation-by-nation basis are available.

Although a small proportion of funding for bilateral development and political/strategic assistance programs results in transfers of U.S. dollars, the services of experts and project management personnel and much of the required equipment is procured from the United States. Section 604 of the Foreign Assistance Act of 1961 (P.L. 87-195; 22 U.S.C. §2151)— often referred to as the "Buy America" provision—limits the expenditure of foreign assistance funds outside the United States, though subsequent amending legislation has loosened the restriction to allow for more expenditures within poor countries receiving assistance. Countries receiving MCC Compact grants are required to follow a modified version of World Bank procurement guidelines that call for open competition, excepting only specific countries subject to sanctions under U.S. law. In addition to the direct benefits derived from aid dollars used for American goods and services, many argue that the foreign aid program brings significant indirect financial benefits to the United States. First, it is argued that provision of military equipment through the military assistance program and food commodities through P.L.480, the Food For Peace program, helps to develop future, strictly commercial, markets for those products. Second, as countries develop economically, they are in a position to purchase more goods from abroad and the United States benefits as a trade partner.

The use of "tied" aid—which is conditional on procurement of goods and services from the donor-country or a limited group of designated countries—has become increasingly disfavored in the international community. Critics of such conditional aid argue that it inhibits a sense of responsibility and support on the part of recipient governments for development projects and impedes the integration of the host country into the global economy [15]. Studies have shown that tying aid increases the costs of goods and services by 15%-30% on average, and up to 40% for food aid, reducing the overall effectiveness of aid flows [16]. Reflecting donor concerns about these findings, the average percent of official bilateral development assistance from donor countries that was tied fell from 70% in 1985 to 15% in 2007. Meanwhile, 31% of U.S. bilateral development assistance in 2007 was tied, down sharply from 55% in 2006 [17].

This is the highest level of tied aid among donor countries, and widely believed to reflect policy makers' perception that maintaining public and political support for foreign aid programs requires ensuring direct economic benefit to the United States. The United States joined other donor nations in committing to reduce tied aid in the Paris Declaration on Aid Effectiveness in March 2005, but the Declaration did not set target goals on tied aid as it did for the other indicators of progress identified in the document [18]

How Does the United States Rank as a Donor of Foreign Aid?

For decades, the United States ranked first among the developed countries in net disbursements of economic aid, or "Official Development Assistance (ODA)" as defined by the international donor community [19] In 1989, for the first time, Japan supplanted the United States as the largest donor. The United States was again the leading donor from 1990 to 1992, and fluctuated between a second and third position from 1993 to 2000. In 2001, it again became the largest contributor and remained in that position in 2007, the most recent year for which data is available, with a commitment of $21.75 billion.

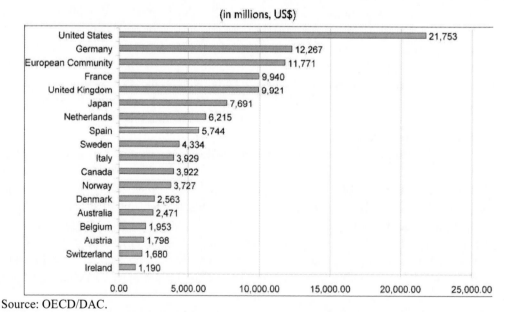

Source: OECD/DAC.

Figure 11. Economic Aid From Major Donors, 2007.

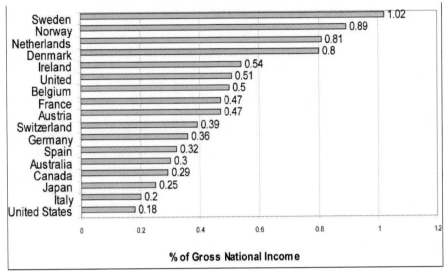

Source: OECD/DAC.

Figure 12. Economic Aid as % of GNI for Major Donors, 2007.

Germany followed at $12.3 billion, the European Community at $11.8 billion, and both France and the United Kingdom at $9.9 billion. Japan, which has significantly scaled back its foreign aid program in recent years, gave $7.7 billion in 2007. As a group, the 22 members of the Organization for Economic Cooperation and Development (OECD)'s Development Assistance Committee (DAC), representing the world's leading providers of economic aid, transferred $103.6 billion in 2007, down slightly in current dollars from $104.4 billion in 2006.

Even as it leads in dollar amounts of aid flows to developing countries, the United States is often among the last when aid transfers by developed country donors are calculated as a percent of gross national income (GNI) [20]. In 2007, as has been the case since 1993, the United States ranked last among major donors at 0.18% of GNI. Sweden ranked first at 1.02% of GNI, while the United Kingdom dispensed 0.51%, France 0.47%, and Germany 0.26%. The average for all DAC members in 2007 was 0.48%, up from .25% in 2003.

DELIVERY OF FOREIGN ASSISTANCE

How and in what form assistance reaches an aid recipient can vary widely, depending on the type of aid program, the objective of the assistance, and the agency responsible for providing the aid.

What Executive Branch Agencies Administer Foreign Aid Programs?

U.S. Agency for International Development

For over 40 years, the bulk of the U.S. bilateral economic aid program has been administered by the U.S. Agency for International Development (USAID). Created by an executive branch reorganization in 1961, USAID became an independent agency in 1999, although its Administrator reports to and serves under the "direct authority and foreign policy guidance" of the Secretary of State. USAID is directly responsible for most bilateral development assistance and disaster relief programs, including economic growth, global health, many democracy programs, and Title II of P.L. 480 (Food for Peace program) food assistance. These programs amounted to $5.138 billion in FY2008. In conjunction with the State Department, USAID manages the ESF, SEED, and FSA programs, amounting to $6.05 billion in FY2008 [21]. USAID's staff in late 2008 totaled 7,291, of which only about 2,692 were U.S. citizen "direct hire" employees. Almost three quarters of USAID staff—about 5,273—are U.S. citizen foreign service employees and foreign nationals working overseas in one of the 84 country missions, six regional offices, and three representational offices to oversee the implementation of hundreds of projects undertaken by thousands of private sector contractors, consultants, and non-governmental organizations [22]

U.S. Department of State

In addition to those programs jointly managed with USAID, the Department of State administers several aid programs directly. Individual offices at State oversee activities dealing with international narcotics control and law enforcement, terrorism, weapons proliferation, non-U.N. peacekeeping operations, refugee relief, and voluntary support for a range of international organizations such as UNICEF. In FY2008, appropriations for these State Department-administered bilateral aid programs totaled about $2.4 billion. State is also home to the Office of the Global AIDS Coordinator, created to manage President Bush's Global AIDS Initiative, which administered $4.6 billion in FY2008 for international HIV/AIDS, tuberculosis, and malaria programs. The funds are channeled through USAID, the Department of Health and Human Services, the Centers for Disease Control, the National Institutes for Health, and other implementing agencies. In addition, State has policy authority, together with the Department of Defense, over the FMF and IMET programs, which are implemented by the DOD's Defense Security Cooperation Agency.

The Director of Foreign Assistance (DFA), a State Department position created in 2006, is charged with coordinating U.S. assistance programs. Until January 2009 when a separate acting DFA was appointed, the DFA served concurrently as the Administrator of USAID. The DFA has authority over most State Department and USAID programs. Though the DFA is also tasked with providing "guidance" to other agencies that manage foreign aid activities, major foreign aid programs, such as the Millennium Challenge Account and the Office of the Global AIDS Coordinator, have remained outside of the DFA's authority.

U.S. Department of Defence

Most military assistance, including Foreign Military Financing (FMF) and International Military Education and Training (IMET), is administered by the Department of Defense in conjunction with the Bureau of Political-Military Affairs in the State Department. The Defense Security Cooperation Agency is the primary DOD body responsible for Foreign Military Financing and related training programs. DOD has also been involved in an expanded range of foreign assistance activities in recent years, providing development assistance to Iraq and Afghanistan through the Commander's Emergency Response Program (CERP) and the Iraq Relief and Reconstruction Fund, and elsewhere through the Defense Health Program, counter-drug activities, and humanitarian and disaster relief activities. While DOD managed about $4.9 billion in traditional military aid in FY2008, other funds appropriated through defense appropriations legislation, and not counted as foreign assistance for the purposes of this report, have been used to carry out state-building development activities, usually in the context of training exercises and military operations, that were once the exclusive jurisdiction of civilian aid agencies.

U.S. Department of Treasury

The Treasury Department administers three foreign aid programs. U.S. contributions to and participation in the World Bank and other multilateral development institutions are managed by Treasury's Under Secretary for International Affairs. Presidentially appointed U.S. executive directors at each of the banks represent the United States' point of view. Treasury also deals with foreign debt reduction issues and programs, including U.S. participation in the Highly Indebted Poor Countries (HIPC) initiative. The Treasury Department further manages a technical assistance program, offering temporary financial advisors to countries implementing major economic reforms and combating terrorist finance activity. For FY2008, funding for activities falling under the Treasury Department's jurisdiction totaled about $1.3 billion.

Millenium Challenge Corporation

A new foreign aid agency was created in February 2004 to administer the Millennium Challenge Account (MCA) initiative. The account is intended to concentrate significantly higher amounts of U.S. resources in a few low- and low-middle income countries that have demonstrated a strong commitment to political, economic, and social reforms. A significant feature of the MCA program is that recipient countries formulate, propose and implement mutually-agreed multi-year U.S.-funded projects known as Compacts. Compacts in the 18 recipient countries selected to date have emphasized construction of infrastructure. The Millennium Challenge Corporation (MCC) is charged with managing this results-oriented, competitive foreign aid delivery mechanism. The MCC is a U.S. government corporation, headed by a Chief Executive Officer who reports to a Board of Directors chaired by the Secretary of State. The Corporation maintains a relatively small staff of about 300. The MCC managed a budget of $1.5 billion in FY2008.

Other Agencies

Other government agencies that play a role in implementing foreign aid programs include the Peace Corps, the Trade and Development Agency (TDA), and the Overseas Private Investment Corporation (OPIC). The Peace Corps, an autonomous agency with an FY2008 budget of $331 million, supports nearly 8,000 volunteers in 76 countries. Peace Corps volunteers work in a wide range of educational, health, and community development projects. TDA finances trade missions and feasibility studies for private sector projects likely to generate U.S. exports. Its budget in FY2008 was $50 million. OPIC provides political risk insurance to U.S. companies investing in developing countries and the new democracies and finances projects through loans and guarantees. It also supports investment missions and provides other pre-investment information services. Its insurance activities have been self-sustaining, but credit reform rules require a relatively small appropriation to back up U.S. guarantees and for administrative expenses. For FY2008, Congress appropriated $71 million to OPIC.

Two independent agencies, the Inter-American Foundation and the African Development Foundation, also administer U.S. foreign aid. Both organizations emphasize grassroots development by providing financial support to local private organizations in developing countries. For FY2008, Congress appropriated $21 million and $29 million, respectively, to the Inter-American Foundation and the African Development Foundation.

What Are the Different Forms in Which Assistance Is Provided?

Most U.S. assistance is now provided as a grant (gift) rather than a loan, but the forms a grant may take are diverse.

Cash Transfers

Although it is the exception rather than the rule, some countries receive aid in the form of a cash grant to the government. Dollars provided in this way support a government's balance-of-payments situation, enabling it to purchase more U.S. goods, service its debt, or devote more domestic revenues to developmental or other purposes. Cash transfers have been made as a reward to countries that have supported the United States in its war on terrorism (Turkey and Jordan in FY2004), to provide political and strategic support (both Egypt and Israel annually for decades after the 1979 Camp David Peace Accord), and in exchange for undertaking difficult political and economic reforms. Countries receiving cash transfers in 2007 were Pakistan ($200 million), Egypt ($284 million), Jordan ($116 million), and Lebanon ($250 million).

Equipment and Commodities

Assistance may be provided in the form of food commodities, weapons systems, or equipment such as generators or computers. Food aid may be provided directly to meet humanitarian needs or to encourage attendance at a maternal/child health care program. Weapons supplied under the military assistance program may include training in their use. Equipment and commodities provided under development assistance are usually integrated with other forms of aid to meet objectives in a particular social or economic sector. For instance, textbooks have been provided in both Afghanistan and Iraq as part of a broader effort to reform the educational sector and train teachers. Computers may be offered in conjunction with training and expertise to fledgling microcredit institutions. In recent years, antiretroviral drugs (ARVs) provided through PEPFAR programs to individuals living with HIV/AIDS have been a significant component of commodity-based assistance.

Economic Infrastructure

Although once a significant portion of U.S. assistance programs, construction of economic infrastructure—roads, irrigation systems, electric power facilities, etc.—was rarely provided after the 1970s. Because of the substantial expense of these projects, they were to be found only in large assistance programs, such as that for Egypt in the 1980s and 1990s, where the United States constructed major urban water and sanitation systems. In the past decade, however, the aid programs in Iraq and Afghanistan have supported the building of schools, health clinics, roads, power plants and irrigation systems. In Iraq alone, more than $10 billion has gone to economic infrastructure. Economic infrastructure is now also supported by U.S.

assistance in a wider range of developing countries through the Millennium Challenge Account. In this case, recipient countries design their own assistance programs, most of which, to date, include an infrastructure component.

Training

Transfer of know-how is a significant part of most assistance programs. The International Military and Educational Training Program (IMET) provides training to officers of the military forces of allied and friendly nations. Tens of thousands of citizens of aid recipient countries receive short-term technical training or longer term degree training annually under USAID's participant training program. More than one-third of Peace Corps volunteers are English, math, and science teachers. Other programs provide law enforcement personnel with anti-narcotics or anti-terrorism training.

Expertise

Many assistance programs provide expert advice to government and private sector organizations. The Treasury Department, USAID, and U.S.-funded multilateral banks all place specialists in host government ministries to make recommendations on policy reforms in a wide variety of sectors. USAID has often placed experts in private sector business and civic organizations to help strengthen them in their formative years or while indigenous staff are being trained. While most of these experts are U.S. nationals, in Russia, USAID has funded the development of locally-staffed political and economic think tanks to offer policy options to that government.

Small Grants

USAID, the Inter-American Foundation, and the African Development Foundation often provide aid in the form of grants that may then be used by U.S. or indigenous organizations to further their varied developmental purposes. For instance, grants are sometimes provided to microcredit organizations which in turn provide loans to microentrepreneurs. Through the USAID-funded Eurasia Foundation, grants are provided to help strengthen the role of former Soviet Union non-governmental organizations in democratization and private enterprise development.

How Much Aid Is Provided as Loans And How Much as Grants? What Are Some Types of Loans? Have Loans Repaid? Why Is Repayment of Some Loans Forgiven?

Under the Foreign Assistance Act of 1961, the President may determine the terms and conditions under which most forms of assistance are provided. In general, the financial condition of a country—its ability to meet repayment obligations—has been an important criterion of the decision to provide a loan or grant. Some programs—such as humanitarian and disaster relief programs—were designed from the beginning to be entirely grant activities.

Loan/Grant Composition

During the past two decades, nearly all foreign aid—military as well as economic—has been provided in grant form. Between 1962 and 1988, loans represented 32% of total military and economic assistance. This figure declined substantially beginning in the mid-1980s, until by FY2001, loans represented less than 1% of total aid appropriations. The de-emphasis on loan programs came largely in response to the debt problems of developing countries. Both Congress and the executive branch supported the view that foreign aid should not add to the already existing debt burden carried by these countries.

Types of Loans

Although a small proportion of total aid, there are several significant USAID-managed programs that provide direct loans or guarantee loans. Under the Israeli Loan Guarantee Program, the United States has guaranteed repayment of loans made by commercial sources to support the costs of immigrants settling in Israel from other countries. Other guarantee programs support low-income housing and community development programs of developing countries and microenterprise and small business credit programs. A Development Credit Authority in which risk is shared with a private sector bank can be used to support any development sector.

Loan Repayment

Between 1946 and 2006, the United States loaned more than $108 billion in foreign aid, and while most foreign aid is now provided through grants, $22.6 billion in loans to foreign governments remained outstanding in 2007 [23]. Most recipients of U.S. loans remain current or only slightly in arrears on debt payments. For nearly three decades, Section 620q of the Foreign Assistance Act (the Brooke amendment) has prohibited new assistance to any country that falls more than one year past due in servicing its debt obligations to the United States. Argentina, Democratic Republic of the Congo, Somalia, Sudan, Syria, and Zimbabwe are countries to which the provision applies as of October 2008 [24]. The President may waive application of this prohibition if he determines it is in the national interest.

Debt Forgiveness

The United States has also forgiven debts owed by foreign governments and encouraged, with mixed success, other foreign aid donors and international financial institutions to do likewise. In total, the United States forgave or reduced about $24.3 billion owed by foreign governments between 1990 and 2007 [25].

In some cases, the decision to forgive foreign aid debts has been based largely on economic grounds as another means to support development efforts by heavily indebted, but reform-minded, countries. The United States has been one of the strongest supporters of the Heavily Indebted Poor Country (HIPC) Initiative. This initiative, which began in the late 1990s and continues in 2008, includes for the first time participation of the World Bank, the International Monetary Fund, and other international financial institutions in a comprehensive debt workout framework for the world's poorest and most debt-strapped nations.

The largest and most hotly debated debt forgiveness actions have been implemented for much broader foreign policy reasons with a more strategic purpose. Poland, during its transition from a communist system and centrally-planned economy (1990—$2.46 billion), Egypt, for making peace with Israel and helping maintain the Arab coalition during the

Persian Gulf War (1990—$7 billion), and Jordan, after signing a peace accord with Israel (1994—$700 million), are examples. Similarly, the United States forgave about $4.1 billion in outstanding Saddam-era Iraqi debt in November 2004, and helped negotiate an 80% reduction in Iraq's debt to Paris Club members later that month [26]

What Are the Roles of Government and Private Sector in Development and Humanitarian Aid Delivery?

Most development and humanitarian assistance activities are not directly implemented by U.S. government personnel but by private sector entities. Generally speaking, government foreign service and civil servants determine the direction and priorities of the aid program, allocate funds while keeping within legislative requirements, ensure that appropriate projects are in place to meet aid objectives, select implementors, and monitor the implementation of those projects for effectiveness and financial accountability. At one time, USAID professionals played a larger role in implementing aid programs, but the affect of budget cuts on personnel and the emergence of private sector alternatives over the past thirty years has led to a shift in responsibilities [27]

Private sector aid implementors, usually employed as contractors or grantees, may be individual personal service contractors, consulting firms, non-profit non-government organizations (NGOs), universities, or charitable private voluntary organizations (PVOs). These carry out the vast array of aid projects in all sectors.

CONGRESS AND FOREIGN AID

Numerous congressional authorizing committees and appropriations subcommittees maintain responsibility for U.S. foreign assistance. Several committees have responsibility for authorizing legislation establishing programs and policy and for conducting oversight of foreign aid programs. In the Senate, the Committee on Foreign Relations, and in the House, the Committee on Foreign Affairs, have primary jurisdiction over bilateral development assistance, ESF and other economic security assistance, military assistance, and international organizations. Food aid, primarily the responsibility of the Agriculture Committees in both bodies, is shared with the Foreign Affairs Committee in the House. U.S. contributions to multilateral development banks are within the jurisdiction of the Senate Foreign Relations Committee and the House Financial Services Committee.

Traditionally, foreign aid appropriations are provided entirely through subcommittees of the Appropriations panels in both the House and Senate. Most foreign aid funds fall under the jurisdiction of the State-Foreign Operations Subcommittees, with food assistance appropriated by the Agriculture Subcommittees. As noted earlier, however, a growing segment of military activities that could be categorized as foreign aid have been appropriated through the Defense Subcommittees in recent years.

What Congressional Committees Oversee Foreign Aid Programs?

The most significant *permanent* foreign aid *authorization* laws are the Foreign Assistance Act of 1961, covering most bilateral economic and security assistance programs (P.L. 87-195; 22 U.S.C. 2151), the Arms Export Control Act (1976), authorizing military sales and financing (P.L. 90-629; 22 U.S.C. 2751), the Agricultural Trade Development and Assistance Act of 1954 (P.L. 480), covering food aid (P.L. 83-480; 7 U.S.C. 1691), and the Bretton Woods Agreement Act (1945) authorizing U.S. participation in multilateral development banks (P.L. 79-171; 22 U.S.C. 286) [28]. In the past, Congress usually scheduled debates every two years on omnibus foreign aid bills that amended these permanent authorization measures. Although foreign aid authorizing bills have passed the House or Senate, or both, on numerous occasions, Congress has not enacted into law a comprehensive foreign assistance authorization measure since 1985. Instead, foreign aid bills have frequently stalled at some point in the debate because of controversial issues, a tight legislative calendar, or executive-legislative foreign policy disputes [29]

In lieu of approving a broad authorization bill, Congress has on occasion authorized major foreign assistance initiatives for specific regions, countries, or aid sectors in stand-alone legislation or within an appropriation bill. Among these are the SEED Act of 1989 (P.L. 101-179; 22 U.S.C. 5401), the FREEDOM Support Act of 1992 (P.L. 102-511; 22 U.S.C. 5801), the United States Leadership Against HIV/AIDS, Tuberculosis, and Malaria Act of 2003 (P.L. 108-25; 22 U.S.C. 7601), the Tom Lantos and Henry J. Hyde United States Global Leadership Against HIV/AIDS, Tuberculosis, and Malaria Reauthorization Act of 2008 (P.L. 110-293), and the Millennium Challenge Act of 2003 (Division D, Title VI of P.L. 108-199).

In the absence of regular enactment of foreign aid *authorization* bills, *appropriation* measures considered annually within the State-Foreign Operations spending bill have assumed greater significance for Congress in influencing U.S. foreign aid policy. Not only do appropriations bills set spending levels each year for nearly every foreign assistance account, State-Foreign Operations appropriations also incorporate new policy initiatives that would otherwise be debated and enacted as part of authorizing legislation.

APPENDIX A. DATA TABLES

Table A-1. Aid Program Composition, FY2008

Aid Program	$s (billions)	% of total aid
Bilateral Development	$10.298	35.5%
Humanitarian	$4.169	14.4%
Multilateral Development	$1.594	5.5%
Economic Political/Security	$7.840	27.1%
Military	$5.068	17.5%
TOTAL	$28.969	100.0%

Source: House and Senate Appropriations Committees and CRS calculations.

Note: Based on appropriated levels in the 151 and 152 subfunction accounts. Table omits operational expense accounts.

**Table A-2. Program Composition, FY1995-FY2008
(current $ in billions, and as% of total aid)**

Fiscal Year	Development/ Humanitarian		Economic Political /Security		Military		Total
1995	$6.539	47.6%	$3.636	26.4%	$3.572	26.0%	$13.747
1996	$5.096	41.4%	$3.689	29.9%	$3.536	28.7%	$12.321
1997	$4.969	41.0%	$3.827	31.6%	$3.333	27.5%	$12.129
1998	$5.575	42.8%	$4.038	31.0%	$3.425	26.3%	$13.038
1999	$6.433	42.1%	$5.352	35.0%	$3.507	22.9%	$15.292
2000	$5.331	33.1%	$5.780	35.9%	$4.998	31.0%	$16.109
2001	$6.365	43.8%	$4.430	30.5%	$3.753	25.8%	$14.548
2002	$6.649	41.3%	$5.557	34.6%	$3.875	24.1%	$16.081
2003	$8.361	34.1%	$9.737	39.7%	$6.399	26.1%	$24.497
2004	$9.520	24.6%	$19.310	49.9%	$9.849	25.5%	$38.679
2004 (w/o Iraq)	$9.520	47.0%	$5.873	29.0%	$4.849	24.0%	$20.242
2005	$11.531	47.9%	$7.027	29.2%	$5.502	22.9%	$24.060
2006	$12.087	50.6%	$6.891	28.9%	$4.902	20.5%	$23.880
2007	$13.784	50.9%	$7.957	29.4%	$5.365	19.8%	$27.106
2008	$16.061	55.4%	$7.840	27.1%	$5.068	17.5%	$28.969

Source: USAID, House and Senate Appropriations Committees, and CRS calculations.

Notes: Based on appropriated levels in the 151 and 152 subfunction accounts. FY2004 without Iraq subtracts $18.4 billion in Iraq Relief and Reconstruction Funds from political-strategic aid—$5 billion from military aid and the rest from political-strategic aid. Table omits operational expense accounts.

Table A-3. Foreign Aid Funding Trends

Fiscal Year	Billions of current US $s	Billions of constant 2008 $s	As % of GDP	As % of total discretionary budget authority
1946	$3.08	$28.38	1.38%	—
1947	$6.71	$56.07	2.75%	—
1948	$3.18	$24.26	1.18%	—
1949	$8.30	$61.27	3.10%	—
1950	$5.97	$48.72	2.03%	
1951	$7.61	$57.12	2.24%	—
1952	$6.81	$50.39	1.90%	—
1953	$4.98	$35.57	1.31%	—
1954	$4.77	$34.76	1.25%	—
1955	$4.10	$30.09	0.99%	—
1956	$4.85	$33.90	1.11%	—
1957	$4.87	$34.07	1.06%	—
1958	$4.01	$27.33	0.86%	—
1959	$5.07	$34.32	1.00%	—
1960	$5.22	$34.61	0.99%	—
1961	$5.48	$35.89	1.01%	—
1962	$6.53	$42.50	1.12%	—
1963	$6.38	$40.77	1.03%	—
1964	$5.27	$33.21	0.79%	—
1965	$5.42	$33.77	0.75%	—
1966	$6.90	$41.75	0.88%	—
1967	$6.34	$37.24	0.76%	—

Table A-3. (Continued)

Fiscal Year	Billions of current US $s	Billions of constant 2008 $s	As % of GDP	As % of total discretionary budget authority
1968	$6.76	$38.17	0.74%	—
1969	$6.64	$35.92	0.67%	—
1970	$6.57	$33.93	0.63%	—
1971	$7.84	$38.72	0.70%	—
1972	$9.02	$43.32	0.73%	—
1973	$9.45	$42.62	0.68%	—
1974	$8.50	$34.97	0.57%	—
1975 [a]	$6.91	$26.20	0.42%	—
1976	$9.11	$32.65	0.47%	—
1977	$7.78	$26.24	0.34%	3.15%
1978	$9.01	$28.42	0.35%	3.47%
1979	$13.85	$39.87	0.50%	5.02%
1980	$9.69	$25.10	0.31%	3.11%
1981	$10.54	$24.91	0.32%	3.09%
1982	$12.32	$27.46	0.35%	3.46%
1983	$14.20	$30.41	0.36%	3.66%
1984	$15.52	$31.85	0.37%	3.66%
1985	$18.13	$35.91	0.41%	3.97%
1986	$16.62	$32.30	0.35%	3.79%
1987	$14.80	$27.76	0.29%	3.32%
1989	$14.85	$25.52	0.26%	3.15
1990	$16.02	$26.13	0.27%	3.22
1991	$17.05	$26.67	0.27%	3.12
1992	$16.43	$24.95	0.25%	3.09
1993	$17.91	$26.41	0.25%	3.42
1994	$17.04	$24.50	0.23%	3.32
1995	$16.14	$22.58	0.21%	3.22
1996	$14.68	$19.94	0.18%	2.93
1997	$13.66	$18.15	0.16%	2.67
1998	$14.69	$19.21	0.16%	2.77
1999	$17.55	$22.44	0.18%	3.02
2000	$16.39	$20.27	0.16%	2.80
2001	$15.33	$18.46	0.15%	2.31
2002	$17.93	$21.24	0.16%	2.44
2003	$22.40	$25.93	0.19%	2.64
2004	$29.69	$33.50	0.24%	3.27
2005	$30.17	$32.92	0.23%	3.06
2006	$27.26	$28.80	0.20%	2.73
2007	$26.08	$26.81	0.20%	2.59
2008	$27.68	$27.68	0.19%	2.40

Source: USAID, Office of Management and Budget, annual appropriations legislation and CRS calculations.

Notes: The data in this table represent obligated funds reported in the USAID Greenbook up through FY2006 (FY2007-FY2008 are appropriations), but the Greenbook accounts included in the total have been adjusted by CRS to allow for accurate comparison over time. CRS has attempted to include only programs that correlate with the traditional foreign assistance budget accounts, excluding, for example, such Greenbook additions as State Department accounts for embassy security and Foreign Service retirement , Cooperative Threat Reduction funds to the former Soviet Union, and certain funds administered by the Department of Defense in Iraq and Afghanistan. FY2008 % of GDP based on 3 Quarter reports.

[a].FY1976 includes both regular FY76 and transition quarter (TQ)funding, and the GDP calculation is based on the average FY76 and TQ GDP.

APPENDIX B. COMMON FOREIGN ASSISTANCE

ACRONYMS AND ABBREVIATIONS

DA	Development Assistance
DOD	Department of Defense
ERMA	Emergency Refugee and Migration Assistance
ESF	Economic Support Fund
FMF	Foreign Military Financing
FSA	FREEDOM (Freedom for Russia and Emerging Eurasian Democracies and Open Markets) Support Act of 1992
GDP	Gross Domestic Product
GNI	Gross National Income
HIPC	Heavily Indebted Poor Country
IBRD	World Bank, International Bank for Reconstruction and Development
IDA	World Bank, International Development Association
IDA	International Disaster Assistance
IMET	International Military Education and Training
IMF	International Monetary Fund
INCLE	International Narcotics Control and Law Enforcement
MCC	Millennium Challenge Corporation
MDBs	Multilateral Development Banks
MRA	Migration and Refugees Assistance
NADR	Non-Proliferation, Anti-Terrorism, Demining and Related Programs
NGO	Non-Governmental Organization
ODA	Official Development Assistance
OECD	Organization for Economic Cooperation and Development
OFDA	Office of Foreign Disaster Assistance
OPIC	Overseas Private Investment Corporation
OTI	Office of Transition Initiatives
PEPFAR	President's Emergency Plan for AIDS Relief
P.L. 480	Food for Peace/Food Aid
PVO	Private Voluntary Organization
SEED	Support for East European Democracy Act of 1989
TDA	U.S. Trade and Development Agency
UNDP	United Nations Development Program
UNICEF	United Nations Children's Fund
USAID	U.S. Agency for International Development

REFERENCES

[1]   Other tools of U.S. foreign policy are the U.S. defense establishment, the diplomatic corps, public diplomacy, and trade policy. American defense capabilities, even if not employed, stand as a potential stick that can be wielded to obtain specific objectives. The State Department diplomatic corps are the eyes, ears, and often the negotiating voice of U.S. foreign policymakers. Public diplomacy programs, such as exchanges like the Fulbright program and Radio Free Europe, project an image of the United States that may influence foreign views positively. U.S. trade policy—through free trade agreements and Export-Import Bank credits, for example—may directly affect the economies of other nations. Foreign aid is probably the most flexible tool—it can act as both carrot and stick, and is a means of influencing events, solving specific problems, and projecting U.S. values.

[2]   Development was again underscored in the Bush Administration's re-statement of the National Security Strategy released on March 16, 2006. Executive Office of the President, *U.S. National Security Strategy 2002 and 2006*, available at [http://www.whitehouse.gov/nsc/nss/2006].

[3]   The framework, representing about 90% of the traditional foreign aid budget in FY2008 (including supplementals), does not include the Millennium Challenge Corporation, Peace Corps, other independent agencies, and international financial institutions. It also excludes non-traditional foreign aid programs, such as DOD-funded activities. While the framework includes the State Department's HIV/AIDS program, it is not under the direct management responsibility of the DFA.

[4]   Most are funded through several accounts. For instance, the objective of Governing Justly and Democratically and each of its individual sectoral elements (see Table 1) are funded through portions of the Development Assistance, SEED, FSA, ESF, and INCLE accounts.

[5]   In the U.S. federal budget, all commonly accepted, traditional foreign aid accounts are subsumed under the 150, international affairs, budget function. The Office of Management and Budget (OMB) has designated development and humanitarian assistance as subfunction 151 and security assistance as subfunction 152. Currently, all traditional foreign aid accounts fall under one of these two subfunctions.

[6]   Because of the unanticipated nature of many disasters, humanitarian aid budget allocations often increase throughout the year as demands arise. Figures listed here include supplemental funds provided at various stages throughout the year as of the end of FY2008.

[7]   The IDA account was previously known as the International Disaster and Famine Assistance account (IDFA).

[8]   Until FY1998, food provided commercially under long-term, low interest loan terms (Title I of P.L. 480) was also included in the foreign assistance account. Because of its increasing export focus, it is no longer considered foreign aid.

[9]   It is important to note that the amount of resources allocated to any single development sector relative to other sectors in any given year is not necessarily a good measure of the priority assigned to that sector. Different types of development activities require varying amounts of funding to have impact and achieve the desired goals. Democracy and governance programs, for example, are generally low-cost interventions that

include extensive training sessions for government officials, the media, and other elements of civil society. Economic growth programs, on the other hand, might include infrastructure development, government budget support, or commodity import financing, activities that require significantly higher resources. What may be a better indicator of changing priorities is to compare funding allocations over time to the same objective or sector.

[10] Of the $18.4 billion provided in FY04 for Iraq from the IRRF, $5 billion was utilized in the same way as military assistance and delegated to DOD for implementation. The remainder was used in ways similar to ESF and, therefore, is considered political-strategic assistance for purposes of this analysis.

[11] FY2008 is the latest year for which reliable data is available, and includes supplemental funds that largely went for activities in Iraq, Afghanistan, and Georgia. Figures do not include Millennium Challenge Corporation Compacts as MCC appropriations are not broken out by recipient country until they are obligated, a one-time event for each country and on a scale that would distort the aid picture in any given year.

[12] Most notably, food aid and certain Department of Defense aid programs are not appropriated in the Foreign Operations measure, while the Export-Import Bank, an activity not considered "foreign aid," is funded in the Foreign Operations annual bill.

[13] Due to changes over time in appropriation "scoring," calculating historic Foreign Operations appropriations that are precisely equivalent to the methodology used currently is virtually impossible. This is especially true since Congress altered, beginning in FY1992, the methodology for "scoring" credit programs. The 30-year estimate noted here compares the FY2004 appropriation level of $44.0 billion (in FY2008 dollars) with total foreign aid obligations of about $40 billion (real terms) in the early 1970s.

[14] The Cargo Preference Act, P.L. 83-644, August 26,1954.

[15] OECD Report on The Developmental Effectiveness of Untied Aid, p.1, available at http://www.oecd.org/dataoecd/5/22/41537529.pdf.

[16] Id., p.1.

[17] See http://stats.oecd.org/wbos/Index.aspx?DatasetCode=TABLE1; 2008 DAC Reporting Documents, Table 7B, provided by Bill McCormick at USAID.

[18] Paris Declaration on Aid Effectiveness: Ownership, Harmonization, Alignment, Results and Mutual Accountability, a product of the High Level Forum on Aid Effectiveness; Paris, France (March 2, 2005).

[19] The OECD Glossary of Statistical Terms defines ODA as "flows of official financing administered with the promotion of economic development and welfare of developing countries as the main objective, and which are concessional in character with a grant element of at least 25%. By convention, ODA flows comprise contributions of donor government agencies, at all levels, to developing countries and to multilateral institutions." ODA does not include military assistance.

[20] Gross National Income (GNI) comprises GDP together with income received from other countries (notably interest and dividends), less similar payments made to other countries.

[21] The State Department generally determines the policy on distribution of funds from these accounts, but the funds are appropriated and attributed to USAID when foreign assistance is reported by obligations.

[22] Semi-Annual USAID Worldwide Staffing Pattern Report, data as of November 30, 2008, Table 1.

[23] U.S. Overseas Loans and Grants (Greenbook) 2006; U.S. Department of the Treasury and the Office of Management and Budget. *U.S. Government Foreign Credit Exposure as of December 31, 2006*, part 1, p. 20.

[24] Information provided by Department of State, F Bureau, 1/6/2009.

[25] U.S. Department of the Treasury and the Office of Management and Budget. *U.S. Government Foreign CreditExposure as of December 31, 2006*, part 1, p. 9.

[26] For more on debt relief for Iraq, see CRS Report RL33376, *Iraq's Debt Relief: Procedure and Potential Implicationsfor International Debt Relief*, by Martin A. Weiss.

[27] Currently there are about 2,400 U.S. direct hire personnel at USAID, down from 3,406 in 1992 and 8,600 in 1962.

[28] Separate permanent authorizations exist for other specific foreign aid programs such as the Peace Corps, the Inter-

[29] American Foundation, and the African Development Foundation.

[30] A few foreign aid programs that are authorized in other legislation have received more regular legislative review.Authorizing legislation for voluntary contributions to international organizations and refugee programs, for example,are usually contained in omnibus Foreign Relations Authorization measures that also address State Department and U.S. Information Agency issues. Food aid and amendments to P.L.480 are usually considered in the omnibus "farm bill" that Congress re-authorizes every five years.

In: Economics, Political and Social Issues …
Editor: Michelle L. Fergusson

ISBN: 978-1-61122-555-6
©2011 Nova Science Publishers, Inc.

SCIENCE, TECHNOLOGY, AND AMERICAN DIPLOMACY: BACKGROUND AND ISSUES FOR CONGRESS[*]

Deborah D. Stine[#]

Science and Technology Policy

ABSTRACT

Science and engineering activities have always been international. Scientists, engineers, and health professionals frequently communicate and cooperate with one another without regard to national boundaries. This report discusses international science and technology (S&T) diplomacy, instances when American leadership in S&T is used as a diplomatic tool to enhance another country's development and to improve understanding by other nations of U.S. values and ways of doing business. According to the National Research Council, five developmental challenges where S&T could play a role include child health and child survival, safe water, agricultural research to reduce hunger and poverty, micro-economic reform, and mitigation of natural disasters.

Title V of the Foreign Relations Authorization Act, FY1979 (P.L. 95-426) provides the current legislative guidance for U.S. international S&T policy. This act states that Department of State (DOS) is the lead federal agency in developing S&T agreements. The National Science and Technology Policy, Organization, and Priorities Act of 1976 (P.L. 94-282) states that the director of the White House Office of Science and Technology Policy (OSTP) is to advise the President on international S&T cooperation policies and the role of S&T considerations in foreign relations.

DOS sets the overall policy direction for U.S. international S&T diplomacy, and works with other federal agencies as needed. Within DOS, the Bureau of Oceans and International Environmental and Scientific Affairs (OES) coordinates international S&T activities. The Science and Technology Advisor to the Secretary of State (STAS) provides S&T advice to the Secretary and the director of the U.S. Agency for International Development (USAID). OSTP acts as a interagency liaison. A number of federal agencies that both sponsor research and use S&T in developing policy are involved in international S&T policy.

A fundamental question is why the United States should invest in international S&T diplomacy instead of domestic research and development (RandD) and science, technology, engineering, and mathematics education (STEM) activities, which are facing budget constraints. If Congress should decide that funding international S&T activities is important, agreeing on a policy goal beyond enhancing the country's development, such

---

[*] Excerpted from CRS Report RL34503 dated February 3, 2009.
[#] E-mail: dstine@crs.loc.gov

as improving U.S. relations with other countries, or enhancing popular opinion of the United States may help set priorities.

Policy options identified for Congress by expert committees who have assessed U.S. international S&T diplomacy efforts include ensuring a baseline of science, engineering, and technical (SET) literacy among all appropriate DOS personnel, increasing the presence overseas of personnel with significant SET expertise, and expanding the Department's engagement within global SET networks through exchanges, assistance, and joint research activities addressing key global issues. Other proposed actions include increasing USAID support that builds S&T capacity in developing countries, and orienting other departments and agencies S&T developing country programs to support the development priorities of the host countries. Another proposal would establish a new U.S. government organization, modeled on the Defense Advanced Research Projects Agency (DARPA) known for its risk-taking and innovation, called the "Development Applications Research Institute" (DARI) to develop and apply innovative technologies to development problems. In all of these efforts, Congress might wish to consider enhancing the prominence of the STAS, and coordination among S&T leaders at OES, STAS, and OSTP.

INTRODUCTION

Scientists, engineers, and health professionals frequently communicate and cooperate with one another without regard to national boundaries. Dating back to the 1700s, Benjamin Franklin and Thomas Jefferson are thought of as the nation's first scientific diplomats [1]. Scientists and inventors themselves, they corresponded with colleagues and brought knowledge back from their visits to Europe to enhance the development and policies of the very young United States. Today, the United States serves the same role for other countries that are in the early stages of development or at a major point of transition. Congress is currently discussing how to maximize the effectiveness of these international science and technology (S&T) policy activities [2]

This report provides an overview of current U.S. international S&T policy; describes the role of the Department of State (DOS), the White House Office of Science and Technology Policy (OSTP), the U.S. Agency for International Development (USAID), and other federal agencies; and discusses possible policy options for Congress. It focuses on international science and technology diplomacy, where American leadership in science and technology is used as a diplomatic tool to enhance another country's development and to improve understanding by other nations of U.S. values and ways of doing business. These efforts could focus on both enhancing a nation's science and technology (S&T) resources, as well as addressing developmental challenges where S&T could play a role. According to the National Research Council, five potential challenges include child health and child survival, safe water, agricultural research to reduce hunger and poverty, micro-economic reform, and mitigation of natural disasters [3]

OVERVIEW OF CURRENT U.S. INTERNATIONAL SCIENCE AND TECHNOLOGY (S&T) POLICY

Title V of the Foreign Relations Authorization Act, Fiscal Year 1979 (P.L. 95-426, 22 U.S.C. 2656a - 22 U.S.C. 2656d, as amended) provides the current legislative guidance for U.S. international S&T policy, and made DOS the lead federal agency in developing S&T agreements [4] In that act, Congress found that the consequences of modern S&T advances are of major significance in U.S. foreign policy—providing many problems and opportunities— meaning that its diplomacy workforce should have an appropriate level of knowledge of these topics. Further, it indicated that this workforce should conduct long-range planning to make effective use of S&T in international relations, and seek out and consult with public and private industrial, academic, and research institutions in the formulation, implementation, and evaluation of U.S. foreign policy.

The National Science and Technology Policy, Organization, and Priorities Act of 1976 (P.L. 94-282) states that the OSTP director is to advise the President on S&T considerations in foreign relations. Further, the OSTP director is to "assess and advise [the President] on policies for international cooperation in S&T which will advance the national and international objectives of the United States." The following sections discuss the international S&T activities of DOS, OSTP, USAID, and other federal agencies.

Department of State (DOS)

DOS sets the overall policy direction for U.S. international S&T diplomacy, and works with other federal agencies, as needed. In its May 2007 strategic plan, DOS and USAID identify the following key S&T diplomatic strategies:

- encourage science and technology cooperation to advance knowledge in areas related to water management;
- promote sharing of knowledge in the international scientific community that will enhance the efficiency and hasten the fruition of U.S. research efforts, andpromote international scientific collaboration;
- strengthen major international collaborations on cutting-edge energy technologyresearch and development in carbon sequestration, biofuels, clean coal powergeneration, as well as hydrogen, methane, and wind power;
- apply research including promotion of technological improvements to foster more sustainable natural resource use, conservation of biodiversity, and resilience to climate change impacts;
- support scientific and technological applications, including biotechnology, that harness new technology to raise agricultural productivity and provide a more stable, nutritious, and affordable food supply; and enhance outreach to key communities in the private sector [5]

DOS uses a variety of tools to implement this strategy, such as formal bilateral S&T cooperation agreements that facilitate international collaboration by federal agencies;

promotion and support of S&T entrepreneurs and innovators; [6] scientist and student exchanges; workshops, conferences, and meetings; public-private partnerships; seed funding for scientific programs and innovation activities; and production of educational materials, including films, websites, posters, and cards [7]. Within the State Department, the Bureau of Oceans and International Environmental and Scientific Affairs (OES) coordinates international S&T activities, and the Science and Technology Advisor (STAS) provides S&T advice to the Secretary of State, DOS staff, and the director of USAID. USAID is an independent federal government agency that, with guidance from DOS, supports developmental and U.S. strategic interests, among other duties.

Bureau of Oceans and International Environmental and Scientific Affairs (OES)

OES coordinates international S&T cooperative activities throughout the federal government [8]. Within OES is the Health, Space, and Science Directorate, which works with federal agencies on S&T policy issues [9]. In addition, some U.S. embassies have bilateral Environment, Science, Technology, and Health foreign service officers. Embassies may host their own country-specific activities such as joint research grants, junior scientist visit grants, events, and workshops. Some have a joint board that includes both scientists from the host country as well as government scientists to oversee these activities [10] There are also "hubs" that focus on environmental issues on a regional basis.

Science and Technology Advisor to the Secretary of State (STAS)

Within the State Department, but distinct from the OES, is the Science and Technology Advisor to the Secretary of State (STAS) [11]. The STAS acts as an advisor for both DOS and USAID. The goals of this office are to enhance the S&T literacy and capacity of DOS; build partnerships with the outside S&T community, within the U.S. government, with S&T partners abroad, and with foreign embassies in the United States; provide accurate S&T advice to DOS; and shape a global perspective on the emerging and "at the horizon" S&T developments anticipated to affect current and future U.S. foreign policy [12]

U.S. Agency for International Development (USAID)

USAID is an independent federal government agency with the goal of supporting transformational development, strengthening fragile states, supporting U.S. geostrategic interests, addressing transnational problems, and providing humanitarian relief [13]. Although independent, USAID's overall foreign policy guidance comes from the Secretary of State. At one time S&T had a major role at USAID. Today, however, S&T capacity, staffing, and funding, particularly in overseas missions, are far less than in the past [14]

White House Office of Science amd Technology Policy (OSTP) and the National Science and Technology Counsil (NSTC)

OSTP, a staff office within the Executive Office of the President (EOP), does not fund domestic or international programs. Rather, the Assistant to the Director for International Relations acts as a liaison: within the EOP, to organizations such as the National Security Council; with federal agencies, including DOS and the international offices of federal agencies such as the National Science Foundation; and with the science liaisons of foreign country embassies in the United States [15]. Within OSTP, the National Science and

Technology Council (NSTC), currently established by Executive Order 12881, coordinates S&T policy across the federal government [16]

Management of international S&T policy issues at OSTP and NSTC has varied among Presidential administrations [17]. During the Clinton Administration, OSTP had a Presidentially-appointed associate director whose primary focus was on international policy. This presidential appointee, along with a DOS presidential appointee, co-chaired a NSTC Committee on International Science, Engineering, and Technology (CISET) that addressed "international science cooperation as it related to foreign policy and the Nation's research and development (RandD) agenda." [18]. In the George W. Bush Administration, rather than an OSTP political appointee focused on international issues, there is a staff member who serves as an assistant to the director for international affairs [19]. Another difference is that rather than focusing an NSTC committee on overall international S&T policy, OSTP coordinates federal international S&T activities through NSTC committees that focus on a particular topic, like nanotechnology, or a specific country, like Brazil [20]

Role of Other Federal Agencies and Nongovernmental Organizations

A number of federal agencies that both sponsor research and use S&T in developing policy are involved in international S&T policy. These include National Science Foundation (NSF), National Institutes of Health, Department of Energy, National Aeronautics and Space Administration (NASA), Department of Agriculture, Environmental Protection Agency, Department of Interior, and others [21].

Federal programs may be formal "top-down" activities focused on the agencies' mission and identified by agency leadership, or "bottom-up" activities identified by scientists and engineers. Examples of "Top-down" activities include the National Oceanic and Atmospheric Administration (NOAA)'s National Environmental Satellite, Data, and Information Service focused on Earth observation data exchange, or the National Institute for Science and Technology (NIST)'s development of uniform measurement standards for ethanol and biodiesel. "Bottom-up" activities often arise from proposals submitted in response to a specific solicitation or as part of a general solicitation for research in their field [22].

ROLE OF CONGRESS

An April 2008 House Committee on Science and Technology Subcommittee on Research and Science Education hearing examined global and domestic benefits from cooperation in science and technology [23]. One fundamental question asked during the hearing was why the United States should support international science diplomacy rather than invest in domestic RandD. Table 1 provides a summary of the Bush Administration's response.

For the United States to be competitive, according to Bush Administration witnesses, it needs to know where the frontier of science is occurring. As other countries increase their investment in higher education and RandD, the top science and engineering research and facilities may not be in the United States, but in other countries. This increases the importance of U.S. investment in international S&T diplomatic activities, said Bush Administration witnesses, including federal programs that support U.S. scientists' collaborations with foreign scientists, and access to the best research facilities in the world, as well as enhancing the international connections of U.S. science and engineering students and leaders. In addition,

U.S. science and engineering higher education and research helps developing countries by enhancing their human resource capacity, and as a result, their ability to achieve long-term development. These international connections can be important, say Bush Administration witnesses, not just for those countries, but in helping the U.S. respond to global challenges such as infectious diseases such as avian flu. Further, according to a Bush Administration witness, international cooperative activities at their agency in almost all instances are conducted on a "no exchange of funds" basis with U.S. funding supporting U.S. scientists and engineers, not those in the cooperating country [24]

Table 1. U.S. Objectives in International Research and Development Programs

1. To maintain and continually improve the quality of U.S. science by applying global standards of excellence. (Performing science to the highest standards)
2. To provide access by U.S. scientists to the frontiers of science without regard to national borders. (Access to the frontiers of science)
3. To increase the productivity of U.S. science through collaborations between U.S. scientists and the world's leading scientists, regardless of national origin. (Access to scientific talent)
4. To strengthen U.S. science through visits, exchanges, and immigration by outstanding scientists from other nations. (Augmentation of scientific human capital)
5. To increase U.S. national security and economic prosperity by fostering the improvement of conditions in other countries through increased technical capability. (Security through technology-based equity)
6. To accelerate the progress of science across a broader front than the U.S. may choose to pursue with its own resources. (Leveraging on foreign science capabilities)
7. To improve understanding by other nations of U.S. values and ways of doing business. (Science diplomacy)
8. To address U.S. interests of such global nature that the U.S. alone cannot satisfy them. (Global support for global scientific issues)
9. To discharge obligations negotiated in connection with treaties. (Science as a tradable asset)
10. To increase U.S. prestige and influence with other nations. (Science for glory)

Source: John Marburger, Director, Office of Science and Technology Policy, "National Science Board Hearing on International Science Partnerships," speech, May 11, 2006. John H. Marburger, Director, OSTP, Response to questions at House Committee on Science and Technology, Subcommittee on Research and Science Education, International Science and Technology Cooperation,110Cong. 2 sess., April 2, 2008, at http://science.house.gov/ publications/hearings_ markups_details.aspx?NewsID=2134.

Some believe, however, that the United States should enhance its international science and technology activities. They believe that such investments are sometimes viewed by policymakers as either "giving away knowledge" or a "humanitarian luxury," when they actually could help all countries to reach common goals such as developing safe and reliable nuclear power, or enhancing all countries' economic development [25]. Others express concerns that although the United States has many programs to promote science and technology in the developing world, such programs have limited due to insufficient financial and human resources at DOS, AID, and OSTP that limit the ability of these agencies to achieve their mission [26]

If Congress should decide that funding international S&T activities is important, agreeing on a policy goal beyond enhancing the country's development, such as improving U.S. relations with other countries, or enhancing popular opinion of the United States may help set priorities. Activities funded might differ depending on those priorities. For example, two possible goals might be (1) improving U.S. relations with the government of a country or in a region, or (2) raising popular opinion of the United States in that country or region. In the case of the first goal, activities might focus on enhancing the foreign government(s) decision-making based on science and engineering information or providing financial or technical aid to a country's science and engineering efforts. In the case of the second goal, activities might focus on a challenge more visible to the public, such as increasing access to water, enhancing agricultural productivity, or obtaining high quality STEM education.

Although the effectiveness of different S&T diplomatic initiatives has not been studied, the State Department contends that some key elements for success are finding areas or programs that (1) break new ground, sometimes in a neglected area of science or development; (2) are educationally and developmentally transformative; (3) address core developmental issues of poverty and human development; (4) promote sustainable uses of natural resources; (5) stimulate job creation and private sector investment; and (6) are collaborative projects with tangible results [27]

Six broad categories of international S&T cooperative activities include (1) agreements; (2) research; (3) facilities and equipment; (4) academic opportunities from primary through post-secondary education; (5) meetings, dialogues, and visits; and (6) private sector activities (see Table 2). International S&T cooperative activities can be multinational, regional, or bilateral. A related question is who might best lead such efforts relative to the desired goal. Options include scientists, engineers, and health professionals at academic institutions, business and industry, and non-governmental organizations; scientists, engineers, and health professionals who work for the federal government; and S&T federal government leaders. Expert committees which have assessed U.S. international S&T diplomacy efforts express concerns about (1) the lack of S&T expertise, presence, and global engagement at DOS, (2) a decline in support for S&T capacity at USAID, (3) a lack of coherent and integrated international S&T policy direction and federal coordination role at OSTP, and (4) insufficient technological research to respond to development challenges. The following sections discuss proposed recommendations to respond to these concerns.

S&T Expertise, Presence and Global Engagement at DOS

The report of the State Department Advisory Committee on Transformational Diplomacy, State Department in 2025 Working Group [28] recommends that the State Department expand its investment in Science, Engineering, and Technology (SET) expertise, presence, and global engagement. The report's specific recommendations include ensuring a baseline of SET literacy among all appropriate Department personnel, increasing the presence overseas of personnel with significant SET expertise, and expanding the Department's engagement within global SET networks through exchanges, assistance, and joint research activities addressing key global issues.

In addition, the report recommends creating a closer connection between the roles of the Assistant Secretary for OES and the STAS to bring senior attention to the full range of SET challenges and opportunities facing the Department. For example, if the Assistant Secretary for OES is a scientist, that person could serve simultaneously as the Science and Technology Advisor to the Secretary of State. Otherwise, the STAS could become the Principal Deputy Assistant Secretary of State (PDAS) in OES [29].

Table 2. International Science and Technology Policy Mechanisms

Agreements
- Formal multinational, regional, and bilateral agreements between the U.S. government and the government of another country.
- Government-level bilateral agreements between a U.S. agency and a research agency of a foreign country that are related to a government-level agreement and provide additional details that define how each agency will cooperate.
- Agency-level bilateral agreements between a U.S. agency and a research agency of a foreign country that are not related to a government-level agreement.
- Agency-level multilateral agreements between a U.S. agency and research agencies of international organization and/or of two or more foreign countries.

Research
- Joint research sponsorship where a U.S. and foreign researcher, group of researchers, or institutions work together.
- Visiting foreign researchers who come to the United States, or U.S. researchers who visit the foreign country.
- Sponsorship of foreign researchers in early stage of their careers.
- Sponsorship of research conducted by a U.S. researcher in a foreign country or a researcher in the foreign country.

Education
- Fellowships, research assistantships, and traineeships.
- Undergraduate and graduate student exchange programs.
- Visiting foreign lecturers who come to the United States, or U.S. researchers who visit the foreign country.
- K-12 science, technology, engineering, and mathematics (STEM) curriculum development and teacher training, methods, and certification.
- Educational materials including films, websites, posters, and cards.

Meetings, Dialogues, and Guidance
- Meetings to exchange ideas.
- Workshops to learn about a science and technology topic.
- Guidance on the application of research and technology.
- Dialogues on how best to harmonize S&T regulatory activities.

Facility, Equipment, Data, and Information
- Facility utilization.
- Equipment provision and lending.
- Data and information measurement, provision, and exchange.

Private Sector
- Promotion and support of S&T entrepreneurs and innovators.
- Public-private partnerships.

Source: Congressional Research Service. Agreements section is based on General Accounting Office, Federal Research: Information on Science and Technology International Agreements, Report Number RCED-99-108, April 1999 at http://www.gao.gov/archive/1999/rc99108.pdf.

S&T Capacity at USAID

A National Research Council (NRC) report recommends Congress and others take action to reverse what they state is the decline in USAID support for building S&T capacity, and strengthen the capabilities of its leadership and program managers in Washington, DC, and in foreign countries on S&T issues. In addition, the report recommends that Congress encourage other departments and agencies to orient their S&T developing country programs to support the development priorities of the host countries, and that USAID take actions to enhance interagency coordination [30]

International S&T Policy Direction and Federal Coordination at OSTP and NSTC

A National Science Board (NSB) report [31] recommends that the United States create a coherent and integrated international science and engineering strategy, balance U.S. foreign and RandD policy, and promote intellectual exchange. In addition, it recommends reestablishing the NSTC Committee on International Science, Engineering, and Technology, and appointing a high-level international S&T policy official in OSTP. Congress, according to NSB, should amend the Government Performance and Results Act to require Federal agencies to address international S&T partnerships. Further, Congress should direct the Department of Commerce, OSTP, DOS, and the Department of Homeland Security to balance U.S. security policies with international science and engineering (SandE) needs. The report also contends it is important to facilitate "brain circulation" as opposed to "brain drain," by supporting study abroad opportunities for American students, streamlining the visa process for foreign scientists, engineers and students, and identifying and increasing the use of U.S. and international facilities for collaborative research [32]

New Institute to Support Technology Research

The United States Commission on Helping to Enhance the Livelihood of People Around the Globe (HELP Commission) was charged in Section 637 of P.L. 108-199 (Consolidated Appropriations Act, 2004) to study, develop, and deliver to the President, Congress, and the Secretary of State actionable proposals to enhance and leverage the efficiency and effectiveness of U.S. foreign assistance to reduce poverty through sustained economic growth and self-sufficiency [33]. One study by several commissioners found the following characteristics of successful efforts:

- Ownership and initiative must be local;
- Partnership is the premise;
- Technology adaptation and adoption matter;
- Leaders and policy must drive toward self-reliance; and
- Continual information loops contribute to learning and adjustments [34]

The study found that some of the most widely acknowledged foreign assistance successes have incorporated the application of technologies including the Green Revolution of the mid-20th century, which they state doubled food production in developing countries, and the presence today of Consultative Group on International Agricultural Research (CGIAR), a partnership of government, nongovernmental organizations, and businesses that support 15 international research centers to provide technical support. Other examples include bednets to reduce malaria, smallpox and polio vaccines, and "smart cards" that provide loans to businesses located in poor areas where no bank is available. The study also indicates that the scientific and technological capacity of developing countries is growing, such as the African Laser Center.

In its report, the Commission proposed the establishment of a new U.S. government organization, modeled on the Defense Advanced Research Projects Agency (DARPA) known for its risk-taking and innovation, [35] called the "Development Applications Research Institute" [36] (DARI). According to the Commission, DARI could "develop and apply innovative technologies to development problems in order to jumpstart research and development aimed at reducing global poverty," and its head could serve as the science advisor to the lead U.S. government official in charge of development policy. The Commission proposed that DARI focus on all relevant development areas including agriculture, health, and education; carry out its work in partnership with development countries to spur the development of local RandD capabilities; and carefully structured to ensure accountability and performance. The cost of DARI, according to the Commission would be $50-100 million per year.

Additional Consideration

If Congress should decide to address the trends described above, additional financial resources and personnel with expertise in S&T may be necessary. If Congress is concerned about a lack of overall international S&T policy direction at OSTP or coordination among the White House and federal agencies as described by the reports above, possible actions include enhancing the prominence of the STAS, and coordination among, S&T leaders at OES, STAS, and OSTP. One option that takes into account all three reports is for the STAS to play a greater role in coordination by appointment to a high-level position within OES as well as chairing a revived CISET. If Congress decides to establish DARI, the STAS might also play a leadership role there as well.

REFERENCES

[1] Silvio A. Bedini, *Thomas Jefferson: Statesman of Science* (New York: Macmillian, 1990). I. Bernard Cohen, *Benjamin Franklin's Science* (Cambridge: Harvard University Press, 1996). Joyce E. Chaplin, *The First Scientific American: Benjamin Franklin and the Pursuit of Genius* (New York: Basic Books, 2007).

[2] See, for example, U.S. Congress, House Committee on Science and Technology, Subcommittee on Research and Science Education, *International Science and*

Technology Cooperation, hearing, 110th Cong., 2nd sess., April 2, 2008, at http://science.house.gov/publications/hearings_markups_details.aspx?NewsID=2134.

[3]   National Research Council, *The Fundamental Role of Science and Technology in International Development: An Imperative for the U.S. Agency for International Development* (Washington, DC: National Academy Press, 2006), at http://www.nap.edu/catalog.php?
record_id=11583.

[4]   According to DOS, science and technology agreements "establish frameworks to facilitate the exchange of scientific results, provide for protection and allocation of intellectual property rights and benefit sharing, facilitate access for researchers, address taxation issues, and respond to the complex set of issues associated with economic development, domestic security and regional stability." See State Department, "List of Umbrella SandT Agreements," at http://www.state.gov/g/oes/rls/fs/2006/77212.htm for more information.

[5]   U.S. Department of State/U.S. Agency for International Development Strategic Plan, Fiscal Years 2007-2012: Transformational Democracy, May 7, 2007, available at http://www.usaid.gov/policy/coordination/
stratplan_fy07-12.pdf.

[6]   This report does not discuss issues related to the promotion and support of technological innovation such as export controls or technology, trade, and security issues. For more information on these issues, see CRS Report RL31832, *The Export Administration Act: Evolution, Provisions, and Debate*, by Ian F. Fergusson, and CRS Report RL32591, *U.S. Terms of Trade: Significance, Trends, and Policy*, by Craig K. Elwell.

[7]   Jeff Miotke, Deputy Assistant Secretary for Science, Space, and Health, OES, DOS, Testimony before the House Committee on Science and Technology, Subcommittee on Research and Science Education, *International Science and Technology Cooperation*,110th Cong. 2nd sess., April 2, 2008, at http://democrats.science.house.gov/
Media/File/Commdocs/hearings/2008/Research/2apr/Miotke_Testimony.pdf.

[8]   For more information, see http://www.state.gov/g/oes/c20049.htm. The FY2008 budget estimate for OES is $31 million. See State Department FY2009 budget justification, available at http://www.state.gov/s/d/rm/rls/statecbj/2009/.

[9]   According to the FY2009 State Department budget justification, the FY2008 budget estimate for this directorate is $4million and includes 24 staff members.

[10]   For an illustration, see http://egypt.usembassy.gov/usegypt/contacts.htm.

[11]   For more information, see Nina Fedoroff, Science and Technology Adviser to the Secretary of State and the Administrator of USAID, Testimony before the House Committee on Science and Technology, Subcommittee on Research and Science Education, *International Science and Technology Cooperation*, 110th Cong. 2nd sess., April 2,2008, at http://democrats.science.house.gov/Media/File/Commdocs/hearings/
2008/Research/2apr/Fedoroff_Testimony.pdf.

[12]   For more information, see http://www.state.gov/g/stas/c6063.htm.

[13]   U.S. Agency for International Development, *USAID Primer: What We Do and How We Do It*, January 2006, at http://www.usaid.gov/about_usaid/PDACG100.pdf.

[14]   National Research Council, The Fundamental Role of Science and Technology in International Development: AnImperative for the U.S. Agency for International

Development   (Washington,   DC: National   Academy   Press,   2006)
athttp://www.nap.edu/catalog.php?record_id=11583. Nina Fedoroff, Science and
Technology Adviser to the Secretary ofState and the Administrator of USAID,
Testimony before the House Committee on Science and Technology,Subcommittee on
Research and Science Education, International Science and Technology
Cooperation,110th Cong. 2ndsess., April 2, 2008, at http://democrats.science.house.gov/
Media/File/Commdocs/hearings/2008/Research/2apr/Fedoroff_Testimony.pdf.

[15] John H. Marburger, Director, OSTP, Testimony before the House Committee on
Science and Technology, Subcommittee on Research and Science Education,
International Science and Technology Cooperation, 110th Cong. 2ndsess., April 2, 2008,
at http://democrats.science.house.gov/Media/File/Commdocs/hearings/2008/Research/
2apr/Marburger_Testimony.pdf.

[16] National Science and Technology Council, at http://www.ostp.gov/cs/nstc.

[17] A Woodrow Wilson Center report identifies what they consider to be the best practices
regarding OSTP and international SandT policy. For more information, see Jennifer Sue
Bond, Mark Schaefer, David Rejeski, Rodney W.Nichols, *OSTP 2.0: Critical Upgrade:
Enhancing Capacity for White House Science and Technology Policymaking:
Recommendations for the Next President* (Washington, DC: Woodrow Wilson
International Center for Scholars, June2008) at http://wilsoncenter.org/news/docs/
OSTP%20Paper1.pdf.

[18] National Science and Technology Council*, 2000 Annual Report*, at http://www.ostp.
gov/pdf/nstc_ar.pdf.

[19] John H. Marburger, Director, OSTP, Testimony before the House Committee on
Science and Technology, Subcommittee on Research and Science Education,
International Science and Technology Cooperation, 110th Cong. 2nd sess., April 2, 2008,
at http://democrats.science.house.gov/Media/File/Commdocs/hearings/2008/Research/
2apr/ Marburger_Testimony.pdf.

[20] Ibid.

[21] A description of federal agency international SandT activities is provided in Jeff
Miotke, Deputy Assistant Secretary for Science, Space, and Health, OES, DOS,
Testimony before the House Committee on Science and Technology, Subcommittee on
Research and Science Education, *International Science and Technology Cooperation*,
110th Cong. 2nd sess., April 2, 2008, at http://democrats.science.house.gov/Media/File/
Commdocs/hearings/2008/Research/2apr/ Miotke_Testimony.pdf.

[22] Ibid.

[23] U.S. Congress, House Committee on Science and Technology, Subcommittee on
Research and Science Education, *International Science and Technology Cooperation*,
hearing, 110th Cong., 2nd sess., April 2, 2008, at http://science.house.gov/ publications/
hearings_markups_details.aspx?NewsID=2134.

[24] Testimony and response to questions by John H. Marburger (OSTP), Arden Bement
(NSF), Nina Fedoroff (STAS), Jeff Mitoke (DOS), and Michael O'Brien (NASA) at
U.S. Congress, House Committee on Science and Technology, Subcommittee on
Research and Science Education, *International Science and Technology Cooperation*,
hearing, 110th Cong., 2nd sess., April 2, 2008, at http://science.house.gov/publications/
hearings_markups_details.aspx?NewsID=2134. A transcript of the hearing is available
from Congressional Quarterly.

[25] See, for example, Rodney W. Nichols, *US Science Office Must Promote Global Collaboration*, Science and Development Network, October 31, 2008 at http://www.scidev.net/en/opinions/us-science-office-must-promote-global-collaboratio. html?utm_source=linkandutm_medium=rssandutm_campaign=en_opinions.

[26] David Dickson, *The World's Poor Deserve Better U.S. Leadership*, Science and Development Network, October 31, 2008, at http://www.scidev.net/en/editorials/the-world-s-poor-deserve-better-us-leadership.html.

[27] Jeff Miotke, Deputy Assistant Secretary for Science, Space, and Health, OES, DOS, Testimony before the House Committee on Science and Technology, Subcommittee on Research and Science Education, *International Science and Technology Cooperation*, 110th Cong. 2nd sess., April 2, 2008, at http://democrats.science.house.gov/ Media/File/Commdocs/hearings/2008/Research/2apr/Miotke_Testimony.pdf.

[28] State Department, *Advisory Committee on Transformational Diplomacy: Final report of the State Department in 2025 Working Group*, at http://www.state.gov/secretary/ diplomacy/99774.htm.

[29] Ibid.

[30] National Research Council, *The Fundamental Role of Science and Technology in International Development: An Imperative for the U.S. Agency for International Development* (Washington, DC: National Academy Press, 2006), at http://www. nap.edu/catalog.php?record_id=11583.

[31] National Science Board, *International Science and Engineering Partnerships: A Priority for U.S. Foreign Policy and Our Nation's Innovation Enterprise*, NSB 08-4 (Arlington, VA: National Science Foundation, 2008), at http://www.nsf.gov/ nsb/publications/2008/nsb084.pdf.

[32] Ibid.

[33] The HELP Commission, "Mission," webpage at http://www.helpcommission.gov/Mission/tabid/53/Default.aspx.

[34] Carol Adelman, Nicholas Eberstadt, Susan Raymond, and Melissa Griswold, *Foreign Assistance: What Works and What Doesn't with Recommendations for Future Improvements*, December 14, 2007 at http://www.helpcommission.gov/portals/0/ HELP_WWWD.pdf.

[35] For more information on DARPA and other similar models, see CRS Report RL34497, *Advanced Research Projects Agency - Energy (ARPA-E): Background, Status, and Selected Issues for Congress*, by Deborah D. Stine.

[36] HELP Commission, *Beyond Assistance: The HELP Commission Report on Foreign Assistance Reform*, December 7, 2007 at http://www.helpcommission.gov/portals/0/Beyond%20Assistance_HELP_Commission _Report.pdf.

In: Economics, Political and Social Issues ...
Editor: Michelle L. Fergusson

ISBN: 978-1-61122-555-6
©2011 Nova Science Publishers, Inc.

STRATEGIC ARMS CONTROL AFTER START: ISSUES AND OPTIONS[*]

Amy F. Woolf[#]
Nuclear Weapons Policy

ABSTRACT

The United States and Soviet Union signed the Strategic Arms Reduction Treaty in 1991; it entered into force in December 1994 and is due to expire in December 2009. The United States and Russia have held several meetings to discuss options for continuing their arms control relationship, but have not agreed on whether to extend START or how to replace it.

START counts each deployed ICBM, SLBM, bomber as a single delivery vehicle under the Treaty limit of 1,600 delivery vehicles and attributes an agreed number of warheads to each deployed delivery vehicle. This attribution rule provides the total number of warheads that count under the 6,000 warhead limit in the Treaty. To verify compliance with START, each side monitors the numbers and locations of ballistic missiles, launchers and heavy bombers deployed by the other country. The parties use a wide variety of means to collect information—or monitor—these forces and activities. Some of these monitoring systems, such as overhead satellites, operate outside the territories of the treaty parties. They also have also been required to exchange copious amounts of data on locations, operations, and technical characteristics of the treaty-limited items. This verification regime has allowed the parties to remain confident in each other's compliance with the Treaty.

The United States and Russia began to discuss their options for arms control after START expired in mid-2006. They have, however been unable to agree on a path forward. Neither side wants to extend START in its current form, as some of the Treaty's provisions have begun to interfere with some military programs on both sides. Russia wants to replace START with a new Treaty that would further reduce deployed forces while using many of the same definitions and counting rules in START. The United States initially did not want to negotiate a new treaty, but, under the Bush Administration, would have been willing to extend, informally, some of START's monitoring provisions. In 2008, the Bush Administration agreed to conclude a new Treaty, with monitoring provisions attached, but this Treaty would resemble the far less formal Strategic Offensive Reductions Treaty that the two sides signed in 2002. In December 2008, the two sides agreed that they wanted to replace START before it expired, but acknowledged that this task would have to be left to negotiations between Russia and the Obama Administration.

---

[*] Excerpted from CRs Report 40084 dated February 12, 2009.

[#] E-mail: awoolf@crs.loc.gov

The United States and Russia could choose from a number of options for the future of their arms control relationship. They could allow START to lapse or they could extend START for five years. They could extend START, then amend it to ease some of the outdated provisions. They could negotiate a new Treaty, or they could pursue less formal arrangements to manage their nuclear forces. Moreover, if a new treaty included further reductions in nuclear weapons, it could use some START definitions and counting rules or the less formal Moscow Treaty declarations.

INTRODUCTION

The United States and Soviet Union signed the Strategic Arms Reduction Treaty (START) on July 31, 1991. After the demise of the Soviet Union in December 1991, the parties signed a Protocol that named the four former Soviet Republics with nuclear weapons on their territory—Ukraine, Belarus, Kazakhstan, and Russia—parties to the Treaty [1]. START entered into force on December 4, 1994. The Treaty was to remain in force for 15 years, unless replaced by a subsequent agreement, and, therefore, will expire on December 5, 2009 [2] According to Article XVII of the Treaty, the parties must meet "no later than one year" before this date to consider whether the Treaty should be extended or allowed to lapse [3]. If the parties agree to extend the Treaty, the extension would last five years, unless START were replaced by a subsequent agreement during that time.

The United States and Russia held several meetings in the latter years of the Bush Administration to discuss the options for continuing their bilateral arms control relationship after START, but have did not reach an agreement on whether to extend START or on how to replace it. The Obama Administration has pledged to resume the discussions, both to extend the monitoring and verification provisions in START and to seek an agreement on further reductions in strategic nuclear weapons. The discussions thus far, along with the statements from Members of Congress and others following the process, reflect not only on the specific issues that may be addressed in a possible follow-on Treaty, but, also on the broader question of what, if any, role arms control should play in future U.S.-Russian relations.

The United States and Soviet Union negotiated START between 1994 and 2001. It contains many detailed definitions and restrictions that not only limit the permitted number of nuclear warheads but also restrain the locations and movement of delivery vehicles carrying nuclear warheads and require extensive exchanges of data about them. Many of these provisions reflect the more competitive relationship between the United States and Soviet Union, and the concerns that drove their inclusion in the Treaty, may no longer seem as important to the U.S.-Russian relationship. Specifically, some in the Bush Administration and the broader foreign policy community have argued that, because the United States no longer structures its nuclear forces in response to a Russian threat, it no longer needs a treaty that restrains and reduces the weapons that make up that threat. They, therefore, question whether the START Treaty, or U.S.-Russian nuclear arms control in general, remain important as tools in the political relationship between the United States and Russia.

Some U.S. critics of arms control have argued that the bilateral arms control process should fade away after START expires. They note that START may have served its purpose by helping to reduce the size of the Russian arsenal after the demise of the Soviet Union and by restraining the permitted operations of the remaining forces, but its reductions have been overtaken by deeper cuts mandated by the Moscow Treaty and the restrictions on Russian forces also serve to restrict the flexibility of U.S. forces. In the current environment, the United States may be better served by maintaining its own freedom of action in deploying and operating its nuclear forces than by retaining START's or similar restraints on U.S. and Russian forces.

Others, however, argue that START remains relevant to the U.S.-Russian relationship and deserves to be either extended or replaced with a similar treaty. In this view, the predictability created by START's well-defined restrictions on Russian and U.S. nuclear forces can benefit both countries. Moreover, continuing this cooperation can help to restore some trust in the relationship between the two nations. In addition, some in Russia still feel threatened by U.S. nuclear weapons and continue to value the restraints provided by arms control treaties.

Some Members of Congress have joined this debate, with several endorsing the view that extending START, and its monitoring and verification provisions, will help improve the relationship between the United States and Russia. For example, Senator Richard Lugar has stated that "the current U.S.-Russian relationship is complicated enough without introducing more elements of uncertainty. Failure to preserve the START Treaty would increase the potential for distrust between the two sides." [4] Some also believe, as Senator Lugar has noted, that the "failure to renew START will be seen worldwide as weakening the international nuclear nonproliferation regime and a further sign to many foreign leaders and experts that U.S. nonproliferation policy is adrift" [5]

Congress has limited influence on the process of seeking a replacement for START. If the United States and Russia amend START, or negotiate a new treaty to replace it, the Senate will have to provide its advice and consent before the parties ratify the Treaty. However, if the two parties do not reach any agreement and START lapses, or if they choose simply to extend START for five years, according to the provision in Article XVII, the Senate would not have to approve or reject the outcome. Nevertheless, Congress can, through resolutions, hearings, and consultations, offer the Administration its views on the future of the START Treaty and the U.S.-Russian arms control process.

This report provides background information about the START Treaty and reviews the discussions about a possible successor to START. It also presents a range of alternatives that the United States and Russia might consider if they choose to follow START with a new framework for the arms control process.

THE START TREATY

Key Provisions

Central Limits

START limits long-range nuclear-capable delivery systems—land-based intercontinental ballistic missiles (ICBMs), submarine-launched ballistic missiles (SLBMs), and heavy bombers—in the United States and the four states of the former Soviet Union. The Treaty limits both the number of delivery systems and the number of warheads carried on these systems.

As Table 1 below indicates, each side can deploy 6,000 "attributed" warheads on no more than 1,600 ballistic missiles and heavy bombers, with no more than 4,900 attributed warheads on land-based and submarine-based ballistic missiles.

Table1. Central Limits in START

Deployed Strategic Nuclear Delivery Vehicles	1,600
Heavy ICBMs	154
Accountable Warheads on Deployed Delivery Vehicles	6,000
Ballistic Missile Warheads	4,900
Warheads on Heavy ICBMs	1,540
Warheads on Mobile ICBMs	1,100
Total Ballistic Missile Throwweight	3,600 metric tons[a]

Source: U.S. Department of State, Text of the Strategic Offensive Reductions Treaty.
    http://www.state.gov/t/ac/ trt/18535.htm.
[a.]This is around 54% of the amount of throwweight deployed on Soviet missiles when the treaty was signed.

Within the aggregate limits on ballistic missile warheads, START also limits each side to no more than 1,540 warheads on heavy ICBMs, which are defined as those with a throwweight greater than 4,350 kilograms, and 1,100 warheads on mobile ICBMs. These two limits are an added effort to restrain forces that the United States feared would provide the Soviet Union with an avenue to exceed the warhead limit. The United States had long sought to use the arms control process to limit, or eliminate, the Soviet monopoly on heavy ICBMs because it believed that the Soviet Union could expand the capabilities of these missiles by deploying them with more or higher yield. The United States did not have any ballistic missiles of this size, and had no plans to develop or deploy them. The Soviet Union initially resisted U.S. pressures to limit these missiles, but eventually agreed to halve their force of 304 SS-18 ICBMs, each of which was deployed with 10 warheads, under START.

As the START negotiations proceeded through the 1980s, the United States also grew concerned about the Soviet deployment of ballistic missiles on mobile launchers. The Soviet Union had begun to deploy single-warhead SS-25 missiles on road-mobile launchers and 10-warhead SS-24 missiles on rail-mobile launchers. The United States considered these missiles both a military and an arms control problem. Because the United States did not think it could locate and track these missiles all the time, it believed it would be difficult to target them during a conflict. Moreover, because the Soviet Union had large land areas where it could operate and conceal these missiles, U.S. negotiators argued that the United States would not be able to monitor mobile ICBM deployments well enough to count the missiles and verify Soviet compliance with the limits in START.

The United States initially proposed that START ban mobile ICBMs, even though it was considering the possible use of mobile launchers for its new 10-warhead Peacekeeper (MX) ICBM and for a prospective small, single-warhead ICBM. But, after the United States and Soviet Union began to consider options for a monitoring and verification regime that might track the numbers of mobile ICBMs, they agreed to limit, rather than ban, these systems. The limited numbers, when combined with location restrictions, notifications prior to movement, data exchanges that identified the numbers of missiles and warheads based at approved locations, and a continuous monitoring regime outside the final assembly facility for one type of mobile ICBM, would help each side count the number of acknowledged mobile ICBMs and complicate efforts to conceal extra missiles or warheads. Even though the United States eventually dropped its plans to deploy mobile ICBMs, it agreed to apply these limits and restrictions to the Peacekeeper (MX) missiles that were deployed in silos.

START also limits the total amount of throwweight on each side's ballistic missiles, to an amount equal to around 54% of the amount of throwweight on Soviet missiles before the Treaty entered into force. Throwweight is the combined weight of the post-boost vehicle, warheads, guidance system, penetration aids, and other equipment found on the front end of a missile. It is considered to be a measure of a missile's destructive capacity because larger missiles with greater throwweight can carry larger or greater numbers of warheads. Hence, this limit was a further effort by the United States to limit the potential for the Soviet Union to add warheads to its missiles in violation of the Treaty's limits. Because Soviet forces deployed when START was signed carried had than three times as much throwweight as U.S. missiles, the United States did not have to reduce its forces to comply with this limit. However, the United States could have exceeded the limit on throwweight if it had deployed new, larger missiles while START remained in force.

Counting Rules

START counts each deployed ICBM and its associated launcher, each deployed SLBM and its associated launcher, and each deployed heavy bomber as a single delivery vehicle under the Treaty limit of 1,600 delivery vehicles. They count regardless of whether they are equipped with nuclear or conventional warheads. They also continue to count under the Treaty limits until the launchers or bombers are eliminated according to the Treaty's detailed elimination procedures. For example, a bomber, such as the B-1, that has been converted to carry conventional weapons continues to count under the Treaty limits. Moreover, an empty missile launcher, either on land or on a ballistic missile submarine, continues to count as if it still holds a missile and the missile still carries the attributed number of warheads, even if the missile system is deactivated or the launcher is converted to another purpose.

The number of warheads *attributed* to each type of missile or bomber is listed in an agreed data base [7]. For the most part, the number of warheads attributed to each type of missile equals the maximum number of warheads that the missile had been tested with and could be equipped to carry when the treaty entered into force. In some cases, however, such as for the U.S. Trident II (D-5) missile, the number of warheads attributed to the missile (8) fell below the maximum number the missile could carry (12). The Soviet SS-18 missile had also been tested with 12 or 14 warheads, but the data base counted it as carrying only 10. The parties adopted this formula of counting delivery vehicles and attributing warheads to each type of delivery vehicle, because, although they sought to reduce warheads, they could not monitor the actual numbers of warheads deployed on the delivery vehicles but could identify and count the large delivery vehicles with their monitoring systems.

The number of warheads attributed to heavy bombers falls far below the maximum number that could be carried on those aircraft. Heavy bombers that are not equipped to carry long-range nuclear-armed air-launched cruise missiles (ALCMs) [8]—such as the U.S. B-1 and B-2 bombers— count as only one warhead under the START limits. This number applies even though these bombers can carry at least 16 bombs and short-range missiles. Further, heavy bombers that are equipped to carry ALCMs count as half of the maximum number of weapons they are permitted to carry. START states that U.S. bombers can be equipped to carry up to 20 ALCMs, but they only count as 10 warheads under the Treaty limit of 6,000 warheads. Russian bombers can be equipped to carry up to 16 ALCMs, and count as only 8 warheads under the Treaty limit.

START allows the United States and Soviet Union to reduce the number of warheads attributed to a particular type of ballistic missile through a process known as "downloading." According to the Treaty, each party can reduce the "attributed number" listed in the data base for up to three types of missiles. If they do this, they must then reduce the number of warheads carried on each missile, and if the number declines by more than 2 warheads, they must replace the platform on the missile that holds the warheads, so that it does not have space for the larger number of missiles. This "downloading" process would allow each country to spread its 4,900 ballistic missile warheads among a greater number of missiles. The countries use short-notice on-site inspections to confirm that the number of warheads actually deployed on a particular missile does not exceed the number of warheads attributed to that type of missile in the data base. The United States has taken advantage of this provision with its Minuteman III and Trident II missiles.

Existing types of missiles cannot be deployed with more warheads than the number attributed to that type of missile in the data base. The number in the data base could only increase if the missile were altered to meet the definition of a "new type" of missile. START bans new types of heavy ICBMs. For smaller missiles, it contains an elaborate definition that is designed to allow the parties to distinguish between modified versions of existing ballistic missiles, which would be subject to the warhead attribution numbers already in the data base, and new types, which would receive a new warhead attribution number. During the negotiations, the parties agreed that the definition would reflect changes in missile characteristics such as the propellant used, the number of stages, its length and diameter, and its throwweight, but they differed on the magnitude of the changes that would define a "new type." The United States feared that, with smaller changes, the Soviet Union would be able to have a missile that was virtually identical to an existing missile declared a new type with a greater number of warheads, and then might secretly backfit the older version with more warheads, as well. This was one of the last issues resolved in the START negotiations [9]

Collateral Constraints

START contains detailed definitions of the items and activities limited by the treaty. The parties have also been required to exchange copious amounts of detailed data on the technical characteristics of the treaty-limited items. The Treaty mandates that the parties locate all strategic forces limited by the Treaty at "declared facilities" which include production, assembly, testing, storage, maintenance, deployment, and elimination facilities. It outlines detailed notifications that must be provided and procedures that must be followed when items move from one location to another. It further defines detailed procedures that the countries must follow when they eliminate weapons limited by the Treaty, or close down facilities that had once housed these items. Designed to reduce ambiguities and minimize the opportunities for dispute, these details provide the "foundation" for the Treaty's verification regime by drawing sharp distinctions between permitted and prohibited forces and activities.

Monitoring and Verification

Verification is the process that one country uses to assess whether another country is complying with an arms control agreement. To verify compliance, a country must determine whether the forces and activities of another country are within the bounds established by the limits and obligations in the agreement. Treaty language forms the core of the verification regime: it describes the limits and obligations the countries must observe and allows them to identify the forces and activities that comply with the terms of the Treaty. The identification of compliant activities also helps a country focus on what it should look for when it collects information about the other country's forces and activities. No verification regime can ensure the detection of all violations, but the START regime is designed to ensure that parties would have a high probability of detecting militarily significant violations.

The parties to a treaty use a wide variety of means to collect information—or monitor—the forces and activities of the other parties. Some of these monitoring systems, such as overhead satellites, operate outside the territories of the treaty parties. But the parties can also cooperate in providing information by exchanging data, displaying treaty-limited items, and allowing on-site inspections. Once they have collected this information, the parties analyze and refine the raw data to help develop a meaningful picture of each other's forces and activities. They then evaluate the results of the monitoring process, compare the observed forces and activities with the expected forces and activities, and determine whether the other party has complied with its obligations under the terms of the Treaty.

To verify compliance with START, each side monitors the numbers and locations of ballistic missiles, launchers and heavy bombers deployed by the other country. To achieve this goal, the countries have had to

- establish the number and location of deployed and stored ballistic missiles and deployed bombers when the Treaty entered into force;
- confirm the technical characteristics of existing types of weapons and establish the measurements for new types of weapons;
- add the number of ballistic missiles and heavy bombers deployed after the treaty entered into force;
- subtract the number of ballistic missiles and heavy bombers eliminated, according to treaty rules, during the life of the treaty;
- track treaty-limited items when they move between declared facilities;
- monitor the armament on permitted systems, to confirm that missiles and bombers are deployed with the numbers and types of warheads permitted by the START data base; and
- monitor ballistic missile flight tests to determine the characteristics of different types of ballistic missiles.

START contains a complex verification regime that is designed to allow the parties to achieve these objectives. Both sides use their own satellites and remote sensing equipment—their National Technical Means of Verification (NTM)—to gather the vast majority of the information each needs to monitor the other country's forces and activities and to determine whether the other country has complied with the limits in START. But the Treaty also contains a number of specific verification provisions that are designed to help the parties gather and confirm the needed information. For example, it bans measures that would interfere with the parties' ability to collect information with their NTM, and requires that they use data exchanges, notifications, and on-site inspections to gather information about forces and activities limited by the Treaty. These measures do not replace monitoring with NTM, but they can add detail to information collected by NTM, enhance a country's confidence in the meaning and reliability of the information, and help deter violations. The Treaty also established the Joint Compliance and Inspection Commission (JCIC), where the parties meet to discuss treaty implementation issues and compliance questions.

Access Measures

START contains several verification measures that allow the countries' NTM to gain access to information about the other country's treaty-limited forces. These measures include a ban on interference with NTM—for example, the parties cannot interfere with the launch or operation of the other side's satellites—and a requirement that they broadcast telemetry, the technical data generated during missile flight tests over open channels. START also bans efforts to conceal forces and activities from NTM and mandates that the parties display treaty limited items under certain circumstances, so that NTM can confirm their locations and some characteristics.

The ban on data denial during missile flight tests was a particularly important feature of START for the United States. Each nation transmits data, known as telemetry, during its flight tests of ballistic missiles. Even without START, each nation monitored the other's missile flight tests to gain information about characteristics such as missile throwweight, launch weight, and the number of reentry vehicles releases tested during the flight. The nations could deny each other access to this data by encrypting it and transmitting it in coded form, recording it during the flight and storing it aboard the missile for recovery after the test, or by jamming and otherwise interfering with the other side's receiving instruments. Because the United States believed that this information would be critical to its efforts to monitor Soviet compliance with START, it insisted that the Treaty contain a complete ban on the denial of data generated during flight tests. Not only must the parties broadcast unencrypted data during the tests, they also agreed to exchange the tapes of data recorded during the flight tests.

Information Exchanges

START mandates that the parties exchange detailed information about the numbers, locations, and characteristics of treaty-limited ballistic missiles and heavy bombers. For the most part, this information confirms information that each country collects with its own NTM. It can provide additional details and help the countries interpret ambiguous or incomplete data. The countries have also had to notify each other when they move ballistic missiles or bombers that are limited by the treaty. These notifications help each country monitor the locations of the other side's permitted systems and detect the possible presence of excess or illegal systems.

On-site Inspections

Under START, the United States and Russia have conducted several different types of on-site inspections. They use these inspections to collect information about permitted systems and activities at declared facilities, but they are not permitted to go "anywhere, anytime" in search of treaty violations. These inspections may not provide much new information that is needed to verify compliance with the Treaty, but can confirm and add detail to information collected by NTM and data exchanges. Further, with the short notice available before many of these inspections, a country would find it difficult to hide evidence of a violation at a declared facility.

START has permitted inspections at all the declared facilities that produce, house, and support ballistic missiles and heavy bombers. The countries use these inspections to confirm information about the number of systems located at each facility. They have also viewed treaty-limited items to confirm information about their characteristics; for example, they can use short-notice inspections to confirm that the number of warheads on a missile does not exceed the number attributed to that type of missile in the data base. Each country has also established permanent monitoring systems around a final assembly facility for one of the other country's mobile ICBMs to help them count mobile ICBMs as they enter the force.

Each of the inspections permitted by the START Treaty is governed by complex and detailed procedures that address everything about the inspection process. These procedures outline, among other things, the airports the inspectors can use when they arrive in the country, the amount of notice they need to give before the start of the inspection, the amount of time the host country has to transport the inspectors to the selected site, the types of equipment the inspectors can use, the amount of time that can transpire during the inspection, and the procedures the inspectors and hosts would use to resolve questions that came up during the visit. These procedures and rules are designed to outline the rights and responsibilities of both parties, and minimize any potential conflict that might occur during inspections, but they also can create conflicts and of their own if questions about procedures come up during the process. Most analysts agree, however, that the START inspection process has had few significant problems over the years.

Synergy in Monitoring and Verification

Each verification provision in START is designed to provide the parties with a distinct source of information about the forces and activities of the other side. They also mesh together in a way that is designed to deter violations and increase confidence in the parties' compliance with the Treaty. For example, much of the data collected during on-site inspections can also be collected by NTM or shared during data exchanges. The inspections essentially confirm expected information. Nevertheless, this redundancy can detect inconsistencies and thereby complicate efforts to hide information and evade Treaty limits. For example, if one party did not notify the other before it moved a treaty-limited item to a different facility, but the other party's NTM detected the movement, the inconsistency might raise questions about whether the first party were trying to hide or conceal an item limited by the treaty. Over time, the START regime has also allowed the parties to collect information that may not be central to the goals of the Treaty but could still add to their understanding of the forces and operations of the other side. Many of the Treaty's supporters argue that this adds confidence and predictability to assessments of the other side's strategic forces.

START Implementation

In September 1990, before START entered into force, the United States had more than 10,500 accountable warheads deployed on nearly 2,250 delivery vehicles [10]. By mid-2008, this number had declined to 5,941 accountable warheads on 1,214 delivery vehicles [11]. Soviet forces had declined from more than 10,000 accountable warheads on 2,500 delivery vehicles in September 1990 to 4,138 accountable warheads on 839 delivery vehicles in mid-2008. All the nuclear warheads from the SS-18 ICBMs and heavy bombers in Kazakhstan had been returned to Russia by May 1995. All the nuclear weapons had been removed from Ukraine's territory by June 1996, and all 81 SS-25 mobile ICBMs had been moved from Belarus to Russia by late November 1996. Ukraine has eliminated all the ICBM silos and heavy bombers that were deployed on its territory. All the parties have also participated in the on-site inspections permitted under the Treaty. They continue to meet, twice each year, in the JCIC. While both the United States and Russia have raised some questions about compliance with the Treaty, both agree that there have been few significant compliance disputes.

THE STRATEGIC OFFENSIVE REDUCTIONS TREATY [12]

In 2001, during its first year in office, the Bush Administration conducted a Nuclear Posture Review to evaluate the size, structure, and role of the U.S. nuclear arsenal. As a part of that review, the Administration determined that the United States could reduce its strategic forces to between 1,700 and 2,000 "operationally deployed nuclear warheads." During a summit meeting with Russia's President Vladimir Putin in November 2001, President Bush announced that the United States would pursue these reductions unilaterally in the next decade, without signing a formal arms control agreement. President Putin indicated that Russia wanted to use the formal arms control process to achieve deeper reductions in nuclear arsenals, and emphasized that the two sides should focus on "reaching a reliable and verifiable agreement" [13]

Within the Bush Administration, Secretary of State Colin Powell supported the conclusion of a "legally binding" arms control agreement. He apparently prevailed over the objections of officials in the Pentagon who reportedly wanted the United States to maintain the flexibility to size and structure its nuclear forces in response to its own needs [14]. Consequently, the United States and Russia signed the Strategic Offensive Reductions Treaty (also known as the Moscow Treaty) on May 24, 2002. It received the advice and consent of the Senate on March 6, 2003 and the approval of the Russian parliament on May 14, 2003; it entered into force on June 1, 2003.

The Moscow Treaty states that the United States and Russia will reduce their "strategic nuclear warheads" to between 1,700 and 2,200 warheads by December 31, 2012 [15]. The text does not define "strategic nuclear warheads" and, therefore, does not indicate whether the parties will count only those warheads that are "operationally deployed," all warheads that would count under the START counting rules, or some other quantity. The text does refer to statements made by Presidents Bush and Putin in November and December 2001, when each outlined their own reduction plans. As a result, the United States and Russia each use their own definition when counting strategic nuclear warheads, and neither uses the START counting rules. The Treaty does not limit delivery vehicles or impose sublimits on specific types of weapons systems. Each party shall determine its own "composition and structure of its strategic offensive arms." In addition, the Treaty does not contain any definitions or descriptions of the types missiles and bombers whose warheads count under the Treaty limits.

In addition, the Moscow Treaty does not contain any monitoring or verification provisions. During the hearings on the resolution of ratification, the Bush Administration noted that the United States and Russia already collect information about strategic nuclear forces under START and during implementation of the Nunn-Lugar Cooperative Threat Reduction Program. At the time, some in Congress questioned whether this information would be sufficient for the duration of the Treaty, since START expires three years ahead of the Moscow Treaty [16]. This break in the time lines is one of the primary reasons why many analysts and Members of Congress believe the two sides should at least extend the monitoring and verification provisions in START through the end of the Moscow Treaty.

PREPARING FOR START EXPIRATION

U.S. – Russian Discussions

In September 2006, U.S. Undersecretary of State Robert Joseph and Russian Deputy Foreign Minister Sergei Kislyak met to initiate a new strategic security dialogue. This dialogue evolved into a series of meetings that addressed a range of issues. START was included, but was not high on the agenda of the meetings. During the first meeting, and at a second one in December 2006, the two sides outlined their goals for the talks. Russia indicated that it wanted to follow START with a new formal treaty that would be "similar in size and complexity to START" and would use many of the same definitions and counting rules as START. Russia also suggested that the two sides establish a regular working group, with meetings chaired at the Assistant Secretary level, to work out the details of this new Treaty. According to a Bush Administration official, the United States had "no appetite for those big, giant documents that try to script every single element of strategic forces." [17]. The Administration emphasized that the United States and Russia no longer needed arms control agreements to manage their strategic relationship. The United States also did not want to set up a working group or negotiate a new Treaty to follow START, and preferred to pursue broader "strategic discussions" within a political framework [18]

In spite of their differences, the United States and Russia agreed that they should continue to implement some of the monitoring and verification provisions in START after the Treaty expired. Russia proposed that they include these verification provisions in a new, legally binding Treaty that would also limit the number of warheads permitted on each side. According to one Russian official, these measures would have to be a part of a legally binding agreement to be permitted by domestic Russian law [19]. The United States, however, argued for a less formal arrangement of transparency and confidence-building measures. These could include voluntary notifications and site visits, but would not contain the detailed procedures and provisions included in START [20]

Although Undersecretary of State Joseph initially rejected the idea, the two sides did hold a series of meetings chaired at the Assistant Secretary level in search of a possible monitoring and verification agreement. They continued to disagree, however, on whether the verification measures should be voluntary or legally binding, and whether they should be attached to a formal treaty that would also limit the numbers of deployed warheads.

In addition to the periodic meetings at the Undersecretary level (Joseph/Kislyak, then Rood/Kislyak) and the working group meetings at the Assistant Secretary level, the United States and Russia held several high level meetings that addressed the future of U.S.-Russian arms control. For example, Secretary of State Condoleezza Rice met with Russia's Foreign Minister Sergey Lavrov in July 2007. Their formal statement after the meeting said that "The United States and Russia reiterate their intention to carry out strategic offensive reductions to the lowest possible level consistent with their national security requirements and alliance commitments." It added that the "Ministers discussed development of a post-START arrangement to provide continuity and predictability regarding strategic offensive forces [21]. But the United States still did not accept Russia's proposal to pursue a formal Treaty.

The U.S. position began to shift later in 2007. Secretary Rice and Secretary of Defense Robert Gates held joint meetings in Moscow with their counterparts in October, and concluded that, although the United States was still seeking something "far less formal than a major treaty" it might accept, according to Secretary Gates, "a binding agreement" preserving some of START, as long as it was "narrowly focused." [22] Nevertheless, the United States continued to reject a formal treaty that would limit the number of nuclear weapons. When Secretary Gates and Secretary Rice traveled to Moscow to discuss START again in March 2008, Secretary Rice argued the current U.S.-Russian relationship does not require "the kind of highly articulated, expensive limitations and verification procedures that attended the strategic arms relationship with the Soviet Union." [23] Russian officials, however, continued to reject the U.S. proposals for an informal "notification" regime.

Presidents Bush and Putin failed to break this stalemate when they met in Sochi, Russia in April 2008. Although they signed a new Strategic Framework that contained a pledge to enact nuclear weapons reductions "to the lowest possible level consistent with our national security requirements and alliance commitments," they failed to agree on the way forward in their arms control relationship. Russia still wanted to negotiate a Treaty based on the START framework; the United States was only willing to codify some verification measures [24]

The talks continued through the spring and summer of 2008, although, according to some news reports they were "irregular and unproductive." [25]. Some reports suggested that the United States might suspend the talks in response to the Russian incursion into Georgia in August, 2008, but both sides agreed the talks were important enough to continue in September and October [26]. Nevertheless, the two sides remained far apart. Russia was unwilling to recede from its call for a formal Treaty with detailed definitions and counting rules; the United States still preferred a less formal agreement that outlined transparency and confidence-building measures. The United State did, however, recognize that Russia would not permit on-site visits without a formal Treaty, so Washington proposed in October 2008 that the two sides attach an informal transparency regime to a legally binding Treaty that essentially reiterated the limits and declarations outlined in the Moscow Treaty. Russia rejected this proposal. In a speech delivered on October 10, Russian President Dmitry Medvedev said that Russia attaches "exceptional importance to concluding a new, legally binding Russian-American agreement on nuclear disarmament" to replace START. He further noted that "what we need is a treaty and not a declaration," which is a reference to the format used in the Moscow Treaty [27].

The United States and Russia, along with representatives from Ukraine, Belarus, and Kazakhstan, met in the JCIC from November 13 through 21, 2008. This forum provided the venue for the formal meeting, mandated by START, where the parties considered whether to extend the Treaty [28]. They did not reach any agreements during this meeting, other than to note that they were leaving the options open for the Obama Administration. The United States and Russia held one final meeting in their series of strategic security discussions on December 15, 2008; bi-lateral arms control was one of many issues on the agenda [29]. They held extensive discussions about the U.S. draft treaty, but they failed to reach agreement on any of the outstanding issues.

U.S. and Russian Proposals

Neither the United States nor Russia believes the two parties should extend the START Treaty. Neither wants to continue to implement all the monitoring and verification provisions included in START; the lengthy and highly detailed lists of procedures and requirements have proven costly and complicated. In some cases, these details were designed to address concerns about the potential for cheating and evasion that no longer exist in the current environment. Moreover, as is noted below, some of the limits and restrictions have begun to interfere with ongoing weapons programs for both nations. A simple extension of START would not reduce these pressures, and, unless the parties could agree on a new Treaty, could remain in force for five years.

Russian Proposals

In a speech to Russian diplomats in June 2006, then-President Vladimir Putin proposed that the United States and Russia begin negotiations to replace START with a new Treaty [30]. Since then, Russia has consistently and repeatedly insisted that the two sides replace START with a treaty that would not only reduce each side's strategic offensive forces to 1,500 warheads, but would count the warheads on all deployed delivery vehicles, as START has done [31] Such an agreement would maintain the predictability and the stability afforded by START, an outcome that would not be possible in the absence of a detailed, legally binding Treaty [32] The new treaty would not need to keep all the provisions of START, but should preserve "the main systematic structure of the agreement," including limitations on delivery vehicles and warhead deployments [33]

Reports indicate that Russia would like the new treaty to relax START's requirements for new types of ballistic missiles. As was noted above, START contains a precise definition of the changes needed to have a new missile counted as a "new type." These provisions were designed to prevent Russia from deploying its SS-25 missile with more than one warhead. But Russia has developed the RS-24 missile, a new variant of its single-warhead SS-27 missile, which is, itself, a variant of the SS-25, and it plans to deploy this new missile with three warheads on each missile [34]. Because the missile does not satisfy the Treaty's "new types" definition, it would be limited to a single warhead under START, and a three-warhead version would violate the Treaty. This missile had its third successful test launch in late November 2008, and recent press reports indicate that Russia now plans to deploy this missile in December 2009, as soon as START expires. Russian officials have indicated that this missile is critical to the future of Russia's strategic forces, not only because it can carry up to three warheads, but also because it will incorporate technologies that would allow it to penetrate U.S. ballistic missile defenses [35]

According to some reports, Russia would also like the new Treaty to ease some of the restrictions that START imposes on mobile ICBMs [36]. Although these restrictions were intended to apply to both parties, the United States has never been affected by them because it never deployed mobile ICBMs. These provisions, including limits on the size of deployment areas, notifications about exercises, and the rights to special on-site inspections after the missiles have dispersed for exercises, were designed to complicate any effort to hide extra missiles within the legal deployments of mobile ICBMs. But they also impinge on the operations of the permitted missiles and add to the costs of operating the systems [37]

Over the years, Russia has also expressed concerns about the U.S. ability to add warheads to its missiles quickly by restoring warheads that had been removed under START's downloading provisions. It may insist that a new Treaty require the United States to replace the platform on all downloaded missiles, instead of just those that have had more than two warheads removed [38]

Russia would like to retain some of START's monitoring and verification provisions, although it would like to make them less costly and cumbersome. For example, the two sides could reduce the numbers of short-notice inspections permitted each year, and replace these inspections with less formal "visits." The parties could also reduce the number of mandatory notifications, which were intended to help each side monitor the numbers and locations of treaty-limited items, and replace them with routine, periodic data exchanges [39]

U.S. Proposals

When U.S. and Russian talks on the future of START began in 2006, the United States expected START to expire and the parties to pursue their own priorities when modernizing and modifying their nuclear forces. However, the participants in the U.S. government were divided on the question of whether to extend START's monitoring provisions. According to some reports, U.S. officials believed the two sides should evaluate whether they even needed to continue to implement these provisions because, even without START, the amount of military cooperation and transparency between them had increased over the years [40]. They further argued that the inspections regime had become too costly and cumbersome for the United States, and could interfere with military operations, without providing certain knowledge about Russian's nuclear forces. Moreover, in the new security environment, the United States no longer needs detailed information about Russian forces; it just needs to understand the general trends and pending changes in force size and structure. Therefore, the two sides need, at most, an informal system with less structured visits and looser inspections.

Others argued that the START regime provides valuable information about Russian forces that is not available elsewhere, while also helping to build confidence and cooperation between the two sides [41]. Further, reports indicate that officials in the U.S. intelligence community have argued that, without START's cooperative monitoring provisions, it will not be able to assess, with confidence, Russia's compliance with the limits in the Moscow Treaty [42]

While the United States has not identified any of the central limits in START that impinge on its current plans and programs, some officials have expressed concerns that an extension of these provisions, or their inclusion in a new Treaty, could affect future plans, such as the possible deployment of conventional warheads on ballistic missiles and the potential deployment of these conventional missiles at sites that are not listed in the Treaty [43]. This concern has emerged as a major roadblock in the recent U.S.-Russian discussions about what type of treaty should follow START [44]. Russia has insisted that the new treaty count the warheads that could be deployed on *all* strategic delivery vehicles, as START did, in part to capture the warheads that could be carried on missiles converted to carry conventional weapons. It wants to count these warheads to limit the U.S. ability to break out of the treaty by converting the missiles back to nuclear warheads [45]. The United States, however, does not want the warheads that could be carried on these missiles to count under the Treaty because it does not want any limits on conventional warheads or any forced trade-offs between numbers of nuclear and conventional warheads.

U.S. officials have also expressed concerns about some of START's monitoring and verification provisions. For example, the Navy has indicated that Russian requests for re-entry vehicle inspections on U.S. ballistic missile submarines can interfere with the scheduled maintenance and operations of the submarines, because the Navy must bring the submarine into port and the missile into a handling facility on the base. The treaty's limits on the number of warheads that can be removed, or downloaded, from Trident submarines might also interfere with the Navy's deployment plans for the future, particularly the United States chooses to remove more warheads from Trident missiles as it continues to reduce the overall number of strategic warheads in its arsenal.

Some in the U.S. government have also argued that START's provisions requiring the exchange of telemetry data during flight tests of ballistic missiles will interfere with U.S. military plans and programs [46]. In particular, the United States uses retired Minuteman II ICBMs as target vehicles during tests of its missile defense capabilities. Because these missiles are still limited by the START Treaty, the United States must provide Russia with all the telemetry generated during these flights. Yet, the data from these tests may reveal information not only about the Minuteman II ICBMs but also about the goals of the flight test and the characteristics of the missile defense interceptors. This concern has been a key issue in discussions about whether, and how, the United States and Russia should extend some of START's monitoring provisions.

The Bush Administration eventually proposed that the two sides replace START with a short, legally binding Treaty similar to the Moscow Treaty and a longer, non-binding appendix on transparency and cooperation. This transparency regime would be far less detailed and complex than START. It would allow for informal visits, without the detailed plans and notifications required by START, and probably would relax the telemetry provisions, or at least exempt Minuteman II flights during missile defense tests from the requirement to broadcast and exchange telemetry. Moreover, as is noted above, the legally binding portion of the U.S. proposal would not contain any of the detailed definitions and counting rules of START; the parties would declare their numbers of deployed warheads, as they do under the Moscow Treaty.

The Obama Administration has not yet outlined any specific proposals for advancing the U.S.-Russian arms control agenda, although it has indicated that it may resume discussions at an early date, and that it has two separate objectives for these discussions. In response to questions posed by the Arms Control Association, then-candidate Obama stated that he would "seek Russia's agreement to extend essential monitoring and verification provisions of START before it expires." He also said that he would seek "real, verifiable reductions in all U.S. and Russian nuclear weapons—whether deployed or nondeployed, whether strategic or nonstrategic.... " [47] Secretary of State Hillary Clinton offered a similar response during her nomination hearings, indicating that the Obama Administration would continue negotiations with Russia to replace START and would seek to negotiate "deep, verifiable reductions in all U.S. and Russian nuclear weapons, whether deployed or non-deployed, strategic or nonstrategic." [48]. During a speech before the Munich Security Conference on February 7, 2009, Vice President Biden also stated that the United States and Russia should cooperate to "renew the verification procedures in the START treaty and then go beyond existing treaties to negotiate deeper cuts in our arsenals." [49]

Press reports indicate that the White House and State Department have begun to hold internal talks on potential arms control proposals [50]. While the statements quoted above do not specify whether the Administration will support a simple extension of START or its replacement with another agreement, it indicates that President Obama is more open to completing formal agreements with Russia, in general, and to negotiating further reductions in U.S. and Russian nuclear forces.

OPTIONS FOR THE FUTURE

The United States and Russia have two distinct issues to consider when they contemplate the future of their arms control relationship. First, what, if anything, should they do within the next year to extend or replace START? And, second, should they seek to negotiate a new treaty to replace the Moscow Treaty before it expires in 2012? Moreover, should the provisions in a new Treaty focus on transparency and confidence-building measures, or should the two nations also seek to impose deeper reductions on their strategic offensive forces?

It is unlikely that the United States and Russia will be able to negotiate and ratify a new Treaty before the end of 2009, even though both sides have said they want to do so. The Obama Administration has to name the senior State Department and Defense Department officials who may craft U.S. policy on arms control and nuclear weapons, develop its negotiating positions for a future arms control treaty; and negotiate and reach agreement on a wide range of issues with Russia. Both sides must present the treaty to their legislatures for advice and consent. Moreover, during its first year in office, the Obama Administration must conduct a Nuclear Posture Review, [51] which could recommend changes in both U.S. nuclear weapons policy and the U.S. force structure. These changes could affect U.S. arms control proposals, but the study will not be completed until early 2010.

The United States and Russia could choose from a number of options for the future of their arms control relationship. They could allow START to lapse or they could extend START for five years. They could negotiate a new Treaty, or they could pursue less formal arrangements to manage their nuclear forces. A new Treaty could include further reductions in nuclear weapons, or it could simply establish a transparency regime that called for continued cooperation in monitoring without further reductions in deployed weapons. In their discussions thus far, the United States and Russia have agreed they do not want to extend START, but they have been unable to agree on what kind of arrangement will follow START, in part because they do not agree on the goals they seek to achieve in their discussions. Hence, this paper will review some of the possible goals for the future of the U.S.-Russian arms control relationship before it reviews the range of options.

Possible Goals

Improving U.S. – Russian Relationship

Many of the public discussions about the future of the U.S.-Russian arms control process focus on whether arms control can help the United States and Russia manage and improve their broader political relationship. As was noted at the beginning of this report, many observers, including some who served in the Bush Administration believe that the U.S.-Russian relationship has evolved to the point where the parties no longer need arms control as a symbol of their cooperation on resolving common security issues. Others, however, including some Members of Congress, believe that START and the arms control process still represent "the foundation of the U.S.-Russian strategic relationship" and a "key basis for trust between the two sides" [52].

Supporting Nuclear Nonproliferations Goals

During the past few years, the public debate over arms control and nuclear weapons has increasingly focused on the role that the U.S.-Russian arms control process can play in furthering broader international nuclear nonproliferation goals. For example, many analysts have argued that a U.S.-Russian agreement to either extend or replace START can demonstrate their commitment to their arms reduction obligations under the Nuclear Nonproliferation Treaty, [53] and can, therefore help strengthen the nonproliferation regime, in general, and help ensure a successful outcome at the 2010 review conference of the NPT. Others, however, argue that the nations who are currently seeking nuclear weapons would not be swayed in their decisions by any steps taken by the United States or Russia, as their nuclear programs derive from their own political and security concerns. Moreover, they note that the United States and Russia have already reduced their Cold-War era nuclear arsenals sharply, without reaping any benefits in their efforts to stem nuclear proliferation.

Restraining Weapons

Many analysts in the United States and officials in the Bush Administration have argued that, in the current security environment, the United States and Russia no longer need to worry about all the details related to the size or structure of the other side's nuclear forces, they just need to understand the general trends [54]. Both have reduced their forces in recent years and neither needs to fear that the other would attack it with its remaining forces. Therefore, they no longer need to negotiate formal treaties to establish and maintain balance between their two force structures. Moreover, these treaties undermine the flexibility that each nation may need to adjusts its forces in response to future threats from emerging adversaries.

Although Russia recognizes that the relationship between the two nations is not as tense as it was during the Cold War, it still sees threats to its security from U.S. policies and programs. Therefore Russia continues to value arms control measures that restrain U.S. forces because these measures provide both stability between the two sides forces and predictability for Russia when it considers how U.S. forces may evolve [55]

Many analysts in the United States also believe that the stability and predictability offered by arms control agreements are valuable enough to offset any limits the treaties may create for U.S. flexibility. Some argue that the process of implementing an arms control treaty, with its communication and cooperation, by itself, is important, so that the parties can avoid misunderstandings while they work together to reduce nuclear forces and nuclear dangers. Others, however, emphasize that the actual limits and restrictions in the treaty, as much as the cooperation to implement them, determine the amount of stability and predictability offered by the treaty. They note that the United States and Soviet Union included many of the detailed provisions in START because both wanted to restrain and reduce the nuclear forces of the other side to reduce the threat from those forces, and both agreed to include detailed monitoring and verification provisions so that they could be more confident about achieving the goal of reducing the threat.

Promoting Transparency and Cooperation

Many have argued that, at least in the near-term, the United States and Russia should seek to replace START with a regime that will ensure transparency and build confidence, even if it does not mandate deeper reductions in nuclear weapons [56]. This type of agreement will ensure that some form of monitoring and verification provisions remains in place after START expires and while the Moscow Treaty remains in force. A confidence-building regime can foster cooperation between the two sides even if the data it provides is not needed to verify compliance with an arms control Treaty. As one observer has noted, START "forces the United States and Russia to communicate," and to interact in ways that can build trust between them [57]. Therefore, an agreement that allowed the parties to continue with data exchanges, notifications, and some inspections, even without further reductions, could prove valuable.

Some argue that the United States and Russia can promote transparency and continue their cooperation without signing a formal arms control agreement. They note that the two sides will continue to cooperate on reducing nuclear dangers through the nonproliferation and threat reduction programs that the United States funds to improve security and eliminate weapons in Russia. These efforts can be bolstered by informal visits to weapons deployment areas and storage facilities. Moreover, some have argued that the formal monitoring and verification provisions in START can create tensions and undermine cooperation with their rigid requirements and stringent rules, which do not allow the parties to adapt their activities when conditions change [58]

SCOPE

Reductions vs Transparency

Some analysts have argued that START provides the United States and Russia with the framework they could use to move quickly to negotiate a comprehensive agreement that would both reduce forces below the Moscow Treaty limits and outline a wide-ranging monitoring and verification regime [59]. This approach would not only satisfy Russia's preference for pursuing deeper reductions in a follow-on to START in the near-term, but would also allow the United States and Russia to demonstrate bold leadership to the international community in the months before the 2010 NPT Review Conference. The two sides may not have time to complete this type of agreement before START expires, but this could still advance the arms control agenda by highlighting their commitment to pursue a Treaty on deep reductions even if START were to lapse in the near-term.

On the other hand, some have argued that a shorter, less detailed document, like the Moscow Treaty, might be sufficient to foster communication and cooperation. Even without specific definitions and restrictions, such a document can still demonstrate the parties' intent to reduce nuclear arms. Further, with fewer detailed restrictions, both sides would be able to maintain the flexibility they might need to alter their forces to meet unanticipated changes in the international security environment. Moreover, the negotiations could probably proceed more quickly than those that sought to produce a lengthy, detailed treaty. The United States and Soviet Union took seven years to negotiate START, but the United States and Russia completed the Moscow Treaty in less than a year.

Linkages

The START Treaty limits only strategic offensive delivery vehicles and the warheads carried by those forces. But the history of U.S.-Soviet arms control negotiations is full of examples where one or the other side has tried to include limits or restrictions on other types of weapons. Over the years, both countries have sought to include some types of limits on their shorter-range non-strategic nuclear weapons in arms control agreements; analysts continue to suggest that these limits are both necessary and inevitable in a future agreement [60].

The two sides have also often linked progress in discussions on missile defense programs with progress on limits on strategic offensive nuclear weapons. This linkage was explicit in the 1970s, when the first Strategic Arms Limitation Talks (SALT I) produced both the Anti-Ballistic Missile Treaty and the Interim Agreement on Offensive Arms. This linkage between offenses and defense remains important to Russia, as is evident in its concerns about the U.S. plans to deploy a missile defense site in Poland and the Czech Republic.

Several analysts have also suggested that future treaties should limit not only deployed warheads, but also the numbers of warheads that each side retains in its stockpile of reserve warheads [61]. While no arms control treaty has ever sought to reduce either nation's stockpile of reserve warheads, as the number of deployed warheads declines further, the number of warheads in storage could create an imbalance if either side could return them to deployment quickly. Moreover, reductions in the numbers of stored warheads, and their consolidation in fewer storage facilities, might ease concerns about the possibility that some might be stolen from insecure storage facilities.

Participants

Although the United States and Soviet Union signed START as a bilateral agreement, it evolved into a multilateral treaty when Belarus, Ukraine, Russia, and Kazakhstan succeeded the Soviet Union as parties to the Treaty. Each of the four former Soviet states is subject to the limits, restrictions, and monitoring provisions in START, even though Russia is the only one with nuclear weapons left on its territory. Each also has a voice and a vote in the deliberations in the Joint Compliance and Inspection Commission established by the Treaty. If the parties agree to extend START, Ukraine, Belarus, and Kazakhstan will remain as parties to the Treaty unless they agree to amend it to include only the United States and

Russia. If the United States and Russia sign a new Treaty, these other three states probably would not be included [62]

Analysts have long suggested that, as the United States and Russia reduce their forces to ever lower levels, they may eventually open up the arms control process to other nuclear weapons states. This was rarely an issue during the Cold War, because the United States and Soviet Union each deployed thousands of warheads on their strategic offensive nuclear weapons. France, Great Britain, and China have deployed just a few hundred warheads each [63]. Most analysts agree that these other nations should not join the process until the United States and Russia reduce to 1,000 or fewer warheads. Hence, as the United States and Russia decide how, or whether, to advance their bilateral arms control agenda, they may also begin to think about when, or whether, to expand the process to include other nuclear nations.

POTENTIAL PATHS

Allow START to Lapse

The United States and Russia could allow START to lapse at the end of 2009. The Bush Administration initially preferred this option because it did not want to continue the formal U.S.-Russian arms control process at all, but also believed that START could lapse without signaling the end of U.S.-Russian nuclear cooperation or even the end of formal arms control. As the Bush Administration eventually suggested, the two sides could agree, without signing a formal Treaty, to continue to implement some of the monitoring provisions in START so that they could both gather information needed to verify compliance with the Moscow Treaty and retain the cooperative relationship that had developed during START's verification process. This path could, however, conflict with Russia's domestic law as it would need to be a party to a legally binding Treaty before it could allow foreigners to have access to sensitive military and nuclear sites [64]. To rectify this problem, the parties might seek to negotiate a separate executive agreement or memorandum of understanding to allow the visits. Alternatively they could, as the Bush Administration suggested, attach the monitoring provisions to a simple treaty document that essentially restated the provisions of the Moscow Treaty.

If the parties allowed START to lapse, and did not have the time to agree on a replacement before December 2009, they could still pursue negotiations on a treaty that would eventually replace both START and the Moscow Treaty. Concerns about the absence of any arms control limits might inspire them to press forward on this task and seek compromises in a short amount of time. Conversely, if the absence of arms control limits did not appear to upset stability or the level of cooperation between the parties, then the pressure to reach a new agreement might diminish. Hence, this path may be attractive to those who believe that the United States and Russia no longer need formal treaties to manage their relationship, but it may appear too risky to those who believe that the arms control process remains an important part of the relationship.

Extend START

Neither the Bush Administration nor the current Russian leadership want to extend START in its present form, particularly for the full five years allowed under the terms of the Article XVII. Yet, this path may be the only one available if the parties want to retain some of the START monitoring and verification provisions in the near term. They could possibly agree to extend START for a shorter period of time, perhaps two years, while they negotiate a new Treaty that would replace START. But this option is not mentioned in the current Treaty, so it might need to be treated as an amendment to the Treaty and require the advice and consent of both nations' legislatures. The U.S. Senate might not object to a short-term extension of START, particularly since several Members have already called on the parties to extend the Treaty's monitoring and verification regime, but Russia's parliament may not be as accepting. The current tensions in the U.S.-Russian relationship, along with ongoing concerns about U.S. plans to deploy missile defenses in Poland and the Czech Republic, could lead some in Russia to question whether any extension of START, with its limits on Russia's ability to modernize its forces and deploy multiple warhead ballistic missiles, serves Russia's interests.

Extend and Amend START

Instead of amending START so that they could extend it for less than the mandated five years, the parties might extend START according to the Treaty provisions, which they could do without seeking approval from their legislatures, then try to amend the Treaty to adjust the provisions that each finds too binding in the current environment. For example, Russia might want to alter the "new types" rule in START, or it might seek a waiver from the rule for the RM-24 missile; the United States might want to alter the provision requiring the exchange of telemetry from missile flight tests, or seek a waiver for retired Minuteman II missiles that are used as missile defense targets. Both sides might want to modify the verification protocol to remove some of the more costly and intrusive requirements, particularly if the parties believe the data they provide is no longer critical to understanding the other side's nuclear forces. Consequently, they might be able to craft a "package" of amendments that would incorporate each side's highest priorities.

Both the United States and Russia would have to submit this package for approval by their legislatures. Some in the U.S. Senate might object to the changes that relieve Russia of some of its obligations, but a package that addressed both nations' concerns might still win the approval of the necessary 67 Senators. The Russian parliament might object to any agreement that extended START without addressing Russia's concerns about U.S. missile defense plans. However, it might, nevertheless, accept an amendment package that addressed some of Russia's concerns with the provisions in START. In addition, if the United States and Russia extended START for five years before negotiating the amendments, the Russian parliament would have to accept either the unmodified extension, or the amendment package.

Replace START

Regardless of whether they allow START to lapse or extend it before December 2009, the United States and Russia could continue negotiations on a new Treaty. If they completed the Treaty before an extended START expired, the new Treaty could replace START, or, if it were similar to the Moscow Treaty, with aggregate limits but no detailed definitions, counting rules, or monitoring provisions, it could run concurrently without substituting for START.

As was noted above, Russia would like the new treaty to be a complete package of further limits on nuclear weapons, detailed definitions and counting rules, and monitoring and verification provisions. The Bush Administration, on the other hand, would have liked the new treaty to essentially replace the Moscow Treaty, with some informal monitoring provisions to offer a measure of transparency and cooperation. A future Treaty could take either of these forms, or it could focus solely on monitoring measures by establishing a legally binding framework for transparency and cooperation not linked to the need to verify compliance with restrictions on nuclear forces and activities.

Further Reductions with START Rules

A new treaty could contain START-style definitions and counting rules, along with deeper reductions in the permitted numbers of warheads. This combination of provisions would continue to reduce U.S. and Russian deployed forces and would also provide transparency and predictability for the future. Without the START-style definitions and counting rules, neither side would be able to confirm that the other has complied with the Treaty's reductions because each will not know what the other side considered to be limited by the treaty.

At the same time, a Treaty that required the United States to reduce its forces below the Moscow Treaty limits of 1,700-2,200 warheads, but also used the START counting rules to calculate the number of warheads attributed to deployed delivery vehicles could force the United States to make hard choices and significant changes in the structure of its nuclear forces. Under START, all deployed delivery vehicles count under the Treaty's limits (Russia has proposed that the same be true in a new agreement); the parties then calculated the number of deployed warheads by multiplying the number of deployed delivery vehicles by a number of warheads listed in the data base for that type of delivery vehicle.

The Moscow Treaty, on the other hand, does not assume all delivery vehicles carry deployed warheads, and allows the parties to exclude those that do not. As a result, the United States does not count the launchers or warheads on 2 of its 14 Trident submarines because they are in overhaul and not "deployed." These would count under the START rules. It also has removed more than 2 warheads from some Trident missiles, without changing the front end of the missile. Under START, these missiles would count as 6 warheads each; in its declaration under the Moscow Treaty, the United States counts only the aggregate number of actual deployed warheads; it does not even have to specify how many warheads are deployed on any given missile or submarine. Moreover, under the Moscow Treaty, the United States counts only the bomber weapons maintained in the active stockpile at U.S. bomber bases. Under START each bomber equipped to carry cruise missiles would count as 20 warheads, regardless of available weapons or actual deployments.

These differences produce striking differences in the number of warheads that count under each Treaty. In May 2008, the United States declared that it had 2,871 operationally deployed strategic warheads that would count against the Moscow Treaty [65]. At the same time, when it exchanged START data with Russia in July 2008, it stated that it had 5,951 warheads attributed to deployed ICBMs, deployed SLBMs, and heavy bombers. Many of these attributed warheads could be eliminated with some accounting changes, [66] but it is clear that under START definitions, the United States would have to count hundreds of warheads that it excludes from the Moscow Treaty total because it does not consider them to be operationally deployed.

To bring its warhead totals down to 1,500 or less, while using definitions and counting rules similar to those in START, the United States could seek to deploy each of its remaining Trident missiles with a smaller number of warheads. However, if START rules apply, a reduction of more than 2 warheads would necessitate the costly replacement of the platform on the post-boost vehicle on each missile. The United States could suggest that the new Treaty relax this rule, but Russia may object as it has been concerned about the U.S. ability to upload its missiles and increase its warheads in a crisis. Russia has long suggested that the parties tighten the downloading rules to minimize the possibility.

As an alternative, the United States could reduce its total warheads by eliminating some of its deployed launchers (bombers, ICBMs, or SLBMs), or even removing one leg of its "strategic triad" from the nuclear force. However, the United States probably would not want to reduce the number of B-52 and B-2 bombers, as these fly conventional missions in ongoing conflicts, so it might have to remove them from the nuclear force altogether. It also might be difficult to reduce the Minuteman fleet of ICBMs below the current number of 450 without also reducing the number of bases and cutting into the number of personnel trained to operate the system. Further, as the number drops, it may be also be difficult to justify the costs associated with retaining the smaller force.

Most experts agree that the Trident submarines are going to be the mainstay of the U.S. nuclear arsenal in the future. But, unless the United States cuts deeply into the other "legs" of its strategic triad, deep reductions in total warheads may require reductions in the number of Trident submarines. If the United States were to reduce its Trident fleet to 10 or fewer submarines, it might not be able to operate out of two bases, as it does now, and retain submarines on patrol in the areas from where they would fire their missiles, in both oceans. Changes in this deployment pattern might require changes in the missions and targets of the submarine fleet. The President and the U.S. military would probably want to consider the implications of these basing and operational changes before deciding whether to accept arms control limits that produce such changes.

Hence, if the United States agrees to replace START with a new Treaty that reduces warheads below the levels in the Moscow Treaty but retains many of the definitions and counting rules of START, it will have to make difficult choices about how to structure and operate its nuclear force.

These decisions are not likely to come easily or quickly, and could delay both the start and the finish of negotiations on a new Treaty.

Further Reductions without START Rules

The complexities detailed above demonstrate why the Bush Administration has been unwilling to follow START with a similar, detailed document. Even those in the Administration who believe that the U.S.-Russian arms control process should continue argue that the two sides should pursue a Treaty that did not contain the level of detail in START.

For example, during a speech before the Carnegie Endowment for International Peace in October 2008, Secretary of Defense Robert Gates said, "I am not sure that agreements that are the size of a telephone book and take years to negotiate are in the interest of either party." He went on to say, "I believe we should go for another agreement with Russia. I believe it could involve further cuts in the number of warheads. I believe we do need the verification provisions. But I think it ought to be an agreement that is shorter, simpler, and easier to adjust to real-world conditions than most of the arms control agreements I've seen over the last 40 years." [67]

A shorter, less detailed Treaty may not, however, provide the level of transparency or predictability sought by many analysts. Under the Moscow Treaty, which is short and contains few details, neither the United States nor Russia has to offer any transparency into the structure of its nuclear forces. Each simply has to declare how many warheads it has deployed on its operational forces. Further, because the Treaty includes no time lines for the reduction process and no definitions of the items limited by the Treaty, neither side can predict with confidence the process or outcome of the other side's reductions. As a result, some argue that, while the shorter negotiations may seem preferable, a shorter Treaty with an absence of details would not necessarily serve the goals of an arms control process that sought to strengthen the relationship between the United States and Russia or to reduce the perceived threats from their nuclear weapons.

Transparency and Confidence Building Measures

Some Members of Congress and analysts outside government have called on the United States and Russia to extend the monitoring regime in START, even if they cannot reach agreement on further reductions in nuclear forces. In a "Dear Colleague" letter circulated in July 2007, Representative Ellen Tauscher, Chair of the House Armed Services Committee, Subcommittee on Strategic Forces, noted the "transparency required by the START verification regime has bred confidence in both Russia and the U.S. enabling cooperation on a range of nuclear arms issues" [68]. As was noted above, Secretary of State Clinton and Vice President Biden both referred to the possibility of extending the monitoring and verification provisions in START.

An agreement that established a transparency regime without imposing any further reductions on nuclear weapons could allow the United States and Russia to sustain their confidence in their knowledge of each other's nuclear weapons deployments. The START regime's extensive exchanges of data about the characteristics of each party's weapons systems provide each party with significant amounts of information that would not have been available, or would have been difficult to acquire, otherwise. The parties can be confident in the accuracy of this data because they have the opportunity to visit the sites and view the weapons themselves. Moreover, START required each party to notify the other when they changed the numbers or locations of strategic systems. Even if the parties have not agreed to limit or reduce their nuclear weapons, they could continue to house their weapons at agreed sites, provide data about their characteristics and capabilities, and provide notifications when they moved them.

Some have also argued that, by continuing to cooperate in monitoring the locations and characteristics of deployed nuclear weapons, the United States and Russia would be better positioned to monitor compliance with the Moscow Treaty. The notifications and data exchanges would continue to inform them about the numbers and locations of missiles and bombers, while on-site visits would give them an opportunity to count the warheads deployed on some missile. These inspections would not, however, provide the parties with an opportunity to calculate all the warheads that would count under the Moscow Treaty. Because START inspections were designed to confirm that the number of warheads deployed on a particular missile did not exceed the number declared in the data base, they do not provide a way to count the total number warheads deployed on the entire force. However, by confirming that the deployed warhead number did not exceed the number in the data base, the inspections could provide the parties with some confidence in the number of warheads they might then use in their calculations of deployed warheads across the force.

CHOOSING A PATH

Although President Obama has stated that he would like the United States and Russia to negotiate deeper reductions in their nuclear weapons, the United States and Russia still may not be on the same path forward in their arms control relationship. They still have to decide what, if anything, to do about START before it expires, and what, if any, type of Treaty they should negotiate to replace START in the longer term. They may agree that the Treaty should contain more details than were included in the Moscow Treaty, but they will still have to decide which of START's counting rules and definitions will continue to apply, whether the new Treaty would ease or tighten the rules governing the downloading of missiles and the deployment of new types of missiles, and which of the Treaty's monitoring and verification provisions they would continue to implement. Moreover, they would have to decide whether to include only deployed warheads, or all deployed and reserve warheads, and whether to link reductions in strategic weapons to other issues, like nonstrategic nuclear weapons or missile defense [69].

Because each side would like some of START to continue and some of it to end, both may find it difficult to reach an agreement on the substance of a new treaty that matches their priorities. On the other, if they balance and offset their differing preferences and priorities they may be able to craft a compromise that provides them with more transparency and predictability than the Moscow Treaty, but less precision than the START Treaty.

REFERENCES

[1]   The leaders in Belarus, Ukraine, and Kazakhstan agreed to eliminate all of the nuclear weapons on their territories and to sign the Nuclear Non-Proliferation Treaty (NPT) as non-nuclear weapons states. These three states have been nuclear free since the late 1990s; all remaining Soviet-era nuclear warheads are deployed in Russia.

[2]   The United States and Russia signed the Strategic Offensive Reductions Treaty (also known as the Moscow Treaty) on May 24, 2002. They do not, however, consider this Treaty to be a successor to START. Article II of the Moscow Treaty specifically states that the START Treaty remains in force. See CRS Report RL31448, *Nuclear Arms Control: The Strategic Offensive Reductions Treaty*, by Amy F. Woolf.

[3]   The Parties did not need to make a decision about the future of START in December 2008, they just needed to meet to consider the question.

[4]   Richard Lugar. Speech at Conference on Defense Against Weapons of Mass Destruction. January 20, 2008.

[5]   Richard Lugar. "Trust Still Needs Verification." *Washington Times*. July 18, 2008. p. 24.

[6]   The full text of the Treaty and its many annexes is available at the U.S. State Department website: http://www.state.gov/t/ac/trt/18535.htm.

[7]   The most recent data base exchanged among the parties to the Treaty can be found at U.S. State Department, Bureauof Verification, Compliance, and Implementation. START Aggregate Numbers of Strategic Offensive Arms.http://www.state.gov/t/vci/rls/prsrl/2008/110337.htm.

[8]   Long-range nuclear-armed air-launched cruise missiles are those with a range of more than 600 kilometers.

[9]   The Soviet Union suggested that a 15% change in throwweight would be enough to distinguish a new type of missile, while the United States wanted a throwweight change of 30% and a change in one other missile characteristic. They eventually agreed to essentially split their differences and defined a new types of missile as one with a 21% change in throwweight and at least a 5% change in the length of the first stage. This would make new types of missiles significantly different from existing types.

[10]   U.S. Arms Control and Disarmament Agency Archives. START Data Base, exchanged September 1, 1990.

[11]   U.S. Department of State. Bureau of Verification, Compliance, and Implementation. Fact Sheet. START Aggregate Numbers of Strategic Offensive Weapons. October 1, 2008.

[12]   The text of this treaty can be found at U.S. Department of State. Bureau of Verification, Compliance, and Implementation. Treaties and Agreements. http://www.state.gov/t/ac/trt/10527.htm.

[13]   The White House, Office of the Press Secretary. Press Conference. President Bush and President Putin Discuss New Relationship. November 13, 2001.

[14]   Jonathan Landay. "Rumsfeld Reportedly Resists Firm Limits on Nuclear Arms," *San Jose Mercury News*. April 27, 2002.

[15]   For details on the substance of the Treaty, see CRS Report RL31448, *Nuclear Arms Control: The Strategic Offensive Reductions Treaty*, by Amy F. Woolf.

[16]   For details, see U.S. Congress, Senate. Committee on Foreign Relations. Hearing. Treaty on Strategic OffensiveReductions. Testimony of Secretary of State Colin Powell. July 9, 2002.

[17]   Sebastian Sprenger. "Nations to Kick off Initiative Against Nuclear Terrorism Next Week. Separate U.S.-Russianmeeting on START expected." *Inside Defense.com*, October 26, 2006.

[18]   Nicholas Kralev. "Russia, U.S. to Discuss START." *Washington Times*. March 6, 2007. p. 1.

[19]   Wade Boese. "U.S., Russia exploring post-START Options." *Arms Control Today*. May 2007.

[20]   Nicholas Kralev. "Russia, U.S. to Discuss START." *Washington Times*. March 6, 2007. p. 1.

[21] U.S. State Department. Office of the Spokesman. Joint Statement by U.S. Secretary of State Condoleezza Rice and Minister for Foreign Affairs of the Russian Federation Sergey Lavrov. July 3, 2007.

[22] Ken Fireman. "Gates, Rice made Last-Minute Offer of New Arms Ideas in Moscow." *Bloomberg News*, October 13, 2007.

[23] Wade Boese. "U.S., Russia at Odds on Key Arms Issues." *Arm Control Today*. April 2008.

[24] Wade Boese. "Bush, Putin Leave Arms Disputes Unsettled." *Arms Control Today*. May 2008.

[25] Wade Boese. "Russia Wants Limits on Prompt Global Strike." *Arms Control Today*. June 2008.

[26] Wade Boese. "U.S.-Russian Strategic Dialogue in Limbo." *Arms Control Today*. October 2008.

[27] Wade Boese. "Bush Administration Sets Russian Arms Talks." *Arms Control Today*. October 2008.

[28] U.S. Department of State. Bureau of Verification, Compliance, and Implementation. Statement by the United States Representative to the Joint Compliance and Inspection Commission for the Strategic Arms Reduction Treaty. Fact Sheet. November, 21, 2008.

[29] U.S. Department of State. Office of the Spokesman. "Acting Under Secretary for Arms Control and International Security John C. Rood To Travel to Moscow for Bilateral Strategic Security Dialogue Talks." Media Note. December 12, 2008.

[30] Wade Boese. "Russia Seeks New Nuclear Accord." *Arms Control Today*, September 2006.

[31] Wade Boese. "Arms Issues Divide U.S. and Russia." *Arms Control Today*. September 2007.

[32] Nikolai Sokov, "START I Replacement: The End of Cold War Disarmament." *PONARS Policy Memo No. 418.*Monterey Institute of International Studies. December 2006.

[33] Arms Control Association, *Interview with Sergey Kislyak, Russian Ambassador to the United States.* December, 2008. http://www.armscontrol.org/act/2008_12/Kislyak Interview.

[34] Pavel Podvig. "Why START is Important." *Bulletin of the Atomic Scientists.* July 3, 2007.

[35] "Russia To Deploy Missile To Counter US Missile Shield Next Year." *London Daily Telegraph.* November 29, 2008.

[36] Anatoli Diakov and Eugene Miasnikov. "ReSTART: The Need for a New U.S.-Russian Strategic Arms Agreement." *Arms Control Today*. September 2006.

[37] Nikolai Sokov. "Review of Disarmament Issues in U.S. Russian Relations." James Martin Center for Nonproliferation Studies, Monterey Institute of International Studies. November, 2007.

[38] Ibid.

[39] Ibid.

[40] David Francis. "Arms Expert Calls for START Verification Extension." *Global Security Newswire*. November 8, 2005.

[41] Carol Giacomo. "U.S. to let START nuclear treaty expire." *Reuters*. May 22, 2007. See also, Jonathan S. Landay."Dispute Delays Arms Control Talks with Moscow." *McClatchy Washington Bureau.* June 18, 2007.

[42] Wade Boese. News Analysis: "The Bush Administration and Verification." *Arms Control Today*, April 2005.

[43] Phil Gardner, Michael George, Vera Lev, and Sandra McMahon. *Extension of the START Treaty?* An SAIC Emerging Issues Project. December, 2005.

[44] Walter Pincus. "U.S., Russia Split over Scope of Arms Treaty Follow-up But Concur on Goal, Negotiator Says."*Washington Post*. December 22, 2008. p. 19.

[45] Russia Concerned by U.S. Position on START, Deputy Foreign Minister Says. *Interfax*, December 19, 2008.

[46] Ibid.

[47] Arms Control Today 2008 Presidential QandA: Democratic Candidate Barack Obama. Arms Control Association. September 24, 2008.

[48] Walter Pincus, "Clinton's Goals Detailed," *Washington Post*, January 19, 2009, p. 17.

[49] The White House, *Remarks by Vice President Biden at 45th Munich Conference on Security Policy*, Washington, D.C., February 7, 2009, http://www.whitehouse.gov/the_press_office/RemarksbyVicePresidentBidenat45thMunichConferenceonSecurityPolicy/.

[50] Barry Schweid, "Obama Admin. Seeks Treaty to Cut U.S., Russia Nukes," *Associated Press*, February 5, 2009.

[51] The mandate for the new Nuclear Posture Review is contained in the FY2008 Defense Authorization Act. (P.L. 110-181, Sec. 1070).

[52] Senator Richard Lugar. "Trust Still Needs Verification." *Washington Times*. July 18, 2008. P. 24.

[53] Jenifer Mackby ad Edward Ifft. "The End of START." *Special to the Washington Post*, April 20, 2007.

[54] Jonathan S Landay. "Dispute Delays Arms Control Talks with Moscow." *McClatchy Washington Bureau.* June 18, 2007.

[55] In a recent interview with the Arms Control Association, Russia's Ambassador to the United States, Sergey Kislyak,who, as Deputy Foreign Minister participated in talks on the future of START, stated that "the mutual constraints provided for in START should not be lost because they do provide stability and are one of the important things that also should be preserved and should not be discarded." See, Arms Control Association, *Interview with Sergey Kislyak,Russian Ambassador to the United States.* December, 2008. http://www.armscontrol.org/act/2008_12/KislyakInterview.

[56] Edward Ifft. "The Future of START." June 11, 2007.

[57] Pavel Podvig. "Why START is Important.*" Bulletin of the Atomic Scientists.* July 3, 2007.

[58] Phil Gardner, Michael George, Vera Lev, and Sandra McMahon. *Extension of the START Treaty?* An SAIC Emerging Issues Project. December, 2005.

[59] Daryl G. Kimball. "START Over." *Arms Control Today*. June 2007.

[60] Oliver Thranert. *U.S. Nuclear Forces in Europe to Zero? Yes, But Not Yet.* Carnegie Endowment for International Peace. December 10, 2008.

[61] President Obama has indicated that he would seek to include limits on weapons in the stockpile in a future armscontrol treaty. See "Arms Control Today 2008 Presidential

QandA: Democratic Candidate Barack Obama." *Arms Control Association*. September 24, 2008.

[62] According to an official with the U.S. State Department, Russia "prefers working bilaterally with the United States on nuclear weapons issues and wants to 'exclude' Belarus, Kazakhstan, and Ukraine from future arrangements." See Wade Boese. "START Decision Put Off to 2009." *Arm Control Today*. December, 2008.

[63] For summaries of the nuclear forces of these nations, see, Robert S. Norris and Hans Kristensen. "Chinese Nuclear Forces, 2008." *Bulletin of the Atomic Scientists*. July/August 2008; Robert S. Norris and Hans Kristensen and Robert S. Norris and Hans Kristensen. "British Nuclear Forces, 2005." *Bulletin of the Atomic Scientists*. November/December, 2005.

[64] Alexei Arbatov and Rose Gottemoeller. "New Presidents, New Agreements? Advancing U.S.-Russian Strategic Arms Control." *Arms Control Today*. July/August 2008.

[65] U.S. Department of State. 2008 Annual Report on Implementation of the Moscow Treaty. Bureau of Verification, Compliance and Implementation. Washington, D.C. May 13, 2008.

[66] For example, this total includes 400 warheads attributed to Peacekeeper missiles. These missiles have been deactivated, but the United States did not eliminate the silos according to START Treaty rules, so the warheads still count. It also excludes up to 768 warheads that could be deployed on four Trident submarines. The U.S. Navy has converted these submarines to carry non-nuclear cruise missiles, but, because it did not remove the launch tubes for the Trident missiles, they still count under START as if each launch tube held one missile and each missile carried either six or eight warheads.

[67] Secretary of Defense Robert Gates. *Nuclear Weapons and Deterrence in the 21st Century*. Carnegie Endowment for International Peace. October 28, 2008. http://www.carnegieendowment.org/files/1028_transcrip_gates_check ed.pdf.

[68] Representative Ellen Tauscher. *Call on the President to Extend the Most Significant Remaining Arms Control Agreement of Our Time*. July 2007.

[69] For a detailed proposal that addresses these issues, see Alexei Arbatov and Rose Gottemoeller. "New Presidents, New Agreements? Advancing U.S.-Russian Strategic Arms Control." *Arms Control Today*. July/August, 2008.

In: Economics, Political and Social Issues ...   ISBN: 978-1-61122-555-6
Editor: Michelle L. Fergusson   ©2011 Nova Science Publishers, Inc.

THE GLOBAL FINANCIAL CRISIS: THE ROLE OF THE INTERNATIONAL MONETARY FUND (IMF)·

Martin A. Weiss[#]
International Trade and Finance

ABSTRACT

This report discusses two potential roles the International Monetary Fund (IMF) may have in helping to resolve the current global financial crisis: (1) immediate crisis control through balance of payments lending to emerging market and less-developed countries and (2) increased surveillance of the global economy through better coordination with the international financial regulatory agencies.

INTRODUCTION

The current global financial crisis, which began with the downturn of the U.S. subprime housing market in 2007, is testing the ability of the International Monetary Fund (IMF), in its role as the central international institution for oversight of the global monetary system.

Though the IMF is unlikely to lend to the developed countries most affected by the crisis and must compete with other international financial institutions [1] as a source of ideas and global macroeconomic policy coordination, the spillover effects of the crisis on emerging and less-developed economies gives the IMF an opportunity to reassert its role in the international economy on two key dimensions of the global financial crisis: (1) immediate crisis management and (2) long-term systemic reform of the international financial system.

The role of the IMF has changed significantly since its founding in July 1944. Late in World War II, delegates from 44 nations gathered in Bretton Woods, New Hampshire to discuss the postwar recovery of Europe and create a set of international institutions to resolve many of the economic issues—such as protectionist trade policies and unstable exchange rates—that had ravaged the international economy between the two world wars. As the global financial system has evolved over the decades, so has the IMF. From 1946 to 1973, the main purpose of the IMF was to manage the fixed system of international exchange rates agreed on at Bretton Woods. The U.S. dollar was fixed to gold at $35 per ounce and all other member

---

[*] Excerpted from CRS Report RL 22976 dated February 4, 2009.
[#] E-mail: mweiss@crs.loc.gov

countries' currencies were fixed to the dollar at different rates. The IMF monitored the macroeconomic and exchange rate policies of member countries and helped countries overcome balance of payments crises with short-term loans that helped bring currencies back in line with their determined value. This system came to an abrupt end in 1973 when the United States floated its currency and subsequently introduced the modern system of floating exchange rates. Over the past three decades, floating exchange rates and financial globalization have contributed to, in addition to substantial wealth and high levels of growth for many countries, an international economy marred by exchange rate volatility and semi-frequent financial crises. The IMF adapted to the end of the fixed-exchange rate system by becoming the lender of last resort for countries afflicted by such crises.

Current IMF operations and responsibilities can be grouped into three areas: surveillance, lending, and technical assistance. Surveillance involves monitoring economic and financial developments and providing policy advice to member countries. Lending entails the provision of financial resources under specified conditions to assist a country experiencing balance of payments difficulties. Technical assistance includes help on designing or improving the quality and effectiveness of domestic policy-making.

WHITHER THE IMF?

The current financial crisis represents a major challenge for the IMF since the institution is not in financial position to be able to lend to the United States or other Western countries affected by the crisis (with the possible exception of Iceland). The IMF's total financial resources as of August 2008 were $352 billion, of which $257 billion were usable resources [2]. The most the IMF ever lent in any one year period (the four quarters through September 1998 at the height of the Asian financial crisis) was $30 billion. The most lent during any two-year period was $40 billion between June 2001-2003 during the financial crises in Argentina, Brazil, Uruguay, and Turkey [3]. The IMF is wholly unequipped to provide by itself the necessary liquidity to the United States and affected industrialized countries. In addition, the United States and other Western countries, along with some Middle Eastern oil states, are the primary contributors to IMF resources, and it is unlikely that these countries would seek IMF assistance. The last time that developed countries borrowed from the IMF was between1976 and1978, when the United Kingdom, Italy, and Spain borrowed from the IMF to deal with the aftershocks of the 1973 increase in oil prices [4].

Since the financial crises of a decade ago, many emerging market economies, largely in response to their criticism of the policy conditions that the IMF required of countries receiving IMF loans, have built up extensive foreign reserve positions in order to avoid having to return to the IMF should such a crisis occur again [5] From a level of around $1.2 trillion in 1995, global foreign exchange reserves now exceed $7 trillion. The IMF tabulates that by the second quarter of 2008, developing countries' foreign reserves were $5.47 trillion compared to $1.43 trillion in the industrialized countries [6].

This reserve accumulation was driven by increasing commodity prices (such as oil and minerals) and large current account surpluses combined with high savings rates in emerging Asian countries [7].

Emerging market foreign reserve accumulation fueled by rising commodity prices and large emerging market trade surpluses, and net foreign direct investment flows has led to a decrease in demand for IMF lending and a weakening in the IMF's budget position. IMF lending peaked in 2003 with IMF credit outstanding totaling $110.29 billion. By September 30, 2008, outstanding IMF loans had decreased by $92.6 billion to $17.72 billion (see also Figure 1) [8].

Since the IMF earns income on the interest paid on its loans, the decrease in demand for IMF's lending led to a budget shortfall in 2007. The IMF is in the process of seeking authorization from national legislatures to sell a portion of gold that the IMF holds in reserve to create an investment fund whose profits can be used to finance IMF operations and delink IMF operations (such as its global surveillance programs) from profit earned on IMF lending. Congress is expected to face a vote in FY2009 on whether or not to authorize this proposal.

The rise of emerging market countries over the past decade, has created new challenges for the IMF. Many emerging market economies argue that their current stake in the IMF does not represent their role in the world economy.

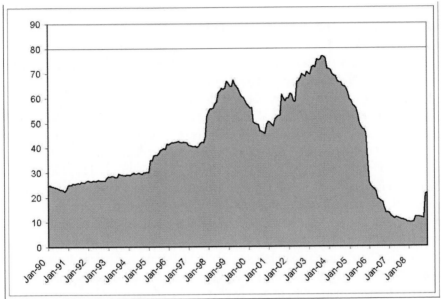

Source: International Monetary Fund Notes: The Special Drawing Right (SDR) is an international reserve asset, created by the IMF in 1969. SDRs are allocated to member countries in proportion to their IMF quotas. The SDR also serves as the unit of account of the IMF and some other international organizations. Its value is based on a basket of key international currencies (the U.S. dollar, Euro, Japanese yen, and pound sterling). The SDR currency value is calculated daily and the valuation basket is reviewed and adjusted every five years.

Figure 1. Outstanding IMF Credit (1990-2008, SDR)

Several countries, particularly in East Asia and South America, believe that their new economic weight and status should afford them a larger quota and a greater voice at the institution. In addition, many poor countries believe that the IMF's quota system is prejudiced against them, giving them little voice even though they are the majority of the IMF's borrowers. In response to these concerns, the IMF embarked in 2006 on a reform process to increase the quota and voice of its emerging market country members [9].

While the IMF has struggled to define its role in the global economy, the global financial crisis has created an opportunity for the IMF to reinvigorate itself and possibly play a constructive role in resolving, or at the least mitigating, the effects of the global downturn, on two fronts: (1) through immediate crisis management, primarily balance of payments support to emerging-market and less-developed countries, and (2) contributing to long-term systemic reform of the international financial system.

IMMEDIATE CRISIS MANAGEMENT

IMF rules stipulate that countries are allowed to borrow up to three times their quota over a three-year period, although this requirement has been breached on several occasions where the IMF has lent at much higher multiples of quota [10]. While many emerging market countries, such as Brazil, India, Indonesia, and Mexico, have stronger macroeconomic fundamentals than they did a decade ago, a sustained decrease in U.S. imports resulting from an economic slowdown could have recessionary effects overseas. Emerging markets with less robust financial structures have been more dramatically affected, especially those dependent on exports to the United States. Increased emerging market default risk can be seen in the dramatic rise of credit default swap (CDS) prices for emerging market sovereign bonds. Financial markets are currently pricing the risk that Pakistan, Argentina, Ukraine, and Iceland will default on their sovereign debt at above 80% [11]. On October 26, the IMF announced a $16.5 billion agreement with Ukraine. On October 27, the IMF announced a $15.7 billion loan to Hungary. On November 19, the IMF announced a $2.1 billion loan to Iceland. On November 24, the IMF announced a $7.6 billion loan to Pakistan [12] On December 23, 2008, the IMF announced a $2.35 billion dollar loan for Latvia. Other potential candidates for IMF loans are Serbia, Kazakhstan, Lithuania, and Estonia [13].

IMF Managing Director Dominique Strauss-Kahn has stressed that the IMF is able and poised to assist with crisis loans. At the IMF annual meetings in October 2008, Managing Director Strauss-Kahn announced that the IMF had activated its Emergency Financing Mechanism (EFM) to speed the normal process for loans to crisis-afflicted countries [14]. The emergency mechanism enables rapid approval (usually within 48-72 hours) of IMF lending once an agreement has been reached between the IMF and the national government. As noted before, while normal IMF rules are that countries can only borrow three times the size of their respective quotas over three years, the Fund has shown the willingness in the past to lend higher amounts should the crisis require extraordinary amounts of assistance.

A second instrument that the IMF could use to provide financial assistance is its Exogenous Shock Facility (ESF). The ESF provides policy support and financial assistance to low-income countries facing *exogenous shocks*, events that are completely out of the national government's control. These could include commodity price changes (including oil and food), natural disasters, and conflicts and crises in neighboring countries that disrupt trade. The ESF was modified in 2008 to further increase the speed and flexibility of the IMF's response. Through the ESF, a country can immediately access up to 25 % of its quota for each exogenous shock and an additional 75% of quota in phased disbursements over one to two years.

On October 29, 2008, the IMF announced that it plans on creating a new three month short-term lending facility aimed at middle income countries such as Mexico, South Korea, and Brazil. The IMF plans to set aside $100 billion for the new Short-Term Liquidity Facility (SLF). In a unprecedented departure from other IMF programs, SLF loans will have no policy conditionality [15]. Under the SLF, countries with track records of sound policies, access to capital markets and sustainable debt burden can draw up to five times their IMF quota for three months and up to two additional three-month periods. To date, no country has drawn on the SLF. For many middle-income countries this is likely due to the associated stigma of accepting IMF assistance. Concerns have also been raised that by creating a new lending mechanism the IMF is dividing potential borrowers into those that qualify for the SLF and those that would be forced to accept regular IMF lending with its associated policy conditionality [16]. To counter this stigma, some analysts have proposed coordinating an SLF package for several countries at the same time. Another option may be to coordinate an SLF loan with the newly created Federal Reserve swap arrangements for developing countries. On the same day that the IMF announced the SLF, the U.S. Federal Reserve approved $30 billion in reciprocal swap arrangements with four emerging-market countries: Brazil, Korea, Mexico, and Singapore.

At the 2009 Davos World Economic Forum, John Lipsky, the IMF's First Deputy Managing Director, said that to be able to effectively lend to all the potential countries affected by the crisis, the IMF should double its lending resources to around $500 billion [17]. In addition to potential resources freed up by the sale of IMF gold reserves, two additional financing options for the IMF are seeking additional capital from its member countries and selling bonds. The government of Japan has agreed to lend the IMF $100 billion dollars and it is reported that the agreement is almost finalized [18]. According to Mr. Lipsky, the Japanese loan would be structured in a way that is similar to two IMF programs: the General Arrangements to Borrow (GAB) and the New Arrangements to Borrow (NAB), which provide up to $50 billion in additional funding if the IMF were to exceed that amount available in its core resources. The second option would be for the IMF to issue bonds, which it has never done in its 60 year history. According to Mr. Lipsky, the IMF bonds would be sold to central banks and government agencies. According to economist and former IMF chief economist Michael Mussa, the United States and Europe blocked attempts by the IMF to issue bonds since it could potentially make the IMF less dependent on them for financial resources and thus less willing to take policy direction from them [19]. However, several other multilateral institutions such as the World Bank and the regional development banks routinely issue bonds to help finance their lending.

The IMF is not alone in making available financial assistance to crisis-afflicted countries. The International Finance Corporation (IFC), the private-sector lending arm of the World Bank, has announced that it will launch a $3 billion fund to capitalize small banks in poor countries that are battered by the financial crisis. The Inter-American Development Bank (IDB) announced on October 10, 2008 that it will offer a new $6 billion credit line to member governments, as well as increase its more traditional lending for specific projects [20]. In addition to the IDB, the Andean Development Corporation (CAF) announced a liquidity facility of $1.5 billion and the Latin American Fund of Reserves (FLAR) has offered to make available $4.5 billion in contingency lines. While these amounts may be insufficient should Brazil, Argentina, or any other large Latin American country need a rescue package, they could be very helpful for smaller countries such as those in the Caribbean and Central America that are heavily dependent on tourism and property investments [21]

In Asia, where countries were left no choice but to accept IMF rescue packages a decade ago, efforts are under way to promote regional financial cooperation, so that governments can avoid having to borrow from the IMF in a financial crisis. One result of these efforts is the Chiang Mai Initiative, a network of bilateral swap arrangements among east and Southeast Asian countries. In addition, Japan, South Korea, and China have backed the creation of a $10 billion crisis fund. Contributions are expected from bilateral donors, the Asian Development Bank (ADB), and the World Bank [22]

Lastly, economic conditions over the past decade have created a new class of bilateral creditors who could challenge the IMF's role as the lender of last resort. The rise of oil prices has created vast wealth among Middle Eastern countries and persistent trade surpluses in Asia have created a new class of emerging creditors. These countries either have the foreign reserves to support their own currencies in a financial crisis, or they are a potential source of loans for other countries.

REFORMING GLOBAL MACROECONOMIC SURVEILLANCE

In addition to revising its emergency lending assistance guidelines to make the IMF's financial assistance more attractive to potential borrowers, there is a role for the IMF to play in the broader reform of the global financial system. Efforts are underway to expand the IMF's ability to conduct effective multilateral surveillance of the international economy. In addition, there are efforts to increase cooperation with the international financial standard setters as the Financial Stability Forum (FSF), the Bank for International Settlements (BIS), as well as in various international working groups such as the Basel Committee on Banking Supervision and the Joint Forum on Risk Assessment and Capital. The deepening interconnectedness of the international economy may call for such increased cooperation between the IMF, which performs global macroeconomic surveillance, and the individual global financial regulatory bodies.

The IMF Articles of Agreement require (Article IV) that the IMF "oversee the international monetary system in order to ensure its effective operation" and to "oversee the compliance of each member with its obligations" to the Fund. In particular, "the Fund shall exercise firm surveillance over the exchange rate policies of member countries and shall adopt specific principles for the guidance of all members with respect to those policies." Countries are required to provide the IMF with information and to consult with the IMF upon its request. The IMF staff generally meets each year with each member country for "Article IV consultations" regarding the country's current fiscal and monetary policies, the state of its economy, its exchange rate situation, and other relevant concerns. The IMF's reports on its annual Article IV consultations with each country are presented to the IMF executive board along with the staff's observations and recommendations about possible improvements in the country's economic policies and practices.

As the global financial system has become increasingly interconnected, the IMF has conducted multilateral surveillance beyond two bi-annual reports it produces, the *World Economic Outlook* and the *Global Financial Stability Report,* four regional reports, and regular IMF contributions to intergovernmental for a and committees, including the Group of Seven and Group of Twenty, and the Financial Stability Forum. These efforts at multilateral surveillance, however, have been criticized as being less than fully effective, too focused on bilateral issues, and not fully accounting for the risks of contagion that have been seen in the current crisis. A 2006 report by the IMF's internal watchdog agency, the Independent Evaluation Office (IEO) found that, "multilateral surveillance has not sufficiently explored options to deal with policy spillovers in a global context; the language of multilateral advice is no more based on explicit consideration of economic linkages and policy spillovers than that of bilateral advice" [23] Participants at an October 2008 IMF panel on the future of the IMF reiterated these concerns, adding that many developed countries have impeded the IMF's efforts at multilateral surveillance by largely ignoring IMF's bilateral surveillance of their own economies and not fully embracing the IMF's first attempt at multilateral consultations on global imbalances in 2006. According to Trevor Manuel, South Africa's Finance Minister, "one has to start from the fundamental view that if you accept public policy and you accept the interconnectedness of the global economy, then you need an institution appropriate to its regulation" [24] Analysts argue, however, that developed countries have long ignored IMF advice on their economic policy, while at the same time pressuring the IMF to use its role in patrolling the exchange rate system to support their own foreign economic goals.

REFERENCES

[1]   Such as the Bank for International Settlements, Financial Stability Forum (FSF), and the Organization for Economic Cooperation and Development (OECD).

[2]   IMF resources that are considered non-usable to finance IMF operations are (1) its gold holdings, (2) the currencies of members that are using IMF resources and are therefore, by definition, in a weak balance of payments or reserve position, (3) the currencies of other members with relatively weak external positions, and (4) other non-liquid IMF assets.

[3]   Brad Setser, "Extraordinary Times," Council on Foreign Relations, September 29, 2008. It is worth noting that the final rescue packages during the Asian crisis totaled many times $30 billion once bilateral assistance was included.

[4]   Oxford Analytica, "IMF reaffirms role in global economy." October 15, 2008.

[5]   Many analysts believe that the tight monetary and fiscal policies that the IMF required of countries accepting IMF loans accentuated the immediate economic impact of the crisis while having marginal impact on the countries' long-term structural reform.

[6]   IMF Currency Composition of Official Foreign Exchange Reserves (COFER) available at http://www.imf.org/external/np/sta/cofer/eng/index.htm.

[7]   Georges Pineau and Ettore Dorruci, "The Accumulation of Foreign Reserves," *European Central Bank*, March 2006.

[8]   Total IMF Credit Outstanding for all members from 1984-2008, available athttp://www.imf.org/external/np/fin/tad/extcred1.aspx.

[9]   For background, see CRS Report RL33626, *International Monetary Fund: Reforming Country Representation*, by Martin A. Weiss.

[10]   The 1997 package for South Korea was 19 times as large as their quota at the IMF.

[11]   David Oakley, "Emerging Nations hit by growing debt fears," *Financial Times*, October 14, 2008.

[12]   Information on ongoing IMF negotiations is available at http://www.imf.org.

[13]   Oxford Analytica, "IMF reaffirms role in the global economy." October 15, 2008.

[14] The EFM was set up in 1995 and has been used on six occasions—in 1997 for the Philippines, Thailand, Indonesia, and Korea; in 2001 for Turkey; and in 2008 for Georgia.

[15] "IMF to Launch New Facility for Emerging Markets Hit by Crisis," *IMF Survey Online*, October 29, 2008.

[16] Edwin Truman, On What Terms is the IMF Worth Funding, *Peterson Institute for International Economics*, December 2008.

[17] "As Contingency, IMF Aims to Double its Lendable Resources," *IMF Survey Magazine: Policy*, February 2, 2008.

[18] "IMF talks to borrow $100 billion from Japan almost completed," *Japan Times*, February 4, 2009.

[19] Bob Davis, "IMF Considers Issuing Bonds to Raise Money," *Wall Street Journal*, February 1, 2009.

[20] Bob Davis, "International Groups Offer Latin America More Loans," *Wall Street Journal*, October 14, 2008.

[21] "QandA: Central American "Exports, Production, Employment" Hit by Crisis" *Inter Press Service News Agency*, October 14, 2008.

[22] Malcolm Moore, "Asia Mounts its own Bank Bailout," *The Daily Telegraph*, October 15, 2008.

[23] Independent Evaluation Office (IEO) of the IMF, *An Evaluation of the IMF's Multilateral Surveillance*, September 1, 2006.

[24] Camilla Anderson, "Future Role of IMF Debated As Financial Crisis Takes Toll," *IMF Survey Online*, October 16, 2008.

In: Economics, Political and Social Issues ...
Editor: Michelle L. Fergusson

ISBN: 978-1-61122-555-6
©2011 Nova Science Publishers, Inc.

CRITICAL INFRASTRUCTURE:
THE NATIONAL ASSET DATABASE[*]

John Moteff
Science and Technology Policy Resources,
Science, and Industry Division

ABSTRACT

The Office of Infrastructure Protection (OIP) in the Department of Homeland Security (DHS) has been developing and maintaining a National Asset Database. The Database contains information on over 77,000 individual assets, ranging from dams, hazardous materials sites, and nuclear power plants to local festivals, petting zoos, and sporting good stores. The presence of a large number of entries of the latter type (i.e. assets generally perceived as having more local importance than national importance) has attracted much criticism from the press and from Members of Congress. Many critics of the Database have assumed that it is (or should be) DHS's list of the nation's *most* critical assets and are concerned that, in its current form, it is being used inappropriately as the basis upon which federal resources, including infrastructure protection grants, are allocated.

According to DHS, both of those assumptions are wrong. DHS characterizes the National Asset Database not as a list of critical assets, but rather as a national asset inventory providing the 'universe' from which various lists of critical assets are produced. As such, the Department maintains that it represents just the first step in DHS's risk management process outlined in the National Infrastructure Protection Plan. DHS has developed, apparently from the National Asset Database, a list of about 600 assets that it has determined are critical to the nation. Also, while the National Asset Database has been used to support federal grant-making decisions, according to a DHS official, it does not drive those decisions.

In July 2006 the DHS Office of the Inspector General released a report on the National Asset Database. Its primary conclusion was that the Database contained too many unusual and out-of-place assets and recommended that those judged to be of little national significance be removed from the Database. In his written response to the DHS IG report, the Undersecretary of DHS did not concur with this recommendation, asserting that keeping these less than nationally significant assets in the Database gave it a situational awareness that will assist in preparing and responding to a variety of incidents.

Accepting the DHS descriptions of the National Asset Database, questions and issues remain. For example, the National Asset Database seems to have evolved away from its origins as a list of critical infrastructures, perhaps causing the differences in perspective on what the Database is or should be. As an inventory of the nation's assets, the National

---

[*] Excerpted from CRS Report RL 33648 dated July 16, 2007.

Asset Database is incomplete, limiting its value in preparing and responding to a wide variety of incidents. Assuring the quality of the information in the Database is important and a never-ending task. If DHS not only keeps the less than nationally significant assets in the Database but adds more of them to make the inventory complete, assuring the quality of the data on these assets may dominate the cost of maintaining the Database, while providing uncertain value. Finally, the information currently contained in the Database carries with it no legal obligations on the owner/operators of the asset. If, however, the Database becomes the basis for regulatory action in the future, what appears in the Database takes on more immediate consequences for both DHS and the owner/operators.

INTRODUCTION

The Office of Infrastructure Protection (OIP) in the Department of Homeland Security (DHS) has been developing and maintaining a National Asset Database. The Database contains information on a wide range of individual assets, from dams, hazardous materials sites, and nuclear power plants to local festivals, petting zoos, and sporting good stores. The presence of a large number of entries of the latter type (i.e. assets generally perceived as having more local importance than national importance) has attracted much criticism from the press and from Members of Congress. Many critics of the Database have assumed that it is (or should be) DHS's list of the nation's *most* critical assets and are concerned that, in its current form, it is being used inappropriately as the basis upon which federal resources, including infrastructure protection grants, are allocated. According to DHS, both of those assumptions are wrong.

The purpose of this report is to discuss the National Asset Database: what is in it, how it is populated, what the Database apparently is, what it is not, and how it is intended to be used. The report also discusses some of the issues on which Congress could focus its oversight. This report relies primarily on a DHS Office of the Inspector General (DHS IG) report, [1] released on July 11, 2006, but makes reference to other government documents as well.

A SHORT REVIEW OF THE DHS IG REPORT

The genesis of the National Asset Database remains somewhat unclear. A list of critical sites was begun in the spring of 2003 as part of Operation Liberty Shield [2]. The list contained 160 assets, including chemical and hazardous materials sites, nuclear plants, energy facilities, business and finance centers, and more. The assets were selected by the newly formed Protective Services Division within the Office of Infrastructure Protection, in what was then called the Information Analysis and Infrastructure Protection Directorate, Department of Homeland Security. The Secretary of DHS asked states to provide additional security for these sites [3]

During the course of the year (2003), DHS continued to collect information on various assets from a variety of sources. By early 2004, DHS had accumulated information on 28,368 assets. Although Operation Liberty Shield was now considered over, the initial list of 160 critical assets, those judged to be in need of additional protection because of their vulnerability and the potential consequences if attacked, grew to 1,849 assets and became known as the Protected Measures Target List [4]. It is not clear when the information being gathered became known as the National Asset Database [5]

By January 2006, according to the DHS IG report, the Database had grown to include 77,069 assets, ranging from nuclear power plants and dams to a casket company and an elevator company. It also contains locations and events ranging from Times Square in New York City to the Mule Day Parade in Columbia Tennessee (which, according to the city's website, draws over 200,000 spectators each year for the week-long event).

The IG report categorized entries in the National Asset Database by critical infrastructure/key resource sector (see Figure 1) [6]. Additionally, the DHS IG report identified some of the entries with more specificity.

For example, the Database contained, at the time, 4,055 malls, shopping centers, and retail outlets; 224 racetracks; 539 theme parks and 163 water parks; 1,305 casinos; 234 retails stores; The DHS gets information for the Database from a variety of sources.

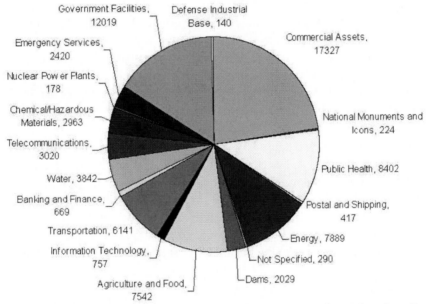

Source: Office of the Inspector General. Department of Homeland Security. Taken from Progress in Developing the National Asset Database.

Figure 1. National Asset Database Entries by Sector.

According to the National Infrastructure Protection Plan (NIPP) [7], sources include existing government and commercially available databases; [8] sector-specific agencies and other federal entities; voluntary submittals by owners and operators; periodic requests for information from states and localities and the private sector; and DHS-initiated studies. The number of assets in the Database is expected to grow as additional information is gathered.

The DHS IG report focused much of its attention on information provided by states and localities as the result of two data requests made by DHS. According to the DHS IG report, the vast majority of the 77,069 entries was collected as a result of those requests.

According to the IG report, the first data call to the states, made by the Office of Domestic Preparedness in 2003, yielded poor quality data [9]. The IG report described the guidance given states and localities as "minimal" [10]. The guidance apparently did tell states, however, to "consider any system or asset that, if attacked, would result in catastrophic loss of life and/or catastrophic economic loss" [11]. As a result, assets such as the petting zoos, local festivals and other places where people within a community congregate, or local assets ostensibly belonging to one of the critical infrastructure sectors, were among the assets reported. According to the IG report, many state officials were surprised to learn that additional assets from their states were added to the Database, which raises additional questions about how the information was collected.

According to the IG report, the second request to the states for critical infrastructure information came from the Office of Infrastructure Protection in July 2004 and was "significantly more organized and achieved better results." [12] Guidance was more specific, as was the information requested. DHS requested information for 17 data fields. Of those, DHS considered the following to be most important: address, owner, owner type, phone, local law enforcement point of contact, and latitude and longitude coordinates [13]. States were also asked to identify those assets that they felt met a level of national significance. Criteria for identifying assets of national significance was provided by DHS. The criteria described certain thresholds, such as refineries with refining capacity in excess of 225,000 barrels per day, or commercial centers with potential economic loss impact of $10 billion or capacity of more than 35,000 people. Although the request was more specific, states were given much leeway as to what to include, and OIP accepted into the Database every submitted asset [14] As a result, additional assets of questionable national significance were added to the Database [15]

The DHS IG report drew two primary conclusions. The first is that the Database contains many "unusual, or out-of-place, assets whose criticality is not readily apparent," [16] while, at the same time, it "may have too few assets in essential areas and may present an incomplete picture" [17]. The second conclusion was that the types of assets that were included and the information provided are inconsistent from state to state, locality to locality. For example, California entries included the entire Bay Area Regional Transit System as a single entry, while entries listed for New York City included 739 separate subway stations [18]

The IG report made 4 recommendations:

- review the National Asset Database for out-of-place assets and assets marked as not nationally significant, and determine whether those assets should remain in the Database;
- provide state homeland security advisers the opportunity to review their assets in the Database to identify previously submitted assets that may not be relevant;
- during future data calls, provide States a list of their respective Database assets to reduce ... duplicate submissions; and
- establish a milestone for the completion of a comprehensive risk assessment of critical infrastructure and key resources and ensure they are accuratelycaptured in the National Infrastructure Protection Plan.

THE NATIONAL ASSET DATABASE: WHAT IT IS AND WHAT IT IS NOT

The National Strategy for Homeland Security recognized that not all assets within each critical infrastructure sector are equally important, and that the federal government would focus its effort on the highest priorities [19]. The National Strategy for the Physical Protection of Critical Infrastructure and Key Assets stated that DHS will develop a methodology for identifying assets with national-level criticality and using this methodology will build a comprehensive database to catalog these critical assets [20] Judging from the criticism leveled at it, many believe the National Asset Database is (or should be) DHS's list of assets critical to the nation.

However, in his written response to the IG report, the Undersecretary for Preparedness, George Foresman, to whom the Office of Infrastructure Protection reports, stated that the National Asset Database is "not a list of critical assets...[but rather] a national asset inventory...[providing] the 'universe' from which various lists of critical assets are produced." [21] According to the National Infrastructure Protection Plan, the National Asset Database is a comprehensive catalog with descriptive information regarding the assets and systems that comprise the nation's critical infrastructure and key resources [22]. The Assistant Secretary for Infrastructure Protection, Robert Stephan, has called the Database a 'phonebook' of 77,000 facilities, assets and systems from across the nation, needed to facilitate more detailed risk analyses [23].

Some may ask why there should be this difference in perception regarding the National Asset Database. One possible explanation is that, as noted above, the National Asset Database started out as the Protected Measures Target List, which was a prioritized list of assets considered critical at the national level. Also, as reported in at least one media source, when asked for its list of critical assets, Members of Congress were shown the expanded list containing the questionable assets [24]. Based on subsequent response, Congressional interest appears focused on a prioritized list.

Also, what is meant by the term "critical infrastructure" continues to generate some confusion. The definition provided in the USA PATRIOT Act and in other policy documents refers to specific assets or systems within a selected set of sectors or categories. However, the term also is used often to identify the sectors and categories themselves. For example, the transportation sector is often called a critical infrastructure, when, according to the statutory definition, only those assets within the transportation sector whose loss would be debilitating to the nation should be called critical infrastructure. Given the varied usage of the term critical infrastructure, the National Infrastructure Protection Plan description of the National Asset Database above, is unclear. Is it a list of assets that are critical, or is it a list of assets that make up each of the critical sectors, with criticality to be determined later?

WHAT ARE ITS INTENDED USES?

There appear to be two primary uses for the Database: as a first step in a prioritization process that eventually will help focus risk reduction activities; and, to provide a degree of situational awareness. According to Assistant Secretary Stephan, the Database "does not drive the Department's funding decisions." [25]

First Step in Identifying Critical Assets and Prioritizing Risk Reduction Activities

Taking an inventory of one's assets is a standard first step for most risk management processes used to prioritize the protection of those assets [26]. The second step is to screen this initial list for those assets considered critical to the organization (or country) using specific criteria. Further analysis is focused on these critical assets. The National Infrastructure Protection Plan establishes DHS's risk management process. According to the NIPP, identifying the assets that comprise the nation's 17 critical infrastructure sectors and key resources within the National Asset Database represents the first step in its process.

As envisioned by the NIPP, DHS will then select those assets from the Database it considers critical to the nation as a whole [27]. If the asset is judged not to be critical from a national perspective, DHS does not require any further information. If the asset does have the potential to be critical, DHS will ask for more information, which includes information that will support further risk and risk mitigation analysis (e.g. vulnerability to specific forms of attack or natural disasters and more detailed analysis of the consequences associated with the loss of the asset, including interdependencies with other assets). Vulnerability, consequences, and threat information then will be integrated to yield a risk score. According to the NIPP, those assets that pose the greatest risk are further analyzed to identify potential risk reduction initiatives, which are then prioritized (i.e. the risk reduction initiatives) based on their cost-effectiveness. Presumably, as additional analysis and information is generated for a particular asset, it will be added, or linked, to the Database. According to the IG report, DHS officials acknowledge that many of the assets currently in the Database "will never be analyzed in depth or used to support any program activity" [28]

According to the Assistant Secretary, DHS had identified about 600 assets that it considers to be critical to the nation, based on its analysis of vulnerability to attack or natural events and the possible consequences [29]. This list is apparently prioritized further [30]. The Assistant Secretary asserted that this shorter list does not contain petting zoos, popcorn factories or other such facilities [31]

While it may be common practice to take an initial inventory of one's assets as a first step in a risk management process, detailed information on individual assets is not necessarily needed to determine their criticality. The presence of gas stations listed in the National Asset Database is a case in point.

Gas stations could be considered a part of the oil and gas infrastructure, a subsector of the energy sector. In assessing the oil and gas infrastructure, one may want to identify, in general, all the assets that make up that infrastructure from production fields, to refineries, to distribution, and all the transport elements in between. Gas stations would be on that list, at the very end of the distribution chain.

In determining which assets are the most critical, one does not need specific information on individual gas stations to determine that the loss of any individual gas station would have a minimal effect on the distribution of gasoline throughout the country, or on the economy, or national public health, beyond the immediate vicinity of the gas station itself. Yet the National Asset Database contains 127 gas stations. Unless these 127 specific gas stations have some unique characteristics (perhaps being located next to an identified critical asset which could be damaged if there were a loss of the gas station), maintaining specific information on those gas stations seems unnecessary to determine their criticality [32]

Situational Awareness

DHS justifies keeping assets that have not been judged as being critical at the national level in the Database as a way to provide a degree of situational awareness [33].

Undersecretary Foresman noted in his response to the IG report that, "Many assets not 'critical' are, in fact, critical depending upon the circumstances...." [34] For example, as noted in the NIPP, "...the information may be used to quickly identify those assets...that may be the subject of emergent terrorist statements or interest or that may be located in the areas of greatest impact from natural disasters." [35]. According to the NIPP, having this information (apparently regardless of the criticality level of the asset) will help inform decisions made regarding preparedness, response, and recovery to a wide range of incidents and emergencies [36] In defense of the contents of the National Asset Database, Assistant Secretary Stephan is quoted as saying: "What happens the very first day that al-Qaeda attacks a convenience store chain times a dozen across the country?...we better have some of those things in the database so that we know what that universe of things is that we have to worry about" [37]

According to the FY2007 Congressional Budget Justification for the Infrastructure Protection and Information Security (IP/IS) Program, [38] the Database will deliver something called the Risk/Readiness Dashboard to DHS management. The budget justification identified the Risk/Readiness Dashboard as a planning and management tool that will eventually fuse threat streams with critical infrastructure vulnerability information and consequences, and will visually present a risk profile for critical infrastructure assets. According to the budget justification, such a capability will provide real-time knowledge that can be used to support rapid decision-making during periods of heightened threats.

Also, while a particular asset may not be critical at the national level, it may still be critical at the state or local level. Since DHS plans to allow many stakeholders eventually (with appropriate clearances) to have selected access to the Database, and the information in it or linked to it, the Database represents a common picture (i.e. a standard format and taxonomy) for all to use [39] Also, according to the Undersecretary, DHS does not support purging the Database of these non-nationally critical assets, because it is important to the Department to be informed about what is important to the states and localities [40]

The statements above raise a number of issues. First, that assets may be critical under some circumstances and not others, or become critical because they have been identified by intelligence as possible targets, seems to conflict with the statutory definition of critical infrastructures. Under the conditions stated above, just about any asset could be considered critical and setting and implementing priorities would become even more complicated than it is now. Many would expect DHS to respond to such intelligence as part of its counter-terrorism efforts, which might include quickly deploying critical infrastructure resources such as sending out vulnerability assessment teams and establishing buffer zone protection plans. However, such efforts seem to lie beyond the fundamental goal of the critical infrastructure protection program, which is to identify those assets most critical to the nation as a whole.

Also, if the National Asset Database is meant to be a comprehensive list of the nation's infrastructure assets, regardless of criticality, it is incomplete. As noted in the previous section, only 127 gas stations are in the Database. There are over 167,000 gas stations in the United States [41]. Similarly, the Database contains only 140 defense industrial base assets, 417 postal and shipping sites, 669 banking and financial assets, and 7,542 agriculture and food assets. According to the *National Strategy for the Physical Protection of Critical Infrastructures and Key Assets*, DHS estimated that there are 250,000 defense industrial firms, 137 million postal and shipping delivery sites, 26,600 FDIC insured institutions, and almost 2 million farms and 87,000 food processing plants [42]. To identify only a few a these assets, perhaps in some states, but not in others, limits the utility of the current National Asset Database to support situational awareness to those relatively few instances where the Database may have the appropriate information.

The position that the National Asset Database holds data on those assets that states and localities have identified as important to them is contradicted by the DHS IG report. According to the report, state officials were repeatedly surprised to learn about the assets that were added as part of the ODP data call and which remain in the Database [43]. The Database includes many assets not selected by the states.

Basis for Allocating Critical Infrastructure Protection Grants

The role that the National Asset Database plays in allocating federal resources to states and localities for infrastructure protection is of obvious interest to Congress. In FY2006, allocations of Urban Area Security Initiative grants saw some significant changes based on new risk calculations by the DHS. A number of cities saw their grant levels drop. Some Members believe that allocations were based on what they consider to be a flawed National Asset Database.

Over the last two grant cycles, according to the DHS IG report, ODP has made increased use of information in the National Asset Database to support its allocation of various critical infrastructure protection grants to states and localities. However, according to the Assistant Secretary, the National Asset Database does not drive DHS's funding decisions. The exception is the Buffer Zone Protection Plan grants, which were initiated to support the protection efforts associated with the original Protected Measures Target List and Operation Liberty Shield.

The relationship between the ODP's grant-making process, the National Asset Database, and the NIPP is not explicitly stated in DHS documents. The NIPP risk assessment process was finalized June 30, 2006, but ODP has had some form of risk assessment process in place for determining initial grant allocations for programs such as the Urban Area Security Initiative since 2003. Also, for the FY2006 cycle, ODP indicated it had evaluated over 120,000 specific infrastructure assets, [44] but the National Asset Database only contained

77,069 assets as of January 2006. It would appear that ODP's grant-making process operates independently from both the National Asset Database and the National Infrastructure Protection Plan [45]

ISSUES

Assuming that the Undersecretary is not changing the definition of critical infrastructure, and accepting DHS's argument that the National Asset Database is not a prioritized list of critical assets, and that it is not the basis for determining grant allocations, two issues remain: the quality of the information contained in the Database; and, whether the value of keeping low criticality assets in the Database warrant the costs associated with maintaining them in the Database. Another potential issue could arise if the current voluntary nature of the Database changes. Congress may ultimately focus its oversight of the National Asset Database on these areas.

Quality

Data quality is always an issue in generating any database. In the case of the National Asset Database, quality includes accuracy, consistency, and completeness. The quality of the information gathered early in the development of the Database has been questioned. For example, early in the evolution of the list, certain electric utility operators were presented with a list of critical electric power assets drawn up by DHS and noticed that some of the entries were not currently in use [46]. Also, one Member of Congress noted that the location for Disneyland was incorrect [47]. According to the IG report, DHS itself determined that the early Protected Measures Target List was unreliable [48]

DHS has taken a number of steps to improve the quality of the information contained in the Database. The IG report noted that during the second data call to the states, DHS hired contractors to put the information it received into a consistent format, to research missing information, and to verify the accuracy of the information. DHS has approved a taxonomy which everyone submitting information can use to categorize and subcategorize assets. DHS plans to use this taxonomy in future data calls. The IG report also stated that DHS intends to use expert panels to review information in their sector of expertise. According the FY2007 budget justification, one of the responsibilities of the Protective Security Advisors [49] is to verify critical infrastructure information.

Of particular concern is the completeness of the information included. Beyond the issue that there appears to be an incomplete inventory of the less than critical assets, as noted above, the IG was particularly concerned that the Database does not include assets that one might conclude should be included. The IG attributed part of this problem to reluctance on the part of private sector owner/operators to share certain information with DHS, notwithstanding the Protected Critical Infrastructure Information Program [50]

Insuring the quality of the information in the Database is likely to require a continuous effort, since quality also implies currency. If a particular site closes, moves, or changes ownership, the changes would logically need to be captured in the Database.

The consideration of quality could include also the accessibility, flexibility, and security of the database. The NIPP suggested that the Database would be accessible to many type of queries, by many types of stakeholders. However, it is not clear that the Database yet has these capabilities. DHS intends to develop a second generation Database, one that includes the integration of vulnerability, risk, threat, and other relevant information. According to the IG report, DHS does not expect the second generation Database to be ready for two more years. In regard to security, the Undersecretary, in his response to the IG report, asserted that the Database currently "exceeds all security and protection standards" [51] Assessing the accuracy of this assertion is beyond the scope of this report.

What to Keep

The IG report asserted that maintaining unusual and out-of-place entries in the Database may:

- complicate efforts to develop a useful database;
- make resource allocation more challenging;
- obscure desired data;
- waste time and money in repeatedly filtering them out of analyses or trying to prioritize them; and
- taint credibility.

The DHS IG report, however, does not explain how these entries would necessarily complicate, challenge, and obscure efforts. While the Database may not yet be as accessible or as searchable as eventually planned, it is not clear why less critical (or more critical) data could not be tagged as such. However, the presence of this data does involve cost in time and resources. At the very least, as discussed above, the information collected on all assets must be entered and verified (even the less critical ones) and missing data also may have to be located. Also, additional costs would likely be incurred if any further analysis (such as vulnerability assessment or more detailed consequence analysis) were done on these entries [52]. The budget justification documents do not present data on how much money DHS spends on the Database, or how that expense is broken down. However, Congress did appropriate $20 million for the Database in FY2006 [53]

While the argument could be made that the costs might be marginal, the DHS IG report noted that, currently, those entries identified as not being critical at the national level outnumber, by 3 to 1, those that are identified as critical at the national level. Currently, DHS considers only 600 assets as being the most critical, indicating that less than critical sites could actually dominate the cost of maintaining the Database.

It is not clear how to evaluate the value of maintaining these non-critical assets in the Database, especially if their numbers are under-represented and the risk associated with them is relatively low.

A Potential Change in Status for the Database

Currently the presence of a particular asset in the Database carries with it no specific obligations on the part of the owner/operator. They are not required by statute or regulation to provide information to the Database, per se, or to take any specific actions as a result of having an asset listed [54]. Information solicited by DHS is voluntarily given. Presumably, publicly available information does not require the permission of the owner/operator for it to be included in the Database. However, if ever having an asset on the National Asset Database carries with it some legal or regulatory requirements, then what is in and not in the Database, or adding or removing assets from it, might result in much greater consequences for both the owners/operators and DHS.

CONGRESSIONAL ACTION

The House of Representatives, as part of the 110th Congress's first 100 hours of legislation, passed H.R. 1, "Implementing the 9/11 Commission Recommendations Act of 2007." Title IX of this act includes a section (Sec. 902) dealing with the National Asset Database. The Section did a number of things. It amended the Homeland Security Act to include the requirement that the Secretary of Homeland Security establish a National Asset Database. It also required the Secretary to establish within this Database a subset of assets that the Secretary determines are most at risk. This subset of assets shall be called the National At-Risk Database. This requirement indicated that the House disagrees with the Undersecretary that the National Asset Database should not include a prioritization of assets.

Section 902 also established a National Asset Database Consortium, made up of representatives from at least two, but no more than four, national laboratories along with officials from other federal agencies with appropriate experience in working with and identifying critical infrastructure. The Consortium is to advise the Secretary on how to identify, generate, organize, and maintain the National Asset Database. In addition, the Secretary is to solicit comments from the Consortium on the appropriateness of the risk methodologies employed by the National Infrastructure Protection Plan and alternative methods for defining risk and identifying specific criteria by which to set priorities. The Secretary is to secure recommendations from the Consortium 60 days after this act is enacted.

The Section also required the Secretary to annually review the Database to examine assets in the Database to determine if the information on these assets is incorrect or if they do not meet national asset guidelines used by the Secretary to determine which assets should remain in the Database. It required the Secretary to remove from the Database any asset whose information is not verifiable or which does not meet the nation asset guidelines. The requirement disagrees with the Undersecretary's position that less-than-nationally-critical assets should remain in the Database.

Also, the Secretary is to provide the Database to states for review and to meet annually with the states to discuss guidelines their submissions of information for the Database. This requirement is in agreement with recommendations made by the Inspector General. Section 902 also required the Secretary to ensure that the information contained in the Database can be organized by sector, state, locality, and region.

Section 902 required the Secretary to report to Congress annually on those assets in the Database considered to be most at risk. The report is to include name, location, and sector of each asset. It is also to include any changes in the criteria used to define or identify critical infrastructure and any changes in the compiling of the Database. It is also to include the extent to which the Database has been used as a tool for allocating resources. It is likely that DHS would classify much of the information specific to particular assets in the Database.

Title XI in the Senate's companion bill, S. 4, "Improving America's Security Act of 2007," also required the Secretary to develop a risk-based prioritized list of critical infrastructure and key resources. The list should consider those assets or systems that, if destroyed or disrupted, by attack or natural catastrophe, would cause significant loss of life, severe economic harm, mass evacuations, or lead to the loss of vital public services. The list should reflect a cross-sector analysis to determine priorities for prevention, protection, recovery, and reconstitution. The act also instructed the Secretary to report to Congress annually the criteria used to create the list, the methodology used to solicit and verify information submitted to the list, and how the list will be used in program activities, including grant making.

No further action on either of these bills has occurred to date [55]

The House version of the FY2008 Department of Homeland Security Appropriations Bill, H.R. 2638, contained report language directing the National Protection and Programs Directorate to remove from the National Asset Database items it deems insignificant, and encouraged the Directorate to provide states and local partners the opportunity to review their assets listed in the Database and to recommend items for removal. The language also stated that the Directorate should clarify its guidance when soliciting information to ensure uniform and accurate information. The Senate version (S. 1644) contained no similar language.

REFERENCES

[1] Department of Homeland Security. Office of the Inspector General. *Progress in Developing the National Asset Database*. OIG-06-04. June 2006.

[2] Operation Liberty Shield was a comprehensive national plan to protect the homeland during U.S. operations in Iraq. For a discussion of some of the other initiatives taken as part of Operation Liberty Shield, see CRS Report RS21475, *Operation Liberty Shield: Border, Transportation, and Domestic Security*, by Jennifer E. Lake.

[3] DHS offered assistance to help protect these sites through its Buffer Zone Protection Plan program. At times the State Homeland Security grants could be used to help pay for overtime of law enforcement officials and National Guardsmen protecting critical sites.

[4] According to testimony by the then Undersecretary for Information Analysis and Infrastructure Protection, a list of 1,700 assets (according to the DHS IG report the actual number was 1,849) was culled from the larger list. However, the DHS IG report implied that the Protected Measures Target List grew independently, to which was added additional information from the states and other sources, leading to a combined list of 28,368 assets, which then grew into the National Asset Database.

[5] In June 2004, the House Appropriations Committee made reference to a Unified National Database of Critical Infrastructure, described as a master database of all

existing critical infrastructures in the country. See, U.S. Congress. House of Representatives. *Department of Homeland Security Appropriations Bill, 2005*. H.Rept. 108-541. p. 92. The comparable Senate Appropriations Committee report (S.Rept. 108-280) made reference to a National Asset Database. The budget request for FY2005 mentions the development of a primary database of the nations critical infrastructure, but gave it no name.

[6]   The statutory definition of critical infrastructure is given in the USA PATRIOT Act (P.L.107-56). It is: "...systems and assets...so vital to the United States that the incapacity or destruction of such systems and assets would have a debilitating impact on security, national economic security, national public health and safety, or any combination of those matters." There are currently 12 sectors of the economy and 5 groups of key resources (dams, commercial assets, government facilities, national monuments, nuclear facilities) that DHS considers as possessing systems or assets that, if lost, may have a critical impact on the United States. 514 religious meeting places; 127 gas stations; 130 libraries; 4,164 educational facilities; 217 railroad bridges; and 335 petroleum pipelines.

[7]   Department of Homeland Security. *National Infrastructure Protection Plan*. Released June 30, 2006. See, [http://www.dhs.gov/xprevprot/programs/editorial_0827.shtm].

[8]   According to the DHS IG report, examples of existing government databases that have contributed to the National Asset Database include the Chemical Sites List (an Environmental Protection Agency database), and the Government Services Administration list of GSA Buildings.

[9]   Department of Homeland Security. Office of the Inspector General. Op. Cit. p. 11. The Office of Domestic Preparedness is now called Grants and Training and is located within the Federal Emergency Management Agency, newly reconstituted by the Post-Katrina Management Reform Act of 2006 (part of the FY2007 DHS appropriation bill). Referred to as ODP throughout this report, it manages the majority of grants to states and localities for homeland security and critical infrastructure protection.

[10]   Ibid p. 8.

[11]   Ibid p. 8. This is similar language used in ODP's Urban Areas Security Initiative grants.

[12]   Ibid. p. 12.

[13]   The collection of personal information in the Database requires DHS to publish a Privacy Impact Assessment. That Assessment can be found at [http://www.dhs.gov/xlibrary/assets/privacy/privacy_pia_nadb.pdf]. A discussion of the Assessment is beyond the scope of this report. Site last visited on July 16, 2007.

[14]   Department of Homeland Security. Office of the Inspector General. Op. cit. p. 6.

[15]   According to the DHS IG report, the Database contains 11,018 entries identified as nationally significant, 32,631 identified as not considered nationally significant, and 33,419 whose significance are undetermined.

[16]   Department of Homeland Security. Office of Inspector General. Op. cit. p. 9.

[17]   Ibid p. 18.

[18]   Other examples of what the DHS IG considered to be inconsistent were: some states listed schools for their sheltering function, some did not; Indiana listed over 8,000 assets, more than states larger in area and population like New York, Texas, and California; and, fewer banking and finance centers are listed for New York than North Dakota.

[19] Office of Homeland Security. *National Strategy for Homeland Security.* July 2002. p. 30.

[20] White House. *The National Strategy for the Physical Protection of Critical Infrastructures and Key Assets.* February 2003. p. 23.

[21] Department of Homeland Security. Office of Inspector General. Op. cit. p. 29.

[22] Department of Homeland Security. *National Infrastructure Protection Plan.* Op. cit. pg159.

[23] See *USA Today*, "Database is Just the 1st Step," by Robert Stephan. July 21, 2006. p. 8A.

[24] See Congressional Quarterly's internet publication, *CQ Homeland Security*, July 29, 2004, at [http://homeland.cq.com/hs/display.do?docid=1278697andsourcetype=31], last viewed July 16, 2007.

[25] *USA Today.* Op. cit.

[26] For a discussion on common basic elements of a risk management process, in the context of critical infrastructure protection, see CRS Report RL32561. *Risk Management and Critical Infrastructure Protection: Assessing, Integrating, and Managing Threat, Vulnerability, and Consequences*, by John Moteff.

[27] As mentioned above, in the second data request to the states, DHS provided some characteristic thresholds by which DHS may assess whether or not an asset is critical at the national level. Also, according to the NIPP, as the various sectors work with their Sector Specific Agencies to develop sector-level protection plans, another source of information for the Database, owners/operators will have a standard form containing a few questions that can assist in determining criticality.

[28] Department of Homeland Security. Office of Inspector General. Op. cit. p. 10.

[29] In more recent testimony, before the Senate Committee on Homeland Security and Governmental Affairs, Ad Hoc Subcommittee on State, Local, and Private Sector Preparedness and Integration, July 12, 2007, the number of such assets has grown to about 2,500. It is not clear how this list of about 600 assets compares with the earlier Protective Measures Target List. Presumably, the list is a subset of the 77,069 assets in the Database and not a parallel list, but that is not clear either.

[30] See, ABC News Internet Ventures, *Government Confirms Much Shorter List of Critical U.S. Locations,* at [http://www.abcnews.go.com/GMA/print?id=2218846]. Site last viewed July 16, 2007.

[31] *USA Today.* Op. cit.

[32] Gas stations of any size or location are not listed in the criteria of what DHS considers to be a nationally significant asset within the oil and gas sector or any other sector or key resource category.

[33] Neither DHS or the IG report use the term "situational awareness" to describe the activities discussed in this section. This is a term CRS believes captures the breadth of the statements made regarding this particular use of the Database.

[34] Department of Homeland Security. Office of Inspector General. Op. cit. p. 29.

[35] Department of Homeland Security. *National Infrastructure Protection Plan.* Op. cit. p.

[36] It is not clear how, or if, the Database was used to inform preparedness and response decisions made during the hurricanes of 2005.

[37] *The Washington Post.* "U.S. Struggles to Rank Potential Terror Targets. Securing All Sites Not Financially Feasible, but Choices Are Fraught With Uncertainty," by Spencer Hsu. July 16, 2006. p. A9.

[38] The IP/IS program supports much of the Department's critical infrastructure protection activities, including its coordinating responsibilities, the National Infrastructure Protection Plan, the Protected Critical Infrastructure Information Program, etc. It is one of the Preparedness Directorate's Budget Activities.

[39] For example, the FY2007 budget justification discussed a program called Constellation, an automated critical asset management system, which would allow law enforcement to inventory, categorize, prioritize, and database critical assets. It also includes a risk assessment system, compatible with the National Asset Database, and allows for automated BZPP development. Constellation was begun in Los Angeles as a pilot program. The program is suppose to expand to other cities during FY2007 and information integrated with the National Asset Database.

[40] Department of Homeland Security. Office of Inspector General. Op. cit. p. 31.

[41] *National Petroleum News.* "Market Facts: Mid-July 2006. 2006 NPN Station Count." p.98.

[42] White House. *The National Strategy for the Physical Protection of Critical Infrastructures and Key Assets.* Op. Cit. p. 9.

[43] Department of Homeland Security. Office of the Inspector General. Op. cit. p. 12.

[44] See, Department of Homeland Security. Office of Grants and Training. *Discussion of the FY2006 Risk Methodology and the Urban Area Security Initiative* located at [http://www.ojp.usdoj.gov/odp/docs/FY_2006_ UASI_Program_Explanation_Paper_011 805.doc], last viewed on July 16, 2007.

[45] According to a conversation with Assistant Secretary Stephan, July 12, 2007, the short list of critical assets is forwarded to the Office of Grants and Training (referred to as ODP in this report), to be incorporated into their modeling exercise.

[46] Based on personal communication with industry official, September 29, 2003.

[47] Quoted by *CQ Homeland Security.* Op. cit.

[48] Department of Homeland Security. Office of Inspector General. Op. cit. p. 16.

[49] Protective Security Advisors are DHS employees stationed in the field to act as liaison with state and local stakeholders.

[50] The Protected Critical Infrastructure Information Program implements the Critical Infrastructure Information Act of 2002, passed as part of the Homeland Security Act, P.L. 107-296, Title I, Subtitle B. The act provides for a variety of protections of critical infrastructure information submitted voluntarily to the Department, including exemption from the Freedom of Information Act (552 U.S.C. 15). For a discussion of the Critical Infrastructure Information Act see, Archived CRS Report RL31762. *Homeland Security Act of 2002: Critical Infrastructure Information Act.*

[51] Department of Homeland Security. Office of Inspector General. Op. cit. p. 32.

[52] While the NIPP suggests that this would not occur, the NIPP also makes reference to (as do the IG report and the FY2007 budget justification) a "national risk profile." The NIPP describes the national risk profile as a high level summary of the aggregate risk and protective status across all sectors. The IG report makes reference to a contractor developed Gross Consequences of Attack tool that would automatically estimate, across a large number of potential targets held in the Database, the consequences associated

with various types of attacks. It is not clear if this includes all entries or just those eventually judged most critical.

[53] U.S. Congress. House of Representatives. *Making Appropriations for the Department of Homeland Security for the Fiscal Year Ending September 30, 2006, and for Other Purposes.* H.Rept. 109-241, accompanying H.R. 2360. p. 71.

[54] Note that the Database may contain information associated with regulations which require submission of the information for other regulatory purposes.

[55] These bills may be combined with other homeland security related legislation. See, Congress Daily PM. "House Will Merge 9/11, Transit Bills And Name Conferees." Monday, July 16, 2007, at [http://nationaljournal.com/pubs/congressdaily/ dj070716.htm#6]. Site last visited July 16, 2007.

In: Economics, Political and Social Issues ...
Editor: Michelle L. Fergusson

ISBN: 978-1-61122-555-6
©2011 Nova Science Publishers, Inc.

CAMPAIGN FINANCE: AN OVERVIEW[*]

Joseph E. Cantor

American National Government,
Government and Finance Division

ABSTRACT

Concerns over financing federal elections have become a seemingly perennial aspect of our political system, long centered on the enduring issues of high campaign costs and reliance on interest groups for needed campaign funds. Rising election costs had long fostered a sense in some quarters that spending was out of control, with too much time spent raising funds and elections "bought and sold." Debate had also focused on the role of interest groups in campaign funding, especially through political action committees (PACs). Differences in perceptions of the campaign finance system were compounded by the major parties' different approaches. Democrats tended to favor more regulation, with spending limits and public funding or benefits a part of past proposals. Republicans generally opposed such limits and public funding.

The 1996 elections marked a turning point in the debate's focus, as it shifted from whether to further restrict already regulated spending and funding sources to addressing election-related activities largely or entirely outside federal election law regulation and disclosure requirements (i.e., soft money). While concerns had long been rising over soft money in federal elections, its widespread and growing use for so-called issue advocacy since 1996 raised questions over the integrity of existing regulations and the feasibility of any limits at all. Following 1996, reform supporters offered legislation whose primary goals were to prohibit use of soft money in ways that could affect federal elections and to bring election-related issue advocacy communications under federal regulation. In both the 105th and 106th Congresses, the House passed the Shays-Meehan bill, but the Senate failed to invoke cloture to allow a vote on the companion McCain-Feingold bill. The 106th Congress did, however, agree on an aspect of campaign reform, in passing P.L. 106-230, to require disclosure by certain tax-exempt political organizations organized under Section 527 of the Internal Revenue Code. Such groups exist to influence elections, but many had not been required to disclose financial activity (to the FEC or IRS).

In the 107th Congress, the Senate passed McCain-Feingold, as amended, and the House passed the companion Shays-Meehan bill, as amended. The Senate then passed the House bill, which was signed into law by President Bush as the Bipartisan Campaign Reform Act of 2002 — BCRA (P.L. 107-155), constituting the first major change to the nation's campaign finance laws since 1979.

In the 2004 elections, more than $400 million was raised and spent by "political organizations" organized under Section 527 of the Internal Revenue Code but outside of federal election law regulation. In response to this perceived circumvention of election

---

[*] Excerpted from CRS Report RL 33580 dated july 31, 2006.

law regulation, the 109th Congress has examined the role of 527 groups in federal elections, and the House has passed legislation to address it.

This report (formerly CRS Issue Brief IB87020) provides an overview of campaign finance law governing federal elections, issues raised in recent years by campaign finance practices, and recent legislative activity and proposals in Congress, with a focus on the current (109th) Congress.

EVOLUTION OF THE CURRENT SYSTEM

Today's federal campaign finance law evolved during the 1970s out of five major statutes and a paramount Supreme Court case. That case not only affected earlier statutes, but it has also continued to shape the dialogue on campaign finance reform.

The 1971 Federal Election Campaign Act (FECA), as amended in 1974, 1976, and 1979, imposed limits on contributions, required disclosure of campaign receipts and expenditures, and set up the Federal Election Commission (FEC) as a central administrative and enforcement agency. The Revenue Act of 1971 inaugurated public funding of presidential general elections, with funding of primaries and nominating conventions added by the 1974 FECA Amendments. The latter also imposed certain expenditure limits, later struck down by the Supreme Court's landmark *Buckley v. Valeo* ruling [424 U.S. 1 (1976)].

In the *Buckley* ruling, the Court upheld the act's limitations on contributions as appropriate legislative tools to guard against the reality or appearance of improper influence stemming from candidates' dependence on large campaign contributions. However, *Buckley* invalidated the act's limitations on independent expenditures, on candidate expenditures from personal funds, and on overall campaign expenditures. These provisions, the Court ruled, placed direct and substantial restrictions on the ability of candidates, citizens, and associations to engage in protected First Amendment free speech rights. The Court saw no danger of corruption arising from large expenditures, as it did from large contributions, and reasoned that corruption alone could justify the First Amendment restrictions involved. Only voluntary limits on expenditures could be sustained, perhaps in exchange for government benefits. Such a plan was specifically upheld in the existing presidential public funding system, as a contractual agreement between the government and the candidate. The Court's dichotomous ruling, allowing limits on contributions but striking down mandatory limits on expenditures, has shaped subsequent campaign finance practices and laws, as well as the debate over campaign finance reform.

In 2002, Congress enacted the Bipartisan Campaign Reform Act (BCRA) of 2002 (popularly known as McCain-Feingold for its Senate sponsors). This statute made the most significant changes in the FECA since the 1970s, featuring higher contribution limits, a ban on the raising of soft money [1] by political parties and federal candidates, and a restriction on broadcast ads by outside groups in the closing days of an election. BCRA's constitutionality was challenged in court but, in a decision that surprised many observers, was essentially upheld by the Supreme Court in its December 10, 2003, ruling in *McConnell v. FEC*.

CAMPAIGN FINANCE PRACTICES AND RELATED ISSUES

From the mid-1970s through at least the late 1990s, the limits on contributions by individuals, political action committees (PACs), and parties, and an absence of congressional spending limits, governed the flow of money in congressional elections. Throughout the 1980s and much of the 1990s, the two paramount issues raised by campaign finance practices were the phenomena of, first, rising campaign costs and the large amounts of money needed for elections and, second, the substantial reliance on PACs as a source of funding.

After 1996, the debate shifted considerably to a focus on the perceived loopholes in existing law (a source of increasing debate since the mid-1980s). The PAC issue was largely supplanted by more fundamental issues of election regulation, with one-time critics finding new appreciation for the limited, disclosed nature of PAC funds. The issue of high campaign costs and the concomitant need for vast resources continues to underlie the debate, but even this was almost overshadowed by concerns over the system's perceived loopholes. Although these practices were (largely) presumably legal, they may have violated the law's spirit, raising a basic question of whether money in elections can, let alone should, be regulated.

Enduring Issues: Campaign Costs and Funding Sources

Increased Campaign Costs. Since first being systematically compiled in the 1970s, campaign expenditures have risen substantially, even exceeding the overall rise in the cost of living. An estimated $540 million was spent on all elections (at all levels) in the U.S. in 1976, [2] rising to some $3.9 billion in 2000 [3] Preliminary estimates from the 2004 elections show that spending on federal elections alone exceeded $3.9 billion [4]

Aggregate costs of House and Senate campaigns increased tenfold between 1976 and 2004, from $115.5 million to $1.16 billion, while the cost of living rose a little more than threefold. Campaign costs for average winning candidates, a useful measure of the real cost of seeking office, showed an increase in the House from $87,000 in 1976 to $1.0 million in 2004; a winning Senate race went from $609,000 in 1976 to $7.0 million in 2004 (not adjusted for inflation).

The above data are cited by many as evidence that our democratic system of government has suffered as election costs have grown to levels often considered exorbitant. Specifically, it is argued that officeholders must spend too much time raising money, at the expense of their public duties and communicating with constituents. The high cost of elections and the perception that they are "bought and sold" are seen as contributing to public cynicism about the political process. Some express concern that spiraling campaign costs have resulted in more wealthy individuals seeking office or determining election winners, denying opportunities for service to those lacking adequate resources or contacts. Others see a correlation between excessive, available money and the perceived increased reliance of sophisticated, often negative, media advertising.

Not all observers view the high cost of elections with alarm. Many insist we do not spend too much on elections and maybe do not spend enough. They contrast the amount spent on elections with that spent by government at all levels, noting that only a fraction of a percent is spent to choose those who make vital decisions on the allocation of tax dollars. Similarly, they contrast costs of elections with those on commercial advertising: the nation's two leading commercial advertisers in 1996, Proctor and Gamble and General Motors, spent more to promote their products that year ($5 billion) than was spent on all U.S. elections [5]. In such a context, these observers contend, the costs of political dialogue may not be excessive.

High election costs are seen largely as a reflection of the paramount role of media in modern elections. Increasingly high television costs and costs of fundraising in an era of contribution limits require candidates to seek a broad base of small contributors — a democratic, but time-consuming, expensive process — or to seek ever-larger contributions from small groups of wealthy contributors. It has been argued that neither negative campaigning nor wealthy candidates are new or increasing phenomena but merely that better disclosure and television's prevalence make us more aware of them. Finally, better-funded candidates do not always win, as some recent elections show.

PACs and Other Sources of Campaign Funds. Issues stemming from rising election expenses were, for much of the 1970s through 1990s, linked to substantial candidate reliance on PAC contributions. The perception that fundraising pressures might lead candidates to tailor their appeals to the most affluent and narrowly "interested" sectors raised perennial questions about the resulting quality of representation of the whole society. The role of PACs, in itself and relative to other sources, became a major issue. In retrospect, however, it appears that the issue was really about the role of interest groups and money in elections, PACs being the most visible vehicle thereof. As discussed below, the PAC issue per se has seemed greatly diminished by recent events, while concerns over interest group money through other channels have grown.

Through the 1980s, statistics showed a significant increase in PAC importance. From 1974 to 1988, PACs grew in numbers from 608 to a high of 4,268, in contributions to House and Senate candidates from $12.5 million to $147.8 million (a 400% rise in constant dollars), and in relation to other sources from 16% of congressional campaign receipts to 34%. While PACs remain a considerable force, data show a relative decline in their role since 1988: the percentage of PAC money in total receipts dropped to 28% in 2004; PAC numbers dropped to 4,040 in 2004; and, after individual giving had been declining vis-à-vis PACs, there has been some increase of late, with individuals giving 72% of Senate and 56% of House receipts in 2004, for example. Still, not all indicators show decline in the PAC role; PAC contributions to candidates rose to $289.1 million in 2004, for example.

Despite some aggregate data on the relative decline of PACs, they still provide a considerable share of election financing for various subgroups. For example, in 2004, House candidates got 35% of their funds from PACs; House incumbents received 41%. To critics, PACs raise troubling issues in the campaign financing debate: Are policymakers beholden to special interests for election help, impairing their ability to make policy choices in the national interest? Do PACs overshadow average citizens, particularly in Members' states and districts? Does the appearance of quid pro quo relationships between special interest givers and politician recipients, whether or not they actually exist, seriously undermine public confidence in the political system?

PAC defenders view them as reflecting the nation's historic pluralism, representing not a monolithic force but a wide variety of interests. These observers see them, rather than overshadowing individual citizens, merely as groups of such citizens, giving voice to many who were previously uninvolved. PACs are seen as promoting, not hindering, electoral competition, by funding challengers in closely contested races. In terms of influencing legislative votes, donations are seen more as rewards for past votes than as inducements to alter future ones. Defenders also challenge the presumed dichotomy between *special* and *national* interest, viewing the latter as simply the sum total of the former. PACs, they argue, afford clearer knowledge of how interest groups promote their agendas, particularly noteworthy in light of the flood of unregulated and undisclosed money since 1996.

Today's Paramount Issues: Perceived Loopholes in Current Law

Interest has intensified, especially since 1996, in campaign finance practices that have been seen by some as undermining the law's contribution and expenditure limits and its disclosure requirements. Although these practices may be legal, they have been characterized as "loopholes" through which electoral influence is sought by spending money in ways that detract from public confidence in the system and that are beyond the scope intended by Congress. Some of the prominent practices have been soft money, election-related issue advocacy, and, most recently, election-related activities by groups operating under Section 527 of the Internal Revenue Code (IRC).

Soft Money. This term has generally been used to refer to money that may influence federal elections (at least indirectly) but is raised and spent outside the purview of federal laws and would be illegal if spent directly on a federal election by a candidate, party, or PAC. The significance of soft money, prior to enactment of BCRA, stemmed from several factors: (1) many states permitted (then and now) direct union and corporate contributions and individual donations in excess of $25,000 in state campaigns, all of which were (and are) prohibited in federal races; (2) under the 1979 FECA Amendments and FEC rulings, such money could be spent by state and local parties in large or unlimited amounts on grassroots organizing and voter drives that could benefit all party candidates; and (3) publicly funded presidential candidates could not spend privately raised money in the general election. In presidential elections through 2000, national parties made extensive efforts to raise money for their state affiliates, partly to boost the national tickets beyond what could be spent directly. The data for 2000 showed some $495 million in soft money was raised by the major parties, nearly double the $262 million raised in 1996.

Issue Advocacy. Although federal law regulates expenditures in connection with federal elections, it has generally used a fairly narrow definition for what constitutes such spending. Prevailing judicial interpretation of Supreme Court precedent, both before and arguably since BCRA, has created a conundrum by permitting regulation of only those communications containing express advocacy, that is, communications containing explicit terms urging the election or defeat of clearly identified federal candidates. By avoiding such terms, groups arguably can promote their views and issue positions in reference to particular elected officials, without triggering the disclosure and source restrictions of the FECA. Such activity, known as issue advocacy, is widely perceived as having the intent of bolstering or detracting from the public image of officials who are also candidates for office. In 1996, an estimated $135 million was spent on issue advocacy, rising to between $275 and $340 million in 1998, and to $509 million in 2000 (although these data do not distinguish between campaign-related and non-campaign-related communications). Also, groups ranging from labor unions to the Christian Coalition promote their policy views through voter guides, which present candidates' views on issues in a way that some see as helpful to some candidates and harmful to others, without meeting the standards for FECA coverage.

527 Political Organizations. In the years leading up to enactment of BCRA and in the wake of its major provisions being upheld by the Supreme Court in December 2003, attention has been increasingly focused on activity by interest groups operating outside the regulatory framework of federal election law. Of particular interest have been groups operating under Section 527 of the Internal Revenue Code, which provides tax-exempt status to organizations it defines as political. In 2000, some groups engaged in election-related issue advocacy aroused controversy when it was revealed that they were operating under Section 527 of the IRC while not being regulated under the FECA. At that time, BCRA was still under consideration, and Congress was enmeshed in the thorny issue of regulating activity that was not express advocacy. Rather than short-circuit that debate and begin yet another on the also complicated issue of differing definitions of *political organization* under the IRC and *political committee* under the FECA, Congress addressed the issue by simply requiring disclosure to the IRS by groups with tax-exempt 527 status.

In 2002, Title II of BCRA addressed the express advocacy issue, but only with regard to broadcast advertisements in the period just prior to federal elections. BCRA was silent regarding interest groups' involvement in such other election-related activities as public communications through non-broadcast methods, broadcasts prior to the last 30 days before a primary or 60 days before a general election, voter identification, and get-out-the-vote and registration drives. These activities loom particularly large in the wake of BCRA's prohibition on national political party use of non-federally permissible funds (i.e., soft money) to pay for voter mobilization activities. With some $425 million reported as having been spent in the 2004 elections by groups with Section 527 status, public attention has shifted to these new patterns of electioneering, raising questions as to whether requiring disclosure to the IRS is sufficient. The following table presents data on spending and receipts of 527s since IRS disclosure was required in 2000. The source, PolicalMoneyLine, examined reports and identified "key groups," those that were clearly federal election-related.

Receipts and Disbursements by Federal-Related 527s: 2000-2004
(dollars in millions)

Election Cycle	Total Spending	Receipts		
		Total	Democratic- oriented 527s	Republican oriented 527s
2000	$89.6	$62.3	$40.6	$21.7
2002	$194.9	$184.9	$105.5	$78.4
2004	$424.8	$421.4	$265.0	$154.1

Source: PoliticalMoneyLine, "key groups" (those that were clearly federal-election related) identified from IRS filings at [http://www.tray.com/cgi-win/irs_ef_527.exe?DoFn=andsYR=2000], site visited Mar. 30, 2006.

POLICY OPTIONS TO ADDRESS CAMPAIGN FINANCE ISSUES

The policy debate over campaign finance laws proceeds from the philosophical differences over the underlying issues discussed above, as well as the more practical, logistical questions over the proposed solutions. Two primary considerations frame this debate. What changes can be made that will not raise First Amendment objections, given court rulings in *Buckley* and other cases? What changes will not result in new, unforeseen, and more troublesome practices? These considerations are underscored by the experience with prior amendments to FECA, such as PAC growth after the 1974 limits on contributions.

Just as the overriding issues centered until recently around election costs and funding sources, the most prominent legislation long focused on controlling campaign spending, usually through voluntary systems of public funding or cost-reduction benefits, and on altering the relative importance of various funding sources. Some saw both concepts primarily in the context of promoting electoral competition, to remedy or at least not exacerbate perceived inequities between incumbents and challengers. Increasingly since the mid-1980s, and particularly since the 1996 elections, concerns over perceived loopholes that undermine federal regulation have led to proposals to curb such practices. Conversely, some proposals have urged less regulation, on the ground that it inherently invites circumvention, while still other proposals have focused exclusively on improving or expanding disclosure.

Addressing the Enduring Issues

Campaign Spending Limits and Government Incentives or Benefits

Until the late 1990s, the campaign reform debate often focused on the desirability of campaign spending limits. To a great extent, this debate was linked with public financing of elections. The coupling of these two controversial issues stemmed from *Buckley's* ban on mandatory spending limits, while allowing voluntary limits, with adherence a prerequisite for subsidies. Hence the notion arose in the 1970s that spending limits must be tied to public benefits, absent a constitutional amendment.

Public funding not only might serve as an inducement to voluntary limits, but by limiting the role of private money, it is also billed as the strongest measure toward promoting the integrity of and confidence in the electoral process. Furthermore, it could promote competition in districts with strong incumbents or one-party domination. Public financing of congressional elections has been proposed in nearly every Congress since 1956 and has passed in several Congresses. The nation has had publicly funded presidential elections since 1976, and tax incentives for political donations were in place from 1972 to 1986.

Objections to public financing are numerous, many rooted in philosophical opposition to funding elections with taxpayer money, supporting candidates whose views are antithetical to those of many taxpayers, and adding another government program in the face of some cynicism toward government spending. The practical objections are also serious: How can a system be devised that accounts for different natures of districts and states, with different styles of campaigning and disparate media costs, and is fair to all candidates — incumbent, challenger, or open-seat, major or minor party, serious or "longshot"?

A major challenge to spending limit supporters has been how to reduce, if not eliminate, the role of public funding in their proposals. Although spending limits may have wide public support, most evidence suggests far less support for public financing. In the 105th through 107th Congresses, the principal reform bills debated on the floor contained neither campaign spending limits nor public funding, reflecting not only the overriding concerns over soft money and issue advocacy but also the changed political climate since the 1970s.

Stemming from the spending limits debate have been proposals to lower campaign costs, without spending limits. Proposals for free or reduced rate broadcast time and postage have received some notable bipartisan support. Such ideas seek to reduce campaign costs and the need for money, without the possibly negative effects of arbitrary limits.

Changing the Balance among Funding Sources

Until the late 1990s, most proposed bills sought, at least in part, to curb PACs' perceived influence, either directly, through a ban or reduced contribution limits, or indirectly, through enhancing the role of individuals and parties. Prior to enactment of BCRA, individuals could give $1,000 per candidate, per election, while most PACs (if they were "multicandidate committees") could give $5,000 per candidate, thus increasing their ability to assist candidates. Furthermore, unlike individuals, there was (and is) no aggregate limit on all contributions in federal elections by a PAC in a given time period, thus further increasing a PAC's opportunity to be involved.

Three chief methods of direct PAC curbs were prominent in proposals advanced through the mid-1990s: banning PAC money in federal elections; lowering the $5,000 limit; and limiting candidates' aggregate PAC receipts. These concepts were included, for example, in all of the bills that the House and Senate voted on in the 101st through 104th Congresses. Although support for such proposals was fueled by a desire to reduce the perceived role of interest groups, each proposal had drawbacks, such as constitutional questions about limiting speech and association rights and the more practical concern over devaluation of the $5,000 limit by inflation since it was set in 1974.

Yet another concern raised during that period was the potential encouragement for interest groups to shift resources to "independent" activities, which are less accountable to voters and more troublesome for candidates in framing the debate. Furthermore, independent advertisements were often marked by negativity and invective. If such prospects gave pause to lawmakers during the 1980s, the surge of financial activity outside the framework of federal election law since 1996 has largely dampened attempts to further limit PACs. The major reform bills in the 105th through 107th Congresses contained no further PAC restrictions.

Partly because of this problem, both before and after 1996, many have looked to more indirect ways to curb PACs and interest groups, such as raising limits on individual or party donations to candidates. These increases have also been proposed on a contingency basis to offset such other sources as wealthy candidates spending large personal sums on their campaigns. As enacted in 2002, BCRA provided both for higher individual contribution limits in general and provisional increases in both individual and party limits to assist candidates opposed by free-spending, wealthy opponents. While higher limits might counterbalance PACs and others and offset inflation, opponents observed that few Americans could afford to give even $1,000, raising age-old concerns about "fat cat" contributors.

House Republicans have pushed to boost the role of individuals in candidates' states or districts, to increase ties between Members and constituents. By requiring a majority of funds to come from the state or district (or prohibiting out-of-state funds), supporters sought to indirectly curb PACs, typically perceived as out-of-state, or Washington, influences.

Support also exists for increasing or removing party contribution and coordinated expenditure limits, based on the notions that the party role can be maximized without leading to influence peddling and on strengthening party ties to facilitate effective policymaking. Opponents note that many of the prominent allegations in 1996 involved party-raised funds.

Closing Perceived Loopholes

Proposals have increasingly addressed perceived loopholes in FECA, and indeed this area was the primary focus of recent reform efforts, culminating in enactment of BCRA in the 107th Congress. This debate underscored a basic philosophical difference between those who favored and opposed government regulation of campaign finances. Opponents said that regulation invited attempts at subterfuge, that interested money would always find its way into elections, and that the most one could do was see that it was disclosed. Proponents argued that while it was hard to restrict money, it was a worthwhile goal, hence one ought to periodically fine-tune the law to correct "unforeseen consequences." Proposed "remedies" stemmed from the latter view (i.e., curtail the practices as they arise).

Soft Money. This issue was one of the key issues addressed by BCRA. Title I provided that national parties and federal candidates or officials, and entities they directly or indirectly establish, finance, maintain, or control, may not solicit, receive, direct, transfer, or spend funds not raised under the limits, prohibitions, and reporting requirements of federal law (i.e., soft money). State and local political parties, and entities they directly or indirectly establish, finance, maintain, or control, may not spend soft money on "federal election activities." The act's so-called Levin amendment, however, allowed for some use of soft money under certain conditions for specified grassroots activities by state and local parties.

Issue Advocacy. The other key issue addressed by BCRA pertained to issue advocacy. The challenge to Congress in addressing this practice, a form of soft money, involved broadening the definition of what constituted federal election-related spending. A 1995 FEC regulation had offered such a definition, using a "reasonable person" standard, but this was struck down by a First Circuit federal court in 1996; this decision was later upheld by an appeals court but was at variance with an earlier Ninth Circuit ruling. The FEC was reluctant to enforce the regulation pending further judicial or legislative action. Earlier versions of what became BCRA (the Shays-Meehan bill, as passed in the 105th and 106th Congresses) sought to codify a definition of "express advocacy" that allowed a communication to be considered as a whole, in context of such external events as timing, to determine if it was election related.

In the final analysis, BCRA adopted a narrower approach, in large measure to enhance its chances of withstanding judicial scrutiny, by incorporating into Title II language initially proposed by Senators Snowe and Jeffords. This title regulates election-related issue advocacy by creating a new term in federal election law, *electioneering communications* (i.e., political advertisements that refer to clearly identified federal candidates, broadcast within 30 days of a primary or 60 days of a general election). Generally, they may not be funded from union or corporate treasuries, and disbursements of over $10,000 and donors of $1,000 or more must be disclosed.

527 Activity. Efforts to address the activity of 527 political organizations that operate outside the regulatory framework of federal election law have been underway in the 109th Congress. Supporters of BCRA offered measures (S. 1053 and H.R. 513) to apply federal election law regulation to 527 groups involved in federal election-related activities. The 527 Reform Act of 2005 would add political organizations under Section 527 of the IRC to the definition of *political committee* under FECA, unless they are involved exclusively in state and local elections. The Senate bill was reported by the Rules and Administration Committee and placed on the Senate's legislative calendar. In response to this proposal, H.R. 1316 (Pence-Wynn) was introduced to address the issue more indirectly, largely by loosening restrictions on individuals, parties, and PACs under the FECA, and in the soft money realm as well. This bill, intended to provide some balance to the role of the 527s, was reported by the House Administration Committee, which later reported H.R. 513 without recommendation. This set the stage for a House floor debate between two bills to address the 527 issue based on diametrically opposed philosophies. On April 5, 2006, the House passed H.R. 513 (Shays-Meehan), as amended, by a 218-209 vote. The text of H.R. 513 was also incorporated into the House Republican leadership's lobby and ethics reform bill — H.R. 4975 (Dreier) — which was passed by the House on May 3, 2006.

LEGISLATIVE ACTION IN CONGRESS

Congress's consideration of campaign finance reform has steadily increased since 1986, when the Senate passed the PAC-limiting Boren-Goldwater amendment, marking the first campaign finance vote in either house since 1979 (no vote was taken on the underlying bill). With Senate control shifting to Democrats in 1986, each of the next four Congresses saw intensified activity, based on Democratic-leadership bills with voluntary spending limits combined with inducements to participation, such as public subsidies or cost-reduction benefits. In the 100th Congress, Senate Democrats were blocked by a Republican filibuster. In the 101st through 103rd Congresses, the House and Senate each passed comprehensive bills based on spending limits and public benefits. Those bills were not reconciled in the 101st or 103rd, while a conference version in the 102nd was vetoed by President George H. W. Bush.

Republicans assumed control in the 104th Congress, and changes in campaign finance laws were not a priority for the new leadership, as many of them had philosophical differences with the most prominent "reform" proposals. A bipartisan bill based on previous Democratic-leadership bills was blocked by filibuster in the Senate, while both Republican- and Democratic-leadership bills — with starkly different approaches — failed to pass in the House. In the 105th Congress, reform supporters succeeded in passing the Shays-Meehan bill in the House (H.R. 2183, as amended). Senate sponsors of its companion McCain-Feingold measure (S. 25, as revised) failed on three occasions to break a filibuster in opposition, and no vote occurred on the bill.

In the 106th Congress, the House again passed the Shays-Meehan bill (H.R. 417). Supporters of the companion McCain-Feingold bill initially introduced S. 26, much the same bill as its final version in the 105th Congress. They later introduced a much narrower version (S. 1593), focusing largely on party soft money but dropping the issue advocacy and other provisions. This version was debated in October 1999 but failed to break a filibuster in opposition. Reform supporters succeeded, however, in enacting a law to require disclosure by tax-exempt political organizations under Section 527 of the Internal Revenue Code.

In the 107th Congress, the long stalemate over campaign finance reform was broken when Congress enacted BCRA. The Senate passed S. 27 (McCain-Feingold) on April 2, 2001, by a vote of 59-41, after a two-week debate which added 22 amendments on the floor and rejected 16 others. The Senate also defeated S.J.Res. 4 (Hollings-Specter), a constitutional amendment to allow mandatory campaign spending limits, by a 40-56 vote on March 26, 2001. Although Senate passage marked a major breakthrough, the measure appeared to be stalled in the House in 2001, when the House rejected (by 203-228) the proposed rule for consideration on July 12. Supporters of Shays-Meehan filed a discharge petition to force reconsideration and, on January 24, 2002, secured the last four needed signatures. On February 13, 2002, the House passed H.R. 2356 (Shays-Meehan) by a 240-189 vote, after including four perfecting amendments and rejecting two substitute and eight perfecting amendments. On March 20, the Senate passed H.R. 2356 by a 60-40 vote, and President Bush signed the measure into law on March 27, as P.L. 107-155. Also in the 107th Congress, P.L. 107-276 was enacted to relieve 527 tax-exempt political organizations that operate at the state and local levels from reporting requirements enacted in 2000 and to improve IRS dissemination of federally filed reports under that law.

The 108th Congress was a transitional one in terms of campaign finance issues, as the political community adjusted to the newly enacted BCRA and watched the courts for rulings on its constitutionality. This matter was settled on December 10, 2003, when the Supreme Court, in *McConnell v. FEC* (549 U.S. 93), upheld the constitutionality of key provisions of BCRA, dealing with soft money and electioneering communications. The issue of 527 political organizations, which emerged as strong forces in the wake of BCRA, occupied some congressional attention, with hearings held on the subject in the House Administration and Senate Rules and Administration Committees and bills introduced by supporters of BCRA to apply federal election law regulation to such groups involved in federal election-related activities.

109th Congress

In the wake of the 2004 elections, when some $425 million was spent by 527 organizations outside federal election law regulation, the 109th Congress has examined the role of 527 groups in federal elections. On March 8, 2005, the Senate Rules and Administration Committee held a hearing on S. 271 (McCain-Feingold-Lott), a bill to require that 527s involved in federal elections comply fully with federal election law, and on April 27, it voted to report the bill, as amended in committee. On May 17, that bill was reported as an original bill — S. 1053 — and placed on the Senate's legislative calendar.

The House Administration Committee held a hearing April 20, 2005, on regulation of 527 organizations, which focused on H.R. 513 (Shays-Meehan), the companion to S. 271 (now S. 1053), and H.R. 1316 (Pence-Wynn). In sharp contrast with the bill reported in the Senate, H.R. 1316 seeks to address the 527 issue indirectly, by loosening restrictions on funding sources within FECA. By so doing, proponents maintain that there would be less of an incentive for political money to flow to 527 groups operating outside the framework of FECA. On June 9, 2005, House Administration voted to report H.R. 1316, as amended; it was reported on June 22 [6]. On June 29, the committee held a markup of H.R. 513 (Shays-Meehan), and ordered it reported (as amended to reflect the sponsors' changes), without recommendation, [7] thus setting the stage for a floor debate on the two contrasting measures.

On April 5, 2006, the House passed H.R. 513 (Shays-Meehan), as amended, by a 218-209 vote. The rule under which it was considered — H.Res. 755 [8] — allowed one floor amendment, by Representative Dreier, to remove political party-coordinated expenditure limits. This was added by voice vote before final passage.

The text of H.R. 513 was also incorporated into the House Republican leadership's lobby and ethics reform bill — H.R. 4975 (Dreier). As introduced, Title VI of the bill incorporated the language of H.R. 513 as reported by the House Administration Committee. In addition, it included one provision unrelated to 527s, to remove the political party-coordinated expenditure limits in 2 U.S.C. §441a(d).

Party-coordinated expenditures refer to expenditures made by a political party in coordination with a candidate's campaign; they have been subject to limits since the 1974 FECA Amendments. The limits are relatively high compared with limits on contributions, with typical House candidates eligible for $74,620 in 2004 and a Senate candidate as much as $3.8 million (in California) that year. Ever since the Supreme Court ruling in *Colorado Republican Federal Campaign Committee v. FEC* (518 U.S. 604 (1996)), which permitted parties to make independent expenditures on behalf of their candidates, the importance of coordinated expenditures has been diminished. The prospect of unlimited independent expenditures has been increasingly appealing to the parties, and it has become common for parties to make both independent expenditures and coordinated expenditures for the same candidates, albeit from at least nominally different departments of a party committee. In 2004, Democratic party committees (federal, state, and local) made $33.1 million in coordinated expenditures and $176.5 million in independent expenditures to promote their federal candidates; Republican party committees made $29.1 million in coordinated expenditures and $88.0 million in independent expenditures.

BCRA had contained a provision to require a party to choose making either independent expenditures or coordinated expenditures, but not both, for one of its nominees; this, however, was one of two BCRA provisions struck down by the Supreme Court in *McConnell v. FEC* (549 U.S. 93(2003)). Hence, while abolishing the limit on coordinated expenditures would appear to allow the parties to spend unlimited amounts on behalf of their candidates, they already have that right, albeit through expenditures that are technically made without any coordination with the favored candidate. Supporters of removing the limits assert that doing so would largely indicate acceptance of the current reality and allow parties to reinforce their direct ties with candidates. Opponents assert that this would send the wrong message to an electorate cynical about the role of money in politics and also that the national parties are now playing a significant role, especially in light of increased hard money limits under BCRA. Nearly $1.5 billion was raised by party committees in the 2004 election cycle (all hard money), more than ever had been raised in combined hard and soft money by the national parties.

Prior to House passage of H.R. 4975, an amendment was included by the House Rules Committee to prohibit leadership PACs' funds from being converted to personal use (as is the case with funds in principal campaign committees). On May 3, 2006, the House passed H.R. 4975, the Lobbying Accountability and Transparency Act of 2006, which included the text of H.R. 513 (Shays-Meehan), as well as the two amendments on leadership PACs and party coordinated expenditures. After passing H.R. 4975, the House substituted it for the text of S. 2349, the Senate-passed version of the bill, to enable a conference with the Senate. The Senate-passed bill does not contain the 527 provisions.

On other 109th Congress issues, a provision allowing leadership PACs to transfer unlimited funds to national parties was added in committee to the Transportation-Treasury-HUD-Judiciary-DC appropriations bill for FY2006 (H.R. 3058). Following a move by BCRA sponsors, the Senate deleted the provision by unanimous consent on October 17, 2005.

Also, the Senate Indian Affairs Committee held a hearing February 8, 2006, to examine rules governing campaign contributions by Indian tribes, in response to large sums of money given in recent elections and concerns over the application of federal campaign finance law thereto. In its final report on its investigation of lobbying and political activities by Indian tribes, the committee recommended requiring Indian tribes making federal election contributions to register with the FEC and improving rules for disclosure of those contributions [9]

The issue of regulation of Internet communications was addressed at a House Administration Committee hearing September 22, 2005. On November 2, the House failed to approve a measure to exempt Internet communications from regulation under federal campaign finance laws. H.R. 1606 (Hensarling) was brought up under suspension of the rules but failed on a 225-182 vote. On March 9, 2006, the House Administration Committee ordered the bill favorably reported, [10] and it was expected to be considered by the House on March 16, but that vote was postponed. On March 27, the FEC approved new regulations to regulate only paid advertisements placed on another's website, thus addressing much of the concern expressed about Internet regulation. On March 29, House Majority Leader Boehner announced that consideration of H.R. 1606 would be postponed indefinitely.

As of July 30, 2006, 49 bills (41 House and 8 Senate) have been introduced in the 109th Congress to change federal campaign finance law.

MAJOR LEGISLATION IN 109TH CONGRESS

H.R. 513 (Shays-Meehan) — 527 Reform Act of 2005. [italicized text indicates amendment added on House floor]

- Includes in the definition of *political committee* any 527 organization, unless it (1) has annual gross receipts of less than $25,000, (2) is a state or local party committee or a political committee of a state or local candidate, (3) is exclusively devoted to non-federal elections or non-election activity, or (4) exists solely to pay certain administrative expenses or expenses of a qualified newsletter; ! the last two exemptions do not apply if the 527 spends money for public communications that promote, support, attack, or oppose a clearly identified federal candidate within one year of the general election in which that candidate is seeking office or for any voter registration or mobilization effort in connection with an election in which a candidate for federal office is on the ballot; ! requires political committees (but not candidate or party committees) that make disbursements for voter mobilization activities or public communications that affect both federal and non-federal elections to generally use at least 50% hard money from federal accounts to finance such activities (but requires that 100% of public communications and voter drive activities that refer to only federal candidates be financed with hard money from a federal account, regardless of whether the communication refers to a political party); ! allows contributions to non-federal accounts making allocations under this provision only by individuals in amounts of up to $25,000 per year; ! states that this act shall have no bearing on FEC regulations, on any definitions of political organizations in Internal Revenue Code, or on any determination of whether a 501(c) tax-exempt organization may be a political committee under FECA;

- provides special expedited judicial review procedures, similar to those in BCRA, for a challenge to the act on constitutional grounds, and allows any Member to bring or intervene in any such case;
- *repeals limits on coordinated expenditures by political parties.*

Introduced February 2, 2005; referred to Committee on House Administration. June 29, 2005, ordered reported as amended without recommendation (H.Rept. 109-181). April 5, 2006, H.Res. 755 (H.Rept. 109-404), allowing vote on H.R. 513 and Dreier amendment, passed House (223-199). April 5, 2006, H.R. 513, with Dreier amendment, passed House (218-209).

H.R. 1316 (Pence-Wynn) — 527 Fairness Act of 2005. [provisions added in committee substitute amendment shown in italics]

- Removes aggregate limit on contributions by individuals; removes limit on party-coordinated expenditures;
- *raises limit on contributions to and by PACs,* and indexes them (*and limit on individual contributions to state parties*) for inflation;
- *allows leadership PACs to transfer unlimited funds to national party committees;*
- *increases annual contribution and expenditure threshold for determining political committee status to $10,000;*
- *bans contributions to 527 groups from foreign nationals;*
- *requires 527 groups now filing financial activity reports with IRS but not FEC to file reports with FEC as well;*
- removes "targeted communications" exception to exemption of 501(c)(4) and 527 organizations from ban on electioneering communications by unions and corporations (i.e., allows 501(c)(4) and 527 corporations to make electioneering communications with funds donated solely by individuals who are citizens or permanent resident aliens);
- extends same authority granted to 501(c)(4) organizations with regard to electioneering communications to 501(c)(5) and 501(c)(6) organizations (typically unions and trade associations);
- states that expenditures made by 501(c)(4), (c)(5), or (c)(6) organizations shall not affect their tax status under Internal Revenue Code;
- removes requirements that trade association solicitations of member corporations' restricted classes have prior approval of the corporations and that no more than one trade association may solicit such classes in a calendar year;

- allows unions, corporations, and trade associations to solicit restricted classes by means other than mail;
- loosens restrictions on state/local parties by allowing use of soft money for voter registration activities in last 120 days of a federal election and for sample ballots in elections with both federal and state/local candidates on ballot;
- *codifies FEC regulation that federal candidates and officeholders may speak at state/local party fundraisers without restriction or regulation;*
- *provides that communications on Internet are not regulated by FECA;*
- *allows federal candidates/officeholders to endorse state/local candidates and appear in their advertisements without this constituting coordinated contributions under FECA.*

Introduced March 15, 2005; referred to Committee on House Administration. Ordered reported from committee, as amended, June 8, 2005. Reported June 22, 2005 (H.Rept. 109-146).

H.R. 4975 (Dreier) — Lobbying Accountability and Transparency Act of 2006. Title VI, Reform of Section 527 Organizations, incorporates text of H.R. 513, as passed by House (see above). In addition, it would prohibit leadership PAC funds from being converted to personal use. Introduced March 16, 2006; jointly referred to Committees on the Judiciary, House Administration, Rules, Government Reform, and Standards of Official Conduct. May 3, 2006, passed House, as amended, including the text of H.R. 513.

S. 1053 (McCain-Feingold-Lott) — 527 Reform Act of 2005. [amendments adopted in Committee in *italics*]

527s:

- Includes in the definition of political committee any 527 organization, unless it: has annual gross receipts of less than $25,000; is a political committee of a state or local party or candidate; exists solely to pay certain administrative expenses or expenses of a qualified newsletter; is composed solely of state or local officeholders and candidates whose voter drive activities refer to state and local candidates but not federal candidates and parties; *is solely involved in voter drive activities, including public communications devoted to such, but does not engage in broadcast, cable, or satellite communications* (Schumer amendment); or is exclusively devoted to elections where no federal candidate is on ballot, or to non-federal elections, ballot issues, or selection of non-elected officials.
- This last exemption does not apply if the 527 spends more than $1,000 for: public communications that promote, support, attack, or oppose a clearly identified federal candidate within one year of the general election in which that candidate is seeking office; or for any voter drive activity conducted by a group in a calendar year, unless: sponsor confines activity solely within one state; (2) non-federal candidates are referred to in all voter drive activities and no federal candidate or party is referred to in any substantive way; (3) no federal candidate or officeholder or national party official or agent is involved in the organization's direction, fundraising, or disbursements; and (4) no contributions are made by the group to federal candidates;

- requires political committees (but not candidate or party committees) that make disbursements for voter mobilization activities or public communications that affect both federal and non-federal elections to generally use at least 50% hard money from federal accounts (or more, if FEC so determines) to finance such activities (but requires that 100% of public communications and voter drive activities that refer to only federal candidates be financed with hard money from a federal account, regardless of whether the communication refers to a political party);
- allows contributions to non-federal accounts making allocations under this provision only by individuals in amounts of up to $25,000 per year (and states that funds in non-federal accounts are not otherwise subject to FECA);
- states that this act shall have no bearing on FEC regulations, on any definitions of political organizations in the IRC, or on any determination of whether a 501(c) tax-exempt organization may be a political committee under FECA;
- provides special expedited judicial review procedures, similar to those in BCRA, for a challenge to the act on constitutional grounds, and allows any Member to bring or intervene in any such case.

Broadcast rates:

- *Makes TV, cable, and satellite lowest unit rate broadcast time non-preemptible, with rates based on comparison with full prior year, and requires such rates be available to national parties for time on behalf of candidates* (Durbin amendment);

PACs:

- *Increases limit on contributions to and by PACs from $5,000 to $7,500;*
- *increases limit on PAC contributions to national parties from $15,000 to $25,000;*
- *indexes these limits for inflation;*
- *allows leadership PACs to transfer unlimited funds to national party committees;*
- *eliminates twice-a-year limit on solicitations by unions/corporations of their restricted classes;*
- *eliminates requirements that trade associations get prior approval of member corporations before solicitations are made to their restricted classes and that corporations may grant approval to only one association in a year* (Bennett amendment);

Other FECA provisions:

- *Provides that communications on the Internet are not regulated by FECA;*
- *indexes, for inflation, limit on contributions by individuals to state and local parties (now $10,000);*
- *increases annual contribution and expenditure threshold for determining political committee status to $10,000* (Bennett amendment).

Original bill ordered reported April 27, 2005, by Committee on Rules and Administration (in lieu of S. 271, which was approved that day by committee, as amended). Placed on legislative calendar May 17, 2005.

FOR ADDITIONAL READING

CRS Report RS21176, *Application of Campaign Finance Law to Indian Tribes*, by L. Paige Whitaker and Joseph E. Cantor.

CRS Report RL31402, *Bipartisan Campaign Reform Act of 2002: Summary and Comparison with Previous Law*, by Joseph E. Cantor and L. Paige Whitaker.

CRS Report 97-1040, *Campaign Financing: Highlights and Chronology of Current Federal Law*, by Joseph E. Cantor.

CRS Report RS21693, *Campaign Finance Law: The Supreme Court Upholds Key Provisions of BCRA in* McConnell v. FEC, by L. Paige Whitaker.

CRS Report RS22272, *Campaign Finance Reform: Regulating Political Communications on the Internet*, by L. Paige Whitaker and Joseph E. Cantor.

CRS Report RL30669, *Campaign Finance Regulation Under the First Amendment:*
Buckley v. Valeo *and Its Supreme Court Progeny*, by L. Paige Whitaker.

CRS Report RL32954, *527 Political Organizations: Legislation in the 109th Congress*, by Joseph E. Cantor and Erika Lunder.

CRS Report RS21716, *Political Organizations Under Section 527 of the Internal Revenue Code*, by Erika Lunder.

CRS Report RL33377, *Tax-Exempt Organizations: Political Activity Restrictions and Disclosure Requirements*, by Erika Lunder.

CRS Report RL32786, *The Presidential Election Campaign Fund and Tax Checkoff: Background and Current Issues*, by Joseph E. Cantor.

REFERENCES

[1]   Soft money (discussed more fully in this report) generally refers to funds that are raised and spent outside the purview of federal election law regulation but which are intended to affect federal elections, at least indirectly.

[2]   Herbert E. Alexander, *Financing the 1976 Election* (Washington: Congressional Quarterly Press, 1979), p. 166.

[3]   Candice J. Nelson, "Spending in the 2000 Elections," in David B. Magleby (ed.), *Financing the 2000 Election* (Washington: Brookings Institution Press, 2002), p. 24.

[4]   Center for Responsive Politics, *'04 Elections Expected to Cost Nearly $4 Billion*, press release, Oct. 21, 2004, [http://www.opensecrets.org/pressreleases/2004/04 spending.asp], site visited July 21, 2006.

[5]   "100 Leaders by U.S. Advertising Spending," *Advertising Age*, Sept. 29, 1997, p. 14.

[6]   U.S. Congress, House Committee on House Administration, *527 Fairness Act of 2005*, report to accompany H.R. 1316, 109th Cong., 1st sess., H.Rept. 109-146 (Washington: GPO, 2005).

[7]   U.S. Congress, House Committee on House Administration, *527 Reform Act of 2005*, report to accompany H.R. 513, 109th Cong., 1st sess., H.Rept. 109-181 (Washington: GPO, 2005).

[8]   U.S. Congress, House Committee on Rules, *Providing for Consideration of H.R. 513, 527 Reform Act of 2005*, report to accompany H.Res. 755, 109th Cong., 2nd sess., H.Rept. 109-404 (Washington: GPO, 2006).

[9]   U.S. Congress, Senate Committee on Indian Affairs, *"Gimme Five": Investigation of Tribal Lobbying Matters*, final report, 109th Cong., 2nd sess., June 22, 2006; at [http://www.indian.senate.gov/public/_files/Report.pdf], site visited July 21, 2006.

[10]   U.S. Congress, House Committee of House Administration, *Online Freedom of Speech Act*, report to accompany H.R. 1606, 109th Cong., 2nd sess., H.Rept. 109-389 (Washington: GPO, 2006).

In: Economics, Political and Social Issues ...
Editor: Michelle L. Fergusson

ISBN: 978-1-61122-555-6
©2011 Nova Science Publishers, Inc.

THE ELECTORAL COLLEGE:
AN OVERVIEW AND ANALYSIS
OF REFORM PROPOSALS[*]

L. Paige Whitaker[1] and Thomas H. Neale[2]
[1]Legislative Attorney American Law Division
[2]Government and Finance Division

ABSTRACT

American voters elect the President and Vice President of the United States indirectly, through an arrangement known as the electoral college system. The electoral college system comprises a complex mosaic of constitutional provisions, state and federal laws, and political party rules and practices.

Although the electoral college system has delivered uncontested results in 46 out of 50 presidential elections since it assumed its present constitutional form in 1804, it has been the subject of persistent criticism and frequent proposals for reform. Reform advocates cite several problems with the current system, including a close or multi-candidate election can result in no electoral college majority, leading to a contingent election in Congress; the current system can result in the election of a President and Vice President who received a majority of electoral votes, but fewer popular votes, than their opponents; the formula for assignment of electoral votes is claimed to provide an unfair advantage for less populous states and does not account for population changes between censuses; and the winner-take-all system used by most states does not recognize the proportional strength of the losing major party, minor party, and independent candidates. On the other hand, defenders assert that the electoral college system is an integral and vital component of federalism, that it has a 92% record of non-controversial results, and that it promotes an ideologically and geographically broad two-party system. They maintain that repair of the electoral college system, rather than abolition, would eliminate any perceived defects while retaining its overall strengths. Proponents of presidential election reform generally advocate either completely eliminating the electoral college system, replacing it with direct popular election, or repairing perceived defects in the existing system. The direct election alternative would replace the electoral college with a single, nationwide count of popular votes. That is, the candidates winning a plurality of votes would be elected; most proposals provide for a runoff election if no candidates received a minimum of 40% of the popular vote. Electoral college reform proposals include (1) the district plan, awarding each state's two at-large electoral votes to the statewide popular vote winners, and one electoral vote to the winning candidates in each congressional district; (2) the proportional plan, awarding electoral votes in states in

---

[*] Excerpted from CRS Report RL30804 dated November 5, 2004.

direct proportion to the popular vote gained in the state by each candidate; and (3) the automatic plan, awarding all of each state's electoral votes directly on a winner-take-all basis to the statewide vote winners. Major reforms of the system can be effected only by constitutional amendment, a process that requires two-thirds approval by both houses of Congress, followed by ratification by three-fourths (38) of the states, usually within a period of seven years. For further information, please consult CRS Report RL32611, The Electoral College: How It Works in Contemporary Presidential Elections, by Thomas H. Neale, and CRS Report RL32612, The Electoral College: Reform Proposals in the 108th Congress, by Thomas H. Neale.

INTRODUCTION: THE ELECTORAL COLLEGE SYSTEM IN BRIEF

The President and the Vice President of the United States are elected indirectly by an institution known as the electoral college. The U.S. Constitution, in Article II, Section 1, Clause 2, as amended by the 12th Amendment, together with a series of implementing federal statutes, [1] provides the broad framework through which electors are appointed and by which they cast votes for the President and Vice President.

Origins of the Electoral College

The method of electing the President and Vice President was the subject of considerable discussion at the Constitutional Convention of 1787. While some delegates favored direct election of the President, others opposed it on the grounds that the people would lack sufficient knowledge of the character and qualifications of presidential and vice presidential candidates to make intelligent electoral decisions. Indirect election of the chief executive, by Congress, the legislatures of the states, or even by electors drawn by lot, enjoyed equally wide or greater support. Moreover, the delegates were reluctant to set uniform national voting standards for federal elections, believing this to be a prerogative of the states. Finally, delegates from less populous states feared that presidential elections might be dominated by a few large states [2]

The Convention settled on a compromise plan: the electoral college system [3]. It provides for the election of the President and Vice President by electors appointed by each state in a manner determined by its legislature. The electors then meet in their respective states to vote. Among its more attractive elements, it removed election from Congress, thus reinforcing separation of powers, acknowledged the federal principle by requiring electoral votes to be cast by state, and made it at least possible that some of the people would be able to vote, albeit indirectly, for the nation's chief executive. For instance, while the Constitution did not mandate popular participation in the selection of electors, neither did it prohibit it, leaving the question to state discretion. In fact, the states moved to provide for direct popular choice of electors by the voters beginning in the late 18th Century. By 1836, only South Carolina's legislature continued to select the state's presidential electors, and since the Civil War, electors have been popularly chosen in all states.

The 12th Amendment

The Constitution originally provided that each elector would cast two votes, for different persons, for President. The person winning the most electoral votes, provided the total was a majority of the total number of electors, would become President; the person winningthe next largest number would become Vice President. There was to be no separate vote for Vice President. This system understandably failed to envision the growth of political parties in the new republic, which would nominate unified tickets of nominees for President and Vice President [4]. The system worked as intended only for the two elections won by George Washington. By 1796, a nascent party system proposed competing candidacies of John Adams and Thomas Pinckney for the federalists, and Thomas Jefferson and Aaron Burr for the anti-federalists or republicans [5]. In each case, the second named candidate was clearly intended to be nominated for Vice President, but because electoral votes were undifferentiated, it was necessary for at least one elector on the winning team to cast a vote for a candidate other than the designated vice presidential nominee, in order to avoid a tie for the presidency.

When Adams and Jefferson again contested the election of 1800, with Burr again as Jefferson's designated vice presidential running mate, the republicans won a solid majority of electors, but failed to have one elector cast his vote for someone other than Jefferson. Jefferson and Burr were thus tied for the presidency, and the election went to the House of Representatives. The electoral college "misfire" threw the nation into its first, and one of its worst, constitutional crises, as federalists and dissident republicans plotted and caballed to deny Jefferson the presidency. The House required 35 deadlocked ballots before the impasse was broken and Jefferson was elected.

The shock of the 1800 election led directly to proposal of the 12th Amendment in 1803 and its speedy ratification in 1804. The system was revised so that electors would cast one vote each for President and Vice President, thus compartmentalizing the two contests. As before, the candidates who gained a majority of electoral votes would be elected President and Vice President; if there were no majority, the House of Representatives would elect the President and the Senate, the Vice President [6]. The 12th Amendment is the most recent constitutional change to the electoral college system.

Electoral Vote Allocation

The total number of electors comprising the electoral college equals the total combined congressional representation of each state (House plus Senate seats), plus three electors representing the District of Columbia [7]. After each decennial census, as the states gain or lose population and, consequently, gain or lose Representatives in the House, the number of electors assigned to each state may change to reflect the new apportionment. Presently, 538 electors are apportioned to the states and the District of Columbia based on: (1) 100 Senators; (2) 435 Representatives; and (3) 3 electors representing the District of Columbia. The current allocation of electoral votes by state, which remains in effect for the 2004 and 2008 presidential elections, follows.

Alabama	9	Kentucky	8	North Dakota	3
Alaska	3	Louisiana	9	Ohio	20
Arizona	10	Maine	4	Oklahoma	7
Arkansas	6	Maryland	10	Oregon	7
California	55	Massachusetts	12	Pennsylvania	21
Colorado	9	Michigan	17	Rhode Island	4
Connecticut	7	Minnesota	10	South Carolina	8
Delaware	3	Mississippi	6	South Dakota	3
District of Columbia	3	Missouri	11	Tennessee	11
Florida	27	Montana	3	Texas	34
Georgia	15	Nebraska	5	Utah	5
Hawaii	4	Nevada	5	Vermont	3
Idaho	4	New Hampshire	4	Virginia	13
Illinois	21	New Jersey	15	Washington	11
Indiana	11	New Mexico	5	West Virginia	5
Iowa	7	New York	31	Wisconsin	10
Kansas	6	North Carolina	15	Wyoming	3

Total: 538 electoral college votes; 270 votes constitute a majority.

State and District of Columbia Appointment of Electors

Under Article II, Section 1, Clause 2 of the Constitution, as amended by the 12th Amendment in 1804, each state is required to appoint electors in the manner directed by its state legislature. In 1961, the 23rd Amendment provided for three electors from the District of Columbia. The Commonwealth of Puerto Rico, Guam, the U.S. Virgin Islands, and American Samoa are not constitutionally entitled to electors, because they are not states.

Appointment Date and Meeting Date of Electors

Article II provides that Congress may determine the date for selecting electors and mandates that the date chosen be uniform throughout the United States [8] Accordingly, Congress, in 1845, enacted federal law establishing the Tuesday after the first Monday in November in every presidential election year as the general election date for the choice of electors [9] Voters also choose U.S. Senators and Representatives and a wide range of state and local officials at this time, which is generally known as national election day. Election day falls on November 2 in 2004. Article II further authorizes Congress to determine the date for the electors to meet and cast their ballots [10] and, hence, federal law provides that on the Monday after the second Wednesday in December following each presidential election, the electors meet at a place designated by each state to vote for the President and Vice President [11]. The electors will meet on December 13 in 2004.

Counting and Certification of Electoral Votes

After the electoral college delegations meet in their states and cast votes for President and Vice President, according to the 12th Amendment and applicable federal law, the certified results are transmitted to Congress and to other designated authorities [12] On January 6, following the election, the Senate and the House of Representatives, with the President of the Senate (the Vice President of the United States) serving as the presiding officer, meet in joint session to count the electoral votes [13]. The presidential and vice presidential candidates receiving a majority of the total number of electoral votes are then declared to be elected President and Vice President [14]

Objections to either individual electoral votes or state electoral vote totals may be made by Members of Congress at the joint electoral vote count session. Such objections must be presented in writing and signed by one Senator and one Representative to be in order. If a valid objection is raised, the session recesses; the Senate returns to its own chamber, and the two houses deliberate separately on the question. Debate is limited to two hours, and each Member is limited to five minutes speaking time on the floor. At the end of the two hours, the House and Senate vote separately on the objection, and the joint session reassembles. If both houses vote to sustain the objection, the electoral vote or votes in question are not counted [15]

Contingent Election [16]

If no candidates for president and/or vice president obtain a simple majority of the electoral votes, according to the 12th Amendment, the newly elected Congress conducts what is referred to as "contingent election": the House of Representatives chooses the President, and the Senate chooses the Vice President [17]. In the House, the President is elected from among the three candidates who received the most electoral votes, with each state (not including the District of Columbia) casting a single vote for President. In 1825, the only occasion on which contingent election was conducted under the 12th Amendment, a majority of votes within multi-memberstate House delegations was required to cast each state vote. In the Senate, the Vice President is elected from among the two candidates who received the most electoral votes, with each Senator casting a single vote. In the House, a majority of 26 or more state votes is required to elect; in the Senate, a majority of 51 or more votes is required to elect [18]

ELECTORAL COLLEGE CRITICISMS
AND CONTROVERSIES

Proponents of presidential election reform cite several shortcomings in the electoral college as justifications for reform or abolition of the current system.

Electoral College Deadlock: Contingent Election

As noted previously in this report, if the presidential and vice presidential candidates fail to receive a simple majority of the electoral college votes, the 12th Amendment provides that the House of Representatives chooses the President and the Senate chooses the Vice President by contingent election [19]. The election of the President by the House of Representatives has happened only once since ratification of the 12th Amendment. On February 9, 1825, the House elected John Quincy Adams as President over Andrew Jackson by a vote of 13 states to 7, with an additional 4 states voting for William H. Crawford [20]. Likewise, election of the Vice President by the Senate has occurred only once. On February 8, 1837, the Senate elected Richard Mentor Johnson as Vice President over Francis Granger by a vote of 33 to 16.

Some commentators have criticized the 1825 presidential contingent election, claiming it created a "constitutional crisis" because the House, according to Jackson supporters, appeared to select a President as part of a political "corrupt bargain" between Adams and Henry Clay, who had been disqualified from the contingent election process because he came in fourth, after Jackson, Adams, and Crawford, in electoral vote totals (recall that the 12th Amendment limits contingent election candidates to the top three electoral vote winners) [21]. Indeed, critics of the contingent election system generally argue that it further removes the choice of President and Vice President from the voters. That is, members of the House and Senate are free to exercise their choice without regard to the winners of the popular vote in their districts, states, or in the nation at large. Moreover, by effectively granting each state an equal vote, the contingent election system fails to account for great differences in population — and the number of votes cast — in the various states. On the other hand, others point out that the 1825 House contingent election resulted in a political backlash that ultimately facilitated Andrew Jackson's successful election four years later. As a result, supporters maintain, the contingent election system has demonstrated that it does function by channeling voter dissatisfaction into subsequent political action [22].

In evaluating the contingent election process, some commentators have suggested that any threshold inquiry requires assessing how often contingent election occurs. That is, if the results of a general election are frequently inconclusive, thereby increasing the likelihood of contingent election, then democratic criteria would require implementing reforms that "bring ... the people into the contingency process" [23]. Indeed, critics of the electoral college system caution that the presence of viable and well-funded third-party or independent presidential candidates, who may be able to garner electoral votes by carrying a plurality of the votes in statewide elections, increases the likelihood of contingent election. The most recent example of a third-party candidate winning electoral votes occurred in 1968 with the minor party candidacy of George C. Wallace, who won 46 electoral college votes in six southern states [24]. Furthermore, critics argue, an extremely close and/or contested presidential election, such as that of 2000, could likewise increase the probability of a contingent election determining the presidency [25]

It is also important to note, when considering the contingent election procedure, that the 12th Amendment does not provide for District of Columbia participation in a contingent election in the House and Senate. While the ratification of the 23rd Amendment in 1961 granted the District of Columbia three votes in the electoral college, the District of Columbia would be effectively disenfranchised in a contingent election, as it is not a state and sends neither Senators nor Representatives to Congress [26]

The Minority President: An Electoral College Misfire

Reform proponents also cite the fact that the current electoral college system can result in the election of a so-called "minority" president, i.e., one who wins a majority of electoral votes, but loses the popular vote. Indeed, in the 1800s, the electoral college system led to the election of three such "minority" presidents, namely, John Quincy Adams in 1824, Rutherford B. Hayes in 1876, and Benjamin Harrison in 1888. In 1824, John Quincy Adams received fewer popular and electoral votes than Andrew Jackson, his major opponent, but was chosen President by contingent election (as noted previously, both ran as Democratic Republicans). In 1876, Republican Rutherford B. Hayes received fewer popular votes than his opponent, Democrat Samuel J. Tilden, but won the election by one electoral vote. In the presidential election of 1888, Republican Benjamin Harrison received fewer popular votes than his major opponent, Democrat Grover Cleveland, but won the election with more electoral college votes [27]

Most recently, for the first time in 112 years, the very closely contested presidential election of 2000 resulted in a President and Vice President who received a majority of electoral votes, but fewer popular votes than the electoral vote runners-up. The popular vote results for that election were: Gore and Lieberman: 50,992,335; for Bush and Cheney: 50,455,156 [28].

A "Small State" Advantage in the Electoral College?

As the composition of the electoral college is based on state representation in Congress, some maintain it is inconsistent with the "one person, one vote" principle [29]. The Constitutional Convention of 1787 agreed on a compromise election plan whereby less populous states were assured of a minimum of three electoral votes, based on two Senators and one Representative, regardless of state population. Since state electoral college delegations are equal to the combined total of each state's Senate and House delegation, the composition of the electoral college thus appears to be weighted in favor of the small states. The two "senatorial" electors and the one "representative" elector to which each state is entitled may advantage smaller states over more populous ones because voters in the smaller states, in effect, cast more electoral votes per voter. For instance, in 2000, voters in Wyoming, the least populous state, cast 218,351 popular votes and three electoral votes for President, or one electoral vote for every 72,784 voters. By comparison, Californians cast 10,965,856 popular votes and 54 electoral votes, or one electoral vote for every 203,071 [30] As a result of this distribution of electoral votes among the states, it is argued that "small" states have an advantage over large states with regard to electoral vote allocation relative to their populations.

While it is generally recognized that small states possess an arithmetical advantage in the electoral college, some observers hold that, conversely, the most populous (large) states enjoy a "voting power" advantage, because they control the largest blocs of electoral votes. For example, voters in more populous states are better able to influence a larger bloc of electoral votes than those in less populous ones, because of the winner-take-all method of allocating electoral votes. Thus, to use the previously cited examples, a voter in Wyoming in 2000 could influence only three electoral votes, whereas a voter in California could influence 54 electoral votes in the same presidential election. According to this argument, known as the "voting power" theory, the electoral college system actually provides an *advantage* to the six most populous states (California, 55 electoral votes; Texas, 34 electoral votes; New York, 31 electoral votes; Florida, 27 electoral votes; and Pennsylvania and Illinois, 21 electoral votes each) and disadvantages all other states and the District of Columbia [31]

An Ethnic Voter Advantage in the Electoral College?

Another theory advanced during debate on electoral college reform centers on the asserted advantage enjoyed by ethnic minority voters. According to this argument, minority voters, e.g., Blacks, Hispanics, and Jews, tend to be concentrated in populous states with large electoral college delegations. By virtue of this concentration, they are presumably able to exert greater influence over the outcomes in such states because they tend to vote overwhelmingly for candidates whose policies they perceive to be favorable to their interests, and thus helping to gain these states and their electoral votes for the favored candidates. These arguments were advanced by the Presidents of the American Jewish Congress and the National Urban League as reasons for their support of the electoral college system during hearings before the Senate Judiciary Committee's Subcommittee on the Constitution as it considered a direct election amendment in 1979 [32]

Current Methods of Allocating Electoral Votes

Under Article II, Section 1, clause 2 of the Constitution, electors are appointed in "such Manner as the Legislature thereof may direct." In interpreting this constitutional provision, the Supreme Court, in the 1892 decision *McPherson v. Blacker*, [33] held that state legislatures have the exclusive power to direct the manner in which presidential and vice presidential electors are appointed. Moreover, aside from Congress having the authority, under this provision, to determine the time of choosing electors and the day on which they vote, the power of the several states is exclusive. Accordingly, a state legislature has the authority to determine, for example, whether its electors will be allocated according to the general ticket system or the district system [34]

The General Ticket or Winner-Take-All System
Presently, 48 states and the District of Columbia (Maine and Nebraska are the exceptions, having adopted the district system) have adopted the winner-take-all method of allocating electors. Under this method, the slate of electors, representing the presidential and vice presidential ticket that wins a plurality of votes in a state is elected on election day in November, and later meets in mid-December as the electoral college to cast all of the state's electoral ballots for the winning presidential and vice presidential candidates [35]

The District System
The states of Maine [36] and Nebraska [37] have adopted the congressional district method of allocating their electors. Under the district system, two electors are chosen on a statewide, at-large basis, and one is elected in each congressional district. Each voter casts a

single vote for President and Vice President, but the votes are counted twice. That is, they are first tallied on a statewide basis and the two at-large elector candidates winning the most votes (a plurality) are elected. The popular votes are also tallied in each district, where the district elector candidate winning the most votes is elected. Proponents of the district system claim that it more accurately reflects differences in support in various parts of a state and does not necessarily "disenfranchise" voters who picked the losing ticket.

The Decennial Census Problem

As the number of electors apportioned to each state is equal to the combined total of its Representatives and Senators in Congress, [38] that number is ultimately dependent upon each state's population. After each decennial census, the 435 Representatives are reapportioned to the states based on their respective populations: some states gain Representatives while other states lose them, in accordance with shifts in population [39]. Therefore, the gain or loss of a state's representation in the House of Representatives affects the size of its electoral college delegation.

The decennial reapportionment of electors fails, however, to account for significant population shifts that often occur during the course of a decade. Thus, the allocation of electoral votes in the 2000 election actually reflected 1990 population distribution among the states. For a period of time, therefore, this situation results in over-representation in the electoral college for some states and under-representation for others. Moreover, the 2000 reallocation of electoral votes came into effect only with the presidential election of 2004, when it was four years out of date. It will be even more less reflective of state population trends for the 2008 election.

The Faithless Elector

Although presidential electors are generally expected to support the candidates in whose name they are chosen, 26 states plus the District of Columbia go one step further and attempt to bind their electors [40] by one of several means: (1) requiring an oath or pledge or requiring the elector to cast a vote for the candidates of the political party he or she represents, all under penalty of law; [41] (2) requiring a pledge or affirmation of support, without any penalty of law; [42] (3) directing electors to support the winning ticket; [43] and (4) directing electors to vote for the candidates of the party they represent [44]. In addition, some state political parties require in their rules that candidates for elector make an affirmation or pledge to support the party nominees.

In its 1952 decision *Ray v. Blair,* the Supreme Court held that it does not violate the Constitution for a political party, exercising state-delegated authority, to require candidates for the office of elector to pledge to support the presidential and vice presidential nominees of the party's national convention [45]. Specifically, the Court found that excluding a candidate for elector because he or she refuses to pledge support for the party's nominees is a legitimate method of securing party candidates who are pledged to that party's philosophy and leadership. According to the Court, such exclusion is a valid exercise of a state's right under Article II, Section 1 of the Constitution, which provides for appointment of electors in such manner as the state legislature chooses [46]. In addition, the Court determined, state imposition of such pledge requirements does not violate the 12th Amendment, [47] nor does it deny equal protection and due process under the Fourteenth Amendment [48]

In *Ray v. Blair,* however, the Court did not rule on the constitutionality of state laws that bind electors, and left unsettled the question of whether elector pledges and penalties for failure to vote as pledged may be constitutionally enforceable. Indeed, in the view of many commentators, based on the text of the Constitution, its structure, and history, statutes binding electors and the pledges that electors make are likely to be constitutionally *unenforceable.* That is, according to some commentators, electors remain free agents who may vote for any candidate they choose [49]. Presidential election reform advocates argue that the free agency status of electors further diminishes democratic involvement in the presidential election process.

Historically, most electors have actually been faithful to the presidential and vice presidential tickets winning the most votes in their respective states. On a number of occasions, however, "faithless electors" have voted for presidential and vice presidential candidates other than those to whom they were pledged, and, in the election of 2000, an elector cast a blank ballot. Contemporary incidents of the "faithless elector," and the one elector who cast a blank ballot, have occurred in the following presidential election years:

1948 — Preston Parks, a Tennessee elector for Harry S. Truman (D), voted for Governor Strom Thurmond (States' Rights) of South Carolina;

1956 — W.F. Turner, an Alabama elector for Adlai E. Stevenson (D), voted for Walter E. Jones, a local judge;

1960 — Henry D. Irwin, an Oklahoma elector for Richard M. Nixon (R), voted for Senator Harry F. Byrd (D) of Virginia;

1968 — Lloyd W. Bailey, a North Carolina elector for Richard M. Nixon (R), voted for George C. Wallace of the American Independent Party;

1972 — Roger MacBride, a Virginia elector for Richard M. Nixon (R), voted for John Hospers of the Libertarian Party;

1976 — Mike Padden, a Washington elector for Gerald R. Ford (R), voted for Governor Ronald Reagan (R) of California;

1988 — Margaret Leach, a West Virginia elector for Michael Dukakis (D), voted for Senator Lloyd Bentsen (D) of Texas; [50] and

2000 — Barbara Lett-Simmons, a District of Columbia elector for Albert Gore, Jr. (D), cast a blank ballot.

Presidential Succession: Between Nomination and Inauguration [51]

During the multistage presidential election process, as set forth in the Constitution and applicable federal statutes, a number of contingencies could occur as a result of the death, disability, or resignation of a prospective president or vice president during the period between nomination and inauguration. Given that the rules of succession may be unclear during certain stages of the process, some commentators have argued that statutory or constitutional reforms are needed in order to provide clarification and avoid dispute.

The first contingency could occur if a candidate nominated by a political party were to die or resign prior to the November election. At that point in the process, since no one has been elected, there is not yet a question of succession under the Constitution or federal law [52]. As a result, the political parties have adopted rules to fill presidential and vice presidential nominee vacancies [53] For example, in 1972, the Democratic Party filled a vacancy when vice presidential nominee Senator Thomas Eagleton resigned at the end of July, and the Democratic National Committee met on August 8 to nominate R. Sargent Shriver as the new vice presidential candidate.

The second could occur if a presidential or vice presidential candidate were to die after election day in November, but before the electors meet to cast their votes in December. This contingency has been the subject of concerned speculation and unsettled debate. Some commentators suggest that the political parties, employing their rules providing for the filling of presidential and vice presidential vacancies, would designate a substitute nominee. Accordingly, the electors, who are predominantly party loyalists, would cast their votes for the substitute nominee, thereby producing the satisfactory result of the election of a candidate from the party that prevailed in November [54]. Other commentators, however, caution that a faithful elector, perhaps complying with a state statutorily mandated pledge, would feel compelled to vote for the decedent, even though precedent suggests that such votes might not be counted by Congress [55]. Due to the arguable indecisiveness of the process, many commentators have urged Congress to enact clarifying federal statutes to address this contingency [56]

Similarly, a third contingency, if a presidential or vice presidential nominee were to die after the electors cast their votes in December, but before Congress counts the electoral votes in January, has also been discussed with uncertainty. Legal scholars suggest that ascertaining the applicable succession process for this contingency turns on when a presidential or vice presidential designate, who has received a majority of the electoral votes, becomes certified "President-elect" or "Vice President-elect." Some commentators, who maintain that presidential and vice presidential designates are considered President and Vice President-elect at this stage in the process, conclude that the 20th Amendment provides clear rules of succession [57]. That is, if at the time the presidential term is set to begin (namely, January 20), the "President elect shall have died," the Vice President-elect shall become President on January 20 [58]. This point of view receives strong support from the language of the 1932 House committee report accompanying the 20th Amendment. Addressing the question of when there is a President elect, the report states:

> It will be noted that the committee uses the term "President elect" in its generally accepted sense, as meaning the person who has received the majority of electoral votes, or the person who has been chosen by the House of Representatives in the event that the election is thrown into the House. It is immaterial whether or not the votes have been counted, for the person becomes the President elect as soon as the votes are cast [59].

Others, however, are doubtful as to whether an official President and Vice President-elect exist prior to the electoral votes being counted and announced by Congress on January 6, and therefore contend that this is also a problematic contingency lacking clear constitutional or statutory direction [60]

The 20th and 25th Amendments clearly address the fourth contingency, whereby a president or vice president-elect dies after Congress counts and certifies the electoral votes, but prior to being inaugurated on January 20. If the President-elect were to die after certification, but before being inaugurated, the Vice President-elect would become President-elect, under the 20th Amendment [61]. The resulting vacancy in the Vice Presidency would then be filled after inauguration by the new President, subject to confirmation by a majority of both houses of Congress, under the 25th Amendment [62]. Likewise, according to the 25th Amendment, if the Vice President-elect were to die after certification, but before inauguration, the vacancy would be filled by the new President after the inauguration, subject to confirmation by a majority of both houses of Congress [63]

Independent and Third-Party versus Major Party Candidates

As it evolved politically and historically under state election laws and major political party rules, the electoral college system has generally favored the major political parties over independent and third-party candidacies. While major party presidential candidates are automatically placed on the ballot, independent and third-party presidential and vice presidential candidates must demonstrate certain levels of popular support to gain access to the November general election ballots in the states and the District of Columbia [64]. Often the independent candidates directly, and the minor parties generally by party committee, appoint or nominate their electors to state election officers to be voted on in the November general election. Moreover, the non-major party candidates must comply with diverse and often complicated nominating petition requirements for ballot positions in these 51 jurisdictions, which generally require a certain number of voter signatures in order to demonstrate that the candidate or party has a reasonable level of support [65].

Historically, no independent, minor party, or third-party presidential candidate has ever won the presidency, although three presidential candidates in past elections did win statewide elections and thus electoral college votes:

1948 — 39 electoral votes for Strom Thurmond (States' Rights Party);
1960 — 15 electoral votes for Harry F. Byrd ("unpledged" Democrat); and
1968 — 46 electoral votes for George C. Wallace (American Independent Party) [66]

Over the last 35 years, however, various federal court decisions have made it easier for minor party and independent candidates for President and Vice President to gain ballot access. For example, in 1968, the Supreme Court in *Williams v. Rhodes*, struck down on equal protection grounds an Ohio election law requiring a new political party to obtain petitions signed by qualified electors totaling15% of the number of ballots cast at the last gubernatorial election and to file them in early February of the presidential election year.

The Court found that Ohio's election laws relating to the nomination and election of presidential and vice presidential electors, which effectively limited general election ballot access to the two major political parties, taken as a whole, were invidiously discriminatory against minor party candidates in violation of the 14th Amendment equal protection clause [67]

Furthermore, during the 1976 presidential election, independent candidate Eugene J. McCarthy challenged the constitutionality of a number of state statutes providing ballot access procedures for independent presidential candidates, many of which the federal courts invalidated on equal protection grounds as being discriminatory to independent presidential candidates [68]. During the 1980 election, independent presidential candidate John B. Anderson still encountered similar obstacles to ballot access and, accordingly, he was able to successfully challenge state election laws in seven states: Florida, [69] Kentucky, [70] Maine, [71] Maryland, [72] New Mexico, [73] Ohio, [74] and North Carolina [75]. Generally, as a result of such challenges, it is now somewhat easier for independent and third party presidential candidates to gain ballot access in the states and the District of Columbia, and, therefore, to wage more competitive campaigns against major party presidential candidates.

ELECTORAL COLLEGE REFORM: THE FOX AND THE HEDGEHOG

The arguments raised in defense of the electoral college, and those arrayed in support of direct popular election, are arguably profoundly different. These basic differences are perhaps summed up in Isaiah Berlin's famous quotation of the Greek poet Archilochus: "the fox knows many things, but the hedgehog knows one big thing." The electoral college's defenders may be likened to Archilochus's fox in that they deploy a wide range of arguments and assertions in support of their position: original intent, tradition, federalism, minority voting power, state voting power (for both populous and less populated states), avoidance of post-election controversies, support of the two-party system, political moderation, and others. Proponents of the direct election alternative more closely resemble the hedgehog in that they focus largely, on the democratic principle of majority rule. "Many things" versus "one big thing": which is more likely to prevail?

History

Since the adoption of the Constitution, the electoral college has been the subject of discussion and controversy. The 12th Amendment, (proposed by Congress on December 9, 1803, and ratified by three-fourths of the several states on July 27, 1804) which prescribes the current electoral voting procedures, has been the only major reform of the electoral college. Since then, in almost every session of Congress, resolutions have been introduced proposing electoral college reform. Indeed, more proposed constitutional amendments have been introduced in Congress regarding electoral college reform than on any other subject. Between 1889 and 2004, approximately 595 such amendments were proposed [76] Generally, most of these resolutions had minimal legislative activity. For some, however, hearings were held and legislative activity occurred, but there was insufficient legislative support to obtain the two-thirds votes of both houses of Congress necessary for approval of a constitutional amendment under Article V [77]

The attempt in Congress that came closest to success occurred after the 1968 presidential election when American Independent party candidate George Wallace won 46 electoral votes, generating concern about the prospect of contingent election or the trading of electoral votes in return for policy concessions. In the 91st Congress (1969-1970), H.J.Res. 681, introduced by Representative Emanuel Celler, proposed to abolish the electoral college and provide for the direct popular election of the President and the Vice President, with a runoff requirement between the two presidential candidates with the highest votes if a 40% margin of the vote was not obtained. This resolution passed the House on September 18, 1969, by a vote of 338-70, but failed to pass the Senate in 1970 due to a filibuster [78]

Likewise, congressional interest increased after the close presidential election in 1976, in which Democratic candidate Jimmy Carter defeated Republican President Gerald R. Ford by a 50.1% popular vote margin and by 297 electoral votes to Ford's 48.0% of the popular vote and 240 electoral votes, with 270 needed to win [79] S.J.Res. 28, introduced by Senator Birch Bayh in the 96th Congress (1979-1980), proposed direct popular election but failed of passage by a Senate vote of 51-48 in 1979 [80] Given the results of the vote, the leadership of the House of Representatives decided not to bring the House version of the proposal to the floor in the 96th Congress. No proposal concerning electoral college reform has come to the floor of either house since that time.

Proposals to reform the electoral college in recent Congresses generally fall into two categories: those that would eliminate the electoral college system entirely, replacing it with direct popular election, and those that seek to repair perceived defects in the existing arrangement. These proposals are examined below.

The Direct Election Plan: Elimination of the Electoral College

In recent decades, the most widely offered proposal to reform the present method of electing the President and Vice President has been the direct election plan. Under this plan, the electoral college would be abolished, and the President and Vice President would be elected directly by popular vote. Most direct election proposals would require that the winning candidates receive at least 40% of the votes cast, and provide for a runoff election between the two presidential and vice presidential tickets receiving the greatest number of popular votes if no candidates receive the requisite percentage [81]

Some direct election plans, however, would not require candidates to win a specific percentage of the vote in order to be elected: more votes, or a plurality, would suffice. Others have proposed that in the event the 40% threshold is not attained, then Congress, meeting in joint session and voting per capita (rather than by states as under current contingent election procedures), would elect the President and Vice President.

Pro and Con Arguments

Proponents of direct election, as noted earlier, may be likened to Archilochus's foxes. They make the argument that their proposal is simple and democratic: the candidates winning the most popular votes would always be elected. Direct election would thus eliminate the possibility of a "minority" President and Vice President, because the candidate winning the most popular votes would always prevail. Further, it would eliminate what they characterize as an even greater potential for distortion of the public will by abolishing the contingent election process. In addition, proponents note that the direct election plan would give every vote equal weight, regardless of the state in which it was cast. It is further noted that the direct election plan would reduce the complications that currently could arise in the event of a presidential candidate's death between election day and the date that the electoral college meets, since the winning candidates would become President and Vice President-elect as soon as the results were certified.

Opponents, Archlochus's foxes, offer many arguments by comparison. They assert that the direct election plan would weaken the present two-party system, and result in the growth of minor parties, third parties, and new parties. Today's two major parties are relatively broadly based both ideologically and geographically, and conduct nationwide presidential campaigns in order to assemble the requisite majority of 270 electoral votes. Similarly, the need to forge national coalitions having a wide appeal has been a contributing factor to the comparative moderation of the two major parties and the governmental stability enjoyed by the nation under the present system. Moreover, it is argued, the growth or emergence of more narrowly focused parties could have a divisive effect on national politics, and result in governance by less stable coalitions similar to those in some parliamentary democracies.

Opponents also contend that a direct election plan would weaken the influence both the smallest and most populous populated states are said to enjoy under the present system, since direct popular election would eliminate the role of states as election units in favor of the single nationwide count under direct presidential election. Thus, each vote would be counted equally under the one person, one vote principle, regardless of the population size of the state in which it was cast [82]. Finally, they question the 40% runoff requirement included in most direct election proposals: how can the concept of a "plurality" President, who may have gained well under half the votes, be justifiable if the chief aim of direct popular election is to elect a President who enjoys a majority of votes?

Other critics of direct election contend that the allocation of electoral votes is a vital component of our federal system. The federal nature of the electoral college system is a positive good, according to its defenders. They assert that the founders of the Constitution intended the states to play an important role in the presidential elections and that the electoral college system provides for a federal election of the President that is no less legitimate than the system of allocating equal state representation in the Senate. Direct popular election, they claim, would be a serious blow to federalism in the United States.

Finally, they note that, as was demonstrated in the presidential election of 2000, close results in a single state in a close election are likely to be bitterly contested. Under direct election, they claim, every close contest in the future could resemble the post-election struggles in 2000, but on a nationwide basis, as both parties would seek to gain every vote. Such rancorous disputes, they argue, could have profound negative effects on political comity in the nation, and possibly even affect the political stability of the federal government.

Electoral College Reform

In contrast to direct popular election, the three proposals described in this section would retain the electoral college, but would repair perceived defects in the existing system. One characteristic shared by all three is the elimination of electors as individual actors in the process. Electoral votes would remain, but they would be awarded directly to candidates. The asserted advantage of this element in these reform plans is that it would eliminate the potential for faithless electors.

The District Plan

The district plan preserves the electoral college method of electing the President and Vice President, with each state choosing a number of electors equal to the combined total of its Senate and House of Representatives delegations. It would, however, eliminate the present general ticket or winner-take-all procedure of allotting a state's entire electoral vote to the presidential and vice presidential candidates winning the statewide vote. Instead, one elector would be chosen by the voters for each congressional district, while an additional two, representing the two "senatorial" electors allocated to each state regardless of population, would be chosen by the voters at large. This plan, which could be adopted by any state, under its power to appoint electors in Article II, Section 1, clause 2 of the Constitution, is currently used by Maine [83] and Nebraska, as noted earlier in this report [84]. Under the district plan, the presidential and vice presidential candidates winning a simple majority of the electoral votes would be elected.

Most district plan proposals provide that, in case of an electoral college tie, the candidates having the plurality of the district electoral votes nationwide — excluding the at-large electoral votes assigned to each state for Senators — would be declared the winners. If the electoral vote count still failed to produce a winner, most proposals advocating the district plan would require the Senate and House of Representatives to meet in joint session to elect the President and Vice President by majority vote, with each Member having one vote, from the three candidate tickets winning the most electoral votes.

On the national level, the district system would have produced somewhat different national electoral college results if it had been in effect in the presidential election of 2000. The blank electoral vote cast in 2000 is not retained, since the district plan would eliminate the office of elector, thus eliminating the possibility of casting a blank vote. Totals for the general ticket and district methods are provided below [85]:

Candidate	General Ticket System	District System
Bush (R)	271	288
Gore (D)	266	250
Blank/Other	1	0
Total	538	538

An example of how the district system would operate in one state of average population, Missouri, with 11 electoral votes, as compared with the winner-take-all or general ticket system, follows [86]. In 2000, under the existing general ticket system, Republican candidates Bush and Cheney won a majority of popular votes in Missouri, and were awarded all 11 of its electoral votes, while Democratic candidates Gore and Lieberman received none. Under the district system, Bush and Cheney would have received a total of eight electoral votes in Missouri in the 2000 election: one for each of the six congressional districts where they received a plurality of popular votes, and two for having won the statewide popular vote. Gore and Lieberman would have won three electoral votes, one for the three congressional districts where they received a popular vote majority [87].

Proponents of the district plan assert that it would more accurately reflect the popular vote results for presidential and vice presidential candidates than the present electoral college method. Moreover, proponents note, by preserving the electoral college, the district plan would not deprive small or sparsely populated states of certain advantages under the present system. That is, each state would still be allocated at least three electoral votes, correlating to its two Senators and its one Representative, regardless of the size of the state's population. The also maintain that in states dominated by one political party, the district plan might also provide an incentive for greater voter participation and an invigoration of the two-party system in presidential elections because it might be possible for the less dominant political party's candidates to carry certain congressional districts [88] Finally, proponents argue that the district plan reflects political diversity within different regions of states, while still providing a two-vote bonus for statewide vote winners.

On the other hand, opponents of the district plan contend that it does not go far enough in reforming the present electoral college method, because the weight of each vote in a small state would still be greater than the weight of a vote in a more populous state. In addition, they note, the district plan would continue to allow the possibility of electing "minority" Presidents and Vice Presidents, who won the electoral vote while losing the popular vote. Some opponents of the district plan further argue that it has the potential to fragment the electoral vote among marginal candidates who may manage to capture a few districts. This, they claim, might actually weaken the present two-party system by encouraging parties that cater to narrow geographical interests or ideological interests that may be concentrated in certain areas.

The Proportional Plan
The proportional plan retains electoral votes, but awards the votes in each state based on the percentage of votes received in each state (regardless of the districts from which the voters come) by the competing candidates. In the interests of fairness and accuracy, most proportional plans divide whole electoral votes into thousandths of votes, that is, to the third decimal point. This variation is known as the strict proportional plan. Another version, the rounded proportional plan, would provide some form of rounding to retain whole electoral votes [89].

Under most proposals advocating the proportional plan, the presidential and vice presidential candidates receiving a simple majority of the electoral vote, or a plurality of at least 40% of the electoral votes, would be elected. Should presidential and vice presidential candidates fail to receive the percentage, most proportional plan proposals provide that the Senate and the House of Representatives would meet and vote in joint session to choose the President and the Vice President from the candidates having the two highest numbers of electoral votes.

Nationwide electoral vote tallies for the presidential election of 2000 under the general ticket and proportional systems are provided below [90].

Candidate	General Ticket System	Proportional System: Strict/Rounded
Bush (R)	271	259.185/263
Gore (D)	267	258.227/269
Blank/Other	1	20.542/6
Total	538	538.004/538

Again using Missouri as an example, in 2000, a strict proportional plan would have awarded 5.547 Missouri electoral votes to Bush/Cheney, 5.179 to Gore/Lieberman, 0.180 to Nader/LaDuke, and 0.095 to other candidates. A rounded proportional plan of the type proposed for Colorado in the 2004 would have yielded six electoral votes for Bush/Cheney, and five for Gore/Lieberman. Nader/LaDuke and other minor party and independent candidates would not have gained sufficient popular votes to qualify for electoral votes under this plan [91]

Proponents of the proportional plan argue that this plan comes the closest of any of the other plans to electing the President and Vice President by popular vote while still preserving each state's electoral college strength. They also note that the proportional plan would make it more unlikely that "minority" presidents — those receiving more electoral votes than popular votes under the present system — would be elected. Proponents also argue that the proportional plan, by eliminating the present winner-take-all system, would give weight to the losing candidates by awarding them electoral votes in proportion to the number of votes they obtained. They also suggest that presidential campaigns would become more national in scope, with candidates gearing their efforts to nationwide popular and electoral vote totals, rather than concentrating on electoral vote-rich populous states.

Opponents of the proportional plan argue that it could undermine and eventually eliminate the present two-party system by making it easier for minor parties, new parties, and independent candidates to compete in the presidential elections by being able to win electoral votes without having to win statewide elections to do so. Further, opponents argue, the states would generally have less importance as units, since the winner-take-all aspect would be eliminated [92]. In close elections, it is asserted, the proportional plan would lead to more frequent instances of electoral vote deadlock, in which neither candidate would gain the necessary majority of electoral votes, if this threshold were retained. Relatedly, opponents question the 40% plurality threshold. If the point of the presidential election is to ascertain the people's choice, should not the winning candidate be required to gain at least a majority (50%) of electoral votes in order to avoid a runoff election or election in Congress?

The Automatic Plan

The automatic plan would amend the present system by abolishing the office of presidential elector and by allocating state electoral votes on an automatic winner-take-all basis to the candidates receiving the highest number of popular votes in a state. Most versions of the automatic plan provide some form of contingent election in Congress in the event no candidate receives a majority of electoral votes. Of the three principal proposals to reform the electoral college, this proposal would result in the least change from the present system of electing the President and the Vice President.

The only change to electoral vote totals in 2000 under the automatic plan would have been elimination of the blank vote cast by a District of Columbia elector. Thus, the tally would have been 271 electoral votes for Bush/Cheney and 267 (as opposed to 266) for Gore/Lieberman.

Proponents of the automatic plan argue that it would maintain the present electoral college system's balance between national and state powers and between large and small states. Proponents note that the automatic plan would eliminate the possibility of the "faithless elector." Furthermore, the automatic plan would preserve the present two-major party system under a state-by-state, winner-take-all method of allotting electoral votes.

Under the present system, minor parties, new parties, and independent candidates have not fared very well in presidential elections, probably due to, *inter alia,* problems such as ballot access procedures, public financing in the general election, and the lack of name recognition and grass-roots organization in comparison to those of the established major parties.

Opponents of the automatic plan argue that it perpetuates many of the perceived inequities inherent in the present electoral college system of electing the President and the Vice President. Opponents also note that under the automatic plan, it would still be possible to elect a "minority" President and Vice President — those receiving more electoral votes than popular votes under the present system [93]. Moreover, it presents the perceived problem that Congress and not the people could still decide the presidency and the vice presidency when a majority of the electoral votes is not obtained.

Reform Proposals Following the 2000 Presidential Election

In the presidential election of 2000, the electoral college system resulted in a President and Vice President who received more electoral votes, but fewer popular votes, than the electoral vote runners-up for the first time in 112 years, a classic case of what some observers identify as an electoral college "misfire." Following the bitterly contested aftermath of this election, and its extraordinarily close electoral vote margin, it was anticipated that Congress would revisit the question of electoral college reform. Reform proposals were duly introduced, but no action was taken during the 107th Congress, nor has any been taken to date on relevant proposals introduced in the 108th Congress [94]. Congressional attention focused instead on proposals for election administration reform, resulting in the passage of P.L. 107-252, the Help America Vote Act (HAVA), in 2002. This act expanded federal involvement in election administration, traditionally a state responsibility, by setting new requirements for improvements in voting systems, providing grants to states to improve voting administration, and establishing the federal Election Administration Commission to administer these programs and monitor state compliance with HAVA's provisions [95]

CONCLUDING OBSERVATIONS: PROSPECTS FOR REFORM

Despite various criticisms and controversies, the electoral college system has endured since the first presidential elections in 1789. Over the past two centuries, it has evolved through the ratification of one constitutional amendment, the 12th, the passage of various federal and state laws, and changing political party practices and traditions. It has delivered the presidency to the popular and electoral vote winners in 46 out of 51 elections since it became operational in 1804, and even in the case of "misfires," that is, cases in which a candidate was elected with a majority of electoral votes but a minority of popular votes, the results it has delivered have been widely, if not universally, accepted as legitimate [96]

Interest in changing or abolishing the electoral college has arguably been dependent, at least in recent decades, on how accurately it has appeared to ratify the voters' choice. During periods when the system seemed to be performing well, there was relatively little impetus for reform, although, as noted earlier, there was nearly always a steady stream of proposals for change.

Following close elections in 1960, 1968, and 1976, however, proposed constitutional amendments providing for direct election were actively considered in the House of Representatives and the Senate in the 91st through 96th Congresses; during these periods of heightened interest, a direct popular election amendment was approved in the House in 1969, [97] and debated, but not approved, in the Senate in 1979 [98]. In neither of these instances, however, did the proposals achieve the momentum necessary to hurdle the difficult challenge faced by all would-be constitutional amendments: approval by two-thirds of the Members of both chambers present and voting, followed by approval in three-fourths of the states.

During the ensuing two decades, the electoral college delivered substantial majorities of electoral votes to the popular vote winners in every presidential election. Once again, the system functioned as its defenders predicted, notwithstanding occasional concerns over close elections and the potential impact of independent or third party candidates, and there was little impetus for change during this period. Curiously, perhaps, the bitterly contested presidential election of 2000, which many observers characterized as an electoral college "misfire," failed to galvanize support for direct popular election or electoral college reform. Anger over the election's outcome seemed more intensely directed against voting system inadequacies and failures in Florida, and by extension, nationwide, that had thrust the election results into uncertainty and contention for over a month. As noted earlier, the Help America Vote Act of 2002, which sought to remedy deficiencies in elections administration technology and procedures, owed its passage largely to these controversies.

The first, and perhaps largest single factor in the electoral college reform equation is Article V of the Constitution, which provides for its amendment, among other things. As noted previously in this report, the founders intentionally made it difficult to alter the nation's fundamental charter, establishing what is the only double requirement of super majorities in the document: a proposed amendment must win proposed by two thirds majorities in both houses of Congress, and must then be approved by three fourths of the states. In practice, the hurdle has been raised even higher, since it is customary to attach a seven-year deadline for ratification of proposed amendments.

Second, most successful attempts to change the Constitution have depended on the stimulus of sudden great events, or have benefitted from the "ripeness" of an idea that had been before the public for many years. Sometimes both factors have contributed to the successful passage and ratification of an amendment. Another common element in successful amendments has generally been a widespread public awareness of a problem to be addressed and a broad national consensus that reform was necessary and desirable. Moreover, such an awareness has usually extended well beyond Congress into the nation at large.

For instance, the only previous constitutional revision of the electoral college, the 12th Amendment, was spurred by a profound constitutional crisis, the events surrounding the presidential election of 1800 [99]. Although "public opinion" in its modern sense can scarcely be said to have existed at the time, America's political elites had been strongly influenced by the election and its aftermath. In this case, Congress acted with considerable dispatch for the era, proposing an amendment less than two years later, in December, 1803. The states moved even more quickly to approve the proposal: the 12th Amendment's ratification process was completed in either June or July of 1804, depending on whether the legislature of New Hampshire or Tennessee is considered to have cast the decisive vote [100]

More recently, proposal and ratification of the 25th and 26th Amendments was facilitated by trends and developments representative of those cited above. The 25th Amendment, which revamped presidential succession procedures, emerged almost directly from the events surrounding the assassination of President John F. Kennedy in 1963, which incontestably stunned and galvanized both Congress and the nation. The vice presidency was vacant for 14 months, with the designated presidential successors during this period being the 71-year-old Speaker of the House of Representatives, John W. McCormack, and the 86-year-old President Pro Tempore of the Senate, Carl F. Hayden. The obvious need for constitutional procedures to replace a Vice President who had succeeded to the presidency, or left office for some other reason, coupled with the shock following President Kennedy's death, led to a broad national consensus for change, both in Congress and among the public. An amendment was proposed to the states on July 6, 1965, and was declared to have been ratified less than 19 months later, on February 23, 1967.

The 26th Amendment, which effectively set 18 as voting age in the United States, had been under consideration in various proposals beginning in the 1940s, and throughout the post-war era, a public consensus favorable to lowering the voting age began to emerge. It is arguable, however, that the great upsurge in political involvement among young people that began with President Kennedy's summons to public service in the early 1960s, and continued, albeit down many different roads, during the Vietnam War and the general cultural upheaval that characterized the latter part of the 1960s, also strongly contributed to the amendment's success. The 26th Amendment was proposed by Congress on March 23, 1971, and was declared to have been ratified less than four months later, on July 10 of the same year.

Notwithstanding the results of the presidential election of 2000, proposals for direct popular election or reform of the electoral college in the subsequent 107th and 108th Congresses never benefitted from a comparable sense of urgency or high level of public awareness and consensus on the need for reform.

Finally, the success of amendments has often depended on the support of congressional leaders who helped guide such proposals to passage by Congress, and proposal to the states. For instance, both the 25th and 26th Amendments enjoyed the approval and very active support of House Judiciary Committee Chairman Emmanuel Celler and Senator Birch Bayh, chairman of the Senate Judiciary Committee's Subcommittee on the Constitution. The cause of electoral college reform has not had such champions since Senator Bayh guided a direct election proposal to the Senate floor in 1979.

Given the high hurdles faced by proposed constitutional amendments, it is arguable that the electoral college system will likely remain in place unless or until its alleged failings become so compelling that large concurrent majorities in the public, the Congress, and the states, are prepared to undertake its reform or abolition.

REFERENCES

[1]   The implementing statutes are codified at 3 U.S.C. §§ 1-17.

[2]   CONGRESSIONAL QUARTERLY,INC.,PRESIDENTIAL ELECTIONS SINCE 1789 1 (2d ed. 1980).

[3]   R. Gordon Hoxie, *Alexander Hamilton and the Electoral System Revisited,* 18 Presidential Studies Q. 717-20 (1987)(arguing that the electoral college represented a

compromise between those advocating direct election of the President and those advocating that state or federal representatives should elect the President).

[4]   The founders feared and deprecated the whole idea of competing political factions, or parties, which they associated with what they viewed as the worst excesses of the British system. In the electoral college, they sought, perhaps ingenuously, to craft a system where electors chosen by, or simplyin touch with, the people would cast non-politically motivated votes for the best candidates for President.

[5]   Adams was elected President, but too many federalist electors cast their second votes for candidates other than Pinckney, so Jefferson came in second in the total number of electoral votes, and was thus elected Vice President. This revealed another unintended consequence of the original constitutional provisions, since Adams and Jefferson, now President and Vice President, were bitter political enemies.

[6]   For additional information on this process, known as contingent election, please consult CRS Report RS20300, *Election of the President and Vice President by Congress: Contingent Election*, by Thomas H. Neale.

[7]   U.S. CONST. amend. XXIII.

[8]   U.S. CONST. art. II, § 1, cl. 3.

[9]   3 U.S.C. § 1. ("The electors of President and Vice President shall be appointed, in eachState, on the Tuesday next after the first Monday in November, in every fourth year succeeding every election of a President and Vice President.") June 25, 1948, ch. 644, 62 Stat. 672.

[10] U.S. CONST. art. II, § 1, cl. 3.

[11] 2 U.S.C. § 7.

[12] 3 U.S.C. §§ 9, 10, 11.

[13] 3 U.S.C. § 15.

[14] *Id.*

[15] For further discussion regarding the electoral vote count session and the objection process, please consult CRS Congressional Distribution Memorandum, *Overview of Electoral College Procedure and the Role of Congress*, by Jack Maskell, available from the author to Members of Congress and congressional staff.

[16] For further discussion regarding the contingent election process, please consult CRS Report RS20300, *Election of the President and Vice President: Contingent Election*, by Thomas H. Neale.

[17] U.S. CONST. amend. XII.

[18] *Id.*

[19] U.S. CONST. amend. XII.

[20] The 1824 presidential election was contested by four candidates: Jackson, who won a plurality of popular and electoral votes, Adams, Crawford, and Henry Clay, all of whom were Democratic Republicans. In contrast, there was only one vice presidential candidate in the election, John C. Calhoun.

[21] Jackson supporters asserted that Adams agreed to nominate Clay for Secretary of State, in return for Clay's support in the contingent election process. William Josephson and Beverly J. Ross, *Repairing the Electoral College,* 22 J. Legis. 145, 149 (1996).

[22] *Id.*

[23] Judith Vairo Best, The Case Against Direct Election of the President, A Defense of the Electoral College 88-89 (1971). The commentator notes, however, that since ratification

of the 12th Amendment, only one contingent election has been necessary and, further, since gradual adoption by the states of the winner-take-all or general ticket system of awarding electoral votes, discussed *infra,* there have been no contingent elections.

[24] *See* discussion of independent and third-party candidacies *infra* pp. 11-13.

[25] For discussion of electoral college procedure if, for example, as the result of a closely contested election, two lists of electors from the same state are presented to the Congress, see CRS Congressional Distribution Memorandum, *Overview of Electoral College Procedure and the Role of Congress*, by Jack Maskell and Paul S. Rundquist , available to Members of Congress and staff from the authors.

[26] "But in choosing the President, the votes shall be taken by *states*" and "the Senate shall choose the Vice-President." U.S. CONST. amend. XII (emphasis added).

[27] NOMINATION AND ELECTION OF THE PRESIDENT AND VICE PRESIDENT, S. Doc. 106-16 at 409 (2000). Some historians suggest that, due to the prevalence of election fraud by both parties, it is difficult to determine which candidate actually won more votes in the 1876 and 1888 contests.

[28] *Congressional Quarterly's Guide to U.S. Elections*, 4th ed. (Washington: CQ Press, 2001), vol. 1, p. 688.

[29] The one person, one vote principle was established by the U.S. Supreme Court in congressional and state legislative reapportionment and redistricting cases in order to insure equal representation for equal numbers of people. *See, e.g., Reynolds v. Sims,* 377 U.S. 533, 568 (1964) and *Wesberry v. Sanders, 376* U.S. 1, 7-18 (1964).

[30] *Congressional Quarterly's Guide to U.S. Elections*, 4th ed., vol. 1, p. 688.

[31] Lawrence D. Longley and James D. Dana, Jr., *The Biases of the Electoral College in the 1990s,* 25 Polity 123-45 (1992).

[32] U.S. Congress, Senate, Committee on the Judiciary, Subcommittee on the Constitution, *Direct Election of the President and Vice President of the United States*, hearings on S.J.Res. 28, 96th Cong., 1st sess, Mar. 27, 30 Apr. 3, 9, 1979 (Washington: GPO, 1979), pp. 163-219.

[33] 146 U.S. 1 (1892).

[34] *Id.* at 35-36.

[35] NOMINATION AND ELECTION OF THE PRESIDENT AND VICE PRESIDENT, S. Doc. 106-16 at 313-94 (2000).

[36] ME. REV. STAT. ANN. tit. 21, § 805.

[37] NEB. REV. STAT. § 32-548.

[38] U.S. CONST. art. II, § 1, cl. 2.

[39] U.S. CONST. art. I, § 2, cl. 3.

[40] For a summary of the state and District of Columbia statutes binding electors votes, *see,* U.S. LIBRARY OF CONGRESS, CONGRESSIONAL RESEARCH SERVICE, STATE STATUTES BINDING ELECTORS'VOTES IN THE ELECTORAL COLLEGE (2000), Memorandum by L. PaigeWhitaker.

[41] New Mexico, North Carolina, Oklahoma, South Carolina, and Washington.

[42] District of Columbia, Florida, Massachusetts, Mississippi, and Oregon.

[43] Alabama, Alaska, Colorado, Maine, Maryland, Montana, Nebraska, Nevada, Vermont, and Wyoming.

[44] California, Connecticut, Hawaii, Michigan, Ohio, Virginia, and Wisconsin.

[45] 343 U.S. 214, 228-231 (1952).

[46] *Id.* at 225-27.

[47] *Id.* at 228-31.

[48] *Id.* at 226, n.14 (distinguishing *Nixon v. Herndon,* 273 U.S. 536 (1927)).

[49] *See, e.g.,* LAWRENCE D. LONGLEY AND NEAL R. PEIRCE, THE ELECTORAL COLLEGE PRIMER 109 (1996)(remarking that "statutes binding electors, or pledges that theymaygive, are unenforceable"); Akhil Reed Amar, *Presidents, Vice Presidents, and Death: Closing the Constitution's Succession Gap,* 48 Ark. L. Rev. 215, 230 (1995)("Notwithstanding some language in *Ray v. Blair,*" Professor Amar acknowledges "real doubts about state laws that attempt to force electors to take legally binding pledges" and further notes that "even if a legal pledge can be required, it is far from clear that any legal sanction could be imposed in the event of a subsequent violation of that pledge"); *But see* Beverly J. Ross and William Josephson, *The Electoral College and the Popular Vote,* 12 J.L. and Politics 665, 745 (1996)(concluding that "state statute-based direct or party pledge binding legislation is valid and should be enforceable.")

[50] Ms. Leach effectively reversed the order of her vote, choosing Senator Bentsen, the vice presidential nominee in 1988, for President, and Governor Dukakis, the presidential nominee, for Vice President.

[51] For additional information, see CRS Archived Report 96-855, *Major Party Candidates for President and Vice President: How Vacancies Are Filled,* by Thomas H. Neale; U.S. LIBRARY OF CONGRESS, CONGRESSIONAL RESEARCH SERVICE, PRESIDENTIAL AND VICE PRESIDENTIAL SUCCESSION: FROM NOMINATION THROUGH INAUGURATION (2000), Memorandum by L. Paige Whitaker.

[52] *See* WALTER BERNS,AFTER THE PEOPLE VOTE:AGUIDE TO THE ELECTORAL COLLEGE 92-93 (Walter Berns ed., American Enterprise Institute Press, 2d ed. 1992).

[53] *See* The Republican National Committee Rules, 2000, Rule No. 9; The Charter and By Laws of the Democratic Party of the U.S., Sept. 25, 1999, Art. III, § 1(c).

[54] *Presidential Succession Between the Popular Election and the Inauguration: Hearing Before the Subcomm. on the Constitution of the Senate Comm. on the Judiciary,* 103d Cong., 2d Sess. 12-13 (1994) [hereinafter *Hearing*] (prepared statement of Walter Dellinger on behalf of the Office of Senate Legal Counsel U.S. Dept. of Justice).

[55] Akhil Reed Amar, *Presidents, Vice Presidents, and Death: Closing the Constitution's Succession Gap,* 48 Ark. L. Rev. 215 (1995), *reprinted in Hearing,* at 217-19 (prepared statement of Akhil Reed Amar, Southmayd Professor, Yale Law School)(advocating that Congress enact federal law clearly providing a succession process in order to address this "time bomb ticking away in our Constitution").

[56] *See, e.g., Id.*

[57] *Hearing, supra* note 47, at 11 (prepared statement of Walter Dellinger).

[58] U.S. CONST. amend. XX, § 3, cl. 1.

[59] U.S. Congress, House *Proposing an Amendment to the Constitution of the United States*, report to accompany S.J.Res. 14, 72nd Cong., 1st sess., Rept. 345 (Washington? GPO?: 1932), p. 6.

[60] *Hearing, supra* note 47, at 39 (prepared statement of Walter Berns, John M. Olin University Professor, Georgetown University; Adjunct Scholar, American Enterprise Institute).

[61] U.S. CONST. amend. XX, § 3, cl. 1.

[62] U.S. CONST. amend. XXV, § 2.

[63] *Id.*

[64] *See* NOMINATION AND ELECTION OF THE PRESIDENT AND VICE PRESIDENT, S. Doc. 106-16, at 310-94 (2000).

[65] *See id.* Further adding to the major party advantage in presidential elections, the federal public financing provisions facilitate the acquisition of public campaign funds for major party presidential candidates, while independent, minor party, and third-party candidates must demonstrate at least a 5% voter support in order to receive any public funds, which are then provided four years later. *See generally,* 26 U.S.C. §§ 9001-9012 (general election presidential public financing provisions); 26 U.S.C. § 9004(a)(2)(A)(B),(3)(eligibility of minor party candidates to receive public funds). While it was argued in the 1976 Supreme Court decision, *Buckley v. Valeo,* 424 U.S.1, 97 (1976), that the presidential public financing provisions were invidiously discriminatory against non-major party candidates in violation of the due process clause of the Fifth Amendment, the *Buckley* Court disagreed since "the Constitution does not require Congress to treat all declared candidates the same for public financing purposes." *Id.* at 97. "The Constitution does not require the Government to 'finance the efforts of every nascent political group' [quoting *American Party of Texas v. White,* 415 U.S. at 794] merely because Congress chose to finance the efforts of the major parties." The Court noted, however, that it was not ruling out a future conclusion that public financing systems invidiously discriminate against non-major parties if such parties could present an appropriate factual demonstration. *Id.* at 97, n.13.

[66] *See* U.S. DEP'T OF COMMERCE, STATISTICAL ABSTRACT OF THE U.S. 72 (115 ed. 1995).

[67] 393 U.S. 23, 28-34 (1968).

[68] *See generally,* COMMITTEE FOR A CONSTITUTIONAL PRESIDENCY, *Progress Report On McCarthy Legal Challenges* (1976).

[69] *Anderson v. Firestone,* 499 F. Supp. 1027 (N.D. Fla. 1980).

[70] *Greaves v. Mills,* 497 F. Supp. 283 (E.D. Ky. 1980), *aff'd* in part and *rev'd* in part, *subnom., Anderson v. Mills,* 664 F.2d 602 (6th Cir. 1981).

[71] *Anderson v. Quinn,* 495 F. Supp. 730 (D. Me. 1980), *aff'd* 634 F.2d 616 (1st Cir. 1980).

[72] *Anderson v. Morris,* 500 F. Supp. 1095 (D. Md. 1980), *aff'd* 636 F.2d 55 (4th Cir. 1980), judgment vacated 658 F. 2d 246 (4th Cir. 1980).

[73] *Anderson v. Hooper,* 498 F. Supp. 898 (D.N.M. 1980).

[74] *Anderson v. Celebrezze,* 499 F. Supp. 121 (S.D. Oh. 1980), *rev'd* 664 F. 2d 554 (6th Cir.1981), *rev'd* 460 U.S. 780 (1983). The Supreme Court held that the restrictive provisions of the Ohio election statutes, requiring early filing deadlines for independent candidates, placed an unconstitutional burden on the voting and associational rights of the independent candidate's supporters. *Id.* at 790-95.

[75] *Anderson v. Babb,* No. 80-561-CIV-5 (E.D. N.C. 1980), *aff'd per curiam* 632 F.2d 300 (4th Cir. 1980).

[76] CONG. REC. index; Legislative Information Service.

[77] LEAGUE OF WOMEN VOTERS OF THE U. S., WHO SHOULD ELECT THE PRESIDENT? 43, 92-95 (1969). The House Judiciary Committee held hearings on proposals to reform the electoral college in 1947, 1949, 1951, and 1969. Likewise, the Senate Subcommittee on Constitutional Amendments held hearings in 1948, 1953, 1955, 1961, 1963, 1966, 1967, and 1969. In the House, between 1947 and 1968, there were four occasions when House Joint Resolutions were reported favorably: 1948 (H.J.Res. 9, Gossett); 1949 (H.J.Res. 2, Gossett); 1950 (S.J.Res. 2, Lodge); and 1951 (H.J.Res. 19, Gossett). Between 1947 and 1968, Senate Joint Resolutions were also reported favorably four times: 1948 (S.J.Res. 200, Lodge); 1949 (S.J.Res. 2, Lodge); 1951 (S.J.Res. 52, Lodge); and 1955 (S.J. 31, Daniel). S. J. Res. 2 (Lodge) passed the Senate by the required two-thirds votes, but the House failed to vote on the Senate Resolution. *Id.*

[78] CONGRESSIONAL QUARTERLY, INC., POWERS OF CONGRESS 279-80 (1976).

[79] U.S. DEP'T OF COMMERCE, STATISTICAL ABSTRACT OF THE UNITED STATES 271 (1995). In 1976, the Democratic presidential and vice presidential candidates received 40,831,000 votes over the Republican presidential and vice presidential candidates, who received 39,148,000 votes. Note that one Ford elector cast his vote for Ronald Reagan. See above under "The Faithless Elector" for further information.

[80] Recall that Article V of the Constitution requires a two-thirds majority vote in both houses to propose constitutional amendments.

[81] A less frequently offered variant would provide for election by a joint session of Congress instead of a runoff election in the event no candidates received a 40% majority.

[82] LEAGUE OF WOMEN VOTERS OF THE U. S., *supra* note 74, at 71-79.

[83] ME. REV. STAT. ANN. tit. 21, § 805.

[84] NEB. REV. STAT. § 32-548.

[85] Computed by CRS. See CRS congressional distribution memorandum, *Alternative Methods to Allocate the Electoral Vote: The Winner-Takes-All, Proportional, and District Systems Compared Using 1992, 1996 and 2000 Data*, by David C. Huckabee. Available to Members of Congress and their staff from the author.

[86] Dividing 50 states and the District of Columbia into the total of 538 electoral votes yields an average of 10.55 electoral votes per jurisdiction.

[87] Huckabee, *Alternative Methods to Allocate the Electoral Vote*, pp. 10-11.

[88] *See* WALLACE S. SAYRE AND JUDITH H. PARRIS, THE BROOKINGS INSTITUTION, VOTING FOR PRESIDENT 102-17 (1970); *see generally* LEAGUE OF WOMEN VOTERS OF THE U.S., *supra* note 74, at 64-66.

[89] For information on a 2004 initiative proposal in Colorado that would have established a rounded proportional plan in that state, please consult CRS Report RL32611, *The Electoral College: How It Works in Contemporary Presidential Elections*, by Thomas H. Neale.

[90] Huckabee, *Alternative Methods to Allocate the Electoral Vote*, p. 11.

[91] Ibid., p. 10.

[92] *See generally* LEAGUE OF WOMEN VOTERS OF THE U.S., *supra* note 74, at 68-71; SAYRE and PARRIS, *supra* note 81, at 118-34.

[93] *See generally* LEAGUE OF WOMEN VOTERS OF THE U.S., *supra* note 74, at 61-64; SAYRE and PARRIS, *supra* note 81, at 90-101.

[94] For further information, please consult CRS Report RL30844, *The Electoral College: Reform Proposals in the 107th Congress*, by Thomas H. Neale, and CRS Report RL32612, *The Electoral College: Reform Proposals in the 108th Congress*, by Thomas H. Neale.

[95] For additional information on the Help America Vote Act and other election-related issues, consult CRS electronic briefing book, *Election Reform*, available to Members of Congress and staff at [http://www.congress.gov/brbk/html/eberf1.shtml]

[96] The anomaly contests included one in which the President was chosen by contingent election (1824), one in which the Vice President was chosen by contingent election (1836), and three occasions in which the electoral college winners received fewer popular votes than the electoral college runners-up (1876, 1888, and 2000).

[97] H.J.Res. 681, 91st Cong., carried in the House on September 18, 1969, by a vote of 338 to 70.

[98] S.J.Res. 28, 96th Cong., was defeated in the Senate on July 10, 1979. The vote was 51 to 48, 15 votes short of the necessary two-thirds majority of Senators present and voting.

[99] See discussion of the 12th Amendment earlier in this report.

[100] U.S. Congress, Senate, *The Constitution of the United States of America: Analysis and Interpretation*, Johnny H. Killian, ed., 99th Cong., 1st sess., S. Doc. 99-16 (Washington: GPO, 1987), p. 29.

In: Economics, Political and Social Issues ...
Editor: Michelle L. Fergusson

ISBN: 978-1-61122-555-6
©2011 Nova Science Publishers, Inc.

THE ELECTORAL COLLEGE: HOW IT WORKS IN CONTEMPORARY PRESIDENTIAL ELECTIONS[*]

Thomas H. Neale

American National Government,
Government and Finance Division

ABSTRACT

When Americans vote for a President and Vice President, they actually vote for presidential electors, known collectively as the electoral college. It is these electors, chosen by the people, who elect the chief executive. The Constitution assigns each state a number of electors equal to the combined total of its Senate and House of Representatives delegations; at present, the number of electors per state ranges from three to 55, for a total of 538, a figure which includes three electors for the District of Columbia. Anyone may serve as an elector, except for Members of Congress, and persons holding offices of "Trust or Profit" under the Constitution. In each presidential election year, a group (ticket or slate) of candidates for elector is nominated by political parties and other groups in each state, usually at a state party convention, or by the party state committee. It is these elector-candidates, rather than the presidential and vice presidential nominees, for whom the people vote in the election held on Tuesday after the first Monday in November (November 2, 2004).

In most states, voters cast a single vote for the slate of electors pledged to the party presidential and vice presidential candidates of their choice. The slate winning the most popular votes is elected; this is known as the winner-take-all, or general ticket, system. Maine and Nebraska use the district system, under which two electors are chosen on a statewide, at-large basis, and one is elected in each congressional district. A second alternative, the proportional system, would award electors to presidential tickets in direct proportion to the percentage votes they received in a particular state. Electors assemble in their respective states on Monday after the second Wednesday in December (December 13, 2004). They are pledged and expected, but not required, to vote for the candidates they represent. Separate ballots are cast for President and Vice President, after which the electoral college ceases to exist for another four years. The electoral vote results are counted and declared at a joint session of Congress, held on January 6 of the year succeeding the election. A majority of electoral votes (currently 270 of 538) is required to win. Constitutional amendments to abolish or reform the electoral college system are regularly introduced in Congress. For information on legislative activity in the current

---

[*] Excerpted from CRS Report RL32611 dated September 28, 2004.

Congress, please see CRS Report RL32612, The Electoral College: Reform Proposals in the 108th Congress, by Thomas H. Neale.

A proposal to establish the proportional system in Colorado will appear on that state's ballot on November 2, 2004. If the voters of that state approve it, and if it is found to be constitutional, Colorado's electoral votes for the current election could be allocated according to this plan.

CONSTITUTIONAL ORIGINS

The Constitutional Convention of 1787 considered several methods of electing the President, including selection by Congress, by the governors of the states, by the state legislatures, by a special group of Members of Congress chosen by lot, and by direct popular election. Late in the convention, the matter was referred to the Committee of Eleven on Postponed Matters, which devised the electoral college system in its original form [1]. This plan, which met with widespread approval by the delegates, was incorporated into the final document with only minor changes. It sought to reconcile differing state and federal interests, provide a degree of popular participation in the election, give the less populous states some additional leverage in the process, preserve the presidency as independent of Congress for election and reelection, and generally insulate the election process from political manipulation.

The Constitution gave each state a number of electors equal to the combined total of its Senate and House of Representatives membership. The electors were to be chosen by the states "in such Manner as the Legislature thereof may direct...." (Article II, section 1). Qualifications for the office were broad: the only persons prohibited from serving as electors are Senators, Representatives, and persons "holding an Office of Trust or Profit under the United States" [2]. In order to forestall partisan intrigue and manipulation, the electors were required to assemble in their respective states and cast their ballots as state units, rather than meet at a central location. At least one of the candidates for whom the electors vote was required to be an inhabitant of another state. A majority of electoral votes was necessary to elect, a requirement intended to insure broad acceptance of a winning candidate, while election by the House was provided as a default method in the event of electoral college deadlock. Finally, Congress was empowered to set nationwide dates for choice and meeting of electors. All the foregoing structural elements of the electoral college system remain in effect currently. The original method of electing the President and Vice President, however, proved unworkable, and was replaced by the 12th Amendment, ratified in 1804 [3]

THE ELECTORAL COLLEGE TODAY [4]

Notwithstanding the founders' efforts, the electoral college system almost never functioned as they intended, but, as with so many constitutional provisions, the document prescribed only the system's basic elements, leaving ample room for development. As the republic evolved, so did the electoral college system, and, by the late 19th century, the following range of constitutional, federal and state legal, and political elements of the contemporary system were in place.

Allocation of Electors and Electoral Votes. The Constitution gives each state a number of electors equal to the combined total of its Senate membership (two for each state) and House of Representatives delegation (currently ranging from one to 53, depending on population). The 23rd Amendment provides an additional three electors to the District of Columbia. The total number of electoral votes per state, based on the 2000 census, ranges from three (for seven states and the District of Columbia) to 55 for California, the most populous state. Table 1 provides current electoral vote allocations by state and D.C. These totals are adjusted following each decennial census in a process called reapportionment, which reallocates the number of Members of the House of Representatives to reflect changing rates of population growth (or decline) among the states. Thus, a state may gain or lose electors following reapportionment, as it gains or loses Representatives, but it always retains its two "senatorial" electors, and at least one more reflecting its House delegation. The current allocation among the states is in effect for the presidential elections of 2004 and 2008; electoral votes will next be reallocated following the 2010 census, and will be in effect for the 2012 election.

Table 1. Electoral Vote Allocation by Jurisdiction, 2004-2008

State	Electors	State	Electors	State	Electors
Alabama	9	Kentucky	8	North Dakota	3
Alaska	3	Louisiana	9	Ohio	20
Arizona	10	Maine	4	Oklahoma	7
Arkansas	6	Maryland	10	Oregon	7
California	55	Massachusetts	12	Pennsylvania	21
Colorado	9	Michigan	17	Rhode Island	4
Connecticut	7	Minnesota	10	South Carolina	8
Delaware	3	Mississippi	6	South Dakota	3
District of Columbia	3	Missouri	11	Tennessee	11
Florida	27	Montana	3	Texas	34
Georgia	15	Nebraska	5	Utah	5
Hawaii	4	Nevada	5	Vermont	3
Idaho	4	New Hampshire	4	Virginia	13
Illinois	21	New Jersey	15	Washington	11
Indiana	11	New Mexico	5	West Virginia	5
Iowa	7	New York	31	Wisconsin	10
Kansas	6	North Carolina	15	Wyoming	3

Popular Election of Electors. Today, all presidential electors are chosen by the voters, but, in the early republic, more than half the states chose electors in their legislatures, thus eliminating any direct involvement by the voting public in the election. This practice changed rapidly after the turn of the 19th century, however, as the right to vote was extended to an ever-wider segment of the population. As the electorate grew, so did the number of persons able to vote for presidential electors, to its present limit of all eligible citizens age 18 or older. The tradition that the voters choose the presidential electors thus became an early and permanent feature of the electoral college system; while the states theoretically retain the constitutional right to choose some other method, this would be extremely unlikely under normal circumstances.

The existence of the presidential electors and the duties of the electoral college are so little noted in contemporary society that most American voters believe that they vote directly for President and Vice President on election day. In fact, they are actually voting for a slate of candidates for the office of elector nominated by a party or other political group, and pledged to support the candidates of that party. Although candidates for elector may be well known persons, such as governors, state legislators, or other state and local officials, they generally receive little recognition as electors. In fact, in most states, the names of individual electors do not appear anywhere on the ballot; instead only those of the various presidential and vice presidential candidates appear, often prefaced by the words "electors for." Moreover, electoral votes are commonly referred to as having "been awarded" to the winning candidate, as if no human beings were involved in the process.

The Electors: Ratifying the Voters' Choice. Presidential electors in contemporary elections are expected, and, in many cases pledged, to vote for the candidates of the party that nominated them. While there is considerable evidence that the founders assumed they would be independent, weighing the merits of competing presidential candidates, the electors have been regarded as agents of the public will since the first decade under the Constitution [5]. They are expected to vote for the candidates of the party that nominated them.

Faithless Electors. Notwithstanding the tradition that electors are bound to vote for the candidates of the party that nominated them, individual electors have sometimes broken their commitment, voting for a different candidate or candidates than those to whom they were pledged; they are known as "faithless" or "unfaithful" electors. Although 24 states seek to prohibit faithless electors by a variety of methods, including pledges and the threat of fines or criminal action, most constitutional scholars believe that electors, once chosen, remain constitutionally free agents, able to vote for any candidate who meets the requirements for President and Vice President [6]. Faithless electors have, however, been few in number (since the 20th century, one each in 1948, 1956, 1960, 1968, 1972, 1976, and 1988, and one blank ballot cast in 2000), and have never influenced the outcome of a presidential election.

The General Ticket System. While the Constitution is silent on the formula for awarding each state's electoral votes, 48 states and the District of Columbia currently use the "general ticket" or "winner-take-all" system. Under this arrangement, each political party or group or independent candidacy eligible to be on the ballot nominates a group ("ticket" or "slate") of elector-candidates equal in number to the state's total number of electors. Voters then cast a single vote for the ticket of electors pledged to the presidential and vice presidential candidates of their choice; the ticket receiving the most votes statewide (a plurality is sufficient) is elected. These people become the electors for that state.

This is how the general ticket system works in a hypothetical state, State A. State A currently has 10 electoral votes, reflecting its two Senators and eight Representatives. The two equally hypothetical major parties, "X" and "Y" each nominate 10 persons for the office of presidential elector, pledged to the presidential and vice presidential candidates of their party. Voters go to the polls and cast a single vote for the ticket of party electors of their choice. Party A's slate of elector-candidates receives 51% of the popular vote; Party B's slate receives 49%. Notwithstanding the closeness of the results, all of Party A's electors are chosen, and Party A's presidential and vice presidential candidates normally receive all the state's electoral votes. Party B gains no electoral votes.

The general ticket system has been favored since the 19th century, as it tends to magnify the winning candidates' victory margin within states, and generally guarantees a national electoral college majority for the winners. It has been criticized on the grounds that it effectively negates the votes for the runners up.

Alternative Systems: The District and Proportional Plans. Two alternative methods for awarding electoral votes which pass the test of constitutionality have long been available to the states. They have historically been promoted as avoiding the alleged failings of the general ticket system [7].

The District Plan. The first is the district plan or system, which has been adopted by Maine and Nebraska. Under the district system, two electors are chosen on a statewide, at-large basis (representing the two "senatorial electors" allotted to each state regardless of population), and one is elected in each congressional district.8 Each voter still casts a single vote for President and Vice President, but the votes are counted twice: first on a statewide basis, with the two at-large elector-candidates who win the most votes (a plurality) elected en bloc, and then again in each district, where the district elector-candidate winning the most votes in each district is elected.

This is how the district system might work in State A. Assume that Party X again receives 51% of the statewide vote, and Party 49%. Party X's candidates for the two statewide (or senatorial) elector offices are thus elected. Assume also that Party X receives a plurality or majority of the popular vote in five of State A's congressional districts, while Party Y wins three of the districts. Under the district plan, the "district" electoral votes would be similarly awarded, so that Party X would receive seven electoral votes, reflecting the statewide electors and the five congressional districts it won, while Party Y would receive the three electors that reflected its congressional district majorities.

The claimed advantage of the district system is that it more accurately reflects differences in support in various parts of a state, and does not necessarily "disenfranchise" voters who picked the losing ticket. For instance, a state that has one or more large cities and a large rural and suburban population with differing political preferences and voting patterns might well split its electoral vote under the district system. Opponents suggest that the district system, with its division of electoral votes within states, would more frequently lead to deadlocked elections in which no candidate receives a majority of electoral votes. Perhaps ironically, however, neither Maine nor Nebraska has split its electoral vote during the time the district system has been in place. In every presidential election, the overall winners also gained the most votes in each congressional district.

The Proportional Plan. The other commonly proposed option is the proportional plan or system, which has never been adopted by a state, but which will be the subject of a proposed Colorado constitutional amendment that will be decided at the November 2, 2004 general election. For further information on the Colorado amendment, see under "Current Developments" later in this report. The proportional plan allocates electors and electoral votes in direct proportion to the number of votes gained by each state. Unlike the district plan, it does not account for geographic voting patterns, but allocates electors on a purely statewide basis. Two variations of the proportional plan exist: the strict proportional plan, which would allocate electoral votes to thousands of electoral votes, that is to the third decimal point, and the rounded proportional plan or system, which would use some method of rounding to allocate only whole electoral votes.

This is how the rounded proportional plan might operate in State A. Party X, once again, receives 51% of the popular vote, and Party Y receives 49%. When these totals are rounded, Party X would be awarded five electors, and Party Y would also gain five electors [9]

Proponents of the proportional system argue that this is the fairest plan, since it most accurately reflects in it selector/electoral vote allocation the preferences of the voters, acting as a statewide political community. The also note that it would provide recognition for new- or third-party candidates that achieve a substantial level of support in a state. Opponents suggest that, like the district system, the proportional plan would more frequently lead to deadlocked elections in which no candidate receives a majority of electoral votes.

Nominating Elector-Candidates: Diverse State Procedures. Nomination of elector-candidates is another of the many aspects of this system left to state and political party preferences. Most states prescribe one of two methods: in 34 states candidates for presidential elector are nominated by state party conventions, while 10 states mandate nomination by the state party's central committee. The remainder uses a variety of methods, including nomination by the governor (on recommendation of party committees), by primary election, and by the party's presidential nominee.

Joint Tickets: One Vote for President and Vice President. General election ballots, which are regulated by state election laws and authorities, offer voters joint candidacies for President and Vice President for each political party or other group. Thus, voters cast a single vote for electors pledged to the joint ticket of the party they represent. They cannot effectively vote for a President from one party and a Vice President from another, unless their state provides for write-in votes.

General Election Day. Elections for all federal elected officials are held on the Tuesday after the first Monday in November in even-numbered years; presidential elections are held in every year divisible by four (November 2, 2004) for the next presidential election). Congress selected this day in 1845 (5 Stat. 721); previously, states held elections on different days between September and November, a practice that sometimes led to multiple voting across state lines, and other fraudulent practices. By tradition, November was chosen because the harvest was in, and farmers were able to take the time needed to vote. Tuesday was selected because it gave a full day's travel between Sunday, which was widely observed as a strict day of rest, and election day [10]. Travel was also easier throughout the north during November, before winter had set in.

The Electors Convene. The 12th Amendment requires electors to meet "in their respective states...." This provision was intended to deter manipulation of the election by having the state electoral colleges meet simultaneously, but keeping them separate. Congress sets the date on which the electors meet (3 U.S.C. 7), which is currently the first Monday after the second Wednesday in December (December 13, 2004). The electors almost always meet in the state capital, usually in the capitol building or state house itself. They vote "by ballot" [11] separately for President and Vice President (at least one of the candidates must be from another state). The results are then endorsed, and copies are sent to the following officials: the Vice President of the United States (in his capacity as President of the Senate); the secretary of state of their state; the Archivist of the United States; and the judge of the federal district court of the district in which the electors met (3 U.S.C. 11). The electors then adjourn, and the electoral college ceases to exist until the next presidential election.

Congress Counts, Ascertains, and Declares the Vote. The final step in the presidential election process (aside from the presidential inaugural on January 20) is the counting, ascertainment, and declaration of the electoral votes in Congress [12]. The House of Representatives and Senate meet in joint session in the House chamber on January 6 of the year following the presidential election, at 1:00 P.M. [13] No debate is allowed in the joint session. The Vice President, who presides in his capacity as President of the Senate, opens the electoral vote certificates from each state, in alphabetical order. He then passes the certificates to four tellers (vote counters), two appointed by each house, who announce the results. The votes are then counted, and the results are announced by the Vice President. The candidates receiving a majority of electoral votes (currently 270 of 538) are declared the winners by the Vice President, an action that constitutes "a sufficient declaration of the persons, if any, elected President and Vice President of the States" (3 U.S.C. 15) [14]

Objections to State Electoral Vote Returns [15]. Objections may be offered to both individual electoral votes and state returns as a whole. Objections must be filed in writing, and be signed by one Senator and one Representative. If an objection is received, and determined to be valid, then the electoral vote count session is recessed. The Senate returns immediately to its chamber, and the two houses of Congress consider the objections separately. By law, these sessions cannot last more than two hours, and no member of either house may speak for more than five minutes. At the end of this period, the houses vote separately to agree or disagree with the objection. The Senate then returns to the House chamber, and the joint session reconvenes. The decisions of the two houses are announced. If both houses agree to the objection, then the electoral vote or votes in question are not counted. Otherwise, the vote or votes stand as submitted, and are counted as such [16]

CURRENT DEVELOPMENTS: THE PROPOSED COLORADO AMENDMENT

On November 2, 2004, voters in Colorado will cast ballots on a proposed state constitutional amendment [17] that would establish a "rounded" version of the proportional system which would be effective with the current election. That is, if the amendment passes, and is not found unconstitutional, it would provide proportional allocation of Colorado's presidential electors for the current, 2004, election. If so, it could have a serious impact on the election outcome, and might lead to challenges as to its constitutionality that could further result in prolonged post-election legal struggle.

Colorado is among the 18 states that provide for the proposal and approval of amendments to their state constitutions by popular vote. In order to place an amendment on the ballot in Colorado, registered voters equal in number to 5% of the number of votes cast for the office of State Secretary of State at the last election must sign petitions. The amendment is then placed on the ballot at the next general election; approval by a majority of those voting is required for passage [18]. On August 13, 2004, Colorado's Secretary of State announced that the proposed amendment had gained sufficient voter signatures to qualify for inclusion on the ballot at the November 2 general election [19].

The amendment would allocate electoral votes and electors based on the popular proportional share of the total statewide ballots cast for each presidential ticket. The percentage of each ticket's vote would then be multiplied by Colorado's electoral vote total, nine. These figures would then be rounded to the nearest whole number of electors and electoral votes, but any ticket that did not receive at least one vote under this method would be eliminated from the total. If the sum of whole electoral votes derived from this computation were to be *greater* than nine, then the ticket receiving at least one whole electoral vote, but fewest popular votes, would have its electoral vote total reduced by one. This process would continue until the computed allocation of votes reached nine. Conversely, if the sum of whole electoral votes awarded after rounding the percentages of popular votes were *less* than nine, then such additional electoral votes as necessary to bring the number up to nine would be allocated to the ticket receiving the most popular votes, until all nine electoral votes were so allocated. In the event of a popular and electoral vote allocation tie (i.e., Candidates A and B each receiving 4.5 electoral votes), then the Secretary of State would determine by lot who would receive the evenly split electoral vote [20].

The amendment includes several additional features.

- In Section 1(f), it states that the voters "by approving this initiative ... understand, desire, and expect that the popular selection of presidential electors is intended to apply retroactively and thus determine the manner in which our state's presidential electors are chosen and our state's votes are cast for the general election of 2004." The apparent retroactive nature of this requirement might be subject to legal challenge, calling into question whether the amendment, if adopted, would apply to the election of 2004, or only to later elections.
- In section 2, it directs that "[e]ach presidential elector shall vote for the presidential candidate and, by ballot, vice-presidential candidate on the presidential ticket of the political party or political organization that nominated that presidential elector." While this requirement would theoretically prohibit faithless electors, as noted earlier in this report, the question of whether the states have the power to so bind their electors remains at issue [21]
- In Section 6, it provides for the determination of which elector-candidates would be elected. Each party or political group would nominate a full slate of nine elector-candidates, and the number of electors allocated to each candidate would be determined by the formula described above. The Colorado Secretary of State would then determine, by lot, which of the elector-candidates would be elected. In other words, if Candidate A received five electoral votes under the proposal, and Candidate B received four, then the Secretary of State would determine by lot which five elector-candidates on Candidate A's ticket would be chosen, and which four would be chosen from Candidate B's ticket.

Implications of the Colorado Amendment. If it were implemented retroactively, as proposed in the preamble, the Colorado amendment could have profound implications for the 2004 presidential contest, particularly if the election proved to be close.

For instance, in 2000, the Republican Bush-Cheney ticket won 50.8% of the popular vote in Colorado, the Democratic Gore-Lieberman ticket won 42.4%, the Green Party Nader-

LaDuke ticket 5.3%, and other candidates won 1.6%. Under the familiar rules of the general ticket system, the Republican nominees gained all eight of Colorado's electoral votes [22]

Proponents of the amendment maintain that awarding the state's electoral votes proportionally would end the general ticket system's alleged disenfranchisement of those whose preferred candidates who received fewer popular votes in the state. Opponents claim that it would reduce Colorado's importance in the electoral process: "It takes Colorado out of play for any presidential election, ... And I think that impacts future decisions on things like potential [military] base closings or federal highway funding allocations." [23]

The proposal also figures in the national political context. If a proportional system like that currently under consideration had been in place in Colorado in 2000, the state's electoral vote results would been different, with the Republican nominees winning five electors in Colorado, and the Democratic nominees three [24]. (The Green Party and minor parties would not have qualified for any electors under the provisions of Amendment 36). The change resulting from the loss of those three electoral votes by the Bush ticket would have reduced its nationwide total to 268. Conversely, the Gore ticket's total would have risen to 269, giving the Democrats a plurality in the electoral college. This would have left Vice President Gore one vote short of an electoral college majority, conceivably leading to contingent election in Congress. These numbers do not, however, account for the single blank electoral vote cast by a District of Columbia elector to the protest the election results. Under the circumstances described above, the said elector might rather have chosen to cast her ballot as instructed, providing the Democratic ticket with the majority of electoral votes required by the Constitution, and thus changing the election's outcome.

Constitutional Questions. Other questions have been raised as to whether this effort to change the allocation formula for Colorado's electoral votes by initiative is constitutional. Specifically, the U.S. Constitution (in Article II, section 1, clause 2) provides that, "Each state shall appoint, in such Manner as the Legislature thereof may direct, a Number of Electors, equal to the whole Number of Senators and Representatives to which the State may be entitled in the Congress...." Since the early years of government under the Constitution, the state legislatures have generally exercised this grant of power by authorizing the voters to choose electors, and they have usually specified the winner-take-all or general ticket system as the means by which the voters' decision is used to allocate electors and electoral votes.

The fact that Colorado's proposed Amendment 36 would alter the formula for awarding electoral votes by *a vote of the people* is the salient issue here. The Colorado legislature's right under Article II to establish a proportional system is not in dispute; the question rather, is, does the Colorado legislature have authority to *subdelegate* its Article II powers to determine and change the existing method of appointing electors to a popular vote? Can the voters of Colorado act in place of, or *as* the state legislature? The Colorado Constitution specifically empowers the people of the state to "to propose laws and amendments to the constitution and to enact or reject the same at the polls independent of the general assembly ..." [25]

Proponents of Amendment 36 could argue that this is sufficient authority to change the allocation of electoral votes by popular vote. Further, it could be argued that the U.S. Constitution's failure to expressly prohibit this procedure, or others like it, provides an implicit endorsement. On the other hand, opponents could arguably assert that the U.S. Constitution clearly delegates this power to the state legislatures, and only the state legislatures [26]. Moreover, commentary on the Colorado amendment by initiative process notes that, "An amendment is not valid just because the people voted for it. The initiative gives the people of a state no power to adopt a constitutional amendment which violates the federal constitution" [27].

A subsidiary question is whether the amendment can be retroactively instituted, as stated in the preamble. Proponents could cite commentary on the initiative device in Colorado notes that, "The initiative and referendum provision is in all respects self-executing. It is not a mere framework, but contains the necessary detailed provisions for carrying into immediate effect the enjoyment of the rights therein established without legislative action." [28] Opponents could argue that the retroactive provision is an attempt at political manipulation of the election results to gain a short term benefit for one candidate, and that it runs contrary to notions of fair play.

These questions might be raised following an extremely close presidential election in 2004, particularly if proportional electoral vote allocation in Colorado appeared to reverse the nationwide results. Legal challenges to the amendment on various grounds would arguably be likely under these circumstances, and might lead to a prolonged and bitter dispute, such as occurred following the 2000 election.

CONCLUDING OBSERVATIONS

The electoral college system has demonstrated both durability and adaptability during more than two centuries of government under the U.S. Constitution. Although its structural elements remain largely unchanged, in operation it has never worked in quite the way the founders anticipated, and has evolved into a patchwork assemblage of constitutional provisions, state laws, political party practices, and enduring traditions. The electoral college system has always had flaws and critics, and it has been the subject of controversy on five occasions, [29] but it has delivered a President and Vice President in 54 elections under the Constitution. Given the high hurdles faced by proposed constitutional amendments, it seems likely to remain in place unless or until its alleged failings become so compelling that large concurrent majorities in the public, the Congress, and the states, are prepared to undertake its reform or abolition.

REFERENCES

[1]   Although the term is not found in the Constitution, the electors have been known collectively as the electoral college since the early days of the republic, an expression that may be misleading, since the college has no continuing existence, never meets in plenary session, and ceases to exist immediately after the electors have performed their function.

[2]   U.S. Constitution, Article II, Section 1. In practice, this formulation also prohibits any person working for the federal government in either a civilian or military capacity from serving as an elector.

[3]   Under the original system, each elector cast two votes for President (for different candidates), and no vote for Vice President. The candidate receiving the most votes was

elected President, provided it was a majority of the number of electors (not electoral votes). The runner up became Vice President.

[4]   For a list of electors in the presidential election of 2000, consult the National Archives at   [http://www.archives.gov/federal_register/electoral_college/members_2000.html]. For information on proposals to reform the electoral college, see CRS Report RL30804, *The Electoral College: An Overview and Analysis of Reform Proposals*, by L. Paige Whitaker and Thomas H. Neale; and CRS Report RL32612, *The Electoral College: Reform Proposals in the 108th Congress*, by Thomas H. Neale.

[5]   Neal Peirce and Lawrence D. Longley, *The People's President: The Electoral College in American History and the Direct Vote Alternative*, rev. ed. (New Haven, CT, 1981: Yale U. Press), pp. 24, 96-101.

[6]   U.S. Congress, Senate, *The Constitution of the United States of America, Analysis and Interpretation*, S. Doc. 99-16, 99th Cong., 1st sess., prepared by the Congressional Research Service (Washington: GPO, 1987), pp. 457-460.

[7]   For information on how electoral votes would have been allocated under the district and proportional plans in the presidential elections of 1992, 1996, and 2000, please consult CRS congressional distribution memorandum *Alternative Methods to Allocate the Electoral Vote: The Winner Take All, Proportional, and District Systems Compared Using 1992, 1996, and 2000 Data*, by David C. Huckabee. Available to Members of Congress and congressional staff from the author.

[8]   Some versions of the district plan would use ad hoc presidential election districts to award these votes, rather than congressional districts, but both Maine and Nebraska, which use the district system, tally their votes by congressional district.

[9]   Given that the strict proportional plan, by providing for fractions of electoral votes, would almost certainly require a U.S. constitutional amendment, and since the proposed Colorado constitutional amendment would establish a rounded proportional system, the strict proportional plan allocation of electoral votes has not been included in this hypothesis.

[10]   In most rural areas, the only polling place was at the county seat, frequently a journey of many miles on foot or horseback.

[11]   12th Amendment; this provision is interpreted to require paper ballots for President and Vice President.

[12]   3 U.S.C. 15-18.

[13]   Congress occasionally sets a different date for the electoral vote count session, particularly in years when January 6 falls on a Sunday.

[14]   If there is no majority, due to a tie or division of the electoral vote among three or more candidates, the President is elected in the House of Representatives, and the Vice President in the Senate by the contingent election process. For further information, see CRS Report RS20300, *Election of the President and Vice President by Congress: Contingent Election*, by Thomas H. Neale.

[15]   3 U.S.C. 15.

[16]   For information on efforts to file objections to electoral vote returns from Florida at the 2001 electoral vote count session, please consult CRS congressional distribution memorandum, *Congressional Objections to Electoral Votes for President*, by Jack Maskell, available to Members of Congress and staff from the author.

[17]   Amendment 36.

[18] Council of State Governments, *The Book of the States*, 2004 edition, vol. 36 (Lexington: KY, The Council of State Governments, 2004), p. 14.

[19] *USA Today.com*, "Colorado Weighs Proportional Electoral Votes, Aug. 16, 2004. at [http://www.usatoday.com/news/politicselections/state/Colorado/2004-08-16-colo-electoral_x.htm] , visited Sept. 3, 2004.

[20] Proposed Colorado Amendment 36, § 2-4.

[21] See elsewhere in this report under "Faithless Electors".

[22] Colorado gained one House seat, and hence, one electoral vote, as a result of the 2000 census, thus raising its current total to nine.

[23] Dan Hopkins, spokesman for CO Governor Bill Owens, quoted in Jo Becker, "Colorado Initiative Could Be Key to Presidential Race," *Washington Post*, Sept. 18, 2004, p. A12.

[24] Results computed by CRS from *America Votes 24: A Handbook of Contemporary American Election Statistics* (Washington: CQ Press, 2001).

[25] Constitution of the State of Colorado, Article V, section 1, clause 1.

[26] See, e.g., *McPherson v. Blacker*, 146 U.S. 1,25 (1892), holding that the word "legislature" in Article II, section 1, clause 2 of the U.S. Constitution operates to limit the states); *Hawke v. Smith*, No. 1, 253 U.S. 221 (1920), (holding that the language of Article V is "plain", and that there is "no doubt in its interpretation" that ratification of amendments is limited to the only two methods specifically granted by the Constitution); but see, *Ohio ex rel. Davis v. Hildebrant*, 241 U.S. 565 (1916), (holding that a referendum did not violate the use of the word "legislature" in Article I, section 4, clause 1 of the Constitution).

[27] *Colorado Revised Statutes, 2003*, vol. 1 (n.p. : LexisNexis, 2003), p. 380.

[28] Ibid., p. 373.

[29] 1800, 1824, 1876, 1888, and 2000.

In: Economics, Political and Social Issues …
Editor: Michelle L. Fergusson

PRESIDENTIAL ELECTIONS
IN THE UNITED STATES: A PRIMER*

Kevin J. Coleman, Joseph E. Cantor and Thomas H. Neale

American National Government, Government and Finance Division

ABSTRACT

This report describes the four stages of the presidential election process: the pre-nomination primaries and caucuses for selecting delegates to the national conventions; the national nominating conventions; the general election; and voting by members of the electoral college to choose the President and Vice President. The report will be updated again for the 2004 presidential election.

SUMMARY

Every four years, Americans elect a President and Vice President, thereby choosing both national leaders and a course of public policy. The system that governs the election of the President combines constitutional and statutory requirements, rules of the national and state political parties, political traditions, and contemporary developments and practices.

As initially prescribed by the Constitution, the election of the President was left to electors chosen by the states. Final authority for selecting the President still rests with the electoral college, which comprises electors from each state equal in number to the state's total representation in the House and Senate. All but two states award electoral votes on a winner-take-all basis to the candidate with a plurality of the state's popular vote.

The process of electing the President is essentially divided into four stages: (1) the prenomination phase, in which candidates compete in state primary elections and caucuses for delegates to the national party conventions; (2) the national conventions—held in the summer of the election year—in which the two major parties nominate candidates for President and Vice President and ratify a platform of the parties' policy positions and goals; (3) the general election campaign, in which the major party nominees, as well as any minor party or independent contenders, compete for votes from the entire electorate, culminating in the popular vote on election day in November; and (4) the electoral college phase, in which the President and Vice President are officially elected.

Presidential elections in recent years differ in several important respects from those held earlier in American history. The first is the far wider participation of voters today in

---

* Excerpted from CRS Report RL30527 dated April 17, 2000.

determining who the party nominees will be; the political parties have in recent years given a much greater role to party voters in the states (in lieu of party leaders) in determining the nominees. The second difference involves the role of the electronic media and, most recently, the Internet, both in conveying information to the voters, and shaping the course of the campaign. Third, the financing of presidential campaigns is substantially governed by a system of public funding in the pre-nomination, convention, and general election phases, enacted in the 1970s in response to increasing campaign costs in an electronic age and the concomitant fundraising pressures on candidates. Thus, contemporary presidential elections blend both traditional aspects of law and practice and contemporary aspects of a larger, more complex, and more technologically advanced society.

This report explains the presidential election process in the United States. It provides general information about Presidential candidates and their campaigns and it reviews the laws, activities, and customs that govern each of the four stages of the process–the primary campaign, the national nominating conventions, the general election, and the electoral college.

Chapteronediscussesthecandidatesthemselves—theirqualificationsforoffice, the procedure for gaining ballot access, the stages of their campaigns, and the protection accorded them by the federal government.

Chapter two focuses on the nomination process, describing the evolution of the current system of primaries and caucuses, the basic structure, methods and rules governing selection of delegates to the nominating conventions, and the major characteristics of the contemporary process.

Chapter three examines the national party conventions, including both their evolution and traditions, and contemporary structure and procedures.

Chapter four focuses on the general election campaign, from the Labor Day "kickoff" to November election day. It offers general comments on widely used campaign methods during this period, examines the important role played by television—through advertising, news coverage, and debates—and provides information on election day itself (how it was selected, polling hours in the states, etc.).

Chapter five provides information on the electoral college, the process by which the President and Vice President are officially elected. It follows the steps in the process of convening the electors and counting their votes, and offers information on past discrepancies between electoral and popular vote leaders. It also discusses possible scenarios for contingent election, in which no candidate receives an electoral majority or when a candidate dies at some stage of the process.

One aspect of the process not examined in this discussion is treated in a companion CRS report on the funding of presidential elections, in particular the system of public financing available since 1976. See CRS Report RS20133, *The Presidential Election Campaign Fund and Tax Checkoff: Background and Current Issues*.

I. Presidential Candidates

Qualifications for the Office of President

Article II, Section 1 of the Constitution specifies that, to be President or Vice President, a person must be a natural-born citizen of the United States, at least 35 years of age, and a resident of the United States for at least 14 years [1]. Most constitutional scholars interpret this language as including citizens born outside the United States to parents who are U.S. citizens under the "natural born" requirement [2] Under the 22nd Amendment, no one may serve more than two full terms, although a Vice President who succeeds to the Presidency and serves less than two full years of the prior incumbent's term may seek election to two additional terms.

Prior Occupations of Presidents

American voters have chosen men of varied backgrounds on the 53 occasions they have gone to the polls to elect a President. All 41 Presidents served the country previously either in government or the military. Of the 24 Presidents who served prior to 1900, seven had been Vice Presidents (three of whom were elected to the Presidency, while four succeeded a deceased incumbent), four were Members of Congress, four were governors, and nine previously held an appointive federal position.

The trend in 20th century presidential elections has favored former Vice Presidents, Governors, and Senators. of 17 20th century Presidents, several served in more than one of these positions.

At the time of their inauguration, one (Eisenhower) had served as a career Army officer; two (Taft and Hoover) had most recently served as cabinet officers; five (Wilson, F.D. Roosevelt, Carter, Reagan, and Clinton) as governors; two (Harding and Kennedy) were Senators; and seven were Vice Presidents. Five of the seven Vice Presidents (T. Roosevelt, Coolidge, Truman, Johnson, and Ford) succeeded on the death or resignation of the incumbent; two Vice Presidents were elected—one (Nixon) as a former and one (Bush) as an incumbent.

The Candidate Field

Before the primaries and conventions, the candidates determine the presidential field. The decline of party leader dominance over the nominating process has resulted in a system whereby self-selected candidates compete in the states for the delegates needed for nomination. The democratization of the nominating process has meant that many candidates enter the race, begin raising money, and organize for the primaries and caucuses well before the election year in order to be competitive. According to the Federal Election Commission, 203 individuals had filed statements of candidacy or had committees file statements of organization for the 2000 presidential election as of January 31, 2000. Just 33 of these individuals had met the Federal Election Campaign Act's (FECA) criteria for candidacies subject to federal election laws, i.e., raising contributions or making expenditures in excess of

$5,000 [2 U.S.C. §431(2)]. In reality, only a small number of these are considered by the media as serious candidates seeking the nomination of the two major parties.

Exploratory Candidacies–Testing the Waters

The formal announcement of candidacy is often preceded by a period in which candidates "test the waters" as unannounced candidates for nomination; this may begin several years before the convention. Likely candidates may form exploratory committees to gauge popular support and to begin developing a base of supporters and contributors, while avoiding some of the legal requirements (such as contribution limits and disclosure of receipts and disbursements) of the FECA. As unofficial candidates who are not technically campaigning for office, persons may raise and spend unlimited amounts of money without registering as candidates with the Federal Election Commission (FEC).

Upon declaration of candidacy, however, the individual must register with the FEC and report all financial activity while testing the waters; these amounts become retroactively subject to all FECA regulations.

Announcement of Candidacy

An individual must file a statement of candidacy with the FEC within 15 days of reaching the law's financial threshold (*i.e.*, $5,000 in receipts or expenditures), and must name a principal campaign committee to receive contributions and make expenditures.

This committee must file a statement of organization with the FEC within ten days after being designated; the statement must identify the committee's title (which includes the candidate's name), the treasurer, bank depositories, and any other committees the candidate has authorized to raise or spend on his or her behalf. Such other committees which the candidate authorizes may raise and spend funds, but they must report such activity through the principal committee.

The timing of the formal announcement is crucial because of its political impact, and also because of the legal and tactical implications. Once a public declaration of candidacy is made, candidates are subject to state and national spending limits if they qualify for and choose to accept public matching funds, and they are subject to the broadcasting provisions of the equal-time rule (47 U.S.C. 315(a)).

Nominations today are usually won during the primary campaign rather than at the convention, and primaries have proliferated and been scheduled earlier in the election year. Because of these developments, competitors are pressed to announce their candidacies much earlier than in years past. Whereas in 1932, Franklin Roosevelt formally announced for the Presidency 156 days before the convention, Michael Dukakis formally announced his candidacy 446 days prior to the 1988 Democratic National Convention. The trend toward earlier, longer campaigns is a hallmark of modern presidential elections.

Qualifying for the Primaries and Caucuses

The guidelines that candidates follow to qualify for primaries and caucuses differ from state to state. In primary states, the Secretary of State (or other chief elections officer) is the authority for listing candidate names on the ballot; in caucus states, the parties oversee the procedures for candidates to gain ballot access (they do not always have to file to be eligible for delegates in caucus states, however).

Candidates generally file a statement of candidacy with the Secretary of State or the party chair at the state level. In some primary states, the Secretary of State may automatically certify for the ballot the names of all major party candidates, those submitted by the party, candidates who have qualified in other states, or candidates who have applied with the FEC or are eligible for federal matching funds.

Presidential candidates may also be required to pay a filing fee, submit petitions, or both. Signatures may be required from a requisite number of voters in each congressional district or from a requisite number of voters statewide.

Party Nominations

The primary season gradually reduces the field of major party candidates. The accelerated pace of the present system winnows out those who fall short of expectations, and hence, find it difficult to raise the money needed to sustain their candidacies. Furthermore, there forms of the past 30 years have changed the dynamics of the nominating process by closely tying the allocation of delegates to electoral performance.

The days when a candidate could compete in a select number of primaries to demonstrate popular appeal have passed: the nomination goes to the candidate who has amassed a majority of delegates in the primaries and caucuses. Party conventions have largely become ratifying bodies that confer the nomination on the candidate who won it in state contests.

The 1976 Republican National Convention was the most recent one at which the determination of a major party's nominee was in any real doubt before the nominating ballots were cast.

The General Election Ballot

The names of the major party nominees for President and Vice President are automatically placed on the general election ballot. Some states also list the names of presidential electors adjacent to the presidential and vice presidential candidates whom they support. Voters mark their ballots once for a party's presidential and vice presidential ticket; electors also cast a single vote in the electoral college for the party ticket. Minor party and independent candidates are also listed on the ballot, if they qualify according to provisions of the state codes, and several such candidates are usually on the ballot in different states.

Secret Service Protection [3]

In the aftermath of the 1968 assassination of Senator Robert Kennedy while he was seeking the Democratic presidential nomination, Congress passed legislation which, for the first time, authorized Secret Service protection of presidential and vice presidential candidates [4]. The law made the Secretary of the Treasury responsible for determining which major candidates are eligible for protection, after consultation with a bipartisan advisory committee comprised of the Majority and Minority Leaders of the Senate, the Speaker and Minority Leader of the House of Representatives, and one additional member to be chosen by the committee. (Spouses of such candidates are also entitled to protection, within 120 days of the general election.) On occasion, candidates have declined protection offered to them.

While the law provides protection for major party presidential and vice presidential nominees in the general election, it does not specify the criteria for determining major candidates in the primary season. However, criteria and standards in the advisory committee's guidelines specify that an eligible individual: (1) is a publicly declared candidate; (2) is actively campaigning nationally and is contesting at least 10 state primaries; (3) is pursuing the nomination of a qualified party (*i.e.*, whose presidential candidate received at least 10% of the popular vote in the prior election); (4) has qualified for public matching funds of at least $100,000, and has raised at least $2 million in additional contributions; and (5) as of April 1 of the election year, has received at least an average of five percent in individual candidate preferences in the most recent national opinion polls by ABC, CBS, NBC, and CNN, or has received at least 10% of the votes cast for all candidates in two same-day or consecutive primaries or caucuses [5].

Notwithstanding this, the Secretary of the Treasury, after consultation with the advisory committee, may provide protection for a candidate even if all of the conditions of the guidelines have not been met.

Secret Service protection for primary candidates generally begins shortly after January 1 of the election year. On occasion, the Secretary of the Treasury has accorded protection to certain candidates earlier than the election year.

II. THE NOMINATION PROCESS

Primaries and caucuses are the initial testing ground for the next President. The primary season plays an essential role in presidential elections by narrowing the field of major party candidates. The nomination is conferred on the candidate who holds a majority of delegates at the party convention, but under the present system for choosing delegates one candidate is likely to emerge with a majority by the end of the primary season, if not sooner, and well before the convention meets.

The Development of the Nominating System

The emergence of the national nominating convention in 1831, in place of the congressional caucus method of choosing nominees, gave the political parties a more democratic means of bestowing nominations, based more closely on popular sentiment. (See Chapter III for detailed information on national nominating conventions.)

Early Delegate Selection Methods

Delegates to the early conventions were either appointed by a party leader or were chosen under a party-run caucus system. While both methods involved more participants than the congressional caucus, in reality they merely shifted control of nominations to the state party leadership, which usually controlled the state's entire delegation. Delegates were chosen in this manner until the beginning of the 20th century when members of the Progressive Party, whose aim was to reform the structure and processes of government, introduced an innovative device called the primary.

Emergence of the Primary

In 1904, Florida became the first state to adopt the primary as a means of choosing delegates to the nominating conventions, and many states followed within the decade. By 1916, 20 Democratic and Republican parties selected delegates in primaries. The primary took democratization of the nominating process a step further by enabling party members to choose the delegates. It was the first large-scale innovation in the process since the introduction of the party convention about 80 years earlier.

Hailed as a triumph of democracy upon its debut, the primary failed to attract many voters, and, in the first half of this century, it never became the principal route to the nomination. In 1912, Theodore Roosevelt won nine of 13 Republican primaries, but his name was not even placed in nomination at the Republican Convention (which instead re-nominated incumbent William Howard Taft, who had won only one primary, but whose forces controlled the party's National Committee).

TheprimarymovementmadelittleprogressintheyearsfollowingthefirstWorld War, and some states abandoned it as the method for choosing delegates. The number of state party primaries in which delegates were chosen stood at around 14 for the next four decades.

Many candidates avoided primaries altogether or ran in a select few, simply to demonstrate their popular appeal. In 1952, Democratic contender Estes Kefauver entered and won 12 of 15 primaries held, only to see the convention turn to Adlai Stevenson, who had not entered any primaries. In 1960, John F. Kennedy demonstrated electability by winning a few selected primaries, but his delegate totals were amassed more by his cultivation of key party leaders and state delegations.

Reform and Revival of the Primary

The violence that marred the 1968 Democratic Convention in Chicago underscored growing discontent in that party with the dominant role played by party leaders in the nomination of candidates. In response, the Democratic National Committee formed the "McGovern-Fraser Commission" to evaluate the delegate selection process and to recommend changes designed to make the system more responsive to rank-and-file party members. The Commission, in 1969, proposed a series of reforms that addressed most aspects of delegate selection, the principal aim of which was to increase popular participation and link it more directly to the selection of delegates. The National Committee accepted nearly all of the Commission's proposals, which were subsequently adopted by the state parties.

Furthermore, some state legislatures, many of them under Democratic control, enacted statutes applicable to both parties which incorporated the Commission's recommendations.

The Commission recommended a series of sweeping changes that addressed nearly every major aspect of delegate selection. It established guidelines for translating public support for candidates into delegate votes and eliminated automatic *ex-officio* delegate slots by calling for the election of all of the delegates to the convention. Guidelines for equal representation of women and minorities were adopted, and devices that vested considerable power in the party leadership (*e.g.*, proxy voting, the unit rule, etc.) were eliminated. The McGovern-Fraser recommendations, as subsequently modified, changed the process for the Democrats, and had an impact as well on the system used by the Republicans, who made changes to respond to perceived public pressure for greater democratization.

Perhaps the principal effect of the reform movement was the revitalization of the primary in determining the choice of party nominees: it was viewed as the most suitable method for encouraging broad participation. In 1968, 37.5% of Democratic delegates were chosen in 17 primary states; the 16 Republican primary states that year sent 34.3% of the delegates to that party's convention. By 1976, the Democrats held primaries in 30 states which selected 72.6% of the delegates, while the Republicans chose 67.9% of their delegates in 28 primary states. The percentage of delegates chosen in states holding primaries has been higher in recent cycles. Under the present schedule for 2000, 85.2% of Democratic delegates (in 38 states and the District of Columbia) and 90.1% of Republican delegates (in 41 states and the District of Columbia) will be selected in states holding primaries.

The resurgence of the primary was accompanied by changes in other aspects of the political landscape which reinforced the importance of primary elections. The media became a full-fledged participant in the nominating process through their extensive coverage of primaries and their role in publicizing primary results.

Candidates are now likely to pick and choose which primaries to contest because delegates are at stake in virtually all of them. Early primaries are especially vigorously contested, particularly by lesser known candidates who seek to gain crucial media coverage and establish campaign momentum; the pace of the entire season has quickened. The nominating process in the post-1968 era thus focused attention once again on the primaries, where nominations today are won or lost.

Assignment and Categorization of Delegates by the National Parties

Allocation of Delegates to the States and Other Jurisdictions
Each party has its own method for assigning delegates (and alternates) to the different states and jurisdictions.

Democrats. The Democratic Party allocates delegates and alternates according to a formula based on population, as measured by electoral college strength and past levels of voting for Democratic presidential candidates in the general election. The Democratic National Committee also awards delegates and alternates to five jurisdictions for which the allocation factor cannot be computed because they do not participate in the presidential election—American Samoa, Democrats Abroad, Guam, Puerto Rico, and the Virgin Islands. Furthermore, the party assigns additional delegate slots for party leaders, former distinguished elected officials, and the entire Democratic membership of the U.S. Senate and House of Representatives.

Republicans. The Republican allocation system assigns three delegates per congressional district and six delegates at-large for every state. It also assigns bonus delegates based on the state's Republican vote in the previous election for President, U.S. Senate, U.S. House of Representatives, and Governor. Delegates to the convention for other jurisdictions are as signed by the Republican National Committee.

Categories of Delegates

Democrats. The Democratic Party has two basic types of delegates, grouped by whether or not they are pledged to support a particular candidate. Furthermore, there are three categories of pledged delegates (which comprise the majority of delegates to the convention) and four categories of unpledged delegates.

Pledged delegates. The allocation formula determines only the number of delegates in the pledged categories:

- District-level base delegates;
- At-large base delegates; and
- Pledged party and elected official delegates.

Of the number of delegates assigned to a state according to the allocation formula, 75 % are assigned at the district level and 25 % are designated at-large. Although district-level and at-large delegates are allocated in the same manner, they are chosen separately at different stages of the process.

Pledged party and elected official delegates represent a 15% addition to the base number of allocated delegates. They are usually chosen in the same manner as the at-large delegates.

Unpledged Delegates. The number of unpledged delegates for a state depends on the number of individuals available in each specified category. Delegate slots are allocated for:

- Former Democratic Presidents and Vice Presidents, former Democratic Majority Leaders of the U.S. Senate, former Democratic Speakers of the U.S. House of Representatives, and all former Chairs of the Democratic National Committee;
- Democratic Governors;
- Members of the Democratic National Committee (DNC), including the State chairs and vice chairs and officers of the DNC; and
- All Democratic Members of the U.S. Senate and House of Representatives.

Republicans. Aside from three congressional district delegates and six at-large delegates assigned to each state under Republican allocation rules, a number of bonus delegates may be awarded for the at-large category as well.

Four and one-half at-large bonus delegates are assigned to each state which cast its electoral votes for the Republican nominee in the previous election. One bonus delegate is allocated to each State in which a Republican was elected to the Senate or the Governorship between the last and the upcoming presidential election. One bonus delegate is also allocated to states in which half the delegation to the House of Representatives is Republican. (In 1996, 15 at-large delegates have been allocated to the District of Columbia, Puerto Rico has been allocated 14 at-large delegates, and four delegates have been allocated each to Guam and the Virgin Islands.)

The national party also awards bonus delegates to states where the primary or caucus is held after mid-March of the election year. In states where the primary or caucus is scheduled between March 15 and April 14, a 5% increase to the national convention delegation is awarded; a 7½% increase is awarded to state parties with contests scheduled between April 15 and May 14; and, a 10% increase is awarded to states where the primary or caucus is held between May 15 and the third Tuesday in June.

State parties have considerable flexibility to determine the means of electing or choosing the district and at-large delegates, according to national party rules.

Delegate Selection Structure

Under the present system for choosing presidential nominees, state parties use two main electoral devices: the primary and the caucus/convention system. State parties combine the two in a variety of ways to choose delegates to the national conventions and the resulting mix of methods accounts for the complexity that characterizes the presidential nominating process. Furthermore, the timing of delegate selection events is determined by either the state legislatures or the state parties, depending on which electoral method is used. Primary dates are usually determined by the legislatures, while caucus events are scheduled by the state's political parties. In large part, this divided authority concerning the choice of method and the timing of delegate selection events explains and perpetuates the inherent complexity of the nominating system.

The Present Mixed System of Presidential Nomination Events

Primaries. A primary is a state-run election for the purpose of nominating party candidates to run in the general election. Presidential primaries perform this function in an indirect manner, because voters elect delegates to a national convention rather than directly selecting presidential candidates.

Most states restrict voting in a primary to party members; these are *closed primary* states. *Open primary* states allow the voter to choose either party's ballot in the voting booth on primary day; none of the open primary states require voter registration by party.

In 1992, more state parties selected delegates in a primary than ever before—34 Democratic and 37 Republican (out of the 50 states and the District of Columbia). In 2000, 39 Democratic and 42 Republican primaries are scheduled in the states and the District of Columbia.

Caucuses and Conventions. A caucus is a meeting of party members or leaders to select nominees for public office and to conduct other party business. In the presidential nominating process, it is often used in combination with a state convention to elect delegates to the national nominating convention.

The caucus/convention process is typically comprised of several tiers, beginning with broad-based meetings of rank-and-file party members, usually at the precinct level. Because of their cumbersome nature, precinct caucuses invariably attract fewer voters than do primaries. Participants must invest substantial time to attend a caucus, in contrast to voting in a primary, and participants usually register their support for a presidential candidate by public declaration (by a show of hands or by gathering in groups according to presidential preference). In some places, caucus participants may vote by ballot for presidential candidates, but, in any event, the process requires face-to-face contact with other participants that is not required when casting a ballot at a polling place.

Once the presidential preference vote is tallied, caucus participants elect representatives for their preference who attend the meeting convened as the next stage in the process. Precinct caucuses are usually followed by county or congressional district meetings, with a smaller number of representatives selected at each stage—based on support for them or the candidate they favor—to go on to the next level. Delegates to the national convention are finally chosen by the representatives to the congressional district caucus or the state convention, or both.

In 2000, both state parties in nine states will select delegates using the caucus process; Democrats scheduled caucuses in three additional states.

Choice of Device for Electing   Delegates. Because primaries are administered by the states, the guidelines and timing are determined by state law; however, a political party may opt out of the primary and select delegates in a caucus process instead. Not all states provide for a presidential primary, in which case both parties use the caucus method and accordingly set their own rules and dates for caucus events. In many primary states, caucuses are a component of the process for choosing delegates as well, but the results of the primary are the crucial factor in determining the division of delegates.

Methods of Selecting Delegates

The principal difference between the parties in choosing delegates is the Democratic Party's requirement that delegate candidates selected in primaries and caucuses state their presidential or uncommitted preference as a condition for election. The Republican Party does not require a declaration of preference and, consequently, Republic and elegates election is less uniform and more dependent upon the different approaches of the state parties.

Democrats. Under the present system, state Democratic parties use one of the following four methods to elect district delegates:

Caucus/convention system. This consists of one to four tiers. As a general rule, grassroots participation is at the first tier, at which representatives to the next tier are elected, and so on. Delegates and alternates are chosen at a district meeting, usually the second or third tier.

Pre-primary caucus. This nominates district delegates, who are subsequently elected on the basis of the vote for President in the primary.

Post-primary caucus. This is held after the primary to elect the number of delegates a presidential candidate has won on the basis of the primary vote.

Two-part primary. This requires that the voter mark the ballot for presidential preference and again for individual delegates within a preference.

District delegates declare a presidential preference or run as uncommitted in the primaries and caucuses. At-large and pledged party and elected official delegates also declare a presidential or uncommitted preference, but they are chosen by the state committee, a committee of elected district delegates, or by the state convention to reflect primary or caucus results.

Republicans. District delegates may be elected in a primary or may be selected by presidential candidates on the basis of the primary vote. They can be chosen in congressional district caucuses, or they may be combined with the at-large delegates and selected as a unit at the state convention.

At-large delegates may be elected by primary voters, chosen by presidential candidates according to the primary vote, selected by the state committee, or, as in most states, chosen at the state convention.

Timing of Delegate Selection Events

With three exceptions, the Democratic Party restricts first-stage delegate selection events to the period between the first Tuesday in March and the second Tuesday in June. Party rules permit three states to hold delegate selection events prior to the first Tuesday in March: the Iowa Democratic Party may conduct its precinct caucuses 15 days earlier; the New Hampshire primary may be held seven days earlier; and the Maine first-tier caucuses may be held two days earlier. These exceptions honor traditional dates for holding primaries and caucuses in New Hampshire, Iowa and Maine that pre-dated the national party's rule that restricts delegate selection contests to a specific period.

For 2000, Iowa was given approval by the DNC to hold its caucuses even earlier, on January 24, and New Hampshire received approval to hold its primary on February 1. Maine Democrats no longer use a caucus process, but elect delegates in a primary (on March 7, 2000).

National rules for the Republican Party state only that participants in caucuses or conventions for the purpose of choosing national convention delegates shall not be elected prior to the official call for the convention. The Party issues the call prior to January 1 of the election year.

The timing of 2000 events appears in table 1, which presents the dates for state primaries and caucuses in chronological order, along with the number of delegates each state sent to the respective conventions.

Table 1. 2000 Presidential Primaries and Caucuses, by Date

Date	State	Method [a] (Primary or Caucus)	Dems	Reps
January 24	Iowa	Caucus	56	25
	Alaska (R)	Caucus	—	23
February 1	New Hampshire	Primary	29	17
February 7-13	Hawaii (R)	Caucus	—	14
February 8	Delaware (R)	Primary [b]	—	12
February 19	South Carolina (R)	Primary [b]	—	37
February 22	Arizona (R)	Primary	—	30
	Michigan (R)	Primary	—	12
February 26	American Samoa (R)	Caucus	—	4
	Guam (R)	Caucus	—	4
	Virgin Islands (R)	Caucus	—	4
February 27	Puerto Rico (R)	Primary	—	14
February 29	North Dakota (R)	Caucus	—	19
	Virginia (R)	Primary	—	56
	Washington (R)	Primary	—	37
March 7	California	Primary	434	162
	Connecticut	Primary	67	25
	Georgia	Primary	92	54
	Hawaii (D)	Caucus	33	—
	Idaho (D)	Caucus	23	—
	Maine	Primary	32	14

Table 1. (Continued)

Date	State	Method [a] (Primary or Caucus)	Dems	Reps
	Maryland	Primary	92	31
	Massachusetts	Primary	118	37
	Minnesota (R)	Caucus	—	34
	Missouri	Primary	92	35
	New York	Primary	294	101
	North Dakota (D)	Caucus	22	—
	Ohio	Primary	170	69
	Rhode Island	Primary	32	14
	Vermont	Primary	22	12
	Washington (D)	Caucus	94	—
	American Samoa (D)	Caucus	6	—
March 9	South Carolina (D)	Caucus	52	—
March 10	Colorado	Primary	61	40
	Utah	Primary	29	29
	Wyoming (R)	Caucus	—	22
March 10-14	Democrats Abroad	Caucus	9	—
March 11	Arizona (D)	Primary b	55	—
	Michigan (D)	Primary b	157	—
March 11-12	Minnesota (D)	Caucus	91	—
March 12	Nevada (D)	Caucus	29	—
March 14	Florida	Primary	186	80
	Louisiana	Primary	74	29
	Mississippi	Primary	48	33
	Oklahoma	Primary	53	38
	Tennessee	Primary	81	37
March 14	Texas	Primary	231	124
March 18	Guam (D)	Caucus	6	—
March 21	Illinois	Primary	189	74
	Nevada (R)	Caucus	—	17
March 25	Wyoming (D)	Caucus	18	—
March 26	Puerto Rico (D)	Primary	59	—
March 27	Delaware (D)	Caucus	22	—
April 1	Virgin Islands (D)	Caucus	6	—
April 4	Kansas	Primary	42	35
	Pennsylvania	Primary	191	78
	Wisconsin	Primary	92	37
April 14-17	Virginia (D)	Caucus	98	—
May 2	Indiana	Primary	88	55
	North Carolina	Primary	103	62
	District of Columbia	Primary	32	15
May 9	Nebraska	Primary	32	30
	West Virginia	Primary	42	18
May 16	Oregon	Primary	58	24
May 23	Arkansas	Primary	48	24
	Idaho (R)	Primary	—	28
	Kentucky	Primary	58	31
June 6	Alabama	Primary	63	44
	Montana	Primary	24	23
	New Jersey	Primary	124	54
	New Mexico	Primary	35	21
	South Dakota	Primary	22	22

[a] The events listed here are the initial step for choosing national convention delegates, at which rank-and-file voters participate. In a primary, Democratic voters mark their ballot either for a presidential candidate (with delegates chosen or allocated afterwards, according to the results) or for both a presidential

candidate and individual delegate candidates. Republican primary voters may have a third option, whereby the voter marks the ballot for individual delegate candidates without an accompanying Presidential candidate preference vote. The caucus process is comprised of several stages (usually three or four), where rank-and-file voters participate at the first stage, to choose participants for the next stage, and so on. National convention delegates are chosen at a later stage, after the initial mass participation event. Under the convention system, a group of participants assembles to choose the national delegates. Convention participants may have been chosen through the caucus process, they may be party officials from throughout the state, or they may have been designated to attend the convention according to some other mechanism. Most state parties adopt a delegate selection system that combines, in some manner, at least two of these methods—the primary, caucus, or convention.

[b] Party-run primaries.

Characteristics of the Contemporary Nominating System

Length of the Campaign

Potential candidates begin organizing their campaigns and raising money a year or more in advance of the primary season in order to be competitive. While the length of the nominating season has remained virtually unchanged, the pre-election maneuvering by candidates may begin shortly after the previous presidential election, and exploratory committees are often in operation one or two years before the election. In 1972, 12 of 15 major party contenders announced their candidacies no earlier than two months preceding January 1 of the election year; in 1988, all 14 major party candidates announced before the election year began (one of whom announced in 1986). For the 2000 election, six candidates had announced by the end of April 1999 and all twelve major party candidates had announced their candidacies (or the formation of their exploratory committees) by September.

The Accelerated Pace

In 1976, the Iowa Republican Party advanced its caucus date to January 19, the same day as Democratic Party caucuses, thereby supplanting the New Hampshire primary in its traditional role as the first two-party delegate selection event of the nominating season. Since then, Iowa and New Hampshire have played an incipient role in narrowing the field of candidates and setting the stage for ensuing primaries and caucuses. Other states have reacted to the influence and attention accorded Iowa and New Hampshire by advancing their dates as well—a phenomenon known as "front-loading."

The 2000 calendar was the most front-loaded ever. The nominating season began in Iowa and New Hampshire, according to tradition, although events in these states took place nearly a month earlier than in past years. The Iowa caucuses were moved to January 24 (from February 21 in 1996) and the New Hampshire primary was scheduled on February 1 (it was held on February 29 in 1996)

Following New Hampshire, Republicans scheduled events in eight states during February. But the most significant change to the calendar was the scheduling of primaries in California, New York, and Ohio on March 7, the first date on which Democrats may hold delegates election events according to national rules (from which Iowa and New Hampshire are exempt). Seven primaries were scheduled on the first Tuesday in March in 1996, mostly in New England states, but the addition of California, New York, and Ohio in 2000 swelled the number of delegates at stake and created a national event with contests taking place in each region of the country. Twelve primaries and caucuses were scheduled for both parties on March 7, 2000, and caucuses for one party or the other were scheduled in an additional four states.

In contrast, delegate selection events had been held in 23 states by the end of March in the 1992 calendar, while in 1976, delegate selection had begun in only seven states by that time.

On March 14, six southern states (Florida, Louisiana, Mississippi, Oklahoma, Tennessee, and Texas) hold primaries on the date previously known as "Super Tuesday." The event was organized by mostly Democratic members of the Southern Legislative Conference in 1988 as a 14-state southern regional primary. "Super Tuesday" offered nearly one-third of the delegates to either convention on a single day, but met with mixed reviews. Some analysts suggested the event achieved its goals, while others said it fell short of expectations. In 1992, five of the states which participated in the 1988 "Super Tuesday" primaries rescheduled their events for later during the campaign season, while Georgia officials moved their primary to the week prior to "Super Tuesday." In 2000, only six of the original 14 states will hold primaries simultaneously on March 14.

Increased Number of Debates

Campaign debates have become an increasingly important aspect of the nominating process in recent years. An unprecedented number occurred during the 1988 primary season: approximately 60 debates (virtually all televised locally or nationally) were held among candidates of one or both parties [6]. For the 2000 election cycle, 19 debates between the Democratic or Republican candidates were held between October 27, 1999 and February 21, 2000, according to the Alliance for Better Campaigns [7]

In general, the increase in debates coincided with a decrease in the number of "straw poll" elections before and during the nominating season; these polls measure candidate popularity among party activists at state conventions but have no bearing on the selection of delegates. To some extent, candidate debates offset one of the most frequently cited criticisms of the process—that the combined influence of the media and the proliferation of primaries (with their mass audience) seem to foster an emphasis on candidate image over substantive issues. Debates will likely continue to play an important role in the pre-nomination period.

III. The Nominating Conventions

National conventions combine three important functions: nomination of candidates for the office of President and Vice President; formulation and adoption of a statement of party principles—the platform; and adoption of rules and procedures governing party activities, particularly the nomination process for presidential candidates in the next election cycle.

Evolution and Traditions of the Party Convention

The first nominating convention by one of what emerged as our two major parties—the Democrats—was held in Baltimore, Maryland, between May 21 and 23, 1832. Nomination by party convention replaced earlier arrangements, which included nomination by both congressional party caucuses, and by state legislatures, which prevailed through 1828.

Historical Developments

The Caucus System. In 1800, Thomas Jefferson was nominated by a caucus comprised of Democratic-Republican Members of Congress. The Federalists chose the same method to renominate President John Adams. Following Jefferson's successful election to the Presidency that year, the Democratic-Republicans continued to use the caucus method until the election of 1820, when incumbent President James Monroe was the unchallenged consensus candidate. The declining Federalists, who relied on meetings of party leaders to nominate their choices after 1800, fielded their last presidential ticket in 1816.

Emergence of the National Party Convention. The election of 1824 brought an end to both the Democratic-Republican-dominated "era of good feeling" and the use of a congressional caucus as a nominating device. Although the Democratic-Republican caucus nominated William Crawford of Georgia as its candidate, three other candidates (John Quincy Adams, Henry Clay, and Andrew Jackson) were also nominated by rival factions within the party. After a bitter contest and an electoral college deadlock, Adams was elected President by the House of Representatives.

A brief transitional period followed, in which state legislative caucuses and conventions and various other methods were used to nominate presidential candidates. In 1832, the three parties contesting the election—Anti-Masonic, Democratic, and National Republican—used national conventions as vehicles for nominating their presidential tickets for the first time. The use of nominating conventions reflected the growing trend toward greater democratic participation which characterized the "Jackson Era."

"King Caucus" had been criticized as being both basically undemocratic and insufficiently reflective of the popular choice of candidates. The national convention, by comparison, was comprised of delegates chosen by party voters, activists and officeholders in each state. It was a natural extension, on the national level, of the party conventions used to nominate elected officials on the county and state levels. The Anti-Masonic Party was the first to use the national convention, which met in Baltimore in September 1831, to choose William Wirt as its candidate; the Democrats and National Republicans followed suit the next year. By 1840, the Democrats and Whigs had adopted the national convention as the standard nominating device, which the major parties have used without exception ever since.

Classic Elements of the National Convention

For over a century, national conventions were often unruly, strongly contested gatherings. It was common for a number of names to be placed in nomination, with no single candidate possessing the requisite number of votes to win on the first ballot.

In 1860, the Democrats were unable to decide on a candidate after ten days and were forced to reconvene six weeks later in another city to finalize their selection. On other occasions, many ballots and extensive political maneuvering were required before a presidential candidate could be nominated. Various party rules and political practices contributed to these characteristics.

The Two-Thirds Rule and Dark-Horse Candidates. A major factor was the Democratic Party requirement, adopted at the 1832 convention and not abandoned until 1936, that the party's nominee receive a two-thirds majority of delegate votes. The record for the number of ballots cast is held by the Democrats, who required 103 ballots to nominate John W. Davis in the 1924 national convention [8].

Fear of dead lock among the most widely-known candidates led to the occasional emergence of a "dark horse" candidate—a minor candidate or party figure who had not originally been thought of as a candidate—as a compromise choice. James K. Polk of Tennessee, nominated by the Democrats in 1844, is often cited as the first dark horse candidate to win nomination. In 1936, the Democrats adopted rules changes requiring only a simple majority for nomination, largely ending the lengthy balloting which had occasionally resulted in the selection of dark horse candidates.

The Smoke-Filled Room. Convention deadlock was not unknown among the Republicans, despite the fact that they required only a simple majority to nominate. At their 1920 convention, Ohio Senator Warren Harding emerged as a compromise candidate on the 10th ballot. According to legend, Harding's nomination was engineered at a secret late-night meeting of party leaders held in a hotel suite, giving rise to an enduring element of national convention lore—selection of the presidential nominee in "the smoke-filled room." The term came to imply choice of a nominee by a small group of party leaders meeting out of the view of public scrutiny.

Favorite Sons. The "favorite son" candidacy is another once-common device which is seen much less frequently in contemporary national conventions. Favorite sons were political figures (often Governors, Senators, or Representatives) who ran for the Presidency, usually campaigning only in their home states, for the purpose of retaining control of state delegations. Once at a convention, the favorite son typically used his delegates as bargaining chips, to influence the party platform, to help secure the nomination for a preferred candidate, to seek future political favors, or to enhance his own prospects as vice presidential nominee.

A 1972 Democratic Party rules change required that candidates secure pledges of support from at least 50 delegates, not more than 20 of whom can be from a single state. This rule, which essentially required candidates to secure at least a modest level of support from a more geographically diverse representation of delegates, further served to reduce the number of names placed in nomination at subsequent conventions. Similarly, current Republican Party rules require that candidates must be able to demonstrate the support of a majority of the delegates from five or more states in order to have their names placed in nomination.

The decline of favorite son candidacies in both parties is also attributed to the changing nature of the pre-convention nomination process: fewer uncommitted delegates are elected in the primaries and caucuses. Moreover, as state and local party leaders gradually lost control of the selection process, they were unable to keep delegates from supporting major candidates for the nomination.

The Modern Convention

Ratifying the Party Choice

Throughout most of the first half of the 20th century, national conventions were frequently the scene of contentious struggles for the presidential nomination. It was not uncommon for a convention to open without a clear favorite and with no candidate holding the votes needed to win the nomination on the first ballot.

Since that time, the choice of nominees has been much less likely to be made at the convention. Although there can be—and frequently are—spirited controversies over rival candidacies, the nominee today is usually known well in advance of the convention, based on an accumulation of a comfortable majority of delegate votes. As a result, the convention now characteristically serves largely to ratify a choice already arrived at by party primaries, caucuses and state conventions.

To a large extent, this change has resulted from a corresponding change in how convention delegates are chosen. Traditionally, most delegates were selected by party leaders and officials. Since World War II, and especially since the 1970s, increased reliance on caucuses and primaries has opened the delegate selection process to larger numbers of party activists and the voting public, effectively wresting control from state and national party professionals. Primary voters usually declare their presidential candidate choice at the same time as they indicate their choice of convention delegates.

Moreover, despite the large numbers of candidates who have entered the race in recent elections (at least when no incumbent was running in a particular party), the increasing length of the primary and caucus season has tended to eliminate weaker candidates, winnowing the field to one or two major contenders. In almost every convention since 1956, one candidate has gone to each party's convention with a clear, strong lead in delegate totals.

The Influence of Television

Since 1952, when full-scale television coverage began, the national convention has been transformed from a gathering of the party faithful to a media event which attracts widespread national interest. Television coverage led to a complete reorganization of scheduling and events. Convention sessions, once primarily conducted during the day, are now largely scheduled for peak viewing hours, in order to attract the widest television audience. The once-leisurely pace of events has been tightened, time-consuming demonstrations are more strictly limited, and lengthy speeches have largely been curtailed or eliminated.

Emphasis has been placed on producing stage-set platforms geared more to television viewers than convention participants. Both parties also make increasing use of professionally produced films on the candidates and the party. Included as an integral part of the convention proceedings, these serve the dual purpose of entertaining delegates and broadcasting a carefully tailored image and message to viewers nationwide.

As of 1992, the three major commercial television networks announced a reduction in convention coverage, citing increased costs and declining viewer interest. More extensive, even "gavel-to-gavel," convention coverage has been provided, however, by the Public Broadcasting System (PBS), Cable News Network (CNN), and C-SPAN.

Planning the Convention

The "Call"

The official "call" to the convention, customarily issued by the national committees of the two major parties some 18 months in advance, announces the dates and site of the national convention. The call also includes information on delegate allocation and rules for deciding disputed delegate credentials. In recent years, the Democrats have included rules governing affirmative action in the delegate selection process, activities of convention committees, and procedures and scheduling for various committees and convention events.

Timing and Location of National Conventions

During the 20th century, national party conventions have come to be held during the summer immediately preceding the opening of the general election campaign for President. Since 1952, all conventions have been held in July or August. In a tradition that dates to 1932, the party out of power has convened first, usually about a month before the party holding the Presidency. In 2000, the Republican National Convention is scheduled to be held from July 31-August 3 in Philadelphia, while the Democrats will meet from August 14-17 in Los Angeles.

In the 19th century, difficulties of travel led to the selection of centrally located cities as convention sites. Baltimore, located midway along the Atlantic seaboard, was a favorite choice in early years. As the center of population moved west, Chicago and other midwestern cities were more frequently selected. With the advent of air travel and further population growth in the west, south, and southwest, a broader range of locations has been considered. Chicago has been host to the greatest number of conventions (11 Democratic and 14 Republican).

Table 2. Democratic and Republican National Party Conventions: 1832-2000

Year	Party	Location	Dates
1832	Democratic	Baltimore	May 21-23
1835	Democratic	Baltimore	May 20-23
1840	Democratic	Baltimore	May 5-6
1844	Democratic	Baltimore	May 27-29
1848	Democratic	Baltimore	May 22-25
1852	Democratic	Baltimore	June 1-5
1856	Democratic	Cincinnati	June 2-6
	Republican	Philadelphia	June 17-19
1860	Democratic	Charleston	April 23-May 3
		Baltimore	June 18-23
	Republican	Chicago	May 16-18
1864	Democratic	Chicago	Aug. 29-31
	Republican	Baltimore	June 7-8
1868	Democratic	New York	July 4-9
	Republican	Chicago	May 20-21
1872	Democratic	Baltimore	July 9-10
	Republican	Philadelphia	June 5-6
1876	Democratic	St. Louis	June 27-29
	Republican	Cincinnati	June 14-16
1880	Democratic	Cincinnati	June 22-24
	Republican	Chicago	June 2-8
1884	Democratic	Chicago	July 8-11
	Republican	Chicago	June 3-6
1888	Democratic	St. Louis	June 5-7
	Republican	Chicago	June 19-25
1892	Democratic	Chicago	June 21-23
	Republican	Minneapolis	June 7-10
1896	Democratic	Chicago	July 7-10
	Republican	St. Louis	June 16-18
1900	Democratic	Kansas City	July 4-6
	Republican	Philadelphia	June 19-21
1904	Democratic	St. Louis	July 6-9
	Republican	Chicago	June 21-23
1908	Democratic	Denver	July 7-10
	Republican	Chicago	June 16-19

Table 2. (Continued)

Year	Party	Location	Dates
1912	Democratic	Baltimore	June 25-July 2
	Republican	Chicago	June 18-22
1916	Democratic	St. Louis	June 14-16
	Republican	Chicago	June 7-10
1920	Democratic	San Francisco	June 28-July 6
	Republican	Chicago	June 8-12
1924	Democratic	New York	June 24-July 9
	Republican	Cleveland	June 10-1
1928	Democratic	Houston	June 26-29
	Republican	Kansas City	June 12-15
1932	Democratic	Chicago	June 27-July 2
	Republican	Chicago	June 14-16
1936	Democratic	Philadelphia	June 23-27
	Republican	Cleveland	June 9-12
1940	Democratic	Chicago	July 15-18
	Republican	Philadelphia	July 24-28
1944	Democratic	Chicago	July 19-21
	Republican	Chicago	June 26-28
1948	Democratic	Philadelphia	July 12-14
	Republican	Philadelphia	June 21-25
1952	Democratic	Chicago	July 21-26
	Republican	Chicago	July 7-11
1956	Democratic	Chicago	Aug. 13-17
	Republican	San Francisco	Aug. 20-23
1960	Democratic	Los Angeles	July 11-15
	Republican	Chicago	July 25-28
1964	Democratic	Atlantic City	Aug. 24-27
	Republican	San Francisco	July 13-16
1968	Democratic	Chicago	Aug. 26-29
	Republican	Miami Beach	Aug. 5-8
1972	Democratic	Miami Beach	July 10-13
	Republican	Miami Beach	Aug. 21-23
1976	Democratic	New York	July 12-15
	Republican	Kansas City	Aug. 16-19
1980	Democratic	New York	Aug. 11-14
	Republican	Detroit	July 14-17
1984	Democratic	San Francisco	July 16-19
	Republican	Dallas	Aug. 20-23
1988	Democratic	Atlanta	July 18-21
	Republican	New Orleans	Aug. 14-18
1992	Democratic	New York	July 13-16
	Republican	Houston	Aug. 17-20
1996	Democratic	Chicago	Aug. 26-29
	Republican	San Diego	Aug. 12-16
2000	Democratic	Los Angeles	Aug. 14-17
	Republican	Philadelphia	Jul. 31-Aug. 3

Source: National Party Conventions, 1831-1988. (Washington, Congressional Quarterly, Inc., 1991.). 283 p.; 1992, 1996, and 2000 data from published sources.

Site Selection. Selection of sites for national party conventions is a lengthy process in which facilities, security arrangements, and level of assistance offered by local governments are all considered by a special committee of the parties' national committees. An incumbent President's choice of location may also be an important factor in his party's decision. State and local governments actively seek conventions due to the economic benefits conferred by the presence of large numbers of delegates, party officials and media representatives, as well as the presumably favorable national publicity generated by a national convention.

The Delegates

Delegates to national political conventions are chosen by various methods, as detailed in Chapter II. The number of delegates is established by the respective party committee and has risen over the years. In 2000, the Democratic National Convention will be comprised of 4,337 delegates and 610 alternates, while the Republicans select 2,066 delegates and an equal number of alternates. A table reflecting the growth in delegate numbers since 1952 follows:

Table 3. Growth of National Convention Delegations: 1952-2000

Year	Democrats	Republicans
1952	1230	1206
1956	1372	1323
1960	1521	1331
1964	2295	1308
1968	2522	1333
1972	3016	1333
1976	3008	2259
1980	3331	1994
1984	3933	2235
1988	4161	2277
1992	4287	2207
1996	4329	1984
2000	4337	2066

Source: James W. Davis, *National Conventions in an Age of Party Reform* (Westport, CN: Greenwood Press, 1983). p. 43. (1952-1980); Republican and Democratic National Committees, for 1984 and 1988; 1992, 1996, and 2000 data from Final Calls.

Convention Organization

National conventions of the Democratic and Republican Parties follow similar patterns of organization.

Permanent Chair

Although conventions of both parties are opened by a temporary presiding officer, election of a permanent chair is usually one of the first points in the order of business. The Permanent Chair, who presides for the balance of the convention, is usually a senior party figure, most often the party leader in the House of Representatives. (Since 1972, the Democrats have required that the permanent chairmanship alternate between the sexes every four years.) In 1996, House Speaker Newt Gingrich (GA) chaired the Republican National Convention, while Senate Minority Leader Tom Daschle (SD) and House Minority Leader Richard Gephardt (MO) co-chaired the Democratic National Convention.

Convention Committees

Committees of the national conventions prepare reports for the conventions on delegate credentials, rules of procedure, and party platforms. The full convention ratifies or amends the respective recommendations from each of these committees.

Permanent Organization. The Permanent Organization Committee, which functions continuously between conventions, has as its primary role the selection of convention officers. As part of its 1972 reforms, the Democrats abolished the Permanent Organization Committee, transferring its duties to the Rules Committee.

Credentials. The Credentials Committees of both parties examine and rule on the accreditation of state delegations to the conventions. In closely contested or unusually acrimonious nomination campaigns, the Credentials Committees occasionally consider conflicting claims for recognition by competing slates of delegates. The Rules and Bylaws Committee of the Democratic National Committee monitors the delegate selection process to ensure party rules are observed.

Rules. The Rules Committees of the two parties recommend procedures under which the national conventions are conducted.

Platform. The first party platform was adopted by the Democrats at their 1840 national convention. The task of drafting the platforms of the two major parties is the responsibility of the Platform Committees, which draft the document for the conventions' approval. Typically, these committees hold hearings around the country prior to the convention at which public views on policy questions are solicited.

The Convention Day-by-Day

Contemporary national conventions are generally held over a four-day period, with both parties observing similar schedules. The proceedings are regularly interspersed with films honoring party figures. A continuing procession of party notables, usually selected to reflect the party's diversity, offer short speeches throughout the proceedings, while clergymen from various denominations offer invocations and benedictions to open and close each session.

The following day-by-day account provides a general overview of the course of events at a typical national convention. Variations in scheduling, both planned and those necessitated by time-consuming floor procedures, are not uncommon.

Day One

The first day of a national convention is generally devoted to routine business. The convention is called to order by the national party chair, the roll of delegations is called, and the temporary chair is elected. Welcoming speeches are delivered by the mayor of the host city and often the governor of the state in which the convention is held. Committee appointments, which have been previously announced, are ratified. The Democrats generally install permanent convention officers at the first session, while the Republicans, in recent years, have completed adoption of credentials, rules, and the party platform before turning over convention proceedings to the permanent chair, usually on the second or third day. The Democratic Convention keynote address is also delivered on the first day of convention proceedings. The Republicans tend to schedule keynote speeches for later in the convention, usually at the second session.

Table 4. Keynote Speakers at National Conventions: 1900-1996

Year	Party	Speaker	State
1900	Democratic	Charles S. Thomas	CO
	Republican	E. O. Woolcott	CO
1904	Democratic	John Sharp Williams	MS
	Republican	Elihu Root	NY
1908	Democratic	Theodore A. Bell	CA
	Republican	Julius C. Burrows	MI
1912	Democratic	Alton B. Parker	NY
	Republican	Elihu Root	NY
1916	Democratic	Martin S. Glynn	NY
	Republican	Warren G. Harding	OH
1920	Democratic	Homer S. Cummings	CT
	Republican	Henry Cabot Lodge	MA
1924	Democratic	Pat Harrison	MS
	Republican	Theodore E. Burton	OH
1928	Democratic	Claude G. Bowers	IN
	Republican	Simeon D. Fess	OH
1932	Democratic	Alben W. Barkley	KY
	Republican	L. J. Dickinson	IA
1936	Democratic	Alben W. Barkley	KY
	Republican	Frederick Steiwer	OR
1940	Democratic	William B. Bankhead	AL
	Republican	Harold E. Stassen	MN
1944	Democratic	Robert S. Kerr	OK
	Republican	Earl Warren	CA
1948	Democratic	Alben W. Barkley	KY
	Republican	Dwight H. Green	IL
1952	Democratic	Paul A. Dever	MA
	Republican	Douglas MacArthur	NY
1956	Democratic	Frank G. Clement	TN
	Republican	Arthur B. Langlie	WA
1960	Democratic	Frank Church	ID
	Republican	Walter H. Judd	MN
1964	Democratic	John O. Pastore	RI
	Republican	Mark O. Hatfield	OR
1968	Democratic	Daniel K. Inouye	HI
	Republican	Daniel J. Evans	WA
1972	Democratic	Reubin Askew	FL
	Republican	Edward W. Brooke	MA
		Richard G. Lugar	IN
		Anne Armstrong	TX
1976	Democratic	John Glenn	OH
		Barbara Jordan	TX
	Republican	Howard H. Baker, Jr.	TN
1980	Democratic	Morris K. Udall	AZ
	Republican	Guy Vander Jagt	MI
1984	Democratic	Mario M. Cuomo	NY
	Republican	Katherine Ortega	NM TX
1988	Democratic	Ann Richards	
	Republican	Thomas Kean	NJ NJ TX
1992	Democratic	Bill Bradley	
		Barbara Jordan	
		Zell Miller	GA
1996	Republican Democratic	Phil Gramm Evan Bayh	TX IN
	Republican	Susan Molinari	NY

Sources: Proceedings of the National Conventions of the Democratic and Republican Parties, 1900-1996.

The Keynote Address

The keynote address sets the themes and tone of the convention and often of the general election campaign to follow. Keynote speakers are usually prominent office holders or party officials, chosen because of their national appeal and speaking ability, or because they may be viewed as "rising stars" in the party.

The keynote address is highly partisan in tone and content. It extols the party record and the incumbent President, when the party holds the White House. It attacks the opposition candidates, policies, and record.

Perhaps the most famous such address was delivered at the 1896 Democratic National Convention by William Jennings Bryan of Nebraska. His passionate attack on the gold standard, coupled with a plea for free silver ("You shall not crucify mankind on a cross of gold") stampeded the convention and led to his own nomination. A list of 20th century keynote speakers follows.

Day Two

Credentials. Routine convention business often spills over into the second day of proceedings, as reports of the credentials, rules, and platform committees are debated and approved by the delegates. While the acceptance of delegate credentials is usually a perfunctory procedure, in some years credentials have been hotly contested as rival slates of delegates from the same state, representing contending factions, were presented.

In 1968, the Democratic National Convention voted to unseat the racially segregated Mississippi Regular Democratic delegation and replace it with the rival, integrated Freedom Democratic delegation. Four years later, in 1972, challenges to both the California and Illinois Democratic delegations resulted in lengthy struggles on the floor. These struggles grew out of infighting between supporters and opponents of candidate George McGovern and focused on whether the delegations had been elected in accordance with newly adopted reform rules. In both cases, the pro-McGovern delegations were seated, helping insure nomination of the South Dakota Senator and constituting a major defeat for more traditional party leaders.

Rules. Adoption of the Rules Committee report, setting convention procedures, is another important function usually completed on the second day of the convention. Consideration of the committee report has occasionally been accompanied by spirited debate, particularly in a close convention when delegates have sought to boost their candidate's chances by securing rules changes.

At the 1976 Republican Convention, supporters of Ronald Reagan unsuccessfully sought a rules change which would have required candidates for the nomination to name their vice presidential running mate before the first ballot. Failure to comply with the proposed rule change would have freed all delegates from their customary pledge to vote for the candidate to whom they were committed on the first round. Reagan supporters hoped that adoption of the rule might force opposing candidate Gerald Ford to name a running mate unacceptable to some of his committed delegates, and thus enhance Reagan's chances of nomination.

Platform. Adoption of the party platform is another task usually completed on the second day of a convention, although consideration of proposed amendments to the Platform Committee draft will occasionally continue into the third day.

The party platform, a statement of principles and policy proposals, is prepared in advance by the Platform Committee, but is sometimes amended on the floor through minority reports. These reports are filed by those who were unsuccessful in incorporating their views into the draft version. Consideration of minority reports by the convention is contingent upon obtaining a threshold level of delegate support.

The process of platform approval has also occasionally led to spirited struggles between contending convention factions, often allied with opposing candidates. In 1984, for instance, candidate Jesse Jackson sought platform 'planks' (statements of distinct party policies) renouncing 'first use' of nuclear weapons, denouncing run off primary elections (deemed discriminatory to black candidates), and embracing the use of quotas to combat racial discrimination, all controversial positions considered by opponents as pushing the party too far to the 'left.' Convention forces loyal to eventual nominee Walter Mondale rejected all three proposals, although compromise language allegedly acceptable to Jackson was eventually adopted.

Platformsareintendedtomaintaintheloyaltyofcommittedpartyactivists,while attracting the support and votes of political independents. As such, they generally avoid proposals which might be interpreted as extreme. On the occasions when party platforms have incorporated allegedly radical proposals of the left or right, they have tended to damage the election chances of the presidential ticket.

Although serving as a statement of principles and intentions, party platforms are not binding. Presidents, once in office, may choose to ignore the pledges made by the party in convention. For example, in 1932, Franklin D. Roosevelt was elected on a platform calling for increased austerity and a balanced budget. Once in office, however, his administration undertook a program of spending measures—the New Deal—intended to stimulate the economy and end the Depression. Furthermore, Republican platforms in 1980, 1984, and 1988 called for a balanced federal budget, but budget deficits throughout this period continued to increase.

Day Three

The third day of national conventions is usually reserved for the nomination of the presidential candidate. In recent years, the nomination is accomplished in one evening, with only one ballot. The last national convention requiring more than one ballot to nominate a presidential candidate was the 1952 Democratic National Convention, in which Adlai Stevenson was chosen on the third round of voting.

The Nominating Speech. Prominent or promising party figures are usually given the task of placing the names of candidates in nomination, followed by a series of seconding speeches. The classic form of nominating speech, which generally included along list of the candidate's strengths and achievements, avoided naming the candidate until the final paragraph. This device, known as "the man who," was intended to postpone the inevitable and time-consuming demonstrations of delegate support which inevitably followed mention of the candidate's name. This classic formulation has largely disappeared from contemporary nomination speeches.

Balloting. Following completion of the nominating and seconding speeches, the role of states is called, by the clerk of the convention, a position usually filled by the permanent secretary of the party's national committee. The tally of delegate votes in each state is announced by the chair of the delegation, often the party's highest ranking elected official in the state. A running count of vote totals is maintained, usually culminating in a "spontaneous" demonstration for the nominee when he or she receives enough votes to go "over the top" to secure the nomination. Following the completion of balloting, the chair usually entertains a motion to demonstrate party unity by making the nomination unanimous by acclamation. In 1984, the Republicans departed from tradition by nominating incumbent President Ronald Reagan and Vice President George Bush in a joint ballot.

Day Four

The fourth day of the convention is usually dominated by the nomination of the vice presidential candidate and the presidential and vice presidential nominees' acceptance speeches.

Nominating the Vice President. In a current practice embraced by both parties, the choice of a vice presidential nominee remains the prerogative of the presidential candidate. Franklin Roosevelt (particularly in 1940 and 1944) is generally regarded as the first President who was able to impose his personal vice presidential choice. In 1948, Republican nominee Thomas Dewey followed suit when he chose Earl Warren as his running mate. Prior to these precedents, party leaders usually chose the vice presidential nominee, often an unsuccessful presidential candidate who had wide support, or who was perceived as adding geographical balance to the ticket.

The concept of ticket balance remains an active element in contemporary nominations, with such factors as geography, age of vice presidential nominee, and political ideology (*i.e.*, a presidential nominee perceived as liberal will often choose a more conservative running mate, and vice versa) figuring in the nominee's choice. That choice is rarely challenged, although a notable deviation from this tradition occurred in 1956, when Democratic nominee Adlai Stevenson encouraged open nominations for Vice President from the convention floor.

A spirited contest ensued, in which Tennessee Senator Estes Kefauver bested a number of challengers on the third ballot, including Senators Albert Gore, Sr.(TN), John F. Kennedy (MA), Hubert Humphrey (MN), and New York Mayor Robert F. Wagner.

Incumbent Presidents seeking reelection usually select their current Vice Presidents as running mates, in the interest of continuity and party unity, although there have been occasional efforts to deny an incumbent Vice President a place on the ticket. For instance, in 1956, some Republican leaders unsuccessfully urged President Eisenhower to replace Vice President Nixon. More recently, in 1976, Vice President Nelson Rockefeller announced that he would not seek the nomination, an action widely interpreted at the time as an effort to preserve party unity by opening the slot for a more conservative candidate and to bolster President Ford's candidacy.

The procedure for nominating the vice presidential candidates mirrors that for the presidential candidates, with the name placed in nomination by a prominent party leader, seconded by others, and followed by a roll call of the states (often a motion to nominate by acclamation occurs in place of the roll call).

Acceptance Speeches. Following his or her nomination, the vice presidential candidate delivers an acceptance speech which is followed by the last major activity of the convention—the presidential nominee's acceptance speech.

Democratic nominee Franklin Roosevelt, in 1932, was the first candidate both to appear at a national convention, and to deliver his acceptance in person. Prior to that time, a committee of party dignitaries customarily visited the candidate to inform him of his nomination. Republican nominee Thomas Dewey inaugurated this practice in the GOP in 1944.

The candidate's acceptance speech ranks with the keynote address as one of the highlights of the convention, and it serves as its finale. It provides an opportunity for the nominee to establish the tone, content, and general themes of the election campaign to come, while providing incumbent Presidents running for reelection with the opportunity to defend their record and seek a renewed mandate from the voters.

Adjournment. Immediately following the nominee's acceptance speech, the presidential nominee is joined on the podium by the vice presidential nominee, their spouses, families, defeated rivals and other party leaders for the traditional unity pose. Shortly afterwards, the convention is adjourned *sine die*.

IV. THE GENERAL ELECTION

Adjournment of the national nominating conventions marks the beginning of the next phase of the presidential election process—the general election campaign. In the months following the conventions, the candidates, parties, and campaign organizations seek to build a winning popular and electoral vote coalition.

Labor Day has traditionally marked the start of the general election campaign. Although party nominees make campaign appearances throughout the summer, scheduling and media advertising begin in earnest in September. Dramatic "kickoff" events seek to draw the greatest possible attention to the national ticket. Democratic nominees traditionally began their campaigns with a large Labor Day rally in Detroit's Cadillac Square. However, in recent years, both parties have varied the site.

Campaign Structure

Immediately following the conventions, the nominees are faced with several tasks. These include uniting the party behind the candidates, establishing a general election campaign organization, and preparing a campaign plan.

Campaign Organizations

In recent years, presidential campaigns have been managed by separate candidate centered organizations, ad-hoc groups assembled for the specific purpose of winning the election. After the conventions, these committees are usually expanded from the nominee's primary organization to include key party professionals and staff from the campaigns of rival contenders for the nomination.

The campaign organization prepares the campaign plan, schedules appearances by the nominees and surrogate campaigners, conducts opposition and survey research, manages the national media campaign, and conducts both voter registration and get-out-the-vote (GOTV) drives. The organization is organized on the national, state, and local levels, overlapping, especially on the local level, existing party structures. The campaign organization seeks to broaden the candidate's appeal beyond committed partisans, bringing his or her message to the largest number of independent voters possible and to dissatisfied members of the other party.

Campaign Plans

Campaign plans detail the strategy and tactics which the campaign organizations and candidates hope will bring a winning combination of electoral and popular votes in the general election. They specify the issues to be emphasized by the nominees and aspects of the candidates' personal image they hope to project to the voters. They include: plans of attack on the platform, issues, and candidates of the opposition; targeting of socioeconomic, ethnic, and religious groups deemed to be most amenable to the campaign message; assessments of the ticket's strengths and weaknesses in various states; and decisions on which geographic areas the candidates should concentrate in order to assemble an electoral college majority.

Campaign plans, while often quite detailed, tend to be flexible. They seek to anticipate possible events, emerging issues, and fluctuations in voter attitudes, allowing candidate and organization activities to be adjusted or "fine tuned" in order to strengthen the ticket as needed and to most effectively allocate resources.

Candidate Activity

The contemporary model of presidential candidates crisscrossing the country on campaign tours, participating in a wide variety of political gatherings, is actually a fairly recent innovation in presidential campaign activity.

Traditional Methods–The Front Porch Campaign

Throughout the 19th century, and well into the 20th, campaigns were conducted largely at grassroots levels by "surrogates"–party leaders and officeholders who spoke for the national ticket. With a few notable exceptions–in 1896, Democratic nominee William Jennings Bryan toured the country by rail in his impassioned, yet unsuccessful, campaign, nominees conducted "front porch campaigns," staying at home, receiving groups of supporters, and issuing occasional statements to the press.

The Modern Campaign Style

Active campaigning by presidential candidates became more common in the 20th century. In 1932, Franklin D. Roosevelt conducted the first modern "whistle stop" campaign, traveling 13,000 miles by train and visiting 36 states. In succeeding elections, the "whistlestop" campaign, in which candidate stoured the country by train, delivering speeches from the rear platforms, became a regular fixture of presidential politics. President Harry Truman apparently holds the record, covering 32,000 miles and averaging 10 speeches a day in his successful 1948 election bid.

During the same period, candidates made increasing use of air travel, another area in which Roosevelt pioneered. In 1932, he flew from New York to Chicago to accept the Democratic nomination, the first candidate to do so in person. Modern presidential campaigns are almost exclusively conducted by air, with the candidates able to cover both coasts in a single day. Air travel enables candidates to touch base in media markets in different parts of the country on the same day, maximizing their television exposure to voters. Sometimes, the candidates' appearances are confined to airport rallies, after which the campaign plane flies to another metropolitan area.

The Rose Garden Campaign

A variation of the front porch campaign survives in contemporary presidential electoral politics. Sitting Presidents running for reelection, seeking both to maximize the advantages of incumbency and to project a "presidential" image, are likely to make use of the "Rose Garden" campaign style. They maintain a limited campaign schedule, while carrying out their duties as President. The incumbent makes well publicized use of the perquisites of the Presidency, including the use of the President's airplane—Air Force One, scheduling frequent announcements and activities at the White House, and delivering grants and other federal benefits in states and localities which, it is hoped, contribute to the reelection effort's success.

Television Dominated Presidential Campaigns

The 1930s and 1940s saw the increasing use of radio as a major campaign communications tool. The advent of widespread commercial television broadcasting in the late 1940s added a further dimension. With its use of compelling video images, TV eventually revolutionized presidential contests. In 1952, Dwight Eisenhower became the first presidential candidate to make systematic use of the new medium, spending almost $2,000,000 on television advertising [9]. The Eisenhower campaign messages, the first created by advertising professionals, were credited with creating a favorable image of the GOP candidate, contributing substantially to his victory.

Since that time, television has come increasingly to dominate presidential election campaigns. Its influence is felt in three separate, but related areas: paid political advertising, news coverage, and candidate debates.

Paid Advertising

Televised political advertising today comprises the largest single expense in any presidential general election campaign. In 1996, more than 60% of the money spent by the Clinton and Dole general election campaigns (by the candidates and national parties) was devoted to electronic media advertising, most all of it for television [10]

Since the advent of broadcast political advertising, first on radio and later TV, candidate messages have grown progressively shorter. The standard 30-minute broadcast speech by a nominee was succeeded by the five-minute spot, which in turn has yielded to the 30- and 60-second messages most common in today's campaigns.

Televised political advertising, which has achieved a high degree of technical sophistication, generally falls into either of two categories: positive or negative. Both approaches are likely to be used, aired in different markets at different times, as dictated by the campaign plan and changing circumstances.

Positive Messages. Positive political advertising seeks to portray the candidate and issues in a favorable light. The candidate, his family, career achievements, and issue identifications are emphasized. If he is an incumbent running for reelection, the achievements of his administration are detailed. Positive campaign spots generally seek to solidify party support and attract undecided voters of either party.

Negative Messages. So-called negative, or comparative, political advertising has been used increasingly in recent years. It conveys or seeks to evoke a basically unfavorable view of the opposing candidate or party, often by means of comparison with the sponsoring candidate.

Negative spots are intended to establish doubts among the public about a candidate or his policies, in hopes of persuading them to vote against that candidate or party, or not to vote at all.

News Coverage

Television news is considered a vital source of free political advertising for presidential candidates. A January 2000 poll conducted for the Pew Research Center for the People and the Press reported that 75% of respondents stated that television was their main source for election campaign news [11]. Campaign managers seek both to keep the nominee in the spotlight and to insure that the candidate is positively portrayed. Day-to-day scheduling is now largely geared to the requirements of TV news broadcasts. Candidate appearances, often airport rallies and political speeches, are timed for inclusion in nightly network and local news broadcasts, the latter aimed at media markets in different regions. At the same time, campaign staff seek to generate large and enthusiastic crowds at these events, to convey the impression of a vital campaign effort which enjoys wide and growing support.

Televised Debates

Political historians long pointed to the Lincoln-Douglas senatorial debates of 1858 as a model for issues to be discussed before the voters. In 1948, the first public debate among presidential candidates was held, between Thomas E. Dewey and Harold Stassen, a radio broadcast in connection with the Oregon Republican presidential primary. In 1952, a joint televised appearance before the League of Women Voters' national convention included several presidential candidates or their representatives, although the event did not constitute a debate. The first televised debate occurred in 1956, between contestants for the Democratic presidential nomination: Adlai Stevenson and Estes Kefauver [12]. The first nationally televised presidential debate among general election contenders was held in1960, and since 1976, these events have become a regular fixture of presidential elections.

The 1960 Debates. In 1960, proposals were advanced for a series of televised debates between the major party nominees in the general election. However, an obstacle to such debates lay in the Federal Communications Commission's (FCC) interpretation of the Federal Communications Act's "equal time" provision a sit applied to political broadcast debates. Under this interpretation, TV networks would be required to give equal time to presidential candidates of the numerous minor parties if they broadcast the Kennedy-Nixon debates. In Public Law 86-677, Congress temporarily suspended the equal time rule for presidential candidates for the duration of the 1960 campaign, paving the way for four debates between John F. Kennedy and Richard M. Nixon, sponsored by the three commercial networks.

Following the 1960 campaign, the FCC returned to strict enforcement of the equal time rule. Furthermore, at least one of the major party candidates in the next three elections (Lyndon Johnson in 1964 and Richard Nixon in 1968 and 1972) expressed reluctance or unwillingness to participate in televised debates.

Presidential Debates Since 1976. Since 1976, televised debates have become a regular, expected feature of presidential campaigns, both in the primary and general elections. In 1975, the FCC reversed its longstanding interpretation of the equal time rule [Aspen Institute, 55 F.C.C.2d 697 (1975)] when it established an exemption for debates by qualified major party candidates as long as they were conducted as bona fide news events, sponsored by non-broadcast entities, and covered in their entirety.

The following year, the League of Women Voters Education Fund, anon-partisan public interest group, sponsored a series of three presidential debates between nominees Jimmy Carter and Gerald Ford, and one vice-presidential debate between their respective running mates, Walter Mondale and Robert Dole.

In 1980, President Jimmy Carter declined to participate in any debate that included Independent John Anderson, whom the League invited based on his public opinion poll standing. The Fund ultimately sponsored two debates, one in which only Anderson and Republican Ronald Reagan participated, and these cond with only Carter and Reagan (Anderson no longer met the Fund's criteria by that point).

In 1983, the FCC modified its earlier ruling when it allowed broadcasters, principally the commercial networks, to sponsor debates. Through 1992, debates generally followed a familiar format: candidates appeared before a panel of journalists, made an opening statement, took questions from the panel, heard rebuttal by the opponent, and generally ended with closing statements.

In 1984, President Ronald Reagan met Democrat Walter Mondale in two debates sponsored by the Fund, while their running mates—George Bush and Geraldine Ferraro—debated in a single meeting. In 1985, in an effort to assert party control over the debates, the Chairs of the Democratic and Republican National Committees collaborated to establish a non-partisan Commission on Presidential Debates. After protracted negotiations, a 1988 agreement called for commission sponsorship of the first of two presidential debates, with the Fund sponsoring the second. Eventually, the Fund withdrawal together, and the Commission sponsored both presidential events and the single vice presidential debate held in 1988.

Table 5. Nationally Televised General Election Debates: 1960-1996

Year	Date	Presidential	Vice Presidential
1960	September 26 October 7 October 13 October 21	Kennedy (D); Nixon (R) Kennedy and Nixon Kennedy and Nixon Kennedy and Nixon	
1976	September 23 October 6 October 15 October 22	Carter (D); Ford (R) Carter and Ford Carter and Ford	Mondale (D); Dole (R)
1980	September 21 October 28	Reagan (R); Anderson (I) Carter (D); Reagan	
1984	October 7 October 11 October 21	Mondale(D); Reagan (R) Mondale and Reagan	Ferraro (D); Bush (R)
1988	September 25 October 5 October 13	Dukakis (D); Bush (R) Dukakis and Bush	Bentsen (D); Quayle (R)
1992	October 11 October 13 October 15 October 19	Clinton (D); Bush (R); Perot (I) Clinton, Bush, and Perot Clinton, Bush, and Perot	Gore (D); Quayle; Stockdale (I)
1996	October 6 October 9 October 16	Clinton (D); Dole (R) Clinton and Dole	Gore (D); Kemp (R)

Sources: Commission on Presidential Debates web site, visited Feb. 17, 2000 [http://www.debates.org/pages/debhis.html].

Debates in 1992 were agreed to after an even longer struggle between Democrats and Republicans, with the plan featuring three presidential and one vice presidential Commission-sponsored debates and including Independents Ross Perot and James Stockdale. The Commission experimented with different formats for each debate, including: moderator and panel of journalists (the traditional format); single moderator and audience questions; moderator and panel of journalists, each responsible for half the time; and single moderator and free-form discussion among participants [13]

In 1996, Bill Clinton (D) and Bob Dole (R) debated once with a single moderator questioning them and then in a town hall meeting in which citizens posed questions. In the vice presidential debate, a single moderator questioned Democrat Al Gore and Republican Jack Kemp.

Role of Televised Presidential Debates. Televised debates now constitute one of the most important elements in presidential electoral politics. They draw what is easily the largest audience of any public activity associated with the election. The final presidential debate of the hotly contested, three-way election of 1992 was watched by an estimated 97 million TV viewers, for example [14].

Candidates devote substantial time and effort in preparing for debates, as it is widely believed that their performance may significantly affect their chances of electoral success. Extensive briefings and rehearsals are conducted, to anticipate questions and issues which may be raised. Careful attention is paid to the nominee's physical appearance, in order to project an appealing, if not "presidential," image.

Survey Research in the Presidential Election Campaign

The use of survey research is an integral aspect of contemporary electioneering. The public watches the fluctuations in candidate match-ups by polling organizations during the campaign, but more important to the campaigns than the "horse race" data are the tracking polls conducted on a continuing basis. These surveys, done by organizations on contract for the campaigns, are designed to identify issues of concern to potential voters, as well as to measure support for the nominee and his running mate among key demographic groups and in different geographical areas.

The tracking polls, along with even more in-depth devices like focus groups (wherein carefully selected groups of representative voters are interviewed for their reactions to the candidates and their messages), provide a source of vital information for campaigns. If support is low among particular social, economic, or ethnic groups, or in certain states, such resources as candidate appearances and political advertising are redirected and targeted to strengthen the campaign where needed. In this way, the candidates seek to change or minimize negative personal images or to emphasize their strengths and achievements, based on trends monitored often on a daily basis.

Election Day

On election day, voters in the 50 states and the District of Columbia cast their ballotsforelectorspledgedtotheirfavoredpresidentialandvicepresidentialnominees. The law establishes the first Tuesday after the first Monday in November for the choice of all federal elective officers. In the interest of convenience and economy, most states and many localities also hold elections on federal election day.

ElectionsforPresidentandVicePresidentareheldeveryfourthyear,inyearsthat are divisible by the number four (*i.e.* 1988, 1992 and 1996). Congressional elections are held on this day every even-numbered year, with those in between presidential contests termed mid-term or off-year elections.

History of Selection
The Constitution originally made no provision for election dates for presidential electors or representatives, delegating the power to establish such times to Congress. In 1845, Congress set a uniform time for holding elections for presidential and vice presidential electors, specifying that such individuals would be chosen on the first Tuesday after the first Monday in November every fourth year (5 Stat. 721). The States, however, were specifically empowered to set different times by legislation. Maine provided the best known exception to the November practice, holding its presidential election on the first Tuesday after the first Monday in September, until 1956. This practice, sometimes regarded as a "bellwether" for the rest of the U.S. gave rise to the not always accurate phrase, "As Maine goes, so goes the Nation." As of 1960, Maine has held its presidential election in conformity with the other states. In 1872, Congress extended the November election day to cover Members of the House of Representatives (17 Stat. 28). In 1915, following ratification of the 17th Amendment to the Constitution (establishing direct popular election of Senators), the same date in November was also designated for Senate elections (38 Stat. 384).

Reasons for Selection. Several reasons are traditionally cited for the selection of November as the time for federal elections. In a largely rural and agrarian America, harvesting of crops was completed by then, and farmers were able to take the time necessary to vote. Travel was also easier before the onset of winter throughout the northern part of the country. Tuesday was chosen partly because it gave a full day's travel time between Sunday (often strictly observed as a day of rest) and voting day. This was considered necessary when travel was either on foot or by horse, and the only polling place in most rural areas was at the county seat. The choice of Tuesday *after* the first Monday prevented elections from falling on the first day of the month, which was often reserved for court business at the county seat.

Polling Hours
Voting hours are regulated by the states. Current polling hours in the 50 states and the District of Columbia, arranged alphabetically by time-zone, are illustrated below. States which fall into two time-zones are denoted by an asterisk (*). The polling hours are local time in each zone, except as noted.

Table 6. Polling Hours in the States and District of Columbia[1]

State	Polls Open	Polls Close	Time Zone
Alabama	no later than 8:00 a.m.	6-8:00 p.m.[2]	Central
Alaska	7:00 a.m.	8:00 p.m.	Alaska
Arizona	6:00 a.m.	7:00 p.m.	Mountain
Arkansas	7:30 a.m.	7:30 p.m.	Central
California	7:00 a.m.	8:00 p.m.	Pacific
Colorado	7:00 a.m.	7:00 p.m.	Mountain

Table 6. (Continued)

State	Polls Open	Polls Close	Time Zone
Connecticut	6:00 a.m.	8:00 p.m.	Eastern
Delaware	7:00 a.m.	8:00 p.m.	Eastern
District of Columbia	7:00 a.m.	8:00 p.m.	Eastern
Florida *	7:00 a.m.	7:00 p.m.	Eastern
Georgia	7:00 a.m.	7:00 p.m.	Eastern
Hawaii	7:00 a.m.	6:00 p.m.	Hawaii
Idaho	8:00 a.m.	8:00 p.m.	Mountain
Illinois	6:00 a.m.	7:00 p.m.	Central
Indiana *	6:00 a.m.	6:00 p.m.	Eastern
Iowa	7:00 a.m.	9:00 p.m.	Central
Kansas *	6-7:00 a.m.	7-8:00 p.m.[3]	Central
Kentucky *	6:00 a.m.	6:00 p.m.	Eastern
Louisiana	6:00 a.m.	8:00 p.m.	Central
Maine	6-10:00 a.m.	8:00 p.m.	Eastern
Maryland	7:00 a.m.	8:00 p.m.	Eastern
Massachusetts	7:00 a.m.	8:00 p.m.	Eastern
Michigan	7:00 a.m.	8:00 p.m.	Eastern
Minnesota	7:00 a.m.	8:00 p.m.	Central
Mississippi	7:00 a.m.	7:00 p.m.	Central
Missouri	6:00 a.m.	7:00 p.m.	Central
Montana	7:00 a.m.	8:00 p.m.[4]	Mountain
Nebraska *	8:00 a.m.	8:00 p.m.	Central
	7:00 a.m	7:00 p.m.	Mountain
Nevada	7:00 a.m.	7:00 p.m.	Pacific
New Hampshire	11:00 a.m.	7:00 p.m.[5]	Eastern
New Jersey	7:00 a.m.	8:00 p.m.	Eastern
New Mexico	7:00 a.m.	7:00 p.m.	Mountain
New York	6:00 a.m.	9:00 p.m.	Eastern
North Carolina	6:30 a.m.	7:30 p.m.	Eastern
North Dakota	7-9:00 a.m.	7-9:00 p.m.[6]	Central
Ohio	6:30 a.m.	7:30 p.m.	Eastern
Oklahoma	7:00 a.m.	7:00 p.m.	Central
Oregon	7:00 a.m.	8:00 p.m.	Pacific
Pennsylvania	7:00 a.m.	8:00 p.m.	Eastern
Rhode Island	6-9:00 a.m.	9:00 p.m.	Eastern
South Carolina	7:00 a.m.	7:00 p.m.	Eastern
South Dakota	7:00 a.m.	7:00 p.m.	Mountain
	8:00 a.m.	8:00 p.m.	Central
Tennessee *	no standard opening[7] time	7:00 p.m.	Central
		8:00 p.m.	Eastern
Texas	7:00 a.m.	7:00 p.m.	Central
Utah	7:00 a.m.	8:00 p.m.	Mountain
Vermont	6-10:00 a.m.	7:00 p.m.	Eastern
Virginia	6:00 a.m.	7:00 p.m.	Eastern
Washington	7:00 a.m.	8:00 p.m.	Pacific
West Virginia	6:30 a.m.	7:30 p.m	Eastern
Wisconsin	7-9:00 a.m.	8:00 p.m.8	Central
Wyoming	7:00 a.m.	7:00 p.m.	Mountain

* States located in two time zones, listed under the eastern most time zone. [1] Local time, except as noted in states which are split between time zones. [2] Polls must be open 10 consecutive hours. [3] Polls

must be open at least 12 consecutive hours between 6:00 a.m. and 8:00 p.m. [4] Polling places with fewer than 200 registered voters may be open from noon-8:00 p.m., or until all registered electors have voted. 5 All polling places open not later than 11:00 a.m. and close not earlier than 7:00 p.m. In cities, the city council sets polling hours at least 30 days prior to the State election day. 6 In precincts where less than 75 votes were cast in the previous election, polls may open at noon. 7 Polls must be open for at least 10 hours. 8 Polls open at 7:00 a.m. in 1st, 2nd, and 3rd class cities; in 4th class cities, towns, and villages, the polls may open between 7:00 a.m. and 9:00 a.m.

Source: The Council of State Governments, The Book of the States, 1998-99 edition (Lexington KY, 1998), p. 163.

V. ELECTORAL COLLEGE AND INAUGURATION

Electoral College

When voters go to the polls on election day, they actually cast their votes for a slate of electors, who are entrusted by the Constitution with election of the President and Vice President. The electors are known collectively as the electoral college [15]

The Electoral College in the Constitution

The question of the manner in which the President was to be elected was debated at great length at the Constitutional Convention of 1787. At one point, the delegates voted for selection by Congress; other proposals considered were for election by: the people at large; governors of the several states; electors chosen by state legislatures, and a special group of Members of Congress chosen by lot. Eventually, the matter was referred to a "committee on postponed matters," which arrived at a compromise: the electoral college system.

Size of the Electoral College and Allocation of Electoral Votes

The electoral college, as established by the Constitution and modified by the 12th and 23rd Amendments, currently includes 538 members: one for each Senator and Representative, and three for the District of Columbia (under the 23rd Amendment of 1961). It has no continuing existence or function apart from that entrusted to it.

Each state has a number of electoral votes equal to the combined numerical total of its Senate and House delegation. Since the size of state delegations in the House of Representatives may change after the reapportionment mandated by the decennial census, the size of state representation in the electoral college has similarly fluctuated. The most recent House reapportionment and reallocation of electoral votes followed the 1990 census, in effect for the 1992, 1996 and 2000 presidential elections. Current electoral vote allocations are listed in table 7.

Qualifications for the Office of Elector

Article II, section 1 of the Constitution provides that, "No Senator or Representative, or person holding an office of trust or profit under the United States shall be appointed an elector." Aside from this disqualification, any person is qualified to be an elector for President and Vice President.

Table 7. Electoral Votes by State: 1992-2000

State	No.	State	No.	State	No.
Alabama	9	Kentucky	8	North Dakota	3
Alaska	3	Louisiana	9	Ohio	21
Arizona	8	Maine	4	Oklahoma	8
Arkansas	6	Maryland	10	Oregon	7
California	54	Massachusetts	12	Pennsylvania	23
Colorado	8	Michigan	18	Rhode Island	4
Connecticut	8	Minnesota	10	South Carolina	8
Delaware	3	Mississippi	7	South Dakota	3
District of Columbia	3	Missouri	11	Tennessee	11
Florida	25	Montana	3	Texas	32
Georgia	13	Nebraska	5	Utah	5
Hawaii	4	Nevada	4	Vermont	3
Idaho	4	New Hampshire	4	Virginia	13
Illinois	22	New Jersey	15	Washington	11
Indiana	12	New Mexico	5	West Virginia	5
Iowa	7	New York	33	Wisconsin	11
Kansas	6	North Carolina	14	Wyoming	3
Total:	538	Required for Election:		270	

Source: U.S. Library of Congress, Congressional Research Service, Electoral Votes Based on the 1990 Census, by David C. Huckabee, CRS Report 91-809 GOV (Washington, November 19, 1991), pp. 2-3.

Nomination of Elector Candidates

The Constitution does not specify procedures for the nomination of candidates for the office of presidential elector. The states have adopted various methods of nomination for elector candidates, of which the two most popular are by state party convention, used in 36 states, and by state party committee, used in 10 states. In practice, elector candidates tend to be prominent state and local officeholders, party activists, and other citizens associated with the party which they are nominated.

A list of elector candidates and those chosen as electors in each state may be obtained from the Secretaries of State (Commonwealth), at the state capital. Lists of electors for 1992 and 1996 and other related information may be obtained from the National Archives and Records Administration's electoral college home page at: [http://www.nara.gov/fedreg/ec-hmpge.html].

Selection of Electors

The Constitution left the method of selecting electors and of awarding electoral votes to the States. In the early years of the Republic, many states provided for selection of electors by the state legislatures. Since 1864, all states have provided for popular election of electors for President and Vice President.

According to practices adopted universally by the states beginning early in the 19th century, popular votes are cast for a unified ticket of party candidates for President and Vice

President. This insures that they will be of the same party, avoiding a source of potential partisan divisiveness in the executive branch.

General ticket system. In 48 states and the District of Columbia, all electoral votes are awarded to the slate that receives a plurality of popular votes in the state. This practice is variously known as the general ticket or winner-take-all system.

The general ticket system usually tends to exaggerate the winning candidates' margin of victory, as compared with the share of popular votes received. For instance, in 1996, Bill Clinton and Al Gore won 49.2% of the popular vote, as compared with 40.7% by Bob Dole and Jack Kemp. The Democrats' electoral vote margin of 379 to 159 was a much higher 70.4% of the total, due to the fact that the Democratic ticket received a plurality vote in 32 States and the District of Columbia.

District system. Currently, Maine and Nebraska provide the only exception to the general ticket method, awarding one electoral vote to the ticket gaining the most votes in each of their congressional districts, and awarding the remaining two (representing their senatorial allotment) to the winners of the most votes statewide. This variation, more widely used in the 19th century, is known as the district system.

The Faithless Elector

The founding fathers intended that individual electors be free agents, voting for the candidates they thought most fit to hold office. In practice, however, electors are not expected to exercise their own judgment, but, rather, to ratify the people's choice by voting for the candidates winning the most popular votes in their state. Despite this understanding, there is no constitutional provision requiring electors to vote as they have pledged. Over the years, a number of electors have voted against the voters' instructions, known as the phenomenon of the unfaithful, or faithless, elector.

Although a number of states have laws which seek to bind the electors to the popular vote winners, the preponderance of opinion among constitutional scholars holds that electors remain free agents. Moreover, all of the seven votes of the faithless electors between 1948 and 1988 were recorded as cast [16]. The most recent occurrence was in 1988, when a West Virginia Democratic elector voted for Lloyd Bentsen for President and Michael Dukakis for Vice President.

Winning the Presidency

The 12th Amendment of the Constitution requires that winning candidates receive an absolute majority of electoral votes (currently 270 of the 538 total).

Counting the Electoral Votes

Once the voters have chosen the members of the electoral college, the electors meet to ratify the popular choices for President and Vice President. The Constitution provides (again, in the 12th Amendment) that they assemble in their respective states. Congress has established (in 3 U.S.C. §8) the first Monday after the second Wednesday in December following their election as the date for casting electoral votes, at such place in each state as the legislature directs.

In practice, the electors almost always meet in the state capital, usually at the State House or Capitol Building, often in one of the legislative chambers. The votes are counted and recorded, the results are certified by the Governor and forwarded to the President of the U.S. Senate (the Vice President).

The electoral vote certificates are opened and counted at a joint session of the Congress, held, as mandated (3 U.S.C. §15), on January 6 following the electors' meeting (or, by custom, on the next day, if it falls on a Sunday); the Vice President presides. Electoral votes are counted by the newly elected Congress, which convenes on January 3. The winning candidates are then declared to have been elected.

Minority Presidents

A major criticism of the electoral college is that it could deny victory to the candidate with the most popular votes, which can occur when one ticket wins the requisite majority of electors but gets fewer popular votes than its opponent(s).

Popular vote winners have failed to win the Presidency on three occasions since adoption of the 12th Amendment: in 1824, 1876, and 1888. In 1824, the electoral vote was split among four candidates, necessitating election by the House of Representatives, which chose the popular vote runner-up. In 1876, due to contested returns from four states, Congress setup an electoral commission, which awarded the disputed votes to the apparent popular vote runner-up, resulting in a one-vote margin in the electoral college. In 1888, the apparent popular vote runner-up won a comfortable electoral college majority. Electoral college 'misfires' are listed below.

Table 8. Presidents Elected Without A Plurality of the Popular Vote

Year	Candidates	Party	Popular Vote	Electoral Vote
1824 [1]	Andrew Jackson	D-R	152,933	99
	John Quincy Adams *	D-R	115,696	84
	William H. Crawford	D-R	46,979	41
	Henry Clay	D-R	47,136	37
1876	Samuel J. Tilden	D	4,287,670	184
	Rutherford B. Hayes *	R	4,035,924	185
1888	Grover Cleveland	D	5,540,365	168
	Benjamin Harrison *	R	5,445,269	233

* Elected

D-R=Democratic Republican; D=Democratic; R=Republican.

[1] Popular returns for 18 states; in 6 states, electors were appointed by the state legislatures.

Source: Peirce and Longley. The People's President, p. 241-242.

Electoral Contingencies

Electoral College Deadlock

The Constitution, in the 12th Amendment, provides for cases in which no slate of candidates receives the required electoral college majority, a process usually referred to as contingent election. Under these circumstances, the House of Representatives elects the

President, choosing from among the three candidates receiving the most electoral votes, with each state casting a single vote [17]

In the course of the usual presidential election, in which only the two major party candidates have a chance of victory, such occurrences are extremely unlikely. In those elections characterized by the emergence of a strong third party candidate (George Wallace in 1968, John Anderson in 1980, and H. Ross Perot in 1992), electoral college deadlock is possible. Only once since adoption of the 12th Amendment, in the four-candidate election of 1824, was the President—John Quincy Adams—elected by the House of Representatives.

If there is no electoral vote majority, election of Vice President is entrusted to the Senate, with each member casting one vote, choosing from the two candidates with the most electoral votes. Only once, in 1837, did the Senate so elect a Vice President—Richard M. Johnson. Although Democratic presidential nominee Martin Van Buren won a clear electoral college majority, votes were cast for two Democratic vice presidential candidates, yielding a three-way contest requiring Senate resolution.

In the event contingent election is necessary, the House has two weeks between counting the electoral votes (January 6) and Inauguration Day (January 20) in which to elect a President. If it is unable to do so during this time, the Vice President-elect, assuming one has been chosen by the electors or the Senate, serves as acting President until the House resolves its deadlock. In the event the Senate has been similarly unable to elect a Vice President, the Speaker of the House of Representatives serves as Acting President until a President or Vice President is elected, but he must resign the offices of both Speaker and Representative in order to so serve. In the event there is no Speaker, or the Speaker fails to qualify, then the President Pro-tempore of the Senate (the longest serving Senator of the majority party) becomes Acting President, under identical resignation requirements.

Death of a Candidate

Before December meeting of electors. In the event a presidential or vice presidential candidate of either party dies or resigns between the convention and the meeting of electors in December, the rules of the major parties provide that their national committees shall meet and fill the vacancy. In the Democratic Party, the replacement nominee is approved by a *per capita* vote of the members of the national committee. For the Republicans, each state delegation to the national committee casts a number of votes equal to its delegation to the national convention [18]

In 1972, the Democratic National Committee selected R. Sergeant Shriver as vice presidential nominee, to replace Senator Thomas Eagleton, who resigned as nominee after the national convention. The Republicans most recently replaced a candidate on the national ticket in 1912, when Vice President James S. Sherman died on October 30. Meeting after the election, the Republican National Committee elected Nicholas M. Butler to receive Republican electoral votes for Vice President.

Between December and January 6. If there is a vacancy due to the death of the President-elect after the electoral votes have been cast in the states, most authorities maintain that the provisions of the 20th Amendment apply: Section 3 specifies that the Vice President-elect becomes President-elect in these circumstances. Some observers, however, maintain that there is no President-elect until the electoral votes are counted by Congress on January 6 of the following year, and that since no *living* candidate received a majority of electoral votes, then the House would elect the President, and the Senate, the Vice President [19]. Other sources dispute this inference, however, maintaining that Congress "has no choice but to count all the ballots provided the 'person' voted for was alive at the time they were cast." [20]. Moreover, this interpretation is corroborated by the House report accompanying the 20th Amendment, which states that "the votes, under the above circumstances, must be counted by Congress . . . . Consequently, Congress would declare that the deceased candidate had received a majority of the votes"[21]. The balance of opinion and precedent thus suggests that electoral votes cast for a deceased candidate would be valid, provided they were cast when the candidate was living.

A final question is whether these provisions would apply if a winning presidential candidate withdrew from consideration after the electoral votes were cast, but before they were counted, as the 20th Amendment cites only the case of a candidate's death. Would Congress count the votes, proclaim the results, and then have the option to declare the position of President-elect vacant? If so, it is then arguable whether the Vice President-elect would become President-elect. On the other hand, it can also be argued that Section 3 of the 20th Amendment provides only for cases in which a President-elect has died, and would not cover other circumstances. In this case, it could be argued that sentence 2 of Section 3 would apply:

> If a President shall not have been chosen before the time fixed for the beginning of his term or *if the President elect shall have failed to qualify* (emphasis added), then the Vice President elect shall act as President until a President shall have qualified.

Under these circumstances, the Vice President-elect would serve only as acting President. While the differences in these two situations may seem to be a "difference without a distinction," it can be argued that it is preferable for the nation to have a duly inaugurated President serving a full term to an acting President whose term of office and constitutional status are largely undefined. This question would appear to merit further legal and constitutional study.

Between January 6 and January 20. If a winning presidential candidate dies *after* Congress has counted the electoral vote, the Vice President-elect becomes President-elect, under the provisions of the 20th Amendment. The new President would then be empowered, under the 25th Amendment, to nominate a person to fill the consequent vacancy in the Vice Presidency. If *both* the President and Vice President-elect die before the inauguration, but after the electoral votes are counted, Congress is then empowered (by the 20th Amendment) to provide by law who shall act as President, or the manner in which a President is to be selected.

Inauguration

Although the President and Vice President were inaugurated on March 4 of the year after their election from 1789 to1933, the 20th Amendment, ratified in 1933 and effective in 1937, changed the commencement date of the presidential term of office to January 20. The purpose of this change, which also moved the start of the congressional term from March 4 to January 3, was to shorten the time between election and inauguration, to eliminate "lame duck" sessions of Congress, in which defeated and retired members had regularly met for a final session after the election.

Sunday Inaugurals

In a tradition dating to the 19th century, Presidents are not publicly inaugurated on Sundays. When January 20 falls on that day, a brief private inauguration is held, usually in the East Room of the White House, with a public ceremony the next day. This occurred most recently in 1985, when President Ronald Reagan was privately installed for his second term on Sunday, January 20, and publicly inaugurated on Monday, January 21. Inauguration Day next falls on a Sunday in the year 2013.

Location of the Inauguration Ceremonies

In a tradition dating to Andrew Jackson's first inaugural in 1829, Presidents were previously installed at outdoor ceremonies at the East Front of the U.S. Capitol (facing the Supreme Court). Vice Presidents were customarily sworn in the Senate Chamber until 1933, when the two ceremonies were held jointly for the first time, a practice which continues.

On seven occasions since 1837, the presidential inaugural has been held elsewhere than the East Front. In 1909, due to inclement weather, William Howard Taft was installed in the Senate Chamber; in 1945, in consideration of the President's health and wartime security demands, Franklin D. Roosevelt was sworn in for his fourth term on the South Portico of the White House; in 1981, 1989, 1993, and 1997, Ronald Reagan, George Bush, and Bill Clinton were inaugurated at the West Front of the Capitol (facing the Mall); and in January 1985, due to inclement weather, President Reagan was publicly installed for his second term in the Capitol Rotunda. The West Front venue appears to have gained wide acceptance since 1981, and may be expected to continue to be the site of future inaugurals, barring unforeseen circumstances.

REFERENCES

[1]   Defined as including the 50 states and the District of Columbia.

[2]   Citizens born in Guam, Puerto Rico, and the U.S. Virgin Islands are legally defined as "natural born" citizens, and are, therefore, also eligible to be elected President, provided they meet qualifications of age and 14 years residence within the United States. Residence in Puerto Rico and U.S. territories and possessions does not qualify as residence within the United States for these purposes. [U.S. Library of Congress, Congressional Research Service, *U.S. Insular Areas and Their Political Development*, by Andorra Bruno and Garrine P. Laney, CRS Report 96-578GOV (Washington: Jun. 17, 1996), pp. 9, 21, 33].

[3]   Frederick Kaiser, Specialist in American National Government, in the CRS Government and Finance Division assisted in preparation of this section.

[4]   P.L. 90-331; 18 U.S.C. §3056.

[5]   Advisory Committee Guidelines for Assignment of Secret Service Protection to Presidential Candidates. U.S. Department of the Treasury, Washington, 2000.

[6]   R.W. Apple, Jr., "Political Debates and Their Impact on The Race," *New York Times*, Apr. 23, 1988. p. 10; In 1992, some 15 debates were held during the primary season, a lower number than 1988, partly because of a greater degree of competition in both parties in the earlier year.

[7]   Glenn Kessler, "In Debates, Sponsor's Can't Lose," *The Washington Post*, Feb. 29, 2000, p. E1.

[8]   The Republican record is held by the 1880 convention, which took 36 ballots to nominate James Garfield.

[9]   Stanley Kelly, *Professional Public Relations and Political Power* (Baltimore: Johns Hopkins Press, 1956), p. 161, 162.

[10] Campaign Study Group, as reported in: Ira Chinoy, "In Presidential Race, TV Ads Were Biggest '96 Cost By Far," *Washington Post*, Mar. 31, 1997, p. A19.

[11] "Audiences Fragmented and Skeptical: The Tough Job of Communicating with Voters," The Pew Research Center for the People and the Press [http:/www.people-press.org/jan00rpt2.htm]

[12] Susan A. Hellweg, Michael Pfau, and Steven R. Brydon, *Televised Presidential Debates: Advocacy in Contemporary America* (NY: Praeger, 1992), pp. 1-3.

[13] Richard L. Berke, "Bush and Clinton Agree on Debates; Plan to Ask Perot." *New York Times*, Oct. 3, 1992, p. 1,9.

[14] Commission on Presidential Debates web site, visited Feb. 17, 2000 [http://www.debates.org/pages/debhis92.html].

[15] For additional information on the contemporary role of the electoral college, see CRS Report RS20273, *The Electoral College: How it Operates in Contemporary Presidential Elections*.

[16] Neal Peirce and Lawrence D. Longley, *The People's President*, rev. ed. (New Haven CT: Yale University Press, 1981), p. 98-101. The vote of the "faithless elector" in 1988 (see below) was also recorded as cast.

[17] For additional information on contingent election, see CRS Report RS20300, *Election of the President and Vice President by Congress: Contingent Election*.

[18] Democratic National Committee. *Rules of Procedure for Filling a Vacancy on the National Ticket*; Rule 27 of the Republican Party.

[19] Walter Berns, ed., *After the People Vote: A Guide to the Electoral College* (Washington: AEI Press, 1992), p. 27,28.

[20] John D. Feerick, *From Failing Hands: The Story of Presidential Succession*, (NY: Fordham Univ. Press, 1965), p. 274.

[21] U.S. Congress, House, Committee on Election of President and Vice President, and Representatives in Congress, *Proposing an Amendment to the Constitution of the United States*, 72nd Cong., 1st sess., H.Rept. 72-345 (Washington: GPO, 1932), p. 5.

In: Economics, Political and Social Issues ...
Editor: Michelle L. Fergusson

ISBN: 978-1-61122-555-6
©2011 Nova Science Publishers, Inc.

ELECTION OF THE PRESIDENT AND VICE PRESIDENT BY CONGRESS: CONTINGENT ELECTION[*]

Thomas H. Neale

American National Government,
Government and Finance Division

ABSTRACT

The 12th Amendment to the Constitution requires that candidates for President and Vice President receive a majority of electoral votes (currently 270 or more of a total of 538) to be elected. If no candidate receives a majority, the President is elected by the House of Representatives, and the Vice President is elected by the Senate. This process is referred to as contingent election. It has occurred only twice since the adoption of the 12th Amendment in 1804: for President in 1825, and for Vice President in 1837. In the House, the President is elected from among the three candidates who received the most electoral votes. Each state casts a single vote for President, and a majority of 26 or more state votes is required to elect. In 1825, the House decided that a majority of votes of Representatives in each state was required to cast the state's vote for a particular candidate, or the state's vote would be forfeit for that round of voting. This and other decisions reached in 1825 would have precedent, but would not be binding in future contingent elections. In cases where a state has only one Representative, that Member decides the state vote. In the Senate, the Vice President is elected from among the two candidates for Vice President who received the most electoral votes, with each Senator casting a single vote. A majority of the whole Senate, 51 or more votes, is necessary to elect. The District of Columbia does not participate in contingent election of either the President or Vice President. Contingent election would be conducted by the newly elected Congress immediately following the joint session (held on January 6 of the year following a presidential election) that counts electoral votes. If the House is unable to elect a President by January 20 (when the new presidential and vice presidential terms begin), the Vice President-elect serves as Acting President until the impasse is resolved. If the Senate is unable to elect a Vice President by January 20, then the Speaker of the House serves as Acting President.

For additional information on the electoral college, consult CRS Reports RS20273, The Electoral College: How it Works in Contemporary Presidential Elections, and RL30804, The Electoral College: An Overview and Analysis of Reform Proposals.

---

[*] Excerpted from CRS Report RS20300 dated January 17, 2001.

ORIGINAL CONSTITUTIONAL PROVISIONS

The Constitution's original provisions (Article II, section 1) required each elector to cast two undifferentiated votes for President—one each for two preferred candidates. There was no separate electoral vote for Vice President. The candidate receiving the most votes was elected President, provided the votes constituted a number equal to a majority of electors, *not* electoral votes. The runner-up was elected Vice President [1]. In the event of a tie vote, or if no candidate received a vote from a majority of electors, the House of Representatives elected the President from among the five candidates receiving the most electoral votes. Voting was by states, with each state casting a single vote.

THE 12TH AMENDMENT

The system's deficiencies became disastrously apparent in the election of 1800,when all Democratic-Republican electors cast one vote each for presidential candidate Thomas Jefferson and vice presidential candidate Aaron Burr, resulting in a tie, and thus requiring contingent election in the House when it met to count the electoral votes on February 11, 1801. A constitutional crisis resulted as Burr supporters allegedly sought support from Federalist Representatives in order to gain the presidency for the vice presidential candidate [2]. Enough Federalists voted for Burr to deny Jefferson a majority in the first round (the vote was eight states for Jefferson, six for Burr, with two states divided). Voting continued in the House for seven days and required 36 ballots before the impasse was broken and Burr's support collapsed. Jefferson's final margin was 10 states to Burr's four, with two remaining divided [3]

Shocked by the election crisis, Congress, in 1803, proposed a constitutional amendment designed to prevent any repetition of the events of 1801. State ratifications followed quickly, and the new, 12th Amendment to the Constitution was declared to be in effect on September 25, 1804. The amendment's provisions, which remain in effect, are summarized as follows.

- The electors cast separate ballots for President and Vice President.
- The votes are opened and counted in a joint session of Congress presided over by the President of the Senate (the Vice President or the President *pro tempore*).
- The person having a majority of votes for each office is elected.
- If no candidate for President gains a majority, then the House votes "immediately, by ballot" for President (contingent election), choosing from among the three candidates who received the most electoral votes. Contingent election would also apply in the case of an electoral vote tie, since a tie vote does not produce a majority.
- A quorum of at least one Representative from two-thirds of the states (34 at present) is necessary for the purposes of contingent election.
- The vote is taken by states, with each state casting a single vote.
- The votes of a majority of states (26 at present) are necessary to elect the President.
- If the House is unable to elect prior to expiration of the presidential term (January 20), then the Vice President, assuming one has been elected, serves as Acting President until a President is chosen.

- If no candidate for Vice President receives a majority of electoral votes, then the Senate elects, choosing between the two candidates receiving the most electoral votes. A quorum of two-thirds of the Senate (67 Members) is necessary for the purposes of contingent election of the Vice President Each Senator casts a single vote. The votes of a majority of the whole Senate (51 or more) are necessary to elect the Vice President.

The amendment made no attempt address the question of which Congress (lame duck or newly-elected) would conduct contingent elections in the future. During this period, electoral votes were cast in January, and counted in February, while congressional and presidential terms expired on March 4. Thus, in 1801, contingent election was conducted by the lame duck House of the 6th Congress, as noted elsewhere in this report. Questions as to the propriety and fairness of this arrangement, by which a Congress controlled by a party repudiated in the immediately preceding elections could choose the President, seem not to have occurred to the framers of the 12th Amendment.

CONTINGENT ELECTION IN 1825: PHILOSOPHY, PROCEDURES, PRECEDENTS

The emergence off our major presidential candidates in the 1824 presidential election led to a fragmentation of the electoral vote, necessitating contingent election of the President by the House of Representatives in 1825. The dominant Democratic-Republicans divided into four largely geographical factions, nominating Andrew Jackson, John Quincy Adams, William H. Crawford, and Henry Clay for President. When no candidate received the requisite majority of electoral votes, a contingent election was conducted in the House on February 9, 1825 [4] The 18th Congress convened its lame duck session in December of 1824, by which time it was already apparent that the House would elect the President, a situation that was complicated by charges from Jackson supporters that Henry Clay had agreed to support the Adams candidacy in the House in return for his appointment as Secretary of State [5]. Spirited debate as to the nature and requirements of contingent election preceded the actual vote. One question concerned the role of individual Representatives. Some asserted that it was the duty of the House to choose Jackson, the candidate who had won a national plurality of the popular and electoral vote. Others believed they should vote for the popular vote winner in their state or district. Another school of opinion suggested that House Members should give prominence to the popular results, but also consider themselves at liberty to weigh the comparative merits of the three candidates. Still others asserted that contingent election was a constitutionally distinct process, triggered by the failure of the people (and the electors) to arrive at a majority. Under this theory, the popular and electoral college results had no bearing or influence on the contingent election process, and Representatives were, therefore, free to consider the merits of the contending candidates without reference to the earlier contest [6]. Given Clay's active support of Adams, the election itself was almost a foregone conclusion: in contrast with 1801, the House required only one ballot to choose Adams, who received 13 state votes, to seven for Jackson and four for Crawford.

While most of the 12th Amendment's provisions are specific, some sections were the subject of further interpretation when the House conducted contingent election in 1825. After days of debate, the House adopted rules of procedure for the impending election that are summarized as follows.

- The House met in closed session, with only stenographers, House officers, Representatives, and Senators present. ! Motions to adjourn were not entertained unless offered and seconded by state delegations, not individual Members.
- State delegations were arranged in the House chamber from left to right in the order in which the roll was called. At the time, the roll began with Maine, proceeded north to south through the original states, and concluded with subsequently admitted states, in order of their entry into the Union.
- Each state delegation received a ballot box, and Representatives cast paper ballots inscribed with the name of the candidate for whom they were voting. A majority of votes of a state delegation was required to cast a vote for any candidate; if there was no majority, the vote was declared "divided" and was forfeit for that round.
- State votes were determined, the results were recorded on two ballots, and deposited in duplicate ballot boxes in the House chamber. The contents were counted by tellers, compared, and reported to the House [7]

These decisions applied only to the rules under which the House of Representatives conducted contingent election of the President in 1825; although they would provide a reference for the House in any future application of the contingent election process, they would not be prescriptive, and could be subject to different interpretations.

CONTINGENT ELECTION IN 1837

An internal dispute in the Democratic Party led to contingent election of the Vice President in the Senate in 1837. Democratic presidential nominee Martin Van Buren won a comfortable electoral vote majority in the 1836 election, but his controversial running mate, Richard Mentor Johnson, split the vote with an "independent" Democratic vice presidential nominee, thus requiring contingent election [8]. Electoral votes were counted on February 8, 1837, in a joint session of the 24th Congress, and the Senate then immediately returned to its own chamber to elect the Vice President. Since the Senate's choice was limited by the 12th Amendment to the two candidates gaining the most electoral votes (rather than three, as required for presidential contingent elections), it chose between Johnson and his leading Whig opponent, Francis Granger. Procedures adopted by the Senate differed from those of the House in 1825: the roll was called in alphabetical order, at which time each Senator gave the name, *vivavoce*, of the person for whom he voted [9] Johnson was elected in the first round of voting, receiving 33 votes to 16 for Granger.

THE 20TH AMENDMENT AND THE PRESIDENTIAL SUCCESSION ACT OF 1947

The contingent election process has been modified in the 20th century by the 20th Amendment to the Constitution, and the Presidential Succession Act of 1947 (61 Stat. 380; 3 U.S.C. 19). Section 1 of the amendment set new expiration dates for congressional and presidential terms, changing the former to January 3 and the latter to January 20. Previously, both terms had expired on March 4. The primary purpose of this change was to eliminate the historical anomaly of lame duck congressional sessions, while also shortening the period between election and inauguration of the President and Vice President by six weeks. A subsidiary purpose, as revealed by the amendment's legislative history, was to remove the responsibility for contingent election from a lame duck Congress [10]. Section 3 restates the 12th Amendment provision that the Vice President acts as President in the event the House is unable to elect a President in the contingent election process. It also empowers Congress to provide by law for situations in which neither a President nor a Vice President "qualifies," (i.e, neither has been elected).

The Presidential Succession Act, among other effects, reinforces this safeguard by naming the Speaker of the House of Representatives to serve as Acting President in such situations, or, alternatively, the President *pro tempore* of the Senate in the event the Speaker is ineligible, or declines, or the speakership is vacant. The Speaker would be required to resign both as Representative and as Speaker to become Acting President. Similarly, the President *pro tempore* would be required to resign both as a Senator and as President *pro tempore* to assume the acting presidency. If both the Speaker and the President *pro tempore* decline the office, or fail to qualify for any reason, then the acting presidency would devolve upon the head of the most senior executive department (Department of State). The other cabinet secretaries would be similarly eligible in the order of their department's seniority [11]

Both the Succession Act and the 20th Amendment specifically limit the service of an Acting President in such circumstances: he holds office only until either a President or Vice President has qualified.

DISTRICT OF COLUMBIA PARTICIPATION

Although the 23rd Amendment empowers citizens of the District of Columbia to vote in presidential elections, the nation's capital is not considered a state for the purposes of contingent election. Thus, the District would not participate in the election, despite the fact that its citizens cast both popular and electoral votes for President and Vice President [12]

CONCLUSION

American presidential elections have generally been dominated by two major parties since the early 19th century, with major party candidates winning a majority of electoral votes in every election since 1836. A popular third party or independent candidacy has the potential of preventing an electoral vote majority, however; such candidacies have emerged in four recent presidential elections (1968, 1980, 1992, and 1996). Furthermore, a contest over election results in Florida in the very closely contested presidential election of 2000 raised the possibility that Florida's electoral votes might be excluded in the electoral vote count session, an action that could have resulted in neither presidential candidate receiving a majority of electoral votes, thus requiring a contingent election. Under either of the above mentioned scenarios, the House and Senate could be called on to elect the President and Vice President in some future election. Barring any comprehensive reform of the presidential election system, such an election would be governed by the provisions of the 12th Amendment.

REFERENCES

[1]   The rise of national political parties that nominated candidates for *both* President and Vice President on a joint ticket doomed the arrangement, which did not anticipate such joint candidacies. In theory, party electors needed to cast one vote for the party presidential candidate, and one for the vice presidential nominee. In order to avoid tying the electoral vote, however, it was necessary for one or more electors to withhold his second vote from the designated vice presidential candidate, a cumbersome arrangement at best.

[2]   The 1800 presidential election was a bitter contest between incumbent President John Adams, representing the Federalists, and his Vice President, Thomas Jefferson, candidate of the Jeffersonian-, or Democratic-Republicans. The results were not in doubt: Jefferson and Burr won 73 electoral votes to Adams's 65 (the Federalist electors had correctly cast one less electoral vote for their vice-presidential candidate, Charles C. Pinckney, who received 64). Further, the contingent election was conducted by a lame duck House session of the 6th Congress, which was controlled by the Federalists. The Democratic-Republicans had gained control of the House in the 1800 congressional elections, but the new 7th Congress did not convene until March 4, 1801.

[3]   Neal R. Peirce and Lawrence D. Longley, *The People's President: The Electoral College in American History and the Direct Vote Alternative*, rev. ed. (New Haven, CT.: Yale University Press, 1981), pp. 35-41.

[4]   The electoral vote totals for President were: Jackson, 99; Adams, 84; Crawford, 41; and Clay, 37. Clay was thus eliminated from the contingent election. Curiously, Vice Presidential candidate John C. Calhoun received an overwhelming electoral vote majority.

[5]   Theodore G. Venetoulis, *The House Shall Choose* (Margate, NJ: Elias Press, 1968), pp. 130-135.

[6]   U.S. Library of Congress, Congressional Research Service, *Election of the President by the House of Representatives and the Vice President by the Senate: Relationship of the Popular Vote for Electors to Subsequent Voting in the House of Representatives in 1801 and 1825 and in the Senate in 1837*, Typed Report, by Joseph B. Gorman (Washington: Nov. 20, 1980), pp. 13-22.

[7]   U.S. Congress, House, *Hind's Precedents of the House of Representatives* (Washington: GPO, 1907), vol.3, pp. 292-293.

[8]   Van Buren won 170 electoral votes to 124 for four Whig candidates; Johnson took 147, while independent Democrat William Smith won 23, and two Whig candidates won 124.

[9]   U.S. Congress, Senate, *Journal of the Senate*, 24th Cong., 2nd sess. (Washington: Gales and Seaton, 1836 [sic]), pp. 229-230.

[10]   U.S. Congress, Senate Committee on the Judiciary, *Report to Accompany S.J. Res. 14, 72nd Congress, 1st Sess.* S. Rept. 26, 72nd Cong., 1st sess. (Washington: GPO, 1932), p. 4.

[11]   For additional information on presidential succession, see: U.S. Library of Congress, Congressional Research Service, *Presidential and Vice Presidential Succession*, by Thomas H. Neale, CRS Report 98-731 GOV (Washington, Aug. 21, 1998).

[12]   U.S. Library of Congress, Congressional Research Service, *Would the District of Columbia Be Allowed to Vote in the Selection of the President by the House of Representatives*, by Thomas B. Ripy, Memorandum (Washington: July 7, 1980), p. 4.

In: Economics, Political and Social Issues …
Editor: Michelle L. Fergusson

ISBN: 978-1-61122-555-6
©2011 Nova Science Publishers, Inc.

NATIONAL CONTINUITY POLICY:
A BRIEF OVERVIEW[*]

R. Eric Petersen

ABSTRACT

On May 9, 2007, President George W. Bush issued National Security Presidential Directive (NSPD) 51, which is also identified as Homeland Security Presidential Directive (HSPD) 20, on National Continuity Policy. The directive updates longstanding continuity directives designed to assure that governing entities are able to recover from a wide range of potential operational interruptions. Executive branch efforts to assure essential operations are similar to those that are broadly integrated into many private sector industries. Government continuity planning also incorporates efforts to maintain and preserve constitutional government, based on the assumption that certain essential activities typically provided by government must be carried out with little or no interruption under all circumstances.

On May 9, 2007, President George W. Bush issued National Security Presidential Directive (NSPD) 51, which is also identified as Homeland Security Presidential Directive (HSPD) 20 (NSPD 51/HSPD 20), on National Continuity Policy.[1] NSPD 51/HSPD 20 updates longstanding continuity policy expressed in various directives issued by previous administrations[2] to assure that governing entities are able to recover from a wide range of potential operational interruptions. Interruptions for which contingency plans might be activated include localized acts of nature, accidents, technological emergencies, and military or terrorist attack-related incidents.

Continuity planning is not unique to government; efforts to assure essential operations are broadly integrated into many private sector industries.[3] As with the private sector, government continuity planning is regarded by some observers as a "good business practice," and part of the fundamental mission of agencies as responsible and reliable public institutions.[4] In the public and private sectors, continuity planning may be viewed as a process that incorporates preparedness capacities ranging from basic emergency preparedness[5] to recovery plans and the resumption of normal operations. Unlike the private sector, however, federal continuity planning also incorporates efforts to maintain and preserve constitutional government, on the assumption that certain essential activities typically provided by government must be carried out with little or no interruption under all circumstances. Examples of those activities include the maintenance of civil authority, support for individuals and firms affected by an incident, infrastructure repair, or other action

---

[*] Excerpted from CRS Report RS22674, dated June 8, 2007.

in support of recovery. Such a response presumes the existence of an ongoing, functional government to fund, support, and oversee recovery efforts.

To support the provision of essential government activities, NSPD 51/HSPD 20 sets out a policy "to maintain a comprehensive and effective continuity capability composed of continuity of operations [6] and continuity of government[7] programs in order to ensure the preservation of our form of government under the Constitution and the continuing performance of national essential functions (NEF) under all conditions." The directive identifies eight NEFs that "are the foundation for all continuity programs and capabilities and represent the overarching responsibilities of the federal government to lead and sustain the Nation during a crisis." These are as follows:

- "Ensuring the continued functioning of government under the Constitution, including the functioning of the three separate branches of government;[8]
- "Providing leadership visible to the Nation and the world and maintaining the trust and confidence of the American people;
- "Defending the Constitution of the United States against all enemies, foreign and domestic, and preventing or interdicting attacks against the United States or its people, property, or interests;
- "Maintaining and fostering effective relationships with foreign nations;
- "Protecting against threats to the homeland and bringing to justice perpetrators of crimes or attacks against the United States or its people, property, or interests;
- "Providing rapid and effective response to and recovery from the domestic consequences of an attack or other incident;
- "Protecting and stabilizing the Nation's economy and ensuring public confidence in its financial systems; and
- "Providing for critical Federal Government services that address the national health, safety, and welfare needs of the United States."

Since operations may be interrupted without warning, NSPD 51/HSPD 20 requires that continuity planning be incorporated into the daily operations of all executive departments and agencies. Executive branch continuity planning emphasizes "geographic dispersion of leadership, staff, and infrastructure to alternate facilities to increase survivability and maintain uninterrupted Government Functions." The directive requires the application of risk management principles "to ensure that appropriate operational readiness decisions are based on the probability of an attack or other incident and its consequences." By mandating planning based on risk analysis, incorporating continuity activities in day-to-day operations, and mandating the utilization of alternate facilities and staffing, the directive appears to incorporate planning assumptions and approaches used widely in the private sector.[9]

MANAGING NATIONAL CONTINUITY POLICY

NSPD 51/HSPD 20 designates the President to lead the activities of the federal government for ensuring constitutional government, and designates the Assistant to the President for Homeland Security and Counterterrorism as the National Continuity Coordinator (NCC). In coordination with the Assistant to the President for National Security

Affairs, and without exercising directive authority, the NCC coordinates the development and implementation of continuity policy for executive branch departments and agencies. In consultation with the heads of appropriate executive departments and agencies, the NCC is required to lead the development of a National Continuity Implementation Plan for submission to the President before August 10, 2007. NSPD 51/HSPD 20 does not explicitly specify the appropriate departments and agencies.

The directive specifies a "Continuity Policy Coordination Committee (CPCC), chaired by a Senior Director from the Homeland Security Council (HSC) staff" appointed by the NCC, and designated as the main day-to-day forum for continuity policy coordination, but also indicates that the NCC will coordinate with the Assistant to the President for National Security Affairs. The directive designates the Secretary of Homeland Security "as the President's lead agent for coordinating overall continuity operations and activities of executive departments and agencies." Other than explicitly denying the NCC the capacity to exercise directive authority, the extent to which any official charged with continuity coordinating responsibilities can enjoin executive branch agencies to comply with their guidance or recommendations is unclear.[10]

NSPD 51/HSPD 20 provides that federal executive branch departments and agencies are "assigned to a category in accordance with the nature and characteristics of its national security roles and responsibilities in support" of the NEFs. Agency leaders are required to execute their respective department or agency COOP plans in response to emergencies that affect their operations. In addition, each agency head is required to appoint a senior accountable official, at the assistant secretary level, as the continuity coordinator for the department or agency; identify and submit to the NCC agency mission essential functions and "develop continuity plans in support of the NEFs and the continuation of essential functions under all conditions;" plan, program, and budget for continuity capabilities; plan, conduct, and support annual tests and training, to evaluate program readiness and ensure the adequacy and viability of continuity plans and communications systems; and support other continuity requirements, "in accordance with the nature and characteristics of the agency's national security roles and responsibilities."

In addition to efforts within the federal executive branch, NSPD 51/HSPD 20 requires the integration of continuity planning with the "emergency plans and capabilities of state, local, territorial, and tribal governments, and private sector owners and operators of critical infrastructure, as appropriate, in order to promote interoperability and to prevent redundancies and conflicting lines of authority," and requires the Secretary of Homeland Security to coordinate that integration "to provide for the delivery of essential services during an emergency."

REFERENCES

[1]   White House, Office of the Press Secretary, *National Security and Homeland Security Presidential Directive* , May 9, 2007, available at [*http://www.whitehouse.gov/news/ releases/2007/05/20070509-12.html*]. The press release provides the text of the directive. Quotes in this report are taken from NSPD 51/HSPD 20, unless an alternate source is identified.

[2]   NSPD 51/HSPD 20 revokes Presidential Decision Directive (PDD) 67, *Enduring Constitutional Government and Continuity of Government Operations*, which was issued by the Clinton Administration on October 21, 1998. PDD 67 replaced National Security Directive (NSD) 69, "Enduring Constitutional Government," issued by President George H. W. Bush, June 2, 1992, which in turn succeeded NSD 37, "Enduring Constitutional Government," issued April 18, 1990. National Security Decision Directive (NSDD) 47, "Emergency Mobilization Preparedness," issued July 22, 1982, and NSDD 55, "Enduring National Leadership," issued September 14, 1982, by President Ronald Reagan, included consideration of continued government operations planning. See Christopher Simpson, *National Security Directives of the Reagan and Bush Administrations: The Declassified History of U.S. Political and Military Policy, 1981-1991* (Boulder, CO: Westview Press), pp. 59, 71, 102-104, and 158-178. Earlier national security directives relating to continuity of government include Presidential Directive (PD) 58, "Continuity of Government," issued June 30, 1980, by President Jimmy Carter; two National Security Decision Memoranda (NSDM) issued by President Richard Nixon, NSDM 201, "Contingency Planning," issued January 5, 1973, and NSDM 8, "Crisis Anticipation and Management," issued March 21, 1969; and two National Security Action Memoranda (NSAM) issued by President John F. Kennedy, NSAM 166, "Report on Emergency Plans and Continuity of the Government," issued June 25, 1962, and NSAM 127, "Emergency Planning for Continuity of Government," issued February 14, 1962. The initial national security document establishing continuity programs appears to be NSC 5521, "NSC Relocation Plan," issued during 1955, by President Dwight D. Eisenhower.

[3]   See for example, CRS Report RL31873, *Banking and Financial Infrastructure Continuity*, by N. Eric Weiss; Cole Emerson, *Planning for Manufacturing Operations*, Disaster Resource.com website, at [*http://www.disaster-resource.com/cgi-bin/article_ search.cgi?id=*

[4]   *%27146%27*]; Buffy Rojas, "Constellation Energy Exemplifies Panning Excellence," *Continuity Insights*, September/October 2006, pp.13-16; Buffy Rojas, "Wal-Mart: Looking Beyond BCP Basics," *Continuity Insights*, March/April 2006, pp. 10-13. Securities Industry and Financial Markets Association (SIFMA) website, *Business Continuity Planning Rules*, available at [http://www.sifma. org/services/business_ continuity/html/

[5]   rules.html]; and AXA UK website, *Business Continuity Guide for Small Businesses*, available at [*http://www.axa4business.co.uk/resources/files/ BizContinuity Guide T1404.pdf*]

[6]   Department of Homeland Security, Federal Emergency Management Agency, Office of National Security Coordination, Federal Preparedness Circular 65, "Federal Executive Branch Continuity of Operations (COOP)," June 15, 2004, available at [*https://www.fema.org/txt/government/ coop/ fpc65_0604.txt*].

[7]   Basic emergency preparedness might include agency evacuation or sheltering plans, employee training, or alert and notification protocols.

[8]   NSPD 51/HSPD 20 identifies continuity of operations (COOP) as "an effort within individual executive departments and agencies to ensure that Primary Mission-Essential Functions continue to be performed during a wide range of emergencies, including localized acts of nature, accidents, and technological or attack-related emergencies."

[9]   NSPD 51/HSPD 20 identifies continuity of government (COG) as "a coordinated effort within the federal government's executive branch to ensure that national essential functions continue to be performed during a catastrophic emergency." A catastrophic emergency is defined as "any incident, regardless of location, that results in extraordinary levels of mass casualties, damage, or disruption severely affecting the U.S. population, infrastructure, environment, economy, or government functions."

[10]   The directive notes "that each branch of the federal government is responsible for its own continuity programs," and requires an official designated by the Chief of Staff to the President to "ensure that the executive branch's COOP and COG policies ... are appropriately coordinated with those of the legislative and judicial branches in order to ensure interoperability and allocate national assets efficiently to maintain a functioning federal government." The legislative branch and the federal judiciary maintain continuity programs consonant with their positions as coequal branches of government. NSPD 51/HSPD 20 does not specify the nature of appropriate coordination with continuity planners in the legislative and judicial branch.

[11]   See The Business Continuity Institute, *Good Practice Guidelines (2005): A Framework for Business Continuity Management* , available at [http://www.thebci.org/goodpractice guidetoBCM.pdf], pp. 21-28, and 30-34; and Disaster Recovery Journal and DRI International, *Generally Accepted Practices For Business Continuity Practitioners*, available at [*http://www.drj.com/GAP/gap.pdf*], pp. 15-53. This document is identified as a draft, dated January 2007, subject to practitioner comment and revision.

[12]   In addition to to NSPD 51/HSPD 20, Executive Order (E.O.) 12656, *Assignment of Emergency Preparedness Responsibilities*, which was issued November 18, 1988, by President Ronald Reagan (53 FR 47491; November 23, 1988), assigns national security emergency preparedness responsibilities to federal departments and agencies. E.O.12656 defines a national security emergency as "any occurrence, including natural disaster, military attack, technological emergency, or other emergency, that seriously degrades or seriously threatens the national security of the United States." E.O. 12656, which appears to remain in force and binding on executive branch departments and agencies, requires agencies to have capabilities to meet essential defense and civilian needs in the event of a national security emergency. Section 202 of E.O. 12656 requires the head of each federal department and agency to "ensure the continuity of essential functions in any national security emergency by providing for: succession to office and emergency delegation of authority in accordance with applicable law; safekeeping of essential resources, facilities, and records; and establishment of emergency operating capabilities." Subsequent sections require each department to carry out specific contingency planning activities in its areas of policy responsibility.

In: Economics, Political and Social Issues …
Editor: Michelle L. Fergusson

ISBN: 978-1-61122-555-6
©2011 Nova Science Publishers, Inc.

THE NATIONAL SECURITY COUNCIL: AN ORGANIZATIONAL ASSESSMENT*

Richard A. Best

National Defense

ABSTRACT

The National Security Council (NSC) was established by statute in 1947 to create an interdepartmental body to advise the President with respect to the integration of domestic, foreign, and military policies relating to the national security so as to enable the military services and the other departments and agencies of the Government to cooperate more effectively in matters involving the national security. Currently, statutory members of the Council are the President, Vice President, the Secretary of State, and the Secretary of Defense; but, at the President's request, other senior officials participate in NSC deliberations. The Chairman of the Joint Chiefs of Staff and the Director of National Intelligence are statutory advisers. In 2007 the Secretary of Energy was added to the NSC membership.

The President clearly holds final decision-making authority in the executive branch. Over the years, however, the NSC staff has emerged as a major factor in the formulation (and at times in the implementation) of national security policy. Similarly, the head of the NSC staff, the National Security Adviser, has played important, and occasionally highly public, roles in policymaking. This report traces the evolution of the NSC from its creation to the present.

The organization and influence of the NSC have varied significantly from one Administration to another, from a highly structured and formal system to loose-knit teams of experts. It is universally acknowledged that the NSC staff should be organized to meet the particular goals and work habits of an incumbent President. The history of the NSC provides ample evidence of the advantages and disadvantages of different types of policymaking structures.

Congress enacted the statute creating the NSC and has altered the character of its membership over the years. Congress annually appropriates funds for its activities, but does not, routinely, receive testimony on substantive matters from the National Security Adviser or from NSC staff. Proposals to require Senate confirmation of the Security Adviser have been discussed but not adopted.

The post-Cold War world has posed new challenges to NSC policymaking. Some argue that the NSC should be broadened to reflect an expanding role of economic, environmental, and demographic issues in national security policymaking. The Clinton Administration created a National Economic Council tasked with cooperating closely with the NSC on international economic matters. In the wake of the 9/11 attacks, the George W. Bush Administration established a Homeland Security Council. Both of

---

* Excerpted from CRS Report RL30840 dated March 31, 2009.

these entities overlap and coordinate with the NSC, but some observers have advocated more seamless organizational arrangements.

INTRODUCTION

The National Security Council (NSC) has been an integral part of U.S. national security policymaking since 1947. Of the various organizations in the Executive Office of the President that have been concerned with national security matters, the NSC is the most important and the only one established by statute. The NSC lies at the heart of the national security apparatus, being the highest coordinative and advisory body within the Government in this area aside from the President's Cabinet. The Cabinet has no statutory role, but the NSC does.

This study reviews the organizational history of the NSC and other related components of the Executive Office and their changing role in the national security policy process. It is intended to provide information on the NSC's development as well as subsequent usage. This study is not intended to be a comprehensive organizational history of all components of the national security policy process nor of the process itself as a whole. Moreover, the high sensitivity and security classification of the NSC's work and organization limit available sources. It is also important to keep in mind the distinction between the NSC's statutory membership (i.e., the President, Vice President, Secretary of State, Secretary of Defense, and Secretary of Energy) and its staff (i.e., the National Security Adviser and his assistants). These two groups have very different roles and levels of influence.

PRE-NSC COORDINATION METHODS

The Need for Interdepartmental Coordination

Successful national security policymaking is based on careful analysis of the international situation, including diplomatic, economic, intelligence, military, and morale factors. Based on a comprehensive assessment, effective government leaders attempt to attain their goals by selecting the most appropriate instrument of policy, whether it is military, diplomatic, economic, based on the intelligence services, or a combination of more than one. Although this approach has been an ideal throughout the history of international relations, prior to World War II, U.S. Presidents, focused primarily on domestic matters, and lacked organizational support to integrate national security policies. They relied instead on ad hoc arrangements and informal groups of advisers. However, in the early 1940s, the complexities of global war and the need to work together with allies led to more structured processes of national security decision making to ensure that the efforts of the State, War, and Navy Departments were focused on the same objectives. There was an increasingly apparent need for an organizational entity to support the President in looking at the multiplicity of factors, military and diplomatic, that had to be faced during wartime and in the early postwar months when crucial decisions had to be made regarding the future of Germany and Japan and a large number of other countries.

Given continuing worldwide responsibilities in the postwar years that involved active diplomacy, sizable military forces, sophisticated intelligence agencies, in addition to economic assistance in various forms, the United States established organizational mechanisms to analyze the international environment, identify priorities, and recommend appropriate policy options. Four decades later, the end of the Cold War saw the emergence of new international concerns, including transnational threats such as international terrorism and drug trafficking, that have continued to require the coordination of various departments and agencies concerned with national security policies.

Past Modes of Policy Coordination

Coordinative mechanisms to implement policy are largely creations of the Executive Branch, but they directly influence choices that Congress may be called upon to support and fund. Congress thus takes interest in the processes by which policies and the roles of various participants are determined. Poor coordination of national security policy can result in calls for Congress to take actions that have major costs, both international and domestic, without the likelihood of a successful outcome. Effective coordination, on the other hand, can mean the achievement of policy goals with minimal losses of human lives while providing the opportunity to devote material resources to other needs.

Throughout most of the history of the United States, until the twentieth century, policy coordination centered on the President, who was virtually the sole means of such coordination. The Constitution designates the President as Commander-in-Chief of the armed forces (Article II, Section 2) and grants him broad powers in the areas of foreign affairs (Article II, Section 2), powers that have expanded considerably in the twentieth century through usage. Given limited U.S. foreign involvements for the first hundred or so years under the Constitution, the small size of the armed forces, the relative geographic isolation of the Nation, and the absence of any proximate threat, the President, or his executive agents in the Cabinet, provided a sufficient coordinative base.

However, the advent of World War I, which represented a modern, complex military effort involving broad domestic and international coordination, forced new demands on the system that the President alone could not meet. In 1916, the Council of National Defense was established by statute (Army Appropriation Act of 1916). It reflected proposals that went back to 1911 and consisted of the Secretaries of War, Navy, Interior, Agriculture, Commerce and Labor. The statute also allowed the President to appoint an advisory commission of outside specialists to aid the Council [1]. The Council of National Defense was intended as an economic mobilization coordinating group, as reflected by its membership—which excluded the Secretary of State. His inclusion would have given the Council a much wider coordinative scope. Furthermore, the authorizing statute itself limited the role of the Council basically to economic mobilization issues. The Council of National Defense was disbanded in 1921, but it set a precedent for coordinative efforts that would be needed in World War II.

The President remained the sole national security coordinator until 1938, when the prewar crisis began to build in intensity, presenting numerous and wide-ranging threats to the inadequately armed United States. The State Department, in reaction to reports of Axis activities in Latin America, proposed that interdepartmental conferences be held with War and Navy Department representatives. In April 1938, Secretary of State Cordell Hull, in a letter to President Franklin Roosevelt, formally proposed the creation of a standing committee made up of the second ranking officers of the three departments, for purposes of liaison and coordination. The President approved this idea, and the Standing Liaison Committee, or Liaison Committee as it was also called, was established, the members being the Under Secretary of State, the Chief of Staff of the Army, and the Chief of Naval Operations. The Standing Liaison Committee was the first significant effort toward interdepartmental liaison and coordination, although its work in the area was limited and uneven. The Liaison Committee largely concentrated its efforts on Latin American problems, and it met irregularly. Although it did foster some worthwhile studies during the crisis following the fall of France, it was soon superseded by other coordinative modes. It was more a forum for exchanging information than a new coordinative and directing body [2].

An informal coordinating mechanism, which complemented the Standing Liaison Committee, evolved during the weekly meetings established by Secretary of War Henry L. Stimson, who took office in June 1940. Stimson arranged for weekly luncheons with his Navy counterpart, Frank Knox, and Cordell Hull, but these meetings also did not fully meet the growing coordinative needs of the wartime government.

In May 1940 President Roosevelt used the precedent of the 1916 statute and established the National Defense Advisory Council (NDAC), composed of private citizens with expertise in specific economic sectors [3] As with the earlier Council of National Defense, NDAC was organized to handle problems of economic mobilization; and by the end of the year it had given way to another organization in a succession of such groups.

During the war, there were a number of interdepartmental committees formed to handle various issues, and, while these did help achieve coordination, they suffered from two problems. First, their very multiplicity was to some degree counter-productive to coordination, and they still represented a piecemeal approach to these issues. Second, and more important, these committees in many cases were not advising the President directly, but were advising his advisers. Although their multiplicity and possible overlapping fit Roosevelt's preferred working methods, they did not represent coordination at the top. Roosevelt ran the war largely through the Joint Chiefs of Staff (JCS), who were then an ad hoc and de facto group, and through key advisers such as Harry Hopkins and James F. Byrnes, and via his own personal link with British Prime Minister Winston Churchill.

The weekly meetings arranged by Stimson evolved, however, into a significant coordinative body by 1945, with the formal creation of the State, War, Navy Coordinating Committee (SWNCC). SWNCC had its own secretariat and a number of regional and topical subcommittees; its members were assistant secretaries in each pertinent department. The role of SWNCC members was to aid their superiors "on politico-military matters and [in] coordinating the views of the three departments on matters in which all have a common interest, particularly those involving foreign policy and relations with foreign nations...." SWNCC was a significant improvement in civilian-military liaison, and meshed well with the JCS system; it did not, however, concern itself with fundamental questions of national policy during the early months of the Cold War [4]. SWNCC operated through the end of the war and beyond, becoming SANACC (State, Army, Navy, Air Force Coordinating Committee) after the National Security Act of 1947. It was dissolved in 1949, by which time it had been superseded by the NSC.

The creation of SWNCC, virtually at the end of the war, and its continued existence after the surrender of Germany and Japan reflected the growing awareness within the Federal

Government that better means of coordination were necessary. The World War II system had largely reflected the preferred working methods of President Roosevelt, who relied on informal consultations with various advisers in addition to the JCS structure. However, the complex demands of global war and the post-war world rendered this system inadequate, and it was generally recognized that a return to the simple and limited prewar system would not be possible if the United States was to take on the responsibilities thrust upon it by the war and its aftermath.

THE CREATION OF THE NSC [5]

Introduction

The NSC was not created independently, but rather as one part of a complete restructuring of the entire national security apparatus, civilian and military, including intelligence efforts, as accomplished in the National Security Act of 1947. Thus, it is difficult to isolate the creation of the NSC from the larger reorganization, especially as the NSC was much less controversial than the unification of the military and so attracted less attention.

Proposals

As early as 1943, General George C. Marshall, Army Chief of Staff, had proposed that the prospect of a unified military establishment be assessed. Congress first began to consider this idea in 1944, with the Army showing interest while the Navy was opposed. At the request of the Navy these investigations were put off until 1945, although by then it was clear to Secretary of the Navy James Forrestal that President Truman, who had come to the White House upon the death of President Roosevelt in April 1945, favored some sort of reorganization. Forrestal believed that outright opposition would not be a satisfactory Navy stance. He also realized that the State Department had to be included in any new national security apparatus. Therefore, he had Ferdinand Eberstadt, a leading New York attorney and banker who had served in several high- level Executive Branch positions, investigate the problem [6]

With respect to the formation of the NSC, the most significant of the three questions posed by Forrestal to Eberstadt, was:

> What form of postwar organization should be established and maintained to enable the military services and other governmental departments and agencies most effectively to provide for and protect our national security?

Eberstadt's response to this question covered the military establishment, where he favored three separate departments and the continuation of the JCS, as well as the civilian sphere, where he suggested the formation of two new major bodies "to coordinate all these [civilian and military] elements." These two bodies he called the National Security Council (NSC), composed of the President, the Secretaries of State and of the three military departments, the JCS "in attendance," and the chairman of the other new body, the National

Security Resources Board (NSRB). Eberstadt also favored the creation of a Central Intelligence Agency (CIA) under the NSC [7]

Eberstadt's recommendations clearly presaged the eventual national security apparatus, with the exception of a unified Department of Defense. Furthermore, it was a central point in Forrestal's plans for holding the proposed reorganization to Navy desires, bringing in the State Department, as he desired, and hopefully obviating the need for some coalescence of the military services. The NSC was also a useful negotiating point for Forrestal with the Army, as Eberstadt had described one of its functions as being the "building up [of] public support for clear-cut, consistent, and effective foreign and military policies." This would appeal to all the service factions as they thought back on the lean and insecure prewar years [8]

War-Navy negotiations over the shape of the reorganization continued throughout 1946 and into 1947. However, some form of central coordination, for a while called the Council of Common Defense, was not one of the contentious issues. By the end of May 1946, agreement had been reached on this and several other points, and by the end of the year the two sides had agreed on the composition of the new coordinative body [9]

Congressional Consideration

The creation of the NSC was one of the least controversial sections of the National Security Act and so drew little attention in comparison with the basic concept of a single military department, around which most of the congressional debate centered.

The concept of a regular and permanent organization for the coordination of national security policy was as widely accepted in Congress as in the Executive. When the NSC was considered in debate, the major issues were the mechanics of the new organization, its membership, assurances that it would be a civilian organization and would not be dominated by the new Secretary of the National Military Establishment, and whether future positions on the NSC would be subject to approval by the Senate [10]

The NSC as Created in 1947

The NSC was created by the National Security Act, which was signed by the President on July 26, 1947. The NSC appears in Section 101 of Title I, Coordination for National Security, and its purpose is stated as follows:

(a) ... The function of the Council shall be to advise the President with respect to the integration of domestic, foreign, and military policies relating to the national security so as to enable the military services and the other departments and agencies of the Government to cooperate more effectively in matters involving the national security.

(b) In addition to performing such other functions as the President may direct, for the purpose of more effectively coordinating the policies and functions of the departments and agencies of the Government relating to the national security, it shall, subject to the direction of the President, be the duty of the Council

(1) to assess and appraise the objectives, commitments, and risks of the United States in relation to our actual and potential military power, in the interest of

national security, for the purpose of making recommendations to the President in connection there with; and

    (2) to consider policies on matters of common interest to the departments and agencies of the Government concerned with the national security, and to make recommendations to the President in connection therewith. . . .

(d) The Council shall, from time to time, make such recommendations, and such other reports to the President as it deems appropriate or as the President may require [11]

The following officers were designated as members of the NSC: the President; the Secretaries of State, Defense, Army, Navy, and Air Force; and the Chairman of the National Security Resources Board. The President could also designate the following officers as members "from time to time:" secretaries of other executive departments and the Chairmen of the Munitions Board and the Research and Development Board. Any further expansion required Senate approval. The NSC was provided with a staff headed by a civilian executive secretary, appointed by the President.

The National Security Act also established the Central Intelligence Agency under the NSC, but the Director of Central Intelligence (DCI) was not designated as an NSC member. The act also created a National Military Establishment, with three executive departments (Army, Navy, and Air Force) under a Secretary of Defense.

Implicit in the provisions of the National Security Act was an assumption that the NSC would have a role in ensuring that the U.S. industrial base would be capable of supporting national security strategies. The Chairman of the National Security Resources Board, set up by the same act to deal directly with industrial base and civilian mobilization issues, was provided a seat on the NSC. Over the years, however, these arrangements proved unsatisfactory and questions of defense mobilization and civil defense were transferred to other federal agencies and the membership of the NSC was limited to the President, Vice President, the Secretary of State and the Secretary of Defense [12] Thus, the need for a coordinative entity that had initially been perceived to center on economic mobilization issues during World War I had evolved to one that engaged the more permanent themes of what had come to be known as national security policy.

The creation of the NSC was a definite improvement over past coordinative methods and organization, bringing together as it did the top diplomatic, military, and resource personnel with the President. The addition of the CIA, subordinate to the NSC, also provided the necessary intelligence and analyses for the Council so that it could keep pace with events and trends. The changeable nature of its organization and its designation as an advisory body to the President also meant that the NSC was a malleable organization, to be used as each President saw fit. Thus, its use, internal substructure, and ultimate effect would be directly dependent on the style and wishes of the President.

THE NATIONAL SECURITY COUNCIL, 1947-2009

The Truman NSC 1947-1953

Early Use. The NSC first met on September 26, 1947. President Truman attended the first session, but did not attend regularly thereafter, thus emphasizing the NSC's advisory role. In his place, the President designated the Secretary of State as chairman, which also was in accord with the President's view of the major role that the State Department should play. Truman viewed the NSC as a forum for studying and appraising problems and making recommendations, but not one for setting policy or serving as a centralized office to coordinate implementation. The NSC met irregularly for the first 10 months. In May 1948, meetings twice a month were scheduled, although some were canceled, and special sessions were convened as needed.

The Hoover Commission. The first review of NSC operations came in January 1949 with the report of the Hoover Commission (the Commission on Organization of the Executive Branch of the Government), which found that the NSC was not fully meeting coordination needs, especially in the area of comprehensive statements of current and long-range policies [13]

The Hoover Commission recommended that better working-level liaison between the NSC and JCS be developed, that the Secretary of Defense become an NSC member, replacing the service secretaries, and that various other steps be taken to clarify and tighten roles and liaison.

1949 Amendments. In January 1949, President Truman directed the Secretary of the Treasury to attend all NSC meetings. In August 1949, amendments to the National Security Act were passed (P.L. 81-216), changing the membership of the NSC to consist of the following officers: the President, Vice President, Secretaries of State and Defense, and Chairman of the National Security Resources Board. This act also designated the JCS as "the principal military advisers to the President," thus opening the way for their attendance, beginning in 1950, even though the Service Secretaries were excluded. In August 1949, by Reorganization Plan No. 4, the NSC also became part of the Executive Office of the President, formalizing a de facto situation.

Subsequent Usage and Evaluation. The outbreak of the Korean War in June 1950 brought greater reliance on the NSC system. The President ordered weekly meetings and specified that all major national security recommendations be coordinated through the NSC and its staff. Truman began presiding regularly, chairing 62 of the 71 meetings between June 1950 and January 1953. The NSC became to a much larger extent the focus of national security decision making. Still, the NSC's role remained limited. Truman continued to use alternate sources of information and advice [14]. As one scholar has concluded:

> Throughout his administration Truman's use of the NSC process remained entirely consistent with his views of its purpose and value. The president and his secretary of state remained completely responsible for foreign policy. Once policy decisions were made, the NSC was there to advise the president on matters requiring specific diplomatic, military, and intelligence coordination [15]

The Eisenhower NSC 1953-1961

President Dwight Eisenhower, whose experience with a well-ordered staff was extensive, gave new life to the NSC. Under his Administration, the NSC staff was institutionalized and expanded, with clear lines of responsibility and authority, and it came to closely resemble Eberstadt's original conception as the President's principal arm for formulating and coordinating military, international, and internal security affairs. Meetings were held weekly and, in addition to Eisenhower himself and the other statutory members, participants often included the Secretary of the Treasury, the Budget Director, the Chairman of the JCS, and the Director of Central Intelligence.

Organizational Changes. In his role as chairman of the NSC, Eisenhower created the position of Special Assistant for National Security Affairs, [16] who became the supervisory officer of the NSC, including the Executive Secretary. The Special Assistant—initially Robert Cutler, a banker who had served under Stimson during World War II—was intended to be the President's agent on the NSC, not an independent policymaker in his own right, and to be a source of advice [17]

Eisenhower established two important subordinate bodies: the NSC Planning Board, which prepared studies, policy recommendations, and basic drafts for NSC coordination, and the Operations Coordinating Board, which was the coordinating and integrating arm of the NSC for all aspects of the implementation of national security policy.

By the end of the Eisenhower Administration, the NSC membership had changed slightly. The National Security Resources Board had been abolished by Reorganization Plan No. 3 in June 1953, and this vacancy was then filled by the Director of the Office of Civil and Defense Mobilization.

In 1956, President Eisenhower, partly in response to recommendations of the second Hoover Commission on the Organization of the Executive Branch of Government, also established the Board of Consultants on Foreign Intelligence Activities in the Executive Office. This board was established by Executive Order 10656 and was tasked to provide the President with independent evaluations of the U.S. foreign intelligence effort. The Board of Consultants lapsed at the end of the Eisenhower Administration, but a similar body, the President's Foreign Intelligence Advisory Board (PFIAB), was created by President Kennedy after the Bay of Pigs failure. PFIAB was itself abolished in 1977, but was resurrected during the Reagan Administration in 1981. Members are selected by the President and serve at his discretion.

Evaluation. The formal structure of the NSC under Eisenhower allowed it to handle an increasing volume of matters. Its work included comprehensive assessments of the country's basic national security strategy, which were designed to serve as the basis for military planning and foreign policymaking. The complexity of NSC procedures under Eisenhower and its lengthy papers led to charges that quantity was achieved at the expense of quality and that the NSC was too large and inflexible in its operations. Critics alleged that it was unable to focus sufficiently on major issue areas [18]. Some observers also held that NSC recommendations were often compromises based on the broadest mutually acceptable grounds from all the agencies involved, leading to a noticeable lack of innovative national security ideas. The Eisenhower NSC did, nonetheless, establish national security policies that were accepted and implemented throughout the Government and that laid the basis for sustained competition with the Soviet Union for several decades.

It may be that the NSC process became overly bureaucratic towards the end of the Eisenhower Administration, perhaps affected by the President's declining health. Hearings by the Senate Government Operations Committee in 1960-61, led by Senator Henry Jackson, produced proposals for a substantial reorientation of this "over-institutionalized" structure, and its replacement by a smaller, less formal NSC that would offer the President a clear choice of alternatives on a limited number of major problems [19]

Some scholars have noted that Eisenhower himself found the lengthy NSC procedures burdensome and argue that many key decisions were made in the Oval Office in the presence of only a few advisers. Nonetheless, Eisenhower saw the NSC process as one which produced a consensus within the Administration which would lead to effective policy implementation. According to this view, the process was largely one of education and clarification [20]. A recent analysis has concluded, that NSC meetings

> brought Eisenhower's thinking into sharper focus by forcing him to weigh it against a range of alternatives that were presented and defended by individuals whose opinions the president took seriously and whose exposure to requisite information and expertise he assured. These individuals, in turn, were educated about the problems in the same way as Eisenhower [21]

The Kennedy NSC, 1961-1963

President John Kennedy, who did not share Eisenhower's preference for formal staff procedures, accepted many of the recommendations of the Jackson Committee and proceeded to dismantle much of the NSC structure, reducing it to its statutory base. Staff work was carried out mainly by the various departments and agencies, and personal contacts and ad hoc task forces became the main vehicles for policy discussion and formulation. The NSC was now one among many sources of advice.

Kennedy's National Security Adviser, McGeorge Bundy, played an important policy role directly under the President. The nature of this position was no longer that of a "neutral keeper of the machinery"; for the first time, the Adviser emerged in an active policymaking role, in part because of the absence of any definite NSC process that might preoccupy him [22]

Kennedy met regularly with the statutory NSC members and the DCI, but not in formal NSC sessions. Studies and coordination were assigned to specific Cabinet officers or subordinates in a system that placed great emphasis on individual responsibility, initiative and action. The Secretary of State, Dean Rusk, was initially seen as the second most important national security official in the President's plans, and Kennedy indicated that he did not want any other organizations interposed between him and Rusk. However, Kennedy came to be disappointed by the State Department's inability or unwillingness to fill this role as the leading agency in national security policy [23]

At the beginning of the Kennedy Administration, the NSC was reportedly cut from seventy-one to forty-eight and "in place of weighty policy papers, produced at regular intervals, Bundy's staff would produce crisp and timely National Security Action Memoranda (NSAMs). The new name signified the premium that would be placed on 'action' over 'planning.'" [24] With an emphasis on current operations and crisis management, special ad hoc bodies came into use. The outstanding example of this was the Executive Committee (ExCom), formed in October 1962 during the Cuban Missile Crisis, which orchestrated the U.S. response to Soviet moves to introduce missiles in Cuba.

Organizational Changes. Kennedy added the Director of the Office of Emergency Planning to the NSC, replacing the Director of the Office of Civil and Defense Mobilization.

It was planned that the new appointee would fill the role originally envisioned for the National Security Resources Board in coordinating emergency management of resources.

The Planning Board and the Operations Control Board were both abolished (by Executive Order 10920) in order to avoid the Eisenhower Administration's distinction between planning and operations. The NSC staff was reduced, and outside policy experts were brought in. Bundy noted that they were all staff officers:

> Their job is to help the President, not to supersede or supplement any of the high officials who hold line responsibilities in the executive departments and agencies. Their task is that of all staff officers: to extend the range and enlarge the direct effectiveness of the man they serve. Heavy responsibilities for operation, for coordination, and for diplomatic relations can be and are delegated to the Department of State. Full use of all the powers of leadership can be and is expected in other departments and agencies. There remains a crushing burden of responsibility, and of sheer work, on the President himself; there remains also the steady flow of questions, of ideas, of executive energy which a strong President will give off like sparks. If his Cabinet officers are to be free to do their own work, the President's work must be done—to the extent that he cannot do its himself—by staff officers under his direct oversight. But this is, I repeat, something entirely different from the interposition of such a staff between the President and his Cabinet officers [25]

Evaluation. Some critics attacked the informality of the system under Kennedy, arguing that it lacked form and direction, as well as coordination and control, and that it emphasized current developments at the expense of planning. As noted, Kennedy himself was disappointed by the State Department, on which he had hoped to rely. In retrospect, Kennedy's system was designed to serve his approach to the presidency and depended upon the President's active interest and continuous involvement. Some critics, both at the time and subsequently, have suggested that the informal methods that the Kennedy Administration adopted contributed to the Bay of Pigs debacle and the confusion that surrounded U.S. policy in the coup against President Diem of South Vietnam in 1963.

The Johnson NSC' 1963-1969

President Lyndon Johnson's sudden accession to power, the need for a show of continuity, and pressures from the upcoming Presidential election all forced Johnson, at least until 1965, to rely heavily on Kennedy's system and personnel, especially as Johnson was less familiar with national security than domestic affairs.

Organizational Changes. Johnson, like Truman, sought out advice from a number of sources other than the NSC and its member departments, although he relied heavily on the Secretaries of State and Defense, Dean Rusk and Robert McNamara.

The institutional system that evolved under Johnson depended heavily on the ability of the State Department to handle the planning and coordination process. This system came about from a study headed by General Maxwell Taylor in 1966 that led to National Security Action Memorandum (NSAM) 341 which concluded that it was necessary to enhance the State Department's role in the policy process and to improve "country team expertise" in Washington, which was felt to be far below that in the various embassies. NSAM 341 led to a new system of interagency committees. The most important of these was the Senior Interdepartmental Group (SIG), whose members were: the Under Secretary of State, Deputy Secretary of Defense, Administrator of the Agency for International Development, DCI, JCS Chairman, Director of the U.S. Information Agency, and the National Security Adviser. In support of the SIG were a number of Interdepartmental Regional Groups (IRGs), each headed by the appropriate Assistant Secretary of State.

Within the NSC itself, structure and membership remained what they had been under Kennedy (with the Office of Emergency Planning changing title to the Office of Emergency Preparedness in 1968), although the title Special Assistant to the President for National Security Affairs was shortened to Special Assistant when Walt W. Rostow replaced Bundy in 1966. This reflected the frequent diversion of the occupant of this position away from NSC affairs to more general concerns.

Evaluation. Johnson's NSC system barely existed as such. The role of the NSC staff was more restricted, and budget and personnel both declined. Key decisions, those especially regarding the war in Vietnam, were made during Tuesday lunches attended by the President, the Secretaries of State and Defense, and a few other invited officials.

Johnson's informal system was not a wholly successful replacement for the highly structured system developed in the Eisenhower Administration. The SIG/IRG system fulfilled neither old functions nor the objectives set forth in NSAM 341. Although this new structure was dominated by the State Department, there was little enthusiasm for the system as a whole on the part of the department's leadership. The State Department did not provide decisive leadership and settled for a system of consensus opinions. Vagueness as to authority in the SIG/IRG system reduced its effect on the bureaucracies. Moreover, there was an insufficient allocation of resources for staff support for the new organization. By 1969, the NSC existed largely in name. Johnson conferred constantly with a wide number of advisers within and outside government; while he respected institutional responsibilities, his own decision making was an intensely personal process.

The Nixon NSC 1969-1974

Experience in the Eisenhower Administration clearly had a formative effect on President Richard Nixon's approach to national security organization. Wanting to switch White House priorities from current operations and crisis management to long-range planning, Nixon revived the NSC. Nixon's NSC staff structure resembled Eisenhower's, with an emphasis on examining policy choices and alternatives, aiming for a number of clear options reaching the highest level, where they would be treated systematically and then effectively implemented. Nixon made it clear that he wanted distinct options presented to him from which he could choose, rather than consensus opinions requiring only acceptance or rejection. Nixon used an NSC framework similar to that set in place by Eisenhower but intended, as much as Kennedy, to give the NSC staff a powerful policy role.

Organizational Changes. While adopting the basic form of the Eisenhower NSC, Nixon streamlined its procedures [26]. The position of Assistant for National Security Affairs was revived, and Henry Kissinger, a Harvard professor and occasional government adviser, was named to fill it. NSC meetings were limited to the statutory members, with Kissinger and the JCS Chairman also sitting in and the DCI attending for intelligence matters. In January 1973, the Office of Emergency Preparedness was abolished along with the NSC seat that originally had belonged to the Chairman of the National Security Resources Board.

Six interdepartmental groups, similar to Johnson's IRGs, formed the NSC's support network, preparing basic studies and developing policy options. However, the influence of the State Department was reduced, and Kissinger's influence soon predominated. Four major new bodies were created:

- Washington Special Action Group (WASAG): headed by Kissinger and designed to handle contingency planning and crises.
- NSC Intelligence Committee: chaired by Kissinger and responsible for providing guidance for national intelligence needs and continuing evaluations of intelligence products.
- Defense Program Review Committee: chaired by Kissinger and designed to achieve greater integration of defense and domestic considerations in the allocation of natural resources. This committee was intended to allow the President, through the NSC, to gain greater control over the defense budget and its implications and policy requirements. As a result of opposition by Defense Secretary Melvin Laird, its role was, however, significantly circumscribed.
- Senior Policy Review Group: chaired by Kissinger, this group directed and reviewed policy studies and also served as a top level deliberative body.

This system had two principal objectives: the retention of control at the top, and the development of clear alternative choices for decision makers.

Evaluation. Most of the criticism of the Nixon NSC centered on the role played by Kissinger. His position in a number of the key committees gave him control over virtually the entire NSC apparatus, leading to charges that the system, for all its efficiency, now suffered from over- centralization, and later from domination by one man.

During Nixon's first term, Kissinger competed with the State Department for control of foreign policy, and soon overshadowed Secretary of State William Rogers. Critics felt that Kissinger stifled dissent within the NSC and the rest of the national security apparatus. Kissinger's venture into "shuttle diplomacy" and the unique circumstances of the Watergate scandal further emphasized his key role. Kissinger's accession to Rogers' position in September 1973, while retaining his National Security Council post, brought renewed criticism of his role. The direct involvement of the NSC Adviser in diplomatic negotiations set a precedent that some observers have criticized as undercutting the established responsibilities of the State Department and as an attempt to orchestrate national security policy beyond the reach of congressional oversight.

Kissinger's predominance derived from his unique intellectual abilities, skill at bureaucratic maneuvering, and the support of a President determined to act boldly in international affairs without being restrained by bureaucratic or congressional inhibitions. It was achieved at a time of profound political differences over foreign policy in which Administration and congressional goals were, on occasion, diametrically opposed. However, under President Nixon, the NSC was restored to a central role in the policy process, acting as the major vehicle and conduit for the formation of national security policy.

The Ford NSC. 1974-1977

President Gerald Ford, who inherited his predecessor's NSC, took no major steps to change the system per se, although Kissinger was replaced as National Security Adviser by Air Force Lt. General Brent Scowcroft in November 1975. The national security policy process continued to be dominated by Kissinger, who retained his position as Secretary of State, an indication of the preeminence he had achieved, as well as a reflection of Ford's limited experience in the conduct of foreign policy prior to his sudden accession.

In June 1975, the Commission on the Organization of the Government for the Conduct of Foreign Policy, also known as the Murphy Commission, issued a report on ways to more effectively formulate and implement foreign policy. Its recommendations dealt in part with the Executive Office of the President and the NSC structure [27].

Implicitly criticizing the expansive role of the NSC staff under Kissinger, the Commission recommended that only the President should have line responsibility in the White House; that staff officials should not themselves issue directives to departmental officials; that, in the future, the National Security Adviser have no other official responsibilities; that the Secretary of the Treasury be made a statutory member of the NSC and that the NSC's scope be expanded to include major international economic policy issues; and that senior officials concerned with domestic policy be invited to NSC meetings when issues with domestic implications were discussed.

The Commission also considered general alternative structures and pointed out their basic advantages and disadvantages. It also noted that,

> Policymaking is not a branch of mechanics; however wisely designed or carefully utilized, no machinery is adequate to assure its results. The selective use of various mechanisms and forums in ways which fit the particular issues, positions, and personalities involved is as much a part of the President's responsibility as is the necessity, finally, to decide the substantive issues [28]

There were no immediate steps taken to implement the Report's recommendations.

Organizational Changes. In February 1976, President Ford issued Executive Order 11905 reorganizing the intelligence community, in response to ongoing investigations in that area. This order, among other things, reaffirmed the NSC's overall policy control over the foreign intelligence community. Some changes were made in the NSC sub-structure, including the abolition of the NSC Intelligence Committee. The so-called 40 Committee of the NSC, which was responsible for covert operations and certain sensitive foreign intelligence operations, was replaced by the Operations Advisory Group. This Executive Order also created the Intelligence Oversight Board in the Executive Office (subsequently disbanded in 1993). It was composed of three civilians and was tasked with reviewing the propriety and legality of the intelligence agencies' operations. In December 1975, Ford vetoed a bill that would have made the Secretary of the Treasury a statutory member of the NSC, saying that the Treasury Secretary is invited to participate in NSC affairs having significant economic and monetary implications, but that there is no need to involve him in all NSC activities [29]

Evaluation. These changes did not detract from the central role that the NSC had achieved under President Nixon. Kissinger's loss of his dual position did not seem to lessen his influence over the policy process, leading critics to charge that this change was largely cosmetic. The new National Security Adviser, Brent Scowcroft, had previously served as Kissinger's deputy on the NSC staff, and was unlikely to challenge Kissinger's pre-eminence. The Ford NSC reflected the close relationship between the President and the Secretary of State, a relationship that itself became a source of controversy both in the Republican primaries of 1976 as well as the ensuing general election. Critics continued to maintain that the Ford Administration decisionmaking was secretive, impervious to congressional input, and out of touch with public opinion.

The Carter NSC 1977-1981 [30]

Under President Jimmy Carter, steps were taken to end the dominant role of the NSC staff and make it a more coequal and cooperating partner with the Departments of State and Defense. The NSC underwent a major reorganization in the new Administration.

Organizational Changes. Upon taking office in January 1977, President Carter issued a directive (PD-2) reorganizing the NSC staff. The avowed purpose of the reorganization was "to place more responsibility in the departments and agencies while insuring that the NSC, with my Assistant for National Security Affairs, continues to integrate and facilitate foreign and defense policy decisions." [31]

The number of NSC staff committees was reduced from seven to two, the Policy Review Committee (PRC) and the Special Coordination Committee (SCC). The functions of these two committees were as follows:

- *Policy Review Committee*: the PRC had responsibility for subjects which "fall primarily within a given department but where the subject also has important implications for other departments and agencies." Examples were "foreign policy issues that contain significant military or other interagency aspects; defense policy issues having international implications and the coordination of the annual Defense budget with foreign policy objectives; the preparation of a consolidated national intelligence budget and resource allocation for the Intelligence Community...; and those international economic issues pertinent to the U.S. foreign policy and security...." [32] Executive Order 12036 of January 24, 1978, added responsibility for the establishment of national foreign intelligence requirements and priorities, and periodic reviews and evaluations of national foreign intelligence products [33] The Vice President, the Secretaries of State and Defense, and the Assistant for National Security Affairs were members of the PRC; the DCI and the Chairman of the JCS also attended. The Secretary of the Treasury, the Chairman of the Council of Economic Advisers, and other officials attended when pertinent topics were being considered. Appropriate Cabinet officers chaired the PRC in accordance with matters being considered; the DCI was chairman when the PRC considered intelligence matters as specified in E.O. 12036. NSC Interdepartmental Groups, which dealt with specific issues at the direction of the President, were under the PRC.
- *Special Coordination Committee:* the SCC dealt with "specific, cross-cutting issues requiring coordination in the development of options and the implementation of Presidential decisions." These included "oversight of sensitive intelligence activities ... arms control evaluation; ... and crisis management." [34] E.O. 12036 gave the

SCC responsibility for sensitive foreign intelligence collection operations and counterintelligence [35]. The SCC thus replaced WASAG and the Operations Advisory Group. Unlike the PRC, the SCC was chaired by the Assistant for National Security Affairs; other members were the Vice President, the Secretaries of State and Defense, and the DCI—or their deputies—and other officials attended when appropriate. When intelligence "special activities" were being considered, the members had to attend, as had the Attorney General, the Chairman of the JCS, and the Director of the Office of Management and Budget (OMB); for counterintelligence activities, the Director of the FBI attended [36]

- The initial emphasis of the NSC's role as a policy coordinator and "think tank" represented a clear reversal of the trend that had developed under Presidents Nixon and Ford. The staff of the NSC was reduced under the Carter Administration, and National Security Adviser Zbigniew Brzezinski established a number of regional and topical offices on the NSC staff that aimed at a more "collegial" approach to staff procedures.

- Although the PRC had a wider charter than the SCC, as a result of the growing importance of crisis management functions and the increasing influence of the National Security Adviser, [37] initiative passed to the SCC and there were fewer PRC meetings.

- *Evaluation.* A rumored rivalry between Brzezinski and Secretary of State Cyrus Vance was not publicly evident during the first year of the Carter Administration, but reports of differences between the two men later increased dramatically as senior Administration officials advised different responses to such questions as Soviet and Cuban activities in Africa and the Iranian hostage question. Towards the end of the Administration, differences between Vance and Brzezinski became pronounced and were widely perceived as contributing to weak and vacillating policies. Carter's Director of Central Intelligence Stansfield Turner later wrote:

National Security Advisers and Secretaries of State and Defense had clashed before, notably under President Nixon when Henry Kissinger was the Adviser. But because Nixon tended to follow Kissinger's advice more often than not, there was no stalemate, and foreign policy moved ahead in innovative ways. However, Jimmy Carter vacillated between Brzezinski and Vance, and they often canceled each other out [38]

Vance, who had strongly opposed the ill-fated effort to rescue the U.S. hostages in Iran, finally resigned and was succeeded by Senator Edmund Muskie in April 1980. Brzezinski's outspokenness and his public role in policymaking became an issue, and led to calls for Senate confirmation of NSC advisers and closer congressional oversight of the NSC staff [39]. There were also reports of infighting between Carter loyalists on the NSC staff and those who had worked for Vice President Walter Mondale, who had been given a major policy role [40]

The Reagan NSC, 1981-1989

Campaigning for the presidency in 1980, Ronald Reagan criticized the divisions of the Carter Administration and promised to restore Cabinet leadership (as, in the 1976 campaign, he had criticized Henry Kissinger's predominant influence in the Ford Administration). Substituting Cabinet leadership for an active NSC proved, however, to be a significant challenge.

Organizational Changes. After extensive delays and bureaucratic infighting, President Reagan signed a Presidential directive (NSDD-2), [41] which enhanced the role of the State Department in national security policymaking and downgraded that of the National Security Adviser. The various NSC sub-committees were to be chaired by State, Defense, and CIA officials, not NSC staff. The Reagan NSC included three Senior Interagency Groups (SIGs)—one for foreign policy, chaired by the Deputy Secretary of State; one for defense, chaired by the Deputy Secretary of Defense; and one for intelligence, chaired by the Director of Central Intelligence. There were also regional and functional interagency groups, chaired by representatives of various Cabinet departments. Crisis management formally became the direct responsibility of the Vice President [42]

This structure, however, had major limitations. Observers and participants portray an absence of orderly decisionmaking and uncertain lines of responsibility. As the Special Review Board (known as the Tower Board) appointed by the President to assess the proper role of the NSC system in the wake of the Iran-Contra revelations, pointedly noted:

> A President must at the outset provide guidelines to the members of the National Security Council, his National Security Adviser, and the National Security Council staff. These guidelines, to be effective, must include how they will relate to one another, what procedures will be followed, what the President expects of them. If his advisors are not performing as he likes, only the President can intervene [43]

The Reagan Administration had a total of six National Security Advisers. Their history is poignant. The first, Richard Allen, did not have direct access to the President, but reported to him through Presidential Counselor Edwin Meese. Allen's tenure was brief; after accusations of influence peddling, he was replaced in January 1982 by Judge William Clark, a longtime Reagan associate who had served since the beginning of the Administration as Deputy Secretary of State. Clark, in turn, resigned in October 1983 to become Secretary of the Interior and his deputy, Robert McFarlane, became National Security Adviser. McFarlane was replaced in January 1986 by his deputy, Vice Admiral John Poindexter, and subsequently pleaded guilty to withholding information from Congress. Poindexter himself was relieved in the context of the Iran-Contra scandal in November 1986, and eventually went on trial for obstructing justice. An effort was made to restore NSC effectiveness under former Ambassador Frank Carlucci, who succeeded Poindexter in December 1986. When Carlucci was appointed Secretary of Defense, he was replaced by Army General Colin Powell in November 1987.

Evaluation. Until the arrival of Carlucci, the Reagan NSC structure lacked a strong, politically attuned National Security Adviser that had characterized Administrations since 1961. It also lacked the administrative structure that existed under Eisenhower, Nixon, Ford, and Carter. The absence of either influential NSC Advisers or effective administrative machinery has been seen by many critics as a major factor contributing to the Iran-Contra misadventures. Allowing NSC committees to be chaired by Cabinet officials tended to reduce the possibility that all sides of a given issue would be laid before the full NSC or the President. The Tower Board noted:

> Most presidents have set up interagency committees at both a staff and policy level to surface issues, develop options, and clarify choices. There has typically been a struggle for the chairmanship of these groups between the National Security Adviser and the NSC staff on the one hand, and the cabinet secretaries and department officials on the other.
>
> Our review of the operation of the present system and that of other administrations where committee chairmen came from the Departments has led us to the conclusion that the system generally operates better when the committees are chaired by the individual with the greatest stake in making the NSC system work.
>
> We recommend that the National Security Adviser chair the senior-level committees of the NSC system [44]

The Reagan Administration, in its efforts to avoid the dominant influence wielded by previous NSC Advisers, fell victim to perpetual bureaucratic intrigues. The efforts of politically weak NSC Advisers, especially McFarlane and Poindexter, to undertake White House initiatives covertly over the strong opposition of senior Cabinet officials and congressional leaders called into question the basic competence of the Administration.

Another aspect of the Reagan NSC that came under heavy criticism was the involvement of NSC staff in covert actions. Although NSC staff efforts to manage certain crises, such as the capture of the Achille Lauro hijackers, were successful, the participation of NSC personnel, especially Lt. Col. Oliver North, in operations run apart from the traditional intelligence apparatus, including efforts to gain the release of American hostages and to supply Nicaraguan insurgents, has been widely censured. Such efforts have been criticized as undercutting the agencies with responsibilities for such operations and which are accountable to congressional oversight committees; secondly, failing to take full advantage of the professional expertise available to the Intelligence Community, and potentially involving the country in misguided ventures. The Iran- Contra Committee recommended that "the members and staff of the NSC not engage in covert actions." [45]

Reagan's final two NSC Advisers, Carlucci and Powell, brought a period of greater stability to NSC operations and both eschewed participation in covert actions. After Poindexter's departure, Carlucci created a Senior Review Group that he himself chaired and that was composed of statutory NSC members (besides the President and Vice President). He also established a Policy Review Group that was chaired by his deputy and composed of second-ranking officials of NSC agencies.

President Reagan's own role in the details of national security policymaking remains unclear. His policies on U.S.-Soviet relations, support for an aggressive struggle against international communism, and the need for strong military forces, including strategic defenses were well- known; such positions provided the overall goals for Administration officials. It is generally acknowledged, however, that unlike some of his predecessors, President Reagan did not himself engage in detailed monitoring of policy implementation. Some maintain that his NSC structure and the absence of strong NSC Advisers led directly to bureaucratic gridlock and ill-advised involvement of the NSC staff in covert actions. Others have concluded that the experience of the Reagan Administration demonstrates that a strong and efficient National

Security Adviser and staff has become essential to national security policymaking, especially if the President himself does not provide detailed direction. The absence of such an Adviser, it is argued, will undermine the development and implementation of effective national security policies. Some subsequent historians, however, give Reagan higher marks for overall national security policy even if his NSC staff was often in flux.

The George H.W. Bush NSC' 1989-1993

The Bush Administration saw the return of Brent Scowcroft as National Security Adviser. His tenure was marked by the absence of public confrontations with Cabinet officers and a close working relationship with the President. National Security Directive 1 (NSD-1) established three NSC sub-groups. The NSC Principals Committee, was composed of the Secretaries of State and Defense, the DCI, the Chairman of the JCS, the Chief of Staff to the President, and the National Security Adviser, who was the chairman. The NSC Deputies Committee, chaired by the Deputy National Security Adviser, was composed of second-ranking officials. There were also a number of NSC Policy Coordinating Committees, chaired by senior officials of the departments most directly concerned with NSC staff members serving as executive secretaries.

The Bush NSC structure most closely resembled that of the Nixon and Ford Administrations in providing for a National Security Adviser chairing most of the key committees. The key differences lay in the personalities involved and the fact that political divisions over foreign policy, while important, lacked some of the emotional heat caused by controversies over Vietnam and Nicaragua. Secretary of State James Baker was a powerful figure in the Administration and a longtime political associate of the President; similarly, Secretary of Defense Dick Cheney himself had White House experience as chief of staff in the Ford Administration and served in a leadership post in the House of Representatives. On occasion, however, Bush did formulate policy within a narrow circle of White House aides [46]

Evaluation. Whether because of the personalities of NSC principals, the structure of NSC committees or the determination among political opponents to concentrate on the domestic economy, the Bush NSC did not come in for the heavy criticisms that were levied against most of its predecessors. Most observers would probably judge that the Bush Administration created a reasonably effective policymaking machinery and avoided the mistakes of some of its predecessors. Arguably, a standard NSC organization had been created. The Administration successfully addressed most issues that resulted from the breakup of the Soviet Union and the unification of Germany along with the conduct of Desert Storm.

The Clinton NSC' 1993-2001

President Clinton came into office with a determination to focus on domestic issues. His Administration sought to emphasize connections between international concerns and the domestic economy in such areas as trade, banking, and environmental standards. Anthony Lake, who had resigned in protest from the NSC Staff in the Nixon Administration and later served in the State Department in the Carter Administration, was appointed National Security

Adviser, and continued in office until he resigned in March 1997. Lake's deputy, Samuel R. Berger, succeeded him, remaining until the end of the Clinton Administration.

With the end of the Cold War, it was widely acknowledged that there was a need for closer integration of national security policy and international economic policy. A major Clinton Administration initiative was the establishment of a National Economic Council (NEC) to coordinate international economic policy which, many observers believed, had usually received short shrift from NSC staffs focused narrowly on diplomatic and security issues. The NEC, initially headed by Robert Rubin who would subsequently become Treasury Secretary in 1995, was charged with coordinating closely with the NSC. To facilitate coordination some NEC staff were "double-hatted" as NSC officials. The close relationship has been credited with enhancing policy coordination at senior White House levels, although, according to some observers, the original promise was not realized as many aspects of international economic and trade policies became parts of major political disputes such as the North American Free Trade Agreement and most-favored-nation status for China [47].

Some observers would have preferred to include a stronger international economic component within the NSC itself, but others have raised strong objections to such an approach on the grounds that national security policymaking, in significant measure the province of diplomats and military officers, is not as closely related to domestic political concerns as international economic policy. Proponents of the latter view argue that economic issues inevitably involve concerns of various domestic groups and the NSC is ill-suited to integrate them into its policymaking processes.

Presidential Decision Directive (PDD) 2, Organization of the National Security Council, issued on January 20, 1993, expanded the NSC to include, in addition to statutory members and advisers, the Secretary of the Treasury, the U.S. Representative to the United Nations, the Assistant to the President for Economic Policy, and the Chief of Staff to the President. The Attorney General attended relevant meetings including those that discuss covert actions. The National Security Adviser determined the agenda of NSC meetings and ensured the preparation of necessary papers.

The Clinton NSC continued the practice of designating the National Security Adviser as chairman of the Principals Committee of Cabinet-level officers. At a lower level, a Deputies Committee was chaired by the Deputy Assistant to the President for National Security Affairs and included representatives of the key Cabinet departments (as well as the Assistant to the Vice President for National Security Affairs). The Deputies Committee was also responsible for day-to-day crisis management.

In addition, provision was made for a system of Interagency Working Groups, (IWG) some permanent, some ad hoc, to be established by the direction of the Deputies Committee and chaired by representatives of the relevant departments, the NEC or the NSC staff. The IWGs convened on a regular basis to review and coordinate the implementation of Presidential decisions in their policy areas.

Evaluation. In general, the Clinton NSC did not see the internecine bureaucratic warfare that had surfaced in earlier administrations. PDD 2 provided for a strong NSC staff. Lake, in his writings on national security policymaking prior to becoming National Security Adviser, reflected a keen appreciation of the disadvantages of bureaucratic infighting. He subsequently recalled that when he came into office, "My model for a national security adviser was that of the behind-the-scenes consensus builder who helped present the communal views of senior advisers to the President." After some months, nonetheless, Lake

> decided to change my approach. I would stay behind the scenes.... And I would do my best always to try to achieve consensus and to make sure that my colleagues' views always had a fair hearing with the President. But I would be less hesitant in voicing my own views when they differed from those of my colleagues, even if it prevented consensus or put me more at odds with them–whether on NATO enlargement, Bosnia, Haiti, or other issues [48]

In 1999, the Clinton NSC staff played an important and influential role in shaping policy regarding Kosovo. Carefully attuned to shifts in U.S. public opinion, Berger, who succeeded Lake as National Security Adviser in March 1997, reportedly focused on the political dimension of policymaking and sought to avoid options that might lead to paralyzing debate in this country or other NATO states. He is reported to have helped the Administration steer a middle course between those who recommended a ground campaign against Serbia and those more ready to compromise with the Yugoslav leadership and, as a result, the Administration maintained a strong sense of unity throughout the Kosovo campaign. One press account suggested that "What may be Berger's distinctive accomplishment is to have put himself so preeminently at the center of decision-making while minimizing the historic antagonisms between national security advisers and secretaries of state and defense." [49]

The George W. Bush NSC' 2001-2009

In February 2001, President George W. Bush issued National Security Presidential Directive-1, Organization of the National Security Council System." The NSPD indicated that the NSC system was to advise and assist the President and "coordinate executive departments and agencies in the effective development and implementation" of national security policies. Among the statutory and other officials to be invited to attend NSC meetings, the Attorney General will be asked to attend meeting pertaining to his responsibilities, both matters within the Justice Department's jurisdiction and those matters arising under the Attorney General's responsibilities in accordance with 28 USC 511 to give advice and opinion on questions of law. The National Security Adviser was charged with determining the agenda, ensuring necessary papers are prepared and recording NSC actions and presidential decisions.

As has been the custom, the Principals Committee of the NSC consists of relevant department heads and relevant advisory officials, and is chaired by the National Security Adviser. When economic issues are on the agenda the National Security Adviser and the Assistant to the President for Economic Policy are to work in concert. The NSC Deputies Committees will be composed of deputy department heads, advisory officials and is chaired by the Deputy National Security Adviser. Lower-level coordination is effected by Policy Coordinating Committees which are to be chaired by appointees of the Secretary of State, another Cabinet level official or the National Security Adviser.

Subsequent to 9/11, the Intelligence Reform and Terrorism Prevention Act (P.L. 108-458) abolished the position of Director of Central Intelligence and established a new position of Director of National Intelligence (DNI) with enhanced authorities over the entire Intelligence Community. The DNI replaced the DCI in NSC-level deliberations.

Several accounts have described the key role of the NSC in undertaking a review of U.S. options in Iraq in late 2006 that resulted in the changes in tactics and force levels that have come to be known as the Surge. Although senior officials in DOD and the State Department were known to be skeptical of increasing troop levels, NSC staffers are reported to have argued that increased numbers of U.S. forces could provide the security to the Iraqi population that would encourage political stabilization. According to these reports, in the end President Bush adopted this approach [50].

Evaluation. Although some observers have argued that Condoleezza Rice, as National Security Adviser in President Bush's first term, allowed the Defense Department to dominate policymaking, especially in regard to Iraq, most acknowledged that she had a good working relationship with the President and was an effective public spokesman for the Administration. Hadley made fewer public appearances but emphasized the importance of the NSC staff monitoring the implementation of NSC decisions. As noted above, he is also credited with organizing a review of Iraq policy that resulted in major changes.

The Obama NSC 2009-

President Obama has designated retired Marine General James L. Jones to serve as National Security Adviser. Jones had previously served as Marine Corps Commandant and as NATO's Supreme Allied Commander. On February 13, 2009, the President signed Presidential Policy Directive-1, Organization of the National Security Council System. The directive lists those who will participate in NSC deliberations, including the Attorney General, the Secretary of Homeland Security, the U.S. Representative to the U.N., and the Counsel to the President. It also makes reference to officials who will be specifically invited to sessions dealing with international economic affairs, homeland security, counterterrorism, and science and technology issues. It describes the membership and duties of the Principals and Deputies Committees, which are to be chaired by the National Security Adviser and the Deputy National Security Adviser, respectively. The Principals Committee will be the "senior interagency forum for consideration of policy issues affecting national security" while the Deputies Committee will "review and monitor the work of the NSC interagency process" and "shall be responsible for day-to-day crisis management." The use of the term "monitor" may indicate a determination to enhance the NSC's ability to oversee implementation of presidential decisions on national security issues. Further management of the development and implementation of national security policies will be overseen by interagency policy committees which shall be established to address specific issues.

OVERVIEW OF CURRENT NSC FUNCTIONS

Largely because of the major influence in policymaking exerted by Kissinger and Brzezinski, the position of National Security Adviser has emerged as a central one. Brzezinski was even accorded Cabinet status—the only National Security Adviser to be thus designated [51] Some observers over the years have argued that the position should be subject to Senate confirmation and that the National Security Adviser should be available to testify before congressional committees as are officials from other Government departments and agencies [52] Others argue that a President is entitled to confidential advice from his immediate staff. They further suggest that making the position subject to confirmation would create confusion in the eyes of foreign observers as to which U.S. officials speak authoritatively on national security policy. This latter argument is arguably undercut, however, by the practice of recent National Security Advisers of appearing on television news programs.

National Security Advisers have come from various professions; not all have had extensive experience in foreign and defense policy. The report of the Committees Investigating the Iran- Contra Affair recommended that the National Security Adviser not be an active military officer [53] although no rationale was given for this recommendation.

A substantial number of NSC staff members over the years have been career military or civil servants with backgrounds in foreign policy and defense issues. A considerable number have been detailed to the NSC staff from various federal agencies, which continue to pay their salaries. This practice has been occasionally criticized as allowing the expansion of the White House staff beyond congressional authorization; nonetheless, the practice has continued with annual reports of the number of personnel involved being made to Appropriations Committees.

Beginning with the Kennedy Administration, a concerted effort was made to bring outside experts into the NSC staff in order to inject fresh perspectives and new ideas into the policymaking process. This effort has been continued to varying extents by successive Administrations. Henry Kissinger made a particular effort to hire academic experts, although some would eventually resign and become bitter critics. The Reagan NSC was occasionally criticized for filling NSC staff positions with political activists. Most of the NSC staff positions in the George H.W. Bush Administration were filled with Government officials. Anthony Lake, President Clinton's first National Security Adviser, argues that the NSC staff

> should be made up of as many career officials as possible, with as much carryover between administrations as can be managed. Its experts should be good (but not necessarily gray) bureaucrats who know how to get things done and how to fight for their views, and who are serving the national interest more than the political interests of their President.

He cautioned that:

> a political appointee whose main credential is work on national security issues in political campaigns will have learned to think about national security issues in a partisan context. The effect of his or her advice is likely to be to lengthen the period of time during which a President, at the outset of a term, tries to make policy on the basis of campaign rhetoric rather than international reality [54]

NSC Executive and Congressional Liaison

The very composition of the NSC, its statutory members, and those who attend meetings on occasion serve to identify those agencies and departments with which the NSC has a regular working relationship. These are the Departments of State and Defense (both the civilian and military staffs), the CIA, the Treasury Department, the Council of Economic Advisers, and a number of other departments as needed. The Director of National Intelligence, who is under the NSC, is responsible for coordinating the nation's foreign intelligence effort. His regular contacts include the CIA, as well as the Defense Intelligence Agency (DIA), the National Security Agency (NSA), the State Department's Bureau of Intelligence and Research (INR), and other elements of the intelligence community. However, these groups are not represented individually in the current NSC structure.

As part of the Executive Office of the President, the NSC does not have the same regular relationship with Congress and its committees that the member departments and agencies have. Most briefings on intelligence matters are undertaken by the CIA and DIA or by the Director of National Intelligence; information on diplomatic and military matters comes primarily from the Departments of State and Defense. As noted above, the President's Assistant for National Security Affairs is not subject to confirmation by the Senate.

Over the years there have been a considerable number of congressional hearings and reports relating to the NSC. However, many have had to do with topics peculiar to a given period: wiretaps against NSC staff members allegedly ordered by Dr. Kissinger, the unauthorized transfer of NSC documents to officials in the Joint Chiefs of Staff, and Watergate. Annual hearings are held concerning the NSC budget, and there have been occasional hearings concerning NSC organization and procedures. Very few of these hearings and reports have served as briefings for Congress on current issues which the NSC might have been considering. NSC appropriations are handled by the Subcommittees on Financial Services and General Government of the House and Senate Appropriations Committees.

As has been noted, Congress's role in NSC matters and its relationship with the NSC are limited. The Senate does not approve the appointment of the National Security Adviser, although it does confirm statutory NSC members Congress does have authority over the designation of those positions that are to have statutory NSC membership, as well as budgetary authority over the NSC. In 2007, as part of the Energy Independence and Security Act of 2007 (P.L. 110-140, section 932) Congress added the Secretary of Energy to the NSC. However, Congress has little direct say in matters of NSC organization, procedure, role, or influence, although a number of hearings on these topics have been held.

The NSC is not a primary and regular source of national security information for Congress. National security information is for the most part provided by those departments and agencies that are represented on the NSC. The NSC, as a corporate entity, rarely testifies before or briefs Congress on substantive questions, although in some Administrations informal briefings have been provided.

The NSC is an organ devoted to the workings of the executive branch in the broad area of national security. Its role is basically that of policy analysis and coordination and, as such, it has been subject to limited oversight and legislative control by Congress. Both in its staff organization and functioning, the NSC is extremely responsive to the preferences and working methods of each President and Administration. It would be difficult to design a uniform NSC structure that would meet the requirements of chief executives who represent a wide range of backgrounds, work styles, and policy agendas although some observers believe that the general pattern established in the final years of the Reagan Administration and followed by successive Presidents is likely to endure. There is unlikely to be a desire to drastically reduce the role of the NSC staff and most observers suggest that elevating the policymaking role of the National Security Adviser at the expense of the Secretary of State leaves Presidents subject to strong criticism.

The NSC and International Economic Issues

The NSC has traditionally focused on foreign and defense policy issues. In the aftermath of the end of the Cold War, many observers argue that the major national security concerns of the United States may no longer be centered on traditional diplomatic and military issues. They suggest, further, that international economic, banking, environmental, and health issues, among others, will be increasingly important to the country's national security. These types of concerns, however, have not been regularly part of the NSC's primary areas of responsibility. The heads of federal agencies most directly concerned with such issues have not been members of the NSC [55]

In the 1970's, Maxwell Taylor, who President Kennedy had appointed Chairman of the JCS, argued that a National Policy Council should replace the NSC and concern itself with broad areas of international and domestic policy [56]. William Hyland, an NSC official in the Reagan Administration, argued in 1980 that

> ... a bad defect in the [NSC] system is that it does not have any way of addressing international economic problems. The big economic agencies are Treasury, to some extent OMB, the Council of Economic Advisers, Commerce, Labor, and Agriculture. They are not in the NSC system, but obviously energy problems, trade, and arms sales are foreign policy issues. Every Administration tries to drag them in, usually by means of some kind of a subcommittee or a separate committee. The committee eventually runs up against some other committee. There is friction, and policies are made on a very ad hoc basis by the principal cabinet officers [57]

In early 1992, Professor Ernest May of Harvard University testified to the Senate Select Committee on Intelligence:

> In the early 1980s, the greatest foreign threat was default by Mexico and Brazil. That could have brought down the American banking system. Despite good CIA analysis and energetic efforts by some NSC staffers, the question did not get on the NSC agenda for more than two years. And then, the policy issues did not get discussed. The agencies concerned with money and banking had no natural connection with either the NSC or the intelligence community. We have no reason to suppose that agencies concerned with the new [post Cold War] policy issues will be any more receptive [58]

In the George H.W. Bush Administration, there remained a strong conviction that defense and foreign policy issues would remain vital and somewhat separate from other interests and that the NSC was the proper forum for them to be addressed. Before he became President Bush's National Security Adviser, Brent Scowcroft stated at a forum on national security policy organization:

> First of all, if there is a consensus ... that the NSC net ought to be spread ever wider, I am not a part of it. There are many things that the NSC system can do better, and it has enough on its plate now. I would not look toward its spreading its net wider [59]

As noted above, the Clinton Administration implemented its determination to coordinate foreign and domestic economic policies more closely. The National Economic Council, established by Executive Order 12835 on January 25, 1993, was designed to "coordinate the economic policy- making process with respect to domestic and international economic issues." Close linkage with the NSC were to be achieved by having the Assistant to the President for Economic Policy also sit on the NSC, supplemented by assigning staff to support both councils. The goal was to ensure that the economic dimensions of national security policy would be properly weighed in the White House decision-making process. Observers consider that cooperation between the NSC and the NEC was productive and contributed to the enhancement of both national security and economic policymaking although one senior NSC official has noted that efforts to deal with the 1997 Asian financial crisis were initially coordinated by U.S. international economic policymakers with little input from national security and foreign policy agencies [60]

The Growing Importance of Law Enforcement Issues

The post-Cold War era has seen a much closer relationship between traditional national security concerns with international issues that have a significant law enforcement component such as terrorism and narcotics smuggling [61]. The increasing intermingling of national security and law enforcement issues could cause major difficulties for the NSC staff and the National Security Adviser who is not a law enforcement official. The Justice Department will inevitably view with concern any incursion into what is regarded as the Attorney General's constitutional responsibilities. The NSC also coordinates with the Office of Drug Control Policy whose responsibilities also encompass both law enforcement and foreign policy considerations.

In dealing with international terrorism or narcotics production and transport from foreign countries, however, diplomatic and national security issues are often involved. Apprehending a terrorist group may require cooperation from a foreign government that has its own interests and concerns. Narcotics production may be entwined in the social and economic fabric of a foreign country to an extent that precludes the country from providing the sort of cooperation that would be expected from a major ally. During the Clinton Administration, the Attorney General's representatives have been included in NSC staff deliberations when law enforcement concerns were involved. Nonetheless, observers note public disagreements between Justice Department and State Department, for instance, regarding cooperation (or the lack thereof) from Saudi Arabia or Yemen. Clearly, the President has constitutional responsibilities for both national security and law enforcement, but the status of any other official to make necessary trade-offs is unclear. Observers suggest that in some future cases the need to establish a single U.S. position may require different ways of integrating national security and law enforcement concerns.

Today's international terrorist threat can encompass not only physical attacks on U.S. physical structures such as the World Trade Center, but also cyber-attacks on critical infrastructures, the computerized communications and data storage systems on which U.S. society has become reliant. Since such systems are in most cases owned and operated by corporations and other commercial entities, the role of the NSC is necessarily constrained. Much depends on law enforcement as well as voluntary cooperation by the private sector. The

Clinton Administration created the position of National Coordinator for Security, Infrastructure Protection, and Counterterrorism who reported to the President through the National Security Adviser [62]. The Intelligence Reform Act of 2004, however, established the National Counterterrorism Center outside the NSC structure.

In dealing with policies related to the protection of critical infrastructures, the National Security Adviser will have an important role, but one inherently different from the traditional responsibilities of the office [63] The position could involve in coordination of responses to threats both in the U.S. and from abroad and among the federal government, the states, and the private sector. It is clear to all observers that such coordination involves much uncharted territory, including a special concern that the National Security Adviser might become overly and inappropriately involved in law enforcement matters.

The Role of the National Security Adviser

The NSC was created by statute, and its membership has been designated and can be changed by statute. The NSC has also been subject to statutorily approved reorganization processes within the executive branch, as when it was placed in the Executive Office by a Reorganization Plan in August 1949. Nonetheless, the NSC has been consistently regarded as a presidential entity with which Congress is rarely involved. The internal organization and roles of the NSC have been changed by Presidents and by National Security Advisers in response to their preferences and these changes have not usually been subject to congressional scrutiny.

The role of the National Security Adviser has, however, become so well established in recent years that Congress has been increasingly prepared to grant the incumbent significant statutory responsibilities. The Foreign Intelligence Surveillance Act and other legislation provides for statutory roles for the National Security Adviser [64]. Executive Orders provide other formal responsibilities. The position has become institutionalized and the exercise of its functions has remained an integral part of the conduct of national security policy in all recent administrations.

Some observers believe that these established duties which extend beyond the offering of advice and counsel to the President will inevitably lead to a determination to include the appointment of a National Security Adviser among those requiring the advice and consent of the Senate. Advice and consent by the Senate is seen as providing a role for the legislative branch in the appointment of one of the most important officials in the federal government. Another cited advantage of this proposal would be the increased order, regularity, and formalization that are involved in making appointments that are sent to the Senate. Proponents argue that this would ultimately provide greater accountability for NSC influence and decisions. Opponents on the other hand, might point to the danger of unnecessary rigidity and stratification of organization and the potential that appointments might be excessively influenced by political considerations.

There is also a potential that the NSC staff might become irrelevant if it loses the trust of a future President or if its procedures become so formalized as to stultify policymaking. Should the Adviser be subject to Senate confirmation, it is argued that an important prerogative of the President to choose his immediate staff would be compromised. In addition, the incumbent could be required or expected to make routine appearances before congressional oversight committees, arguably undermining the primary purpose of the National Security Adviser which is to provide the President with candid advice on a wide range of issues, often on an informal and confidential basis.

One historian has summed up the role of the National Security Adviser:

> The entire national security system must have confidence that the [National Security Adviser] will present alternate views fairly and will not take advantage of propinquity in the coordination of papers and positions. He must be able to present bad news to the president and to sniff out and squelch misbehavior before it becomes a problem. He must be scrupulously honest in presenting presidential decisions and in monitoring the implementation process. Perhaps most important, he must impart the same sense of ethical behavior to the Staff he leads [65]

In a recent assessment, two informed observers listed tasks for which the Adviser and staff uniquely are responsible:

- Staffing the president's daily foreign policy activity: his communications with foreign leaders and the preparation and conduct of his trips overseas;
- Managing the process of making decisions on major foreign and national security issues; -Driving the policymaking process to make real choices, in a timely manner;
- Overseeing the full implementation of the decision the president has made [66]

The increasing difficulties in separating national security issues from some law enforcement and international economic concerns has led some observers to urge that the lines separating various international staffs at the White House be erased and that a more comprehensive policymaking entity be created.

It is argued that such reforms could most effectively be accomplished without legislation [67].

The Project for National Security Reform (PNSR) a nonpartisan task force that has studied the structure of national policymaking has made a number of far-reaching proposals for expanding the role of a national security director and combining the National Security Council and the Homeland Security Council [68] Such proposals raise complex questions, including the role of congressional oversight. Whereas Congress has traditionally deferred to White House leadership in national security matters, to a far greater extent than in international economic affairs, there might be serious questions about taking formal steps to place resolution of a wide range of international policies, including economic and law enforcement issues, in the hands of officials who receive little congressional oversight.

Proposals such as those of the Project on National Security Reform that have been made to enhance the role of the National Security Adviser will probably include consideration of new options for congressional oversight of the National Security Staff. It is likely, in any event, that Congress will continue to monitor the functioning of the staff and the Adviser in the context of U.S. policymaking in a changing international environment.

SELECTED BIBLIOGRAPHY

The most comprehensive source concerning the genesis and development of the NSC through 1960 is contained in a collection of hearings, studies, reports and recommendations complied by Senator Henry M. Jackson and published as U.S. Congress. Senate. Committee on Government Operations. Subcommittee on National Policy Machinery. Organizing for National Security, 3 Vols. 86th and 87th Congress. Washington, Government Printing Office. [1961]. Presidential memoirs are also valuable.

Other useful sources are:

Anderson, Dillon. "The President and National Security." *Atlantic Monthly*, January 1966.

Bock, Joseph G. "The National Security Assistant and the White House Staff: National Security Policy Decisionmaking and Domestic Political Considerations, 1947-1984." *Presidential Studies Quarterly*, Spring 1986. Pp. 258-279.

Bowie, Robert R. and Richard H. Immerman. *Waging Peace: How Eisenhower Shaped an Enduring Cold War Strategy*. New York: Oxford University Press. 1998.

Brown, Cody M. *The National Security Council: A Legal History of the President's Most Powerful Advisers*. Washington: Project for National Security Reform.2008.

Brzezinski, Zbigniew. *Power and Principle: Memoirs of the National Security Adviser, 19 77-1981*. New York: Farrar, Straus, Giroux. 1983.

"The NSC's Midlife Crisis". *Foreign Policy*, Winter 1987-1988. Pp. 80-99.

Bock, Joseph G., and Clarke, Duncan L. "The National Security Assistant and the White House Staff: National Security Policy Decisionmaking and Domestic Political Considerations, 1947- 1984." *Political Science Quarterly*, Spring 1986. Pp. 258-279.

Brown, Cody M. *The National Security Council: A Legal History of the President's Most Powerful Advisers*. Washington: Project for National Security Reform. 2008.

Bumiller, Elisabeth. *Condoleezza Rice: An American Life: A Biography*. New York: Random House. 2007.

Caraley, Demetrios. *The Politics of Military Unification*. New York: Columbia University Press. [1966].

Clark, Keith C., and Laurence S. Legere, eds. "The President and the Management of National Security". Report for the Institute for Defense Analyses. New York: Praeger. [1966]. See especially pp. 55-114.

Commission on the Organization of the Executive Branch of the Government. *National Security Organization*. Washington: Government Printing Office. [1949].

Commission on the Organization of the Government for the Conduct of Foreign Policy. *Report*. Washington: Government Printing Office. [1975].

Cutler, Robert. *No Time for Rest*. Boston: Little, Brown. 1966.

"The Development of the National Security Council". Foreign Affairs, April 1956. Pp. 441- 58.

Daalder, Ivo H., and Destler, I.M. *In the Shadow of the Oval Office: Profiles of the National Security Advisers and the Presidents They Served—from JFK to George W. Bush.* New York: Simon and Schuster. 2009.

Destler, I.M. "Can One Man Do?" *Foreign Policy*, Winter 1971-72. Pp. 28-40.

"National Security Advice to U.S. Presidents: Some Lessons from Thirty Years." *World Politics*, January 1977. Pp. 143-76.

Presidents, Bureaucrats and Foreign Policy: The Politics of Organization. Princeton: Princeton University Press. [1972].

Lake, Anthony; and Gelb, Leslie H. *Our Own Worst Enemy: The Unmaking of American Foreign Policy*. New York: Simon and Schuster. 1984.

Falk, Stanley L., and Theodore W. Bauer. "The National Security Structure." Washington: Industrial College of the Armed Forces. [1972].

Greenstein, Fred I. and Richard H. Immerman. "Effective National Security Advising: Recovering the Eisenhower Legacy." *Political Science Quarterly*, Fall 2000. Pp. 335-345.

Haig, Alexander M., Jr. Caveat: Realism, Reagan, and Foreign Policy. New York: Macmillan. 1984.

Hammond, Paul Y. "The National Security Council as a Device for Interdepartmental Coordination: An Interpretation and Appraisal". *American Political Science Review*, December 1960. Pp. 899-910.

Humphrey, David C. "NSC Meetings during the Johnson Presidency". *Diplomatic History*, Winter 1994. Pp. 29-45.

Hunter, Robert E. *Organizing for National Security*. Washington: Center for Strategic and International Studies. 1988.

Inderfurth, Karl F. and Johnson, Loch K., eds. *Decisions of the Highest Order: Perspectives of the National Security Council*. Pacific Grove, CA: Brooks/Cole Publishing Co. 1988.

Johnson, Robert H. "The National Security Council: The Relevance of its Past to its Future". *Orbis*, Fall 1969. Pp. 709-35.

Kissinger, Henry A. *White House Years*. Boston: Little, Brown. 1979. ——*Years of Renewal*. New York: Simon and Schuster. 1999. ——Years of Upheaval. Boston: Little, Brown. 1982.

Kolodziej, Edward A. "The National Security Council: Innovations and Implications". *Public Administration Review*. November/December 1969. Pp. 573-85.

Korb, Lawrence J. and Hahn, Keith D., eds. *National Security Policy Organization in Perspective*. Washington: American Enterprise Institute. 1981.

Laird, Melvin R. *Beyond the Tower Commission*. Washington: American Enterprise Institute. 1987.

Lake, Anthony. *6 Nightmares*. Boston: Little, Brown. 2000. ——*Somoza Failing*. Boston: Houghton Mifflin. 1989.

Lay, James S., Jr. "National Security Council's Role in the U.S. Security and Peace Program". *World Affairs*, Summer 1952. Pp. 33-63.

Leacacos, John P. "Kissinger's Apparat". *Foreign Policy*, Winter 197 1-72. Pp. 3-27.

Lord, Carnes. "NSC Reform for the Post-Cold War Era," *Orbis*, Summer 2000. Pp. 433-450.

McFarlane, Robert C. "Effective Strategic Policy." *Foreign Affairs*, Fall 1988. Pp. 33-48.

with Richard Saunders and Thomas C. Shull. "The National Security Council: Organization for Policy Making." *Proceedings of the Center for the Study of the Presidency*. Vol. 5. 1984. Pp. 261-273.

Head, Richard G., and Frisco W. Short. *Crisis Resolution, Presidential Decision Making in the Mayaguez and Korean Confrontations*. Boulder, CO: Westview Press. 1978.

Menges, Constantine C. *Inside the National Security Council: The True Story of the Making and Unmaking of Reagan's Foreign Policy*. New York: Simon and Schuster. 1988.

Mulcahy, Kevin V. and Crabb, Cecil V. "Presidential Management of National Security Policy Making, 1947-1987". In *The Managerial Presidency*, ed. by James P. Pfiffner. Pacific Grove, CA: Brooks/Cole. 1991. Pp. 250-264.

Nelson, Anna Kasten. "President Truman and the Evolution of the National Security Council." *Journal of American History*, September 1985. Pp. 360-378.

"The 'Top of the Policy Hill': President Eisenhower and the National Security Council." *Diplomatic History*, Fall 1983. Pp. 307-326.

Nixon, Richard M. *U.S. Foreign Policy for the 1970's: A New Strategy for Peace*. Washington: Government Printing Office. [1970].

U.S. Foreign Policy for the 1970's: The Emerging Structure of Peace. Washington: Government Printing Office. [1971].

U.S. Foreign Policy for the 1970's: Building for Peace. Washington: Government Printing Office. [1972].

Powell, Colin L. "The NSC System in the Last Two Years of the Reagan Administration". *The Presidency in Transition*. Ed. by James P. Pfiffner and R. Gordon Hoxie. New York: Center for the Study of the Presidency, 1989. Pp. 204-218.

Prados, John. *Keepers of the Keys: A History of the National Security Council from Truman to Bush*. New York: William Morrow. 1991.

Rothkopf, David. *Running the World: the Inside Story of the National Security Council and the Architects of American Power*. New York: Public Affairs.2004.

Rostow, Walt Whitman. *The Diffusion of Power: An Essay in Recent History*. New York: Macmillan. 1972.

Sander, Alfred D. "Truman and the National Security Council, 1945-1947". *Journal of American History*, September 1972. Pp. 369-388.

Schlesinger, Arthur, Jr. "Effective National Security Advising: A Most Dubious Precedent." *Political Science Quarterly*, Fall 2000. Pp. 347-351.

Shoemaker, Christopher C. *The NSC Staff: Counseling the Council*. Boulder, CO: Westview Press. 1991.

Souers, Sidney W. "Policy Formulation for National Security". *American Political Science Review*, June 1949. Pp. 534-43.

Steiner, Barry H. "Policy Organization in American Security Affairs: An Assessment". *Public Administration Review*, July/August 1977. Pp. 357-67.

Thayer, Frederick C. "Presidential Policy Process and 'New Administration': A Search for Revised Paradigms". *Public Administration Review*, September/October 1971. Pp. 552-61.

U.S. Congress. Senate. Committee on Government Operations. Subcommittee on National Security and International Operations. *The National Security Council: New role and structure*. 91st Congress, 1st session. Washington: Government Printing Office. 1969.

Select Committee on Secret Military Assistance to Iran and the Nicaraguan Opposition. House of Representatives. Select Committee to Investigate Covert Arms Transactions with Iran. 100th Congress, 1st session. *Report of the Congressional Committees Investigating the Iran- Contra Affair with Supplemental, Minority, and Additional Views*, Senate Report 100-216/House Report 100-433. Washington: Government Printing Office. 1987.

Committee on Government Operations. Subcommittee on National Security and International Operations. *The National Security Council: Comment by Henry Kissinger*. March 3, 1970. 91st Congress, 2d Session. Washington: Government Printing Office. 1970.

U.S. Department of State. "The National Security System: Responsibilities of the Department of State." *Department of State Bulletin*, February 24, 1969. Pp. 163-66.

U.S. President's Special Review Board. *Report of the President's Special Review Board*. Washington: Government Printing Office. 1987.

West, Bing. *The Strongest Tribe: War, Politics and the Endgame in Iraq*. New York. Random House. 2008.

Yost, Charles W. "The Instruments of American Foreign Policy," *Foreign Affairs*, October 1971. Pp. 59-68.

Zegart, Amy B. *Flawed by Design: the Evolution of the CIA, JCS, and NSC*. Stanford, CA: Stanford University Press, 1999.

Note: Many of the above entries contain numerous footnotes that identify a wealth of primary and secondary sources too numerous to include here. Of special interest are the oral interviews of former NSC staff personnel conducted from 1998 to 2000 as part of the National Security

Council Project undertaken by the Center for International and Security Studies at Maryland and the Brookings Institution; transcripts are available at http://www.cissm.umd.edu/projects/nsc.php. Also useful is the transcript of "A Forum on the Role of the National Security Adviser," cosponsored by the Woodrow Wilson International Center for Scholars and the James A. Baker III Institute for Public Policy of Rice University, available at http://wwics.si.edu/news/docs/nsa.pdf.

APPENDIX A. NATIONAL SECURITY ADVISERS

Table A-1. National Security Advisers, 1953-2009

Robert Cutler	March 23, 1953	April 2, 1955
Dillon Anderson	April 2, 1955	September 1, 1956
Robert Cutler	January 7, 1957	June 24, 1958
Gordon Gray	June 24, 1958	January 13, 1961
McGeorge Bundy	January 20, 1961	February 28, 1966
Walt W. Rostow	April 1, 1966	January 20, 1969
Henry A. Kissinger	January 20, 1969	November 3, 1975
Brent Scowcroft	November 3, 1975	January 20, 1977
Zbigniew Brzezinski	January 20, 1977	January 21, 1981
Richard V. Allen	January 21, 1981	January 4, 1982
William P. Clark	January 4, 1982	October 17, 1983
Robert C. McFarlane	October 17, 1983	December 4, 1985
John M. Poindexter	December 4, 1985	November 25, 1986
Frank C. Carlucci	December 2, 1986	November 23, 1987
Colin L. Powell	November 23, 1987	January 20, 1989
Brent Scowcroft	January 20, 1989	January 20, 1993
W. Anthony Lake	January 20, 1993	March 14, 1997
Samuel R. Berger	March 14, 1997	January 20, 2001
Condoleezza Rice	January 22, 2001	January 25, 2005
Stephen Hadley	January 26, 2005	January 20, 2009
James L. Jones	Janua 009	Present

REFERENCES

[1] Paul Y. Hammond, "The National Security Council as a Device for Interdepartmental Coordination: An Interpretation and Appraisal," *American Political Science Review*, December, 1960, p. 899; U.S. Bureau of the Budget, *The United States at War* (Washington: Government Printing Office, 1946), p. 2.

[2] Mark Skinner Watson, *Chief of Staff: Prewar Plans and Preparations* (Washington: Office of the Chief of Military History, 1950), pp. 89-9 1, 93-94.

[3] R. Elberton Smith, The Army and Economic Mobilization (Washington: Office of the Chief of Military History, 1959), pp. 103-04, 109-10; Bureau of the Budget, *The United States at War*, pp. 22-25, 44, 50-51.

[4] Ray S. Cline, *Washington Command Post: The Operations Division* (Washington: Office of the Chief of Military History, 1951), pp. 326-27; John Lewis Gaddis, *The United States and the Origins of the Cold War* (New York, Columbia University Press, 1972), p. 126; U.S. Department of State, *Foreign Relations of the United States*, 1944, v. I: *General* (Washington: Government Printing Office, 1966), pp. 1466-70.

[5] One of the best studies on the creation and development of the NSC through the Eisenhower Administration, including hearings, studies, reports, recommendations and articles, can be found in U.S. Congress, Senate, 86th and 87th Congress, Committee on Government Operations, Subcommittee on National Policy Machinery, *Organizing for National Security*, 1961, 3 vols.

[6] Demetrios Caraley, *The Politics of Military Unification* (New York: Columbia University Press, 1966), pp. 23-44; Walter Millis, ed., *The Forrestal Diaries* (New York: The Viking Press, 1951), pp. 62-63.

[7] Caraley, *The Politics of Military Unification*, pp. 40-41; see also Jeffrey M. Dorwart, *Eberstadt and Forrestal: A National Security Partnership, 1909-1949* (College Station, TX: Texas A and M University Press, 1991), especially pp. 90-107.

[8] Ibid., pp. 86-87, 91; Hammond, "The NSC as a Device for Interdepartmental Coordination," pp. 900-01.

[9] Caraley, *Politics of Military Unification*, pp. 136-37; Millis, *Forrestal Diaries*, p. 222.

[10] The congressional debate over the National Security Act is summarized in Caraley, *Politics of Military Unification*, pp. 153-82; on the NSC, see p. 161. Examples of congressional opinion can be found throughout the lengthy debate. Some representative comments can be found in the *Congressional Record*, v. 93, July 7, 1947, p. 8299, and July 9, 1947, pp. 8496-97, 8518, 8520.

[11] 50 USC 402.

[12] More specific information on the history of the transfers of defense mobilization and civil defense authorities may be found in Sections 402 and 404 of *U.S. Code Annotated*, Title 50 (St. Paul, MN: West Publishing Co., 1991).

[13] The Commission on the Organization of the Executive Branch of the Government. *National Security Organization* (Washington: Government Printing Office, 1949), especially pp. 15-16, 74-76.

[14] Walter Millis, *Arms and the State* (New York: The Twentieth Century Fund, 1958), pp. 255, 388.

[15] Anna Kasten Nelson, "President Truman and the Evolution of the National Security Council," *Journal of American History*, September 1985, p. 377.

[16] This position has been a continuing one, although its title has varied over the years (Special Assistant for National Security Affairs, Assistant to the President for National Security Affairs, National Security Adviser). An adviser or an assistant to the President arguably has a position of greater independence from congressional oversight than the incumbent of a position established by statute; see Richard Ehlke, "Congressional Creation of an Office of National Security Adviser to the President," reprinted in U.S. Congress, 96th Congress, 2d session, Senate, Committee on Foreign Relations, The National Security Adviser: Role and Accountability, Hearing, April 17, 1980, pp. 133-135. The position of National Security Adviser is to be distinguished from the position of Executive Secretary of the NSC, which was created by statute but has, since the beginning of the Eisenhower Administration, been essentially an administrative and logistical one. National Security Adviser positions are funded not as part of the NSC but as part of the White House Office, reflecting the incumbent's status as that of an adviser to the President.

[17] Frederick C. Thayer, "Presidential Policy Processes and 'New Administration': A Search for Revised Paradigms," *Public Administration Review*, September/October 1971: 554. Robert H. Johnson, "The National Security Council: The Relevance of its Past to Its Future," *Orbis*, v. 13, Fall 1969: 715; Robert Cutler, *No Time for Rest* (Boston: Little, Brown, 1966).

[18] Some Eisenhower-era NSC documents are reprinted in the State Department's *Foreign Relations of the United States* series, especially in volumes dealing with National Security Affairs; microfilm copies of declassified NSC documents have been made available by a commercial publisher, University Publications of America, Inc. NSC documents are usually highly classified; while some are subsequently declassified and released to the public (although not necessarily in the *Federal Register* or other official publications series), others have been withheld. Some observers have criticized this situation; see Harold C. Relyea, "The Coming of Secret Law," *Government Information Quarterly*, May 1988, pp. 106-112; U.S. General Accounting Office, "The Use of Presidential Directives to Make and Implement U.S. Policy," Report No. GAO/NSIAD-92-72, January 1992.

[19] The hearings and reports of this study are cited in note 5.

[20] See Anna Kasten Nelson, "The 'Top of Policy Hill': President Eisenhower and the National Security Council," *Diplomatic History*, Fall 1983, p. 324; also, Stephen E. Ambrose, *The President* (New York: Simon and Schuster, 1984), pp. 345, 509.

[21] Robert R. Bowie and Richard H. Immerman, *Waging Peace: How Eisenhower Shaped an Enduring Cold War Strategy* New York: Oxford University Press, 1998), p. 258. Recent support for the Eisenhower system is given in Fred I. Greenstein and Richard H. Immerman, "Effective National Security Advising: Recovering the Eisenhower Legacy," *Political Science Quarterly*, Fall 2000; criticism is renewed in Arthur Schlesinger, Jr., "Effective National Security Advising: A Most Dangerous Precedent," *Political Science Quarterly*, Fall 2000.

[22] Thayer, "Presidential Policy Processes and 'New Administration,'" p. 555.

[23] Arthur M. Schlesinger, Jr., *A Thousand Days: John F. Kennedy in the White House* (Boston: Houghton Mifflin, 1965), pp. 406-47; see especially pp. 412-13, 426, 430-32.

[24] Kai Bird, *The Color of Truth: McGeorge Bundy and William Bundy: Brothers in Arms* (New York: Simon and Schuster, 1998), p. 186.

[25] McGeorge Bundy to Henry M. Jackson, September 4, 1961, reprinted in *Organizing for National Security*, I, 1338

[26] Much of the documentary basis of the Nixon NSC effort is provided in U.S., Department of State, *Foreign Relations of the United States, 1969-1976*, Vol. II, *Organization and Management of U.S. Foreign Policy, 1969-1972* (Washington, DC: Government Printing Office, 2006).

[27] Commission on the Organization of the Government for the Conduct of Foreign Policy, Report (Washington, Government Printing Office, 1975).

[28] Ibid., p. 37.

[29] Veto of a Bill to Amend the National Security Act of 1947, January 1, 1976, *Public Papers of the Presidents: Gerald R. Ford* 1976-1977 Vol. I (Washington: Government Printing Office, 1979), p. 1-2.

[30] For the Carter NSC, see Presidential Directive/NSC-1 and NSC-2, January 20, 1977; Executive Order 12036, January 24, 1978; Zbigniew Brzezinski, *Power and Principle: Memoirs of the National Security Adviser, 1977-1981* (New York: Farrar, Straus, Giroux, 1983).

[31] Presidential Directive/NSC-2, January 20, 1977; see also Statement by White House Press Secretary, January 22, 1977, *Public Papers of the Presidents, Jimmy Carter*, 1977, Vol. I (Washington: Government Printing Office, 1977), p. 8.

[32] Presidential Directive/NSC-2.

[33] Executive Order 12036, January 24, 1978, Section 1-2.

[34] Presidential Directive/NSC-2. January 20, 1977.

[35] Executive Order 12036, January 24, 1978, Section 1-3.

[36] Executive Order 12036, January 24, 1978, Sections 1-302 to 1-304 inclusive.

[37] See Christopher C. Shoemaker, *The NSC Staff: Counseling the Council* (Boulder, CO: Westview Press, 1991), pp. 51-57.

[38] Stansfield Turner, *Terrorism and Democracy* (Boston: Houghton Mifflin, 1991), p. 58.

[39] See *National Security Adviser: Role and Accountability*.

[40] Brzezinski acknowledges but discounts the reports that Mondale had imposed certain staff members on him; see *Power and Principle*, pp. 74-78.

[41] Reprinted in *Public Papers of the Presidents, Ronald Reagan*, 1982, Vol. I (Washington: Government Printing Office, 1983), pp. 18-22.

[42] *Public Papers of the Presidents, Ronald Reagan*, 1981 (Washington: Government Printing Office, 1982), p. 285.

[43] U.S., President's Special Review Board, *Report of the President's Special Review Board* (Washington: Government Printing Office, 1987), pp. V-1-V-2. The Board consisted of former Senator John Tower, former Secretary of State Edmund Muskie and former (and future) National Security Adviser Brent Scowcroft. It is often referred to as the Tower Board.

[44] Ibid., p. V-5.

[45] U.S. Congress. Senate. Select Committee on Secret Military Assistance to Iran and the Nicaraguan Opposition. House of Representatives. Select Committee to Investigate Covert Arms Transactions with Iran. 100th Congress, 1st session. *Report of the Congressional Committees Investigating the Iran-Contra Affair with Supplemental, Minority, and Additional Views*, Senate Report 100-216/House Report 100-433, November 1987, p. 425. The Committee added that, "By statute the NSC was created to

provide advice to the President on national security matters. But there is no express
statutory prohibition on the NSC engaging in operational intelligence activities." Ibid.

[46] See Robert G. Sutter, "American Policy Toward Beijing, 1989-1990: the Role of
      President Bush and the White House Staff," *Journal of Northeast Asian Studies*,
      Winter 1990.

[47] The NEC was established by Executive Order 12835 on January 25, 1993; on the NEC
      see Kenneth I. Jester and Simon Lazarus, *Making Economic Policy: An Assessment of
      the National Economic Council* (Washington: Brookings Institution Press, 1997) and
      I.M. Destler, *The National Economic Council: A Work in Progress* (Washington:
      Institute for International Economics, 1996).

[48] *6 Nightmares* (Boston: Little, Brown, 2000), pp. 131,131-132.

[49] John F. Harris, "Berger's Caution Has Shaped Role of U.S. In War," *Washington Post*,
      May 16, 1999, p. A24.

[50] See Linda Robinson, *Tell Me How This Ends: General David Petraeus and the Search
      for a Way Out of Iraq* (New York: Public Affairs, 2008), pp. 26-36; Bing West, *The
      Strongest Tribe: War, Politics, and the Endgame in Iraq* (New York: Random House,
      2008), pp. 197-207; Ivo H. Daalder and I.M. Destler, *In the Shadow of the Oval
      Office: Profiles of the National Security Advisers and the Presidents they Served from
      JFK to George W. Bush* (New York: Simon and Schuster, 2009), pp. 294-297.

[51] "Cabinet status" is not recognized in law, but is a distinction conferred by the President.
      See Ronald C. Moe, *The President's Cabinet*, CRS Report No. 86-982GOV,
      November 6, 1986, p. 2.

[52] There are differing views regarding linkage between Senatorial confirmation and an
      obligation to testify before congressional committees; see, for instance, Zbigniew
      Brzezinski, "NSC's Midlife Crisis," *Foreign Policy*, Winter 1987-1988, p. 95; also,
      the Prepared Statement of Thomas M. Franck printed in *The National Security
      Adviser: Role and Accountability*, pp. 40-41. For additional background, see CRS
      Report RL3 1351, *Presidential Advisers' Testimony Before Congressional Committees:
      An Overview*, by Harold C. Relyea and Todd B. Tatelman.

[53] Report of the Congressional Committees Investigating the Iran-Contra Affair, p. 426.

[54] *6 Nightmares*, pp. 261-262.

[55] There are other White House-level coordinative bodies, such as the Office of
      Management and Budget, the Council of Economic Advisers, the Office of the United
      States Trade Representative, and the Council on Environmental Quality, that do deal
      with such issues.

[56] Maxwell D. Taylor, *Precarious Security* (New York: W.W. Norton, 1976), pp. 113-116.

[57] Quoted in Lawrence J. Korb and Keith D. Hahn, eds., *National Security Policy
      Organization in Perspective* (Washington: American Enterprise Institute, 1980), p. 11

[58] Ernest R. May, Statement for the Senate Select Committee on Intelligence, March 4,
      1992; see also May's article, "Intelligence: Backing into the Future," *Foreign Affairs*,
      Summer 1992, especially pp. 64-66.

[59] Quoted in Korb and Hahn, eds., *National Security Policy Organization in Perspective*, p.
      34.

[60] James Steinberg, "Foreign Policy: Time to Regroup," *Washington Post*, January 2,
      2001, p. A15.

[61] See CRS Report RL30252, *Intelligence and Law Enforcement: Countering Transnational Threats to the U.S.*, by Richard A. Best Jr.

[62] See CRS Report RL30153, *Critical Infrastructures: Background, Policy, and Implementation*, by John D. Moteff.

[63] It has been noted that the original membership of the National Security Council included officials responsible for mobilization planning, but those offices were subsequently merged into others and are no longer represented on the NSC. The need for national mobilization to sustain a global war effort is not considered a high priority in the post-Cold War world. (See Carnes Lord, "NSC Reform in the Post-Cold War Era," Orbis, Summer 2000, pp. 449-500.) The inclusion of such officials did, nonetheless, reflect the determination of the drafters of the National Security Act that the NSC have a wide mandate in protecting the nation's security interests and one that could extend into the private sector.

[64] The Foreign Intelligence Surveillance Act of 1978, as amended, requires that applications for orders for electronic surveillance for foreign intelligence purposes include a certification regarding the need for such surveillance by the Assistant to the President for National Security Affairs (or someone else designated by the President)(50 USC 1804 (a)(7)); a similar requirement exists for applications for physical searches (50 USC 1823(a)(7)). The Assistant to the President for National Security Affairs is also assigned as chairman of two NSC committees–the Committee on Foreign Intelligence (50 USC 402(h)(2)(D)) and the Committee on Transnational Threats (50 USC 402(i)(2)(E)). These assignments were made as part of the FY1997 Intelligence Authorization Act (P.L. 104-293); in signing it, President Clinton stated his concerns about the provisions relating to the establishment of the two NSC committees: "Such efforts to dictate the President's policy procedures unduly intrude upon Executive prerogatives and responsibilities. ("Statement on Signing the Intelligence Authorization Act for Fiscal Year 1997," October 11, 1996, *Weekly Compilation of Presidential Documents*, October 14, 1996, p. 2039). Other legislation placed the National Security Adviser on the President's Council on Counter-Narcotics (21 USC 1708(b)(1)(O)) and the Director of National Drug Control policy is required to work in conjunction with the Adviser "in any matter affecting national security interests." (21 USC 1703(b)(10)).

[65] Shoemaker, *NSC Staff: Counseling the Council*, p. 115.

[66] Ivo H. Daalder and I.M. Destler, *In the Shadow of the Oval Office: Profiles of the National Security Adviser and the Presidents They Served—From JFK to George W. Bush* (New York: Simon and Schuster, 2009), pp. 318-319.

[67] See Steinberg, "Foreign Policy: Time to Regroup."

[68] For further background, see the PNSR website, http://www.pnsr.org. See also CRS Report RL34455. *Organizing the U.S. Government for National Security: Overview of the Interagency Reform Debates.*

In: Economics, Political and Social Issues ...
Editor: Michelle L. Fergusson

ISBN: 978-1-61122-555-6
©2011 Nova Science Publishers, Inc.

STATE, FOREIGN OPERATIONS APPROPRIATIONS: A GUIDE TO COMPONENT ACCOUNTS[*]

Curt Tarnoff and Kennon H. Nakamura
Foreign Affairs

ABSTRACT

The State, Foreign Operations, and Related Programs appropriations legislation provides annual funding for almost all of the international affairs programs generally considered as part of the 150 International Affairs Budget Function (the major exception being food assistance). In recent years, the legislation has also served as a vehicle for Congress to place conditions on the expenditure of those funds, and express its views regarding certain foreign policy issues.

This report briefly discusses the legislation generally and then provides a short description of the various funding accounts as they appear in Division H, "Department of State, Foreign Operations, and Related Programs Appropriations Act, 2009," of the Omnibus Appropriations Act, 2009 (P.L. 111-8).

INTRODUCTION

The Department of State, Foreign Operations, and Related Programs (State, Foreign Operations) appropriations bill provides annual appropriations for the vast majority of international affairs programs generally considered as part of the 150 International Affairs Budget Function [1]. The State Department portion makes up about one-third of the funding, and the Foreign Operations portion—often called the "foreign aid" bill—makes up the remainder of the funds appropriated [2].

Among the areas covered by the State, Foreign Operations appropriations legislation, and explained below, are the Department of State and the U.S. Agency for International Development's (USAID) operating accounts, both assessed and voluntary U.S. contributions to international organizations and peacekeeping operations, U.S. non-military international broadcasting, bilateral and multilateral U.S. foreign economic assistance, assistance to foreign militaries, anti-narcotics funding, and funding for the Peace Corps, the Millennium Challenge Corporation, and the many other programs operated primarily by the Department of State and USAID through which the United States engages with the world to protect and advance U.S. national interests. Beyond providing funds, the appropriations bills, in recent years, also have

---

[*] Excerpted from CRS Report R40482 dated March 30, 2009.

been an important vehicle in conditioning the use of these funds and stating congressional views regarding foreign policy issues.

There are, however, several funding areas that are not covered by the State, Foreign Operations appropriations legislation that might be considered international affairs activities. These programs would include P.L. 480 and other food assistance, included in the 150 account but funded by the Agriculture appropriations bill. While the State Department and USAID sponsor nearly four-fifths of U.S. and foreign participants in educational and cultural exchange programs, other government agencies are responsible for the remaining participants in such programs, including, for example, the short-term exchange of scientists program at the National Cancer Institute. The Department of Defense's Commander's Emergency Response Program (CERP) supports reconstruction needs in Iraq and Afghanistan and its "Section 1206" authority supports the strengthening of foreign military capacities. These other-agency programs are funded through their own agency appropriations measures.

While the appropriation of funds is an authority reserved for the Congress by the Constitution, the two-step authorization/appropriations process is established by House and Senate rules; and the authorization of appropriations is intended to provide guidance to appropriators as to a general amount and under what conditions funding might be provided to an agency or program [3]. However, in the case of the State Department and foreign assistance programs, it is prescribed by law that legislation authorizing appropriations is required before the appropriations can be made [4]. These provisions have been waived in the years that Congress has not enacted authorizations [5]

Within the appropriations legislation, account names have changed over the years and new accounts have been added. In FY2008, for example, the International Disaster and Famine Assistance account became the International Disaster Assistance account. In the FY2009 bill, the Former Soviet Union account was combined with the Eastern Europe and Baltic States account to form a new Europe, Eurasia, and Central Asia account. In the FY2006 bill, a new Democracy Fund was established. The overall organization of the legislation may change as well. The FY2009 bill added a new title (Title II), specifically for USAID operations.

In the FY2009 Omnibus Appropriations Act (P.L. 111-8), the State Department, Foreign Operations, and Related Programs appropriations legislation (Division H) is divided into seven titles:

Title I	Department of State and Related Agencies
Title II	United States Agency for International Development
Title III	Bilateral Economic Assistance
Title IV	International Security Assistance
Title V	Multilateral Assistance
Title VI	Export and Investment Assistance
Title VII	General Provisions

This report briefly explains the different accounts in the order they are presented in the FY2009 State, Foreign Operations appropriations legislation.

ACCOUNT DESCRIPTIONS

TITLE I—DEPARTMENT OF STATE AND RELATED AGENCIES

Title I provides funds for (1) the personnel, operations, and programs of the Department of State; (2) U.S. participation in international organizations, such as the United Nations as well as small commissions such as the International Boundary and Water Commission between the United States and Mexico; (3) U.S. government, non-military-international broadcasting; and (4) several U.S. non-governmental agencies whose purposes also help promote U.S. interests abroad, and other U.S. commissions and interparliamentary groups more directly related to U.S. foreign policy initiatives such as the U.S. Commission on International Religious Freedom.

Administration of Foreign Affairs

The Administration of Foreign Affairs account category provides for the personnel, operations, and programs of the Department of State as well as the construction and maintenance of its facilities around the world.

Diplomatic and Consular Programs (D&CP)

Diplomatic and Consular Programs is the operating account of the Department of State. It includes salaries for all its employees; funding for the operations of the Office of the Secretary, the deputy secretaries, and the under secretaries; funding for the operations of the various regional, functional, and administrative bureaus and their programs associated with the conduct of foreign policy; "non-bricks-and-mortar" security including funds for a guard force, armored vehicles, security training, and electronic and other technical security systems; telecommunications; medical care; transportation and travel; and training.

Civilian Stabilization Initiatives (CSI)

CSI seeks to improve and maintain an U.S. civilian capability to assist fragile and failed states that are coming out of crisis and conflict situations to stabilize and rebuild the country and its society. While the George W. Bush Administration requested funding for the Civilian Stabilization Initiatives to be fully under the Department of State, Congress divided funding of CSI through both the State Department and USAID.

Working in the State Department, the Coordinator for Reconstruction and Stabilization (S/CRS), is to coordinate the U.S. government interagency response. Along with the funds identified for USAID to provide for the USAID's component to the Civilian Stabilization Initiative, S/CRS is to recruit, organize, train, equip, and deploy if necessary a three-layer Civilian Response Corp—the Active Response Corps, and the Standby Response Corps from

17 federal agencies and the Department of Defense, and the larger Civilian Reserve Corps from the private sector.

Capital Investment Fund (CIF)

The Capital Investment Fund was created in 1994 to provide for purchasing information technology and other capital equipment to ensure efficient management, coordination, and communications.

Office of the Inspector General (OIG)

This account funds the State Department's Office of the Inspector General, which conducts independent audits, inspections, and investigations of the programs and offices of Department of State and the Broadcasting Board of Governors (BBG).

Educational and Cultural Exchange Programs

With funds appropriated to this account, the State Department manages U.S. educational exchanges, such as the Fulbright and Humphrey Fellowships, and citizen exchanges, such as the International Visitors Leadership Program, and the Sports United and Youth Exchange programs that focus on middle and high school students. Cultural exchange programs include sending the *Neo Classic Blues Duo* to Ghana and Togo to perform and discuss blues melodies from the 1920s and 1930s and sending the Harlem Gospel Choir to perform in Lebanon.

Representation Allowances

Funding for the Representation Allowances account provides partial reimbursement to Ambassadors, Principal Officers, and some Foreign Service for costs associated with maintaining vital contacts in the host country where they are assigned.

Protection of Foreign Missions and Officials

The U.S. Diplomatic Security Service permanently or intermittently protects international organizations and foreign missions and officials in New York City and elsewhere in the United States.

Embassy Security, Construction, and Maintenance (ESCM)

The Embassy Security, Construction and Maintenance account is divided in two parts: (1) On-going Operations, which funds the general maintenance and support of U.S. State Department facilities both in the United States and abroad, and (2) Worldwide Security (WWS) Upgrades, which funds the construction and security upgrades of embassy and facilities around the world.

Emergencies in the Diplomatic and Consular Services

The Emergencies account addresses unexpected events, such as the evacuation of U.S. diplomats and their families from an embassy, medical evacuations, and travel expenses related to natural disasters. This account also pays for rewards for information related to international terrorism, narcotics-related activities, and war crimes tribunals.

Buying Power Maintenance Account

The Buying Power Maintenance account helps the Department of State manage exchange rate losses in the cost of its overseas operations.

Repatriation Loan Program

The Repatriation Loan Program allows the U.S. government to provide funds, on a loan basis, to U.S. citizens abroad who become destitute and are unable to fund their return to the United States.

Payment to the American Institute in Taiwan (AIT)

The American Institute in Taiwan acts as an unofficial U.S. consulate. The account supports a contract providing for salaries, benefits, and other expenses associated with maintaining the Institute.

Foreign Service Retirement and Disability Fund

The Fund is a mandatory expense that covers the U.S. government's portion of maintaining the retirement program for the Foreign Service and Foreign Service Nationals/Locally Hired Employees. Contributions to this fund are made by both the employee and the hiring agency.

INTERNATIONAL ORGANIZATIONS

Through the two accounts in the International Organizations category, the United States meets its assessed obligations to the many international organizations and peacekeeping efforts that the United States supports.

Contributions to International Organizations (CIO)

The International Organizations account under the Department of State funds the assessed U.S. contributions to the United Nations (U.N.) and U.N. system organizations, Inter-American organizations, and various regional organizations to which the United States belongs through U.S. law, treaty, or convention. U.S. contributions to organizations funded through the CIO account generally provide about 25% of each organization's budget.

Contributions for International Peacekeeping (CIPA)

The International Peacekeeping account funds assessments on the United States for the 16 current U.N. Peacekeeping operations around the world and two ongoing War Crimes Tribunals regarding Yugoslavia and Rwanda. U.S. contributions generally provide about 27% of the various organizations' budgets.

INTERNATIONAL COMMISSIONS

Accounts under the International Commissions category were established by treaties and agreements that the President ratified with the advice and consent of the Senate. The accounts provide funding for the U.S. portion of the salaries and programs of the following bilateral and multilateral commissions:

- International Boundary and Water Commission between the United States and Mexico,
- International Fisheries Commissions,
- Border Environment Cooperation Commission,
- International Joint Commission (between the U.S. and Canada), and
- International Boundary Commission (between the U.S. and Canada).

BROADCASTING BOARD OF GOVERNORS (BBG)

The nine-member Broadcasting Board of Governors supervises and funds all non-military, U.S. government international broadcasting. Operating in 60 languages, these broadcasts include Voice of America (VOA), Broadcasting to Cuba (Radio and TV Marti), Radio Free Europe/Radio Liberty (RFE/RL), Radio Free Asia (RFA), and the Middle East

Broadcasting Network (MBN), which includes Alhurra, Alhurra-Iraq, Alhurra-Europe, and Radio Sawa. The broadcasting category is generally divided into the following two accounts:

International Broadcasting Operations

The Operations account funds the operations of the BBG and all U.S. government, non-military international broadcasts, including salaries and benefits of management, administrative staff, broadcasters, and reporters; contracts with surrogate broadcasters such as Radio Free Asia; provision of office and broadcasting studio facilities; transitioning to new communications methods such as greater use of the Internet; and other operating expenses.

Broadcasting Capital Improvements

The Capital Improvements account supports maintenance of the BBG from broadcast station repair to the building of new antennas.

RELATED PROGRAMS

Under this category, funds are provided to several non-governmental organizations that have objectives that are similar to views and positions advocated by the United States in its foreign policy.

These non-governmental organizations provide educational programs, exchanges, and grants to organizations in foreign countries promoting democracy, rule of law, economic development, open markets, literacy, women's rights, and many similar objectives.

Most of these organizations are nonprofit organizations and receive funding from both the U.S. government, through appropriated funds, and through private donations.

The Asia Foundation

The Foundation seeks to strengthen democratic processes and institutions in Asia, open markets, and improve U.S.-Asian relations.

United States Institute of Peace (USIP)

The U.S. Institute of Peace mission is to promote international peace through educational programs, conferences, and workshops, professional training, applied research, and dialogue facilitation in the United States and abroad.

International Center for Middle Eastern-Western Dialogue

The Center convenes policy discussion meetings, and develops programs of cooperative study for those working on issues related to the growth of civil society and democratic institutions, and the peaceful resolution of differences among the countries of the Middle East and between the countries of the Middle East and Western nations.

Eisenhower Exchange Fellowship Program

The Exchange Program brings professionals who are rising leaders in their countries to the United States and sends their U.S. counterparts abroad with a custom-designed program for each participant to make contacts and learn about the other's country and work environment.

Israeli-Arab Scholarship Program (IASP)

The IASP funds scholarships for Israeli Arabs to attend institutions of higher education in the United States.

The Center for Cultural and Technical Interchange between East and West (East-West Center)

The East-West Center promotes understanding and cooperation among the governments and peoples of the Asia/Pacific region and the United States.

National Endowment for Democracy (NED)

NED is a private, non-profit organization established to support democratic institutions in over 90 countries.

OTHER COMMISSIONS

The Commissions and groups in the Other Commissions category of the State, Foreign Operations legislation, are organizations that are established by an Act of Congress to advance certain U.S. objectives in the international arena. In the Federal Budget submission to the Congress, these organizations are listed under the legislative Branch Boards and Commissions, but are funded through the State, Foreign Operations legislation.

The funding meets the operational and programmatic requirements of these organizations.

Commission for the Preservation of America's Heritage Abroad

The Commission seeks to purchase, restore, or preserve endangered cultural sites in Eastern and Central Europe important to the heritage of U.S. citizens, and seeks help from other governments in this effort.

Commission on International Religious Freedom (CIRF)

In consultation with the State Department, the Commission seeks to promote international religious freedom.

Commission on Security and Cooperation in Europe (CSCE)

The Commission oversees the work of the Organization on Security and Cooperation in Europe (OSCE), particularly in the area of humanitarian affairs.

Congressional-Executive Commission on the People's Republic of China

The Commission monitors China's compliance with international human rights agreements and standards.

United States-China Economic and Security Review Commission

The Commission monitors, investigates, and submits to Congress an annual report and recommendations on the national security implications of the bilateral trade and economic relationship between the United States and the People's Republic of China.

United States Senate-China, United States Senate-Russia Interparliamentary Groups

This account supports the participation of U.S. Senators in the United States Senate-China Interparliamentary Group and the United States Senate-Russia Interparliamentary Group.

TITLE II—UNITED STATES AGENCY FOR INTERNATIONAL DEVELOPMENT (USAID)

This title provides operational funds for USAID, an independent agency directly responsible for most bilateral development assistance and disaster relief programs, many of which are funded in Title III.

U.S. Agency for International Development Operating Expenses (OE)

The Operating Expense account funds the operational costs of USAID including salaries and benefits, overseas and Washington operations, human capital initiatives, security, and information technology maintenance and upgrades.

Civilian Stabilization Initiative

The Civilian Stabilization Initiative, a portion of which is also funded under the Department of State Title I, here supports the hiring and training of USAID personnel and prepositioning of equipment for the standby response corps, the rapid "surge" element of any deployment to address emergency stabilization needs.

Capital Investment Fund

A program begun in FY2003, the Capital Investment Fund supports USAID construction of facilities overseas, with an emphasis on improving security and enhancing information technology.

USAID Office of Inspector General

This account supports operational costs of USAID's Inspector General office, which conducts audits and investigations of USAID programs.

TITLE III—BILATERAL ECONOMIC ASSISTANCE

Under this title, funds are appropriated in support of U.S. government departments and independent agencies conducting humanitarian, development, and other programs meeting U.S. foreign policy objectives throughout the world.

Funds Appropriated to the President

Funds in this category of appropriations are provided chiefly through USAID or in close association with the Department of State.

Global Health and Child Survival (GHCS)

The Global Health and Child Survival account supports multiple health programs conducted by USAID and the Department of State through funding of two major elements:

Child Survival and Health Programs (CSH)

Managed by USAID, appropriations in the CSH sub-account fund programs focused on combating infectious diseases such as HIV/AIDS; malaria; tuberculosis; maternal and child health; vulnerable children; and family planning and reproductive health.

Global HIV/AIDS Initiative (GHAI)

Managed by the Office of the Global AIDS Coordinator (OGAC) in the Department of State, the Global HIV/AIDS Initiative sub-account is the largest source of funding for the President's Emergency Plan for AIDS Relief (PEPFAR). The account also supports part of the U.S. contribution to the multilateral organization, the Global Fund to Fight AIDS, Tuberculosis and Malaria.

Development Assistance (DA Account)

Managed by USAID, the Development Assistance account funds programs in agriculture, private sector development, microcredit, water and sanitation, education, environment, democracy and governance, among others.

International Disaster Assistance (IDA)

Managed by the USAID Office of Foreign Disaster Assistance, the account aids nations struck by natural and manmade disasters and emergencies. It was previously referred to as the International Disaster and Famine Assistance account (IDFA).

Transition Initiatives

The Transition Initiatives account supports the activities of USAID's Office of Transition Initiatives (OTI), a program launched in 1994 to bridge the gap between disaster and development aid. It supports flexible, short-term assistance projects in transition countries that are moving from war to peace, civil conflict to national reconciliation, or where political instability has not yet erupted into violence and where conflict mitigation might prevent the outbreak of such violence.

Development Credit Authority (DCA)

Managed by USAID, the Development Credit Authority provides for the administrative costs of several USAID credit programs, including loan guarantees that allow private banks to finance housing shelter projects, water and sanitation systems, and microcredit and small enterprise development programs.

Economic Support Fund (ESF)

The Economic Support Fund uses economic assistance to advance U.S. strategic goals in countries of special importance to U.S. foreign policy. Funding decisions are made by the State Department; programs are managed by both USAID and the State Department.

Democracy Fund

The Fund supports democratization programs run by the State Department's Bureau of Democracy, Human Rights and Labor (DRL), and USAID's Office of Democracy and Governance.

International Fund for Ireland

This activity supports the Anglo-Irish Accord and efforts to spur economic and commercial development in Northern Ireland.

Assistance for Europe, Eurasia, and Central Asia

This new account combines two formerly separate accounts into one.
The two accounts were:

Assistance for Eastern Europe and the Baltic States

This account is commonly known as the SEED Act account (Support for East European Democracy), its authorizing legislation (P.L. 101-179). Since 1989, USAID, under the guidance of the State Department, channeled most U.S. economic assistance to Eastern Europe through this regional program.

Assistance for the Independent States of the Former Soviet Union

This account is commonly known as the FREEDOM Support Act account (Freedom for Russia and Emerging Eurasian Democracies and Open Markets Support Act), its authorizing legislation (P.L. 102-511). Through this regional program, launched in 1992, USAID and multiple other agencies, under the guidance of the State Department, extended economic aid to the 12 countries of the former Soviet Union.

Department of State

International Narcotics Control and Law Enforcement (INCLE)

The INCLE account funds international counternarcotics activities; anti-crime programs, including trafficking in women and children; and rule of law activities, including support for judicial reform. The INCLE account includes funds to support the U.S.-Mexico Mérida Initiative to enhance bilateral and regional cooperation to combat drug trafficking and organized crime.

Andean Counterdrug Initiative (ACI)

The Andean Counterdrug Initiative, created in FY2000 as the Plan Colombia account, supports a multi-year counternarcotics effort in the Andean region, providing assistance for both drug interdiction and alternative development.

Nonproliferation, Anti-terrorism, Demining, and Related programs (NADR)
This account funds a variety of State Department-managed activities aimed at countering weapons proliferation and terrorism and promoting demining operations in developing nations.

Migration and Refugee Assistance (MRA)
The Migration and Refugee Assistance program supports refugee relief activities worldwide and, in some cases, helps resettle refugees.

Emergency Refugee and Migration Assistance (ERMA) Fund
ERMA holds funds that can be drawn upon quickly in times of refugee emergencies. Appropriations replenish resources to this account.

Independent Agencies

Peace Corps
The Peace Corps sends U.S. volunteers to developing countries to provide technical aid and to promote mutual understanding on a people-to-people basis.

Millenium Challenge Corporation (MCC)
Established in 2004, the MCC supports large-scale, multi-year development projects designed and implemented by recipient countries, which are selected on the basis of their commitments to good governance, investment in health and education, and support for economic freedom.

Inter-American Foundation (IAF)
The IAF, an independent agency, finances small-scale enterprise and grassroots self-help activities aimed at helping poor people in Latin America.

African Development Foundation (ADF)
The ADF, an independent agency, finances small-scale enterprise and grassroots self-help activities aimed at helping poor people in Africa.

Department of the Treasury

International Affairs Technical Assistance
This technical assistance program supports financial advisors to countries seeking help in implementing economic reforms and improving financial management of government resources. In addition, funds have been used to address terrorist financing activities.

Debt Restructuring
This account provides funds to reduce, and in some cases forgive, debts owed to the U.S. by poor countries, especially those in Africa and the small economies in Latin America and

the Caribbean. In recent years, funds have supported the U.S. commitment to the Heavily Indebted Poor Country (HIPC) Initiative.

TITLE IV — INTERNATIONAL SECURITY ASSISTANCE

Funds Appropriated to the President

Peacekeeping Operations (PKO)
Unlike the Title I Contributions to Peacekeeping Activities (CIPA) account, which provides assessed funds for peacekeeping forces, the PKO account provides voluntary support for multilateral efforts in conflict resolution, including the training of African peacekeepers and funding operations of the Multinational and Observers Mission in the Sinai.

International Military Education and Training (IMET)
Through IMET, the United States provides military training to selected foreign military and civilian personnel. The State Department and the Department of Defense share policy authority, and the Department of Defense implements this program.

Foreign Military Financing (FMF) Program
The Foreign Military Financing Program supports U.S. overseas arms transfers on a grant basis. The State Department and the Department of Defense share policy authority, and the Department of Defense implements this program.

TITLE V — MULTILATERAL ECONOMIC ASSISTANCE

Funds Appropriated to the President

Under this category, funds are provided through the Department of State to international organizations, including the United Nations.

International Organizations and Programs (IO&P)
This account provides voluntary donations to support the programs of international agencies involved in a range of development, humanitarian, and scientific activities, including the U.N. Development Program (UNDP), U.N. Environment Program (UNEP), U.N. Children's Fund (UNICEF), and U.N. Population Fund (UNFPA).

International Financial Institutions
Under this category, funds are provided through the Department of the Treasury to a wide range of multilateral financial institutions, which offer loans—both "soft" (i.e., concessional) and "hard" (i.e., near-market rate)—and some grants to developing countries and private sector entities in those countries. Not all international financial institutions require or receive U.S. contributions from year to year [6]

Global Environment Facility (GEF)

Cosponsored by the UNDP, UNEP, and the World Bank, the GEF makes grants to help developing countries deal with global environmental problems.

World Bank: International Development Association (IDA)

As the World Bank's "soft loan" window, IDA lends at concessional rates to low-income countries. The International Bank for Reconstruction and Development (IBRD) is the World Bank window that provides loans on near-market terms to promote economic development primarily in middle-income countries, based largely on bond sales. Another World Bank window, the International Finance Corporation (IFC), makes loans and equity investments to promote growth of productive private enterprise in developing nations.

Enterprise for the Americas Multilateral Investment Fund (MIF)

The MIF is a multi-donor trust fund providing technical and financial assistance to help countries in Latin America and the Caribbean reform their investment policies in order to attract foreign investment. It resides within the Inter-American Development Bank, which promotes economic and social development in Latin America and the Caribbean by providing near-market rate loans through its ordinary capital account and concessional loans to the poorest nations through its Fund for Special Operations (FSO). The Inter-American Investment Corporation (IIC), makes loans and equity investments to promote the growth of private enterprise.

Asian Development Fund (ADF)

The ADF is the "soft loan" window of the Asian Development Bank (ADB), which finances economic development programs in Asia and the Pacific.

African Development Fund (AfDF)

The African Development Fund (AfDF) lends on concessional terms to low-income sub-Saharan African countries. It resides within the African Development Bank (AfDB), which lends at near- market rates, with special emphasis on agriculture, infrastructure and industrial development.

International Fund for Agricultural Development (IFAD)

IFAD is a multilateral financial institution helping developing countries increase agricultural productivity and income, improve nutritional levels, and integrate into larger markets.

TITLE VI—EXPORT AND INVESTMENT ASSISTANCE

Export-Import Bank

The Export-Import Bank issues loan guarantees and insurance to commercial banks that make trade credits available to American exporters. The Bank also extends direct loans to U.S. businesses, especially those whose counterparts abroad receive foreign government-subsidized trade credits.

Overseas Private Investment Corporation (OPIC)

OPIC offers political risk insurance, guarantees, and investment financing to encourage U.S. firms to invest in developing countries.

Trade and Development Agency (TDA)

The TDA finances feasibility studies and other project-planning services for major development activities in developing countries, to support economic development and to promote U.S. exports.

TITLE VII— GENERAL PROVISIONS

Under the General Provisions title are limitations and prohibitions on assistance, notification and reporting requirements, and more detailed funding mandates for specific accounts in other titles of the legislation.

REFERENCES

[1]   International Affairs is one category of the various components of the federal budget designated by the Office of Management and Budget (OMB). Each category represents a major objective and operation of the Federal Government. Each function and sub-function is assigned a three digit code. International affairs is 150. Subfunction 151 encompasses International development and humanitarian assistance. Accounts under the International Commissions category of the legislation are the exception—they are part of the 300 Natural Resources Budget Function.

[2]   Until the 110th Congress, the State Department and Foreign Operations portions of the bill were developed in different Appropriations subcommittees and considered as separate bills.

[3]   CRS Report RS20371, Overview of the Authorization-Appropriations Process, by Bill Heniff Jr.

[4]   See sec. 15 of the State Department Basic Authorities Act of 1956 (22 U.S.C. 2680) and sec. 10 of the Foreign Military Sales Act amendments, 1971 (22 U.S.C. 2412).

[5]   For example, see sec. 7023 of the FY2009 Omnibus Appropriations Act, Division H (P.L. 111-8). Most foreign operations program appropriations have not been authorized since 1985

[6]   Among those that sometimes receive funding but for which there was no request or appropriation in FY2009 are:
       World Bank Multilateral Investment Guaranty Agency (MIGA). MIGA encourages private investment in developing countries by offering insurance against noncommercial risks such as expropriation.
       European Bank for Reconstruction and Development (EBRD). The EBRD lends at near-market rates to help East European and former Soviet states adopt market

economies. Private sector and privatizing public sector firms receive substantial amounts of EBRD lending.

North American Development Bank (NADBank). The NADBank is governed by the United States and Mexico as part of the North American Free Trade Agreement (NAFTA). It began lending in 1996 to finance environmental infrastructure projects along the U.S./Mexico border, as well as community adjustment and investment activities in both nations.

In: Economics, Political and Social Issues ...
Editor: Michelle L. Fergusson

ISBN: 978-1-61122-555-6
©2011 Nova Science Publishers, Inc.

THE BUDGET RESOLUTION AND SPENDING LEGISLATION*

Megan Suzanne Lynch#
Congress and Legislative Process

ABSTRACT

The budget resolution sets forth aggregate levels of spending, revenue, and public debt. It is not intended to establish details of spending or revenue policy and does not provide levels of spending for specific agencies or programs. Instead, its purpose is to create enforceable parameters within which Congress can consider legislation dealing with spending and revenue.

The spending policies in the budget resolution encompass two types of spending legislation: discretionary spending and direct (mandatory) spending. Discretionary spending is controlled through the appropriations process. Appropriations legislation is considered each fiscal year and provides funding for numerous programs such as national defense, education, and homeland security. Direct spending, alternately, is provided for in legislation outside of appropriations acts. Direct spending programs are typically established in permanent law and continue in effect until such time as revised or terminated by another law.

During the week of March 23, 2009, both the House Budget Committee and the Senate Budget Committee approved their respective versions of a FY20 10 budget resolution. The budget resolution establishes congressional priorities by dividing spending among the 20 major functional categories of the federal budget. These 20 categories do not correspond to the committee system by which Congress operates, and as a result these spending levels must be "crosswalked" to the House and Senate committees having jurisdiction over both discretionary and direct spending. These amounts are known as 3 02(a) allocations and hold committees accountable for staying within the spending limits established by the budget resolution.

Each Appropriations Committee is responsible for subdividing its 302(a) allocation among its 12 subcommittees. These allocations, referred to as 302(b) subdivisions, establish the maximum amount that each of the 12 appropriations bills can spend.

It is inevitable that Members will consider the impact on particular programs or agencies when they consider a budget resolution. While the budget resolution does not allocate funds among specific agencies or programs, congressional assumptions or desires underlying the amounts set forth in the functional categories are frequently communicated through the budget resolution. Report language accompanying the budget resolution, as well as certain provisions in the budget resolution, can sometimes express non-binding programmatic assumptions and desires.

---

* Excerpted from CRS Report R40472 dated March 27, 2009.
# E-mail: mlynch@crs.loc.gov

Budget resolutions also often include procedural provisions such as reserve funds or reconciliation instructions. These provisions may also reflect underlying program assumptions or desires of Congress.

INTRODUCTION

The Constitution grants Congress the power of the purse and provides that "No money shall be drawn from the Treasury, but in Consequence of Appropriations made by Law" [1]. It does not, however, establish any specific procedures by which Congress must consider spending legislation. Instead, Congress has developed rules and practices that govern consideration of spending and other budgetary legislation under each chamber's constitutional authority to " ... determine the Rules of its Proceedings" [2].

It is under this authority that the procedures in the Congressional Budget Act of 1974 were created [3]. The Congressional Budget Act established the basic framework that is used today for congressional consideration of budget and fiscal policy. It provides for the annual adoption of a concurrent resolution on the budget as a mechanism for coordinating congressional budgetary decision making [4].

The budget resolution creates enforceable parameters with which spending, revenue, and debt legislation must be consistent. It is not a law. It is not signed by the President nor can it be vetoed. Instead, its purpose is to establish a framework within which Congress considers legislation dealing with spending and revenue.

The budget resolution is not intended to establish details of spending or revenue policy. Instead, details of such policy are to be included in legislation reported from the committees with legislative jurisdiction subsequent to the adoption of the budget resolution. All spending or revenue legislation reported from legislative committees, however, is expected to be consistent with the levels and priorities agreed to in the budget resolution.

The spending policies in the budget resolution encompass two types of spending legislation: discretionary spending and direct (or mandatory) spending. Discretionary spending is controlled through the appropriations process. Appropriations legislation is considered annually for the fiscal year beginning October 1. Appropriations legislation provides funding for numerous activities such as national defense, education, and homeland security, as well as general government operations [5].

Direct spending, alternately, is provided for in legislation outside of appropriations acts. Direct spending programs are typically established in permanent law that continue in effect until such time as they are revised or terminated by another law. The actual annual cost of direct spending is not determined by Congress. It is instead dictated by formulas within the legislation providing for the program. The overall cost of a program depends on the eligibility requirements and benefits set forth in the legislation. These criteria determine who will be eligible to receive benefits and how much benefit they will receive. Only by altering these formulas can Congress adjust how much money will be spent.

THE BUDGET RESOLUTION

Content

The budget resolution sets forth levels for new budget authority, outlays, revenue, and public debt for the budget year and four outyears [6]. The levels in the budget resolution deal with aggregates, not programmatic spending details. Assumptions concerning some major programs may be discussed in the reports accompanying the budget resolution, but these assumptions are not in the form of legislative language and are not binding on the committee of jurisdiction.

Rather than including levels of spending for specific agencies or programs, the budget resolution establishes congressional priorities by dividing spending among the 20 major functional categories of the federal budget [7]. These 20 functional categories do not correspond to the committee system by which Congress operates. As a result, the spending levels in the 20 functional categories are allocated, or "crosswalked," to the House and Senate committees having jurisdiction over discretionary spending (appropriations committees) and direct spending (legislative committees). These "crosswalked" totals appear in the joint explanatory statement of the conference report on the budget resolution and are referred to as 3 02(a) allocations [8]. These 3 02(a) amounts hold committees accountable for staying within the spending limits established by the budget resolution.

Programmatic Assumptions

It is inevitable that Members will consider the impact on particular programs or agencies when they consider a budget resolution. Each committee is required to submit its "views and estimates" with information on the preferences and legislative plans of that committee regarding budget matters to help the Budget Committee determine spending levels for each of the functional categories.

While the budget resolution does not allocate funds among specific agencies or programs, assumptions underlying the amounts set forth in the functional categories are frequently discussed in the reports accompanying the budget resolution.

For example, the committee print accompanying the budget resolution for FY2009 included the following language:

> The Committee-reported resolution assumes approximately $2 billion for the Department of Energy's Energy Efficiency and Renewable Energy program. The funding level is $738 million above the President's request and would accommodate significant increases for programs such as wind, solar, geothermal, biomass and biorefinery RandD, hydrogen, and vehicle/building technologies. This funding level would also provide $450 million for the Weatherization Assistance Program, a program which was zeroed out in the President's budget [9]

Report language, however, is not binding on the committees with jurisdiction over spending and revenue.

In addition to report language, certain provisions often included in the budget resolution may indicate programmatic assumptions or desires. Budget resolutions frequently include "Sense of the Congress" language expressing the assumptions or desires of one or both chambers for certain programs to receive priority in funding.

For example, the budget resolution for FY2009 included language concerning sense of the Congress on service members' and veterans' health care:

> It is the sense of the Congress that—
>
> (1) the Congress supports excellent health care for current and former members of the United States Armed Services— they have served well and honorably and have made significant sacrifices for this Nation;
>
> (2) this resolution provides $48,202,000,000 in discretionary budget authority for 2009 for Function 700 (Veterans Benefits and Services), including veterans' health care, which is $4,940,000,000 more than the 2008 level, $3,654,000,000 more than the Congressional Budget Office's baseline level for 2009, and $3,284,000,000 more than the President's budget for 2009; and also provides more discretionary budget authority than the President's budget in every year after 2009; [10]

Budget resolutions may also include "Policy" statements [11]. These statements sometimes include language indicating that spending levels in the budget resolution assume certain policies will be carried out. For example,

> It is the policy of this resolution that ...
> (5) TRICARE fees for military retirees under the age of
> 65 should not be increased as the President's budget proposes; [12]

Neither "Sense of the Congress" provisions nor "Policy" statements are binding on the committees with jurisdiction over spending and revenue.

Budget resolutions often include procedural provisions, such as reserve funds or reconciliation instructions. These provisions often indicate underlying program assumptions or desires of Congress. (Further information on reserve funds and reconciliation instructions is provided below.)

Formulation of the Budget and the Budget Cycle

Federal budgeting is a cyclical activity. The President submits a budget request to Congress early in the calendar year. Congressional committees then hold hearings where they hear testimony from OMB officials, presidential advisors, and agencies who defend the President's budget recommendations.

Committees then submit their "views and estimates" to the Budget Committee of their respective chamber. A committee's "views and estimates" provide the Budget Committees with information on the preferences and legislative plans of that committee regarding budget matters within its jurisdiction. House and Senate Budget Committees then consider and report a budget resolution.

Table 1. Congressional Budget Process Timetable

Deadline	Action to be completed
First Monday in February [13]	President submits his budget.
February 15	CBO submits report to Budget Committees.
Six weeks after President's budget is submitted	Committees submit views and estimates to Budget Committees.
April 1	Senate Budget Committee reports concurrent resolution on the budget.
April 15	Congress completes action on concurrent resolution on the budget.
May 15	Annual appropriations bills may be considered in the House.
June 10	House Appropriations Committee reports last annual appropriations bill.
June 15	Congress completes action on reconciliation legislation.
June 30	House completes action on regular appropriations bills.
October 1	Fiscal year begins.

Source: Sec. 300 of the Budget Act.

The Congressional Budget Act establishes a timetable for the consideration of budgetary legislation. This timetable provides various target dates that reflect when certain actions typically occur. Once the budget resolution is adopted, chambers may consider appropriations bills and any other spending and revenue legislation consistent with the budget resolution.

DISCRETIONARY SPENDING

The 3 02(a) allocations made to the House and Senate Appropriations Committees reflect their jurisdiction over all discretionary spending. These allocations hold the appropriations committees accountable for staying within the spending limits established by the budget resolution. In recent years, budget resolutions have also sometimes included explicit spending limits on discretionary spending [14].

Both the House and Senate Appropriations Committees have 12 subcommittees. Each of these subcommittees is responsible for reporting one regular appropriations bill. Sometimes these bills are packaged together in what is referred to as an omnibus appropriations act.

Once an Appropriations Committee has received its 3 02(a) allocation, it then subdivides the committee allocation among its subcommittees as soon as practicable after the budget resolution has been adopted. These suballocations are known as 302(b) subdivisions [15]. The appropriations committees may make allocations among subcommittees, even if they do not correspond with the levels set forth in the functional categories of the budget resolution. Section 3 02(c) of the Budget Act provides a point of order against the consideration of any appropriations measures before the Appropriations Committee reports its subdivisions.

The appropriations committees are then required to report these subdivisions to their respective chambers. The appropriations committees may revise the 3 02(b) subdivisions anytime during the appropriations process to reflect actions taken on spending legislation. If an appropriations committee does adjust the subdivisions among subcommittees, it must inform its respective chamber of the new levels by issuing a new 302(b) subdivision report.

After extensive hearings, each of the subcommittees reports one of the regular appropriations bills to its respective full appropriations committee. Then, the full Appropriations Committee reports the bill to its respective chamber.

Section 302(f) of the Budget Act prohibits consideration of any measure or amendment that would cause the 302(a) or 302(b) allocations to be exceeded. Since appropriations subcommittees usually report their bills at the maximum level of spending, amendments offered to the appropriations bill on the floor are often vulnerable to being ruled out of order since they would cause the spending to exceed the 302(b). [16]

This rule, combined with other rules and practices, makes it difficult to rearrange spending priorities within an appropriations bill through amendments on the floor. A separate amendment (or amendments) to reduce spending would need to be agreed upon prior to, or in conjunction with, one that would increase spending for an agency or program in order to offset that increase. [17]

DIRECT SPENDING

House and Senate legislative committees also receive 3 02(a) allocations that reflect their jurisdiction over direct spending programs. Any legislation reported by these committees must be consistent with these allocations [18]. As with discretionary spending, Section 302(f) prohibits the consideration of any measure or amendment that would cause the 3 02(a) allocation to be exceeded.

Reconciliation

Points of order can effectively limit spending that results from appropriations acts or new entitlement legislation to levels consistent with the budget resolution, but are not an effective control on spending that results from existing laws providing direct spending. As a result, Congress has established the reconciliation process as a way to instruct committees to develop legislation to change current revenue or direct spending laws so that these programs conform with policies established in the budget resolution [19]

The reconciliation process is an optional two-stage process in which instructions are included in the budget resolution. Reconciliation instructions are in the form of a directive to a specific committee to recommend legislative changes. These instructions are specific and include (1) the committee responsible for making the change, (2) the dollar amount of the change, and (3) the period over which this change should be measured. Reconciliation instructions also include a deadline for the committee to submit such recommendations. For example, the budget resolution for FY2006 included the following reconciliation instruction:

(a) SUBMISSIONS TO SLOW THE GROWTH IN MANDATORY SPENDING- (1) Not later than September 16, 2005, the House committees named in paragraph (2) shall submit their recommendations to the House Committee on the Budget. After receiving those recommendations, the House Committee on the Budget shall report to the House a reconciliation bill carrying out all such recommendations without any substantive revision. (2) INSTRUCTIONS-

(A) COMMITTEE ON AGRICULTURE- The House Committee on Agriculture shall report changes in laws within its jurisdiction sufficient to reduce the level of direct spending for that committee by $173,000,000 in outlays for fiscal year 2006 and $3,000,000,000 in outlays for the period of fiscal years 2006 through 2010 [20]

Many changes in direct spending programs have been a result of reconciliation legislation. For example, the instructions in the above example resulted in Title I of the Deficit Reduction Act of 2005 (P.L. 109-171), a reconciliation act. Other titles of that measure included language to make changes in Medicare (Title V), Medicaid and SCHIP (Title VI), and LIHEAP (Title IX). Similarly, reconciliation acts in other years have included titles making changes in diverse direct spending programs as well.

The reconciliation process begins when Congress includes reconciliation instructions in a budget resolution directing one or more committees to recommend changes in current law to achieve the levels of direct spending, revenues, or the debt limit agreed to in the budget resolution. Committees respond to these instructions by drafting legislative language to meet their specified targets. The legislative language recommended by committees is packaged "without any substantive revision" into one or more reconciliation bills by the House and Senate Budget Committees. If only a single committee is instructed to recommend reconciliation changes then those changes are reported directly to its respective chamber. Once reported, reconciliation legislation is considered under special procedures on the House and Senate floor.

RESERVE FUNDS

Spending allocations may be revised subsequent to the adoption of the budget resolution if provided for in the budget resolution. Congress frequently includes provisions referred to as "reserve funds" in the annual budget resolution, which provide the chairs of the House and Senate Budget Committees the authority to adjust the committee spending allocations if certain conditions are met.

Typically these conditions consist of legislation dealing with a particular policy being reported by the appropriate committee or an amendment dealing with that policy being offered on the floor. Once this action has taken place, the Budget Committee chairman submits the adjustment to his respective chamber.

Reserve funds frequently require that the net budgetary impact of the specified legislation be deficit neutral. Deficit-neutral reserve funds provide that a committee may report legislation with spending in excess of its allocations, but require the excess amounts be "offset" by equivalent amounts.

The Budget Committee chairman may then increase the committee spending allocations by the appropriate amounts to prevent a point of order under Section 302 of the Budget Act. For example, the budget resolution for FY2009 included the following language providing for a deficit-neutral reserve fund concerning San Joaquin River restoration and Navajo nation water rights settlements:

> In the House, the Chairman of the Committee on the Budget may revise the allocations, aggregates, and other appropriate levels in this resolution for any bill, joint resolution, amendment, or conference report that would fulfill the purposes of the San Joaquin River Restoration Settlement Act or implement a Navajo Nation water rights settlement and other provisions authorized by the Northwestern New Mexico Rural Water Projects Act by the amounts provided in such measure if such measure would not increase the deficit or decrease the surplus for the period of fiscal years 2008 through 2013 or for the period of fiscal years 2008 through 2018 [21]

Reserve funds are not always required to be deficit-neutral. They may, instead, allow the levels of spending set forth in the budget resolution to be exceeded, as long as the policy legislation meets the conditions of the reserve fund. In some instances, the increases authorized by a reserve fund are limited to specified amounts.

ACKNOWLEDGMENTS

This report draws from materials authored by Bill Heniff Jr, Robert Keith, James Saturno, and Sandy Streeter.

REFERENCES

[1]   U.S. Constitution, Article I, Section 9.
[2]   U.S. Constitution, Article 1, Section 5.
[3]   P.L. 93-344 as amended.
[4]   For more information on the budget process generally, see CRS Report 98-72 1, *Introduction to the Federal Budget Process*, by Robert Keith.
[5]   For more information on the appropriations process see CRS Report 97-684, *The Congressional Appropriations Process: An Introduction*, by Sandy Streeter.
[6]   Under Section 30 1(a) of the Budget Act, four outyears is the minimum required, although the budget resolution may cover more than four. For example, the budget resolution for FY2002 (H.Con.Res. 83, 107th Congress) covered 10 outyears.
[7]   These amounts are not enforced by points of order. For more information on functional categories see CRS Report 98- 280, *Functional Categories of the Federal Budget*, by Bill Heniff Jr.
[8]   These totals are named after Section 302(a) of the Budget Act (Titles I-IX of P.L. 93-344, 88 Stat. 297-332) as amended, which requires that the total budget authority and outlays set forth in the budget resolution be allocated to each House and Senate committee that has jurisdiction over specific spending legislation

[9]   U.S. Congress. Senate Committee on the Budget. *Committee Print to Accompany S. Con.Res. 70.* 110th Cong., 1st sess. S.Prt. 110-039 (Washington: GPO, 2008) p. 9.

[10]   S.Con.Res. 70 (110th Congress), Sec. 511.

[11]   S.Con.Res. 70 (1 10th Congress), Title IV.

[12]   S.Con.Res. 70 (1 10th Congress), Sec. 402

[13]   For information on Presidential budget submission during years of transition, see CRS Report RS20752, Submission of the President's Budget in Transition Years, by Robert Keith.

[14]   For example, see S.Con.Res. 70 (110th Congress), Sec. 312.

[15]   These totals are named after Section 3 02(b) of the Budget Act which requires that the Appropriations Committees suballocate 302(a) allocations among their respective subcommittees.

[16]   Such points of order may be waived by a special rule reported from the Rules Committee or by unanimous consent in the House. In the Senate, points of order may be waived by unanimous consent or by a 3/5 vote of Senators duly sworn and chosen (60 if no vacancies).

[17]   In the House, Rule XXI, clause 2(f) provides that " ... it shall be in order to consider en bloc amendments proposing only to transfer appropriations among objects in the bill without increasing the levels of budget authority or outlays in the bill. When considered en bloc pursuant to this paragraph, such amendments may amend portions of the bill not yet read for amendment ... and shall not be subject to a demand for division of the question." For more information on offsets in the House, see CRS Report RL3 1055, *House Offset Amendments to Appropriations Bills: Procedural Considerations*, by Sandy Streeter.

[18]   When Congress considers new revenue or direct spending legislation, CBO estimates the amount of revenues or outlays that would ensue if the measure were enacted. For revenues CBO uses estimates prepared by the Joint Committee on Taxation. These numbers are then measured against the baseline.

[19]   For more information on the reconciliation process, see CRS Report 98-814, *Budget Reconciliation Legislation: Development and Consideration*, by Bill Heniff Jr.

[20]   H.Con.Res. 95 (109th Congress), Sec. 201.

[21]   S.Con.Res. 70 (110th Congress), Sec. 216.

In: Economics, Political and Social Issues …
Editor: Michelle L. Fergusson

THE FEDERAL DEPOSIT INSURANCE CORPORATION (FDIC): EFFORTS TO SUPPORT FINANCIAL AND HOUSING MARKETS[*]

Darryl E. Getter[#] and Oscar R. Gonzales

Financial Economics
Economic Development Policy

ABSTRACT

The Federal Deposit Insurance Corporation (FDIC) was established as an independent government corporation under the authority of the Banking Act of 1933, also known as the Glass- Steagall Act (P.L. 73-66, 48 Stat. 162, 12 U.S.C.), to insure bank deposits.

This report discusses recent actions taken by the FDIC in support of financial and housing markets, which include restoration of the Deposit Insurance Fund, the development of the Temporary Liquidity Guarantee Program, efforts to reduce foreclosures, and establishment of the proposed Public-Private Investment Fund. Legislation such as H.R. 786 (introduced by Representative Barney Frank); H.R. 1106, Helping Families Save Their Homes Act of 2009 (introduced by Representative John Conyers, Jr., with 24 co-sponsors); and S. 541, The Depositor Protection Act of 2009 (introduced by Senator Christopher Dodd with 12 co-sponsors) have also been introduced to increase the effectiveness of the FDIC's efforts to respond to recent market weaknesses.

BRIEF OVERVIEW OF FDIC FUNCTIONS

Deposit Insurance

The Federal Deposit Insurance Corporation (FDIC) was established as an independent government corporation under the authority of the Banking Act of 1933, also known as the Glass- Steagall Act, to insure bank deposits [1] State bank insurance systems were pioneered in the 19th century, and Congress had proposed legislation then to develop a federal bank deposit insurance system. It was not until 1933, however, that the FDIC was established as the first national deposit insurance system. The most severe banking crisis in the nation's history led to the failure of 9,000 banks between the stock market crash of October 1929 and

---

[*] Excerpted from CRS Report R40413 dated March 27, 2009.
[#] E-mail: dgetter@crs.loc.gov

March 1933 [2] In the first months of 1933 alone, over 4,000 banks failed [3]. One year after the establishment of the FDIC, only 9 banks of the remaining 13,000 insured financial institutions in the U.S. became insolvent [4]

An important issue during the early years after the establishment of the FDIC was the determination of the appropriate level of deposit insurance coverage. If the level of deposit insurance was insufficient, it was feared that this may still result in bank runs. Bank deposits were originally insured up to $2,500 in January 1934, but given the continued failure of banks, Congress saw the need to temporarily double deposit insurance to $5,000 by June of the same year. A year later, the $5,000 temporary increase was made permanent.

Over time, financial and economic disruptions were often associated with bank failures and changes in deposit insurance, as Congress considered options and alternatives to stabilize financial markets [5]. In 1950, after the post-war boom led to an economic decline which resulted in additional bank failures, the $5,000 deposit insurance limit was increased to $10,000 by Congress. The recession of the early 1 960s resulted in bank failures, and in 1966, Congress instituted a 50% increase in deposit insurance, bringing the deposit insurance limit to $15,000. Three years later, in 1969, the deposit insurance limit was increased to $20,000 and to $40,000 in 1974. By 1980, the deposit insurance limit stood at $100,000 and remained at that level until 2008. Table 1 outlines changes in FDIC bank deposit insurance from 1934 to 2008.

The FDIC insures demand deposit (non-interest bearing) accounts, interest bearing checking accounts, money market deposit accounts, savings accounts, and certificates of deposit [6]. The FDIC also insures traditional and Roth Individual Retirement Accounts (IRAs) [7] Bank deposits and individual retirement accounts in the same bank for the same individual are insured separately by the FDIC. The Federal Deposit Insurance Reform Act, which was enacted on February 8, 2006, raised the limit on IRA insurance from $100,000 to $250,000 [8] Annuities, which are similar to traditional Individual Retirement Accounts, are not insured by the FDIC [9]

Table 1. Brief History of FDIC Deposit Insurance 1934-2008

Date	Bank Deposit Insurance Limit
January 1934	$2,500
June 1934	$5,000 (temporary increase)
1935	$5,000 (permanent increase)
1950	$10,000
1966	$15,000
1969	$20,000
1974	$40,000
1980	$100,000
2008	$250,000 (temporary increase until 12/31/2009)

Source: Christine Bradley, A Historical Perspective on Deposit Insurance, Federal Deposit Insurance Corporation, FDIC Banking Review, Washington, DC, December 2000, p. 6-17, http://www.fdic.gov/bank/analytical/banking/ 2000dec/brv 1 3n2_1 .pdf.

Notes: Figures do not include insurance for Individual Retirement Accounts (IRAs), which are currently insured up to $250,000 per account.

Resolution of Bank Failures

When a bank is insolvent or has failed, the FDIC follows a purchase and assumption (P&A) process [10]. The FDIC will close the bank and seek purchasers of bank assets (performing loans) that are also willing to assume the liabilities (insured deposits). Typically, most depositors have access to their insured funds within one business day after the bank closure. With certain deposits, such as 40 1(k) accounts and retirement accounts, which are insured at $250,000, additional time is required to make an insurance determination. The FDIC estimates that this should not be longer than several days. In some situations, depositors may receive a portion of their uninsured funds depending on the sale of the failed bank's assets, which may take one or two years [11].

The FDIC administered 25 bank failures from January to December 2008. In comparison, 16 banks failed in the first two months of 2009 [12]. A list of the largest banks that failed in 2008 is presented in Table A-1. The table also shows that the Deposit Insurance Fund (DIF), the fund which holds the premiums collected from member institutions and is then used to pay depositors, may lose between $12 billion to $17 billion as a result of bank failures in 2008 [13]. Large losses to the DIF are likely to come from IndyMac Bank, Downey Savings and Loan, PFF Bank and Trust, Franklin Bank, and First National Bank of Nevada. The recent increase in bank failures has resulted in a decline in the DIF from over $50 billion in 2006 to an estimated $35 billion in 2009. The FDIC has a $30 billion line of credit from the U.S. Treasury in case funds from the DIF are not immediately available to meet the demands of a bank closure [14]

EFFORTS TO SUPPORT FINANCIAL AND HOUSING

MARKETS [15]

Increase in Deposit Insurance

The Emergency Economic Stabilization Act of 2008 temporarily raised deposit insurance until December 31, 2009 [16]. Under the new 2008 deposit insurance limits, an individual checking account may be covered up to $250,000 and an Individual Retirement Account may be covered for $250,000. An individual having both of these accounts would receive total coverage of $500,000 in a single bank. In the 111th Congress, H.R. 786 (Representative Barney Frank) proposed to make the increase in deposit insurance permanent [17]

Support of the Deposit Insurance Fund

The FDIC is required by statute to set the designated reserve ratio (DRR) for the DIF, which is defined as the ratio of total deposits insured relative to funds in the DIF, so that it stays within the range of 1.15 to 1.50 percent [18]. Given the recent increase in deposit insurance coverage to $250,000 and simultaneous rise in bank failures, as previously discussed, the DIF has fallen below the required reserve ratio range [19] The FDIC is required to set a restoration plan in motion to restore the fund to its statutorily mandated range. On October 7, 2008, the FDIC announced a plan to restore the DIF by the end of 2013 [20]. Under the plan, deposit insurance would increase its assessments by 7 basis points beginning January 1, 2009. In the second quarter of 2009, riskier institutions would be asked to pay higher insurance rates relative to less risky institutions.

The FDIC has taken further actions in 2009 to support the DIF. On February 3, 2009, the FDIC asked Congress to increase its line of credit from the U.S. Treasury from $30 billion to $100 billion [21]. Consequently, H.R. 1106, Helping Families Save Their Homes Act of 2009 (Representative John Conyers, Jr., et al.) has a provision to increase the FDIC's borrowing authority from $30 billion to $100 billion from the U.S. Treasury [22] S. 541, The Depositor Protection Act of 2009 (Senator Christopher Dodd et al.), has provisions to permanently increase the FDIC's borrowing authority to $100 billion and temporarily increase it up to $500 billion until December 31, 2010 [23]

The FDIC announced modifications to its original restoration plan on February 27, 2009 [24] The time horizon deemed necessary to accumulate the DRR level for the DIF fund was extended from the initial five years to seven years [25] The risk-based deposit insurance rates charged to reflect differences in bank risk, scheduled to begin in the second quarter of 2009, were announced. The FDIC also announced an emergency special assessment of 20 basis points that would be imposed on member banks on June 30, 2009, and collected on September 30, 2009.

Temporary Liquidity Guarantee Program

On October 14, 2008, the FDIC announced the creation of the Temporary Liquidity Guarantee Program (TLGP) to encourage liquidity in the banking system [26]. One component of the program guarantees senior unsecured debt issued on or before June 30, 2009. Such debt structures include commercial paper, interbank funding debt, promissory notes, and any unsecured portion of secured debt. The guarantee would remain in effect until June 30, 2012, even if the maturity of these obligations extends beyond that date. On March 17, 2009, the debt guarantee portion of the TLGP program was extended from June 30, 2009, to October 31, 2009. Also, a surcharge would be imposed on any debt issued on or after April 1, 2009, with a maturity date of one year or more [27]. The other component of the program insures all non-interest-bearing deposit accounts, primarily payroll processing accounts used by businesses, which often exceed the $250,000 deposit insurance limit [28]

Financial institutions eligible for participation in the TLGP program include entities insured by the FDIC, bank holding and financial holding companies headquartered in the United States, and savings and loan companies under section 4(k) of the Bank Holding Company Act (12 U.S.C. 1843). Although the TLGP is a voluntary program, eligible financial institutions were automatically registered to participate unless they had requested not to be by November 12, 2008. Eligible entities could also opt out of one or both of the program components.

After the first 30 days, institutions that remain in the program pay insurance fees [29]. To insure senior unsecured debt, the FDIC is assessing an annualized fee corresponding to 75 basis points. A 10-basis-point surcharge will be applied for non-interest-bearing deposit accounts above the $250,000 deposit insurance limit. According to testimony by the FDIC's

Deputy to the Chairman, of 8,300 FDIC-insured institutions, almost 7,000 have opted in to the transaction account guarantee program, and nearly 7,100 banks and thrifts and their holding companies have opted into the debt guarantee program [30]

Foreclosure Mitigation Efforts

The FDIC is working with several foreclosure mitigation initiatives. The chairman of the FDIC serves as a member of the Oversight Board of the HOPE for Homeowners Program (H4H) [31]. The H4H program was established to allow distressed borrowers to refinance their mortgages into loans insured by the Federal Housing Administration [32]. As a member of the Oversight Board, the FDIC, along with the U.S. Department of the Treasury and the Department of Housing and Urban Development, sets underwriting standards and requirements for H4H program participants [33]

When the FDIC closed IndyMac Bank, F.S.B., Pasadena, California, on July 11, 2008, an estimated 653,000 first lien mortgages were transferred to the FDIC under receivership. Approximately 60,000 mortgage loans were more than 60 days past due, in bankruptcy, or in foreclosure. The FDIC suspended most foreclosure actions for loans owned by IndyMac to evaluate how best to modify loans. On August 20, 2008, the FDIC announced a loan modification program to systematically modify troubled residential loans for borrowers with mortgages owned or serviced by IndyMac Federal. In addition, the FDIC sent letters encouraging more than 2,000 IndyMac borrowers to refinance through FHA. Afterwards, the FDIC has published the FDIC Loan Modification Program guide, based upon its loan modification program for IndyMac, to serve as a framework to assist bankers, servicers, and investors with this process [34].

On February 18, 2009, the Homeowner Affordability and Stability Plan (HASP) was unveiled to help prevent foreclosures by modifying loans of borrowers unable to refinance as a result of declining home prices [35]. Financial institutions receiving assistance under HASP would be required to implement loan modification plans consistent with the loan modification guidance developed jointly by the FDIC and the Treasury. The FDIC would provide a partial guarantee, linked to declines in a home price index, to holders of mortgages modified under HASP. The partial guarantee program, funded with $10 billion, is known as the Home Price Decline Reserve Payment program. The FDIC will be jointly responsible for oversight of the HASP program with the Treasury, the Federal Reserve, and the Department of Housing and Urban Development. Quarterly meetings between these agencies are required by HASP. The plan requires overseers to provide regular reports on outcomes of HASP and its impact over mortgage market conditions.

Public-Private Investment Fund (PPIF)/Legacy Loan Program

In conjunction with the U.S. Treasury and the Federal Reserve, the FDIC is currently working to create a Public-Private Investment Fund (PPIF) to acquire real-estate related "legacy" or distressed assets [36]. The FDIC would provide oversight over the PPIF Legacy Loan program, which specifically targets the purchase of distressed whole loans off the balance sheets of depository institutions [37] The FDIC will approve the asset pools from the participating banks and conduct the reverse auctions that will be conducted to establish prices for the pools [38]. The pools would be sold if the participating banks agree to the prices. The FDIC would also provide guarantees for the PPIF asset pools. Such guarantees would arguably enhance the liquidity of these pools and, therefore, their attractiveness to potential investors.

APPENDIX. LARGEST FDIC BANK CLOSINGS, 2008

Table A- 1. Largest Banks Closed by the FDIC in 2008 Amounts in millions of dollars, ranked by total deposits

Bank Name	Closing Date	Estimated Assets as of Closing Date	Estimated Deposits as of Closing Date	Estimated Cost to FDIC DIF as of Closing Date
Washington Mutual Bank, Henderson, NV and Washington Mutual Bank FSB, Park City, UT	September 25, 2008	$307,000	$188,000	Unspecified
IndyMac Bank, Pasadena, CA	July 11, 2008	$32,000	$19,000	$4,000 to $8,000
Downey Savings and Loan, Newport Beach, CA	November 21, 2008	$12,800	$9,700	$2,400
Franklin Bank, SSB, Houston, TX	November 7, 2008	$5,100	$3,700	$1,400 to $1,600
First National Bank of Nevada, Reno, NV	July 25, 2008	$3,400	$3,000	$862
PFF Bank and Trust, Pomona, CA	November 21, 2008	$3,700	$2,400	$2,100
Silver State Bank, Henderson, NV	September 5, 2008	$2,000	$1,700	$450 to $550
Integrity Bank, Alpharetta, GA	August 29, 2008	$1,100	$974	$250 to $350
The Columbian Bank and Trust, Topeka, KS	August 22, 2008	$752	$622	$60
The Community Bank, Loganville, GA	November 21, 2008	$681	$611	$200 to $240

Source: FDIC, http://www.fdic.gov/BANK/HISTORICAL/BANK/index.html. Estimated costs to the Deposit Insurance Fund are available in individual press releases for each bank.

REFERENCES

[1] P.L. 73-66, 48 Stat. 162, 12 U.S.C. See Christine Bradley, *A Historical Perspective on Deposit Insurance*, Federal Deposit Insurance Corporation, FDIC Banking Review, Washington, DC, December 2000, p. 3, http://www.fdic.gov/ bank/analytical/banking/2000dec/brv13n2_1.pdf.

[2] FDIC, A *History of the FDIC 1933-1983: the First Fifty Years*, Washington, DC, 1983, http://www.fdic.gov/bank/ analytical/firstfifty/.

[3] Remarks of Martin J. Gruenberg, Vice Chairman Federal Deposit Insurance Corporation (FDIC), *The International Role of Deposit Insurance,* The Exchequer Club, Washington, D.C., November 14, 2007 at http://www.fdic.gov/news/news/speeches/archives/2007/chairman/spnov1407.html.

[4] To fund deposit insurance, the FDIC established a Temporary Federal Deposit Insurance Fund (TFDIF). The TFDIF charged 13,201 banks insurance premiums. Of these, 12,987 were commercial banks and 214 were mutual savings banks. These represented 90 percent of all commercial banks and 36 percent of all mutual savings banks. The TFDIF changed into the permanent Deposit Insurance Fund in 1935 and the FDIC was allowed to borrow from the Treasury to cover funding due to emergency needs.

[5] For an overview of the relationship of financial disruptions and deposit insurance, see Sebastian Schich, "Financial Crisis: Deposit Insurance and Related Financial Safety Net Aspects", Financial Market Trends, OECD, 2008, available at http://www.oecd.org/dataoecd/36/48/41894959.pdf. The report also outlines four pillars for a safety net in financial systems, including bank deposit insurance, failure resolution, prudential regulation and supervision, and lender of last resort. For deposit insurance levels in different countries, see Sebastian Schich, "Financial Turbulence: Some Lessons Regarding Deposit Insurance," Financial Market Trends, OECD, 2008, page 66, available at http://www.oecd.org/ dataoecd/32/54/41420525.pdf.

[6] In addition, the FDIC insures Money Market Deposit Accounts, which are savings accounts that allow a limited number of checks to be written each month, Negotiable Orders of Withdrawal (NOW), and outstanding cashiers' checks. See CRS Report RL33036, *Federal Financial Services Regulatory Consolidation: An Overview*, by Walter W. Eubanks.

[7] The FDIC also insures the following retirement accounts: Keogh retirement accounts for the self-employed, 457 Plan retirement accounts for state government employees, and employer-sponsored defined contribution plan retirement accounts that are self-directed, which are primarily 40 1(k) accounts and include SIMPLE 40 1(k) accounts, Simplified Employee Pension (SEP) IRAs, and Savings Incentive Match Plans for Employees (SIMPLE) IRAs. See CRS Report RS2 1987, *When Financial Businesses Fail: Protection for Account Holders*, by Walter W. Eubanks.

[8] P.L. 109-171, 110 Stat. 9.

[9] The FDIC does not insure stocks, bonds, mutual funds, money market funds, life insurance policies, annuities, or municipal securities, even if these products were purchased from an insured bank. The FDIC does not insure the contents of safe deposit boxes, losses due to theft or fraud at the bank, losses due to accounting errors, and

investments backed by the U.S. government, such as Treasury securities and Savings Bonds. See Federal Deposit Insurance Corporation, *FDIC Consumer News - Spring 2001*, FDIC, Washington, DC, 2001, http://www.fdic.gov/CONSUMERS/ consumer/ news/cnspr01/cvrstry.html

[10] See Federal Deposit Insurance Corporation, Managing the Crisis: The FDIC and RTC Experience 1980-1 994 (Washington, DC: Federal Deposit Insurance Corporation, 1998) at http://www.fdic.gov/bank/historical/managing/ contents.pdf.

[11] FDIC, FDIC Consumer News , Fall 2008 – Special Edition: Your New, Higher FDIC Insurance Coverage, Washington, DC, 2008, http://www.fdic.gov/consumers/ consumer/news/cnfall08/misconceptions.html.

[12] For a complete list see http://www.fdic.gov/BANK/HISTORICAL/BANK/index.html.

[13] These preliminary estimates are computed by the FDIC, and they may be found by going to the FDIC's failed bank list and viewing the press releases for each failed bank.

[14] For more detailed information concerning FDIC authority, see CRS Report RL34657, *Financial Institution Insolvency: Federal Authority over Fannie Mae, Freddie Mac, and Depository Institutions*, by David H. Carpenter and M. Maureen Murphy.

[15] See Sheila Bair, "Statement of Sheila C. Bair, Chairman, Federal Deposit Insurance Corporation on Turmoil in the U.S. Credit Markets: Examining Recent Regulatory Responses to the Committee on Banking, Housing and Urban Affairs, U.S. Senate," October 23, 2008, available at http://www.fdic.gov/news/news/speeches/archives/2008/ chairman/spoct2308.html

[16] P.L. 110-343. See also CRS Report RL34730, *Troubled Asset Relief Program: Legislation and Treasury Implementation*, by Baird Webel and Edward V. Murphy

[17] H.R. 786, Section 1.

[18] P.L. 109-171, The Federal Deposit Insurance Reform Act of 2005 (the Reform Act). See http://www.fdic.gov/deposit/insurance/initiative/index.html for highlights regarding coverage of the law and a link to the Reform Act.

[19] See statement made by John Bovenzi, Deputy to the Chairman and Chief Operating Officer of the FDIC, to the House Financial Services Committee on Februrary 3, 2009, at http://www.fdic.gov/news/news/speeches/chairman/ spfeb0309.html.

[20] See http://www.fdic.gov/news/news/press/2008/pr08094.html.

[21] See http://www.fdic.gov/news/news/speeches/chairman/spfeb0309.html.

[22] H.R. 1106, Section 204.

[23] S. 541, Section 2.

[24] See http://www.fdic.gov/news/news/press/2009/pr09030.html.

[25] H.R. 786, Section 2 proposed to extend the restoration period to eight years.

[26] See the initial announcement at http://www.fdic.gov/news/news/press/2008/pr08100.html. See http://www.fdic.gov/news/news/press/2008/pr08105.html, which provides further details of the program.

[27] See http://www.fdic.gov/news/news/press/2009/pr09041.html.

[28] Monthly reports on debt issuance under the TLGP program may be found at http://www.fdic.gov/regulations/ resources/tlgp/reports.html.

[29] The list of institutions requesting not to participate in the TLGP program is available at http://www.fdic.gov/ regulations/resources/TLGP/optout.html.

[30] John F. Bovenzi, *Statement of John F. Bovenzi, Deputy to the Chairman and Chief Operating Officer, Federal Deposit Insurance Corporation on Promoting Bank Liquidity and Lending Through Deposit Insurance, Hope for Homeowners, and Other Enhancements before the Committee on Financial Services; U.S. House of Representatives*, February 3, 2009, http://www.fdic.gov/news/news/speeches/chair man/spfeb0309.html.

[31] P.L. 110-289, The Housing and Economic Recovery Act of 2008, Title IV, Sections 1401-1404.

[32] See CRS Report RL34623, *Housing and Economic Recovery Act of 2008*, coordinated by N. Eric Weiss.

[33] See http://www.fdic.gov/news/news/speeches/archives/2008/chairman/spsep1708.html.

[34] Available at http://www.fdic.gov/consumers/loans/loanmod/FDICLoanMod.pdf.

[35] Available at http://www.treasury.gov/press/releases/tg33.htm.

[36] See http://www.fdic.gov/news/news/press/2009/pr_fsb.html and http://www.fdic.gov/llp/index.html.

[37] A separate PPIF program would be established for the purchase of legacy securities, which are held by banks, insurance companies, pension funds, mutual funds, and funds held in retirement accounts. See Treasury announcement at http://www.treasury.gov/press/releases/tg65.htm.

[38] See http://www.fdic.gov/llp/LLPfaq.pdf and CRS Report RL34707, *Auction Basics: Background for Assessing Proposed Treasury Purchases of Mortgage-Backed Securities*, by D. Andrew Austin.

In: Economics, Political and Social Issues ...
Editor: Michelle L. Fergusson

ISBN: 978-1-61122-555-6
©2011 Nova Science Publishers, Inc.

IMMIGRATION: POLICY CONSIDERATIONS RELATED TO GUEST WORKER PROGRAMS[*]

Andorra Bruno

ABSTRACT

At present, the United States has two main programs for temporarily importing low-skilled workers, sometimes referred to as guest workers. Agricultural guest workers enter through the H-2A visa program, and other guest workers enter through the H-2B visa program. Employers interested in importing workers under either program must first apply to the U.S. Department of Labor for a certification that U.S. workers capable of performing the work are not available and that the employment of alien workers will not adversely affect the wages and working conditions of similarly employed U.S. workers. Other requirements of the programs differ.

The 109th Congress revised the H-2B program in the FY2005 Emergency Supplemental Appropriations Act (P.L. 109-13). Among the changes, a temporary provision was added to the Immigration and Nationality Act (INA) to exempt certain returning H-2B workers from the H-2B annual numerical cap. The FY2007 Department of Defense authorization P.L. 109-364) extended this exemption through FY2007. Other bills before the 109th Congress proposed to make changes to the H2A program (S. 359/H.R. 884, H.R. 3857, S. 2087, Senate-passed S. 2611), the H-2B program (S. 278, H.R. 1587, S. 1438, S. 1918), and the "H" visa category generally (H.R. 3333), and to establish new temporary worker visas (S. 1033/H.R. 2330, S. 1438, S. 1918, H.R. 4065, Senate-passed S. 2611). Some of these bills also would have established mechanisms for certain foreign workers to become U.S. legal permanent residents (LPRs). None of these bills were enacted. President George W. Bush proposed a new, expanded temporary worker program in January 2004 when he announced his principles for immigration reform. In a May 2006 national address on comprehensive immigration reform, he reiterated his support for a temporary worker program.

Guest worker bills before the 110th Congress include proposals to reform the H2A program (S. 237/S. 340/H.R. 371, S. 1639, H.R. 1645) and the H-2B program (S. 1639), and to establish new temporary worker visas (S. 330, S. 1639, H.R. 1645). Some of these bills also would establish mechanisms for certain foreign workers to become LPRs.

The current discussion of guest worker programs takes place against a backdrop of historically high levels of unauthorized migration to the United States. Supporters of a large-scale temporary worker program argue that such a program would help reduce unauthorized immigration by providing a legal alternative for prospective foreign workers. Critics reject this reasoning and instead maintain that a new guest worker program would likely exacerbate the problem of illegal migration.

---

[*] Excerpted from CRS Report RL32044, dated June 27, 2007.

The consideration of any proposed guest worker program raises various issues, including how new program requirements would compare with those of the H-2A and H-2B programs, how the eligible population would be defined, and whether the program would include a mechanism for participants to obtain LPR status.

INTRODUCTION

In 2001, the United States and Mexico began Cabinet-level talks on migration. Although the details of these discussions were not made public, two issues — legalization and a temporary worker program — dominated media coverage. The talks lost momentum after the terrorist attacks of September 11, 2001, as the Bush Administration focused its attention on security-related matters. A temporary worker program (not limited to Mexico), however, remains of interest to some Members of Congress and Administration officials. Various bills to reform existing programs for foreign temporary workers and to create new temporary worker programs have been introduced in recent Congresses. Among them, in the 110th Congress, is S. 1639, which would provide for comprehensive immigration reform. In January 2004, the Bush Administration outlined a proposal for a new temporary worker program. The President reiterated his support for a temporary worker program in a May 2006 national address. The temporary worker programs under discussion presumably would cover largely low-skilled workers.

BACKGROUND

The term *guest worker* has typically been applied to foreign temporary low-skilled laborers, often in agriculture or other seasonal employment. In the past, guest worker programs have been established in the United States to address worker shortages during times of war. During World War I, for example, tens of thousands of Mexican workers performed mainly agricultural labor as part of a temporary worker program. The Bracero program, which began during World War II and lasted until 1964, brought several million Mexican agricultural workers into the United States. At its peak in the late 1950s, the Bracero program employed more than 400,000 Mexican workers annually.[1]

The Immigration and Nationality Act (INA) of 1952, as originally enacted,[2] authorized a temporary foreign worker program known as the H-2 program. It covered both agricultural and nonagricultural workers who were coming temporarily to the United States to perform temporary services (other than services of an exceptional nature requiring distinguished merit and ability) or labor. Aliens who are admitted to the United States for a temporary period of time and a specific purpose are known as nonimmigrants. The 1986 Immigration Reform and Control Act (IRCA)[3] amended the INA to subdivide the H-2 program into the current H-2A and H-2B programs and to detail the admissions process for H-2A workers. The H-2A and H-2B visas are subcategories of the larger "H" nonimmigrant visa category for temporary workers[4]

CURRENT PROGRAMS

The United States currently has two main programs for importing temporary low-skilled workers. Agricultural workers enter through the H-2A program and other temporary workers enter through the H-2B program.[5] The programs take their names from the sections of the INA that established them — Section 101(a)(15)(H)(ii)(a) and Section 101(a)(15)(H)(ii)(b), respectively. Both programs are administered by the Employment and Training Administration (ETA) of the U.S. Department of Labor (DOL) and U.S. Citizenship and Immigration Services (USCIS) of the U.S. Department of Homeland Security (DHS).[6]

H-2A Program

The H-2A program allows for the temporary admission of foreign workers to the United States to perform agricultural work of a seasonal or temporary nature, provided that U.S. workers are not available. An approved H-2A visa petition is generally valid for an initial period of up to one year. An alien's total period of stay as an H-2A worker may not exceed three consecutive years.

Employers who want to import H-2A workers must first apply to DOL for a certification that (1) there are not sufficient U.S. workers who are qualified and available to perform the work; and (2) the employment of foreign workers will not adversely affect the wages and working conditions of U.S. workers who are similarly employed. As part of this labor certification process, employers must attempt to recruit U.S. workers and must cooperate with DOL-funded state employment service agencies (also known as state workforce agencies) in local, intrastate, and interstate recruitment efforts. Employers must pay their H-2A workers and similarly employed

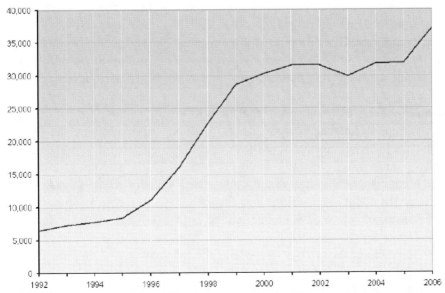

Source: CRS Presentation of data from U.S. Department of State, Bureau of Consular Affairs.

Figure 1. H-2A Visas Issued, FY1992-FY2006.

U.S. workers the highest of the federal or applicable state minimum wage, the prevailing wage rate,[7] or the adverse effect wage rate (AEWR).[8] They also must provide workers with housing, transportation, and other benefits, including workers' compensation insurance.[9] No health insurance coverage is required.[10]

Both growers and labor advocates criticize the H-2A program in its current form. Growers complain that the H-2A program is overly cumbersome and does not meet their labor needs. Labor advocates argue that the program provides too few protections for U.S. workers.

H-2A Visas Issued

The H-2A program, which is not subject to numerical limits, has grown significantly since 1992. One way to measure the program's growth is to consider changes in the number of H-2A visas issued annually by the Department of State (DOS).[11] As illustrated in figure 1, the number of H-2A visas issued increased from 6,445 in FY1992 to 30,201 in FY2000. H-2A visa issuances remained at about 30,000 annually until FY2006, when, according to preliminary data, 37,149 H-2A visas were issued. The H-2A program, however, remains quite small relative to total hired farm employment, which stood at about 1.1 million in 2005, according to the Department of Agriculture's National Agricultural Statistics Service.[12]

H-2B Program

The H-2B program provides for the temporary admission of foreign workers to the United States to perform temporary non-agricultural work, if unemployed U.S. workers cannot be found. Foreign medical graduates coming to perform medical services are explicitly excluded from the program. An approved H-2B visa petition is valid for an initial period of up to one year. An alien's total period of stay as an H-2B worker may not exceed three consecutive years.[13]

Like prospective H-2A employers, prospective H-2B employers must first apply to DOL for a certification that U.S. workers capable of performing the work are not available and that the employment of alien workers will not adversely affect the wages and working conditions of similarly employed U.S. workers. H-2Bemployers must pay their workers at least the prevailing wage rate. Unlike H-2A employers, they are not subject to the AEWR and do not have to provide housing, transportation,[14] and other benefits required under the H-2A program.

In January 2005, USCIS proposed regulations to streamline the H-2B petitioning process, which would significantly alter procedures.[15] Among other changes, the proposed rule would eliminate the requirement that prospective H-2B employers file for a labor certification from DOL in most cases. Instead, employers seeking H-2B workers in areas other than logging, the entertainment industry, and professional athletics would include certain labor attestations as part of the H-2B petition they file with USCIS. According to the proposed rule, this H-2B attestation process would be similar to the process currently used for H-1B professional specialty workers.[16]

A key limitation of the H-2B visa concerns the requirement that the work be temporary. Under the applicable immigration regulations, work is considered to be temporary if the employer's need for the duties to be performed by the worker is a one-time occurrence, seasonal need, peakload need, or intermittent need.[17] According to DOL data on H-2B labor certifications, top H-2B occupations in recent years, in terms of the number of workers certified, included landscape laborer, forestry worker, maid and housekeeping cleaner, and construction worker.

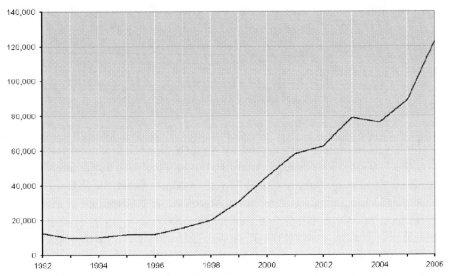

Source: CRS Presentation of data from U.S. Department of State, Bureau of Consular Affairs.

Figure 2. H-2B Visas Issued, FY1992-FY2006.

H-2B Visas Issued and the Statutory Cap

Unlike the H-2A visa, the H2B visa is subject to a statutory numerical limit. Under the INA, the total number of aliens who may be issued H-2B visas or otherwise provided H-2B status during a fiscal year may not exceed 66,000.[18] This cap does not apply to all H-2B petitions. Petitions for current H-2B workers to extend their stay, change their terms of employment, or change or add employers do not count towards the cap. As shown in figure 2, the number of H-2B visas issued by DOS dipped from 12,552 in FY1992 to 9,691 in FY1993 and then began to increase steadily.[19]

In FY2003, DOS issued 78,955 H-2B visas, and in FY2004, it issued 76,169 H2B visas. While for various reasons not all visas issued during a fiscal year necessarily count against that year's cap or, in some cases, any year's cap, USCIS acknowledged that the H-2B cap was exceeded in FY2003. With respect to the FY2004 cap, USCIS announced on March 10, 2004, that it had received a sufficient number of H-2B petitions to meet that cap. On January 4, 2005, it announced that it had received a sufficient number of H-2B petitions to meet the FY2005 cap.

Following the enactment of new H-2B provisions as part of the FY2005 Emergency Supplemental Appropriations Act for Defense, the Global War on Terror, and Tsunami Relief (P.L. 109-13),[20] USCIS announced that on May 25, 2005, it would start accepting additional petitions for H-2B workers for FY2005.[21] Under P.L. 109-13, for FY2005 and FY2006, returning H-2B workers counted against the annual 66,000 cap during any one of the three prior fiscal years were not to be counted again. USCIS determined that approximately 35,000 previously approved H-2B workers for FY2005 qualified as returning workers who, under P.L. 109-13, were exempt from that year's cap, opening up 35,000 slots for other H-2B workers. Employers were able to file FY2005 petitions for new H-2B workers to fill those slots, as well as for cap-exempt returning H-2B workers. According to preliminary data, 89,135 H-2B visas were issued in FY2005 and 122,541 H-2B visas were issued in FY2006. According to DOS, 50,854 of the FY2006 H-2B visas were issued to cap-exempt returning H-2B workers. The John Warner National Defense Authorization Act for FY2007 (P.L. 109-364) extends through FY2007 the provision exempting returning H-2B workers from the H-2B annual cap.

UNAUTHORIZED IMMIGRATION

The current discussion of guest worker programs has been prompted, in part, by the continued high levels of illegal, or unauthorized, immigration to the United States and related deaths along the U.S.-Mexican border. Analyses by the Pew Hispanic Center based on data from the Current Population Survey (CPS) and other sources estimate that the unauthorized resident alien population totaled 10.3 million in March 2004, 11.1 million in March 2005, and 11.5 to 12 million in March 2006, and that since 2000, this population has grown at an average annual rate of more than 500,000 per year.[22] DHS's estimates of the unauthorized alien population and its growth are somewhat lower. Based on data from the 2004 American Community Survey and other sources, DHS estimates that there were 10.5 million unauthorized aliens residing in the United States in January 2005 and that the unauthorized resident population grew at an average annual rate of 408,000 during the 2000-2004 period.[23]

Mexico remains the largest source country for unauthorized immigration. According to the Pew Hispanic Center, the unauthorized Mexican population in the United States stood at about 6.2 million in 2005, comprising 56% of the total unauthorized population. DHS estimates that there were nearly 6 million unauthorized Mexicans residing in the United States in 2005, comprising 57% of the total unauthorized population. With respect to migrant deaths, data from the United States Border Patrol indicate that more than 300 migrants died at the U.S.-Mexican border each year from FY2000 through FY2004 and that there were 472 migrant deaths at the border in FY2005.[24]

UNAUTHORIZED WORKERS

Unauthorized workers are a subpopulation of the total unauthorized alien population. According to the March 2006 report by the Pew Hispanic Center, there were an estimated 7.2 million unauthorized workers in the U.S. civilian labor force in March 2005.[25] These workers represented about 4.9% of the labor force. In some occupations and industries, however, their share of the labor force was considerably higher. The report states:

> Unauthorized workers are employed in a variety of occupations throughout the labor force, although the distribution of the unauthorized workforce across occupations differs from that of native-born workers.
> Unauthorized workers are notably underrepresented in white-collar occupations.... On the other hand, unauthorized migrants are much more likely to be in major occupation groups that require little education or do not have licensing requirements.[26]

Unauthorized aliens are also overrepresented in certain industries relative to their share of the overall labor force. Table 1 presents data from the Pew Hispanic Center report on industries with high concentrations of unauthorized workers. Unauthorized aliens accounted for between 10% and 21% of workers in the industries shown.

Supporters of a large-scale guest worker program contend that such a program would help reduce unauthorized immigration by providing a legal alternative for prospective foreign workers. Critics reject this reasoning and instead maintain that a guest worker program would likely exacerbate the problem of illegal immigration; they argue, for example, that many guest workers would fail to leave the country at the end of their authorized period of stay.

Table 1. Estimates of Unauthorized Employment in Selected Industries, 2005

Industry Group	Unauthorized Workers (in Industry)
Private Households	21%
Food Manufacturing	14%
Agriculture	13%
Furniture Manufacturing	13%
Construction	12%
Textile, Apparel, and Leather Manufacturing	12%
Food Services	12%
Administrative and Support Services	11%
Accommodation	10%

Source: Jeffrey S. Passel, Size and Characteristics of the Unauthorized Migrant Population in the U.S., Pew Hispanic Center, March 7, 2006.

LEGISLATION IN THE 105ᵀᴴ-107ᵀᴴ CONGRESSES

Major guest worker legislation introduced in the 105th, 106th, and 107th Congresses was limited to the H-2A program. No major nonagricultural guest worker bills were offered.[27] In the 105th Congress, for example, a Senate-approved amendment to S. 2260, an FY1999 Departments of Commerce, Justice, and State appropriations bill, would have replaced the existing labor certification process with a new set of procedures for importing H-2A workers. It would have established a system of agricultural worker registries containing the names of eligible U.S. agricultural workers. Employers interested in importing H-2A workers would first have applied to DOL for the referral of U.S. workers through a registry search. If a sufficient number of workers were not found, the employer would have been allowed to import H-2A workers to cover the shortfall. The Senate measure also would have changed wage and other requirements. The provision was not enacted.

Provisions to establish a system of worker registries and to change existing H2A-related requirements were likewise included in two H-2A reform proposals introduced in the 106th Congress (S. 1814/H.R. 4056[28] and H.R. 4548). In addition, S. 1814/H.R. 4056 would have established a two-stage legalization program, under which farm workers satisfying specified work requirements could have obtained temporary resident status and then legal permanent resident (LPR) status. Although formal congressional consideration was limited to a Senate

Immigration Subcommittee hearing, S. 1814/H.R. 4056 became the basis of a bipartisan compromise on foreign agricultural workers. That agreement, however, fell apart at the end of the 106th Congress. H.R. 4548, the other reform bill before the 106th Congress, differed from S. 1814/H.R. 4056 in that it sought to establish a pilot H-2C alien agricultural worker program to supplement, rather than replace, the H-2A program. H.R. 4548 also did not include a legalization program. H.R. 4548 was reported by the House Judiciary Committee in October 2000, but saw no further action.

Like S. 1814/H.R. 4056 in the 106th Congress, key bills before the 107th Congress coupled significant H-2A reform with legalization. S. 1161 and S. 1313/H.R. 2736 would have streamlined the process of importing H-2A workers, particularly for jobs covered by collective bargaining agreements. With respect to legalization, both proposals would have allowed foreign agricultural workers who met specified work requirements to adjust to LPR status through a two-stage process like that in S. 1814/H.R. 4056. The requirements for adjustment of status in S. 1313/H.R. 2736 differed from those in S. 1161, with the latter being more stringent. Among the other major differences between the proposals, S. 1161 would have eased existing wage requirements, while S. 1313/H.R. 2736 would have mandated a study of the wage issue. No action beyond committee referral occurred on either proposal.

LEGISLATION IN THE 108TH CONGRESS

Bills to reform the H-2A program, the H-2B program, and the "H" visa category generally, as well as bills to establish new guest worker programs, were introduced in the 108th Congress. Some of these bills would have enabled certain workers to obtain LPR status. No action beyond committee referral occurred on any of the bills.

Congressional committees held related hearings during the 108th Congress. The House Agriculture Committee held a hearing on the potential impact of recent guest worker proposals on the agricultural sector, and the House Judiciary Committee's Subcommittee on Immigration, Border Security, and Claims held a hearing on the impact of guest workers on U.S. workers. In the Senate, the Judiciary Committee's Subcommittee on Immigration, Border Security, and Citizenship held hearings on evaluating a guest worker proposal and on border security under a guest worker program.

S. 1645/H.R. 3142 and S. 2823

The Agricultural Job Opportunity, Benefits, and Security Act of 2003 (AgJOBS Act; S. 1645/H.R. 3142) would have overhauled the H-2A agricultural worker program. It was introduced, respectively, by Senator Craig for himself and a bipartisan group of cosponsors and by Representative Cannon for himself and Representative Berman. Like the major H-2A reform bills before the 107th Congress, S. 1645/H.R. 3142 would have streamlined the process of importing H-2A workers, particularly for jobs covered by collective bargaining agreements. Under S. 1645/H.R. 3142, prospective H-2A employers would have had to file applications with DOL containing certain assurances. In the case of a job covered by a collective bargaining agreement, the employer would have had to assure, among other things, that there was an applicable union contract and that the bargaining representatives of the employer's employees had been notified of the filing of the application for H-2A workers. An employer interested in filling a job not covered by a collective bargaining agreement would have been subject to a longer list of required assurances. Among these, the employer would have had to assure that he or she would take specified steps to recruit U.S. workers and would provide workers with required benefits, wages, and working conditions. Both groups of employers would have had to assure that the job was temporary or seasonal and that the employer would offer the job to any equally qualified, available U.S. worker who applied. Unless an employer's application was incomplete or obviously inaccurate, DOL would have certified within seven days of the filing date that the employer had filed the required application.

S. 1645/H.R. 3142 further proposed to make changes to the H-2A program's requirements regarding minimum benefits, wages, and working conditions. Among these proposed changes, the adverse effect wage rate (discussed above) would have remained at the January 2003 level for three years after the date of enactment, and employers would have been permitted to provide housing allowances, in lieu of housing, to their workers if the governor of the relevant state certified that adequate housing was available.

Under S. 1645/H.R. 3142, an H-2A worker's initial period of employment could not have exceeded 10 months. The worker's stay could have been extended in increments of up to 10 months each, but the worker's total continuous period of stay, including any extensions, could not have exceeded three years.

In addition to these H-2A reform provisions, S. 1645/H.R. 3142 would have established a two-stage legalization program for agricultural workers. To obtain temporary resident status, the alien worker would have had to establish that he or she performed at least 575 hours, or 100 work days, of agricultural employment in the United States during 12 consecutive months in the 18-month period ending on August 31, 2003, and meet other requirements. To be eligible to adjust to LPR status, the alien would have had to perform at least 2,060 hours, or 360 work days, of agricultural work in the United States between September 1, 2003, and August 31, 2009, and meet other requirements. Existing numerical limits under the INA would not have applied to adjustments of status under the bill.[29]

On September 21, 2004, Senator Craig introduced a modified version of S. 1645 for himself and Senator Kennedy. The revised bill, S. 2823, was very similar to S. 1645, but there were substantive differences in the two bills' legalization provisions. Among these differences, S. 2823 contained a new provision stating that aliens acquiring temporary resident status under the bill would not be eligible for certain federal public benefits until five years after they obtained permanent resident status.[30]

H.R. 3604

Like S. 1645/H.R. 3142, the Temporary Agricultural Labor Reform Act of 2003 (H.R. 3604) proposed to overhaul the H-2A agricultural worker program. It was introduced by Representative Goodlatte for himself and more than 30 co-sponsors.

H.R. 3604 would have streamlined the process of importing H-2A workers. Prospective H-2A employers would have had to file applications with DOL containing certain assurances, including that the job was temporary or seasonal; the employer would provide workers with required benefits, wages, and working conditions; the employer had made positive efforts to recruit U.S. workers; and the employer would offer the job to any equally qualified, available U.S. worker who applied. Unless an employer's application was incomplete or obviously inaccurate, DOL would have certified within seven days of the filing date that the employer had filed the required application.

H.R. 3604 would have made changes to current H-2A requirements regarding minimum benefits, wages, and working conditions. Under H.R. 3604, H-2A employers would have had to pay workers the higher of the prevailing wage rate or the applicable state minimum wage; they would not have been subject to the adverse effect wage rate (discussed above). With respect to housing, employers could have provided housing allowances, in lieu of housing, to their workers if the governor of the relevant state certified that adequate housing was available.

Under H.R. 3604, an H-2A worker's initial period of employment could not have exceeded 10 months. The worker's stay could have been extended in increments of up to 10 months each, but the worker's total continuous period of stay, including any extensions, could not have exceeded two years. H.R. 3604 would not have established a mechanism for agricultural workers to obtain LPR status.

S. 2185

Another H-2A reform bill, introduced by Senator Chambliss, was the Temporary Agricultural Work Reform Act of 2004 (S. 2185). It was similar, but not identical, to H.R. 3604. S. 2185 would have streamlined the process of importing H-2A workers. Prospective H-2A employers would have had to file applications with DOL containing certain assurances, including that the job was temporary or seasonal; the employer would provide workers with required benefits, wages, and working conditions; the employer had attempted to recruit U.S. workers using the state workforce agency; and the employer would offer the job to any equally qualified, available U.S. worker who applied. Unless an employer's application was incomplete or obviously inaccurate, DOL would have certified within 15 days of the filing date that the employer had filed the required application.

S. 2185 proposed to change current H-2A requirements concerning minimum benefits, wages, and working conditions. Under S. 2185, H-2A employers would have had to pay workers the higher of the prevailing wage rate or the applicable state minimum wage. In lieu of offering housing, they could have provided housing allowances if the governor of the relevant state certified that adequate housing was available.

S. 2185 did not contain provisions regarding the period of admission, extension of stay, or maximum period of stay of H-2A workers. It also would not have established a mechanism for agricultural workers to obtain LPR status.

S. 2010

The Immigration Reform Act of 2004: Strengthening America's National Security, Economy, and Families (S. 2010), introduced by Senator Hagel for himself and Senator Daschle, would have reformed the H-2B nonimmigrant visa. The bill would have eliminated the current restriction that H-2B workers can perform only temporary service or labor, and instead would have required that they perform "shortterm service or labor, lasting not more than 9 months." S. 2010 also proposed a new H-2C visa for temporary workers coming to perform "labor or services, other than those occupation classifications" covered under the H-2A, H-2B, or specified high-skilled visa categories, if qualified U.S. workers could not be found.

Both the H-2B and H-2C categories would have been numerically limited. In each of the five fiscal years following issuance of final implementing regulations, the H-2B program would have been capped at 100,000. The cap would have then reverted back to the current 66,000 level. The H-2C program would have been capped at 250,000 in each of the five fiscal years following issuance of final implementing regulations. After these five years, the H-2C program would have terminated.

S. 2010 would have subjected both the H-2B and H-2C programs to a broad set of requirements covering recruitment, application procedures, and worker protections, among other issues. Prior to filing an application with DOL for H-2B or H-2C workers, prospective employers would have had to take specified steps to recruit U.S. workers, including posting the job on DOL's online "America's Job Bank" and with local job banks, and would have had to offer the job to any qualified, available U.S. worker who applied. In the application to DOL, the employer would have had to attest to various items, including that he or she was offering wages to H2B or H-2C workers that were the greater of the prevailing wage rate or the actual wage paid by the employer to other similarly employed and qualified workers, and that he or she would abide by all applicable laws and regulations relating to the rights of workers to organize. DOL would have reviewed the application and required documentation for completeness and accuracy, and issued a determination not later than 21 days after the filing date.

The initial period of admission for an H-2B worker could not have exceeded nine months in a one-year period. An H-2B worker's total period of admission could not have exceeded 36 months in a four-year period. The initial period of admission for an H-2C worker could not have exceeded two years and could have been extended for an additional period of up to two years. An H-2C worker's total period of admission could not have exceeded four years.

S. 2010 would have enabled H-2B and H-2C nonimmigrants to obtain LPR status. Employment-based *immigrant* visas would have been made available to these nonimmigrants without regard to existing numerical limits under the INA. An employment-based petition could have been filed by an employer or any collective bargaining agent of the alien, or after the alien had been employed in H-2B or H-2C status for at least three years, by the alien. In addition, S. 2010 would have established a legalization program for certain unauthorized aliens in the United States.

S. 2381/H.R. 4262

The Safe, Orderly, Legal Visas and Enforcement Act of 2004 (S. 2381/H.R. 4262) was introduced, respectively, by Senator Kennedy for himself and Senators Feingold and Clinton and by Representative Gutierrez for himself and a group of cosponsors. Known as the "S.O.L.V.E. Act," the measure would have reformed the H-2B nonimmigrant visa. It would have eliminated the current restriction that H-2B workers can perform only temporary service or labor, and instead would have required that they perform "short-term service or labor, lasting not more than 9 months." S. 2381/H.R. 4262 also proposed a new H-ID visa for temporary workers coming to perform "labor or services, other than those occupation classifications" covered under the H-2A or specified high-skilled visa categories, if qualified U.S. workers could not be found.

Both the H-2B and H-1D categories would have been numerically limited. The H-2B program would have been capped at 100,000 annually, an increase from the current annual limit of 66,000. The H-1D program would have been capped at 250,000 annually.

S. 2381/H.R. 4262 would have subjected both the H-2B and H-1D programs to a broad set of requirements covering recruitment, application procedures, and worker protections, among other issues. Prior to filing an application with DOL for H-2B or H-1D workers, prospective employers would have had to take specified steps to recruit U.S. workers, including posting the job on DOL's America's Job Bank and with local job banks, and would have had to offer the job to any qualified, available U.S. worker who applied. In the application to DOL, the employer would have had to attest to various items. Among these were that the employer was offering to H-2B or H-1D workers the prevailing wage, to be determined as specified in the bill. The employer also would have had to abide by all applicable laws and regulations relating to the rights of workers to organize. DOL would have reviewed the application and required documentation for completeness and accuracy, and issued a determination not later than 10 working days after the filing date.

The initial period of admission for an H-2B worker could not have exceeded nine months in a one-year period. An H-2B worker's total period of admission could not have exceeded 40 months in the aggregate. The initial period of admission for an H-1D worker could not have exceeded two years and could have been extended for two additional periods of up to two years each. An H-1D worker's total period of admission could not have exceeded six years.

S. 2381/H.R. 4262 would have enabled H-2B and H-1D nonimmigrants to obtain LPR status. Employment-based *immigrant* visas would have been made available to these nonimmigrants without numerical limitation. An employment-based petition could have been filed by an employer, or after the alien had been employed in H-2B or H-1D status for at least two years, by the alien. In addition, S. 2381/H.R. 4262 would have established a legalization program for certain unauthorized aliens in the United States.

H.R. 3534

The Border Enforcement and Revolving Employment to Assist Laborers Act of 2003 (H.R. 3534), introduced by Representative Tancredo for himself and several cosponsors, proposed to amend the INA's "H" visa category generally. It would have eliminated the current subcategories, including the H-2A and H-2B visas, and replaced them with a single category covering aliens coming temporarily to the United States to perform skilled or unskilled work if qualified U.S. workers were not available.

An employer interested in importing "H" workers would have filed an application with DOL. Prior to doing so, the employer would have been required to post a job announcement on an Internet-based job bank that the bill would have directed DOL to create. Among other requirements of the program, the employer would have had to offer wages at least equal to the prevailing wage rate and would have had to provide "H" workers with health insurance.

H nonmimmigrants could only have been admitted from abroad. They would have applied to be added to a database of workers and would have had to remain in their home countries until an approved employer wanted to hire them. Their period of authorized admission could not have exceeded 365 days in a two-year period. After the two-year period, H nonimmigrant visas could have been renewed. H nonimmigrants would not have been permitted to change or adjust to any other nonimmigrant or immigrant status.

Under H.R. 3534, however, the proposed guest worker program would not have been implemented until the Secretary of Homeland Security, in consultation with the Attorney General and the Secretary of State, had made certain certifications to Congress. The Secretary of Homeland Security would have had to certify, among other items, that all noncitizens legally in the United States and all aliens authorized to enter the country had been issued biometric, machine-readable travel or entry documents, and that the number of aliens who overstayed nonimmigrant visas, but were not removed from the United States, was less than 5,000.

S. 1387

The Border Security and Immigration Reform Act of 2003 (S. 1387), introduced by Senator Cornyn, would have authorized new temporary worker programs under the INA for seasonal and nonseasonal workers. S. 1387 would have established a new "W" nonimmigrant visa category for these workers, which would not have been subject to numerical limits. The W-1 visa would have covered seasonal workers, and the W-2 visa would have covered nonseasonal workers. Under the proposal, the Secretary of Homeland Security and the Secretary of State would have jointly established and administered guest worker programs with foreign countries that entered into agreements with the United States. The bill would have directed the Secretary of Homeland Security, in cooperation with the Secretary of State and the participating foreign governments, to establish a database to monitor guest workers' entry into and exit from the United States and to track employer compliance.

In order to import workers through the new programs, employers would have had to file an application with DOL. As part of the application, the employer would have had to request an attestation from DOL that there were not sufficient U.S. workers who were qualified and available to perform the work, and that the hiring of alien workers would not adversely affect the wages and working conditions of similarly employed U.S. workers. The employer also would have needed to provide various assurances in the application, including that the employer would offer the job to any equally qualified, available U.S. worker who applied; would advertise the job opening in a local publication; and would pay workers at least the higher of the federal or applicable state minimum wage. Unless an employer's application was incomplete or obviously inaccurate, DOL would have certified within 14 days of the filing date that the application had been filed. Beginning 12 months after enactment, employers would have been subject to increased penalties for knowingly employing unauthorized aliens.

The authorized period of stay for a W-1 seasonal worker could not have exceeded 270 days per year. Such a worker could have reapplied for admission to the United States each year. The initial authorized period of stay for a W-2 nonseasonal worker could not have exceeded one year, but could have been extended in increments of up to one year each; a W-2 worker's total period of stay could not have exceeded three consecutive years. Unauthorized workers in the United States would have had 12 months from enactment to apply for the program.

Among the other provisions, the bill would have created investment accounts for the guest workers, into which the Social Security taxes paid by them and by their employers on their behalf would have been deposited. The investment accounts would have been the sole property of the guest workers. In most cases, however, distributions of account funds could have been made only after the workers had permanently left the guest worker program and returned to their home countries.

Under S. 1387, guest workers could have applied for U.S. legal permanent residency only after they had returned to their home countries. Their applications would have been evaluated based on a point system to be established by the Secretary of Homeland Security. The bill did not propose a legalization mechanism for guest workers outside of existing channels, and according to Senator Cornyn's office, guest workers would have had to meet all the relevant requirements under current law.[31]

S. 1461/H.R. 2899

The Border Security and Immigration Improvement Act (S. 1461/H.R. 2899), introduced, respectively, by Senator McCain and by Representative Kolbe for himself and Representative Flake, would have established two new temporary worker visas under the INA — the H-4A and H-4B visas. S. 1461/H.R. 2899 would have placed no numerical limit on the H-4A or H-4B visas.

The H-4A visa would have covered aliens coming to the United States to perform temporary full-time employment. An employer interested in importing H4A workers would have had to file a petition with DHS. DHS could only have approved the petition once it determined that the employer had satisfied recruitment requirements, including advertising the job opportunity to U.S. workers on an electronic job registry established by DOL and offering the job to any equally qualified U.S. worker who applied through the registry. The employer also would have had to attest in the petition that he or she: would use the employment eligibility confirmation system established by the bill to verify the alien workers' identity and employment authorization; would provide the alien workers with the same benefits, wages, and working conditions as other similarly employed workers; and did not and would not displace U.S. workers during a specified 180-day period. Aliens granted H-4A status would have been issued machine-readable, tamper-resistant visas and other documents containing biometric identifiers.

An H-4A worker's initial authorized period of staywould have been three years, and could have been extended for an additional three years. S. 1461/H.R. 2899 also would have enabled H-4A nonimmigrants to adjust to LPR status. Petitions for employment-based *immigrant* visas could have been filed by an H-4A worker's employer, or by the H-4A worker, if he or she had maintained H-4A status for at least three years. Employment-based *immigrant* visas would have been made available to H-4A workers adjusting status without numerical limitation.

The H-4B visa established by the bill would have covered aliens unlawfully present and employed in the United States since before August 1, 2003. An H-4B alien's authorized period of stay would have been three years. The alien could have applied to change to H-4A status or another nonimmigrant or immigrant category, but such a change of status could not have taken place until the end of the three years. H-4B employers would have been required to use the employment eligibility confirmation system mentioned above and to comply with specified requirements applicable to H-4A employers, including providing benefits, wages, and working conditions to H-4B workers equal to those provided to other similarly employed workers.

H.R. 3651

The Alien Accountability Act (H.R. 3651), introduced by Representative Issa, would have authorized a new "W" nonimmigrant visa category under the INA for unauthorized aliens. The category would have covered aliens unlawfully present in the United States on December 8, 2003, as well as aliens residing in foreign contiguous territory who had been habitually unlawfully present in the United States during the six-month period ending on December 8, 2003. In order to be eligible for W status, the alien would first have had to register with DHS. Employment would not have been a strict requirement for W status, but the alien would have had to demonstrate an adequate means of financial support. The new category would have sunset six years after the first alien was granted W status.

The initial period of authorized admission of a W nonimmigrant would have been one year and could have been renewed up to five times in one-year increments. H.R. 3651 would not have established a special mechanism for W nonimmigrants to adjust to LPR status. It, however, would not have precluded them from doing so if they satisfied the applicable requirements under current law.

LEGISLATION IN THE 109TH CONGRESS

As in the 108th Congress, bills were introduced in the 109th Congress to reform the H-2A and H-2B programs, to reform the "H" visa category, and to establish new temporary worker visas. An amendment based on one of the H-2B bills (S. 352/H.R. 793) was enacted as part of the FY2005 Emergency Supplemental Appropriations Act for Defense, the Global War on Terror, and Tsunami Relief (P.L. 109-13). Subsequently, the John Warner National Defense Authorization Act for FY2007 (P.L. 109-364) extended one of the temporary H-2B provisions in P.L. 109-13.

As discussed below, the Comprehensive Immigration Reform Act of 2006 (S. 2611), as passed by the Senate, would have reformed the H-2A program and established a new guest worker program for nonagricultural workers. During consideration of the Border Protection, Antiterrorism, and Illegal Immigration Control Act of 2005 (H.R. 4437) by the House Judiciary Committee and on the House floor, efforts were made to add guest worker programs and language expressing support for a guest worker program, but they were unsuccessful. H.R. 4437, as passed by the House, did not contain any guest worker provisions.

The 109th Congress also held a number of hearings on immigration issues relevant to a guest worker program. The House Judiciary Committee's Subcommittee on Immigration, Border Security, and Claims held hearings on employment eligibility verification and work site enforcement. The Senate Judiciary Committee's Subcommittee on Immigration, Border Security, and Citizenship held hearings on immigration reform issues, including the establishment of a new guest worker program. The full Senate Judiciary Committee held hearings on comprehensive immigration reform, at which two major reform proposals (S. 1033/H.R. 2330 and S. 1438) were discussed.

S. 352/H.R. 793 and Related H-2B Legislation

The Save Our Small and Seasonal Businesses Act (S. 352/H.R. 793),[32] introduced respectively by Senator Mikulski and Representative Gilchrest for themselves and bipartisan groups of cosponsors, proposed to revise the H-2B program. During Senate consideration of the FY2005 Emergency Supplemental Appropriations bill (H.R. 1268) in April 2005, Senator Mikulski offered a floor amendment based on S. 352/H.R. 793. On April 19, 2005, the Senate adopted the Mikulski Amendment, as modified, by a vote of 94 to 6, and the amendment was included in the enacted measure (P.L. 109-13) as Division B, Title IV.

The H-2B title of P.L. 109-13 caps at 33,000 the number of H-2B slots available during the first six months of a fiscal year. It also requires DHS to submit specified information to Congress on the H-2B program on a regular basis, imposes a new fraud-prevention and detection fee on H-2B employers, and authorizes DHS to impose additional penalties on H-2B employers in certain circumstances. In addition, the H-2B title of P.L. 109-13 contains a temporary provision, initially scheduled to expire at the end of FY2006, that keeps aliens who have been counted toward the H2B cap in any of the past three years from being counted again. The John Warner National Defense Authorization Act for FY2007 (P.L. 109-364; §1074) extends this returning H-2B worker exemption through FY2007. Thus, aliens who have been counted toward the H-2B cap in FY2004, FY2005, or FY2006 are not to be counted toward the FY2007 cap.

S. 2611

In March 2006, the Senate Judiciary Committee considered an immigration measure by Chairman Specter, known as the Chairman's mark. Among its many provisions, this measure, as amended and approved by the Committee, proposed to reform the H-2A program and establish a new guest worker program for nonagricultural workers. The Committee-approved measure evolved into the Comprehensive Immigration Act of 2006 (S. 2611), which the Senate passed, as amended, on May 25, 2006 on a vote of 62 to 36.

Title VI, Subtitle B of S. 2611 contained provisions on agricultural workers. These provisions were similar to those in the Agricultural Job Opportunities, Benefits, and Security Act of 2005 (AgJOBS Act; S. 359/H.R. 884), discussed below. Like S. 359/H.R. 884, Title VI, Subtitle B of S. 2611 would have streamlined the process of importing H-2A workers, particularly for jobs covered by collective bargaining agreements. Prospective H-2A employers would have had to file applications with DOL containing certain assurances. In the case of a job covered by a collective bargaining agreement, the employer would have had to assure, among other things, that there was an applicable union contract and that the bargaining representatives of the employer's employees had been notified of the filing of the application for H-2A workers. An employer interested in filling a job not covered by a collective bargaining agreement would have been subject to a longer list of required assurances. Among these, the employer would have had to assure that he or she would take specified steps to recruit U.S. workers and would provide workers with required benefits, wages, and working conditions. Both groups of employers would have had to assure that the job was temporary or seasonal and that the employer would offer the job to any equally qualified, available U.S. worker who applied. Unless an employer's application was incomplete or obviously inaccurate, DOL would have certified within seven days of the filing date that the employer had filed the required application.

Title VI, Subtitle B of S. 2611 would have made changes to the H-2A program's requirements regarding minimum benefits, wages, and working conditions. Among these proposed changes, the adverse effect wage rate (discussed above) would have remained at the January 2003 level for three years after the date of enactment, and employers would have been permitted to provide housing allowances, in lieu of housing, to their workers if the governor of the relevant state certified that adequate housing was available. An H-2A worker's initial period of employment could not have exceeded 10 months. The worker's stay could have been extended in increments of up to 10 months each, but the worker's total continuous period of stay, including any extensions, could not have exceeded three years.

Title VI, Subtitle B of S. 2611 also proposed a legalization program for agricultural workers. This program followed the basic design of the legalization program in S. 359/H.R. 884, but included different work and other requirements and used different terminology. Under the program in S. 2611, the Secretary of DHS would have conferred "blue card status" (akin to S. 359/H.R. 884's temporary resident status)[33] on an alien worker who had performed at least 863 hours, or 150 work days, of agricultural employment in the United States during the 24-month period ending on December 31, 2005, and met other requirements. No more than 1.5 million blue cards could have been issued during the five-year period beginning on the date of enactment. To be eligible to adjust to LPR status, the alien in blue card status would have had to, among other requirements, perform either at least 575 hours of U.S. agricultural work per year for the five years after enactment, or at least 863 hours of U.S. agricultural work per year for three of the five years after enactment. Existing numerical limits under the INA would not have applied to adjustments of status under the bill.[34]

Title IV, Subtitle A of S. 2611 proposed to establish a new H-2C nonagricultural guest worker visa, which, as amended on the Senate floor, would have been capped at 200,000 annually. The H-2C visa would have covered aliens coming temporarily to the United States to perform temporary labor or services other than the labor or services covered under the H-2A visa or other specified visa categories. A prospective H-2C employer would have had to file a petition with DHS. In the petition the employer would have had to attest to various items, including that the employer was offering wages to H-2C workers that were the greater of the prevailing wage rate for the occupational classification in the area of employment or the actual wage paid by the employer to other similarly employed and qualified workers; and that there were not sufficient qualified and available U.S. workers to perform the work. Prior to filing the petition, the prospective employer also would have been required to make efforts to recruit U.S. workers in accordance with DOL regulations. To be eligible for H-2C status, the alien would have needed to have evidence of employment and meet other requirements.

An H-2C worker's initial authorized period of stay would have been three years, and could have been extended for an additional three years. H-2C aliens could not have changed to another nonimmigrant visa category. As in S. 1438 (discussed below), an H-2C alien who failed to depart the United States when required to do so would have been ineligible for any immigration relief or benefit, except for specified forms of humanitarian relief. At the same time, H-2C nonimmigrants in the United States could have applied to adjust to LPR status. Petitions for employment-based *immigrant* visas could have been filed by an H-2C worker's employer or, if the H-2C worker had maintained H-2C status for a total of four years, by the worker.

S. 359/H.R. 884

The Agricultural Job Opportunities, Benefits, and Security Act of 2005 (AgJOBS Act; S. 359/H.R. 884) proposed to overhaul the H-2A agricultural worker program. The bills were introduced, respectively, by Senator Craig and Representative Cannon for themselves and bipartisan groups of cosponsors. S. 359/H.R. 884 was very similar to the AgJOBs bills before the 108th Congress (S. 1645/H.R. 3142, S. 2823). Like these bills, S. 359/H.R. 884 would have streamlined the process of importing H-2A workers, particularly for jobs covered by collective bargaining agreements. Prospective H-2A employers would have had to file applications with DOL containing certain assurances. In the case of a job covered by a collective bargaining agreement, the employer would have had to assure, among other things, that there was an applicable union contract and that the bargaining representatives of the employer's employees had been notified of the filing of the application for H-2A workers. An employer interested in filling a job not covered by a collective bargaining agreement would have been subject to a longer list of required assurances. Among these, the employer would have had to assure that he or she would take specified steps to recruit U.S. workers and would provide workers with required benefits, wages, and working conditions. Both groups of employers would have had to assure that the job was temporary or seasonal and that the employer would offer the job to any equally qualified, available U.S. worker who applied. Unless an employer's application was incomplete or obviously inaccurate, DOL would have certified within seven days of the filing date that the employer had filed the required application.

S. 359/H.R. 884 would have made changes to the H-2A program's requirements regarding minimum benefits, wages, and working conditions. Among these proposed changes, the adverse effect wage rate (discussed above) would have remained at the January 2003 level for three years after the date of enactment, and employers would have been permitted to provide housing allowances, in lieu of housing, to their workers if the governor of the relevant state certified that adequate housing was available.

Under S. 359/H.R. 884, an H-2A worker would have been admitted for an initial period of employment not to exceed 10 months. The worker's stay could have been extended in increments of up to 10 months each, but the worker's total continuous period of stay, including any extensions, could not have exceeded three years.[35]

In addition to these H-2A reform provisions, S. 359/H.R. 884 would have established a two-stage legalization program for agricultural workers. To obtain temporary resident status, the alien worker would have had to establish that he or she had performed at least 575 hours, or 100 work days, of agricultural employment in the United States during 12 consecutive months in the 18-month period ending on December 31, 2004, and meet other requirements.

To be eligible to adjust to LPR status, the alien would have had to perform at least 2,060 hours, or 360 work days, of agricultural work in the United States during the six years following the date of enactment, and meet other requirements. Existing numerical limits under the INA would not have applied to adjustments of status under the bills.[36]

H.R. 3857

The Temporary Agricultural Labor Reform Act of 2005 (H.R. 3857), an H-2A reform bill introduced by Representative Goodlatte on behalf of himself and a group of cosponsors, was a revision of a bill of the same name that he had introduced in the 108th Congress. H.R. 3857 would have streamlined the process of importing H-2A workers. Prospective H-2A employers would have had to file petitions with DHS containing certain attestations; they would not have filed applications with DOL as they currently do. Employers would have had to attest that the job was temporary or seasonal; that they would provide workers with required benefits, wages, and working conditions; that they had made efforts to recruit U.S. workers; and that they would offer the job to any equally qualified, available U.S. worker who applied. Unless an employer's application was incomplete or obviously inaccurate, DHS would have adjudicated the petition within seven days of the filing date.

H.R. 3857 would have changed current H-2A requirements regarding minimum benefits, wages, and working conditions. Under the bill, H-2A employers would have had to pay workers the higher of the prevailing wage rate or the applicable state minimum wage; employers would not have been subject to the adverse effect wage rate (discussed above). With respect to housing, employers could have provided allowances, in lieu of housing, to their workers if the governor of the relevant state certified that adequate housing was available.[37]

Under H.R. 3857, an H-2A worker would have been admitted for an initial period of employment not to exceed 10 months. The worker's stay could have been extended in increments of up to 10 months each, but the worker's total continuous period of stay, including any extensions, could not have exceeded 20 months.

S. 2087

The Agricultural Employment and Workforce Protection Act of 2005 (S. 2087), introduced by Senator Chambliss, would have reformed the H-2A program. It would have eliminated the current limitation that H-2A nonimmigrants can perform only temporary or seasonal work and would have broadened the definition of agricultural labor or services for purposes of the H-2A visa to cover labor or services relating to such activities as dairy, forestry, landscaping, and meat processing. Like S. 359/H.R. 884 and H.R. 3857, S. 2087 proposed to streamline the process of importing H-2A workers. As under H.R. 3857, a prospective H-2A employer would have filed a petition with DHS containing certain attestations. Among them, the employer would have had to attest that he or she: would provide workers with required benefits, wages, and working conditions; had made efforts to recruit U.S. workers; and would offer the job to any equally qualified, available U.S. worker who applied. Unless the petition was incomplete or obviously inaccurate, DHS would have approved or denied it not later than seven days after the filing date.

Also like S. 359/H.R. 884 and H.R. 3857, S. 2087 would have changed current H-2A requirements regarding minimum benefits, wages, and working conditions. Under S. 2087, H-2A employers would have had to pay workers the higher of the prevailing wage rate or the applicable state minimum wage; employers would not have been subject to the adverse effect wage rate (discussed above). As under both S. 359/H.R. 884 and H.R. 3857, employers could have provided housing allowances, in lieu of housing, to their workers if the governor of the relevant state certified that adequate housing was available. Under S. 2087, an H-2A worker would have been admitted for an initial period of employment of 11 months. The worker's stay could have been extended for up to two consecutive contract periods.

H.R. 3857 would not have established a mechanism for agricultural workers to obtain LPR status.

Unlike S. 359/H.R. 884 and H.R. 3857, S. 2087 would have established subcategories of H-2A nonimmigrants. It would have defined a "Level II H-2A worker" as a nonimmigrant who had been employed as an H-2A worker for at least three years and worked in a supervisory capacity. The bill would have made provision for an employer of a Level II H-2A worker, who had been employed in such status for not less than five years, to file an application for an employment-based adjustment of status for that worker. Such a Level II H-2A worker could have continued working in such status until his or her application was adjudicated. Under the bill, an "H-2AA worker" would have been defined as an H-2A worker who participated in the cross-border worker program the bill would have established. These H-2AA workers would have been allowed to enter and exit the United States each work day in accordance with DHS regulations.

In addition, the bill would have established a blue card program through which the Secretary of DHS could have conferred "blue card status" upon an alien, including an unauthorized alien, who had performed at least 1,600 hours of agricultural employment for an employer in the United States in 2005 and met other requirements. An alien could have been granted blue card status for a period of up to two years, at the end of which the alien would have had to return to his or her home country. Aliens in blue card status would not have been eligible to change to a nonimmigrant status or adjust to LPR status.

S. 278

The Summer Operations and Seasonal Equity Act of 2005 (S. 278), introduced by Senator Collins, would have made changes to the numerical limits under the H-2B program. It would have required that at least 12,000 of the total number of H-2B slots available annually (currently, 66,000) be made available in each quarter of each fiscal year. It would have exempted an alien who had been counted toward the annual H-2B numerical limit within the past three years from being counted again. Both of these provisions would have expired at the end of FY2007. S. 278 also would have required DHS to submit specified information to Congress on the H-2B program on a regular basis.

H.R. 1587

H.R. 1587, introduced by Representative Tancredo for himself and several cosponsors, would have raised the H-2B cap and placed new requirements on the H2B program. It would have increased to 131,000 the number of aliens who could be issued H-2B visas or otherwise provided H-2B status annually. Not more than half of these slots, or 65,500, would have been available during the first six months of a fiscal year. H.R. 1587 would have added new recruitment-related requirements for prospective H-2B employers, and would have mandated H-2B employer participation in the Basic Pilot program, an electronic employment eligibility verification system.

H.R. 1587 also would have imposed new requirements on H-2B nonimmigrants. Among them, these aliens could no longer have been accompanied by family members.

S. 1918

The Strengthening America's Workforce Act of 2005 (S. 1918), introduced by Senator Hagel, contained guest worker provisions similar to those in the bill he introduced in the 108th Congress. S. 1918 would have revised the H-2B visa and eliminated the current restriction that H-2B workers can perform only temporary service or labor. Instead, the bill would have required workers to perform "shortterm service or labor, lasting not more than nine months." S. 1918 also would have established a new H-2C visa for temporary workers coming to perform "labor or services, other than those occupation classifications" covered under the H-2A, H-2B, or specified high-skilled visa categories. The H-2B visa would have been capped at 100,000 annually, and the H-2C visa would have been capped at 250,000 annually.

S. 1918 would have subjected the H-2B and H-2C programs to a broad set of requirements concerning recruitment, application procedures, and worker protections, among other issues. Prior to filing an application with DOL for H-2B or H-2C workers, prospective employers would have had to take specified steps to recruit U.S. workers, including authorizing DOL to post the job on the online America's Job Bank and on local job banks. Employers also would have had to offer the job to any qualified, available U.S. worker who applied. In the application to DOL, the employer would have had to attest to various items. Among these were that the employer would offer wages to H-2B or H-2C workers that were the greater of the prevailing wage rate or the actual wage paid by the employer to other similarly employed and qualified workers, and that the employer would abide by all applicable laws and regulations relating to the rights of workers to organize. DOL would have reviewed the application for completeness and accuracy and issued a determination not later than 21 days after the filing date.

The initial period of admission for an H-2B worker could not have exceeded nine months in a one-year period. An H-2B worker's total period of admission could not have exceeded 36 months in a four-year period. The initial period of admission for an H-2C worker could not have exceeded two years and could have been extended for an additional period of up to two years. An H-2C worker's total period of admission could not have exceeded four years.

S. 1918 would have enabled H-2B and H-2C nonimmigrants to obtain LPR status. Employment-based *immigrant* visas would have been made available to these nonimmigrants without regard to existing numerical limits under the INA. An employment-based petition could have been filed by an alien's employer or collective bargaining agent or, after the alien had been employed in H-2B or H-2C status for at least three years, by the alien.

H.R. 3333

The Rewarding Employers that Abide by the Law and Guaranteeing Uniform Enforcement to Stop Terrorism Act of 2005 (H.R. 3333), introduced by Representative Tancredo, contained temporary worker provisions similar to those in the bill he had introduced in the 108th Congress. H.R. 3333 would have eliminated all the current "H" visa subcategories, including the H-2A and H-2B visas, and replaced them with a single "H" visa covering aliens coming temporarily to the United States to perform skilled or unskilled work. There would have been no cap on the H visa.

An employer interested in employing H nonimmigrants would have had to recruit U.S. workers by posting the job opportunity on America's Job Bank and would have had to offer the job to any equally qualified U.S. worker who applied. The employer would have had to file an application with DOL containing certain assurances, including that he or she had complied with the recruitment requirements.

Prospective H nonimmigrants, who could only have been admitted from abroad, would have had to apply to be included in a database of workers, which DOL would have been tasked with establishing and maintaining. Once an employer's application had been approved, DOL would have provided the employer with a list of possible job candidates from the database. Aliens admitted on H visas could not have changed to another nonimmigrant status or been adjusted to LPR status in the United States.

Under H.R. 3333, the new H visa program could not have been implemented until the Secretary of Homeland Security made certain certifications to Congress, including that a congressionally mandated automated entry-exit system was fully operational[38] and that at least 80% of aliens who overstayed their nonimmigrants visas were removed within one year of overstaying.

S. 1033/H.R. 2330

The Secure America and Orderly Immigration Act (S. 1033/H.R. 2330) was introduced, respectively, by Senator McCain and Representative Kolbe for themselves and bipartisan groups of cosponsors. It was discussed at the Senate Judiciary Committee hearings on comprehensive immigration reform held in July 2005 and October 2005. Its guest worker and legalization provisions were similar in some respects to provisions in bills from the 108th Congress, including S. 1461/H.R. 2899, S. 2010, and S. 2381/H.R. 4262. S. 1033/H.R. 2330 would have established two new temporary worker visas under the INA — the H-5A and H-5B visas. It would have capped the H-5A visa initially at 400,000, and established a process for adjusting the cap in subsequent fiscal years based on demand for the visas. It would have placed no cap on the H-5B visa.

The H-5A visa would have covered aliens coming temporarily to the United States *initially* to perform labor or services "other than those occupational classifications" covered under the H-2A or specified high-skilled visa categories. Prospective H-5A nonimmigrants would have filed visa applications on their own behalf. Employers would not have filed petitions with DHS for them, as they currently do to employ other nonimmigrant workers. Under S. 1033/H.R. 2330, the Secretary of State could have granted an H-5A visa to an alien who demonstrated an intent to perform work covered by the visa. To be eligible for H-5A status, an alien would have needed to have evidence of employment and to meet other requirements. Before hiring a prospective H-5A worker, an employer would have had to post the job opportunity on a DOL electronic job registry to recruit U.S. workers. H-5A employers also would have been required to comply with all applicable federal, state, and local laws, and to use an employment eligibility confirmation system, to be established by the Social Security Administration, to verify the employment eligibility of newly hired H-5A workers.

An H-5A worker's initial authorized period of stay would have been three years, and could have been extended for an additional three years. Under S. 1033/H.R. 2330, H-5A nonimmigrants in the United States could have adjusted to LPR status. Petitions for employment-based *immigrant* visas could have been filed by an H-5A worker's employer or, if the H-5A worker had maintained H-5A status for a total of four years, by the worker.

The H-5B visa established by the bill would have covered aliens present and employed in the United States since before May 12, 2005. Aliens lawfully present in the United States as nonimmigrants on that date would not have been eligible for H-5B status. An H-5B alien's authorized period of stay would have been six years. At the end of that six-year period, the alien could have applied to adjust to LPR status, subject to various requirements. Such adjustments of status would not have been subject to numerical limitations.

S. 1438

The Comprehensive Enforcement and Immigration Reform Act of 2005 (S. 1438) was introduced by Senator Cornyn for himself and Senator Kyl. Like S. 1033/H.R. 2330, it was discussed at the Senate Judiciary Committee hearings on comprehensive immigration reform held in July 2005 and October 2005. It would have established a new "W" temporary worker visa under the INA. S. 1438 would not have placed a cap on the W visa, but would have authorized DOL to do so in the future based on the recommendations of a task force the bill would have established. In addition, S. 1438 would have amended the INA to authorize DHS to grant a new status — Deferred Mandatory Departure (DMD) status — to certain unauthorized aliens in the United States. It would have placed no limit on the number of aliens who could have received that status.

The W visa would have covered aliens coming temporarily to the United States to perform temporary labor or service other than that covered under the H-2A or specified high-skilled visa categories. S. 1438 would have repealed the H-2B visa category. Prospective W nonimmigrants would have filed applications on their own behalf. Employers would not have filed petitions with DHS on behalf of W workers, as they currently do to employ other nonimmigrant workers. Under S. 1438, the Secretary of State could have granted a W visa to an alien who demonstrated an intent to perform eligible work. To be eligible for W status, the alien would have needed to have evidence of employment, among other requirements. An employer interested in hiring a W nonimmigrant would have had to apply for authorization to do so through an Alien Employment Management System to be established by DHS. Before an employer could have been granted such authorization, he or she would have had to post the position on a DOL electronic job registry and offer the position to any equally qualified U.S. worker who applied. S. 1438 would have made it mandatory for all employers, including W employers, to verify the employment eligibility of new hires through an electronic system. Current electronic employment eligibility verification is conducted through the largely voluntary Basic Pilot program.

A W nonimmigrant's authorized period of stay would have been two years, and could *not* have been extended. After residing in his or her home country for one year, however, an alien could have been readmitted to the United States in W status. An alien's total period of admission as a W nonimmigrant could not have exceeded six years. These stay limitations would not have applied to aliens who spent less than six months a year in W status, or who commuted to the United States to work in W status but resided outside the country. S. 1438 would have made W nonimmigrants ineligible to change to another nonimmigrant status and would not have provided them with any special mechanism to obtain LPR status. Furthermore, a W nonimmigrant who did not depart the United States when required to do so would have been ineligible for any immigration benefit or relief, except for specified forms of humanitarian relief.

Aliens present in the United States since July 20, 2004, and employed since before July 20, 2005, could have applied to DHS for Deferred Mandatory Departure (DMD) status. Aliens lawfully present in the United States as nonimmigrants would not have been eligible. DHS could have granted an alien DMD status for a period of up to five years. Employers interested in employing aliens granted DMD status would have had to apply for authorization through the Alien Employment Management System mentioned above. Aliens in DMD status could not have applied to change to a nonimmigrant status or, unless otherwise eligible under INA §245(i), to adjust to LPR status.[39] Aliens who complied with the terms of DMD status and departed prior to its expiration date would not have been subject to the INA provision that bars previously unlawfully present aliens from being admitted to the United States for 3 or 10 years, depending on the length of their unlawful stay.[40] If otherwise eligible, these aliens could immediately have sought admission as nonimmigrants or immigrants. However, they would not have received any special consideration for admission. Aliens granted DMD status who failed to depart prior to the expiration of that status would have been ineligible for any immigration benefit or relief, except for specified forms of humanitarian relief, for 10 years.

H.R. 4065

The Temporary Worker Registration and Visa Act of 2005 (H.R. 4065), introduced by Representative Osborne, would have established a process for registering aliens who had been continuously unlawfully present and employed in the United States since January 1, 2005. Eligible aliens would have applied for this registration, which would have been valid for six months. Registered aliens would have been given work authorization and would have been eligible for a new "W" temporary worker visa established by the bill. To obtain a W visa, a registered alien would have had to apply at a consular office in his or her home country not later than six months after his or her registration was approved. H.R. 4065 would have placed no numerical limit on the W visa.

The initial period of authorized admission for a W nonimmigrant would have been three years and could have been extended in three year increments without limit.

H.R. 4065 would have required that W nonimmigrants be continuously employed but would have placed no restriction on the type of work they could perform. W nonimmigrants would not have been prohibited from changing to another nonimmigrant classification or adjusting to LPR status. H.R. 4065, however, would have made no special provision for them to do so.

LEGISLATION IN THE 110TH CONGRESS

Bills have been introduced in the 110th Congress to reform the H-2A program and the H-2B program and to establish new temporary worker visas. The House Judiciary Committee's Subcommittee on Immigration, Citizenship, Refugees, Border Security, and International Law also has held hearings related to guest worker programs.

S. 237/S. 340/H.R. 371

The Agricultural Job Opportunities, Benefits, and Security Act of 2007 (AgJOBS Act; S. 237/S. 340/H.R. 371) proposes to overhaul the H-2A agricultural worker program. The Senate bills were introduced by Senator Feinstein and have a bipartisan group of cosponsors. The House companion was introduced by Representative Berman and also has bipartisan cosponsorship. The provisions of the AgJOBS Act of 2007 are similar to those included in S. 2611, as passed by the Senate in the 109th Congress (discussed above).

The AgJOBS Act of 2007 would streamline the process of importing H-2A workers, particularly for jobs covered by collective bargaining agreements. Prospective H-2A employers would have to file applications with DOL containing certain assurances. In the case of a job covered by a collective bargaining agreement, the employer would have to assure, among other things, that there is an applicable union contract and that the bargaining representatives of the employer's employees have been notified of the filing of the application for H-2A workers. An employer interested in filling a job not covered by a collective bargaining agreement would be subject to a longer list of required assurances. Among these, the employer would have to assure that he or she will take specified steps to recruit U.S. workers and will provide workers with required benefits, wages, and working conditions. Both groups of employers would have to assure that the job is temporary or seasonal and that the employer will offer the job to any equally qualified, available U.S. worker who applies. Unless an employer's application is incomplete or obviously inaccurate, DOL would have to certify within seven days of the filing date that the employer had filed the required application. The employer could then file a petition with DHS for H-2A workers.

The AgJOBS Act of 2007 would likewise make changes to the H-2A program's requirements regarding minimum benefits, wages, and working conditions. Among these proposed changes, the adverse effect wage rate (discussed above) would remain at the January 2003 level for three years after the date of enactment, and employers would be permitted to provide housing allowances, in lieu of housing, to their workers if the governor of the relevant state certifies that adequate housing is available. An H-2A worker's initial period of employment could not exceed 10 months. The worker's stay could be extended in increments of up to 10 months each, but the worker's total continuous period of stay, including any extensions, could not exceed three years.

The AgJOBS Act of 2007 also proposes a legalization program for agricultural workers similar to that included in S. 2611, as passed by the Senate in the 109th Congress. Under the program, the Secretary of DHS would grant "blue card status" to an alien worker who had performed at least 863 hours, or 150 work days, of agricultural employment in the United States during the 24-month period ending on December 31, 2006, and meets other requirements. No more than 1.5 million blue cards could be issued during the five-year period beginning on the date of enactment. To be eligible to adjust to LPR status, the alien in blue card status would have to, among other requirements, perform either at least 100 workdays of U.S. agricultural work per year for the five years after enactment, or at least 150 workdays of U.S. agricultural work per year for the three years after enactment.[41] Existing numerical limits under the INA would not apply to adjustments of status under the bill.[42]

H.R. 1645

The Security Through Regularized Immigration and a Vibrant Economy Act of 2007 (STRIVE Act; H.R. 1645), introduced by Representative Gutierrez for himself and a bipartisan group of cosponsors, includes the AgJOBS Act of 2007 (described above) as Title VI, Subtitle C. In addition, Title IV of H.R. 1645 proposes to establish a new H-2C temporary worker program. The new H-2C visa would cover aliens coming temporarily to the United States to initially perform temporary labor or services other than the labor or services covered under the H-2A visa or other specified visa categories. A prospective H-2C employer would have to file a petition with DOL. In the petition the employer would have to attest to various items, including that the employer is offering wages to H-2C workers that are the greater of the prevailing wage rate for the occupational classification in the area of employment or the actual wage paid by the employer to other similarly employed and qualified workers; and that there are not sufficient qualified and available U.S. workers to perform the work. In most cases, prior to filing the petition, the prospective employer also would have to make efforts to recruit U.S. workers, as specified in the bill. To be eligible for H-2C status, the alien would need to have evidence of employment and meet other requirements.

An H-2C worker's initial authorized period of stay would be three years, and could be extended for an additional three years. H-2C nonimmigrants in the United States could apply to adjust to LPR status. Petitions for employment-based *immigrant* visas could be filed by an H-2C worker's employer or, if the alien had been employed as an H-2C worker for a total of five years, by the worker.

S. 330

The Border Security and Immigration Reform Act of 2007 (S. 330), introduced by Senator Isakson, would establish a new W temporary worker program for agricultural or nonagricultural workers. The guest worker provisions are in Title III, §302 of the bill. An employer interested in importing W workers would first apply to DOL for labor certification. After receiving certification, the employer would file an application with DHS, as required by DHS. Aliens who have been unlawfully employed in the United States since January 1, 2007, could participate in the new program if they apply for registration and meet other requirements, as set forth in §301 of the bill. W visas would be issued for an initial period of up to two years and could be renewed for an unlimited number of two-year terms. The guest worker and registration provisions in S. 330 would not take effect, however, until after the Secretary of DHS certifies that specified border security and enforcement-related measures authorized under other titles of the bill are fully operational.

S. 1639

S. 1639, introduced by Senator Kennedy, is based on S.Amdt. 1150, as amended on the Senate floor in late May and early June 2007.[43] Among its many provisions, S. 1639 would repeal the H-2B program, reform the H-2A program, and establish new guest worker programs. The Senate began consideration of S. 1639 in late June 2007.

Agricultural Workers

The H-2A reform provisions are in Title IV, Subtitle B of S. 1639. These provisions are similar to those in S. 237/S. 340/H.R. 371 before the 110th Congress, and in S. 2611, as passed by the Senate in the 109th Congress (these proposals are discussed above). Section 404 of S. 1639 would streamline the process of importing H-2A workers, particularly for jobs covered by collective bargaining agreements. Prospective H-2A employers would have to file applications with DOL containing certain assurances. In the case of a job covered by a collective bargaining agreement, the employer would have to ensure, among other things, that there is an applicable union contract and that the bargaining representatives of the employer's employees have been notified of the filing of the application for H-2A workers. An employer interested in filling a job not covered by a collective bargaining agreement would be subject to a longer list of required assurances.

Among these, the employer would have to ensure that he or she will take specified steps to recruit U.S. workers and will provide workers with required benefits, wages, and working conditions. Both groups of employers would have to ensure that the job is temporary or seasonal and that the employer will offer the job to any equally qualified, available U.S. worker who applies. Unless an employer's application is incomplete or obviously inaccurate, DOL would have to certify within seven days of the filing date that the employer had filed the required application. The employer could then file a petition with DHS for H-2A workers.

Section 404 of S. 1639 would likewise make changes to the H-2A program's requirements regarding minimum benefits, wages, and working conditions. Among these proposed changes, the adverse effect wage rate (discussed above) would remain at the January 2003 level for three years after the date of enactment, and employers would be permitted to provide housing allowances, in lieu of housing, to their workers if the governor of the relevant state certifies that adequate housing is available. Unlike in S. 237/S. 340/H.R. 371 in the 110th Congress and in S. 2611, as passed by the Senate in the 109th Congress, an H-

2A worker's maximum continuous period of authorized status would be 10 months. The worker could not again apply for admission to the United States as an H-2A worker until he or she had been outside the country for a period of time, as specified.

In addition to these H-2A reform provisions, S. 1639 proposes a legalization process for agricultural workers in Title VI, Subtitle C. Under Section 622, the Secretary of DHS would grant a Z-A nonimmigrant visa to an alien worker who had performed at least 863 hours, or 150 work days, of agricultural employment in the United States during the 24-month period ending on December 31, 2006, and meets other requirements, including payment of a $100 fine. No more than 1.5 million Z-A visas could be issued. Spouses or minor children of Z-A nonimmigrants would be eligible for Z-A dependent visas, which would not be subject to a numerical limit. Not later than eight years after enactment, Z-A nonimmigrants would have to either renew the alien's Z visa status or apply to adjust to LPR status. With respect to the latter option, the Secretary of DHS would adjust the status of a Z-A alien to that of an LPR if specified requirements are met. The alien would have to perform either at least 100 workdays of U.S. agricultural work per year for the five years after enactment, or at least 150 workdays of U.S. agricultural work per year for the three years after enactment.[44] The other requirements would include payment of a $400 fine and payment of applicable federal taxes. The Z-A nonimmigrant would have to file the application for adjustment of status in person with a U.S. consulate abroad. Existing numerical limits under the INA would not apply to adjustments of status of Z-A or Z-A dependent aliens under the bill.[45]

Y Nonimmigrants

Title IV, Subtitle A of S. 1639 proposes to establish a new Y temporary worker visa category. The Y-1 visa would cover aliens coming temporarily to the United States to perform temporary labor or services other than the labor or services covered under specified nonimmigrant visas for high-skilled workers and others. The Y-1 visa program would sunset after five years. The Y-2 visa would cover aliens coming temporarily to the United States to perform seasonal nonagricultural labor or services.[46] The Y-3 visa would cover the spouses or children of Y-1 or Y-2 aliens. A prospective employer of Y nonimmigrants would have to file an application for labor certification with DOL that includes attestations regarding U.S. worker protections, wages, and other items. The employer would have to make efforts to recruit U.S. workers prior to filing the labor certification application. After receiving certification from DOL, the employer would file a petition with DHS to import Y workers.

Y-1 nonimmigrants would be granted a period of admission of two years. This period could be extended for two additional two-year periods.[47] Between each two-year period of admission, however, the alien would have to be physically present outside the United States for 12 months. Y-2B nonimmigrants[48] would be granted a period of admission of 10 months. Following this period, they would need to be physically present outside the United States for two months before they could be readmitted to the country in Y status. There would be no limit on the number of times a Y-2B nonimmigrant could be so readmitted.

Section 409 of S. 1639 proposes annual numerical limits on the Y visas. The annual cap on the Y-1 visa would be 200,000. The Y-3 visa would be capped at 20% of the Y-1 visa annual limit The Y-2 visa would be capped at 100,000 for the first fiscal year. In subsequent years, the cap would increase or decrease based on demand for the visas, subject to a maximum cap of 200,000. In addition, §409 would establish an exemption from the Y-2B cap for workers who have been present in the United States as Y-2B aliens in any one of the three fiscal years preceding the start date of the new petition.

Z Nonimmigrants

S. 1639 also would establish another new nonimmigrant category (the Z category) for certain alien workers in the United States. Although the Z category would not be a traditional nonimmigrant worker category and would provide a mechanism for certain unauthorized aliens to legalize their status,[49] aliens granted Z status would have work authorization (and some Z aliens would be required to be employed full-time) and may perform the same type of lower-skilled work as guest workers. Under Section 601 of S. 1639, the Secretary of DHS could permit Z aliens to remain lawfully in the United States under specified conditions.

The Z-1 classification would cover aliens who have been continuously physically present in the United States since January 1, 2007, and are employed. The Z-2 and Z-3 classification would cover specified family members of Z-1 aliens, where the family members have been continuously physically present in the United States since January 1, 2007. An alien making an initial application for Z-1 status would have to pay a $1,000 penalty, as well as a $500 penalty for each alien seeking Z-2 or Z-3 status as the Z-1 applicant's derivative. Section 601 of S. 1639 would provide for certain applicants for Z status to receive probationary benefits in the form of employment authorization pending final adjudication of their applications. The period of admission for a Z nonimmigrant would be four years. Provided that the Z nonimmigrant continued to be eligible for nonimmigrant status and met additional specified requirements, the alien could seek an unlimited number of four-year extensions of the period of admission. There would be no limitation on the number of aliens who could be granted Z-1, Z-2, or Z-3 status.

The Secretary of DHS could adjust the status of a Z nonimmigrant to LPR status if specified requirements are met. Among the requirements for a Z-1 nonimmigrant to adjust status, the alien would need to have an approved immigrant petition; file an adjustment of status application in person at a U.S. consulate abroad; and, if the alien is a head of household, pay a $4,000 penalty at the time of submission of the immigrant petition.

BUSH ADMINISTRATION PROPOSAL

On January 7, 2004, President Bush outlined an immigration reform proposal, at the center of which was a new temporary worker program.[50] The President featured this proposal in his 2004, 2005, and 2006 State of the Union addresses. According to a 2004 White House fact sheet on the proposal, the temporary worker program would "match willing foreign workers with willing U.S. employers when no Americans can be found to fill the jobs." The program, which would grant participants legal temporary status, would initially be open to both foreign workers abroad and unauthorized aliens within the United States. At some future date, however, it would be restricted to aliens outside the country. The temporary workers' authorized period of stay would be three years and would be renewable for an unspecified period of time. Temporary workers would be able to travel back and forth between their home countries and the United States, and, as stated in the background briefing for reporters, would "enjoy the same protections that American workers have with respect to wages and employment rights." The proposal also called for increased workplace enforcement of immigration laws.

The proposal would not establish a special mechanism for participants in the temporary worker program to obtain LPR status. According to the fact sheet, the program "should not permit undocumented workers to gain an advantage over those who have followed the rules." Temporary workers would be expected to return to their home countries at the end of their authorized period of stay, and the Administration favored providing them with economic incentives to do so. As stated in the fact sheet:

> The U.S. will work with other countries to allow aliens working in the U.S. to receive credit in their nations' retirement systems and will support the creation of tax-preferred savings accounts they can collect when they return to their native countries.

Although it does not include a permanent legalization mechanism, the program would not prohibit temporary workers from applying for legal permanent residency under existing immigration law.

According to the Administration, the proposed temporary worker program should support efforts to improve homeland security by controlling the U.S. borders. The fact sheet states that "the program should link to efforts to control our border through agreements with countries whose nationals participate in the program," but does not elaborate further on this issue.

At the October 2005 Senate Judiciary Committee hearing on comprehensive immigration reform, Labor Secretary Elaine Chao reiterated the Administration's support for the immigration reform ideas that President Bush outlined in January 2004.[51] She did not offer a detailed legislative proposal and did not take a position on any of the pending immigration reform bills. Secretary Chao described the Administration's plan as having three components — border security, interior enforcement, and a temporary worker program — and not allowing "amnesty." She maintained that "an improved temporary worker program will enhance border security and interior enforcement by providing a workable and enforceable process for hiring foreign workers."

Both in her written testimony and in responses to Senators' questions, Secretary Chao made some general statements about the type of temporary worker program the Administration favors. She made reference to "streamlining the process so that willing workers can efficiently be matched with employers ... [when] there are no willing U.S. workers." Although she did not describe this streamlined process, she did state that private for-profit or nonprofit organizations could play a role in matching employers and workers. She also explained that under the President's temporary worker program, prospective employers would be subject to labor certification, as they currently are under the H-2A and H-2B programs. In describing how the President's program would overcome problems in existing guest worker programs, Secretary Chao referred generally to "a technologically advanced new system" through which "workers will have visa documentation that clearly establishes their eligibility to work" and "employers will have access to a verification system that enables them to quickly check the eligibility and verify the identity of potential employees."

On May 15, 2006, during Senate consideration of immigration reform legislation,[52] President Bush gave a national address on immigration reform. He voiced support for comprehensive immigration reform that accomplished five objectives, including creation of a temporary worker program. The President maintained that a temporary worker program was needed to secure U.S. borders, another of his five objectives. The President outlined the type of program he favors, as follows:

> I support a temporary worker program that would create a legal path for foreign workers to enter our country in an orderly way, for a limited period of time. This program would match willing foreign workers with willing American employers for jobs Americans are not doing. Every worker who applies for the program would be required to pass criminal background checks. And temporary workers must return to their home country at the conclusion of their stay.

POLICY CONSIDERATIONS

Issues raised in connection with temporary worker programs — such as U.S. economic development, Mexican economic development, law enforcement, and worker protections — coupled with the U.S. experience with the H-2A and H-2B programs, suggest policy issues likely to arise in the evaluation of guest worker proposals.

Comparison of Program Requirements

A new guest worker program could include agricultural workers or nonagricultural workers or both. It could replace or supplement one or both of the existing H-2A and H-2B programs. The assessment of any proposed program would likely include a comparison of the requirements of the proposed and existing programs, especially in the case of a new program covering both agricultural and nonagricultural workers since current H-2A and H-2B requirements vary considerably.

The area of wages provides an example. Under the H-2B program, employers must pay their workers at least the prevailing wage rate. Employers importing agricultural workers through the H-2A program are subject to potentially higher wage requirements. As explained above, they must pay their workers the highest of the minimum wage, the prevailing wage rate, or the AEWR. Therefore, a new guest worker program that covered both agricultural and nonagricultural workers and included a unified wage requirement would represent a change in existing wage requirements for employers.

Eligible Population

A guest worker program could be limited to aliens within the country (many of whom presumably would be unauthorized aliens) or to aliens outside the country or could include both groups. The possible participation of illegal aliens in a guest worker program is controversial. Some parties would likely see their inclusion as rewarding lawbreakers and encouraging future unauthorized immigration, especially if the program enabled some participants to obtain LPR status. The option of excluding unauthorized aliens has raised another set of concerns. Some observers maintain that a large guest worker program limited to new workers could leave unauthorized aliens in the United States particularly vulnerable to exploitation by unscrupulous employers. More generally, many who view a guest worker program as a means of addressing the unauthorized alien problem see the inclusion of unauthorized aliens as integral to any proposal.

Another eligibility question is whether the program would be limited to nationals of certain countries. The Bush Administration began discussion of a guest worker program with Mexico in 2001 as part of binational migration talks, and some immigration experts maintain that "there are very good reasons for crafting a special immigration relationship with Mexico, given its propinquity, its historical ties and NAFTA."[53] Some immigrant advocacy groups, however, have argued that it would be unfair to single out Mexicans for special treatment, especially if legalization were part of the agreement.[54]

Legalization of Program Participants

The issue of whether to include a legalization or *earned adjustment* program as part of a guest worker proposal is controversial. *Earned adjustment* is the term used to describe legalization programs that require prospective beneficiaries to "earn" LPR status through work and/or other contributions. Some see permanent legalization as an essential element of a guest worker proposal,[55] while others oppose the inclusion of any type of LPR adjustment program. In the current debate, reference is often made to two legalization programs established by the Immigration Reform and Control Act (IRCA) of 1986: (1) a general program for unauthorized aliens who had been continually resident in the United States since before January 1, 1982; and (2)

President Bush was asked in July 2001 whether an immigration proposal under consideration at the time to legalize the status of some unauthorized Mexicans would be expanded to cover immigrants from other countries. The President responded, "We'll consider all folks here," but did not provide further details. See Edwin Chen and Jonathan Peterson, "Bush Hints at Broader Amnesty," *Los Angeles Times*, July 27, 2001, Part A, part 1, p. 1. a special agricultural worker (SAW) program for aliens who had worked at least 90 days in seasonal agriculture during a designated year-long period.[56] Approximately 2.7 million individuals have adjusted to LPR status under these programs.[57]

Recent H-2A reform bills suggest a willingness on the part of some policymakers to establish an earned adjustment program, at least for agricultural workers. A key set of questions about any legalization mechanism proposed as part of a guest worker program would concern the proposed legalization process and associated requirements. Major H-2A reform proposals introduced in the 107th Congress (S. 1313/H.R. 2736 and S. 1161), for example, would have established similarly structured earned adjustment programs for agricultural workers. Under both proposals, workers who had performed a requisite amount of agricultural work could have applied for temporary resident status. After satisfying additional work requirements in subsequent years, they could have applied for LPR status. The applicable requirements in the proposals, however, differed significantly. For temporary resident status, S. 1313/H.R. 2736 would have required the alien to have performed at least 540 hours, or 90 work days, of agricultural work during a 12month period. S. 1161 would have required at least 900 hours, or 150 work days, of agricultural work during a similar period. To qualify for adjustment to LPR status, S. 1313/H.R. 2736 would have required at least 540 hours, or 90 work days, of agricultural work in each of three years during a four-year period. S. 1161 would have required at least 900 hours, or 150 work days, of agricultural work in each of four years during a specified six-year period.

Various issues and concerns raised in connection with such earned adjustment proposals for agricultural workers may be relevant in assessing other guest worker legalization programs. Among these issues is the feasibility of program participants' meeting the applicable requirements to obtain legal status. S. 1161, for example, was criticized for incorporating work requirements for legalization that, some observers said, many agricultural workers could not satisfy. It also has been argued that multiyear work requirements could lead to exploitation, if workers were loathe to complain about work-related matters for fear of being fired before they had worked the requisite number of years. A possible countervailing set of considerations involves the continued availability of workers for low-skilled industries, such as agriculture, meat packing, and services industries. Some parties have expressed a general concern that a quick legalization process with light work requirements could soon deprive employers of needed workers, if some newly legalized workers were to leave certain industries to pursue more desirable job opportunities.

Treatment of Family Members

The treatment of family members under a guest worker proposal is likely to be an issue. Currently, the INA allows for the admission of the spouses and minor children of alien workers on H-2A, H-2B and other "H" visas who are accompanying the worker or following to join the worker in the United States. In considering any new program, one question would be whether guest workers coming from abroad could be accompanied by their spouses and children.

If the guest worker program in question were open to unauthorized aliens in the United States, the issue of family members would become much more complicated. Relevant questions would include the following: Would the unauthorized spouse and/or minor children of the prospective guest worker be granted some type of legal temporary resident status under the program? If not, would they be expected to leave, or be removed from, the country? If the program had a legalization component, would the spouse and children be eligible for LPR status as derivatives of the guest worker?

The treatment of family members became a significant issue in the 1986 legalization programs described above. As enacted, IRCA required all aliens to qualify for legalization on their own behalf; it made no provision for granting derivative LPR status to spouses and children. Legalized aliens, thus, needed to file immigrant visa petitions on behalf of their family members. These filings were primarily in the family preference category covering spouses and children of LPRs (category 2A) and had the effect of lengthening waiting times in this category.[58] To partially address the increased demand for visa numbers, the Immigration Act of 1990[59] made a limited number of additional visa numbers available for spouses and children of IRCA-legalized aliens for FY1992 through FY1994. It also provided for temporary stays of deportation and work authorization for certain spouses and children of IRCA-legalized aliens in the United States.

As suggested by the experience of the IRCA programs, the treatment of family members in any guest worker program with a legalization component could have broad implications for the U.S. immigration system. Even in the absence of a legalization component, however, the treatment of family members in a guest worker program could have important ramifications. With respect to the program itself, for example, it could affect the willingness of aliens to apply to participate.

Labor Market Test

A key question about any guest worker program is the type of labor market conditions that would have to exist, if any, in order for an employer to import alien workers.[60] Under both the H-2A and H-2B programs, employers interested in hiring foreign workers must first go through the process of labor certification. Intended to protect job opportunities for U.S. workers, labor certification entails a determination of whether qualified U.S. workers are available to perform the needed work and whether the hiring of foreign workers will adversely affect the wages and working conditions of similarly employed U.S. workers. As described above, recruitment is the primary method used to determine U.S. worker availability. While there is widespread agreement on the goals of labor certification, the process itself has been criticized for being cumbersome, slow, and ineffective in protecting U.S. workers.[61]

A proposed guest worker program could retain some form of labor certification or could establish a different process for determining if employers could bring in foreign workers. As described above, past legislative proposals to reform the H-2A program sought to overhaul current labor certification requirements by, for example, establishing a system of worker registries. Another option suggested by some in H2A reform debates is to adopt the more streamlined labor market test used in the temporary worker program for professional specialty workers (H-1B program). That test, known as labor attestation, requires employers to attest to various conditions. Some argue that labor attestation is inadequate for unskilled jobs without educational requirements. Assuming that protecting U.S. workers remained a policy priority, the labor market test incorporated in any guest worker program would need to be evaluated to determine whether it would likely serve this purpose.

Numerical Limits

Related to the issues of labor market tests and U.S. worker protections is the question of numerical limitations on a guest worker program. A numerical cap provides a means, separate from the labor market test, of limiting the number of foreign workers. Currently, as explained above, the H-2A program is not numerically limited, while the H-2B program is capped at 66,000 annually. Like the H-2B program, other capped temporary worker programs have fixed statutory numerical limits. By contrast, a guest worker program that was outlined by former Senator Phil Gramm during the 107th Congress, but never introduced as legislation, included a different type of numerical cap — one that would have varied annually based on regional unemployment rates. According to the program prospectus released by Senator Gramm:

Except for seasonal work, the number of guest workers permitted to enroll would be adjusted annually in response to changes in U.S. economic conditions, specifically unemployment rates, on a region-by-region basis.

Numerical limitations also are relevant in the context of unauthorized immigration. Some view a temporary worker program as a way to begin reducing the size of the current unauthorized alien population and/or future inflows. In light of the estimated current size and annual growth rate of the unauthorized population, it could be argued that a guest worker program would need to be sizeable to have any significant impact. On the other hand, critics contend that a guest worker program, especially a large one, would be a counterproductive means of controlling unauthorized immigration. In their view, temporary worker programs serve to increase, not reduce, the size of the unauthorized population.

Enforcement

Another important consideration is how the terms of a guest worker program would be enforced. Relevant questions include what types of mechanisms would be used to ensure that employers complied with program requirements. With respect to the H-2A program, for example, the INA authorizes the Labor Secretary to —

> take such actions, including imposing appropriate penalties and seeking appropriate injunctive relief and specific performance of contractual obligations, as may be necessary to assure employer compliance with terms and conditions of employment ...[62]

A related question is whether the enforcement system would be complaint-driven or whether the appropriate entity could take action in the absence of a specific complaint.

Another enforcement-related question is what type of mechanism, if any, would be used to ensure that guest workers departed the country at the end of their authorized period of stay. Historically, the removal of aliens who have overstayed their visas and thereby lapsed into unauthorized status, but have not committed crimes, has not been a priority of the U.S. immigration system. Some have suggested that a large scale guest worker program could help address the problem of visa overstaying and unauthorized immigration generally by severely limiting job opportunities for unauthorized aliens. Others doubt, however, that large numbers of unauthorized residents would voluntarily leave the country; as explained above, they argue instead that a new guest worker program would likely increase the size of the unauthorized alien population as many guest workers opted to overstay their visas.

Other ideas have been put forth to facilitate the departure of temporary workers at the end of their authorized period of stay. One suggestion is to involve the workers' home countries in the guest worker program. Another option is to create an incentive for foreign workers to leave the United States by, for example, withholding or otherwise setting aside a sum of money for each worker that would only become available once the worker returned home. In evaluating any such financially based incentive system, it may be useful to consider, among other questions, how much money would be available to a typical worker and whether such an amount would likely provide an adequate incentive to return home.

Homeland Security

A final consideration relates to border and homeland security, matters of heightened concern since the terrorist attacks of September 11, 2001. Supporters of new temporary worker programs argue that such programs would make the United States more secure. They cite security-related benefits of knowing the identities of currently unknown individuals in the country and of legalizing the inflow of alien workers and thereby freeing border personnel to concentrate on potential criminal and terrorist threats. Opponents reject the idea that guest worker programs improve homeland security and generally focus on the dangers of rewarding immigration law violators with temporary or permanent legal status. Security concerns may affect various aspects of a temporary worker program. Possible security-related provisions that may be considered as part of a new guest worker program include special screening of participants, monitoring while in the United States, and issuance of fraud-resistant documents.

CONCLUSION

The question of a new guest worker program is controversial. A key reason for this is the interrelationship between the recent discussion of guest worker programs and the issue of unauthorized immigration. The size of the current resident unauthorized alien population in the United States, along with continued unauthorized immigration and related deaths at the U.S.-Mexico border, are major factors cited in support of a new temporary worker program. At the same time, the importance of enforcing immigration law and not rewarding illegal aliens with any type of legalized status are primary reasons cited in opposition to such a program. It would seem that some bridging of this gap on the unauthorized alien question — perhaps in some of the areas analyzed above — would be a prerequisite to gaining broad support for a guest worker proposal.

REFERENCES

[1]   For additional information on these historical programs, see U.S. Congress, Senate Committee on the Judiciary, *Temporary Worker Programs: Background and Issues*, committee print, 96th Cong., 2nd sess., February 1980.

[2]   Act of June 27, 1952, ch. 477, codified at 8 U.S.C.§1101 *et seq.* The INA is the basis of current immigration law.

[3]   P.L. 99-603, November 6, 1986.

[4]   For an overview of the INA's nonimmigrant visa categories, see CRS Report RL31381, *U.S. Immigration Policy on Temporary Admissions*, by Ruth Ellen Wasem, and Chad C. Haddal.

[5]   While H-2B workers are, for the most part, low skilled, the H-2B program is not limited to workers of a particular skill level and has been used to import a variety of workers, including entertainers and athletes.

[6]   Prior to March 1, 2003, the H-2A and H-2B programs were administered by ETA and the Immigration and Naturalization Service (INS) of the Department of Justice. The

Homeland Security Act of 2002 (P.L. 107-296, November 25, 2002) abolished INS and transferred most of its functions to DHS as of March 1.

[7]   The prevailing wage rate is the average wage paid to similarly employed workers in the occupation in the area of intended employment. Additional information about prevailing wages is available at [*http://www. foreignlaborcert.doleta.gov/wages.cfm*].

[8]   The AEWR is an hourly wage rate set by DOL for each state or region, based upon data gathered by the Department of Agriculture in quarterly wage surveys. For 2006, the AEWR ranges from $7.58 for Arkansas, Louisiana, and Mississippi to $9.99 for Hawaii. See CRS Report RL32861, *Farm Labor: The Adverse Effect Wage Rate (AEWR)*, by William G. Whittaker.

[9]   Required wages and benefits under the H-2A program are set forth in 20 C.F.R. §655.102.

[10] H-2A workers, like nonimmigrants generally, are not eligible for federally funded public assistance, with the exception of Medicaid emergency services. For further information on alien eligibility for federal benefits, see CRS Report RL31114, *Noncitizen Eligibility for Major Federal Public Assistance Programs: Policies and Legislation*, by Ruth Ellen Wasem (Hereafter cited as CRS Report RL31114); and CRS Report RL31630, *Federal Funding for Unauthorized Aliens' Emergency Medical Expenses*, by Alison M. Siskin.

[11] There is no precise measure available of the number of the aliens granted H-2A status in any given year. While visa data provide an approximation, these data are subject to limitations, among them that not all H-2A workers are necessarily issued visas and not all aliens who are issued visas necessarily use them to enter the United States.

[12] For additional discussion, see CRS Report RL30395, *Farm Labor Shortages and Immigration Policy*, by Linda Levine.

[13] Included in this three-year period is any time an H-2B alien spent in the United States under the "H" (temporary worker) or "L" (temporary intracompany transferee) visa categories.

[14] While not subject to the broader transportation requirements of the H-2A program, H-2B employers are required by law to pay the reasonable costs of return transportation abroad for an H-2B worker who is dismissed prior to the end of his or her authorized period of stay.

[15] The proposed USCIS rule is available at [*http://a257.g.akamaitech.net/7/257/2422/01jan20051800/edocket.access.gpo.gov/2005/05-1240.htm*].   DOL   has published a companion proposal, which is available at [*http:// a257.g.akamaitech.net/7/257/2422/01jan20051800/edocket.access.gpo.gov/2005/05-1222.htm*].

[16] For information on the H-1B nonimmigrant classification, see CRS Report RL30498, *Immigration: Legislative Issues on Nonimmigrant Professional Specialty (H-1B) Workers*, by Ruth Ellen Wasem.

[17] For definitions of these types of need, see 8 C.F.R. §214.2(h)(6)(ii).

[18] See INA §214(g)(1)(B).

[19] There is no precise measure available of the number of the aliens granted H-2B status in any given year. While visa data provide an approximation, these data are subject to limitations, among them that not all H-2A workers are necessarily issued visas and not all aliens who are issued visas necessarily use them to enter the United States.

[20] See discussion below of S. 352/H.R. 793 in the 109th Congress.

[21] U.S. Department of Homeland Security, U.S. Citizenship and Immigration Services, "USCIS to Accept Additional H-2B Filings for FY2005 and FY2006," public notice, May 23, 2005.

[22] Jeffrey S. Passel, *Estimates of the Size and Characteristics of the Undocumented Population*, Pew Hispanic Center, March 21, 2005; Jeffrey S. Passel, *Size and Characteristics of the Unauthorized Migrant Population in the U.S.; Estimates Based on the March 2005 Current Population Survey*, Pew Hispanic Center, March 7, 2006 (hereafter cited as Passel, *Size and Characteristics of the Unauthorized Migrant Population in the U.S.*, March 7, 2006). These reports are available at [*http://pewhispanic.org/ topics/ index.php?TopicID=16*].

[23] U.S. Department of Homeland Security, Office of Immigration Statistics, *Estimates of the Unauthorized Immigrant Population Residing in the United States: January 2005*, by Michael Hoefer, Nancy Rytina, and Christopher Campbell, August 2006.

[24] For further information on migrant deaths, see CRS Report RL32562, *Border Security: The Role of the U.S. Border Patrol*, by Blas Nuñez-Neto.

[25] Passel, *Size and Characteristics of the Unauthorized Migrant Population in the U.S.*, March 7, 2006, at [*http://pewhispanic.org/ reports/report.php? ReportID=61*].

[26] Ibid., pp. 10-11.

[27] During the 107th Congress, former Senator Phil Gramm released a preliminary proposal for a new U.S.-Mexico guest worker program that would have covered both agricultural and nonagricultural workers, but he did not introduce legislation.

[28] Although S. 1814 and H.R. 4056 are not identical, they are treated as companion bills for the purposes of this discussion because they are highly similar.

[29] For a discussion of the U.S. system of permanent admissions, including numerical limits, see CRS Report RL32235, *U.S. Immigration Policy on Permanent Admissions*, by Ruth Ellen Wasem. (Hereafter cited as CRS Report RL32235.)

[30] For information on noncitizen eligibility for federal public benefits, see CRS Report RL31114.

[31] This description of S. 1387 is based on both the bill text and clarifications provided by Sen. Cornyn's office by telephone on July 22, 2003. Some clarifying language may need to be added to the bill.

[32] Although S. 352 and H.R. 793 are not identical, they are treated as companion bills here because they are nearly identical and none of their differences are substantive. The full short title of S. 352 is Save Our Small and Seasonal Businesses of 2005.

[33] The blue card status proposed under this bill is different than the blue card status proposed in S. 2087 (discussed below).

[34] For information on numerical limits, see CRS Report RL32235.

[35] Separate provisions in S. 359/H.R. 884 would have established a two-stage legalization program for agricultural workers.

[36] For information on numerical limits, see CRS Report RL32235.

[37] H.R. 3857 would not have established a mechanism for agricultural workers to obtain LPR status.

[38] For information on the entry-exit system issue, see CRS Report RL32234, *U.S. Visitor and Immigrant Status Indicator Technology (US-VISIT) Program*, by Lisa M. Seghetti and Stephen R. Viña.

[39] For an explanation of INA §245(i), see CRS Report RL31373, *Immigration: Adjustment to Permanent Resident Status Under Section 245(i)*, by Andorra Bruno.

[40] INA §212(a)(9)(B). This ground of inadmissibility, known as the "3 and 10 year bars," applies to aliens who have been unlawfully present in the United States for more than 180 days and who then depart or are removed.

[41] A "work day" is defined in the legislation as a day in which the individual is employed for at least 5.75 hours in agricultural employment.

[42] For information on numerical limits, see CRS Report RL32235.

[43] S.Amdt. 1150, the bipartisan compromise proposal for immigration reform, was proposed by Senator Kennedy as an amendment in the nature of a substitute to S. 1348. (The text of S.Amdt. 1150 appears in "Text of Amendment Submitted Monday, May 21, 2007," *Congressional Record*, daily edition, vol.153 (May 24, 2007), pp. S6625-S6687.) S. 1348, the Comprehensive Immigration Reform Act of 2007, was introduced by Senate Majority Leader Reid as the marker for Senate debate on comprehensive immigration reform; it is based on S. 2611, as passed by the Senate in the 109th Congress (discussed above).

[44] A "work day" is defined in the legislation as a day in which the individual is employed for at least 5.75 hours in agricultural employment.

[45] For information on numerical limits, see CRS Report RL32235.

[46] S. 1639 § 403(a) would define an alien admitted to the United States under the new Y-2 nonimmigrant classification as a "Y-2B nonimmigrant" or "Y-2B worker."

[47] Y-1 nonimmigrants who are accompanied by family members in Y-3 status would be limited to one additional two-year period.

[48] S. 1639 § 403(a) would define an alien admitted to the United States under the new Y-2 nonimmigrant classification as a "Y-2B nonimmigrant" or "Y-2B worker."

[49] While Z status would be available to otherwise eligible unauthorized aliens in the United States, unlawful status would not be an explicit requirement for Z status. Instead, to be eligible for Z status under §601, an alien could *not* have been lawfully present in the United States on January 1, 2007, or on the date of application for Z status under any nonimmigrant classification or any other immigration status made available under a treaty or other multinational agreement ratified by the Senate.

[50] The Administration did *not* offer a detailed legislative proposal. Some materials on the Administration proposal, however, are available on the White House website. The President's January 7, 2004, remarks on the proposal are available at [*http://www.whitehouse.gov/news/releases/ 2004/01/print/20040107-3.html*]. A fact sheet on the proposal, entitled *Fair and Secure Immigration Reform* is available at [*http://www. whitehouse.gov/news/releases/2004/01/print/20040107-3.html*]. The transcript of a January 6, 2004 background briefing for reporters is available at [*http://www.whitehouse.gov/news/releases/2004/01/print/20040106-3. html*].

[51] Secretary Chao's written testimony is available at [*http://judiciary.senate. gov/hearing .cfm?id=1634*].

[52] See above discussion of S. 2611 in the 109th Congress.

[53] Comment of T. Alexander Aleinikoff, Migration Policy Institute. Quoted in Eric Schmitt, "The Nation: Separate and Unequal; You Can Come In. You Stay Out," *New York Times*, July 29, 2001, Section 4, p. 5.

[54] President Bush was asked in July 2001 whether an immigration proposal under consideration at the time to legalize the status of some unauthorized Mexicans would be expanded to cover immigrants from other countries. The President responded, "We'll consider all folks here," but did not provide further details. See Edwin Chen and Jonathan Peterson, "Bush Hints at Broader Amnesty," *Los Angeles Times*, July 27, 2001, Part A, part 1, p. 1.

[55] For example, in an August 2001 letter to President Bush and Mexican President Vicente Fox setting forth the Democrats' immigration principles, then-Senate Majority Leader Thomas Daschle and then-House Minority Leader Richard Gephardt stated that "no migration proposal can be complete without an earned adjustment program."

[56] P.L. 99-603, November 6, 1986. The general legalization program is at INA §245A, and the SAW program is at INA §210.

[57] Certain individuals who had not legalized under the general program and were participants in specified class action lawsuits were given a new time-limited opportunity to adjust to LPR status by the Legal Immigration Family Equity Act (LIFE; P.L. 106-553, Appendix B, Title XI, December 21, 2000) and the LIFE Act Amendments (P.L. 106-554, Appendix D, Title XV, December 21, 2000).

[58] See CRS Report RL32235.

[59] P.L. 101-649, November 29, 1990.

[60] Questions about the existence of industry-wide labor shortages are outside the scope of this report. For a discussion of the shortage issue with respect to agriculture, see CRS Report RL30395, *Farm Labor Shortages and Immigration Policy*, by Linda Levine. Also see CRS Report 95-712, *The Effects on U.S. Farm Workers of an Agricultural Guest Worker Program*, by Linda Levine.

[61] See U.S. Department of Labor, Office of Inspector General, *Consolidation of Labor's Enforcement Responsibilities for the H-2A Program Could Better Protect U.S. Agricultural Workers*, Report Number 04-98-004-03-321, March 31, 1998.

[62] INA §218(g)(2).

In: Economics, Political and Social Issues …
Editor: Michelle L. Fergusson

THE COMMITTEE ON FOREIGN INVESTMENT IN THE UNITED STATES (CFIUS)[*]

James K. Jackson

ABSTRACT

The Committee on Foreign Investment in the United States (CFIUS) is comprised of 12 members representing major departments and agencies within the federal Executive Branch. While the group generally operates in relative obscurity, the proposed acquisition of commercial operations at six U.S. ports by Dubai Ports World in 2006 placed the group's operations under intense scrutiny by Members of Congress and the public. Prompted by this case, some Members of the 109th and 110th Congresses have questioned the ability of Congress to exercise its oversight responsibilities given the general view that CFIUS's operations lack transparency. Other Members revisited concerns about the linkage between national security and the role of foreign investment in the U.S. economy. Some Members of Congress and others argued that the nation's security and economic concerns have changed since the September 11, 2001 terrorist attacks and that these concerns were not being reflected sufficiently in the Committee's deliberations. In addition, anecdotal evidence seemed to indicate that the CFIUS process is not market neutral, instead a CFIUS investigation of an investment transaction may be perceived by some firms and by some in the financial markets as a negative factor that adds to uncertainty and may spur firms to engage in behavior that is not optimal for the economy as a whole.

As a result of the attention focused on the Dubai Ports World transaction, Members of Congress introduced more than two dozen measures on foreign investment in the 109th Congress. These measures reflected various levels of unease with the broad discretionary authority Congress has granted CFIUS. In the 1st session of the 110th Congress, Congresswoman Maloney introduced H.R. 556, the National Security Foreign Investment Reform and Strengthened Transparency Act of 2007, on January 18, 2007. The measure was approved by the House Financial Services Committee on February 13, 2007 with amendments, and was approved with amendments by the full House on February 28, 2007 by a vote of 423 to 0. On June 13, 2007, Senator Dodd introduced S. 1610, the Foreign Investment and National Security Act of 2007. On June 29, 2007, the Senate adopted S. 1610 in lieu of H.R. 556 by unanimous consent. On July 11, 2007, the House accepted the Senate's version of H.R. 556 by a vote of 370-45 and sent the measure to the President.

---

[*] Excerpted from CRS Report RL33388, dated July 23, 2007.

BACKGROUND

The Committee on Foreign Investment in the United States (CFIUS) is an interagency committee that serves the President in overseeing the national security implications of foreign investment in the economy. Since it was established by an Executive Order of President Ford in 1975, the committee has operated in relative obscurity.[1] According to a Treasury Department memorandum, the Committee originally was established in order to placate Congress, which had grown concerned over the rapid increase in Organization of the Petroleum Exporting Countries (OPEC) investments in American portfolio assets (Treasury securities, corporate stocks and bonds), and to respond to concerns of some that much of the OPEC investments were being driven by political, rather than by economic, motives.[2]

Thirty years later, public and congressional concerns about the proposed purchase of commercial port operations of the British-owned Peninsular and Oriental Steam Navigation Company (P and O)[3] in six U.S. ports by Dubai Ports World (DP World)[4] sparked a firestorm of criticism and congressional activity during the 109th Congress concerning CFIUS and the manner in which it operates. Some Members of Congress and the public argued that the nation's economic and national security concerns have been fundamentally altered as a result of the September 11, 2001 terrorist attacks on the United States and that these changes require a reassessment of the role of foreign investment in the economy and in the nation's security. As a result of the attention by both the public and Congress, DP World officials announced that they would sell off the U.S. port operations to an American owner.[5] On December 11, 2006, DP World officials announced that a unit of AIG Global Investment Group, a New York-based asset management company with $683 billion in assets, but no experience in port operations, would acquire the U.S. port operations for an undisclosed amount.[6]

Members of Congress introduced more than 25 bills in the 2nd session of the 109th Congress that would have addressed various aspects of foreign investment since the proposed DP World transaction. The Congressional session ended before a Conference Committee could be convened to work out differences between the measures. Overall, the measures can be grouped into four major areas: those that dealt specifically with the proposed DP World acquisition; those that focused more generally on foreign ownership of U.S. ports, especially if the foreign entity is owned or controlled by a foreign government; those that would have amended the CFIUS process; and those that would amend the Exon-Florio process (explained below). Six bills focused primarily on CFIUS and displayed a range of responses by some Members of Congress. These bills are examined in more depth later in this report. In the 1st session of the 110th Congress, Members approved measures that will amend the CFIUS process to provide greater oversight by Congress and increased reporting by the Committee on its decisions. In addition, the measures broaden the definition of national security and require greater scrutiny by CFIUS of certain types of foreign direct investments. The measures demonstrate the concern that some Members have with the way CFIUS has operated and with the lack of transparency in the CFIUS review process that some Members believe has hampered Congress's ability to exercise its oversight responsibilities.

ESTABLISHMENT OF CFIUS

President Ford's 1975 Executive Order established the basic structure of CFIUS, and directed that the "representative"[7] of the Secretary of the Treasury be the chairman of the Committee. The Executive Order also stipulated that the Committee would have "the primary continuing responsibility within the Executive Branch for monitoring the impact of foreign investment in the United States, both direct and portfolio, and for coordinating the implementation of United States policy on such investment." In particular, CFIUS was directed to: (1) arrange for the preparation of analyses of trends and significant developments in foreign investments in the United States; (2) provide guidance on arrangements with foreign governments for advance consultations on prospective major foreign governmental investments in the United States; (3) review investments in the United States which, in the judgement of the Committee, might have major implications for United States national interests; and (4) consider proposals for new legislation or regulations relating to foreign investment as may appear necessary.[8]

President Ford's Executive Order also stipulated that information submitted "in confidence shall not be publicly disclosed" and that information submitted to CFIUS be used "only for the purpose of carrying out the functions and activities" of the order. In addition, the Secretary of Commerce was directed to perform a number of activities, including

1. obtaining, consolidating, and analyzing information on foreign investment in the United States;
2. improving the procedures for the collection and dissemination of information on such foreign investment;
3. the close observing of foreign investment in the United States;
4. preparing reports and analyses of trends and of significant developments in appropriate categories of such investment;
5. compiling data and preparing evaluation of significant transactions; and
6. submitting to the Committee on Foreign Investment in the United States appropriate reports, analyses, data, and recommendations as to how information on foreign investment can be kept current.

The Executive Order, however, raised questions among various observers and government officials who doubted that federal agencies had the legal authority to collect the types of data that were required by the order. As a result, Congress and the President sought to clarify this issue, and in the following year President Ford signed the International Investment Survey Act of 1976.[9] The act gave the President clear and unambiguous authority" to collect information on "international investment." In addition, the act authorized "the collection and use of information on direct investments owned or controlled directly or indirectly by foreign governments or persons, and to provide analyses of such information to the Congress, the executive agencies, and the general public."[10]

By 1980, some Members of Congress had come to believe that CFIUS was not fulfilling its mandate. Between 1975 and 1980, for instance, the Committee had met only ten times and seemed unable to decide whether it should respond to the political or the economic aspects of foreign direct investment in the United States.[11] One critic of the Committee argued in a congressional hearing in 1979 that, "the Committee has been reduced over the last four years to a body that only responds to the political aspects or the political questions that foreign investment in the United States poses and not with what we really want to know about foreign investments in the United States, that is: Is it good for the economy?"[12]

From 1980 to 1987, CFIUS investigated a number of foreign investments, mostly at the request of the Department of Defense. In 1983, for instance, a Japanese firm sought to acquire a U.S. specialty steel producer. The Department of Defense subsequently classified the metals produced by the firm because they were used in the production of military aircraft, which caused the Japanese firm to withdraw its offer. Another Japanese company attempted to acquire a U.S. firm in 1985 that manufactured specialized ball bearings for the military. The acquisition was completed after the Japanese firm agreed that production would be maintained in the United States. In a similar case in 1987, the Defense Department objected to a proposed acquisition of the computer division of a U.S. multinational company by a French firm because of classified work engaged in by the computer division. The acquisition proceeded after the classified contracts were reassigned to the U.S. parent company.[13]

THE "EXON-FLORIO" PROVISION

In 1988, amid concerns over foreign acquisition of certain types of U.S. firms, particularly by Japanese firms, Congress approved the Exon-Florio provision. This statute grants the President the authority to block proposed or pending foreign acquisitions of "persons engaged in interstate commerce in the United States" that threaten to impair the national security. Congress directed, however, that before this authority can be invoked the President is expected to believe that other U.S. laws are inadequate or inappropriate to protect the national security, and that he must have "credible evidence" that the foreign investment will impair the national security.

By the late 1980s, Congress and the public had grown increasingly concerned about the sharp increase in foreign investment in the United States and the potential impact such investment might have on the U.S. economy. In particular, the proposed sale in 1987 of Fairchild Semiconductor Co. by Schlumberger Ltd. of France to Fujitsu Ltd. of Japan touched off strong opposition in Congress and provided much of the impetus behind the passage of the Exon-Florio provision. The proposed Fairchild acquisition generated intense concern in Congress in part because of general difficulties in trade relations with Japan at that time and because some Americans felt that the United States was declining as an international economic power as well as a world power. The Defense Department opposed the acquisition because some officials believed that the deal would give Japan control over a major supplier of computer chips for the military and would make U.S. defense industries more dependent on foreign suppliers for sophisticated high-technology products.[14]

Although Commerce Secretary Malcolm Baldridge and Defense Secretary Casper Weinberger failed in their attempt to have President Reagan block the Fujitsu acquisition, Fujitsu and Schlumberger called off the proposed sale of Fairchild.[15] While Fairchild was acquired some months later by National Semiconductor Corp. for a discount,[16] the Fujitsu-Fairchild incident marked an important shift in the Reagan Administration's support for unlimited foreign direct investment in U.S. businesses and boosted support within the Administration for fixed guidelines for blocking foreign takeovers of companies in national security-sensitive industries.[17]

In 1988, after three years of often contentious negotiations between Congress and the Reagan Administration, Congress passed and President Reagan signed the Omnibus Trade and Competitiveness Act of 1988.[18] The Exon-Florio provision, which was included as Section 5021 of that act, fundamentally transformed CFIUS. The provision originated in bills reported by the Commerce Committee in the Senate and the Energy and Commerce Committee in the House, but the measure was transferred to the Banking Committee as a result of a dispute over jurisdictional responsibilities.[19]

Part of Congress's motivation in adopting the Exon-Florio provision apparently arose from concerns that foreign takeovers of U.S. firms could not be stopped unless the President declared a national emergency or regulators invoked federal antitrust, environmental, or securities laws. Through the Exon-Florio provision, Congress attempted to strengthen the President's hand in conducting foreign investment policy, while providing a cursory role for itself as a means of emphasizing that, as much as possible, the commercial nature of investment transactions should be free from political considerations. Congress also attempted to balance public concerns about the economic impact of certain types of foreign investment with the nation's long standing international commitment to maintain an open and receptive environment for foreign investment.

Furthermore, Congress did not intend to have the Exon-Florio provision alter the generally open foreign investment climate of the country or to have it inhibit foreign direct investments in industries that could not be considered to be of national security interest. At the time, some analysts believed the provision could potentially widen the scope of industries that fell under the national security rubric. CFIUS, however, is not free to establish an independent approach to reviewing foreign investment transactions, but operates under the authority of the President and reflects his attitudes and policies. As a result, the discretion CFIUS uses to review and to investigate foreign investment cases reflects policy guidance from the President. Foreign investors are also constrained by legislation that bars foreign direct investment in such industries as maritime, aircraft, banking, resources and power.[20] Generally, these sectors were closed to foreign investors prior to passage of the Exon-Florio provision in order to prevent public services and public interest activities from falling under foreign control, primarily for national defense purposes.

Through Executive Order 12661, President Reagan implemented provisions of the Omnibus Trade Act. In the Executive Order, President Reagan delegated his authority to administer the Exon-Florio provision to CFIUS,[21] particularly to conduct reviews, to undertake investigations, and to make recommendations, although the statute itself does not specifically mention CFIUS. As a result of President Reagan's action, CFIUS was transformed from a purely administrative body with limited authority to review and analyze data on foreign investment to one with a broad mandate and significant authority to advise the President on foreign investment transactions and to recommend that some transactions be blocked. Presently, the Committee consists of twelve members, including the Secretaries of State, the Treasury, Defense, Homeland Security, and Commerce; the United States Trade Representative; the Chairman of the Council of Economic Advisers; the Attorney General; the Director of the Office of Management and Budget; the Director of the Office of Science and Technology Policy; the Assistant to the President for National Security Affairs; and the Assistant to the President for Economic Policy.[22]

Procedures

According to the Exon-Florio provision, CFIUS has 30 days to decide after it receives the initial formal notification by the parties to a merger, acquisition, or a takeover, whether to investigate a case as a result of its determination that the investment "threatens to impair the national security of the United States." If during this 30 day period all of the members of CFIUS conclude that the investment does not threaten to impair the national security, the review is terminated. If, however, at least one member of the Committee determines that the investment does threaten to impair the national security CFIUS can proceed to a 45-day investigation. At the conclusion of the investigation or the 45-day review period, whichever comes first, the Committee can decide to offer no recommendation or it can recommend that the President suspend or prohibit the investment. The President is under no obligation to follow the recommendation of the Committee to suspend or prohibit an investment.

Factors for Consideration

The Exon-Florio provision includes a short list of factors the President *may* consider in deciding to block a foreign acquisition. These factors are also considered by the individual members of CFIUS as part of their own review process to determine if a particular transaction threatens to impair the national security. This list includes the following elements:

1. domestic production needed for projected national defense requirements;
2. the capability and capacity of domestic industries to meet national defense requirements, including the availability of human resources, products, technology, materials, and other supplies and services;
3. the control of domestic industries and commercial activity by foreign citizens as it affects the capability and capacity of the U.S. to meet the requirements of national security;
4. the potential effects of the transactions on the sales of military goods, equipment, or technology to a country that supports terrorism or proliferates missile technology or chemical and biological weapons; and
5. the potential effects of the transaction on U.S. technological leadership in areas affecting U.S. national security.

The first two factors emphasize the national defense aspects of foreign acquisitions, while the other three factors highlight national security implications of such investment. No clear definition is provided in the legislation for what constitutes "national security" or foreign "control," but CFIUS' regulations state that control is, "the power, whether or not exercised, to formulate, determine, direct, or decide important matters relating to the entity."[23] While national security might be interpreted broadly to include a range of economic issues, neither Congress nor the Administration attempted to define the term. Treasury Department officials have indicated that during an Exon-Florio review or investigation each CFIUS member is expected to apply that definition of national security that is consistent with the representative agency's specific legislative mandate.[24]

The Treasury Department has provided some guidance to firms deciding whether they should notify CFIUS of a proposed or pending merger, acquisition, or takeover. The guidance states that proposed acquisitions that need to notify CFIUS are those that involve "products or key technologies essential to the U.S. defense industrial base." This notice is not intended for firms that produce goods or services with no special relation to national security, especially toys and games, food products, hotels and restaurants, or legal services. CFIUS has indicated that in order to assure an unimpeded inflow of foreign investment it would implement the statute "only insofar as necessary to protect the national security," and "in a manner fully consistent with the international obligations of the United States."[25]

As originally drafted, the Exon-Florio provision also would have applied to joint ventures and licensing agreements in addition to mergers, acquisitions, and takeovers. Joint ventures and licensing agreements subsequently were dropped from the proposal because the Administration and various industry groups argued that such business practices are generally beneficial arrangements for U.S. companies. In addition, they argued that any potential threat to national security could be addressed by the Export Administration Act[26] and the Arms Control Export Act.[27]

Confidentiality Requirements

The Exon-Florio provision also codified confidentiality requirements that are similar to those that appeared in Executive Order 11858 by stating that any information or documentary material filed under the provision may not be made public "except as may be relevant to any administrative or judicial action or proceeding."[28] The provision does state, however, that this confidentiality provision "shall not be construed to prevent disclosure to either House of Congress or to any duly authorized committee or subcommittee of the Congress." The Exon-Florio provision requires the President to provide a written report to the Secretary of the Senate and the Clerk of the House detailing his decision and his actions relevant to any transaction that was subject to a 45-day investigation.[29] As presently written, there is no requirement for CFIUS or the President to notify or otherwise inform Congress of cases it reviews or of the outcome of any investigation.

TREASURY DEPARTMENT REGULATIONS

After extensive public comment, the Treasury Department issued its final regulations in November 1991 implementing the Exon-Florio provision.[30] These regulations created an essentially voluntary system of notification by the parties to an acquisition and they allow for notices of acquisitions by agencies that are members of CFIUS. Despite the voluntary nature of the notification, firms largely comply with the provision because the regulations stipulate that foreign acquisitions that are governed by the Exon-Florio review process that do not notify the Committee remain subject indefinitely to divestment or other appropriate actions by the President. Under most circumstances, notice of a proposed acquisition that is given to the Committee by a third party, including shareholders, is not considered by the Committee to constitute an official notification. The regulations also indicate that notifications provided to the Committee are considered to be confidential and the information is not released by the Committee to the press or commented on publicly.

THE "BYRD AMENDMENT"

In 1992, Congress amended the Exon-Florio statute through Section 837(a) of the National Defense Authorization Act for Fiscal Year 1993 (P.L. 102-484). Known as the "Byrd" amendment after the amendment's sponsor, the provision requires CFIUS to investigate proposed mergers, acquisitions, or takeovers in cases where two criterion are met:

1. the acquirer is controlled by or acting on behalf of a foreign government; and
2. the acquisition results in control of a person engaged in interstate commerce in the United States that could affect the national security of the United States.[31]

This amendment came under intense scrutiny by the 109th Congress as a result of the DP World transaction. Many Members of Congress and others believed that this amendment required CFIUS to undertake a full 45-day investigation of the transaction because DP World was "controlled by or acting on behalf of a foreign government." The DP World acquisition, however, exposed a sharp rift between what some Members apparently believed the amendment directed CFIUS to do and how the members of CFIUS were interpreting the amendment. In particular, some Members of Congress apparently interpreted the amendment to direct CFIUS to conduct a mandatory 45-day investigation if the foreign firm involved in a transaction is owned or controlled by a foreign government. Representatives of CFIUS argued that they interpret the amendment to mean that a 45-day investigation is discretionary and not mandatory. In the case of the DP World acquisition, CFIUS representatives argued that they had concluded as a result of an extensive review of the proposed acquisition prior to the case being formally filed with CFIUS and during the 30-day review that the DP World case did not warrant a full 45-day investigation. They conceded that the case met the first criterion under the Byrd amendment, because DP World was controlled by a foreign government, but that it did not meet the second part of the requirement, because CFIUS had concluded during the 30-day review that the transaction "could not affect the national security."[32]

CFIUS SINCE EXON-FLORIO

Recent information indicates that the number of cases reviewed by CFIUS has declined since the late 1990s. In part, the decline reflects the slowdown in foreign investment activity in the United States generally that occurred between 1998 and 2003, as indicated in Table 1. Based on the number of transactions per year, acquisitions of U.S. firms by other U.S. firms has accounted for the largest share of all merger and acquisition (M and A) transactions over the past ten years. This share fell from 76% of all U.S. M and A transactions in 1996 to 71.7% in 2006, but that was up from a low of 68% recorded in 2001. The share of M and A activity attributed to foreign firms acquiring U.S. firms in 2006 accounts for 14.6% of all such transactions, up from 9% in 1996.

Table 1. Merger and Acquisition Activity in the United States, 1996-2006

	Total Number of Mergers and Acquisitions	U.S. Firms Acquiring U.S. Firms	Non-U.S. Firms Acquiring U.S. Firms	U.S. Firms Acquiring Non-U.S. Firms
1996	7,347	5,585	628	1,134
1997	8,479	6,317	775	1,387
1998	10,193	7,575	971	1,647
1999	9,173	6,449	1,148	1,576
2000	8,853	6,032	1,264	1,557
2001	6,296	4,269	923	1,104
2002	5,497	3,989	700	808
2003	5,959	4,357	722	880
2004	7,031	5,084	813	1,134
2005	7,600	5,463	977	1,160
2006	8,203	5,853	1,074	1,276

Source: *Mergers and Acquisitions*, February 2007.

In addition to a lower overall level of investment activity, the lower case load experienced by CFIUS may reflect the impact of an informal CFIUS review process that has developed over time. This process gives firms the opportunity to reconsider their investments if they believe they could face a difficult CFIUS review or if they believe the transaction could be subjected to a formal 45-day investigation with its potentially negative connotations regarding national security concerns. In addition, some observers argue that the case load diminished following the September 11, 2001 terrorists attacks on the United States due to the organization of the Department of Homeland Security (DHS), which has participated actively in the CFIUS process and has raised security concerns. These concerns may have caused some firms to reconsider their investment transactions before they had progressed very far in the formal CFIUS process in order to avoid a long and involved investigation by DHS.[33]

As a consequence of the confidential nature of the CFIUS review of any proposed transaction, there are few official sources of information concerning the Committee's work to date. For the most part, information concerning individual transactions that have been reviewed by CFIUS or any final recommendations that have been issued by CFIUS have come from announcements released by the companies involved in a transaction and not by CFIUS. According to one source,[34 CFIUS has received more than 1,500 notifications since 1988, of which it conducted a full investigation of 25 cases. Of these 25 cases, thirteen transactions were withdrawn upon notice that CFIUS would conduct a full review and twelve of the remaining transactions cases were sent to the President. Of these twelve transactions, one was prohibited.[35]

IMPACT OF THE EXON-FLORIO PROCESS ON CFIUS

The DP World case exposed a number of important aspects of CFIUS' operations that apparently were not well known or understood by the public in general. As already indicated, the Exon-Florio provision stipulates a three-step process: the formal notification to CFIUS and a 30-day review; a 45-day investigation for those transactions that raised national security concerns during the 30-day review and for those in which the concerns were not resolved during the review period; and a 15-day Presidential determination stage for those transactions that were determined after the 45-day review to pose an impairment to national security. Over time, however, this process apparently has evolved to include an informal fourth stage of unspecified length of time that consists of an unofficial CFIUS determination prior to the formal filing with CFIUS. This type of informal review has developed because it likely serves the interests of both CFIUS and the firms involved in an investment transaction. According to Treasury Department officials, this informal contact enables "CFIUS staff to identify potential issues before the review process formally begins."[36]

Firms that are party to a transaction apparently benefit from this informal review in a number of ways. For one, it allows firms additional time to work out any national security concerns privately with individual CFIUS members. Secondly, and perhaps more importantly, it provides a process for firms to avoid risking the potentially negative publicity that could arise if a transaction were to be blocked or otherwise labeled as impairing U.S. national security interests. For some firms, public knowledge of a CFIUS investigation has had a negative effect on the value of the firm's stock price.

After a lengthy review by CFIUS in 2000 of Verio, Inc., a U.S. firm that operates websites for businesses and provides internet services, was acquired by NTT Communications of Japan. Verio's stock price reportedly fell during the CFIUS investigation as a result of uncertainty in the market about prospects for the transaction. The CFIUS review was instigated by the FBI, which had expressed concerns during the initial review stage that the majority interest of the Japanese government in NTT could give it access to information regarding wiretaps that were being conducted on email and other Web-based traffic crossing Verio's computer system. After completing its investigation, however, CFIUS did not recommend that President Clinton block the transaction.

The potentially negative publicity that can be associated with a CFIUS investigation of a transaction apparently has had a major impact on the transactions CFIUS has investigated. Since 1990, nearly half of the transactions CFIUS investigated were terminated by the firms involved, because the firms decided to withdraw from the transaction rather than face a negative determination by CFIUS. In 2006, for instance, the prospects of a CFIUS investigation apparently was the major reason the Israeli firm Check Point Software Technologies decided to call off its proposed $225 million acquisition of Sourcefire, a U.S. firm specializing in security appliances for protecting a corporation's internal computer networks. In addition, the decision by the China National Offshore Oil Company (CNOOC) to drop its proposed acquisition of Unocal oil company in 2005 was partly due to concerns by CNOOC about an impending CFIUS investigation of the transaction.

For CFIUS members, the informal process is beneficial because it gives them as much time as they feel is necessary to review a transaction without facing the time constraints that arise under the formal CFIUS review process. This informal review likely also gives the CFIUS members added time to negotiate with the firms involved in a transaction to restructure the transaction in ways that address any potential security concerns or to develop other types of conditions that members of CFIUS feel are appropriate in order to remove security concerns.

The DP World acquisition demonstrated how this informal CFIUS process can operate in reviewing a proposed foreign investment transaction. According to officials involved in the review, DP World officials contacted the Treasury Department in early October 2005 to informally discuss their proposed transaction. Treasury officials directed DP World to consult with the Department of Homeland Security and in November the Treasury officials requested an intelligence assessment from the Director of National Intelligence. Staff representatives from all of the CFIUS members met on December 6, 2005 to discuss the transaction, apparently to determine if there were any security concerns that had not been addressed and resolved during the two-month long informal review of the proposed transaction.

Ten days after that meeting, DP World filed its official notification with CFIUS, which distributed the notification to all of the CFIUS members and to the Departments of Energy and Transportation. During this process, the Department of Homeland Security apparently negotiated a letter of assurances with DP World that addressed some outstanding concerns about port security. On the basis of this letter and the lack of any remaining concerns expressed by any member of CFIUS or other agencies that were consulted, CFIUS completed its review of the transaction on January 17, 2006 and concluded that the transaction did not threaten to impair the national security and therefore that it did not warrant a 45-day investigation.[37]

ACTIONS IN THE 109TH CONGRESS

Following the public attention that focused on the DP World transaction in mid-February 2006, Members of Congress introduced more than two dozen bills that related directly or closely to the proposed transaction. The bills range in focus from blocking the DP World transaction to revamping the CFIUS process. These measures can be grouped into four major areas: those that deal specifically with the proposed Dubai Ports World acquisition; those that focus more generally on foreign ownership of U.S. ports, especially if the foreign entity is owned or controlled by a foreign government; those that would amend the CFIUS process; and those that would amend the Exon-Florio process. On the whole, a broad range of measures would increase reporting requirements on CFIUS to keep key congressional leaders apprised of the Committee's actions. In some measures, Congress would have the authority to intercede in a transaction that had been approved by CFIUS, to override the CFIUS action, and to block a transaction.

The first measures that were introduced were directed at stopping the DP World acquisition from occurring and at requesting CFIUS to undertake a full 45-day investigation of the transaction. For instance, S.J.Res. 32, introduced February 27, 2006 and H.J.Res. 79, introduced February 28, 2006 express congressional disapproval of the proposed acquisition and direct CFIUS to conduct a full 45-day review of the transaction and to brief Members of Congress on the results of the investigation.

On March 8, 2006, the House Appropriations Committee attached an amendment (H.Amdt. 702) to a supplemental appropriations bill for defense activities in Afghanistan and Iraq and emergency relief for the victims of Hurricane Katrina (H.R. 4939) that effectively would have nullified the actions of CFIUS regarding the DP World transaction. The amendment would have withheld the use of any funds to approve or "otherwise allow the acquisition of leases, contracts, rights, or other obligations of P and O Ports by Dubai Ports World." In addition, the amendment would have prohibited Dubai Ports World from acquiring any leases, contracts, rights, or other obligations in the United States of P and O

Ports by Dubai Ports World or "any other legal entity affiliated with or controlled by Dubai Ports World." The measure passed by a vote of 62 to 2 in the Committee.[38] The following day, DP World officials announced that they would sell off the newly-acquired U.S. port operations to an American owner.[39] On March 16, 2006, the measure passed the full House by a margin of 348 to 71 after an attempt the previous day failed by a vote of 377 to 38 to remove the ban on Dubai Ports World from the measure.[40]

Such other measures as H.R. 4813 and H.R. 4917 would have placed new reporting requirements on CFIUS to inform Congress when it initiates a 45-day investigation of a proposed acquisition, merger, or takeover. H.R. 4917 also would have expressed a sense of Congress that CFIUS be moved from operating out of the Treasury Department to the Department of Homeland Security. Since CFIUS is entirely a creation of Executive Order and operates exclusively for and on behalf of the President, it is unclear how much of an impact this measure would have had on the actions of the President.

Other measures addressed various concerns some Members of Congress expressed relative to the current CFIUS process. In particular, some Members voiced their dissatisfaction with the broad discretion CFIUS has to determine which transactions it subjects to a 45-day investigation. Also, some Members apparently were dissatisfied with the discretion CFIUS uses to interpret the Byrd Amendment. Other Members introduced measures to shift the leadership of CFIUS from the Treasury Department to the Department of Homeland Security and to limit CFIUS's discretion in investigating certain kinds of transactions, because some Members argued that the Treasury Department acted to limit the number of transactions CFIUS investigates in order to promote the Department's traditional position of supporting an open and unobstructed investment process. Other measures would have left unchanged the basic structure of CFIUS, but would have instituted CFIUS as a matter of statute to strengthen Congressional oversight of the Committee's operations.

The following measures focused most specifically on the Committee on Foreign Investment in the United States and the proposed changes to the existing CFIUS process.

H.R. 4929

H.R. 4929 was introduced by Representative Sabo on March 9, 2006. This measure would have amended the Exon-Florio process to limit CFIUS' discretion to investigate foreign investment transactions by mandating that an investigation must occur for any proposed or pending merger, acquisition, or takeover by any foreign person that could result in foreign control of any person engaged in interstate commerce in the United States. The measure also attempted to prod the administration into investigating more investment cases by requiring that the President must find that a transaction "will not threaten" to impair the national security of the United States in order for any proposed or pending merger, acquisition, or takeover of a person engage in interstate commerce in the United States by a foreign person to occur. The measure would have limited somewhat the President's discretion by changing the statute to indicate that the President's ability to act is based on findings that "shall be based on credible evidence" that leads the President to believe that a) the foreign interest "might" take action that threatens to impair the national security, and b) other provisions of law are appropriate to protect the national security. During an investigation, the measure would have required that those factors that the President is required to consider in investigating a proposed or pending transactions would be the same as those that currently are specified in the Exon-Florio provision.

H.R. 5337

H.R. 5337 was introduced by Representative Blunt on May 10, 2006. The measure was approved unanimously by the full House without amendment on July 26, 2006. The measure would have established the Committee on Foreign Investment in the United States as a matter of statute and would have amended the current procedures for a CFIUS review and investigation. The measure would have amended the current statute regarding national security by indicating that national security is construed "so as to include those issues relating to 'homeland security,' including its application to critical infrastructure." The measure also would have provided for a "National Security Review and Investigation," and would have required the President to take any "necessary" actions in connection with the transaction to protect the national security of the United States under certain conditions. The measure also would have addressed one concern about CFIUS's actions by granting CFIUS the authority to negotiate, impose, or enforce any agreement or condition with the parties to a transaction in order to mitigate any threat to the national security of the United States.

S. 1797

S. 1797 was introduced by Senator Inhofe on September 29, 2005. This measure reflected long-standing displeasure with CFIUS that pre-dates the Dubai Ports World transactions. The measure would have amended the Exon-Florio process by giving CFIUS 60 days instead of the present 30 days to decide if a pending investment requires a mandatory 45-day investigation. In addition, the measure would have provided for a congressional role in the CFIUS process by allowing the Chairman and Ranking Member of the Senate Banking Committee and the House Financial Services Committee to request a full 45-day investigation of investments that fall under the Byrd Amendment and would provide that the results of any such investigation be sent to the President and the Senate Banking Committee and the House Financial Services Committee.

S. 2380

On March 7, 2006, Senator Dodd introduced S. 2380, which would have addressed concerns among some Members who argued that CFIUS has not been viewing national security concerns broadly enough when reviewing and investigating proposed investment transactions. As a result of these concerns, this measure would have restricted CFIUS's discretion in investigating proposed investment transactions by adding a new national security review. The measure also would have amended the Exon-Florio process to require that only the President or the Secretary of the Treasury, with the concurrence of the Secretary of Homeland Security and the Secretary of Defense acting on the President's behalf, could determine that a proposed merger, acquisition, or takeover did not threaten to impair the national security and, therefore, would not have required a 45-day investigation. In such cases, either the President or members of CFIUS acting on his behalf would have been required to certify this conclusion in writing. In addition, any person controlled by or acting on behalf of a foreign government that is a party to a proposed merger, acquisition, or takeover of any U.S. critical infrastructure would have been required to notify the President or his designee.

S. 2400

On March 13, 2006, Senator Collins introduced S. 2400 that would have altered appreciably the current Exon-Florio process and would have expanded the current national security review to include "homeland security." Most importantly, the measure would have transferred the function for reviewing mergers, acquisitions and takeovers to the Secretary of Homeland Security. The measure would have established the Committee for Secure Commerce, which was to be comprised of the heads of those executive departments, agencies, and offices that the President determines to be appropriate and would have included the Director of National Intelligence. The President would have been allowed to exercise his authority under this provision "only if the President finds:" that there is credible evidence that leads the President to believe that the foreign interest exercising control might take action that threatens to impair the national security or homeland security; or that other provisions of law do not provide adequate and appropriate authority for the President to protect the national security or homeland security.

S. 3549

On June 21, 2006, Senator Shelby introduced S. 3549; the measure was passed, with amendments, by the full Senate on July 26, 2006. This measure would have amended the Exon-Florio provision to provide for greater congressional oversight over the review process and to reduce the discretion of CFIUS to review certain types of investments. The measure would have required CFIUS to review any proposed or pending transaction that resulted in a) the control of a person (business) engaged in interstate commerce if the foreign person is a foreign government or is acting on behalf of a foreign government or b) if the transactions could have resulted in control of any "critical infrastructure" if CFIUS determined that there would have been "any possible impairment to national security."

The chairman and vice-chairman of CFIUS, in consultation with the Secretaries of State, Commerce, Energy, the Chairman of the Nuclear Regulatory Commission, and the DNI would have been required to develop and implement a system of assessing individual countries according to three standards: (1) adherence to nonproliferation control regimes, including treaties and multilateral supply guidelines; (2) record on cooperating in counter-terrorism efforts; and (3) potential for transshipment or diversion of technologies with military applications, including an analysis of national export control laws and regulations. Similar to the current statute, the measure would have granted the President the authority to take what action he deems to be appropriate to suspend or to prohibit any transaction which would result in the control of any "critical infrastructure" of a person (entity) engaged in interstate commerce in the United States.

ACTIONS IN THE 110TH CONGRESS

H.R. 556

Congresswoman Maloney introduced H.R. 556, the National Security Foreign Investment Reform and Strengthened Transparency Act of 2007, on January 18, 2007.[41] The measure was approved by the House Financial Services Committee on February 13, 2007 with amendments, and was approved with amendments by the full House on February 28, 2007 by a vote of 423 to 0.

H.R. 556 attempted to address congressional concerns by establishing CFIUS by statutory authority, thereby giving Congress a direct role in determining the makeup and operations of the Committee. The measure would have had the Secretary of the Treasury continue to serve as the Chairman of CFIUS, despite the misgivings of some Members, and the Secretary Homeland Security and the Secretary of Defense serve as Vice Chairmen. In other respects, the bill would have retained the basic structure of the Committee as it presently exists, except that it would have added the Secretary of Energy as a permanent member of CFIUS

According to the measure, the Committee would have operated under the same time frame that currently exists with 30 days allotted for a review, 45 days for an investigation and 15 days for the President to make his determination. The President would have retained his authority as the only officer with the authority to suspend or prohibit certain types of foreign investments. The measure also would have placed additional requirements on firms that resubmit a filing after previously withdrawing a filing before a full review had been completed.

In H.R. 556, no review or investigation would have been considered to be complete until it had been approved by a majority of the members of CFIUS and signed by the Secretary of the Treasury and the Secretary of Homeland Security to ensure that principal members of CFIUS were aware of all reviews and investigations completed by CFIUS. The bill would have required CFIUS to review all 'covered" foreign investment transactions to determine whether a transaction threatened to impair the national security. A covered foreign investment transaction is defined as any merger, acquisition, or takeover which results in "foreign control of any person engaged in interstate commerce in the United States."

For a more detailed presentation of this measure, see CRS Report RL33856, *Exon-Florio Foreign Investment Provision: Overview of H.R. 556*, by James K. Jackson.

The measure would have placed increased requirements on CFIUS to review investment transactions in which the foreign entity is owned or controlled by a foreign government. It is unclear, however, to what extent the bill would have altered the current process. The measure would have explicitly required CFIUS to review all investment transactions in which the foreign entity is owned or controlled by a foreign government, but the measure would not have amended or altered the current statute in the area that has been the source of recent differences between CFIUS and Congress. In particular, the current statute states that the President, and through him CFIUS, can use the Exon-Florio process "only if" he finds that there is "credible evidence" that a foreign investment will impair national security. As a result, CFIUS has determined, as was the case in the Dubai Ports transaction, that if the Committee does not have credible evidence that an investment will impair the national security that it is not required to undertake a full 45-day investigation. It is possible that CFIUS could continue to operate in this manner, regardless of the passage of the measure.

In addition, if CFIUS had investigated all foreign investment transactions in which the foreign person is owned or controlled by a foreign government, foreign investors may well have regarded it as an important policy change by the United States toward foreign investment. As previously stated, the current system presumes that foreign investment transactions are acceptable and provide a positive contribution to the economy. As a result, the burden is on the members of CFIUS to prove that a particular transaction is a threat to national security. H.R. 556, however, might have been interpreted to presume that investment transactions in which the foreign entity is owned or controlled by a foreign government are a threat to the nation's security simply because of the relationship to the foreign government and, therefore, might have required the firms to prove that they are not a threat. Although the number of investment transactions a year in which the foreign investor is associated with a foreign government is small compared with the total number of foreign investment transactions, foreign investors and foreign governments likely would have viewed this as a significant change in the traditional U.S. approach to foreign investment.

The bill attempted to increase the role of congressional oversight by requiring greater reporting by CFIUS on its actions either during or after it completed reviews and investigations and by increasing reporting requirements on CFIUS. H.R. 556 would have required the Secretary of the Treasury, the Secretary of Homeland Security, and the Secretary of Commerce to sign and approve any review or investigation. In those cases in which the foreign person involved in an investment transaction is owned or controlled by a foreign government, a majority of the members of CFIUS would have been required to approve the transaction and the President and the chair and vice chairs of CFIUS would have been required to sign off on investments in which at least one member of CFIUS did not agree with the decision of the majority to approve the transaction.

The measure would have required CFIUS to provide Congress with a greater amount of detailed information about its operations. H.R. 556 would have required CFIUS to notify specified Members at the conclusion of any investment investigation and to report annually to Congress. H.R. 556 also would have provided for greater reporting on and increased authority for CFIUS to negotiate provisions with the foreign firms involved in investment transactions to mitigate the impact of the transaction. Under current statutes, CFIUS has no authority to negotiate such agreements with firms and it is not clear that it has any authority to enforce such agreements. H.R. 556 would have provided for a process to track the agreements and to report the progress of such agreements and any changes to the agreements to the members of CFIUS and to the President.

The measure also would have amended the current statute regarding the meaning of national security and would have placed additional requirements on CFIUS regarding national security reviews. The bill would have explicitly required the Director of National Intelligence to conduct reviews of any investment that posed a threat to the national security. The bill also provided for additional factors the President and CFIUS would have been required to use in assessing foreign investments. In particular, the bill would have added implications for the nation's critical infrastructure as a factor for reviewing or investigating an investment transaction.

S. 1610

S. 1610, the Foreign Investment and National Security Act of 2007, was introduced on June 13, 2007 by Senator Dodd. On June 29, 2007, the Senate adopted S. 1610 in lieu of H.R. 556 by unanimous consent. On July 11, 2007, the House accepted the Senate's version of H.R. 556 by a vote of 370-45 and sent the measure to the President. The measure establishes CFIUS by statutory authority and has the Secretary of the Treasury continue to serve as the Chairman of CFIUS. The measure reduces the official number of members of CFIUS, but grants the President the authority to appoint temporary members on a case-by-case basis. The measure has the Committee operate under the same time frame that currently exists with 30 days allotted for a review, 45 days for an investigation, and 15 days for the President to make his determination. The President retains his authority as the only officer with the authority to suspend or prohibit certain types of foreign investments, and the measure places additional requirements on firms that resubmitted a filing after previously withdrawing a filing before a full review is completed.

S. 1610 requires CFIUS to investigate all "covered" foreign investment transactions to determine whether a transaction threatens to impair the national security, or the foreign entity is controlled by a foreign government. A covered foreign investment transaction is defined as any merger, acquisition, or takeover which results in "foreign control of any person engaged in interstate commerce in the United States." The measure also requires an investigation if the transaction would result in control of any "critical infrastructure that could impair the national security."

The Senate measure places increased requirements on CFIUS to review investment transactions in which the foreign entity is owned or controlled by a foreign government, but it provides for exceptions from the requirement to investigate transactions in which the foreign party is controlled by a foreign government. S. 1610, similar to H.R. 556, allows CFIUS to exclude a transaction from an investigation if the Secretary of the Treasury and certain other specified officials determine that the transaction will not impair the national security. It is somewhat unclear, however, how this change will mesh with the current process. The measure does not amend or alter the current statute in the area that has been the source of recent differences between CFIUS and Congress. In particular, the current statute states that the President, and through him CFIUS, can use the Exon-Florio process "only if" he finds that there is "credible evidence" that a foreign investment will impair national security. As a result, CFIUS has determined, as was the case in the Dubai Ports transaction, that if the Committee does not have credible evidence that an investment will impair the national security that it is not required to undertake a full 45-day investigation.

S. 1610 increases the role of congressional oversight by requiring greater reporting by CFIUS on its actions either during or after it completes reviews and investigations and by increasing reporting requirements on CFIUS. The measure also requires CFIUS to provide Congress with a greater amount of detailed information about its operations. It also provides for greater reporting on and increased authority for CFIUS to negotiate provisions with the foreign firms involved in investment transactions to mitigate the impact of the transaction. S.

1610 provides for a process to track such mitigation agreements and to report the progress of such agreements and any changes to the agreements to the members of CFIUS and to the President.

S. 1610 amends the current statute regarding the meaning of national security and places additional requirements on CFIUS regarding national security reviews. The measure explicitly requires the Director of National Intelligence to conduct reviews of any investment that poses a threat to the national security and it provides for additional factors the President and CFIUS are required to use in assessing foreign investments. In particular, the bill adds implications for the nation's critical infrastructure as a factor for reviewing or investigating an investment transaction.

S. 1610 amends the current factors the President and the Committee use to evaluate mergers, acquisitions, or takeovers. In particular, the measure changes the status of the factors to be considered from being discretionary (may) to being required (shall) in evaluating a transaction. S. 1610 add transactions identified currently under the fourth factor by the Secretary of Defense as "posing a regional military threat" to the interests of the United States.

In addition, S. 1610 adds seven new factors to the five that currently exist. These new factors are:

1. whether the transaction has a security-related impact on critical infrastructure in the United States:
2. the potential effects on United States critical infrastructure, including major energy assets;
3. the potential effects on United States critical technologies;
4. whether the transaction is a foreign government-controlled transaction;
5. in those cases involving a government-controlled transaction, a review of (A) the adherence of the foreign country to nonproliferation control regimes, (B) the foreign country's record on cooperating in counter-terrorism efforts, (C) the potential for transshipment or diversion of technologies with military applications;
6. the long-term projection of the United States requirements for sources of energy and other critical resources and materials; and
7. such other factors as the President or the Committee determine to be appropriate.

S. 1610 makes the United States immune from any liability for any losses or expenses incurred by the parties to an investment transaction as a result of actions taken by CFIUS if the entities did not submit a written notification to CFIUS or if the transaction was completed prior to the completion of a CFIUS review or investigation.

S. 1610 grants CFIUS, and a designated lead agency, the authority to negotiate, impose, or enforce any agreement or condition with the parties to a transaction in order to mitigate any threat to the national security of the United States. Such agreements are to be based on a "risk-based analysis" of the threat posed by the transaction. Also, if a notification of a transaction is withdrawn before any review or investigation by CFIUS can be completed, the measure grants the Committee the authority to take a number of actions. In particular, the Committee could develop (1) interim protections to address specific concerns about the transaction pending a re-submission of a notice by the parties; (2) specific time frames for resubmitting the notice; and (3) a process for tracking any actions taken by any party to the transaction.

In S. 1610, CFIUS must designate a lead agency to negotiate, modify, monitor, and enforce agreements in order to mitigate any threat to national security. The measure requires the federal entity or entities involved in any mitigating agreement to report to CFIUS on any modification to any agreement or condition that had been imposed and to ensure that "any significant" modification is reported to the Director of National Intelligence and to any other federal department or agency that "may have a material interest in such modification." S. 1610 requires such reports to be filed with the Attorney General.

S. 1610 requires CFIUS to develop a method for evaluating the compliance of firms that had entered into a mitigation agreement or condition that was imposed as a requirement for approval of the investment transaction. Such measures, however, are required to be developed in such a way that they allow CFIUS to determine that compliance is taking place without also: 1) "unnecessarily diverting" CFIUS resources from assessing any new covered transaction for which a written notice had been filed; and 2) placing "unnecessary" burdens on a party to a investment transaction.

S. 1610 requires CFIUS to report annually to Congress on any reviews or investigations that it had conducted during the prior year. Each report must include a list of all reviews and investigations that had been conducted, information on the nature of the business activities of the parties involved in an investment transaction, information about the status of the review or investigation, and information on any withdrawal from the process, any roll call votes by the Committee, any extension of time for any investigation, and any presidential decision or action taken under the Exon-Florio provision. In addition, CFIUS must report on trend information on the number of filings, investigations, withdrawals, and presidential decisions or actions that were taken. The report also must include cumulative information on the business sectors involved in filings and the countries from which the investments originated; information on the status of the investments of companies that withdrew notices and the types of security arrangements and conditions CFIUS used to mitigate national security concerns; the methods the Committee used to determine that firms were complying with mitigation agreements or conditions; and a detailed discussion of all perceived adverse effects of investment transactions on the national security or critical infrastructure of the United States.

Relative to critical technologies, S. 1610 requires CFIUS to include in its annual report an evaluation of any credible evidence of a coordinated strategy by one or more countries or companies to acquire U.S. companies involved in research, development, or production of critical technologies in which the United States is a leading producer. The report also must include an evaluation of possible industrial espionage activities directed or directly assisted by foreign governments against private U.S. companies aimed at obtaining commercial secrets related to critical technologies.

In addition, the Senate measure requires the Secretary of the Treasury, in consultation with the Secretary of State and the Secretary of Commerce to conduct a study on investment in the United States, particularly in critical infrastructure and industries affecting national security by: (1) foreign governments, entities controlled by or acting on behalf of a foreign government, or entities of foreign countries which comply with any boycott of Israel; (2) foreign governments, entities controlled by or acting on behalf of a foreign government, or entities of foreign countries which do not ban organizations designated by the Secretary of State as foreign terrorist organizations.

S. 1610 also requires the Inspector General of the Department of the Treasury to investigate any failure of CFIUS to comply with requirements for reporting that were imposed prior to the passage of this measure and to report the findings of this report to the Congress. In particular, the report must be sent to the chairman and ranking member of each committee of the House and the Senate with jurisdiction over any aspect of the report, including the Committee on International Relations, the Committee on Financial Services, and the Committee on Energy and Commerce of the House. S. 1610 also requires the chief executive officer of any party to a merger, acquisition, or takeover to certify in writing that the information contained in the written notification to CFIUS fully complied with the requirements of the Exon-Florio provision and that the information was accurate and complete. This written notification must also include any mitigation agreement or condition that was part of a CFIUS approval.

CONCLUSIONS

The proposed DP World acquisition of P and O, while of arguably little economic impact on the U.S. economy, could affect public policy on foreign investment that relates to issues of corporate ownership, foreign investment, and national security in the U.S. economy. The transaction revealed significant differences between Congress and the Administration over the operations of CFIUS and over the objectives the Committee should be pursuing. In addition, the transaction demonstrated that neither Congress nor the Administration has been able thus far to define clearly the national security implications of foreign direct investment. This issue likely reflects differing assessments of the economic impact of foreign investment on the U.S. economy and differing political and philosophical convictions among Members and between the Congress and the Administration.

The incident also focused attention on the informal process firms use to have their investment transactions reviewed by CFIUS prior to a formal review. According to anecdotal evidence, some firms apparently believe that the CFIUS process is not market neutral, but that it adds to market uncertainty that can negatively affect a firm's stock price and lead to economic behavior by some firms that is not optimal for the economy as a whole. Such behavior might involve firms expending a considerable amount of resources to avoid a CFIUS investigation, or deciding to terminate a transaction that would improve the optimal performance of the economy in order to avoid a CFIUS investigation. While such anecdotal evidence does not provide enough evidence to serve as the basis for developing public policy, it does raise a number of concerns about the possible impact of the CFIUS process on the market and the potential costs of redefining the concept of national security relative to foreign investment.

The focus by Congress on the Committee has also shown that the DP World transaction, in combination with other recent unpopular foreign investment transactions, has exacerbated dissatisfaction among some Members of Congress over the operations of CFIUS. In particular, some Members are displeased with the way the Committee uses its discretionary authority under the Exon-Florio provision to investigate certain foreign investment transactions. Congress is changing the current process to require more frequent contact between the Committee, which generally operates without much public or congressional attention, and the Congress. Congress also has expanded its oversight role over the Committee.

The DP World transaction also revealed that the September 11, 2001 terrorist attacks may have fundamentally altered the viewpoint of some Members of Congress regarding the role of foreign investment in the economy and over the impact of such investment on the national security framework. These observers argue that this change requires a reassessment of the role of foreign investment in the economy and of the implications of corporate ownership of activities that fall under the rubric of critical infrastructure. As a result, Congress amended the CFIUS process to enhance Congress's oversight role while it reduced somewhat the discretion of CFIUS to review and investigate foreign investment transactions in order to have CFIUS investigate a larger number of foreign investment cases. In addition, the DP World transaction has focused attention on long-unresolved issues concerning the role of foreign investment in the nation's overall security framework and the methods that are being used to assess the impact of foreign investment on the nation's defense industrial base and homeland security.

Most economists agree that there is little economic evidence to conclude that foreign ownership, whether by a private entity or by an entity that is owned or controlled by a foreign government, has a measurable impact on the U.S. economy. Others may argue that such firms pose a risk to national security or to homeland security, but such concerns are not within the purview of this report. Similar issues concerning corporate ownership were raised during the late 1980s and early 1990s when foreign investment in the U.S. economy increased rapidly. There are little new data, however, to alter the conclusion reached at that time that there is no definitive way to assess the economic impact of foreign ownership or of foreign investment on the economy. Although some observers have expressed concerns about foreign investors who are owned or controlled by foreign governments acquiring U.S. firms, there is little confirmed evidence that such a distinction in corporate ownership has any effect on the economy as whole.

For most economists, the distinction between domestic- and foreign-owned firms, whether the foreign firms are privately owned or controlled by a foreign government, is sufficiently small that they would argue that it does not warrant placing restrictions on the inflow of foreign investment. Nevertheless, foreign direct investment does entail various economic costs and benefits. On the benefit side, such investments bring added capital into the economy and potentially could add to productivity growth and innovation. Such investment also represents one repercussion of the U.S. trade deficit. The deficit transfers dollar-denominated assets to foreign investors, who then decide how to hold those assets by choosing among various investment vehicles, including direct investment. Foreign investment also removes a stream of monetary benefits from the economy in the form of repatriated capital and profits that reduces the total amount of capital in the economy. Such costs and benefits likely occur whether the foreign owner is a private entity or a foreign government.

REFERENCES

[1]   Executive Order 11858 (b), May 7, 1975, 40 F.R. 20263.
[2]   U.S. Congress. House. Committee on Government Operations. Subcommittee on Commerce, Consumer, and Monetary Affairs. *The Operations of Federal Agencies in*

Monitoring, Reporting on, and Analyzing Foreign Investments in the United States. Hearings. 96th Cong., 1st sess., Part 3, July 30, 1979. Washington, U.S. Govt. Print. Off., 1979. p. 334-335. (Hereafter cited as, *The Operations of Federal Agencies*, part 3.)

[3]   Peninsular and Oriental Steam Company is a leading ports operator and transport company with operations in ports, ferries, and property development. It operates container terminals and logistics operations in over 100 ports and has a presence in 18 countries.

[4]   Dubai Ports World was created in November 2005 by integrating Dubai Ports Authority and Dubai Ports International. It is one of the largest commercial port operators in the world with operations in the Middle East, India, Europe, Asia, Latin America, the Carribean, and North America.

[5]   Weisman, Jonathan, and Bradley Graham, "Dubai Firm to Sell U.S. Port Operations," *The Washington Post*, March 10, 2006. p. A1.

[6]   King, Neil Jr., and Greg Hitt, Dubai Ports World Sells U.S. Assets — AIG Buys Operations that Ignited Controversy As Democrats Plan Changes. *The Wall Street Journal*, December 12, 2006. P. A1.

[7]   The term "representative" was dropped by Executive Order 12661, December 27, 1988, 54 FR 780.

[8]   Executive Order 11858 (b), May 7, 1975, 40 F.R. 20263.

[9]   P.L. 94-472, Oct 11, 1976; 22 USC 3101.

[10]   P.L. 94-472, Oct 11, 1976; 22 USC Sec. 3101(b).

[11]   U.S. Congress. House. Committee on Government Operations. *The Adequacy of the Federal Response to Foreign Investment in the United States.* Report by the Committee on Government Operations. H.Rept. 96-1216, 96th Cong., 2nd sess., Washington, U.S. Govt. Print. Off., 1980. 166-184.

[12]   *The Operations of Federal Agencies*, part 3, p. 5.

[13]   U.S. Congress. House. Committee on Energy and Commerce. Subcommittee on Commerce, Consumer Protection, and Competitiveness. *Foreign Takeovers and National Security.* Hearings on Section 905 of H.R. 3. 100th Cong., 1st sess., October 20, 1987. Testimony of David C. Mulford. Washington, U.S. Govt., Print., Off., 1988. p. 21-22.

[14]   Auerbach, Stuart. Cabinet to Weigh Sale of Chip Firm. *The Washington Post*, March 12, 1987. p. E1.

[15]   Sanger, David E. Japanese Purchase of Chip Maker Canceled After Objections in U.S. *The New York Times*, March 17, 1987. p. 1.

[16]   Pollack, Andrew. Schlumberger Accepts Offer. *The New York Times*, September 1, 1987. p. D1.

[17]   Kilborn, Peter T. Curb Asked On Foreign Takeovers. *The New York Times*, March 18, 1987. p. D1.

[18]   P.L. 100-418.

[19]   Testimony of Patrick A. Mulloy before the Committee on Banking, Housing, and Urban Affairs, October 20, 2005.

[20]   CRS Report RL33103, *Foreign Investment in the United States: Major Federal Restrictions,* by Michael V. Seitzinger.

[21]   Executive Order 12661 of December 27, 1988, 54 F.R. 779.

[22] Executive Order 11858 of May 7, 1975, 40 F.R. 20263 established the Committee with six members: the Secretaries of State, the Treasury, Defense, Commerce, and the Assistant to the President for Economic Affairs, and the Executive Director of the Council on International Economic Policy. Executive Order 12188, January 2, 1980, 45 F.R. 969, added the United States Trade Representative and substituted the Chairman of the Council of Economic Advisors for the Executive Director of the Council on International Economic Policy. Executive Order 12661, December 27, 1988, 54 F.R. 779, added the Attorney General and the Director of the Office of Management and Budget. Executive Order 12860, September 3, 1993, 58 F.R. 47201, added the Director of the Office of Science and Technology Policy, the Assistant to the President for National Security Affairs, and the Assistant to the President for Economic Policy. Executive Order 13286, Section 57, February 28, 2003 added the Secretary of Homeland Security.

[23] Regulations Pertaining to Mergers, Acquisitions, and Takeover by Foreign Persons. 31 CFR Sec. 800.

[24] Senate Armed Services Committee, Briefing on the Dubai Ports World Ports Deal, February 23, 2006.

[25] Ibid.

[26] 50 U.S.C. App. Sec. 2401, as amended.

[27] 22 U.S.C. App. 2778 et seq.

[28] 50 U.S.C. Appendix Sec. 2170(c)

[29] 50 U.S.C. Appendix Sec. 2170(g).

[30] Regulations Pertaining to Mergers, Acquisitions, and Takeovers by Foreign Persons. 31

[31] F.R. Part 800.

[32] P.L. 102-484, October 23, 1992.

[33] Briefing on the Dubai Ports World Deal before the Senate Armed Services Committee, February 23, 2006.

[34] Marchick, David. Testimony Before the House Financial Services Committee, March 1, 2006.

[35] CFIUS, *The Washington Post*, July 3, 2005. p. F3.

[36] Auerbach, Stuart. "President Tells China to Sell Seattle Firm." *The Washington Post*, February 3, 1990. p. A1; and Benham, Barbara. "Blocked Takeover Fuels Foreign Policy Flap." *Investor's Daily*, February 8, 1990. p. 1.

[37] Testimony of Robert Kimmett, Briefing on the Dubai Ports World Deal before the Senate Armed Services Committee, February 23, 2006.

[38] *Ibid*.

[39] Hulse, Carl, "In Break with While House, House Panel Rejects Port Deal," *The New York Times*, March 9, 2006. p. A1.

[40] Weisman, Jonathan, and Bradley Graham, "Dubai Firm to Sell U.S. Port Operations," *The Washington Post*, March 10, 2006. p. A1.

[41] *Washington Trade Daily*, March 17, 2006. p. 3.

In: Economics, Political and Social Issues …
Editor: Michelle L. Fergusson

IMMIGRATION OF FOREIGN WORKERS: LABOR MARKET TESTS AND PROTECTIONS[*]

Ruth Ellen Wasem[#]
Immigration Policy

ABSTRACT

Economic indicators confirm that the economy is in a recession. Historically, international migration ebbs during economic crises; e.g., immigration to the United States was at its lowest levels during the Great Depression. While preliminary statistical trends hint at a slowing of migration pressures, it remains unclear how the current economic recession will effect immigration. Addressing these contentious policy reforms against the backdrop of economic crisis sharpens the social and business cleavages and narrows the range of options.

Even as U.S. unemployment rises, some employers maintain that they continue to need the "best and the brightest" workers, regardless of their country of birth, to remain competitive in a worldwide market and to keep their firms in the United States. While support for increasing employment-based immigration may be dampened by the economic recession, proponents argue that the ability to hire foreign workers is an essential ingredient for economic growth.

Those opposing increases in foreign workers assert that such expansions—particularly during an economic recession—would have a deleterious effect on salaries, compensation, and working conditions of U.S. workers. Others question whether the United States should continue to issue foreign worker visas (particularly temporary visas) during a recession and suggest that a moratorium on such visas might be prudent.

The number of foreign workers entering the United States legally has notably increased over the past decade. The number of employment-based legal *permanent* residents (LPRs) grew from under 100,000 in FY1994 to over 250,000 in FY2005, and stood at 163,176 in 2007. The number of visas for employment-based *temporary* nonimmigrants rose from just under 600,000 in FY1994 to approximately 1.4 million in FY2007. In particular, "H" visas for temporary workers tripled from 98,030 in FY1994 to 424,369 in FY2007.

The Immigration and Nationality Act (INA) bars the admission of any alien who seeks to enter the U.S. to perform skilled or unskilled labor, unless it is determined that (1) there are not sufficient U.S. workers who are able, willing, qualified, and available; and (2) the employment of the alien will not adversely affect the wages and working conditions of similarly employed workers in the United States. The foreign labor certification program in the U.S. Department of Labor (DOL) is responsible for ensuring

---

[*] Excerpted from CRS Report RL 33977 dated March 20, 2009.
[#] E-mail: rwasem@crs.loc

that foreign workers do not displace or adversely affect working conditions of U.S. workers.

In the 110th Congress, Senate action on comprehensive immigration reform legislation, which included substantial revisions to employment-based immigration, stalled at the end of June 2007 after an intensive floor debate. The House, however, did not act on comprehensive legislation in the 110th Congress. During his time in the Senate, President Barack Obama supported comprehensive immigration legislation that reformed employment-based immigration. Similar views have been expressed by Secretary of Homeland Security (and former Arizona Governor) Janet Napolitano.

The 111th Congress addressed one element of this issue in §1611 of P.L. 111-5, the American Recovery and Reinvestment Act of 2009, which requires companies receiving Troubled Asset Relief Program (TARP) funding to comply with the more rigorous labor market rules of H-1B dependent companies if they hire foreign workers on H-1B visas. This report does not track legislation and will be updated if policies are revised.

INTRODUCTION

Economic indicators confirm that the economy is in a recession. Historically, international migration ebbs during economic crises (e.g., immigration to the United States was at its lowest levels during the Great Depression). While preliminary statistical trends hint at a slowing of migration pressures, it remains unclear how the current economic recession will effect immigration. Addressing these contentious policy reforms against the backdrop of economic crisis sharpens the social and business cleavages and narrows the range of options.

Even as U.S. unemployment rises, some employers maintain that they continue to need the "best and the brightest" workers, regardless of their country of birth, to remain competitive in a worldwide market and to keep their firms in the United States. While support for increasing employment-based immigration may be dampened by the economic recession, proponents argue that the ability to hire foreign workers is an essential ingredient for economic growth.

Those opposing increases in foreign workers assert that such expansions—particularly during an economic recession—would have a deleterious effect on salaries, compensation, and working conditions of U.S. workers. Others question whether the United States should continue to issue foreign worker visas (particularly temporary visas) during a recession and suggest that a moratorium on such visas might be prudent.

Key Elements

The Immigration and Nationality Act (INA) bars the admission of a prospective immigrant who seeks to enter the United States to perform skilled or unskilled labor, unless the Secretary of Labor provides a certification to the Secretary of State and the Attorney General [1]. Specifically, the Secretary of Labor must determine that there are not sufficient U.S. workers who are able, willing, qualified, and available at the time of the alien's application for an LPR visa and admission to the United States and at the place where the alien is to perform such skilled or unskilled labor. The Secretary of Labor must further certify that the employment of the alien will not adversely affect the wages and working conditions of similarly employed workers in the United States [2]. The foreign labor certification program in the U.S. Department of Labor (DOL) is responsible for ensuring that foreign workers do not displace or adversely affect working conditions of U.S. workers. Under current law, DOL adjudicates *labor certification* applications (LCA) for permanent employment-based immigrants.

As discussed in more detail below, many of the foreign nationals entering the United States on a temporary basis for employment are *not* subject to a labor market test (i.e., demonstrating that there are not sufficient U.S. workers who are able, willing, qualified, and available), and as a result, their employers do not file LCAs with the DOL. There are several groups of temporary foreign employees, however, that are covered by labor market tests. The DOL adjudicates the streamlined LCA known as *labor attestations* for temporary agricultural workers, temporary nonagricultural workers, and temporary professional workers. Foreign labor certification is one of the "national activities" within the Employment and Training Administration (ETA) [3]

Brief History of Labor Certification

Congress passed the contract labor law of 1885, known as the Foran Act, which made it unlawful to import aliens for the performance of labor or service of any kind in the United States [4]. That bar on employment-based immigration lasted until 1952, when Congress enacted the Immigration and Nationality Act (INA), a sweeping law also known as the McCarran-Walters Act that brought together many disparate immigration and citizenship statutes and made significant revisions in the existing laws [5]. The 1952 Act authorized visas for aliens who would perform needed services because of their high educational attainment, technical training, specialized experience, or exceptional ability [6]. Prior to the admission of these employment-based immigrants, however, the 1952 Act required the Secretary of Labor to certify to the Attorney General and the Secretary of State that there were not sufficient U.S. workers "able, willing, and qualified" to perform this work and that the employment of such aliens would not "adversely affect the wages and working conditions" of similarly employed U.S. workers [7]. This provision in the 1952 Act established the policy of labor certification. The major reform of INA in 1965 included language that obligated the employers to file labor certification applications (LCAs) [8]

Within DOL, the former Bureau of Employment Security first administered labor certification following enactment of the policy in 1952. After the abolishment of Employment Security in 1969, the Manpower Administration handled labor certification. In 1975, the Manpower Administration became the Employment and Training Administration (ETA), and ETA continues to oversee the labor certification of aliens seeking to become legal permanent residents (LPRs). Currently, foreign labor certification is one of the "national activities" within ETA.

The current statutory authority that conditions the admission of employment-based immigrants on labor markets tests is found in the grounds for exclusion portion of the INA. It denies entry to the United States of aliens seeking to work without proper labor certification. The labor certification ground for exclusion covers aliens coming to live as LPRs [9]. The INA specifically states:

Any alien who seeks to enter the United States for the purpose of performing skilled or unskilled labor is inadmissible, unless the Secretary of Labor has determined and certified to the Secretary of State and the Attorney General that—(I) there are not sufficient workers who are able, willing, qualified (or equally qualified in the case of an alien described in clause (ii)) and available at the time of application for a visa and admission to the United States and at the place where the alien is to perform such skilled or unskilled labor, and (II) the employment of such alien will not adversely affect the wages and working conditions of workers in the United States similarly employed [10]

The law also details additional requirements and exceptions for certain occupational groups and classes of aliens, some of which are discussed below.

PERMANENT EMPLOYMENT-BASED ADMISSIONS

Immigrant admissions and adjustments to for legal permanent resident (LPR) status are subject to a complex set of numerical limits and preference categories that give priority for admission on the basis of family relationships, needed skills, and geographic diversity. The INA establishes a statutory worldwide level of 675,000 LPRs annually, but this level is flexible and certain categories of LPRs are excluded from, or permitted to exceed, the limits. This permanent worldwide immigrant level consists of the following components: 480,000 family-sponsored immigrants; 140,000 employment-based preference immigrants; and 55,000 diversity immigrants [11]

The employment-based preference categories are

- *first preference*: priority workers who are persons of extraordinary ability in the arts, sciences, education, business, or athletics; outstanding professors and researchers; and certain multinational executives and managers;
- *second preference*: members of the professions holding advanced degrees or persons of exceptional ability;
- *third preference*: skilled workers with at least two years training, professionals with baccalaureate degrees, and unskilled workers in occupations in which U.S. workers are in short supply;
- *fourth preference*: special immigrants who largely consist of religious workers, certain former employees of the U.S. government, and undocumented juveniles who become wards of the court; and
- *fifth preference*: investors who invest at least $1 million (or less money in rural areas or areas of high unemployment) to create at least 10 new jobs.

In 1990, Congress had amended the INA to raise the level of employment-based immigration from 54,000 LPR visas to more than 143,000 LPR visas annually. That law also expanded two preference categories into five preference categories and reduced the cap on unskilled workers from 27,000 to 10,000 annually. Although there have been major legislative proposals since the mid-1990s to alter employment-based immigration, these preference categories remain intact [12]

Currently, annual admission of employment-based preference immigrants is limited to 140,000 plus certain unused family preference numbers from the prior year. As Figure 1 displays, LPR admissions for the first, second and third employment-based preferences have exceeded the ceilings in recent years [13].

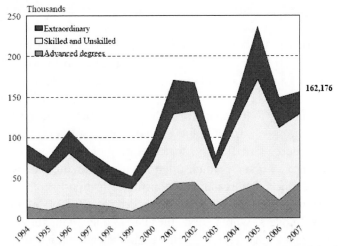

Source: CRS analysis of data from the DHS Office of Immigration Statistics and the former INS.
Note: The 25,911 Chinese who adjusted under the Chinese Student Protection Act from 1994 to 1996 are not depicted even though they were counted under the "Skilled and Unskilled" category.

Figure 1. Permanent Employment-based Admissions for 1st, 2nd, and 3rd Preferences, 1994-2007.

In 2003, however, processing delays—largely due to the reorganization of immigration functions as the Department of Homeland Security (DHS) was established— reduced the number of LPRs to only 705,827. Because DHS' U.S. Citizenship and Immigration Services Bureau (USCIS) was only able to process 161,579 of the potential 226,000 family-sponsored LPRs in FY2003, an extra 64,421 LPR visas rolled over to the FY2004 employment-based categories and created the spike depicted in Figure 1.

Employers who seek to hire prospective immigrant workers petition with the USCIS. An eligible petitioner (in this instance, the eligible petitioner is the U.S. employer seeking to employ the alien) must file an I-140 for the alien seeking to immigrate. USCIS adjudicators determine whether the prospective LPR has demonstrated that he or she meets the qualifications for the particular job as well as the INA employment-based preference category [14].

In terms of employment-based immigration, decisions of the Board of Immigration Appeals (BIA) have significantly effected the implementation of the law by offering clarification of the statutory language. While DOL draws on regulations that govern its role, the USCIS is more often guided through BIA decisions and procedures spelled out in the former Immigration and Naturalization Service's Operations Instructions.

LPR Labor Certification Process

Employment-based immigrants applying through the *second* and *third* preferences must obtain labor certification [15]. The intending employer may not file a Form I-140 with USCIS unless the intending employer has obtained this labor certification, and includes the approved LCA with the Form I-140.

Occupations for which the Secretary of Labor has already determined that a shortage exists and U.S. workers will not be adversely affected are listed in Schedule A of the regulations [16]. Conversely, occupations for which the Secretary of Labor has already determined that a shortage does not exist and that U.S. workers will be adversely affected are listed in Schedule B [17]. If there is not a labor shortage in the given occupation as published in Schedule A, the employer must submit evidence of extensive recruitment efforts in order to obtain certification.

Several elements are key to the approval of the LCA. Foremost are findings that there are not "available" U.S. workers or, if there are available workers, the workers are not "qualified." Equally important are findings that the hiring of foreign workers would not have an adverse affect on U.S. workers, which often hinges on findings of what the prevailing wage is for the particular occupation and what constitutes "similarly employed workers." [18]

Prior to the Program Electronic Review Management (PERM) regulations (which are discussed below), employers would first file an "Application for Alien Employment Certification" (ETA 750 form) with the state Employment Service office in the area of intended employment, also known as state workforce agencies (SWAs) [19]. The SWAs did not have the authority to grant or deny LCAs; rather, the SWAs processed the LCAs.

They also had a role in recruitment as well as gathering data on prevailing wages and the availability of U.S. workers. They then forwarded the LCA along with their report to the regional ETA office [20].

DOL summarized the labor certification process to hire immigrant workers prior to the implementation of PERM as follows:

> ... requires employers to file a permanent labor certification application with the SWA serving the area of intended employment and, after filing, to actively recruit U.S. workers in good faith for a period of at least 30 days for the job openings for which aliens are sought. Job applicants are either referred directly to the employer or their resumes are sent to the employer. The employer has 45 days to report to either the SWA or an ETA backlog processing center or regional office the lawful job-related reasons for not hiring any referred qualified U.S. worker..... If, however, the employer believes able, willing, and qualified U.S. workers are not available to take the job, the application, together with the documentation of the recruitment results and prevailing wage information, is sent to either an ETA backlog processing center or ETA regional office.
>
> There, it is reviewed and a determination made as to whether to issue the labor certification based upon the employer's compliance with applicable labor laws and program regulations.
>
> If we determine there are no able, willing, qualified, and available U.S. workers, and the employment of the alien will not adversely affect the wages and working conditions of similarly employed U.S. workers, we so certify to the DHS and the DOS by issuing a permanent labor certification [21]

Prior to the implementation of the procedural reforms discussed below, DOL acknowledged a backlog of more than 300,000 LCAs for permanent admissions in 2003 and projected an average processing time of 3½ years before an employer would receive a determination. At that time, DOL noted further that some states had backlogs that would lead to processing times of five to six years [22]

Program Electronic Review Management (PERM)

The Program Electronic Review Management (PERM) regulations were published on December 27, 2004, after initially being proposed in May 2002. The stated goals of PERM are to streamline the labor certification process and reduce fraudulent filings. Now all LCAs for aliens becoming LPRs are processed through PERM.

Rather than SWAs receiving the LCAs, all PERM applications are processed by national processing centers (NPCs). There are currently NPCs in Chicago and Atlanta. With the exception of their role in determining prevailing wages and maintaining the job orders, the SWAs have been removed from the LCA adjudication process. To further streamline the process, PERM offers a 10-page attestation-based form that may be submitted electronically (i.e., using web-based forms and instructions) or mailed to one of the NPCs [23]

In additional to centralized filing, PERM requires the employer to register so that they receive a personal identification number (PIN) and password. PERM also identifies employers by their federal employer identification number.

Recruitment must be completed prior to filing the labor certification, but the documentation for recruitment does not need to be submitted with the "Application for Permanent Employment Certification" (ETA Form 9089). Employers must attest that they met the mandatory recruitment requirements for all applications, which are

- two Sunday newspaper job advertisements;
- state workforce agency job order;
- internal posting of job; and
- in-house media (if applicable).

There are specified exceptions to these recruitment requirements—notably those involving college or university teachers selected through competitive recruitment and Schedule A occupations. The recruitment documentation may be specifically requested by the Certifying Officers (COs) through an audit letter. Audit letters may be issued randomly or triggered by information on the form.

PERM recruitment requirements also differentiate between professional and non-professional occupations. Professional occupation is defined in the final rule as "an occupation for which the attainment of a bachelor's or higher degree is a usual education requirement." If the application is for a professional occupation, the employer must conduct three additional steps that the employer chooses from a list published in the regulation [24]

As a result of these regulatory reforms, DOL predicted that its COs will adjudicate PERM applications within 45-60 days. Since PERM provides specific recruitment and documentary requirements, less discretion is given to the COs to determine whether the recruitment requirements are met. Upon adjudication of an application, the CO will have three choices:

- certify the application,
- deny the application, or
- issue an audit letter.

According to the latest available data, PERM handled a total of 98,753 LCAs in FY2007, and 85,112 (86.2%) were approved [25]

TEMPORARY EMPLOYMENT-BASED ADMISSIONS

Overview

Currently, there are 24 major nonimmigrant (i.e., aliens who the United States admits on a temporary basis) visa categories, and 72 specific types of nonimmigrant visas issued. These visa categories are commonly referred to by the letter and numeral that denote their subsection in the INA.[26]. Several visa categories are designated for employment-based temporary admission. The term "guest worker" is not defined in law or policy and typically refers to foreign workers employed in low-skilled or unskilled jobs that are temporary [27] While a variety of temporary visas—by their intrinsic nature—allow foreign nationals to be employed in the United States, the applications for these visas do not trigger the requirement for an LCA filing under §212(a)(5). Under current law, only employers hiring workers through the H visa categories are required to file an LCA, as discussed more fully later in the report.

Temporary Workers [28]

The major nonimmigrant category for temporary workers is the H visa, and an LCA is required for the admission of an H visa holder. The current H-1 categories include professional specialty workers (H-1B) and nurses (H-1C). Temporary professional workers from Canada and Mexico may enter according to terms set by the North American Free Trade Agreement (NAFTA) on TN visas. There are two visa categories for temporarily importing seasonal workers, that is, guest workers: agricultural guest workers enter with H-2A visas and other seasonal/ intermittent workers enter with H-2B visas. The law sets numerical restrictions on annual admissions of the H-1B (65,000), the H-1C (500), and the H-2B (66,000); however, most H-1B workers enter on visas that are exempt from the ceiling. There is no limit on the admission of H-2A workers.

Multinational Executive and Specialist Employees and International Investors

Intracompany transferees who are executive, managerial, and have specialized knowledge, and who are employed with an international firm or corporation are admitted on the L visas. The prospective L nonimmigrant must demonstrate that he or she meets the qualifications for the particular job as well as the visa category. The alien must have been employed by the firm for at least six months in the preceding three years in the capacity for which the transfer is sought. The alien must be employed in an executive capacity, a managerial capacity, or have specialized knowledge of the firm's product to be eligible for the L visa. The INA does not require firms who wish to bring L intracompany transfers into the United States to demonstrate that U.S. workers will not be adversely affected order to obtain a visa for the transferring employee.

Aliens who are treaty traders enter on E-1 visas, whereas those who are treaty investors use E-2 visas. An E-1 treaty trader visa allows a foreign national to enter the United States for the purpose of conducting "substantial trade" between the United States and the country of which the person is a citizen. An E-2 treaty investor can be any person who comes to the United States to develop and direct the operations of an enterprise in which he or she has invested, or is in the process of investing, a "substantial amount of capital." Both these E-class visas require that a treaty exist between the United States and the principal foreign national's country of citizenship [29]

The E-3 treaty professional visa is a temporary work visa limited to citizens of Australia. It is usually issued for two years at a time. Occupationally, it mirrors the H-1B visa in that the foreign worker on an E-3 visa must be employed in a specialty occupation [30]

Cultural Exchange

Whether a cultural exchange visa holder is permitted to work in the United States depends on the specific exchange program in which they are participating. The J visa includes professors, research scholars, students, foreign medical graduates, camp counselors and au pairs who are in an approved exchange visitor program. Participants in structured exchange programs enter on Q-1 visas. Q-2 visas are for Irish young adults from specified Irish border counties in participating exchange programs.

Outstanding and Extraordinary

Persons with extraordinary ability in the sciences, arts, education, business, or athletics are admitted on O visas, whereas internationally recognized athletes or members of an internationally recognized entertainment group come on P visas. Generally, the O visa is reserved for the highest level of accomplishment and covers a fairly broad set of occupations and endeavors, including athletics and entertainers. The P visa has a somewhat lower standard of achievement than the O visa, and it is restricted to a narrower band of occupations and endeavors. The P visa is used by an alien who performs as an artist, athlete, or entertainer (individually or as part of a group or team) at an internationally recognized level of performance and who seeks to enter the United States temporarily and solely for the purpose of performing in that capacity. The law allows individual athletes to stay in intervals up to 5 years at a time, up to 10 years in total.

Religious Workers

Aliens working in religious vocations enter on R visas. The regulations define religious occupation as "an activity which relates to a traditional religious function." USCIS has proposed regulations further defining "religious denomination" to clarify that it applies to a religious group or community of believers governed or administered under some form of common ecclesiastical government. Under the proposed rule, the denomination must share a common creed or statement of faith, some form of worship, a formal or informal code of doctrine and discipline, religious services and ceremonies, established places of religious worship, religious congregations, or comparable indicia of a bona fide religious denomination [31]

Trends in Temporary Employment-Based Visas

As Figure 2 illustrates, the issuances of temporary employment-based visas have risen steadily over the past decade. In FY2007, there were 1.1 million temporary employment-based visas issued [32]. The H and TN visas evidenced largest increase—333,868 more visas issued in 2007 than in 1994. During the period 1994-2007, the category with the largest percentage increase were also the H and NAFTA workers (340.6%). The R visas also evidenced a noteworthy increase of 216.7%. The E and L visas rose by 144.3% over this period, followed by the O and P visas, which increased by 104.5%.

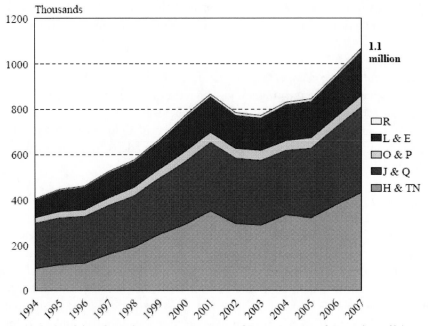

Source: CRS analysis of data from the U.S. Department of State, Bureau of Consular Affairs.

Figure 2. Temporary Employment-based Visas Issued, 1994-2007.

These data are from the Department of State Consular Affairs Bureau, which reports the number of visas issued annually by category. As noted above, many of these visas are valid for several years and may be used for multiple entries into the United States. While visa data offer a measure of labor market demand for a given year, they do not reflect the actual number of temporary employment-based foreign workers in the United States any given year.

Admissions data from the DHS Office of Immigration Statistics (OIS) offer a different perspective on foreign temporary workers in Figure 3. These data indicate that foreign temporary employment-based visa holders entered the United States approximately 1.9 million times in FY2007. That the OIS admissions number is almost twice that of the visa issuances number is due to the fact that many of these visas are multiple entry for multiple years. It is not surprising that the percentage of Hs, Ls, and Es are disproportionately larger in the OIS data than the Consular Affairs data because H, L, and E visas are typically valid for longer periods of time than some of the other temporary employment-based visas. The OIS admission data do not reflect the actual number of temporary employment-based foreign workers in the United States any given year.

LABOR MARKET TESTS FOR WORKERS FOR H VISAS

Prospective employers of H-1B, H-2A, and H-2B workers (approximately one-third of the temporary foreign workers in the United States) must apply to the Secretary of Labor for labor certification before they can file petitions with DHS to bring in foreign workers [33]. Similarly with LCAs for LPRs, the determinations for H workers are made by DOL's Employment and Training Administration (ETA) on behalf of the Secretary or Labor. The INA requires that employers apply for a certification that there are not sufficient U.S. workers who are qualified and available to perform the work; and the employment of foreign workers will not adversely affect the wages and working conditions of U.S. workers who are similarly employed. As summarized below, the particular employer requirements to obtain labor certification differ under the three visas. H-2A and H-2B LCAs include an offer of employment. This job offer, which describes the terms and conditions of employment, is used in the recruitment of U.S. workers and H-2A or H-2B workers, as relevant. Under the H-2a and H-2B labor certification processes, as revised by regulations effective in January 2009, prospective employers must engage in specified recruitment activities filing the LCA [34]

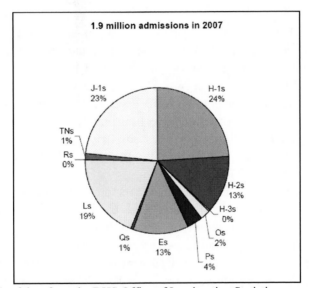

Source: CRS analysis of data from the DHS Office of Immigration Statistics.
Notes: The E visa category includes spouses and children; all other visa categories depict only the principal nonimmigrant.

Figure 3. Temporary Admissions for Selected Employment-based Visas.

H-1B Visas and Labor Attestation

The largest number of H visas are issued to temporary workers in specialty occupations, known as H-1B nonimmigrants [35]. The regulations define a "specialty occupation" as requiring theoretical and practical application of a body of highly specialized knowledge in a field of human endeavor including, but not limited to, architecture, engineering, mathematics, physical sciences, social sciences, medicine and health, education, law, accounting, business specialties, theology, and the arts, and requiring the attainment of a bachelor's degree or its equivalent as a minimum [36]. The prospective H-1B nonimmigrants must demonstrate to the USCIS that they have the requisite education and work experience for the posted positions. After DOL approves the labor attestation, USCIS processes the petition for the H-1B nonimmigrant (assuming other immigration requirements are satisfied) for periods up to three years. An alien can stay a maximum of six years on an H-1B visa.

The H-1B labor attestation, a three-page application form, is a streamlined version of the labor certification application (LCA) and is the first step for an employer wishing to bring in an H-1B professional foreign worker. As noted above, the attestation is a statement of intent rather than a documentation of actions taken [37]. In LCA's for H-1B workers, the employer must attest that the firm will pay the nonimmigrant the greater of the actual wages paid other employees in the same job or the prevailing wages for that occupation; the firm will provide working conditions for the nonimmigrant that do not cause the working conditions of the other employees to be adversely affected; and that there is no applicable strike or lockout. The firm must provide a copy of the LCA to representatives of the bargaining unit or—if there is no bargaining representative—must post the LCA in conspicuous locations at the work site [38]

H-1B Dependent
The law requires that employers defined as H-1B dependent (generally firms with at least 15% of the workforce who are H-1B workers) meet additional labor market tests [39]. These H-1B dependent employers must also attest that they tried to recruit U.S. workers and that they have not displaced U.S. workers in similar occupations within 90 days prior or after the hiring of H-1B workers. Additionally, the H-1B dependent employers must offer the H-1B workers compensation packages (not just wages) that are comparable to U.S. workers [40]. Employers recruiting the H-1C nurses must attest similarly to those recruiting H-1B workers, with the additional requirement that the facility attest that it is taking significant steps to recruit and retain U.S. registered nurses [41]

The American Recovery and Reinvestment Act of 2009 (also known as H.R. 1, the "Stimulus Act," P.L. 111-5) requires companies receiving Troubled Asset Relief Program (TARP) funding to comply with the more rigorous labor market rules [42]. Specifically, §1611 of P.L. 111-5 requires companies receiving TARP funding to follow the labor recruitment and attestation rules of H-1B dependent companies if they wish to hire foreign workers on H-1B visas. It does not, however, place any additional restrictions on companies receiving TARP funding that have other temporary foreign workers such as L-1s with specialized product knowledge or E-3 professional workers, or those petitioning for employment-based LPRs.

H-2A Visas and Labor Certification [43]
The H-2A program provides for the temporary admission of foreign agricultural workers to perform work that is itself temporary in nature, provided U.S. workers are not available. In contrast to the H-1B and H-2B nonimmigrant visas, the H-2A visa is not subject to numerical restrictions. An approved H-2A visa petition is generally valid for an initial period of up to one year. An H-2A worker's total period of stay may not exceed three consecutive years.

The INA provisions pertaining to the H-2A visa requires that employers conduct an affirmative search for available U.S. workers and that DOL determine that admitting alien workers will not adversely affect the wages and working conditions of similarly employed

U.S. workers [44]. The new regulations have replaced employer submitted recruitment documentation with an attestation-based process similar but not identical to the H-1B attestations [45]. Under the threat of penalties including fines and revocation of certification, employers are required to attest that they have fully complied with all program requirements [46]. Under the new regulations, employers of H2A workers may filed unnamed petitions that specify only the number of positions sought (i.e., not identifying the alien workers by name) [47]

On March 17, 2009, however, DOL published a Notice of Proposed Suspension of the H-2A Final Rule and is soliciting public comment for a 10-day period. According to DOL, all employers are expected to comply with the regulations effective as of January 17, 2009. Subsequent actions taken in response to the Notice of Proposed Suspension will be published later in the *Federal Register* [48]

Required Benefits for H-2A Workers

Beyond the procedural requirements mentioned above, the H-2A visa has requirements aimed at protecting the alien H-2A workers from exploitive working situations and preventing the domestic work force from being supplanted by alien workers willing to work for sub-standard wages. The H-2A visa requires employers to provide their temporary agricultural workers the following benefits.

- Employers must pay their H-2A workers and similarly employed U.S. workers the highest of the federal or applicable state minimum wage, the prevailing wagerate, or the adverse effect wage rate (AEWR) [49]. The employer must provide the worker with an earnings statement detailing the worker's total earnings, the hours of work offered, and the hours actually worked.
- The employer must provide transportation to and from the worker's temporaryhome, as well as transportation to the next workplace when that contract is fulfilled.
- The employer must provide housing to all H-2A workers who do not commute. The housing must be inspected by DOL and satisfy the appropriate minimumfederal standards.
- The employer must provide the necessary tools and supplies to perform the work (unless it is generally not the practice to do so for that type of work).
- The employer must provide meals and/or facilities in which the workers can prepare food.
- The employer must provide workers' compensation insurance to the H-2Aworkers.

H-2A workers, however, are exempt from the Migrant and Seasonal Agricultural Worker Protection Act that governs agricultural labor standards and working conditions as well as from unemployment benefits (Federal Unemployment Tax Act) and Social Security coverage (Federal Insurance Contributions Act). Farm workers in general lack coverage under the National Labor Relations Act provisions that ensure the right to collective bargaining.

H-2B Visas and Labor Certifications [50]

The H-2B program provides for the temporary admission of foreign workers to the United States to perform temporary non-agricultural work, if unemployed U.S. workers cannot be found. The work itself must be temporary. Under the applicable immigration regulations, work is considered to be temporary if the employer's need for the duties to be performed by the worker is a one-time occurrence, seasonal need, peakload need, or intermittent need [51]. The statute does not establish specific skills, education or experience required for the visa, with some exceptions [52]. Foreign medical graduates coming to perform medical services are explicitly excluded from the program. An approved H-2B visa petition is generally valid for an initial period of up to 10 months [53] An alien's total period of stay as an H-2B worker may not exceed three consecutive years [54]. Regulations that became effective January 19, 2009, revise the definition of temporary or seasonal job for one occurrence lasting less than 10 months to one occurrence lasting up to three years, reportedly so that additional sectors of the economy (e.g., construction firms and shipyards) could use H-2B workers. Under the new regulations, employers of H-2B workers may filed unnamed petitions that specify only the number of positions sought (i.e., not identifying the individual aliens) [55].

Like prospective H-2A employers, prospective H-2B employers must apply to DOL for a certification that U.S. workers capable of performing the work are not available and that the employment of alien workers will not adversely affect the wages and working conditions of similarly employed U.S. workers [56]. Under the new regulations, H-2B employers attest that they tried to recruit U.S. workers at prevailing wages [57]. Unlike H-2A employers, they are not subject to the AEWR and do not have to provide housing, transportation, [58] and other benefits required under the H-2A program.

Table 1 summarizes key labor market tests for employers to meet and immigration-related protections for workers that are required for the admission of the foreign temporary workers. For employers seeking H temporary workers, only two labor market elements apply to all: (1) some form of a comparable wage requirement and (2) some affirmation that the working conditions for similarly employed U.S. workers will not be adversely affected.

INVESTIGATING AND ENFIRCING LCAS

The INA does not delineate a standard policy to investigate and enforce violations of the LCAs, and the statutory authority for such investigations and enforcement actions varies across visa categories. The enforcement responsibilities for violations of these adverse effect provisions, however, are variously assigned to the Department of Homeland Security (DHS) or the Department of Justice (DOJ) as well as to DOL.

As discussed at the outset of this report, the INA requires the Secretary of Labor to certify that the employment of an employment-based LPR will not adversely affect the wages and working conditions of similarly employed workers in the United States [59]. The DOL Certifying Officer (CO) who learns that an LCA for an employment-based LPR is possibly fraudulent refers that case to DHS or DOJ for investigation [60]. Presumably, DOJ and DHS could also investigate such cases as document fraud under §274C of the INA [61]. DOL has the authority to revoke the LCA if an employer is subsequently found in violation. DOL also may debar an employer for three years if the employer is found to have violated the LCA requirements [62]

Table 1. Summary of Foreign Temporary Worker Labor Market Tests and Protections

Requirements	H-1B Professional	H-1B Dependent	H-2A Agricultural	H-2B Non-agricultural
Efforts to recruit U.S. workers	no	yes	yes	yes
Offering comparable or prevailing wages	yes	yes	yes	yes
Offering comparable benefits	no	yes	no	no
U.S. working conditions not adversely affected	yes	yes	yes	yes
No strikes or lockouts of U.S. workers	yes	yes	yes	yes
Protection from retaliation	yes	yes	yes	no
Lay-off protections for U.S. workers	no	yes	yes	no
Work site postings of intent to hire foreign workers	yes	yes	no	no
Housing, insurance and transportation	no	no	yes	no
Numerical caps	65,000 plus exceptions		no	66,000

Source: CRS summary of INA §212(a)(5), §212(g), §212(n), §218(b) and (c)(4); 8 C.F.R §214.2; and 20 C.F.R. §655-Subparts A, B.

In the case of H-1B labor attestation, however, the Secretary of Labor has statutory authority to investigate and enforce LCA violations of H-1B petitions, which she has delegated to the Administrator of the Wage and Hour Division (WHD) [63] More precisely, the WHD is charged with investigating the complaints [64].The WHD Administrator may assess back wages and benefits for the H-1B worker, civil penalties against the employer, and other administrative remedies [65]. If an employer is found to have willfully violated the INA, the WHD may conduct random investigations of that employer over the next five years. A DOL administrative law judge would decide the case if the employer charged with an H-1B violation requests a hearing. The WHD is also responsible for informing ETA and USCIS of employer violations. It is DHS, however, that has the authority to charge a fee of $500 to H-1B (and L visa) employers for H-1B visa (and L visa) fraud detection and prevention.

The INA provisions governing the enforcement of LCAs for H-2A workers offer yet another approach. "The Secretary of Labor is authorized to take such actions, including imposing appropriate penalties and seeking appropriate injunctive relief and specific performance of contractual obligations, as may be necessary to assure employer compliance with terms and conditions of employment under this section" [66]. The INA authorizes appropriated funding for DOL to carry out these actions [67]. The Secretary of Labor has delegated this enforcement authority to the WHD.[68]

DHS has the investigative and enforcement authorities for H-2B labor certifications. The INA authorizes the DHS to charge a fee of $150 to H-2B employers for fraud detection and prevention [69]. The Secretary of DHS may delegate to the Secretary of Labor, with the agreement of the Secretary of Labor, any of the authority given to the Secretary of DHS given to impose administrative remedies (including civil monetary penalties in an amount not to exceed $10,000 per violation) for H-2B violations. The H-2B violations cited are substantial failure to meet the LCA conditions or a willful misrepresentation of a material fact in the LCA [70]. DOL recently promulgated regulations that state that DHS had formally delegated this authority to impose penalties to the WHD as part of an revision in H-2B procedures. The new regulations have added post-adjudication audits that WHD will conduct as well procedures for penalizing employers who fail to comply the LCAs [71]

RESOURCES FOR FOREIGN LABOR CERTIFICATION

Funding the LCA and Approval Process

As Figure 4 shows, funding for foreign labor certification has fluctuated over the past dozen years despite the steady upward trends in employment-based immigration (Figure 1 and Figure 2).

In 1997, DOL projected that its backlog of applications for permanent LCAs would grow from 40,000 to 65,000 during FY1998. By 2003, however, the backlog of LCAs for permanent admissions was 300,000, and DOL projected an average processing time of three and a half years before an employer received a determination. The Bush Administration sought and received funding increases in FY2004 and FY2005 to reduce the backlog of LCAs that were pending at that time [72]. PERM's online filings are also credited with reducing the LCA processing times. The conference report on the FY2008 Consolidated Appropriations Act (P.L. 110-161) included $42.2 million "to improve the timeliness and quality of processing applications under the foreign labor certification program" [73].

Until the implementation of PERM, state workforce agencies (SWAs) were funded to handle LCA processing with appropriations from the "national activities" account of ETA's Employment Services. As Figure 4 illustrates, Congress has increased the funding for the federal administration of LCAs to reflect the shift in workload as well as backlog issues.

Although over 90% of the funding for USCIS comes from fees for providing adjudication and naturalization services that are deposited into the Examinations Fee Account, [74] Congress has not specifically authorized DOL to collect fees to cover the costs of processing LCAs. The Clinton Administration sought authority in 1997 to charge a user fee that employers would pay to offset the cost of processing the LCAs, but Congress opted not to do so [75]. The George W. Bush Administration had unsuccessfully sought authority to use a portion of the H-1B education and training fees for the processing of LCAs [76]

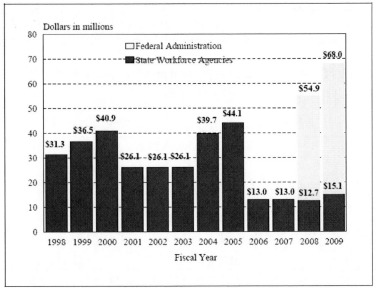

Source: U.S. Department of Labor, Budget Justification of Appropriation Estimates for Committee on Appropriations, FY2006-FY2009; U.S. Congress, House Committee on Appropriations, Consolidated thst Appropriations Act, 2008, H. R. 2764, P.L. 110-161, Division G, committee print, 110th Cong., 1st sess; and Explanatory language accompanying H.R. 1105, Congressional Record, February 23, 2009.

Figure 4. Appropriated Funding to ETA for Foreign Labor Certification FY1998-FY2009.

Funding the LCA Enforcement Activities

There are very limited data available on funding for enforcing the LCAs and investigating those employers who hire temporary foreign workers. DOL is allocated one-third of the total receipts DHS obtains from employers for the H-1B and L visa fraud detection and prevention fee of $500 per employee that has been collected since FY2005 [77]. The fee of $150 per H-2B employee also goes into the same visa fraud detection and prevention account [78] As presented in Table 2, DOL's estimated share of the total Fraud Prevention and Detection Fee Accounts has been $31 million in recent years. However, DOL reportedly used only $6.7 million in FY2007, $5.5 million in FY2008 and an estimated $5.5 million in FY2009 for H-1B and L visa fraud investigation activities [79]

During the George W. Bush Administration, DOL sought to use a portion of these H-1B and L visa funds for "self-directed" investigations aimed at industries that were more likely to employ low-wage, foreign workers. When Congress did not revise INA §286(v) to permit H-1B and L visas investigation fees to be used to fund investigations for low-skilled employment, the funds were rescinded [80]. Although the DOL has not provided detailed data on how much of the H-1B, H-2B, and L visas investigation fees it did not expend, the conference report on the FY2008 Consolidated Appropriations Act (P.L. 110-161) states:

> The amended bill includes a rescission of $102,000,000 in unobligated funds collected pursuant to section 286(v) of the Immigration and Nationality Act. The House and the Senate proposed a rescission of $70,000,000; however, information received from

the Department of Labor indicates that receipts in this account allow a higher amount to be rescinded while still ensuring that the $5,500,000 the Department estimates it will use in fiscal year 2008 under current authority remains available [81]

Table 2.Amounts from the Fraud Prevention and Detection Fees Allocated to DOL, FY2005-FY2009

Dollar Amount is in Thousands of Dollars

Budget Year	Estimated Share of Fees	Amount Reported Used
FY2005	26,175	NA
FY2006	31,000	NA
FY2007	31,000	6,700
FY2008	31,000	4,700
FY2009 (estimate)	31,000	5,500

Source: U.S. Department of Labor, Budget Justification of Appropriation Estimates for Committee on Appropriations, FY2006-FY2009, Volume II, Employment Standards Administration.

Notes: The estimates of total share of fees are matched with the U.S. Citizenship and Immigration Services' Congressional Budget Justifications, FY2006-FY2009, because INA §212(n) allocates that agency the same portion of the fees collected as DOL.

DOL's *Budget Justification of Appropriation Estimates for Committee on Appropriations*, Volume II, however, reported that only $30,000,000 was rescinded in FY2008 [82]. It is unclear at this time what accounts for this difference in FY2008, but it has been addressed further in the FY2009 appropriation. The report language accompanying the recently enacted Omnibus Appropriations Act, 2009 (H.R. 1105, P.L. 111-8) stated the following:

> The bill includes a rescission of $97,000,000 in unobligated funds collected pursuant to section 286(v) of the Immigration and Nationality Act. Sufficient funds will remain to ensure that the Department of Labor will be able to continue its enforcement activities under the current legislative authority [83]

The INA authorizes appropriated funding for DOL to enforce the LCAs for H-2A workers [84] Detailed funding data are not available to determine how much, if any, funds have been requested and appropriated to DOL for this specific activity in recent years [85]

SELECTED ISSUES

Many criticize the foreign labor certification process, both from the perspective of employers and employees (native-born as well as foreign-born workers). Employers often describe frustration with the process, labeling it as unresponsive to their need to hire people expeditiously. Representatives of U.S. workers question whether it provides adequate safeguards and assert that employers find ways to "end run" the lengthy process. Others point out that certain professional employees such as L intracompany transferees with specialized knowledge or E-3 professional workers from Australia are not appreciably different from H-

1B workers, yet only employers of the latter are required to file LCA attestations. Advocates for temporary foreign workers, in turn, maintain that they remain caught up in the long wait for visas to become LPRs, leaving them vulnerable to exploitation by those employers who promise to petition for them. The issues that follow are illustrative of the multifaceted aspects of this debate.

Certification Versus Attestation

Many argue that the labor market tests in the INA in their current forms are insufficiently flexible, entail burdensome regulations, and may pose potential litigation expenses for employers. Proponents of these views support extensive changes—particularly moving from labor certification based upon documented actions (i.e., evidence of recruitment advertisements) to a streamlined attestation of intent. These advocates of streamlining maintain it would increase the speed with which employers could hire foreign workers and reduce the government's role in delaying or blocking such employment.

Others maintain that the streamlined attestation process may be adequate for employers hiring H1B workers because those foreign workers also must meet rigorous educational and work experience requirements, but that an attestation process would be an insufficient labor market test for jobs that do not require a baccalaureate education and skilled work experience [86]. They express concern that PERM regulations have undermined the integrity of labor market tests for the LPR process. Opponents of the new H-2A and H-2B regulations argue that they weaken government protections for vulnerable domestic and foreign workers in industries known exploitative working conditions and for lax enforcement of the minimum wage [87]

Some recommend opting for a streamlined attestation process in which employers who have collective bargaining agreements with their U.S. workers would be afforded expedited consideration. Proponents of this position argue that collective bargaining agreements would enable the local labor-management partnerships to develop the labor market test for whether foreign workers are needed [88]

Protections for U.S. Workers

Some allege that employers prefer foreign workers because they are less demanding in terms of wages and working conditions and that an industry's dependence on temporary foreign workers may inadvertently lead the brightest U.S. students to seek positions in fields offering more stable and lucrative careers [89]. Many cite the GAO studies that document abuses of H-1B visas and recommend additional controls to protect U.S. workers [90].

Some have warned that PERM and other intent-based attestations are more likely to foster non-meritorious applications than the prior system because they hinge on self-reporting by the employers and that such attestations provide inadequate protections for workers currently in the U.S. labor market. Others have expressed concern that the Certifying Officers (COs) are relatively unfamiliar with the local labor markets and that this centralized decision-making might adversely affect U.S. workers. The AFL-CIO has maintained that a thorough manual review of labor certification applications is, at times, the sole protection of American workers [91].

DOL argues that the COs possess sufficient knowledge of local job markets, recruitment sources, and advertising media to administer the program appropriately. DOL maintains that it will handle the non-meritorious applications by adjusting the audit mechanism in the new system as needed. The Bush Administration further pointed out that it retained authority under the regulations to adjust the audit mechanism—increasing the number of random audits or changing the criteria for targeted audits—as necessary to ensure program integrity. Many practitioners observe that under PERM, employers must recruit more intensively and boost their salary offers [92]

Fraudulent Claims

Many observers argue that PERM and other intent-based attestations are more susceptible to fraudulent filings. The American Council of International Personnel (ACIP), for example, has argued that PERM's audit and enforcement procedures would not act as effective deterrents to fraud and misrepresentation. One of the SWAs commenting on the proposed PERM rule stated the incidence of fraud and abuse of the current system suggests a need for tighter controls, rather than a process that relies on employer self-attestations [93].

In terms of its evaluations of the LCA process for H-1B workers in particular, GAO reported that the H-1B petitions had potential for abuses. GAO has issued studies that recommended more controls to protect workers, to prevent abuses, and to streamline services in the issuing of H-1B visas. GAO concluded that the DOL has limited authority to question information on the labor attestation form and to initiate enforcement activities [94].

Most recently, an investigation by USCIS's Office of Fraud Detection and National Security (FDNS) discovered that 13% of the H1B files sampled were fraudulent and another 7% had technical violations of the law [95]

DOL asserts that critics underestimate the process' capacity to detect and deter fraud, though the department acknowledges labor certification fraud to be a serious matter. DOL maintains the COs will review applications upon receipt to verify whether the employer-applicant is a bona fide business entity and has employees on its payroll. DOL has promised to aggressively pursue methods to identify those applications that may be fraudulently filed.

The Bush Administration reportedly considered a plan to cross-check the employer's federal employer identification number with other available databases [96]

Enforcement Tools

A few practitioners assert that PERM fails in achieving the objectives of the law because, as they argue, it functions as only an enforcement mechanism for the relatively small subset of employers who are required to file LCAs [97]. They further point out that most LPRs working in the United States entered on visas not subject to labor market tests [98]. These observers conclude that PERM in particular and labor certification in general neither protects U.S. workers nor facilitates employers who need workers.

Another view is that PERM's streamlining reforms serve to enhance enforcement. According to DOL Assistant Secretary Emily Stover DeRocco, "Technology allows us to strengthen our overall program's integrity and provide better customer service." One practitioner characterizes PERM as "a step in the right direction to move these cases through and do it in a timely fashion." [99]

Small Business Concerns

Some have expressed the concern that the INA's labor market tests favor large companies and unduly affect small businesses because they lack the in-house legal and human resource specialists who can complete and track the LCAs. They point to the PERM regulations in which certain types of aliens are ineligible: small business investors (who also do not qualify as fifth preference investors); employees in key positions who previously worked for affiliated, predecessor, or successor entities; and alien workers who are so inseparable from the sponsoring employer the employer would be unlikely to continue in operations without the foreign national [100]. DOL points out that a small business investor is not an occupational category. The Administration further states that some foreign workers with special or unique skills might be eligible for labor certification under the basic process. In terms of alien workers who are "so inseparable from the sponsoring employer that the employer would be unlikely to continue in operation without the alien," DOL has long held the position that if a job opportunity is not open to U.S. workers, labor certification will be denied [101]

Subcontractors and Multinational Companies

Over the years, the media has aired stories of U.S. workers who have been laid off and replaced by foreign workers who are employed by subcontractors. In many of these accounts, the subcontractor provides the foreign worker fewer benefits than the displaced U.S. workers. In some instances, the displaced workers reportedly have been asked to train their foreign replacements [102]. The additional requirements for H-1B dependent employers are expressly aimed at discouraging subcontractors who recruit H-1B workers from placing the worker with another employer who had recently laid off U.S. workers [103]. However, multinational firms have the option of substituting employees on the L visa for those on the H-1B visa.

Some employers argue that they will not be able to stay in business without expedient access to the contingent workers supplied by subcontractors, some of whom are foreign nationals with the requisite skills. These contingent workers meet the need for a specialized, seasonal, intermittent or peak-load workforce that is able to adapt with the market forces. They express concern that labor market tests for visas may limit the flexibility of firms that are hiring the caliber of workers necessary to stay competitive in the global marketplace [104]

Some observers have expressed concern that intra-company transferees on L-1 visas should be admitted only after a determination that comparable U.S. personnel are not adversely affected, particularly in the cases of foreign nationals entering as mid-level managers and specialized personnel. They argue that the L-1 visa currently gives multinational firms an unfair advantage over U.S.-owned businesses by enabling multinational corporations to bring in lower-cost foreign personnel [105]

Supporters of current law governing intra-company transfers argue that it is essential for multinational firms to be able to assign top personnel to facilities in the United States on an "as needed basis" and that it is counterproductive to have government bureaucrats delay these transfers to perform labor market tests. They warn these multinational firms will find it too burdensome and unprofitable to do business in the United States [106]

Unemployment Statistics and Other Economic Triggers

The option of using unemployment rates and other economic indicators to determine what occupations and sectors might import foreign workers has arisen several times over the past few decades. During the legislative debate leading up to the Immigration Act of 1990, supporters of this alternative argued that it would be a more objective basis to govern employment-based immigration and would place the priorities of the national economy ahead of individual employer preferences.

At that time, however, leading government economists acknowledged that they did not have labor force and other economic data available to make such determinations. The option of using national and regional unemployment data to regulate foreign worker admissions arose most recently during the debate over comprehensive immigration reform in the 110th Congress. Echoing earlier arguments, proponents also maintained such triggers would afford better protections for U.S. workers. Opponents asserted that adoption of such policies would prompt some firms to relocate to areas in which they had access to foreign workers, further harming U.S. workers in locations with higher unemployment.

CONCLUSION

The legal entry of foreign workers into the United States has been governed by the same basic provisions since 1952, with some policy adjustments along the way. Over a decade ago, the Commission on Immigration Reform estimated that the labor certification process costs employers in administrative, paperwork, and legal fees a total of $10,000 per immigrant [107].

As is apparent in the analysis above, the current set of provisions and policies are visa-specific and yield various standards and thresholds for different occupations and sectors of the economy. There are, however, common critiques underlying the recruitment of foreign workers with specialized expertise as well as workers with no skills. Legislation that would reform the INA may provide an opportunity to revise and update the labor market tests; on the other hand, a consensus on the labor market tests may also be hurdle to enacting immigration reform.

REFERENCES

[1] The administration of immigration and citizenship policy was reorganized by Homeland Security Act of 2002 (P.L. 107-296), and the Secretary of Homeland Security now oversees this function that the INA assigns to the Attorney General.

[2] INA §212(a)(5).

[3] DOL is charged with other immigration-related responsibilities. Most notably, the Wage and Hour Division in DOL is tasked with ensuring compliance with the employment eligibility provisions of the INA as well as labor standards laws, such as the Fair Labor Standards Act, the Migrant and Seasonal Worker Protection Act, and the Family and Medical Leave Act.

[4] 23 Stat. 332.

[5] The McCarran-Walters Act (P.L. 82-414).

[6] §203(a)(1) of P.L. 82-414.

[7] §212(a)(14) of P.L. 82-414.

[8] *Interpreter Releases*, "The Lawyer's Guide to §212(a)(5)(A): Labor Certification from 1952 to PERM," by Gary Endelman, Oct. 11, 2004.

[9] LCAs are not required for aliens who are coming as priority workers, investors, refugees, or family-based immigrants.

[10] §212(a)(5) of INA; §1182(a)(5) 8 USC.

[11] CRS Report RL32235, *U.S. Immigration Policy on Permanent Admissions*, by Ruth Ellen Wasem.

[12] CRS Report 96-149, *Immigration: Analysis of Major Proposals to Revise Family and Employment Admissions*, by Joyce C. Vialet and Ruth Ellen Wasem.

[13] For an explanation of these trends, see CRS Report RL32235, *U.S. Immigration Policy on Permanent Admissions*, by Ruth Ellen Wasem.

[14] § 203(b) of INA; 8 U.S.C. § 1153.

[15] Certain second preference immigrants who are deemed to be "in the national interest" are exempt from laborcertification.

[16] 20 C.F.R. Part 656.

[17] 20 C.F.R. Part 656.

[18] §212(a)(5)(A) of INA.

[19] Employers also file immigration petitions with USCIS on behalf of the aliens they are recruiting and pay fees for each petitions they file.

[20] These forms are available at http://www.foreignlaborcert.doleta.gov/, accessed March 16, 2009.

[21] *Federal Register*, vol. 69, no. 247, Dec. 27, 2004, p. 77325.

[22] CRS Report RS21520, *Labor Certification for Permanent Immigrant Admissions*, by Ruth Ellen Wasem.

[23] The new form, Application for Permanent Employment Certification (ETA Form 9089), is available at http://www.foreignlaborcert.doleta.gov/form.cfm , accessed on Apr. 23, 2007. DOL does not permit employers to submit applications by facsimile.

[24] *Federal Register*, vol. 69, no. 247, Dec. 27, 2004, pp. 77325-77421.

[25] U.S. Department of Labor ETA Office of Foreign Labor Certification, *Permanent Labor Certification Program (PERM) Disclosure Data* , February 26, 2008, http://www.foreignlaborcert.doleta.gov/pdf/PERM_Data_FY07_Announcement.pdf.

[26] For a fuller discussion and analysis, see CRS Report RL31381, *U.S. Immigration Policy on Temporary Admissions*, by Chad C. Haddal and Ruth Ellen Wasem.

[27] Some of the earliest nonimmigrant categories enacted are the C visa for aliens traveling through the United States en route to another destination and the D visa for alien crew members on vessels or aircraft. Those foreign nationals with D visas are typically employed by the carrier and those on C visas may be traveling as part of their employment.

[28] See CRS Report RL30498, *Immigration: Legislative Issues on Nonimmigrant Professional Specialty (H-1B) Workers*, by Ruth Ellen Wasem; and CRS Report RL32044, *Immigration: Policy Considerations Related to Guest Worker Programs*, by Andorra Bruno.

[29] See CRS Report RL32030, *Immigration Policy for Intracompany Transfers (L Visa): Issues and Legislation*, by Ruth Ellen Wasem; and CRS Report RL33844, *Foreign Investor Visas: Policies and Issues*, by Chad C. Haddal.

[30] §501 of P.L. 109-13, the Emergency Supplemental Appropriations Act for Defense, the Global War on Terror, and Tsunami Relief, 2005.

[31] U.S. Citizenship and Immigration Services, "Special Immigrant and Nonimmigrant Religious Workers," 72 *Federal Register* 20442, April 25, 2007.

[32] For a detailed analysis, see Table 2 in CRS Report RL31381, *U.S. Immigration Policy on Temporary Admissions*, by Chad C. Haddal and Ruth Ellen Wasem.

[33] D-1 crew members on foreign vessels are generally forbidden to perform longshore work at U.S. ports. There is an exception in which an employer must file an attestation stating that it is the prevailing practice for the activity at that port, there is no strike or lockout at the place of employment, and that notice has been given to U.S. workers or their representatives. Another exception allows D-1 crewmen to perform longshore activities in the State of Alaska, if the employer also has made a bona fide request for and has employed U.S. longshore workers who are qualified and available in sufficient numbers from contract stevedoring companies, labor organizations recognized as exclusive bargaining representatives of United States longshore workers, and private dock operators. 20 CFR Part 655, SubpartsF and G.

[34] U.S. Department of Labor Employment and Training Administration, "Labor Certification Process and Enforcement for Temporary Employment in Occupations Other Than Agriculture or Registered Nursing ," 73 *Federal Register* 78019-78069, December 19, 2008.

[35] Portions of this section draw on CRS Report RL30498, *Immigration: Legislative Issues on Nonimmigrant Professional Specialty (H-1B) Workers*, by Ruth Ellen Wasem. (Hereafter cited as CRS Report RL30498,*Nonimmigrant Professional Specialty (H-1B) Workers*.)

[36] 8 C.F.R. §214.2(h)(4). Law and regulations also specify that fashion models deemed "prominent" may enter on H-1B visas.

[37] Attestation was part of a compromise package on H-1B visa that included annual numerical limits in the Immigration Act of 1990 (P.L. 101-649). See CRS Report RL30498, *Immigration: Legislative Issues on Nonimmigrant Professional Specialty (H-1B) Workers*, by Ruth Ellen Wasem.

[38] INA §212(n); 8 C.F.R. §214.2(h)(4). For a further discussion of labor attestations, see CRS Report RL30498, *Immigration: Legislative Issues on Nonimmigrant Professional Specialty (H-1B) Workers*, by Ruth Ellen Wasem.

[39] Title IV of P.L. 105-277 defined H-1B dependent employers as firms having 25 or less employees, of whom at least 8 are H-1Bs; 26-50 employees of whom at least 13 are H-1Bs; at least 51 employees, 15% of whom are H-1Bs; excludes those earning at least $60,000 or having masters degrees. CRS Report 98-531, *Immigration: Nonimmigrant H-1B Specialty Worker Issues and Legislation*, by Ruth Ellen Wasem.

[40] INA §212(n).

[41] CRS Report RS20164, *Immigration: Temporary Admission of Nurses for Health Shortage Areas (P.L. 106-95)*, by Joyce Vialet.

[42] For a discussion of TARP, see CRS Report R40224, *Troubled Asset Relief Program and Foreclosures*, by N. EricWeiss et al.

[43] For a fuller discussion of labor certification for H-2A temporary foreign workers, see CRS Report RL32044, *Immigration: Policy Considerations Related to Guest Worker Programs*, by Andorra Bruno.

[44] INA §101(a)(15)(H)(ii)(a), §218(a)(1), (d)(1);

[45] U.S. Department of Labor Employment and Training Administration, "Temporary Agricultural Employment of H2A Aliens in the United States; Modernizing the Labor Certification Process and Enforcement," 73 *Federal Register,* December 16, 2008. Prior to these rules, the process was similar but not identical to the labor certification process required of employers who seek to bring in workers as permanent, employment-based immigrants (discussed above). In a 1998 audit, the Labor Department's Office of the Inspector General concluded that "the H-2A certification process is ineffective. It is characterized by extensive administrative requirements, paperwork and regulations that often seem dissociated with DOL's mandate of providing assurance that American workers' jobs are protected." *Consolidation of Labor's Enforcement Responsibilities for the H-2A Program Could Better Protect U.S. Agricultural Workers*, Report 04-98-004-03-321, Mar. 31, 1998.

[46] Prior to January 19, 2009, the effective date of the new regulations, the application must have included a copy of the job offer used to recruit U.S. and H-2A workers. Under the old regulations, a prospective H-2A employer had to submit a plan for conducting independent, positive recruitment of U.S. workers as part of the LCA, and had to engage in such recruitment until the foreign workers have departed for the employer's place of work. H-2A employers' recruitment responsibilities had included assisting the Employment Service system in the preparation of local, intrastate, and interstate job orders; placing newspaper and/or radio advertisements; and contacting farm labor contractors, migrant workers, and other workers in other areas of the state or country. 20 CFR §655.100; §655.101(a), (b); §655.103.

[47] U.S. Department of Labor Employment and Training Administration, "Temporary Agricultural Employment of H2A Aliens in the United States; Modernizing the Labor Certification Process and Enforcement," 73 *Federal Register,* December 16, 2008.

[48] Department of Labor Employment and Training Administration and Wage and Hour Division, "Temporary Employment of H–2A Aliens in the United States," 74 *Federal Register* 11408-11440, March 17, 2009.

[49] For a more complete explanation of this provision and how it works, CRS Report RL34739, *Temporary Farm Labor:The H-2A Program and the U.S. Department of Labor's Proposed Changes in the Adverse Effect Wage Rate (AEWR)*, by Gerald Mayer.

[50] This section is drawn, in part, from CRS Report RL32044, *Immigration: Policy Considerations Related to Guest Worker Programs*, by Andorra Bruno.

[51] For definitions of these types of need, see 8 C.F.R. §214.2(h)(6)(ii).

[52] 8 CFR §214.2(h). There are special requirements for professional athletes, for example. See CRS congressional distribution memorandum, *Temporary Admission of Foreign Professional Athletes*, by Ruth Ellen Wasem, Feb. 15, 2005 (available upon request from the author).

[53] See 8 C.F.R. §214.2(h)(9)(iii)(B).

[54] Included in this three-year period is any time an H-2B alien spent in the United States under the "H" (temporary worker) or "L" (temporary intracompany transferee) visa categories.

[55] U.S. Department of Labor Employment and Training Administration, "Labor Certification Process and Enforcement for Temporary Employment in Occupations Other Than Agriculture or Registered Nursing ," 73 *Federal Register* 78019-78069, December 19, 2008; and U.S. Department of Homeland Security U.S. Citizenship and Immigration Services, "Changes to Requirements Affecting H-2B Nonimmigrants and Their Employers," 73 *Federal Register* 78103, December 19, 2008. These rules also permit the Secretary of Homeland Security, in consultation with the Secretary of State to designate nationals of certain countries for receipt of H-2B visas.

[56] Prior to January 19, 2009, the effective date of the new regulations, DOL policy guidance on the H-2B labor certification process required a prospective H-2B employer to advertise the job opportunity in a newspaper or other appropriate publication for three consecutive days and to provide the SWA with proof of publication; and to document that union and other recruitment sources were contacted.

[57] U.S. Department of Labor Employment and Training Administration, "Labor Certification Process and Enforcement for Temporary Employment in Occupations Other Than Agriculture or Registered Nursing ," 73 *Federal Register* 78019-78069, December 19, 2008.

[58] While not subject to the broader transportation requirements of the H-2A program, H-2B employers are required by law to pay the reasonable costs of return transportation abroad for an H-2B worker who is dismissed prior to the end of his or her authorized period of stay.

[59] INA §212(a)(5).

[60] 20 C.F.R. § 656.31(b).

[61] CRS Report RL34007, *Immigration Fraud: Policies, Investigations, and Issues*, by Ruth Ellen Wasem; and, CRS Report RL32657, *Immigration-Related Document Fraud: Overview of Civil, Criminal, and Immigration Consequences*, by Yule Kim and Michael John Garcia.

[62] 20 C.F.R. § 656.31(f).

[63] The Wage and Hour division is located in the Employment Standards Division of DOL.

[64] 20 C.F.R. § 655.800 implementing INA §212(n) and (t).

[65] 20 C.F.R. § 655.810 implementing INA §212(n) and (t).

[66] §218(g) of the INA.

[67] §218(g) of the INA.

[68] U.S. Department of Labor Employment and Training Administration, "Labor Certification Process and Enforcement for Temporary Employment in Occupations Other Than Agriculture or Registered Nursing ," 73 *Federal Register*78019-78069, December 19, 2008; and U.S. Department of Homeland Security U.S. Citizenship and Immigration Services, "Changes to Requirements Affecting H-2B Nonimmigrants and Their Employers," 73 *Federal Register*78103, December 19, 2008.

[69] P.L. 109-13, §403; 8 U.S.C. §1184(c). This provision states that fraud collection and prevention fees should also go towards "programs and activities to prevent and detect fraud pertaining to H-2B visa petitions.

[70] §214(c)(14) of the INA.

[71] U.S. Department of Labor Employment and Training Administration, "Labor Certification Process and Enforcement for Temporary Employment in Occupations Other Than Agriculture or Registered Nursing ," 73 *Federal Register*78019-78069, December 19, 2008.

[72] *FY1998 Budget Justifications of Appropriations Estimates for Committee on Appropriations*, vol. 1, SUIESO-28.

[73] U.S. Congress, House Committee on Appropriations, *Consolidated Appropriations Act, 2008, H. R. 2764, P.L. 110-161, Division G*, committee print, 110th Cong., 1st sess., p.1472.

[74] 286 of the Immigration and Nationality Act. 8 U.S.C. 1356.

[75] U.S. Department of Labor, *FY1998 Budget Justifications of Appropriations Estimates for Committee on Appropriations*, vol. 1, SUIESO-28.

[76] CRS Report RL31973, *Programs Funded by the H-1B Visa Education and Training Fee, and Labor Market Conditions for Information Technology (IT) Workers*, by Linda Levine and Blake Alan Naughton.

[77] P.L. 108-447, Division J, Title IV, Subtitle B, §426.

[78] §286(v) of the INA; 8 U.S.C. §1356(v).

[79] U.S. Department of Labor, *FY2009 Budget Justification of Appropriation Estimates for Committee on Appropriations*, Volume II, Employment Standards Administration, 2008.

[80] U.S. Department of Labor, *FY2009 Budget Justification of Appropriation Estimates for Committee on Appropriations*, Volume II, Employment Standards Administration, 2008.

[81] U.S. Congress, House Committee on Appropriations, *Consolidated Appropriations Act, 2008, H. R. 2764, P.L. 110-161, Division G*, committee print, 110th Cong., 1st sess., p. 1473.

[82] U.S. Department of Labor, *FY2009 Budget Justification of Appropriation Estimates for Committee onAppropriations*, Volume II, Employment Standards Administration, 2008.

[83] Explanatory language accompanying H.R. 1105, *Congressional Record,* February 23, 2009, pp. H2162-H2167.

[84] §218(g) of the INA.

[85] Explanatory language accompanying H.R. 1105, stated: "Due to concern about the Department's new requirement for State Workforce Agencies to assume the responsibility for employment verification in the H-2A agricultural workers program, the Secretary is directed to provide a report to the Committees on Appropriations of the

House of Representatives and the Senate within 90 days of the enactment of this Act on the costs to States and legal basis for imposing this responsibility on a mandatory basis." *Congressional Record,* February 23, 2009, pp. H2162-H2167.

[86] For example, see AFL-CIO Legislative Alert, letter to U.S. Senators from William Samuel, Oct. 19, 2005.

[87] Susan Ferriss, "Bush administration makes last-minute changes in farmworker hiring," *The Sacramento Bee*, December 11, 2008. The Southern Poverty Law Center (SPLC) called conditions for many H-2B workers "close to slavery," citing unsavory recruiters, abusive employers and substandard wages. Nicolle Gaouette, "Guest workers in U.S. say they are being exploited," *Los Angeles Times*, June 12, 2008.

[88] For example, see the "H-2A Reform and Agricultural Worker Adjustment Act of 2001" S. 1313/H.R. 2736 introduced in the 107th Congress.

[89] CRS Report RL30140, *An Information Technology Labor Shortage? Legislation in the 106th Congress*, by Linda Levine; and CRS Report 98-462, *Immigration and Information Technology Jobs: The Issue of Temporary Foreign Workers*, by Ruth Ellen Wasem and Linda Levine.

[90] For example, see AFL-CIO Legislative Alert, letter to U.S. Senators from William Samuel, Oct. 19, 2005.

[91] *Federal Register*, vol. 69, no. 247, Dec. 27, 2004, pp 77325-77421.

[92] *Federal Register*, vol. 69, no. 247, Dec. 27, 2004, pp 77325-77421.

[93] *Federal Register*, vol. 69, no. 247, Dec. 27, 2004, pp 77325-77421.

[94] U.S. General Accounting Office, *H-1B Foreign Workers: Better Controls Needed to Help Employers and Protect Workers*, GAO/HEHS-00-157, Sept. 2000; and U.S. General Accounting Office, *H-1B Foreign Workers: Better Tracking Needed to Help Determine H-1B Program's Effects on U.S. Workforce*, GAO-03-883 Sept. 2003.

[95] USCIS Office of Fraud Detection and National Security, *H-1B Benefit Fraud and Compliance Assessment*, Washington, D.C., September 2008.

[96] *Federal Register*, vol. 69, no. 247, Dec. 27, 2004, pp 77325-77421.

[97] *Interpreter Releases,* "The Lawyer's Guide to §212(a)(5)(A): Labor Certification from 1952 to PERM," by GaryEndelman, Oct. 11, 2004.

[98] In FY2004, a total of 155,330 LPRs were employment-based preference immigrants (including spouses and children), comprising 16.4% of all LPRs that year.

[99] *Business Dateline*, "The U.S. Labor Department unveils a streamlined path," by William T. Quinn (quoting WilliamMcAlvanah), Apr. 4, 2005.

[100] *Federal Register*, vol. 69, no. 247, Dec. 27, 2004, pp 77325-77421.

[101] *Federal Register*, vol. 69, no. 247, Dec. 27, 2004, pp 77325-77421.

[102] In 1995, the DOL Inspector General found widespread abuses of the H-1B program, and former Secretary of Labor Robert Reich argued for changes in the H-1B provisions so DOL could take action against employers who displace U.S. workers with nonimmigrants.

[103] CRS Report 98-531, *Immigration: Nonimmigrant H-1B Specialty Worker Issues and Legislation*, by Ruth Ellen Wasem.

[104] CRS Report RL30072, *Temporary Workers as Members of the Contingent Labor Force*, by Linda Levine; and CRS Report RL30498, *Immigration: Legislative Issues on Nonimmigrant Professional Specialty (H-1B) Workers*.

[105] The DHS Office of the Inspector General found potential vulnerabilities and abuses in the L-1 visa for intracompany transferees that bear on labor market protections for U.S. workers; U.S. Department of Homeland Security, Office of Inspector General, *Review of Vulnerabilities and Potential Abuses of the L-1 Visa Program*, OIG 06-22, Jan. 2006.

[106] U.S. Congress, Senate Committee on the Judiciary, Subcommittee on Immigration, Citizenship and Border Security, *The L-1 Visa and American Interests in the 21st Century Global Economy,* hearings, 108th Cong., 1st sess., July 29, 2003; and U.S. Congress, House Committee on Foreign Relations, *L Visas: Losing Jobs Through Laissez-faire Policies?* hearings, 108th Cong., 2nd sess., Feb. 4, 2004.

[107] *Congressional Record*, vol. 142, Statement of Senator Ted Kennedy, Apr. 15, 1996, p. S3287.

In: Economics, Political and Social Issues …
Editor: Michelle L. Fergusson

ISBN: 978-1-61122-555-6
©2011 Nova Science Publishers, Inc.

CHINA'S HOLDINGS OF U.S. SECURITIES: IMPLICATIONS FOR THE U.S. ECONOMY[*]

Wayne M. Morrison[1][45] and Marc Labonte[2]
[1]Asian Trade and Finance
[2]Macroeconomic Policy

ABSTRACT

Given its relatively low savings rate, the U.S. economy depends heavily on foreign capital inflows from countries with high savings rates (such as China) to help promote growth and to fund the federal budget deficit. China has intervened heavily in currency markets to limit the appreciation of its currency, especially against the dollar. As a result, China has become the world's largest and fastest growing holder of foreign exchange reserves (FER). China has invested a large share of its FER in U.S. securities, which, as of June 2008, totaled $1,205 billion, making China the 2nd largest foreign holder of U.S. securities (after Japan). These securities include long-term (LT) Treasury debt, LT U.S. agency debt, LT U.S. corporate debt, LT U.S. equities, and short-term debt.

U.S. Treasury securities are issued to finance the federal budget deficit. Of the public debt that is privately held, about half is held by foreigners. As of December 2008, China's Treasury securities holdings were $727 billion, accounting for 23.6% of total foreign ownership of U.S. Treasury securities, making it the largest foreign holder of U.S. Treasuries (replacing Japan in September 2008).

Some U.S. policymakers have expressed concern that China might try to use its large holdings of U.S. securities, including U.S. public debt, as leverage against U.S. policies it opposes. For example, in the past, some Chinese officials reportedly suggested that China could dump (or threaten to dump) a large share of its holdings to prevent the United States from imposing trade sanctions against China over its currency policy. Other Chinese officials reportedly stated that China should diversify its investments of its foreign exchange reserves away from dollar-denominated assets to those that offer higher rates of returns. The recent global financial crisis has heightened U.S. concerns that China might reduce its U.S. asset holdings.

A gradual decline in China's holdings of U.S. assets would not be expected to have a negative impact on the U.S. economy (since it could be matched by increased U.S. exports and a lower trade deficit). However, some economists contend that attempts by China to unload a large share of its U.S. securities holdings could have a significant negative impact on the U.S. economy (at least in the short run), especially if such a move sparked a sharp depreciation of the dollar in international markets and induced other foreign investors to sell off their U.S. holdings as well. In order to keep or attract that

---

[*] Excerpted from CRS Report RL34314 dated march 5, 2009.
[45] E-mail: wmorrison@crs.loc.gov

investment back, U.S. interest rates would rise, which would dampen U.S. economic growth, all else equal. Other economists counter that it would not be in China's economic interest to suddenly sell off its U.S. investment holdings. Doing so could lead to financial losses for the Chinese government, and any shocks to the U.S. economy caused by this action could ultimately hurt China's economy as well.

The issue of China's large holdings of U.S. securities is part of a larger debate among economists over how long the high U.S. reliance on foreign investment can be sustained, to what extent that reliance poses risks to the economy, and how to evaluate the costs associated with borrowing versus the benefits that would accrue to the economy from that practice.

INTRODUCTION

Because of its low savings rate, the United States borrows to finance the federal budget deficit and its capital needs in order to enjoy healthy economic growth. It therefore depends on countries with high savings rates, such as China, to invest some of its capital in the United States.

China's central bank is a major purchaser of U.S. assets, largely because of its exchange rate policy. In order to limit the renminbi's (China's currency) appreciation against the dollar, China's central bank must purchase U.S. dollars [1]. This has led China to amass a huge level of foreign exchange reserves (FER); these totaled $1.95 trillion as of December 2008. Rather than hold dollars, which earn no interest, the Chinese central government has converted some level of its FER holdings into financial securities. Since foreign exchange holdings facilitate trade and prevent speculation against their currency, the central bank also holds securities from other foreign countries. The United States is a major destination of China's overseas investment. China is the second largest holder of U.S. securities, which include U.S. Treasury securities that are used to finance the federal budget deficit. Some U.S. policymakers have expressed concern that China's large holdings of U.S. securities may pose a risk to the U.S. economy should China stop purchasing those securities or attempt to divest itself of a large share of its holdings. In addition, China's FER are expected to continue to grow rapidly in the near future, potentially continuing (and possibly increasing) China's role as a major buyer of U.S. securities.

The recent financial crisis in the United States and the Administration's proposed plans to purchase troubled assets is expected to cost the government hundreds of billions of dollars, at least initially. This will require a substantial level of new government borrowing, some of which will likely be financed by foreign investors. China could be a major purchaser of new U.S. government debt.

This report examines the importance to the U.S. economy of China's investment in U.S. securities, as well as U.S. concerns over the possibility that China might unload a large share of those holdings, the likelihood that this would occur, and the potential implications such action could have for the U.S. economy. The report concludes that a large sell-off of Chinese Treasury securities holdings could negatively affect the U.S. economy, at least in the short-run. As a result, such a move could diminish U.S. demand for Chinese products and thus could lower China's economic growth as well. The issue of China's large holdings of U.S. securities is part of a broader question that has been raised by many economists: What are the implications of the heavy U.S. reliance on foreign investment to maintain healthy economic growth and to finance the budget deficit? [2]

CHINA'S FOREIGN EXCHANGE RESERVES

As indicated in Table 1, China's foreign exchange reserves have increased sharply in recent years, both in absolute terms and as a percent of gross domestic product (GDP). These rose from $216 billion in 2001 to $1,528 billion in 2007, to $1,946 billion as in 2008. China's reserves as a percent of GDP grew from 15.3% in 2001 to 45% in 2008 – an unusually high level for a large economy.

A listing of the world's top five holders of FER as of December 2008 is shown in Table 2. Not only was China by far the world's largest FER holder, its accumulation of additional reserves from 2006-2008 ($878 billion) was significantly larger than the combined FER increases of the other four major holders – Japan, Russia, Taiwan, and India [3]. According to the IMF, as of June 2008, China accounted for 26.2% of the world's FER [4]

Table 1. China's Foreign Exchange Reserves: 2001- 2008

Year	Billions of U.S. Dollars	As a % of Chinese GDP
2001	215.6	16.3
2002	291.1	20.0
2003	403.3	24.6
2004	609.9	31.6
2005	818.9	36.5
2006	1,068.5	40.2
2007	1,528.2	45.2
2008	1,946.0	45.0

Source: Global Insight and Chinese State Administration of Foreign Exchange.
Note: Year-end values.

Table 2. Top 5 Holders of Foreign Exchange Reserves and Changes to Holdings From 2006-2008

Country	Reserves (billions of U.S. dollars)			
	2006	2007	2008	Change in Reserves: 2006-2008
China	1,068.5	1,528.2	1,946.0	877.5
Japan	879.7	948.4	1,003.3	123.6
Russian Federation	295.3	386.2	406.2	110.9
Taiwan	266.1	270.0	291.7	25.6
India	170.2	266.6	246.6	76.4

Sources: EIU Database, IMF International Financial Statistics, and Central Bank of the Republic of China (Taiwan).
Note: Ranked according to total holdings as of December 2008.

CHINA'S HOLDING OF U.S. SECURITIES [5]

China's central bank is a major purchaser of U.S. financial securities because of its exchange rate policy. In order to mitigate the renminbi's appreciation against the dollar, the central bank must purchase dollars. Rather than hold dollars, which earn no interest, the Chinese central government has converted some level of its foreign exchange holdings into financial securities. Since foreign exchange holdings facilitate trade and prevent speculation against their currency, the central bank also holds securities from other foreign countries.

There are no official estimates of what share of China's foreign reserves are held in dollar-denominated assets (assets that were bought with dollars and are cashed in dollars), but the Treasury Department conducts an annual survey of foreign portfolio holdings of U.S. securities by country, and reports data for the previous year as of the end of June [6]. The report does not distinguish between government and private holdings of U.S. securities. U.S. securities include long-term (LT) U.S. Treasury securities, LT U.S. government agency securities, [7] LT corporate securities (some of which are asset-backed), equities (such as stocks), and short-term debt [8]

According to the latest Treasury survey of portfolio holdings of U.S. securities (issued in February 2009), China's total holdings as of June 2008 were $1,205 billion, which were $283 billion (or 31%) larger than June 2007 levels, and were nearly five times 2003 levels (see Figure 1).[9] These increases were significantly more than that of any other major foreign holder [10]

As indicated in Table 3, China was the second largest foreign holder of U.S. securities, after Japan as of June 2008 [11] China may have become the largest foreign holder in late 2008 or early 2009. China's main holdings were in LT government agency securities and LT Treasury securities. This appears to indicate that the Chinese government has been pursuing a relatively low-risk investment strategy. In contrast, most of the United Kingdom's securities holdings were in corporate debt and equities. China's holdings of U.S. securities accounted for 11.7% of total foreign holdings of U.S. securities as of June 2008 (up from 9.4% as of June 2007). Although the Chinese government does not make public the dollar composition of its foreign exchange holdings, many analysts estimate this level to be around 70%. [12] If this figure is correct, China's holdings of U.S. securities may have reached $1.36 trillion or higher as of December 2008 [13].

It is not clear to what extent China's investments have gone into U.S. sub-prime mortgage securities, but they are likely to be small relative to their total investments. As seen in Table 3, China has invested $527 billion in long-term agency securities, most—but not all—of which is likely to be debt issued by Fannie Mae and Freddie Mac. *The South China Morning Post* (September 25, 2008) estimated that Chinese banks held $9.8 billion in U.S. sub-prime loans at the end of 2007 and $25 billion in Fannie Mae and Freddie Mac securities as of June 30, 2008. Whatever risk China faced from its holdings of Freddie Mac and Fannie Mae mortgage-backed securities was greatly reduced in September 2008 when these two institutions were placed in conservatorship by the Federal Government and thus have government backing. The Bank of China (one of China's largest state-owned commercial banks) reportedly had the largest exposures to U.S. sub-prime mortgage-backed securities among any banks in Asia when the financial crisis began. However, it reported that holdings of such securities as a share of its total investment securities portfolio were reduced from 3.5% in March 2008 to 1.4% in October 2008 [14].

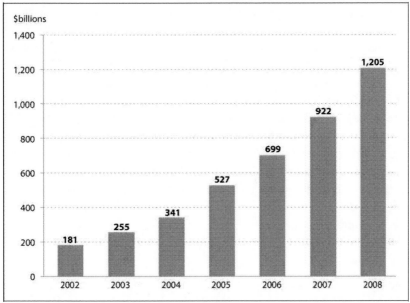

Source: U.S. Treasury Department, Preliminary Report On Foreign Holdings Of U.S. Securities At End-June 2008.

Figure 1. China's Holdings of U.S. Securities: June 2002-June 2008 $billions.

Table 3. Top Three Foreign Holders of U.S. Securities as of June 2008 ($ billions)

Type of Security	Total	LT Treasury	LT Government Agency	LT Corporate	Equities	Short Term
Japan	1,250	568	270	148	199	66
China	1,2051	522	527	26	100	30
United Kingdom	864	45	26	394	376	24
World Total	10,324	2,210	1,464	2,820	2,969	861
Change in China's Holdings over June 2007	283	55	151	-2	71	7
China's Holdings as a Percent of World Total (%)	11.7	23.6	36.0	0.9	3.4	3.5

Source: U.S. Treasury Department, Preliminary Report on Foreign Portfolio Holdings of U.S. Securities as of June 30, 2008, February 2009.

Note: LT securities are those with no stated maturity date (such as equities) or with an original term to maturity date of more than one year. Short term securities have a maturity period of less than one year.

U.S. data indicate Chinese holdings of U.S. agency debt from June 2007 to June 2008 increased by $151 billion (all of this increase was in asset-backed securities) and accounted for over half of China's increased holdings of total U.S. securities in 2008 [15]. China's new purchases of new agency debt were bigger than that of any other foreign country over this one year period. China is by far the largest foreign owner of U.S. agency debt, accounting for 36% of total foreign holdings (up from 29% as of June 2007). The second biggest category of new U.S. securities holdings in 2008 was in equities, which increased by $71 billion.

It is not yet clear how the U.S. sub-prime and financial crisis and ensuing global financial crisis has affected China's purchases of U.S. securities, especially since the extent of these crises became more apparent after June 2008 [11]. For example, in September 2008, Fannie Mae and Freddie Mac were placed in conservatorship by the Federal Government. Press reports indicate that China, which is believed to hold a large amount of Freddie Mac and Fannie Mae securities, was greatly concerned over the financial safety of its holdings when it became clear in July 2008 that both institutions were in serious financial trouble. The U.S. government takeover of Freddie Mac and Fannie Mae provided explicit U.S. government backing to these securities.

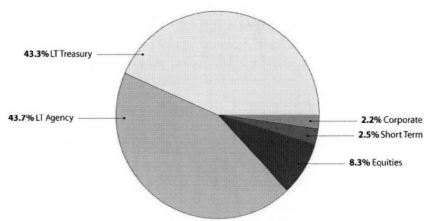

Source: Department of Treasury. Note: LT stands for long-term debt.

Figure 2. Composition of China's Holdings of U.S. Securities as of June 2008.

China's Ownership of U.S. Treasury Securities [16]

U.S. Treasury securities are the main vehicle the U.S. government uses to finance the federal debt, which totaled $10.0 trillion at the end of September 2008. Of this amount, 47% was held by U.S. government trust funds and 53% was privately held. Of the total level of privately-held U.S. Treasury securities ($5.3 trillion), foreigners owned 54% of the total ($2.9 trillion) [17]. China's holdings of U.S. Treasury securities holdings (as of September 2008) accounted for 11.0% of total private holdings (including foreign governments and citizens) of U.S. Treasury securities and 5.9% of total U.S. public debt securities (combined public and private) [18]. Table 5 lists the top five major foreign holders of U.S. Treasury securities as of December 2008. China was the largest holder of U.S. Treasury Securities (overtaking Japan in September 2008) at $724 billion; it was the 7th largest holder in December 1997 [19].

Over the past few years, China has become a major purchaser of Treasury securities. From December 2002 to December 2008, China's share of total foreign holdings of U.S. Treasury securities rose from 9.6% to 23.6%. From December 2007 to December 2008, China's holdings increased by $250 billion (or 52.3%), by far the largest dollar increase of any country. China accounted for 34.4% of net new holdings of U.S. Treasury securities in 2008.

In comparison, Japan's holdings rose by $46.1 billion. China's purchases of U.S. Treasury securities were relatively large in September and October 2008, at $44.5 billion and $65.9 billion, respectively. This may in part reflect a movement by China (and other foreign investors) away from purchases of U.S. agency asset-backed securities (such those issued by Fannie Mae and Freddie Mac) to more "safe" U.S. Treasury securities (especially short-term securities).

Table 4. China's Holdings of U.S.Treasury Securities: 2002-2008 Year-End

	2002	2003	2004	2005	2006	2007	2008
China's Holdings ($billions)	118.4	159.0	222.9	310.0	396.9	477.6	727.4
Holdings as a % of Total Foreign Holdings	9.6%	10.4%	12.1%	15.2%	18.9%	20.3%	23.6%

Source: U.S. Treasury Department.

U.S. CONCERNS OVER CHINA'S LARGE HOLDINGS OF U.S. SECURITIES

Some U.S. policymakers have expressed concern over China's large holdings of U.S. securities, including Treasury securities, contending that China could use it as a political tool against the United States. To illustrate, an August 7, 2007 article in the *Telegraph* (an online British newspaper) cited interviews with officials from two leading Chinese government think tanks who reportedly stated that China had the power to make the dollar collapse (if it chose to do so) by liquidating large portions of its U.S. Treasury securities holdings if the United States imposed trade sanctions to force a renminbi revaluation, and that the threat to do so could be used as a "bargaining chip"[20]. The article prompted concern among many U.S. policymakers, including Senator Chuck Grassley, who, in an August 9, 2007 letter to the Chinese ambassador to the United States (Zhou Wenzhong), called the comments "dangerous" and a factor in why the United States "is right to be concerned with China's currency practices." The letter asked the Chinese government to confirm that "the comments do not reflect the official position of the Chinese government" [21]. In response, the Chinese ambassador wrote to Senator Grassley on August 13, 2007, that "China does not have a plan to drastically adjust the structure of its foreign reserves" [22]. In addition, China's *Xinhua News Agency* on August 13, 2007, quoted an unnamed official at the People's Bank of China as stating that "dollar-denominated assets, including U.S. government securities, are an important component in China's foreign exchange reserve investment portfolio," and that China was "a responsible investor."

Table 5. Major Foreign Holders of U.S. Treasury Securities: December 2007 and December 2008

	Dec 2007	Dec 2008	Dec 2007-Dec 2008 Change in the Value of its Holdings	Holdings as a Share of Total Foreign Holdings as of Dec 2008 (%)
China	477.6	727.4	249.8	23.6
Japan	579.9	626.0	46.1	20.3
Caribbean Banking Centers[a]	117.4	197.5	80.1	6.4
Oil Exporters	137.9	186.2	48.3	6.3
United Kingdom	157.9	130.9	-27.0	4.3
Total Foreign Holdings	2,351.1	3,076.9	725.8	100.0

Source: Department of Treasury, Major Foreign Holders of Treasury Securities Holdings, February 27, 2008.

[a.]Oil exporters include Ecuador, Venezuela, Indonesia, Bahrain, Iran, Iraq, Kuwait, Oman, Qatar, Saudi Arabia, the United Arab Emirates, Algeria, Gabon, Libya, and Nigeria.

Note: *Data are based on surveys which are done annually or biannually. A new survey may often significantly revise data of a previous survey. Thus, time series data should be viewed with caution.

Numerous reports have appeared in the media citing various Chinese officials who, in the past, have claimed or hinted at government plans to reduce its holdings of U.S. Treasury securities for economic reasons. For example, on September 29, 2007, the Chinese government officially launched the state-owned *China Investment Corporation,* which Chinese officials state was created to better manage its foreign exchange reserves. It reportedly will initially manage over $200 billion of China's reserves, making it one of the world's largest sovereign wealth funds. Some contend the creation of this entity could signal Chinese plans to diversify away from relatively low-yielding assets, such as Treasury securities, and perhaps dollar-denominated assets in general [23] On November 7, 2007, Cheng Siwei, the vice chairman of the Chinese National People's Congress, reportedly made remarks that the Chinese government "will favor stronger currencies over weaker ones, and will readjust accordingly." The media claimed that his remarks were a major factor in sparking a sharp decline of the dollar against the euro in international currency markets that day [24]. However, on November 14, 2007, Yi Gang, assistant governor of the People's Bank of China, was quoted as saying that "the U.S. dollar is the main currency in our reserves and that policy remains very firm," and said that statements by other officials to the contrary were "opinions" [25]

Some U.S. policymakers have recently raised concerns that China, for economic reasons (such as concerns over the safety of its current holdings of U.S. securities), might seek to liquidate such assets or significantly cut back on purchases of new securities. These fears have been heightened as a result of the U.S. sub-prime mortgage crisis and the subsequent global financial crisis [26].

At a press conference during her visit to China on February 21, 2009, Secretary of State Hillary Rodham Clinton brought up this issue, stating that she appreciated "greatly the Chinese government's continuing confidence in the United States treasuries."

WHAT IF CHINA REDUCES ITS HOLDINGS OF U.S. SECURITIES? [27]

As the previous data illustrate, China has accumulated large holdings of U.S. assets in recent years. These accumulations are the result of U.S. borrowing to finance its large trade deficit with China (the gap between U.S. exports and Chinese imports). All else equal, Chinese government purchases of U.S. assets increases the demand for U.S. assets, which reduces U.S. interest rates.

If China attempted to reduce its holdings of U.S. securities, they would be sold to other investors (foreign and domestic), who would presumably require higher interest rates than those prevailing today to be enticed to buy them. One analyst estimates that a Chinese move away from long-term U.S. securities could raise interest rates by as much as 50 basis points [28]. Higher interest rates would cause a decline in investment spending and other interest-sensitive spending. All else equal, the reduction in Chinese Treasury holdings would cause the overall foreign demand for U.S. assets to fall, and this would cause the dollar to depreciate. If the value of the dollar depreciated, the trade deficit would decline, as the price of U.S. exports fell abroad and the price of imports rose in the United States [29]. The magnitude of these effects would depend on how many U.S. securities China sold; modest reductions would have negligible effects on the economy given the vastness of U.S. financial markets.

Since China held $1,205 billion of U.S. government assets as of June 2008 (and possibly $1.4 trillion at the end of 2008), any reduction in its U.S. holdings could potentially be large. If there were a large reduction in its holdings, the effect on the U.S. economy would still depend on whether the reduction were gradual or sudden. It should be emphasized that economic theory suggests that a *slow decline* in the trade deficit and dollar would not be troublesome for the overall economy. In fact, a slow decline could even have an expansionary effect on the economy, if the decrease in the trade deficit had a more stimulative effect on aggregate demand in the short run than the decrease in investment and other interest-sensitive spending resulting from higher interest rates. Historical experience seems to bear this out—the dollar declined by about 40% in real terms and the trade deficit declined continually in the late 1980s, from 2.8% of GDP in 1986 to nearly zero during the early 1990s. Yet economic growth was strong throughout the late 1980s.

A potentially serious short-term problem would emerge if China decided to *suddenly* reduce their liquid U.S. financial assets significantly. The effect could be compounded if this action triggered a more general financial reaction (or panic), in which all foreigners responded by reducing their holdings of U.S. assets. The initial effect could be a sudden and large depreciation in the value of the dollar, as the supply of dollars on the foreign exchange market increased, and a sudden and large increase in U.S. interest rates, as an important funding source for investment and the budget deficit was withdrawn from the financial markets. The dollar depreciation would not cause a recession since it would ultimately lead to a trade surplus (or smaller deficit), which expands aggregate demand [30] (Empirical evidence suggests that the full effects of a change in the exchange rate on traded goods takes time, so the dollar may have to "overshoot" its eventual depreciation level in order to achieve a significant adjustment in trade flows in the short run.) [31]. However, a sudden increase in interest rates could swamp the trade effects and cause (or worsen) a recession. Large increases in interest rates could cause problems for the U.S. economy, as these increases reduce the market value of debt securities, cause prices on the stock market to fall, undermine efficient financial intermediation, and jeopardize the solvency of various debtors and creditors. Resources may not be able to shift quickly enough from interest-sensitive sectors to export sectors to make this transition fluid. The Federal Reserve could mitigate the interest rate spike by reducing short-term interest rates, although this reduction would influence long-term rates only indirectly, and could worsen the dollar depreciation and increase inflation.

The likelihood that China would suddenly reduce its holdings of U.S. securities is questionable because it is doubtful that doing so would be in China's economic interests. First, a large sell-off of China's U.S. holdings could diminish the value of these securities in international markets, which would lead to large losses on the sale, and would, in turn, decrease the value of China's remaining dollar-denominated assets [32]. This would also occur if the value of the dollar were greatly diminished in international currency markets due to China's sell-off [33]. Second, such a move would diminish U.S. demand for Chinese imports, either through a rise in the value of the renminbi against the dollar or a reduction in U.S. economic growth (especially if other foreign investors sold their U.S. asset holdings, and the United States was forced to raise interest rates in response) [34] According to some estimates, nearly one quarter of Chinese exports went to the United States in 2008. A sharp reduction of U.S. imports from China could have a significant impact on China's economy, which heavily depends on exports for its economic growth (and is viewed by the government as a vital source of political stability) [35]. Finally, any major action by the Chinese government that destabilized (or further destabilized) the U.S. economy (whether deliberate or not) could provoke "protectionist" sentiment in the United States against China.

CONCLUDING OBSERVATIONS

Many economists argue that concerns over China's holdings of U.S. securities represent part of a broader problem for the U.S. economy, namely its dependence on foreign saving to finance its investment needs and federal budget deficits [36]. The large U.S. current account deficit (the manifestation of the high U.S. saving/investment gap) cannot be sustained indefinitely because the U.S. net foreign debt cannot rise faster than GDP indefinitely [37]. Some economists argue that at some point foreign investors may view the growing level of U.S. foreign debt as unsustainable or more risky, or they may no longer view U.S. securities as offering the best return on their investment, and shift investment funds away from U.S. assets, thus forcing U.S. interest rates to rise to attract needed foreign capital. This would result in higher interest rates and lower investment rates, all else equal, which would reduce long-term growth [38]. Other economists contend that, although the low U.S. savings rate is a problem, the U.S. current account deficit and high levels of foreign capital flows to the United States are also reflections of the strength of the U.S. economy and its attractiveness as a destination for foreign investment, and therefore discount the likelihood that foreign investors will suddenly shift their capital elsewhere [39].

The United States continues to press China to make its currency policy more flexible so that the renminbi will appreciate more significantly against the dollar and to adopt policies that promote domestic consumption as a major source of China's economic growth (as opposed to export and fixed investment-led growth that has resulted from China's currency policy) [40]. This is viewed as a major step towards reducing global trade imbalances, including the large U.S.-China trade imbalance. However, in order for that to occur, the United States must also boost its level of savings in the long run. If China consumed more and saved less, it would have less capital to invest overseas, including in the United States. Thus, if the United States did not reduce its dependence on foreign savings for its investment needs, and China reduced its U.S. investments, the United States would need to obtain investment from other countries, and the overall U.S. current account balance would likely remain relatively unchanged.

Some U.S. policymakers have expressed hope that China will increase its U.S. debt holdings in order to help the Federal government pay for its financial rescue plan and future stimulus packages [41]. But others have expressed concern that becoming more reliant on Chinese purchases of U.S. debt would increase China's political leverage over the United States and may make it more difficult for the United States to induce China to appreciate its currency more quickly and to make other needed reforms to its economy. Some analysts contend that economic factors in China, such as decreased exports and foreign direct investment flows to China, may sharply limit its accumulation of additional foreign exchange reserves, which in turn could slow or halt China's purchases of U.S. securities.

REFERENCES

[1]   China's accumulation of foreign exchange reserves has also occurred because of large annual current account trade surpluses, high levels of foreign direct investment in China, and inflows of "hot money" from overseas investors who anticipate that the Chinese government will appreciate the renminbi in the near future. For additional information, see CRS Report RL32165, *China's Currency: Economic Issues and Options for U.S. Trade Policy*, by Wayne M. Morrison and Marc Labonte.

[2]   For a discussion of the implications of a possible global sell-off of U.S. securities, see CRS Report RL34319, *Foreign Ownership of U.S. Financial Assets: Implications of a Withdrawal*, by James K. Jackson.

[3]   China overtook Japan in 2006 to become the world's largest holder of FER.

[4]   Total reserves for all countries in June 2008 were estimated at $6,894.1 billion. Worldwide, 41% of reserves were held in dollar-denominated assets.

[5]   For additional information on foreign ownership of U.S. securities, see CRS Report RL32462, *Foreign Investment in U.S. Securities*, by James K. Jackson.

[6]   Note, Treasury's annual survey does not include data on foreign direct investment (FDI) in the United States, which measures foreign ownership or investment in U.S. businesses. China's total FDI in the U.S. at the end of 2007 was $1.1 billion (on a historical cost basis), according the U.S. Bureau of Economic Analysis. Since these types of assets cannot be liquidated rapidly, they are not included in this report.

[7]   Agency securities include both federal agencies and government-sponsored enterprises created by Congress (e.g., Fannie Mae and Freddie Mac) to provide credit to key

sectors of the economy. Some of these securities are backed by assets (such as home mortgages).

[8]   LT securities are those with no stated maturity date (such as equities) or with an original term to maturity date of more than one year. Short-term debt includes U.S. Treasury securities, agency securities, and corporate securities with amaturity date of less than one year.

[9]   Data on China's holdings of U.S. securities exclude holdings by Hong Kong (which totaled $147 billion as of June 20080 and Macao. These entities, though part of China, are reported separately by Treasury.

[10]   In comparison, Japan's holdings grew by only $53 billion.

[11]   According to the Treasury Department, data on foreign holdings of U.S. securities should be treated with caution, due to the difficulty in obtaining accurate information on the *actual* foreign owners of U.S. securities. For example, chains of foreign financial intermediaries may be involved in the custody or management of these securities.

[12]   See testimony of Brad Setser, Senior Economist, Roubini Global Economics and Research Associate, Global Economic Governance Programme, University College, Oxford, before the House Budget Committee, *Foreign Holdings of U.S. Debt: Is our Economy Vulnerable?*, June 26, 2007, p. 11. In addition, the *People's Daily Online* (August 28, 2006) estimated China's dollar holdings to total FER at 70%.

[13]   Some analysts contend that the Chinese government undercounts the total level of its foreign exchange reserves and thus, its holdings of U.S. securities could be even higher.

[14]   The Bank of China either reduced its holdings or wrote off the losses.

[15]   For a general discussion of foreign ownership of U.S. debt, see CRS Report RS22331, *Foreign Holdings of Federal Debt*, by Justin Murray and Marc Labonte.

[16]   U.S. Treasury Department, Financial Management Service, *Ownership of Federal Securities*, available athttp://www.fms.treas.gov/ bulletin/index.html.

[17]   Although yields on U.S. Treasury securities are relatively low compared to other types of investment, they are also considered to be relatively low in risk. Thus they are viewed by many central banks to be a safe investment for their FER.

[18]   Treasury constantly revises its estimates of foreign holdings of U.S. securities. On February 27, 2009, it made substantial revisions to its previously released monthly data for 2008 (which was issued on February 17, 2009). The new data raised estimates for China's holdings of U.S. Treasury securities in December 2008 from $696 billion (old estimate) to $727 billion. However, Treasury does not revise its data from previous years. Thus, comparisons of historical Treasury data should be viewed with caution.

[19]   The Telegraph, *China Threatens 'Nuclear Option' of Dollar Sales*, August 7, 2007.

[20]   See text of letter at http://grassley.senate.gov/public/.

[21]   Letter reprinted in *Inside U.S. Trade*, August 13, 2007.

[22]   Others are concerned that China will attempt to use the fund to purchase major U.S. companies. See the New Yorker, *Sovereign Wealth World*, November 26, 2007. According to the article, "were China's fund so inclined, it could buy Ford, G.M., Volkswagen, and Honda, and still have a little money left over for ice cream."

[23]   *Bloomberg News*, November 8, 2007.

[24]   *China Daily*, November 15, 2007.

[25] See CRS Report RL34742, *The Global Financial and Economic Crisis: Analysis and Policy Implications*, coordinated by Dick K. Nanto.

[26] From the perspective of the macroeconomic effects on U.S. investment, interest rates, and so on, it does not matter what type of U.S. security is purchased when foreign capital flows to the United States. Thus, Chinese purchases of all types of U.S. securities (not just Treasury securities) should be considered when attempting to understand the impact China's investment decisions have on the U.S. economy.

[27] Testimony of Brad Setser before the House Budget Committee, *Foreign Holdings of U.S. Debt: Is our Economy Vulnerable?*, June 26, 2007. Brad Setser is Senior Economist, Roubini Global Economics, and Research Associate, Global Economic Governance Programme, University College, Oxford. Setser does not detail how much U.S. debt he assumes China would sell to reach his estimate.

[28] The extent that the dollar declined and U.S. interest rates rose would depend on how willing other foreigners were to supplant China's reduction in capital inflows. A greater willingness would lead to less dollar depreciation and less of an increase in interest rates, and vice versa.

[29] A sharp decline in the value of the dollar would also reduce living standards, all else equal, because it would raise the price of imports to households. This effect, which is referred to as a decline in the terms of trade, would not be recorded directly in GDP, however.

[30] Since the decline in the dollar would raise import prices, this could temporarily increase inflationary pressures. The effect would likely be modest, however, since imports are small as a share of GDP and import prices would only gradually rise in response to the fall in the dollar.

[31] Since there are many other holders of U.S. assets, it is possible that if China believed a decline in asset values was

[32] imminent, it could minimize its losses by dumping its U.S. assets first, however.

[33] Selling off U.S. dollar assets could cause the renminbi to appreciate against the dollar, which would lower the value of remaining U.S. assets since the assets are dollar-denominated.

[34] In addition, if a "dollar collapse" occurred, U.S. imports from other major trade partners would decline, which could slow their economies. This in turn could weaken their demand for Chinese products.

[35] Although a falling dollar may harm China's short-term growth via reduced Chinese exports (and export sector-related employment), it would also improve China's terms of trade with the United States, raising China's overall consumption since it could now spend less to acquire the same amount of American goods (which would also create jobs in other sectors of the economy because of increased consumer purchasing power).

[36] Nations (such as the United States) that fail to save enough to meet their investment needs must obtain savings from other countries with high savings rates (such as China). By obtaining resources from foreign investors for its investment needs, the United States is able to enjoy a higher rate of consumption than it would if investment were funded by domestic savings alone. The inflow of foreign capital to the United States is equivalent to the United States borrowing from the rest of the world. The only way the United States can borrow from the rest of the world is by importing more than it exports, which produces a trade (and current account) deficit.

[37] The current account deficit rose from $389.4 billion in 2002 to $811.5 billion in 2006, and as a percent of GDP, it increased from 4.4% to 6.1%, respectively. The Economist Intelligence Unit estimates that the current account deficit as a percent of GDP 5.3% in 2007 and to 4.8% in 2008.

[38] See CRS Report RL33186, *Is the U.S. Current Account Deficit Sustainable?*, by Marc Labonte.

[39] See Council of Economic Advisors, Economic Report of the President, *The U.S. Capital Surplus*, February 2006, p. 144.

[40] In November, the Chinese government announced it would implement a two-year $586 billion stimulus package, mainly dedicated to infrastructure projects.

[41] See CRS Report RS22984, *China and the Global Financial Crisis: Implications for the United States*, by Wayne M. Morrison.

INDEX

B

C

D

E

F

G

H

J

K

L

Q

R

S

T

U

V

W